A Psychotherapy for the People

How did psychoanalysis come to define itself as being different from psychotherapy? How have racism, homophobia, misogyny, and anti-Semitism converged in the creation of psychotherapy and psychoanalysis? Is psychoanalysis psychotherapy? Is psychoanalysis a "Jewish science"?

Inspired by the progressive and humanistic origins of psychoanalysis, Lewis Aron and Karen Starr pursue Freud's call for psychoanalysis to be a "psychotherapy for the people." They present a cultural history focusing on how psychoanalysis has always defined itself in relation to an "other." At first, that other was hypnosis and suggestion; later it was psychotherapy. The authors trace a series of binary oppositions, each defined hierarchically, which have plagued the history of psychoanalysis. Tracing reverberations of racism, anti-Semitism, misogyny, and homophobia, they show that psychoanalysis, associated with phallic masculinity, penetration, heterosexuality, autonomy, and culture, was defined in opposition to suggestion and psychotherapy, which were seen as promoting dependence, feminine passivity, and relationality. Aron and Starr deconstruct these dichotomies, leading the way for a return to Freud's progressive vision, in which psychoanalysis, defined broadly and flexibly, is revitalized for a new era.

A Psychotherapy for the People will be of interest to psychotherapists, psychoanalysts, clinical psychologists, psychiatrists—and their patients—and to those studying feminism, cultural studies, and Judaism.

Lewis Aron is the Director of the New York University Postdoctoral Program in Psychotherapy and Psychoanalysis. He is author and editor of numerous articles and books on psychotherapy and psychoanalysis, including *A Meeting of Minds* and the *Relational Perspectives Book Series*. He was one of the co-founders of the journal *Psychoanalytic Dialogues* and has served as President of the Division of Psychoanalysis (39) of the American Psychological Association, and founding President of the International Association for Relational Psychoanalysis and Psychotherapy (IARPP). He is co-founder and co-chair of the Sándor Ferenczi Center at the New School for Social Research, and he practices and leads numerous study groups in New York City and Port Washington, NY.

Karen Starr is the author of *Repair of the Soul: Metaphors of Transformation in Jewish Mysticism and Psychoanalysis*. She is adjunct faculty and supervisor at The Graduate Centre, CUNY, and Long Island University. She is on the Editorial Board of the *Psychoanalysis and Jewish Life Book Series*. She is a candidate at the New York University Postdoctoral Program in Psychotherapy and Psychoanalysis, and a recipient of the Ruth Stein Prize. She is in private practice in New York City.

RELATIONAL PERSPECTIVES BOOK SERIES

LEWIS ARON & ADRIENNE HARRIS
Series Editors

The Relational Perspectives Book Series (RPBS) publishes books that grow out of, or contribute to, the relational tradition in contemporary psychoanalysis. The term *relational psychoanalysis* was first used by Greenberg and Mitchell (1983) to bridge the traditions of interpersonal relations, as developed within interpersonal psychoanalysis, and object relations, as developed within contemporary British theory. But, under the seminal work of the late Stephen Mitchell, the term *relational psychoanalysis* grew and began to accrue to itself many other influences and developments. Various tributaries—interpersonal psychoanalysis, object relations theory, self psychology, empirical infancy research, and elements of contemporary Freudian and Kleinian thought—flow into this tradition, which understands relational configurations between self and others, both real and fantasied, as the primary subject of psychoanalytic investigation.

We refer to the relational tradition, rather than to a relational school, to highlight that we are identifying a trend, a tendency within contemporary psychoanalysis, not a more formally organized or coherent school or system of beliefs. Our use of the term *relational* signifies a dimension of theory and practice that has become salient across the wide spectrum of contemporary psychoanalysis. Now under the editorial supervision of Lewis Aron and Adrienne Harris, the Relational Perspectives Book Series originated in 1990 under the editorial eye of the late Stephen A. Mitchell. Mitchell was the most prolific and influential of the originators of the relational tradition. He was committed to dialogue among psychoanalysts and he abhorred the authoritarianism that dictated adherence to a rigid set of beliefs or technical restrictions. He championed open discussion, comparative and integrative approaches, and he promoted new voices across the generations.

Included in the Relational Perspectives Book Series are authors and works that come from within the relational tradition, extend and develop the tradition, as well as works that critique relational approaches or compare and contrast it with alternative points of view. The series includes our most distinguished senior psychoanalysts along with younger contributors who bring fresh vision.

RELATIONAL PERSPECTIVES BOOK SERIES
LEWIS ARON & ADRIENNE HARRIS
Series Editors

RELATIONAL PERSPECTIVES BOOK SERIES

LEWIS ARON & ADRIENNE HARRIS
Series Editors

RELATIONAL PERSPECTIVES BOOK SERIES

LEWIS ARON & ADRIENNE HARRIS
Series Editors

LEWIS ARON & ADRIENNE HARRIS
Series Editors

A Psychotherapy for the People

Toward a Progressive Psychoanalysis

Lewis Aron and Karen Starr

Routledge
Taylor & Francis Group

NEW YORK AND LONDON

First published 2013
by Routledge
711 Third Avenue, New York, NY 10017

Simultaneously published in the UK
by Routledge
27 Church Road, Hove, East Sussex BN3 2FA

*Routledge is an imprint of the Taylor & Francis Group, an informa
business*

Library of Congress Cataloging in Publication Data
Aron, Lewis.
  A psychotherapy for the people : toward a progressive
  psychoanalysis / Lewis Aron and Karen Starr.
     p. cm.
  1. Psychoanalysis.   2. Psychotherapy.   I. Starr, Karen E.
  II. Title.
RC501.2.A76 2012
616.89'17—dc23   2012025384

ISBN: 978-0-415-52998-3 (hbk)
ISBN: 978-0-415-52999-0 (pbk)
ISBN: 978-0-203-09805-9 (ebk)

Typeset in Garamond
by RefineCatch Limited, Bungay, Suffolk, UK

Printed and bound in the United States of America
by Edwards Brothers, Inc.

For my children, Benjamin, Raphi, and Kirya—L. A.

For those I hold dear—K. S.

Contents

Preface

Inspired by the progressive and humanistic origins of psychoanalysis, we begin this book, fittingly, with the words of its founder, Sigmund Freud. Freud's stirring appeal to his followers, made just before the end of World War I, vividly captures his hope and optimism for the ability of psycho-analysis to improve the conditions of the lower classes. Freud called for what we view as a "progressive" psychoanalysis, urging the establishment of free clinics and the provision of "psychotherapy for the people." He stated,

> At present we can do nothing for the wider social strata, who suffer extremely seriously from neuroses . . . it is possible to foresee that at some time or other the conscience of society will awake and remind it that the poor man should have just as much right to assistance for his mind as he now has to the life-saving help offered by surgery; and that the neuroses threaten public health no less than tuberculosis, and can be left as little as the latter to the impotent care of individual members of the community. When this happens, institutions or out-patient clinics will be started, to which analytically-trained physicians will be appointed, so that men who would otherwise give way to drink, women who have nearly succumbed under their burden of privations, children for whom there is no choice but between running wild or neurosis, may be made capable, by analysis, of resistance and of effi-cient work. Such treatments will be free. It may be a long time before the State comes to see these duties as urgent. Present conditions may delay its arrival even longer. Probably these institutions will first be started by private charity. Some time or other, however, it must come to this. We shall then be faced by the task of adapting our technique to the new conditions. I have no doubt that the validity of our psycho-logical assumptions will make its impression on the uneducated too, but we shall need to look for the simplest and most easily intelligible ways of expressing our theoretical doctrines. We shall probably discover that the poor are even less ready to part with their neuroses than the rich, because the hard life that awaits them if they recover

offers them no attraction, and illness gives them one more claim to social help. Often, perhaps, we may only be able to achieve anything by combining mental assistance with some material support, in the manner of the Emperor Joseph. It is very probable, too, that the large-scale application of our therapy will compel us to alloy the pure gold of analysis freely with the copper of direct suggestion; and hypnotic influence, too, might find a place in it again, as it has in the treatment of war neuroses. But, whatever form this *psychotherapy for the people* may take, whatever the elements out of which it is compounded, its most effective and most important ingredients will assuredly remain those borrowed from strict and untendentious psycho-analysis.

(Freud 1918b, pp. 167–168)

Freud envisioned a time when psychoanalysis would be made widely available to the public, not in its "pure" form, but as a practical alloy, provided free of charge to the poor and uneducated. Indeed, as Danto (2005) has documented, Freud's progressive vision led to the development of free psychoanalytic clinics around the world. Given the conservative and isolationist turn of mainstream psychoanalysis in America in the 1950s, the active endorsement of social activism and political engagement by Freud and the early analysts is often overlooked. In our book, *A Psychotherapy for the People: Toward a Progressive Psychoanalysis*, we call for a return to Freud's humanistic vision, the renewal of psychoanalysis' progressive spirit, and for a broader and more inclusive attitude toward its definition and application. We will show that after Freud's death, psychoanalysis unfortunately and mistakenly defined itself in opposition to psychotherapy, narrowing its focus and unduly restricting its scope. Throughout this book, we will be deconstructing the psychoanalysis versus psychotherapy binary, as well as the many other binaries within which psychoanalysis has historically been caught. We use the term "progressive" as a "third" or mediating term, one that enables us to challenge traditional dichotomous categories and to transcend binary thinking. To clarify our use of the term "progressive" with regard to psychoanalysis, let's first briefly examine the ways in which it has been employed in other disciplines.

Progressivism is defined as a political movement advocating progress, change, improvement, and reform. The Progressive Movement was started in the late 19th and early 20th centuries by urban settlement workers involved in helping those facing harsh conditions at home and at work improve their circumstances. Emerging as a response to the vast changes brought about by industrialization, progressivism provided an alternative to the conservative reaction to social and economic problems, and also— despite being associated with left-wing politics—to the more radical streams of Communism and Anarchism. Note that in politics, the term

Planting

Place compressed planting disk in the container you are using to plant the bulb and add approximately 2 cups of warm water. Fluff up the potting mix with a fork. Add more water if necessary. Place your bulb into the potting mix, pointed end up, so the top of the bulb is 1-2" above the soil.

Placement & Watering

Place the bulb in a warm, bright location. Sunlight is necessary for the development of the stems. Water sparingly until the stem appears, then as the bud & stem appear, gradually water more. Keep the soil moist. The Amaryllis will start to bloom in 8 weeks.

After care

Remove faded flowers and flower stalks. Plant the amaryllis in the garden once night-time temp. is above 50° and daytime temp. is consistently warm, and fertilize. Remove from garden in September and cut off the leaves. Store the bulbs in a cool, dry place for 6 weeks. Then, pot the bulb again. This plant will grow for many years!

El plantar

Coloque el disco que planta comprimido en el envase que usted está utilizando plantar el bulbo y agregar aproximadamente 2 tazas de agua caliente. Pelusa encima de la mezcla del encapsulamiento con una bifurcación. Agregue más agua si es necesario. Coloque su bulbo en el suelo, extremo acentuado para arriba, así que la tapa del bulbo es 1-2" sobre el suelo.

Colocación y riego

Coloque el bulbo en una localización brillante en la temperatura ambiente. La luz del sol es necesaria para el desarrollo de los vástagos. Riegue escasamente hasta que aparece el vástago, después como el brote y el vástago aparezca, riegue gradualmente más. Mantenga el suelo húmedo. El Amaryllis comenzará a florecer en 8 semanas.

Después de cuidado

Quite las flores y los tallos descoloridos de la flor. Plante el amaryllis en la temperatura de la noche del jardín adentro una vez. está sobre 50° y la temperatura del día. es constantemente caliente, y fertiliza. Quite de jardín en septiembre y corte las hojas. Almacene los bulbos en un lugar fresco, seco por 6 semanas. Entonces, pot el bulbo otra vez. ¡Esta planta crecerá por muchos años!

Soil level	Nivel del suelo
Plant bulb up to its neck.	Bulbo de la planta hasta su cuello.
Keep soil moist throughout the blooming time.	Mantenga el suelo húmedo.
Don't damage the roots.	No dañe las raíces.

progressivism was not used to denote the binary opposite of conservatism. Rather, it was used as a third term, mediating the dichotomy of liberal versus conservative.

In music, Progressive Rock pushed the technical and compositional boundaries of Rock 'n' Roll, extending the limits of its musical structures and content. In music, as in politics, the term progressive was not meant to refer to the polar opposite of classical, but rather to the frequent incorporation of elements from classical, jazz, and world music. Progressive Rock transcended and challenged the older binary categories.

Similarly, Progressive Judaism includes many diverse Jewish movements— Liberal, Reform, Conservative, and Reconstructionist—embracing pluralism, modernity, equality, and social justice as its core values. The term progressive is not intended to be the opposite of conservative, classical, or orthodox, but rather to be inclusive and extend the boundaries of prior dichotomous schools.

Like Freud, we are advocating for psychoanalysis as a "psychotherapy for the people," envisioning it as a broad discipline having many forms of application. Challenging the binary of psychoanalysis versus psychotherapy, we call instead for a progressive psychoanalysis, one that draws upon the humanistic vision of its founders. To make our case, we present a cultural history of psychoanalysis, examining how psychoanalysis came to define itself so rigidly, and how it has been burdened by being situated within a complex array of binary oppositions.

We purposely do not tell our story in a straightforward linear fashion. Instead, we give our historical account of the development of psychoanalysis by drawing upon Freud's nonlinear concept of *Nachträglichkeit*, or "retroactiveness." Freud wrote to his friend Wilhelm Fliess,

> I am working on the assumption that our psychical mechanism has come into being by a process of stratification: The material present in the form of memory-traces being subjected from time to time to a *re-arrangement* in accordance with fresh circumstances—to a *re-transcription*.
>
> (1986a, p. 207)

Freud's understanding of the development of the individual was never simple or linear. For Freud, the past and present mutually influence one another. Later events lead to the reworking of earlier events, affecting subsequent development. Throughout his writing, Freud depicted the mind as stratified in layers, and the analyst as archeologist, digging from the surface to the depths. However, he did not mean that memory was buried underground like an artifact preserved in its original form, waiting to be dug up. Rather, Freud viewed memory as a fluid entity that was constantly changing and being reworked over time. He referred to this dynamic as *Nachträglichkeit*, translated in English as "afterwardness" or "deferred action," and in French as "après coup."

This phenomenon is usually associated with the impact of trauma, experience that cannot be assimilated. In the contemporary language of psychoanalysis and trauma studies, trauma is often described as leading to dissociated or unformulated experience. What undergoes deferred revision is not the memory of the experience per se; rather what was impossible to assimilate in the first place is now reworked and integrated. New life circumstances or developmental maturation enables the individual to gain access to new levels of meaning in order to integrate earlier experience. Freud most frequently used the concept of *Nachträglichkeit* in the context of the development of sexuality. For example, he believed the Wolfman's dream at age four reworked memories of parental intercourse from much earlier in childhood, which had not been traumatic at that earlier age but became so with his maturing sexuality. Similarly, the biphasic development of sexuality, first in childhood and then again in adolescence lends itself to the reworking of deferred action. This is an ongoing, not a terminal process.

The concept of *Nachträglichkeit* also provides us with a nonlinear understanding of history, and can be applied to the history of the development of psychoanalysis itself. We will use *Nachträglichkeit* as an organizing framework, showing how early experiences in the development of psychoanalysis were reworked in a later chapter of its history, leading to a particular development that was not simply the inevitable result of the initial experience alone. The reworking of the early experience by later events led to a particularly skewed development, reflecting psychoanalysis' traumatic history. We will examine the context in which psychoanalysis was created, the traumatic impact of this context on its creator, and the way in which the effects of this trauma reverberated within psychoanalytic theory. Because the story weaves in on itself, it is best to read this book from beginning to end, rather than delving into a particular chapter out of context.

Psychoanalysis was born of trauma, developed in the context of Freud's strong identification as a Jew, living in a viciously anti-Semitic milieu. Its development cannot be fully understood without attending to the traumatic impact of the virulent anti-Semitism surrounding Freud and his followers, in which the Jewish body was the target of anti-Semitic ridicule and disparagement. Intrinsic to the scientific, anthropological, and evolutionary discourse of the time was the racial model of the Jew, who was seen as having innate biological and psychological traits that distinguished him from the non-Jew. The most salient visible characteristic marking the Jew as racially different was circumcision. Although circumcision was also practiced by non-Jews, being circumcised had come to be equated disparagingly with being Jewish. In the German vernacular of Freud's era "*judischen*," "to make a Jew," was a commonly used metonym for "to circumcise." In accordance with Lamarckian doctrine, it was a widely held belief that circumcision, which was an acquired characteristic, could become an inherited trait. Circumcision was a favorite topic of controversy in scientific debates about biological inheritance. As European anti-Semitism intensified, circumcision, originally a signifier of religious difference, became the centerpiece of discussions about racial difference, including Jewish effeminacy, primitivity, degeneracy, and disease.

Freud's complicated reactions to anti-Semitism were incorporated into the character of psychoanalysis itself. It is easier to understand why Freud constructed the Oedipus complex as the nucleus of neurosis and castration anxiety as bedrock when we understand that his people, Jews, were accused of being neurotic and perverse because of generations of incest, and Jewish men were viewed as castrated and effeminate because they were circumcised. Jews in German society were marginal. Having no real homeland of their own, they occupied a position at a crossroads, between two worlds. As a westernized Jew, Freud, too, was marginal, situated at the crossroads of his Jewish racial and German cultural identities. It is no coincidence that Freud was preoccupied with border crossings.

These traumatic origins are significant when considering the development of psychoanalysis in America, particularly in the "golden years" of the 1950s and 1960s, when psychoanalysis was at its height, considered an elite medical specialty suitable only for an elite group of patients. During this period, the orthodox psychoanalytic mainstream defined psychoanalysis as distinct from, and in opposition to, psychotherapy. The immigration of Jewish psychoanalysts fleeing Europe after Hitler's rise to power had a major impact on the development of psychoanalysis in America. As they joined with their American colleagues, these émigré analysts, having suffered devastating losses, reshaped American psychoanalysis. Much of what became American psychoanalytic orthodoxy resulted from its traumatic European origins. Note that we are not claiming that Freud's Jewishness or the émigré experience is the sole explanation for why psychoanalysis developed as it did; however, we do believe that these are important and previously under-emphasized factors that must be illuminated.

Since that time, there have emerged multiple schools of psychoanalytic thought. Psychoanalytic theory and clinical practice have been greatly influenced by cultural studies and critical theory; in particular, by feminist theory, which has led to major changes in psychoanalytic thinking. We draw heavily upon this scholarship throughout this book in our deconstruction of the binaries within which psychoanalysis has been structured.

If we told this story in linear sequence, as a timeline from pre-Freud to Freud, to the transportation of psychoanalysis to America, leading up to our contemporary situation, we would be giving a decisively false impression. Such a chronologically told story would give the implication of inevitability, of one event leading to the other in a simple causal sequence. A chronological narrative might suggest that Freud's incorporation into psychoanalysis of certain defensive attitudes in reaction to anti-Semitism in fin de siècle Vienna led to particular beliefs among his followers, who brought these attitudes with them to America, influencing developments after World War II. This would be misleading: Freud's texts, attitudes, and beliefs had multiple potentials and could have led in many directions. We present the history of the development of psychoanalysis not as inevitable, but as what in contemporary terms might be referred to as "softly assembled" (Harris, 2005), having many possible trajectories. The immigration of Jewish refugees and their joining with American analysts led to elaborations in which some of these potentials in Freud's work were developed and others were not. Some of Freud's attitudes toward women, suggestion, primitivity, and neurosis were highlighted and made more extreme in America, whereas other attitudes, such as his passion for the non-medicalization of psychoanalysis and its democratization (via free clinics), were de-emphasized or even dismissed.

For this reason, we will begin our story seemingly in the middle, by examining the state of psychoanalysis in America leading up to and following World War II. Only after we explain the definitive shape taken by psychoanalysis after the war, will we return to Freud and his early experiences. Our hope is to create a sense of movement and flux in order to highlight the ways in which what remained unintegrated in Freud's work, what was dissociated precisely because it was traumatic, was reworked and revised by a new generation of already traumatized Jewish analysts, living once again under conditions of trauma. What came to be known as "Freudian" in America was in fact not identical with Freud's own theories or practices, nor was it an inevitable development of what he started. Rather, psychoanalysis in America underwent a *Nachträglich* development; it was twisted and reshaped into a traumatic symptom. We will show that because it was situated within the context of prejudice and hierarchically organized binary oppositions, psychoanalysis incorporated into its structure the problematic legacy of anti-Semitism, racism, misogyny, and homophobia. We will argue that a progressive psychoanalysis must search for the remnants of these biases, and must systematically rework theories and practices whose development was influenced by these often hidden underlying assumptions. In sum, we are presenting an archeology of psychoanalysis, a genealogy of its layered and traumatized convulsions, rather than simply a linear history.

Freud was caught between his German cultural identity and his Jewish ethnicity—between two worlds, situated at the edges of society. In many respects, Freud was "optimally marginal." We will argue that psychoanalysis is at its best when it is marginal or monstrous. Our hope is to provide the background for envisioning a new psychoanalysis for the 21st century, a progressive psychoanalysis that moves beyond old polarities and adapts to our changed world, while remaining true to the revolutionary and humanistic spirit of Freud and his followers: a "psychotherapy for the people."

Acknowledgments

Both of us are members of the community of the New York University Postdoctoral Program in Psychotherapy and Psychoanalysis, our intellectual and professional home. It is within the nurturing, stimulating, progressive, and thought-provoking environment of Postdoc that the ideas in this book were generated and still continue to develop. We thank all of our colleagues for their enthusiastic support of our work and our intellectual and professional growth.

In addition to Postdoc, we have benefited from friends, colleagues, and the lively discussions at the Division of Psychoanalysis (39) of the American Psychological Association and the International Association for Relational Psychoanalysis and Psychotherapy (IARPP).

Over the years, a number of colleagues have either read selections of what eventually became this book or discussed the ideas with us in some depth. We would like to thank especially: Galit Atlas-Koch, Deborah Berry, Celia Brickman, Ann D'Ercole, Muriel Dimen, Adrienne Harris, Steven Kuchuck, Amy Lieberman, Ann Pellegrini, Andrea Recarte, Peter L. Rudnytsky, Jeremy Safran, and Paul Wachtel.

Thank you to Dustin Kahoud for his invaluable editorial assistance. Dustin's responsiveness and attention to detail were essential to completing the final stages of this work. We thank Kirsten Buchanan, Kate Hawes, Kristopher Spring, and the staff of Taylor & Francis for bringing this book to fruition.

We thank our patients for all they have taught us.

From Lewis Aron:

I have been consumed with the thoughts elaborated here for at least the past eight years. About three years ago, I had the inspired idea of asking Karen Starr to join me in undertaking the writing of this book. Karen's collaboration has been essential to realizing this project. She has not only been a pleasure to work with and an expert writer and editor, but she has made decisive and incisive contributions to the overall argument. I look forward to ongoing collaboration with her.

A special thanks to Adrienne Harris, with whom I have co-edited the Relational Perspective Book Series, for her longstanding support, friendship, enthusiasm, and love.

I want to thank the numerous participants in my weekly study/reading groups who have actively discussed and contributed to my thinking over these years.

I dedicate this book with much love to my children Benjamin, Raphi, and Kirya. I thank my wife Jane for giving me the time and space to pursue my scholarly passions.

From Karen Starr:

It has been my great pleasure to collaborate with Lewis Aron on this project for the past three years. Lew is a generous and enthusiastic mentor and study partner, always welcoming a good argument. I have immensely enjoyed learning from him and with him. Researching, developing, and writing this book has been an extraordinary psychoanalytic education in itself, and I am greatly appreciative of the opportunity to be immersed in the history, cultural background, and critical debates of our profession.

A special thank you to Jill Bresler, Alice Cheyer, Barry Cohen, Elaine Epps, Caryl Frohlich, Dodi Goldman, Ed and Debbie Horowitz, Janice Kalin, Alan Kintzer, Sam Kintzer, Arielle Shanok, and Joan Viscardi, whose steadfast friendship, love, and support have sustained me throughout this project.

A book imparts knowledge, but it is life that gives understanding. To my children, Jenna, Rachel, and Benjie, may you grow to be like Sarah, Rebecca, Rachel, and Leah, like Ephraim and like Menashe, and may life give you understanding.

Chapter 1

Introduction

A Psychotherapy for the People

In this book we argue for a progressive and humanistic vision of psychoanalysis. We will show that to its detriment, American psychoanalysis has historically defined itself by contrasting itself with its other—psychotherapy—thereby limiting its own range and scope. We call for a broader and more flexible definition, one that has practical implications for how psychoanalysis and psychoanalytic therapy are theorized, taught, and practiced, and that includes psychoanalysis as a social and humanistic enterprise. When asked by Anthony Molino whether psychoanalysis was a dinosaur, close to extinction, Christopher Bollas wittily remarked, "Psychoanalysis just has to survive 'the psychoanalytic movement' " (Molino, 1997, p. 59). In its efforts to preserve the purity of its methods and protect the status of its practitioners, the psychoanalytic movement has threatened itself with its own extinction. As Stephen Mitchell cautioned,

> It is tempting to preserve the purity of one's practice and work only with patients—generally other mental health practitioners—(or else the very wealthy) who will play it the traditional way—four times a week, the couch, free association and interpretation, and so on, but that is not feasible for most practitioners. Even if it were, it would be hard to avoid a sense of bad faith, that one is preserving one's purity at the price of turning away people seeking help.
>
> (1991, pp. 150–151)

This book is about how psychoanalysis has historically been defined and how it might be understood in the 21st century. We present a cultural and intellectual history that supports our thesis that psychoanalysis has always defined itself in opposition to something else, something it viewed as "other." In its early years, that "other" was suggestion. Psychoanalysis was not hypnosis and its results were not based on suggestion. In the years following World War II and through the 1950s, the psychoanalytic establishment officially defined psychoanalysis as a sub-specialty of psychiatry and as distinct from psychotherapy. These were "the halcyon years" of psychoanalysis in America, the era of consensus (Wallerstein, 1995), "the golden age" (Coser, 1984, p. 47). Viewed as the most scientific form of psychological treatment, psychoanalysis rose to the height of its prestige and popularity. Analysts had lengthy waiting lists and few free hours, and psychoanalysis was one of the highest paid medical specialties in the country (Hale, 1995).

Leo Rangell memorably articulated the consensus leading to these definitions:

> The two disciplines [psychoanalysis proper and psychoanalytic psycho-therapy], at far ends of a spectrum, are qualitatively different from each other, though there is a borderland of cases between them. An analogous comparison can be made to the fact that conscious is different from unconscious. *Day is different from night, though there is dusk; and black from white, though there is gray.*
> (Quoted by Wallerstein, 1995, p. 81; see Rangell, 1954, p. 737, emphasis added)

This masterful piece of rhetoric illustrates how analysts of this era chose to emphasize the differences between psychoanalytically-oriented psy-chotherapy, sometimes referred to as psychodynamic psychotherapy, in contrast to "standard," "classical," or "proper" psychoanalysis. These analysts knew there were many areas of overlap between the two modes. They knew that elements of psychotherapy were always implicated in psychoanalysis proper, and that psychoanalytic psychotherapists used many aspects of standard psychoanalysis. And yet, "day is different from night, though there is dusk." They chose to emphasize the differences rather than highlight the similarities and gray areas. Psychotherapy and psychoanalysis were not just differentiated—they were polarized. Defining psychoanalysis in opposition to psychotherapy set up two poles "at far ends of a spectrum," creating two disciplines, rather than one discipline with a variety of applications. This polarization has been detrimental to all aspects of psychoanalytic theory, practice, and education.

Following World War II and through the 1950s, these postulates dovetailed with the American valuation of self-reliance and the heroic image of the lone cowboy riding off into the sunset. Psychoanalytic values were aligned with polarized notions of masculinity versus femininity and heterosexuality versus homosexuality. Homosexuality was treated as psychopathology and homosexuals were not admitted to psychoanalytic institutes. The cowboy riding off into the sunset was not yet envisioned as being on *Brokeback Mountain* (Ang Lee, 2005). Analysis was defined as superior to psychotherapy as masculinity was to femininity, autonomy to dependence, heterosexual to homosexual, and phallic to castrated. Psychoanalysis led to internal structural change, creating a strong agent, while psychotherapeutic change was devalued as being due only to relational factors, leaving the patient with structural deficits.

Historically, suggestibility was associated with primitivity, degeneracy, women, hysterics, neurotics, and Jews (Brickman, 2003). Considered the product of advanced European civilization, the autonomous individual required renunciation and hence, abstinence (Van Herik, 1982). The issue of suggestion raised serious problems for Freud. He needed to eliminate suggestion in order to make his findings objective, scientific, and universal, rather than idiosyncratically Jewish (Gilman, 1993a, b; Frosh, 2005). In America, suggestion and suggestibility were associated with interpersonal influence and dependence. If you improved because of interpersonal influence or reliance on your relationship with your therapist, you were not helped to be as autonomous as you might be. Under the domination of ego psychology, the principle of ego autonomy became the rationale for determining which interventions defined psychoanalysis. Heinz Hartmann's championing of ego autonomy was in keeping with American values and the European idealization of the autonomous individual. It was believed that the analyst should rely almost exclusively on interpretation so the patient would do as much of the analytic work as possible: the patient's exercise of his own ego muscles would lead to structural change. An analyzable patient was one who could tolerate the analyst's doing very little; an analysis was complete when the patient could analyze himself with the analyst no longer necessary. In short, self-reliance, independence, and autonomy constituted the requisite conditions for analyzability, the analytic process, and the goals of analysis. In contrast, everything involving suggestion was viewed as dependence; all relational factors were reduced to suggestion. If a patient seemed to get better because of reliance on the therapist, a transference cure, it was considered superficial, external behavioral change, rather than deep, internal structural change, because the patient remained dependent rather than becoming autonomous.

Binaries proliferate. Psychoanalysis was historically associated with deep change, psychotherapy with superficial change; psychoanalysis with internal change, psychotherapy with external change; psychoanalysis with insight, psychotherapy with support. Psychoanalysis was for more psychologically developed, analyzable patients, while psychotherapy was for less developed, un-analyzable patients. Psychoanalysis was civilized, psychotherapy primitive. Psychoanalysis required frustration tolerance, impulse control, long-term planning, and postponement of gratification. These were all functions associated with white, middle class values, and so psychoanalysis was White and wealthy in contrast to psychotherapy, which was for those without such values or finances—Blacks, minorities, and the poor. Altman wrote,

> Since . . . the definition of ego strength occurs in a cultural context, the culturally or socioeconomically different patient, if accepted into analytic work at all, is not likely to get the elite version of the treatment. The elite status of psychoanalysis as a treatment modality is thus protected by reserving the "pure gold" for elite patients. The hierarchical class structure of society is thereby replicated in the analytic subculture.
>
> (1995, p. 45)

This gives troublesome new meaning to the phrase "Day is different from night, though there is dusk; and black from white, though there is gray."

Psychoanalysis proper was viewed as pure, while all other uses were considered applied. Of course, psychoanalysis proper was just as much the application of a theory and method as was psychoanalytic art criticism, child analysis, or analytic group therapy. But it was as if the analytic community accepted the fiction that the original method was uncontaminated, an application of a pure practice. Psychoanalysis was defined as pure gold, while psychotherapy was tainted with copper. This polarization aligned with the traditional splits between pure and applied science, theory and practice, abstract and concrete. All of these binaries lined up with masculine versus feminine, civilized versus primitive, and in anti-Semitic Europe, with Christian or Aryan versus Jew (Jews were thought too concrete to be good scientists). Internal and intrapsychic, psychoanalysis was about understanding one's own mind, whereas psychotherapy was about solving external problems. Psychiatric medicine, which dominated psychoanalysis in "the golden years," was largely male, whereas the "salvation army" of women social workers was left to solve concrete problems. Danto (2009) has documented this split between psychoanalysis and social work in terms of the division of labor between men and women, as well as the tendency for psychoanalysts in America to be less radical and eschew social and political action. Cushman (2009) has argued that this unbridgeable chasm between the individual and the social resulted from the Cartesian split between spirit and matter, mind and body. In post-World War II America, psychoanalysis valorized depth, inner life, internalization, and the bounded individual self.

We add the following to this argument: the dichotomy between psychoanalysis proper and psychotherapy is one of a series of polarities built into the structure of psychoanalytic thought. That which is social, cultural, political, interactional, and interpersonal, because they set limits on the individual's autonomy and self-contained independence, leave us vulnerable. These factors are culturally marked as feminine, and so were split off and projected onto psychotherapy. From the point of view of the mainstream psychoanalysis of that classic era, they were "not-me" phenomena. These polarities are based on the split between civilized and primitive, mature and immature, Oedipal and pre-Oedipal, conflict and deficit, guilt and shame, science and magic, cure and care. We will show that psycho-analysis is situated in the midst of a hierarchical division of binaries into male/female, heterosexual/homosexual, white/black, and gentile/Jew. This is why we find racism, misogyny, anti-Semitism, and homophobia to be surprisingly relevant to the fundamentals of psychoanalysis.

Treatment versus Care

In the modern era, treatment and cure have been associated with science, progress, intervention, and accountability, whereas care has been relegated to the intangibles of relationship, morale, support, and palliative gestures. Consistent with an era that emphasizes fast, pragmatic results, empirical support, cost-effectiveness, and measurable outcomes, treatment is assigned the status of science, subject to metrics, whereas care is devalued as being personal and relational, unmeasurable and intangible. Rooted in a long history of gender discrimination and misogyny, especially within medi-cine, which for centuries was an all male profession, treatment is cast as scientific, assertive, penetrative, and essentially male, while care, associ-ated with resignation and passivity, is marked as female. Common gender stereotypes and gender bias, as well as their related aspects—misogyny, homophobia, racism, and anti-Semitism—continue to haunt psychological theory and practice, with adverse effects.

Since its inception, professional medicine was almost exclusively the province of men; this remained true in America until the 1960s. With the modernization of medicine, doctors became intent on presenting them-selves as providing effective treatment, in contrast to nurses, who provided only care. Care was primarily what the male physician had to offer before the invention of modern medical science. But as the doctor came to see himself as a member of a new elite—a scientific, progressive, and highly educated profession—he diagnosed, prescribed, and treated using modern medical interventions and instrumentation, becoming uninterested in wasting his time simply providing care or support. Feminist historians Ehrenreich and English wrote,

> Healing, in its fullest sense, consists of both curing and caring, doctoring and nursing. The old lady healers of an earlier time had combined both functions, and were valued for both. (For example, midwives not only presided at the delivery, but lived in until the new mother was ready to resume care of her children.) But with the devel-opment of scientific medicine, and the modern medical profession, the two functions were split irrevocably. Curing became the exclusive province of the doctor; caring was relegated to the nurse.
>
> (1973, p. 651)

We will show that psychoanalysis aligned itself with the masculine-oriented medical model of treatment, relegating care and all that was associated with the feminine to the purview of psychotherapy.

Autonomy versus Relationality

Taking into consideration the above binaries, the very idea of "relational psychoanalysis" was historically quite literally an oxymoron. To the extent that a treatment relied on relational factors, it was by definition psychotherapy and not psychoanalysis. Let us be clear: we do not envision a simple reversal, in which contemporary psychoanalysis should value relationality over autonomy. Rather, in our view, psychoanalysis must be dialectical, valuing relationality and autonomy, agency and communion. The very name "relational" psychoanalysis can be misleading if it is thought to exclude agency or individuality. Stephen Mitchell's understanding of relational psychoanalysis was dialectical, transcending the one-sided usage of the term relational. He never intended a relational psychoanalysis to omit consideration of individual subjectivity. In clarifying what he meant by a "two-person psychology," Mitchell and Aron (1999) wrote, "These emergent properties of the dyad exist in dialectical relation to the individual subjectivities of the patient and the analyst" (p. xv). An excellent example of Mitchell's (1997) usage of this dialectic notion of autonomy and relationality is his statement, "Personal autonomy is not something that antedates interaction with others, but an emergent property of interactive processes, not something that can be sheltered from influence, but something that grows *through* influence" (p. 21). Relational psychoanalysis is an attempt to move beyond simple binary reversals, to find freeing options when faced with immobilizing deadlocks, both in theory construction and clinical practice. However, our call for a progressive psychoanalysis is not a brief on behalf of relational psychoanalysis or any other school of psychoanalysis. Mitchell's comparative, integrative, and dialectic sensibility remains his most enduring and inspiring legacy (Aron, 2003, 2005).

Years ago, one of us had an experience worth relating directly in the first person: I (Lewis Aron) had just completed my psychoanalytic training at the NYU Postdoctoral Program in Psychotherapy and Psychoanalysis. I was with my mentor, Donald Kaplan, a highly regarded Freudian analyst from New York. At the time, I was not yet on faculty. A young graduate of the program, I had thrown my hat in with the relationalists. Don, with whom I continued to have a wonderful relationship, never stopped teasing me about my becoming more relational in my thinking. We were with a group of the Freudian faculty and were all getting into an elevator; it was very casual and jovial. We were in the elevator, and I don't exactly remember what led to the remark, but Don was talking to me about "you relationalists," in front of the faculty, who were all men. He said (laughing),

"You relationalists, come on, you just want to hold hands, you don't wanna fuck." At the time, I didn't have the presence of mind or the maturity to respond quickly, but this joke captures everything that was wrong with the way psychoanalysis was defined. Psychoanalysis was a masculine phallic thing, in contrast to psychotherapy, which included everything that was degraded, castrated, and devalued, because of its emphasis on the relationship. For the Freudian faculty at that time, relational psychoanalysis and other "deviations" such as "neo-Freudian revisionism" or Kohutian self-psychology were "perversions" of psychoanalysis. Their practitioners were viewed as doing psychotherapy rather than psychoanalysis.

We write as clinicians and educators of clinical psychologists and psychoanalytic therapists. Our goal is not to trace history for its own sake or to make an intellectual contribution suitable only for academic purposes. We believe the future of our profession hangs in the balance. The binaries we have identified continue to haunt contemporary psychoanalysis. On a practical demographic level, psychoanalysis has changed from being an almost exclusively male to a predominantly female profession. Gender and the women's movement have played a significant role in the theoretical shift from the dominance of classical theory to the ascendance of relational and other revisionist theory. Yet underlying prejudices remain deeply embedded in our fundamental concepts. They must be exposed and subjected to radical critique.

In the golden age of psychoanalysis, there was a good deal of consensus about what psychoanalysis was and how it should be defined. But in 1985, as psychoanalysis was breaking up into multiple schools, Roy Schafer introduced the methodology of comparative psychoanalysis, which had not before been necessary. As long as psychoanalysts were able to say that an alternative theory was "not psychoanalysis" but a deviation, there was no need for comparative psychoanalysis. Considering what might be meant in a contemporary age about "wild analysis," Schafer recognized that with the shift to multiple perspectives, what it meant to be wild had become relative to one's orientation. He emphasized, "our ideas of sound technique and appropriate lines of interpretation are necessarily defined by contrast with what is not acceptable" (Schafer, 1985, pp. 275–276). With the proliferation of multiple theoretical models, psychoanalysis can only be defined in the context of a comparative methodology. We suggest that rather than teaching the either/or approach of psychoanalysis or "not psychoanalysis," or psychoanalysis versus psychotherapy, or psychoanalysis versus "wild analysis," all psychoanalysis be taught comparatively.

We are not alone in arguing that psychoanalysis and psychoanalytic education should be more inclusive. But no one has systematically shown how psychoanalysis was defined in contrast to psychotherapy, or why the two have been viewed as incompatible and contradictory. The implications are profound. By stressing the similarities among its various applications, we can make psychoanalysis much more amenable to integration, attracting clinicians who think psychoanalytically even though they do not conduct psychoanalysis "proper" (four or five times per week, using the couch). In this regard, we are pursuing suggestions made by Emanuel Berman (2004a) who argued, "the core of psychoanalytic training is not the teaching of any specific technique or any specific theoretical model but the development of a unique state of mind and of particular sensitivities . . ." (p. 228). While we may differ from Roy Schafer (1983) in precisely what constitutes the "analytic attitude," we would still argue that psychoanalytic education must transmit the analytic attitude to new generations of analysts. As Berman contends, while exploration of the differences between psychoanalysis and psychotherapy is of interest, at a time when all psychodynamic approaches are under attack, "an overemphasis on such inner dividing lines may serve the narcissism of small differences while neglecting the crucial contemporary debate about legitimacy and value of psychoanalytic treatment as a whole" (p. 228). We have often felt that the bickering among psychoanalysts about what "counts" as psychoanalysis, what theory, how many times per week, whether or not the couch is used, what school of thought is included or excluded, is nothing more than rearranging the chairs on the Titanic as the ship is sinking. Ours is not one more effort to shift the chairs. We believe the ship needs to turn in a very different direction.

We argue for a broad definition of psychoanalysis that encompasses the full range of its theories, applications, and methodologies. This includes "psychoanalysis proper" and "psychoanalytic therapy," as well as what has generally been thought of as "applied psychoanalysis;" not only the several times per week clinical analysis of private practice but also the full range of clinical, educational, and social applications in the community and inner cities of America.

The Dialectics of Marginality

In his intellectual history of psychoanalysis in America, Paul Stepansky (2009) refers to *Psychoanalysis at the Margins*. He suggests that like homeopathy, osteopathy, and other forms of alternative health care, psychoanalysis is no longer a part of American mainstream medicine. Stepansky does not point to this marginalization with disparagement but rather suggests that life at the margins of medicine may have its advantages. We agree, but argue even more forcefully that it is at the margins where psychoanalysis thrives and where it is best ethically located. Throughout this book we show how psychoanalysis is at its best when it transcends a variety of binaries, maintaining the position of what has sometimes been called "thirdness," or a dialectical approach. We demonstrate that Freud and the early analysts were at the margins of their society. Being at the margins gave them their edge and allowed for the invention and development of psychoanalysis. Being at the margins is what allows for reflexive self-awareness, the ability to look at oneself as both subject and object, without being caught up in one pole or the other (see Aron, 2000).

The term "optimal marginality" was first used by the sociologist Neil McLaughlin (2001) in a study of Erich Fromm, who was at the margins of mainstream psychiatry, psychology, and psychoanalysis, a non-medical, non-orthodox, Marxist analyst and émigré. Building on McLaughlin's conceptualization, Bos, Park, and Pietikainen (2005) showed how Freud and the early analysts, as well as psychoanalysis as a profession, could each be understood as "optimally marginal." While it might seem that the very idea of marginality implies its polarization from the center, Bos, Park and Pietikainen found that marginality was itself a dynamic and dialectical process because the center and margins mutually influence and define each other. The marginalizer and the marginalized are bound by a common understanding of what constitutes the mainstream; thus marginality involves a surprising degree of cooperation between the center and the margins. Marginality is used strategically to achieve certain goals. Stepansky (2009) acknowledges that marginalization can encourage innovation and group cohesion and suggests that one might speak of "optimal marginality" or advocate the "dialectical interaction" between marginal forces and the mainstream (p. 13). These terms do not signify depreciated outsider status. Optimal or dialectical marginality are terms that best express the position of Freud and many of the early analysts. In fact, dialectical marginality is a more accurate description of psychoanalysis throughout its history, with the exception of the years immediately following World War II in the United States, in which it achieved a peculiar insider status. We show that this so-called golden age was actually a short-lived symptom—a manic defense against loss and vulnerability. We support optimal or dialectical marginality by demonstrating the configuration of binaries within which psychoanalysis has too often been trapped.

The status of psychoanalysis as a cohesive discipline has always been in some question, but the doubts have intensified in recent decades as psychoanalysis has become increasingly diverse in its theorizing. Some have celebrated theoretical pluralism as a sign of health and vitality, a defeat of authoritarianism and intellectual monopolization, and an indication of creativity and generativity. To others, this diversity is a worrisome signal of fragmentation, further evidence of the field's crisis and decline. Stepansky maintains that psychoanalysis is no longer a cohesive profession, but rather "a loose federation of psychoanalytic subcommunities" (p. xi), whose proponents no longer see the world the same way. He argues that this "fractionation" has coincided with the dramatic contraction and marginalization of the field in the wake of managed care, competition from other therapies, the expansion of psychopharmacology, and demands for empirical research (p. xvii).

In accord with our effort to deconstruct binaries, we do not view theoretical pluralism as exclusively a symptom of fragmentation and fragility, nor do we believe it should be idealized as a signal of health and vitality. Rather it is a natural or understandable stage in the development of psychoanalysis, following a long period of domination by ego-psychology, but one that needs to be balanced by coherence and gradual integration before new challenges arise. Binary thinking, or what analysts call "splitting," is not in and of itself pathological, but a necessary step in development, a transitional way of managing tensions before integration is possible. In other words, we believe there should be a continuing dialectic between coherence and diversification.

We also approach the debate about theoretical pluralism in broadly cultural terms. America, like many areas of the world, is currently witnessing serious apprehension about immigration, assimilation, and diversity. Issues of multiculturalism and pluralism dominate the country's concerns. Similarly, psychoanalytic theory and practice are highlighting issues of multiplicity of the self and the connection of multiple self-states to fragmentation and dissociation. This concern with the ancient problem of "the one and the many," coherence and multiplicity, unity and diversity, assimilation and pluralism, is a cultural phenomenon that is being expressed on the many levels of the individual mind and its psychopathology, the nation and its demographics, and theoretical pluralism and professional and interdisciplinary relations.

Examining our internal debates about the unitary cohesive "self" versus "multiplicity" or "multiple self-states" by taking into account social assimilation versus multiculturalism is simply one small example of the relevance of context to an understanding of seemingly clinical matters. Psychoanalysts have too often approached the study of basic concepts without reference to the world beyond, as if applying an intrapsychic methodology or a one-person psychology to their investigation, much as they traditionally studied the individual mind in isolation without attending to its social and interpersonal framework. When some, like Franz Alexander in the 1950s, tried to bring in the sociocultural-economic context, they were dismissed as attempting to bypass the scientific arguments. In recent years, when giving accounts of the development of relational theory within its social and political context, we have been accused of "reducing" theoretical differences to "nothing but politics" (Aron, 1996a). However, our aim is to situate that debate contextually so it can be better understood.

As co-authors of this book we have joined together out of a shared love and concern for the future of psychoanalytic therapy and the profession of psychoanalysis. We are at different phases of our careers and bring two very different perspectives to this work. One of us is the director of the New York University Postdoctoral Program in Psychotherapy and Psychoanalysis, the largest psychoanalytic training program in the country.

The other is a candidate in that program, active on the recruitment committee. Together we approach this topic with a good deal of experience in teaching, supervising, and mentoring, and leadership of and participation in local, national, and international psychoanalytic institutes and organizations. We have a realistic up-close understanding of the present-day concerns of graduate students, the experience of current candidates, and the professional considerations of the next generation of psychoanalysts. In presenting our work together as collaboration, we evoke Bion's (1962) notion of "binocular vision," the constant conjunction of multiple vertices (points of view) that leads to common sense. Our hope is that by bringing together our different perspectives, and by trying to speak the truth of our experiences, we can approach a challenging topic with what is often uncommon: common sense.

The marriage of two points of view produces a third, more integrated view, a new product, an unknown; this happens in all areas of human activity. Our approach is thoroughly deconstructive in that we examine how fundamental concepts in psychoanalysis are structured along the lines of a binary—incompatible, mutually exclusive dichotomies. We try to break down these binaries by attending to what Derrida (1976) called "undecidables," those gray areas, shadows, and ghosts that do not fit neatly into established categories. In recent years, psychoanalysts have been calling these undecidables as they coalesce into a new structure "the third" (Ogden, 1994; Aron and Benjamin, 1999; Benjamin, 2004; Aron, 2006), while others have preferred speaking in terms of paradox (Ghent, 1992) and dialectics (Hoffman, 1998). Contemporary psychoanalysis has tried to move from an either/or to a both/and approach in an attempt to move beyond being caught in doer/done to, push/pull tugs of war. We will pay particular attention to the ways in which psychoanalysis and psychotherapy, as well as numerous key psychoanalytic concepts, became structured along binary either/or lines.

Psychoanalysis is thriving. Psychoanalysis is dying. Must it be one or the other? We reject this dichotomy too. Psychoanalysis is vital, growing, expanding, and thriving, while it is also in serious decline. Psychoanalytic books continue to be published and new psychoanalytic journals continue to appear. Institutes continue to teach; our urban centers often have at least two competing institutes. Students still apply for training with excitement and enthusiasm. Psychoanalysis still turns people on. And yet, viewed from another angle, psychoanalysis has clearly suffered from decline in status and demand, fewer applicants to our institutes, fewer patients, greater competition, less reimbursement, higher demands for empirical research, less support in departments of psychology, and almost none in psychiatry. Sales of psychoanalytic books are at an all-time record low. How do we understand this seemingly contradictory observation? How can psychoanalysis survive? How can it once again flourish?

We believe we have an answer: While psychoanalysis continues to be the best promise we have for a humanistic, engaged therapeutic pursuit of meaning and relationship, what went wrong is that psychoanalysis in America became arrogant, self-protective, self-serving, and increasingly narrow and limited. Its strategy was to define itself in idealistic terms, as pure and classic. It was very careful to differentiate itself by way of contrast even with the most analytic of psychotherapies. Some felt that to do anything less would be to obscure important differences and water down psychoanalysis; with the best of intentions they sought to be precise and scientific. But behind this rationale was also the need to protect the higher income and status of the psychoanalytic profession. We believe this narrowing of definition—and along with it, of practice, flexibility, and identity—led to the decline of interest in psychoanalysis. Interest in psychotherapy has not declined, but the vast majority of psychotherapists are no longer interested in such a narrow and seemingly rigid approach to treatment.

Psychoanalytic Harms

If psychoanalysis is going to transform itself, it must begin by acknowledging its errors. During its decades of dominance, psychoanalysis did not always use its power wisely. Haughty and arrogant, it caused harm to individuals, communities, and large segments of the population.[1] For example, some analysts treated homosexuality and "perversion" in the hope of "conversion." Others thought of these "conditions" as not analyzable as "these people" were by definition prone to action and "acting out" their impulses and so could not be analyzed. Homosexuals were not accepted for psychoanalytic training. Consider these public remarks by Ralph Roughton (2002), who had "come out" only five years earlier, after a lifetime of hiding his homosexuality for fear it would ruin his career as an analyst.

> As we now welcome the new, respected [homosexual] colleagues who are beginning to theorize that experience, *we should pause to acknowledge the injustice and pain that we psychoanalysts created for generations of gay men and women*. Unknown numbers of them were intimidated by the reality of discrimination and did not apply to become candidates. Some did apply and were rejected when they revealed their homosexuality. Others of my vintage made painful internal compromises to become

---

1 We recognize that sexual boundary violations by analysts have caused a great deal of harm to patients. However, we will not address this issue here, as sexual boundary violations can occur in any doctor–patient relationship, and our specific focus is on harms unique to psychoanalysis.

psychoanalysts; we paid the price of maintaining a false front, with its blunting of authenticity and stunting of creativity.

Several years ago, I met with a group of gay psychiatrists at the American Psychiatric Association to explain our new policy of nondiscrimination, expecting it to be received as good news. But the pain and rage in some of those who had once wanted to be analysts were intense. As one man said, with barely controlled tears and anger, "You have to understand; people's lives were affected."

Our profession was also affected. Think of the tragic deprivation that we purchased for ourselves by denying qualified people the chance to become psychoanalytic contributors, simply because they were gay. Even when our profession held very wrong ideas about female development, we did not exclude women from becoming analysts. In contrast, prior to the 1990s, there were no openly gay voices among our membership to challenge our errors—only the protesting voices from the couch, which were too easily dismissed as resistance.

(2002, pp. 735–736, emphasis added)

In these lines, Roughton addresses the harm to the profession and professionals. But he goes on to discuss the harm to all people—not only to homosexuals but also to "straight" men and women who were encouraged in their homophobia, directed toward others and themselves. How much was the public hurt by psychoanalysts who, under the guise of science, publicly, arrogantly, and condescendingly spouted homophobic and outright hateful attitudes? How much harm was done to others because we were left with a developmental theory that was incomplete and inaccurate, as we had inadequate data because of these practices? Wasn't it harmful to everyone that analysts believed they could distinguish between "perversion" and "normal" sexuality? If an analyst sitting behind the couch decides at some point in an analysis that you are too "perverted" to be analyzable and so cuts you off, tells you to sit up, and that you need to be referred out for psychotherapy, is it any big surprise that they find "castration anxiety" in your associations?

Psychoanalysis encouraged women to accept that sexual feelings and impulses were normal at a time when many women did not believe that to be so. It encouraged many women to enter the field and celebrated many women as leading psychoanalytic contributors. We do not question the value or benefits of psychoanalysis, but here we address the harm it caused. How much harm was caused to women who were told by their analysts and by analytic authorities that clitoral masturbation was immature? How many women were encouraged to stay home rather than work because of the use and misuse of analytic theories of gender and sexuality? How much harm was caused to people's marriages and families because analysts, endorsed by the authority of Freud and science, used analytic theory to encourage conservative and stereotyped gender norms? How much harm was caused to men whose own gender and sexual biases were reinforced by conservative analytic attitudes?

Psychoanalysis' premise of a psychological cause for almost every ailment caused serious harm to families. Many parents were led to believe or were told outright that their children's difficulties, such as autism, learning disabilities, and behavioral problems, were caused by parental psychopathology and that the parents needed individual psychoanalytic treatment. Parents of children with developmental disturbances that were not yet well understood (for example, a child who today would be diagnosed with Asperger's) were told that the child's difficulties resulted from the parents' marital conflicts or individual pathology. Psychoanalysis blamed parents for children's schizophrenia (recall the famous "schizophrenogenic mother") and autism ("icebox parents").

What harm was caused to people with regard to such clinical psychoanalytic notions as "analyzability"? We know of people, some of whom are now prominent analysts, who were told they were "unanalyzable" and should seek help from a supportive psychotherapist. They were told to sit up, the analysis was over; they were not analyzable and needed to be referred. People were told, for example, that anyone who was deeply religious could not be analyzable because they were too dependent and irrational. Analysts, following Freud, could be passionately anti-religious while believing that this was simply a scientifically objective observation. Freud's Enlightenment ideal of science saw it as liberating the individual from the illusion of religion. Religious belief was "a lost cause," a "childhood neurosis" (Freud, 1927, p. 53). Consider this statement by Otto Fenichel, from his 1939 classic *Problems of Psychoanalytic Technique*, a text that influenced the theory and practice of psychoanalysis for decades—even to our own day:

> It has been said that religious people in analysis remain uninfluenced in their religious philosophies since analysis itself is supposed to be philosophically neutral. I consider this not to be correct. Repeatedly I have seen that with the analysis of the sexual anxieties and with maturing of the personality, the attachment to religion has ended.
>
> (Fenichel, 1939, p. 89)

How many analysts discouraged their patients from using other forms of treatment, including medication? Patients were told that to consult another therapist was "acting out." They were told that to join a psychotherapy group would interfere with their analysis, as would use of psychiatric medication. Analysts discouraged patients from utilizing 12-step programs such as AA. Analysts who ran groups in addition to seeing patients in individual analysis could be shunned or viewed as not doing authentic analysis.

It was the Osheroff case that eventually led to changes with regard to psychoanalysts and the use of medication. Raphael Osheroff, a medical doctor, was hospitalized for severe depression in the early 1980s at Chestnut Lodge, the famous psychoanalytically-oriented hospital in Maryland, the professional home of analysts such as Frieda Fromm-Reichmann and Harold Searles. He was treated with analytic psychotherapy but without medication. After seven months with no improvement, his family transferred him to Silver Hill hospital, where he received antidepressants and recovered within a few weeks. Osheroff returned to his practice and then sued Chestnut Hill for failure to treat him properly. The case was settled out of court. While no legal precedent was established, the case had an enormous impact on psychoanalytically-oriented psychiatry. From then on, treating a depressive patient without medication left a practitioner vulnerable to charges of malpractice. This case may be seen as a turning point, a professional wake-up call ushering in an era when psychoanalysts would have to consider that without empirical validation they could be accused of offering patients less than standard care. Psychoanalysts were put on notice (Paris, 2005). The Osheroff case also raises questions about how long to continue with any therapeutic procedure if the patient does not seem to be responding. Certainly, at least some patients have been harmed because analysts did not forthrightly discuss their lack of progress, along with various options the patient should consider. While it is now quite common to treat patients using a team approach, for example encouraging a patient to participate in a Dialectical Behavior Therapy group, or to take psychiatric medication while in individual analytic treatment, there was a time when this was discouraged out of fear it would split and complicate the transference.

How many patients were treated in analysis for years because they had peptic ulcers, which were thought to be psychosomatic disorders? In the 1980s, doctors discovered the bacteria that usually cause ulcers; since then, most people are easily treated with antibiotics. Of course, we do not blame analysts for trying to help ulcer patients when in fact stress can play a contributing role, and of course we cannot be responsible for discoveries that have not yet been made. What we can criticize is the arrogance with which pronouncements of psychological causes for physical ailments were made and inflicted on patients.

There are other groups of people that psychoanalysis has harmed over the decades. We have in mind other therapists, non-analysts, those using other modalities such as group and family therapy, as well as those using other orientations such as behavioral, Gestalt, or Jungian approaches. While in positions of dominance, analysts could easily treat those from other schools or traditions with condescension and devaluation. What would it have been like to practice Gestalt therapy or cognitive-behavioral therapy only to have those in power dismiss your work as superficial, anti-intellectual, or as simply manipulation, not to mention as "perversions" of "real" treatment? Is it any surprise that there are mental health professionals who have been glad to see psychoanalysis brought down a few pegs? The analysts who dominated the psychoanalytic mainstream did not treat the so-called "dissidents" with any greater respect. They too were dismissed and derided. How many colleagues were hurt? How many enemies were made?

We want to emphasize a key point with regard to all of these harms. None of the above changed because analysts learned from analytic experience that they should change their ways. The improvements did not come about by analysts listening to each other's case reports or comparing cases using "analytic methodology." Analytic case presentations did not lead to the realization that homosexuality should not be treated as pathology. They did not lead to a reevaluation of our theories of gender and sexuality or to the decision to stop blaming parents for their children's autism, schizophrenia, or learning disabilities.

Rather, all these developments came about because analysts lost some of their power within medicine, psychiatry, and the culture at large. With that loss of power came protests and challenges, sometimes supported by scientific evidence. The American Psychoanalytic Association did not approve a non-discrimination policy for homosexuality because there was new scientific evidence that homosexuality was not pathology—there never had been any scientific evidence establishing that it was to begin with! They changed their attitudes because society changed, more and more people were disillusioned with psychoanalysis, and there were increasingly vehement protests. This turnabout in psychoanalytic theorizing can best be understood in terms of what Foucault called power-knowledge.

> Knowledge linked to power not only assumes the authority of "the truth" but has the power to make itself true. All knowledge, once applied in the real world, has effects, and in that sense at least, "becomes true." Knowledge, once used to regulate the conduct of others, entails constraint, regulation and the disciplining of practice. Thus, there is no power relation without the correlative constitution of a field of knowledge, nor any knowledge that does not presuppose and constitute at the same time, power relations.
>
> (1977, p. 27)

Is it really any wonder that we perpetually hear of "the crisis of psychoanalysis"?

Toward a Progressive Psychoanalysis

Erich Fromm (1970), in his book *The Crisis of Psychoanalysis*, attributed the crisis to the ascension of ego-psychology, which he criticized as being a conformist dilution of European psychoanalysis. Although written more than 40 years ago, the opening lines of his book sound as though they might have been penned today:

> Contemporary psychoanalysis is passing through a crisis which superficially manifests itself in a certain decrease in the number of students applying for training in psychoanalytic institutes, and also in the number of patients who seek help from the psychoanalyst. Competing therapies have emerged in recent years which claim to have better therapeutic results and to require much less time and hence, of course, much less money. The psychoanalyst, who ten years ago was considered by the urban middle class to have the answer to its mental anguish, is now put on the defensive by psychotherapeutic competitors and is losing his therapeutic monopoly.
>
> (Fromm, 1970, p. 12)

We have been deeply influenced by Fromm, who argued that some orthodoxy kept the appearance of an original teaching but lost its essential spirit. Fromm advocated for a revision of Freud's teachings that would adapt them to new problems and situations, while paradoxically, more faithfully maintaining and perpetuating their radical spirit. This dialectical view argues that the revisionist (or reconstructionist) may be more faithful to the spirit of the original than the orthodox. Our argument for a more open and inclusive definition of psychoanalysis may appear radical and may seem to some as though it abandons the specificity of psychoanalytic education and practice, but we view our approach as a return to the early analysts' open, free, innovative, humanistic, social-activist, and more progressive spirit.

How should psychoanalysis respond to its crisis? Several suggestions have been made. Kernberg (1986, 1996, 2000, 2006, 2007, 2010), in a series of penetrating writings about psychoanalytic education, has argued in favor of a combined model of university and art academy as the most promising path. He calls for a more diverse student body, the freedom to challenge authority, and a spirit of scientific inquiry. Yet Kernberg (1999) continues to base his recommendations on a careful delineation of the differences between psychoanalysis, psychoanalytic psychotherapy, and supportive therapy. As he admits, these distinctions do not hold up for those from relational, self-psychological, or interpersonal orientations. Kernberg's model only works by excluding large numbers—perhaps the majority—of American psychoanalysts! This is an excellent example of the troubled intersection of theoretical pluralism, the definition of psychoanalysis in contrast to psychoanalytic therapy, and psychoanalytic education. Does it really make sense in today's world to base a definition of psychoanalysis and the structure of psychoanalytic education on a theoretical model that excludes many if not most psychoanalysts, or for that matter, on a model that excludes even minority groups of practicing analysts?

Reeder (2004) makes clear that even within the IPA, "Psychoanalytic institutions must in time accept that in the future, analyses taking place more than three times per week will most probably be the exception" (p. 232).

He calls on institutes to affiliate with a university in the teaching of interdisciplinary courses; giving students more choice in curriculum; making room for more independent study; and giving them access to courses on quantitative and qualitative research that might be useful in communicating with third-party financiers and other institutions that psychoanalysis will depend on in the future. Like Kernberg, Reeder calls for greater diversity among students, both geographically and in terms of academic background. Aligning himself with the findings of Kirsner's (2000) study of the culture, organization, and group dynamics of four American psychoanalytic institutes, Reeder has called for the abolishment of the training analysis system while maintaining a completely independent personal analysis as a requirement for candidates. Although Reeder was addressing international psychoanalysis, he writes, "What is respected in the United States tends to deposit as authority in Europe" (p. 73).

Yet another option that has been suggested is the broadening of psycho-analysis beyond psychoanalytic training as a clinical specialty, transforming it into the academic university-based discipline of Psychoanalytic Studies. Providing an overview of Psychoanalytic Studies in British universities, Stanton and Reason (1996) suggest there is fear among psychoanalysts that such a university-based, non-clinical program of education would blur the lines between "clinical" and "applied" psychoanalysis. Once again, these authors trace the roots of this fear to transformations in the mental health field that have hurt psychoanalysis, especially reduction in session frequency, which weakens the clinical distinctiveness of psychoanalysis. Nevertheless, for proponents of Psychoanalytic Studies, there is an important shift from psychoanalytic cure to psychoanalytic education. "Universities provide the educational and research environment where psychoanalytic studies can survive—the alternative is inward-looking, antiquated and small-scale institutions inevitably marked by a siege mentality" (Hall, 1996, p. 72). They argue that it would free psychoanalytic education from the inhibiting worries of training clinician practitioners and the accompanying responsibility to the public.

Emanuel Berman's writings on psychoanalytic education have been particularly influential for us. Berman (2004a) called for increased innovation and democratization of the educational process; teaching a broad spectrum of psychoanalytic psychotherapeutic techniques in addition to standard psychoanalysis; relating psychoanalytic education to the humanities and social sciences; and paying particular attention to the influence on psychoanalytic theory and practice of specific cultural, gender, national, and racial issues in order to understand the total reality of patients. He outlined many of the problems created on a practical level when candidates treat a patient in psychoanalysis for their institute requirements. For example, the patient may need to cut back on frequency and then the candidate is caught in a bind, where they may need the patient to continue attending more frequently to meet their own educational requirements, and so the patient's needs and interests may not receive first priority. Berman does not minimize the differences between seeing a patient more or less frequently, but he does argue that for educational purposes, we are better off emphasizing the similarities between various forms of psychoanalytic therapy rather than differences. An advantage of emphasizing similarities over differences is that it facilitates psychotherapy integration. Paul Wachtel's (1987, 2008, 2011) work is a model for the kind of psychoanalysis we are arguing for here. His broad approach has enabled him to integrate various modalities such as individual, couple, group and family, various schools of psychotherapy from behavioral to cognitive to psychoanalytic, and various orientations within psychoanalysis. Wachtel does not downplay the differences among these modalities. Rather, his broad approach to understanding psychoanalysis allows him to include their contributions into his own integration. Wachtel's (1983, 1999, 2002) progressive definition of psychoanalysis also encourages a passionate social activism, including contributions to the study of poverty, class, race, culture, economics, and politics. This definition promotes a politically responsible psychoanalysis and prepares future psychoanalysts to adapt psychoanalysis to new challenges.

Historically in America, mainstream psychoanalytic associations did not actively support community psychiatry. No viable tradition of community psychoanalysis was established, even though numerous analysts contributed as individuals. The mainstream associations did not put their resources and prestige into supporting community psychoanalysis because it was not the individual "pure" clinical psychoanalysis with which they had defined themselves as a medical sub-specialty. We are deeply moved by the work of our colleague, Neil Altman (1995, 2010), who in *The Analyst in the Inner City* makes the strongest case for an expanded vision of psychoanalysis that goes well beyond the practice and the clinic to include child, adolescent, family, group, and community levels of intervention across race, class, and cultural lines. This is precisely the progressive approach to psychoanalysis that should be taught in our institutes, without the hindrance of differentiating community psychoanalysis from some narrow, so-called "pure" version that retains its exalted status.

Elizabeth Danto (2005) has carefully documented the passionate social activism of Freud and the early psychoanalysts. Freud, Wilhelm Reich, Erik Erikson, Karen Horney, Erich Fromm, and Helene Deutsch were not just private practitioners concerned with psychoanalysis as a prestigious sub-specialty of psychiatry. They were out to change the world! They viewed psychoanalysis as a movement for social change and education, and as a challenge to conventional politics, social mores, and sexuality. Individually and as a group, they were dedicated to the free clinic movement established to provide "psychotherapy for the people" (Freud, 1919d, p. 168). Danto shows that in psychoanalysis' initial revolutionary years, the early psychoanalysts did not split themselves off from child analysis, group work, short-term treatments, trauma therapy, educational reform, or social and political movements. Psychoanalysis *was* psychotherapy, not its other. Unfortunately, this humanistic tradition of social activism and community psychoanalysis was left behind in Europe when psychoanalysis rose to its heights in America following World War II. If psychoanalysis is to survive, this progressive tradition must be reestablished and brought into the mainstream.

Let's get right to the heart of our thesis as it relates to the present and future of psychoanalysis. We believe that psychoanalysis is a discipline, comparable to literature, physics, law, or medicine. We do not think the word should be used solely to describe a particular treatment strategy; rather, we believe it should be used to describe a broad field of study that takes into account the psychology of unconscious factors. We have no objection to referring to three, four, or five times per week treatment using the couch as "psychoanalysis proper" or "formal psychoanalysis" if these terms help people differentiate between one form of application and another. We would argue, however, that if one is using well-developed psychoanalytic ideas to work with a patient less frequently, then applying psychoanalysis in that way is just as much a utilization of psychoanalysis as any other approach. We are not in any way devaluing the benefits of increased frequency or use of the couch for some patients, at some times, in some settings, with some therapists. Nor are we in any way suggesting that all therapy is the same, that differences are unimportant, or even that they are less important than we used to think. It certainly makes a difference whether someone is seen alone, in a group, or in a family context. It matters whether they sit face to face or use the couch, go for a walk with their therapist (as Freud sometimes did) or conduct a therapy on horseback (as Ferenczi did). Our point is not to diminish the significant differences between therapeutic approaches. What we are suggesting is that within the scope of the discipline of psychoanalysis, there is a wide range of ways of helping people, all of which may be legitimately referred to as applications of psychoanalysis.

The traditionally troubled relations between psychoanalysis and the university have their origins in the problems faced by Freud and his Jewish followers in the 1890s when confronted with the anti-Semitism of the Austrian government, which controlled the medical school system of academic advancement. We describe how the development of psychoanalysis originated with a small group of Jews who surrounded Freud in Vienna. These Jews often went into medicine precisely because it was a "free" profession that promised upward mobility. Medicine offered them the opportunity to pursue a livelihood outside of the public institutions, hospitals, and universities that denigrated and excluded them. An often overlooked aspect of its early history is that the rise of psychoanalysis was due to the efforts of a number of men, including Freud, Abraham, Jones, and Ferenczi, among others, who harbored unfulfilled academic ambitions. The psychoanalytic movement offered these men a framework for conducting research and scholarship, teaching, developing journals, and acquiring organizational positions outside of academia. The disconnection of psychoanalysis from the university has played a significant role in the schismatic tradition of psychoanalysis in the context of a parochial and doctrinaire private institute structure.

We began this introductory chapter by identifying ourselves as affiliated with the New York University Postdoctoral Program in Psychotherapy and Psychoanalysis, one of very few programs of psychoanalysis housed within the graduate school of a major university. Lewis Aron is a graduate of this program and has served as its director since 1998. For over 30 years, since he began as a student in 1980, this has been his major professional home and affiliation. Karen Starr is a candidate in the program, having begun her analytic training in 2008, following the publication of her book, *Repair of the Soul: Metaphors of Transformation in Jewish Mysticism and Psychoanalysis* earlier that year. She has been actively involved in teaching psychoanalytic ideas to graduate students and in recruitment for the program, and is intimately familiar with the challenges of psychoanalytic education and of attracting new candidates. It is relevant for us to review the particular context in which we work and have absorbed psychoanalysis. We believe that our experience at NYU Postdoc, as it is called, has direct bearing on the arguments we make here. NYU Postdoc has 50 years of experience in trying to solve the problems of psychoanalytic education we have been discussing. The program has always downplayed the demarcation of psychotherapy from psychoanalysis, recognizing their differences, but emphasizing the continuities between them. Because a candidate entering the program brings relevant experience as a therapist, we have always treated candidates as colleagues, adult professionals who already have pertinent experience. This stands in stark contrast to institutes that emphasize the sharp difference between psychoanalysis and psychotherapy. Those more traditional institutes view the candidate's previous experience in psychotherapy as an obstacle that must be overcome on the way to being an analyst! Reeder (2004) asserted that in his study of numerous psychoanalytic institutes:

> One almost always structures seminars as if one were teaching children, with a fixed curriculum and a specified quantum of knowledge to

be acquired. Seldomly does one take after the model of the university and let the candidates compile their own theoretical seminar by choosing from a menu of available courses.

(2004, p. 142)

Kernberg (2000) too, spoke of the infantilization of candidates as well as of the cocoon-like isolation of our educational institutions from intellectual developments in other disciplines. We contend that this infantilization of candidates is a direct result of separating psychoanalysis from psychotherapy. NYU Postdoc is situated within New York University, housed within the graduate school among other fundamental disciplines. A university is the ideal setting for an in-depth investigation of varying orientations. Following the academic tradition and the empirical, open-minded approach of psychology, we can analyze the contrasting metapsychological assumptions of differing theories, compare clinical constructs such as transference, countertransference, and resistance, and contrast different therapeutic approaches and rationales for differing "techniques." As we have seen, it is just this emphasis Roy Schafer highlighted by coining the term "comparative psychoanalysis."

At NYU Postdoc, it has remained a matter of principle that students not be required to declare allegiance to a particular point of view, leaving them free to explore the various offerings in the program as a whole. It was fully anticipated that by the time candidates received their certificates they would have developed a systematic theory, a therapeutic approach derived from their theory, and hopefully, a respect for points of view differing from their own. It was precisely because we agreed with the importance of the candidates' personal analysis that we protected that experience by accepting as personal analysts graduates of other training institutes who have been in practice five years after graduation. In contrast to most other programs, we do not designate "training analysts." As a result, candidates may choose analysts from among our graduates or the graduates of other institutes. The ultimate test of the success of any analysis (for training purposes) is to determine how well the candidate works with their patients and this has to be judged by the supervisors and faculty. Increasingly, the Program has become better integrated with the graduate school and with the University as a whole, offering colloquia, conferences, and courses with other departments, culminating in an NYU Humanities Initiative grant for ongoing interdisciplinary Freud Studies, led by Lewis Aron.

Why is this background relevant? First, it explains how we come to psychoanalysis with an appreciation for and commitment to diversity and a multiplicity of viewpoints. We have spent years immersed in an institution where the faculty has never been able to agree on a monolithic definition of psychoanalysis. The differences between psychoanalysis and intensive psychotherapy have never been highlighted, although of course individual faculty have their own understanding of the advantages and disadvantages of such factors as frequency and the couch. Rather than fit a student into our mold, from the start, we were more concerned with helping the individual use psychoanalysis in a way that best expressed their own individuality, talents, and proclivities. Our assumption was that each candidate would reinvent psychoanalysis for himself or herself and develop a methodology suited for their work with patients in whatever setting and modality they chose.

At NYU Postdoc we do require that a candidate see patients and have their own personal analysis at least three sessions per week. We do this for two reasons. First, it is a compromise among a large faculty with multiple points of view, some of whom completely reject defining psychoanalysis by session frequency. The faculty agreed to live with a three session per week compromise for didactic purposes, so that students would not be caught up in faculty conflict. Second, in recent years, this compromise has allowed us to meet the criteria for accreditation by the Accreditation Council for Psychoanalytic Education (ACPE). We agreed that having such accreditation would be useful for our profession and that NYU Postdoc should support such accreditation, even if not all our faculty agreed with these definitions or criteria.

In some ways our experience at Postdoc has limitations that should be kept in mind. Our candidates come to us already having attained doctoral level degrees and are already state-licensed mental health professionals, usually psychologists. This affords us the luxury of offering a wide range of courses and assuming a high level of clinical competence. We are not in the position of having to evaluate whether or not one of our candidates should be allowed to treat the public—they all are already qualified to treat the public when they enter the program. In addition, postdoctoral education takes our candidates an average of 10 to 12 years to complete, allowing us much greater opportunity to offer courses covering in great depth a wide range of clinical as well as "applied" subjects. We recognize that other psychoanalytic institutes, particularly those educating candidates who have no prior clinical experience and who are not already licensed mental health providers, or even those training candidates with much less clinical experience, must devote a much higher percentage of their educational curriculum to the fundamentals of clinical practice. Yet we would still make the case for a broad approach that does not split off learning about a variety of orientations, modalities, and contexts.

Psychoanalysis: Is it Toast?

A few years ago, *The New York Times Book Review* titled an article "Psychoanalysis: Is It Science or Is It Toast?" The phrasing of that forced choice, science or toast, implies there are no other options that will allow us to survive. So, are we toast? We think not. With all the criticisms and problems, the bottom line is that patients want and need therapists who will listen to them in depth. That is what psychoanalysts do. We listen to people in depth, over an extended period of time, with great intensity. We listen to what they say and don't say, to what they say in words and through their bodies and enactments. We listen to them by listening to ourselves, to our minds, our reveries, and our own bodily reactions. We listen to their life stories and to the story they live with us in the room. We attend to their past, present, and future. We listen to what they already know or can see about themselves, and for what they don't yet know or can't see in themselves. Psychoanalysis is a depth psychology. Despite the claims of managed care, people still want to be listened to in depth and always will. That's why there will always be patients who want and need an analytic approach and why there will always be therapists who want to learn it.

When psychoanalysts speak of "diversity," "multiplicity," and "tolerance," they are usually referring to theoretical pluralism, but we'd like to discuss the issue of diversity within psychoanalysis in other terms, with regard to ethnicity, race, culture, class, religion, gender, and sexuality. A discussion of these issues is essential to the future of psychoanalysis, if psychoanalysis is to remain alive and vibrant. Locally in the New York metropolitan area, and nationally across the United States and North America, psychoanalysis continues in many respects to be homogenous. Although there are notable exceptions, psychoanalysis is overwhelmingly white. The percentage of Jews who participate in psychoanalytic organizations remains dramatically higher than the statistical representation of Jews in the overall population. We have repeatedly heard both private and public comments about the Jewishness of psychoanalysis. These include a non-Jewish friend who describes himself as an honorary Jew because he is an analyst surrounded by Jews; analysts joking about being in a "Jewish profession," anticipating bagels and lox at a professional brunch; and a candidate who confesses to feeling anxious in class because she assumes that everyone else is Jewish, while she is not. We have heard complaints that meetings are often held on Friday evenings when observant Jews cannot attend due to Sabbath travel restrictions, and we have heard from others that Friday evening meetings are a natural alternative to going to Sabbath services! Some Christians in the community have noted feeling excluded by the overwhelming number of expressions of Jewish holiday wishes and discussions about the Jewish history of psychoanalysis.

Marie Hoffman (2011) has written an important scholarly account of contemporary psychoanalytic concepts, arguing that ideas within the relational model can be traced to the Christian narrative. In her view, the relational language of identification, surrender, and gratitude replicate the religious language of incarnation, crucifixion, and resurrection. Hoffman believes that the anti-religious fervor of Freud's writing and the long history of pathologizing religious belief among psychoanalysts have turned the Christian community away from psychoanalysis. She contends that psychoanalysis, which has for so long been dominated by Jewish analysts, has not successfully reached out to Christians and so, at least in America, it has unnecessarily remained a sociologically Jewish discipline. Her book is a significant attempt to reach out to a Christian audience.

We argue that the homogeneity of American psychoanalysis is not limited to religion. At NYU Postdoc, we have established a Committee on Ethnicity, Race, Culture, Class, and Language (CERCCL). We provide several scholarships to promote diversity by supporting students from underrepresented populations within the psychoanalytic profession, as well as assisting those who serve diverse populations. We have had some limited success in recruiting a handful of diverse faculty. Unfortunately, our well-intentioned efforts to recruit a diverse group of students have so far yielded only minimal results.

We have learned from experience that we are drawing from a restricted pool of potentially diverse applicants. As only about 10 percent of graduate students in psychology are considered diverse, the population we draw from is quite homogeneous to begin with. That psychoanalytic psychology is a postdoctoral specialty is a mixed blessing. On one hand, we receive applications from outstanding, highly educated people whom we believe will go on to make significant scholarly and clinical contributions to our profession. On the other hand, limiting our potential candidates to those who have earned a doctoral degree perpetuates the lack of diversity within our training institute. Only a small percentage of those who go on for doctoral degrees are ethnically and racially diverse, a phenomenon that is directly tied to finances and class status. Obtaining a doctoral-level education in psychology is extremely costly. Finding a job in the profession is challenging not only because of the scarcity of positions but also because it takes additional time following completion of the doctoral degree to obtain a state license. It is just at this time that "younger" professionals might likely consider going on for advanced postdoctoral education. In addition to tuition costs, which are especially high in a university setting, there are the costs of personal analysis and clinical supervision and consultation, as well as the enormous commitment of hours that could otherwise be used to support a fledgling practitioner. Embarking on a psychoanalytic education with its associated time and money commitments immediately upon graduation and licensing is a challenging prospect. Therefore, many people wait several years. Such an educational trajectory means we have largely an older profession. The cost of analytic training makes it difficult to diversify the class base of psychoanalytic candidates and skews the age range of analysts upward. Perhaps new licensing laws that create psychoanalysis as an independent profession will attract a wider range of applicants, even if at the cost of lowering the entry-level degree from the doctorate to the master's level. Or perhaps at some point, university-based psychoanalytic programs will award a doctoral-level degree in psychoanalysis itself.

All of these factors contribute to the composition of the community of psychoanalytic psychologists as a largely white, upwardly mobile middle-class, older, and disproportionately Jewish (relative to the distribution of Jews in the general American population) profession. In contrast, some demographics of the profession have changed quite drastically. From the inception of psychoanalysis, most psychoanalysts were men. In fact, the earliest analysts were all men (who treated mostly women) and Freud had to veto a proposal by his Viennese colleagues to officially limit membership in their new society to men, as was done by numerous professional organizations at the time (Gay, 1988). Almost two decades have passed since Ilene Philipson (1993), then a sociologist, now a clinical psychoanalyst, wrote *On the Shoulders of Women: The Feminization of Psychotherapy*. Philipson documented the drastic shift in the demographics of the mental health professions, demonstrating that women began entering the profession at a dramatically rapid rate just as the number of men declined. She showed that the practice of psychotherapy was transforming into a predominantly female profession. Philipson argued that these changing demographics had significant implications for theory and practice. It was no accident that relational theory established itself as dominant in the field just as it was becoming a women's profession. If women were the "other" in the traditional "classical" paradigm, then in some ways, men become "other" within a relational model. As the field was devalued and became less financially lucrative, opportunities were presented for women to enter; but as they did, its status further declined.

As psychoanalysis has changed from being a male-dominated profession to one increasingly dominated by women, it has also shifted from being primarily heterosexual (or at least appearing to be) to being open to and accepting of gay, lesbian, bisexual, and trans therapists. A recent issue of *Psychoanalytic Dialogues* featured an article by an openly transsexual psychoanalyst-in-training (Hansbury, 2011). As far as we know, until recently there were very few reports of psychoanalytic treatment of transsexuals—trans people had very good reasons to avoid analysts. Not long ago, psychoanalytic institutes did not accept homosexual candidates, let alone transsexual candidates. Within our own postdoctoral program, there have been various movements to confront and address bias. Over the years, we made a conscious effort to make room for more women on faculty and leadership positions, to reach out to a more racially diverse faculty, and to be receptive to openly gay and lesbian analysts. With each step, it was not simply a matter of attracting a few token individuals, but rather a concerted effort to open up discussion and root out underlying biases in our teaching and presentation. Considering that we pride ourselves on being among the most radically open-minded and democratic of psychoanalytic institutes, the fact that it took us until the

1990s to organize a movement for gay/lesbian inclusion is a testament to the highly conservative nature of American psychoanalytic culture, with its tendency to pathologize the culturally non-normative. Psychoanalysis cannot and should not remain white, Jewish, elitist, urban, or tied exclusively to private practice. If it is going to survive it needs to become increasingly accessible, broadly applied, and diverse.

A young African-American graduate student asks why she should consider investing time and money pursuing postdoctoral analytic education when there is little likelihood she can conduct four or five times a week individual treatment within her own community. An enthusiastic young Latino psychologist who practices in a community health center asks what benefit there would be in his coming for psychoanalytic training when he is determined to reach out to larger numbers of people than he could possibly reach with a psychoanalytic approach. These psychologists might even think of themselves as "psychodynamically-oriented," but would not necessarily want to invest time and money in learning to do psychoanalysis proper. These are exactly the students we want to attract to our program and to psychoanalysis. The vast majority of psychoanalysts today have little opportunity to practice formal psychoanalysis, but psychoanalysis, defined broadly, can make a significant contribution to psychotherapy and to community mental health. We are familiar with the argument that a psychotherapist should learn psychoanalysis because the training will enrich their work even if they never practice formal psychoanalysis. While that is true, as far as it goes, we do not think it goes very far! Most therapists will not spend four, five, and more years of their lives, at significant expense, studying a specialty they will never practice, just for enrichment. This rationale just doesn't hold up. If psychoanalysis in its traditional form is not workable, then let's change it so that it remains sustainable. We can retain its spirit, its essence, while modifying the form in which it is applied.

Steven Stern (2009) hit the nail on the head in saying, "There is an essential, mutually constituting relationship between a profession's name and its clinical practice. Surgeons operate, family lawyers practice family law and teachers teach" (p. 639). Stern is right to point out that in the field of psychoanalysis there has been a breach in this relationship, since so many psychoanalysts no longer believe that what they are doing with their patients is psychoanalysis. For how long will people think of themselves as psychoanalysts if they are in fact not doing what they believe to be psychoanalysis? A profession is defined by a scope of practice, not by a particular technique or procedure. We psychoanalysts have identified our professional status, our very definition of our profession, with one particular technique, one treatment approach. That this is so is confirmed by the fact that, for decades, psychoanalytic institutes refrained from teaching psychoanalytic therapy because they were concerned it would interfere with the analyst's education and analytic identity. One's background as a competent analytic therapist was actually thought to be an interference with learning psycho-analysis rather than an asset.

Freud wrote,

> Psycho-analytic activity is arduous and exacting; it cannot well be handled like a pair of glasses that one puts on for reading and takes off when one goes for a walk. As a rule psycho-analysis possesses a doctor either entirely or not at all.
>
> (1933, pp. 152–153)

An analytic attitude is like this pair of glasses, a way of viewing the world. All that we do while maintaining an analytic attitude is an aspect of psycho-analysis, without elevating one specific application to the status of "pure" and denigrating another application as "applied." They are ALL applied uses of psychoanalysis. The fact that Freud developed his own application of psychoanalysis in the way he did was in some respects an accident of his being a private practitioner. But psychoanalysis has a long history of free clinics, as well as social activism, and it is critical to recall that for a long time psychoanalysis was as much a social movement, a movement for reform in education, social policy, and culture as it was a treatment method (Danto, 2005). Freud (1926b) was appalled by the thought of psychoanalysis being relegated to being nothing but a handmaiden of psychiatry, writing, "we do not consider it at all desirable for psycho-analysis to be swallowed up by medicine and to find its last resting-place in a text-book of psychiatry under the heading 'Methods of Treatment'" (p. 248). Psychoanalysis remains much more than a specific treatment technique. It is a view of the world.

A Psychoanalysis for the People

In the 1950s, at the height of its success in America, psychoanalysis made a choice. That choice was to define itself narrowly in order to maximize its status and prestige. A sharp divide was erected between psychoanalysis on one side and the dynamic psychotherapies on the other. It was thought this would keep the treatment pure, as it had been in Europe, and that it would justify high fees and the high cost of training. It seemed like a good thing for psychoanalysis to be an elite medical subspecialty. This strategy won out over those leaders who had a much more open vision. William Menninger and Franz Alexander lost their bid for psychoanalysis to present itself to the public as a broad-spectrum approach; instead, it became a high-cost, high-class, elitist, exclusive practice for an exclusive clientele. If that is what it remains then it doesn't deserve public support, nor will it attract the most idealistic and committed followers. The early analysts were not mainstream, high-income professionals; they were intellectuals, yes, but they were marginal, barely eked out a living, and that includes Freud himself for many years. They were optimally marginal, as psychoanalysis should be.

Marginality leaves one vulnerable. Being in touch with our vulnerability fuels our moral and ethical sensibility. In its grandiosity, psychoanalysis dissociated its vulnerability by projecting it onto other psychotherapies and onto patients, leaving it and its practitioners overly identified with the heroic and masterful. We suggest that the vulnerable/invulnerable binary is a dynamic structure in need of deconstruction. Homogeneity is dangerous for any discipline. Diversity is key. If our faculty, students, and patient pool truly represent the demographics of our country, psychoanalysis will be forced to adapt and grow.

As Jews and psychoanalysts, we have a particular interest in the intersection of psychoanalysis and Jewish life. We are proud of the monumental contributions Jews have historically made to psychoanalysis, and of the contemporary contributions of so many Jewish analysts. Nevertheless— and we do not view this as a contradiction—we are hopeful that psychoanalysis will not remain a predominantly Jewish science. We do not want psychoanalysis to end up as a course of study mainly taught within departments of Jewish Studies as a modern form of Midrash, although this may be one legitimate way of conceiving it. We retain enough of the Enlightenment Jewish universalism that was so important to Freud to hope with him that psychoanalysis will be widely applicable, adapted by different peoples, cultures, and languages, and that it will emerge in different forms. Will psychoanalysis survive? Yes. But it will not, nor should it, look like it used to. Psychoanalysis as we knew it, as it once dominated departments of psychiatry and inspired the emergence of clinical psychology, is long dead. If, on the other hand, we are willing to consider that psychoanalysis can transform itself, then we can envision a more hopeful future for its continued study, practice, and influence. Visualizing the future of psychoanalysis requires a readiness to see its continuing influence in a form that appears unfamiliar, an experience that can best be described as "uncanny." If we are willing to envision a psychoanalysis for its time, a "psychotherapy for the people," a progressive psychoanalysis that is not our grandfathers' psychoanalysis, then it can have a thriving future.

Chapter 2

Binaries, Polarities, and Thirds

It has been said there are two types of people—those who divide the world into two categories and those who do not. This tongue-in-cheek statement speaks to the truth of our all-too-human tendency to simplify the ambiguities of psychic life by splitting, resorting to either-or solutions, creating dualities, and privileging one side over the other. Speaking of gender polarization, Jane Gallop (1982) wrote, "all polar oppositions share the trait of taming the anxiety that specific differences provoke" (p. 93). Polarization, like splitting, is a way of managing anxiety. It is not inherently pathological, but a necessary step in development. Anxiety discourages thirdness, a perspective from which binary oppositions can be broken down or deconstructed. Psychoanalysis has been plagued by polarized thinking, which has shaped both the development of its theory and its clinical practice. We will review a variety of ways in which contemporary psychoanalysts have attempted to utilize a dialectical approach as a solution to polarization. We will trace this emphasis on dialectics to contemporary currents in postmodernism, deconstruction, feminism, and postcolonial studies, and show the relevance of these interdisciplinary connections for psychoanalysis, in order to pave the way for our later discussion of how psychoanalysis came to define itself in opposition to psychotherapy.

According to F. Scott Fitzgerald,

> The test of a first-rate intelligence is the ability to hold two opposed ideas in the mind at the same time, and still retain the ability to function. One should, for example, be able to see that things are hopeless and yet be determined to make them otherwise.
>
> (1936, p. 69)

Similarly, Ogden (2009) wrote, "Sanity involves a capacity for generating and maintaining a multiplicity of perspectives from which to view/experience one's life in the real world (including the reality of one's own personality)" (p. 97). Deconstructing binaries by examining equivocal cases is one way of thinking about the value of tolerating ambiguity. According to Philip Reiff (1966), "a tolerance of ambiguity is the key to what Freud considered the most difficult of all personal accomplishments" (p. 57).

Freud's genius and his capacity for maintaining complexity often enabled him to transcend the many dualities he created. Yet psychoanalysis has not always been able to move beyond the dichotomies from which it originated. In an examination of Freud's cognitive style, Holt (1989) demonstrated that Freud had a tendency to think in terms of opposed binary concepts, presenting almost all of his major ideas in matched opposing pairs. Consider the following sampling: conscious versus unconscious; ego instincts versus libidinal instincts; narcissistic versus object libido; life versus death instincts; activity versus passivity; ego versus external world; pleasure versus unpleasure; masculine versus feminine; autoplastic versus alloplastic; fantasy versus reality; free versus bound cathexes; primary versus secondary process; narcissistic versus transference neuroses; analyzable versus unanalyzable; phallic versus castrated. Holt noted, "Freud was overfond of dichotomies, even when his data were better conceptualized as continuous variables" (p. 68). The origin of binary choices may be traced back to our earliest decision making, as can be seen in the following quote from Freud's paper on negation, which may be read as explaining binary thinking in terms of repression. Freud wrote,

> The function of judgement is concerned in the main with two sorts of decisions . . . Expressed in the language of the oldest—the oral—instinctual impulses, the judgement is: "I should like to eat this", or "I should like to spit it out"; and, put more generally: "I should like to take this into myself and to keep that out." That is to say: "It shall be inside me" or "it shall be outside me".
>
> (1925b, pp. 236–237)

In other words, in tracing binaries, Freud said that our first choice is whether to spit or swallow, and all follows from that!

Holt demonstrated that in his effort to move beyond simple dichotomies, Freud often "softened" dualities by introducing a third term or maintaining that one term was derived from the other. Holt referred to these softening strategies as "dialectical dualism" (pp. 42–43). For example, Freud softened the duality of id/ego by introducing the superego and positing that ego was an outgrowth of id. Yet he often tended to reduce the three terms back to two opposing positions. This served him well in his emphasis on conflict and ambivalence in psychic life, but left his theory structured around sets of binaries. Another of Freud's strategies was his "complemental series" (Freud, 1917, p. 347), which allowed for the simultaneous consideration of opposing terms, and which he applied to the dualities of heredity and environment, normal and abnormal. In the complemental series, two opposing poles complement one another in inverse proportion. For example, Freud maintained that in understanding the etiology of neurosis we do not need to choose between constitutional and experiential causes, endogenous and exogenous factors, fixation and frustration. Instead, the two factors vary in inverse ratio to one another; for example, a strong fixation requires only a minimal trauma. Yet the complemental series still advocates binary opposition, in which both terms operate together but inversely—more of one term (heredity) means less of the other (trauma). While this allows for a consideration of the relevance of both terms, it is hardly dialectical. A dialectical formulation would recognize that nature and nurture not only work together but also define and constitute one another. The binary must be examined from a third perspective. Much to his credit, Freud was at times able to brilliantly transcend polarized thinking. His formulation of *heimlich* and *unheimlich* in "The 'Uncanny'" (1919e), for example, involves two terms that appear to be polar opposites. Freud demonstrated that upon close examination, each of these terms moves toward having the same meaning. (See Chapter 14 for a detailed discussion.)

This dualistic tendency in Freud's theorizing led to much of the later criticism of his metapsychology, in which dichotomies abound. Freud's metapsychology was based on an energic model of the mind. The tendency of the psychic apparatus toward discharge or inhibition of discharge led to the idea of unbound versus bound, or freely mobile versus tonic energies, where the freely mobile energy seeks discharge and the bound energy inhibits discharge. In this view, the freer and more plastic the instinctual system, the greater the need for structure to inhibit the discharge. The notion of unbound versus bound energy, or energy versus structure, led to Freud's formulation of primary versus secondary process, unconscious versus conscious, drive versus defense, id versus ego. Fairbairn's (1944) attempt to deconstruct the difference between energy and structure, to show that they were one and the same and not opposed, was at the heart of his critique of Freudian metapsychology. Yet by concluding that libido was object-seeking rather than pleasure-seeking, Fairbairn perpetuated yet another problematic binary opposition. We even speculate that Freud's conception of primary process as a realm in which contradictions do not exist was a reflection of his conscious logical theorizing in terms of opposed binary oppositions.

A key binary in both developmental thinking about the etiology of psychopathology and clinical consideration of the role of the analyst was the question of whether a drive was gratified or frustrated. For many years, analysts considered parental behavior almost exclusively in terms of whether the parent was too frustrating or gratifying, as if these were the only choices in viewing the problem of the patient's childhood. Similarly, Mitchell (1988) pointed out that the focus on whether the analyst was being too frustrating or gratifying avoided a more nuanced examination of other qualities of the therapeutic relationship.

Binary Oppositions in Contemporary Psychoanalysis

In their classic *Object Relations in Psychoanalytic Theory*, Greenberg and Mitchell (1983) differentiated between the drive-structure and relational-structure models of mind, a dichotomy central to their comparative psychoanalysis. Struck by "the deeper divergence" between the two models (p. 398) and profoundly influenced by Isaiah Berlin's analysis of the history of political theory, Greenberg and Mitchell applied Berlin's thinking to the history of psychoanalytic theory.

Of Russian-Jewish origin, Isaiah Berlin was a British social and political theorist, philosopher, and historian of ideas, regarded as one of the leading thinkers of the 20th century and the foremost liberal scholar of his generation. His best-known work, *Two Concepts of Liberty*, was presented in 1958 as his inaugural lecture at Oxford. In this classic essay, Berlin differentiated two broad traditions of political philosophy. The first, closely associated with the political philosophies of Hobbes and Locke, viewed the function of the state as enacting laws that prevented interference with individual fulfillment. The state provided what Berlin called "negative liberty." The second tradition, traced from Aristotle through Rousseau, Hegel, and Marx, began with the assumption that the individual could only achieve satisfaction within a social community. One only becomes fully human through recognition by, and participation with, others. The state provides a necessary positive function, not only protecting individuals from interference with their individual satisfactions, but also providing a regulated social network, what Berlin called "positive liberty."

Greenberg and Mitchell understood Berlin to have argued that these two opposing political philosophies were incompatible and mutually exclusive visions of the role of government. Berlin granted that both concepts of liberty represent valid human ideals, and both forms of liberty are necessary in any free and civilized society. These differing concepts showed the plurality and incompatibility of human values, and he emphasized the need to distinguish between, rather than conflate them. According to Greenberg and Mitchell, Berlin argued that attempts to combine these two models were unsuccessful because they rested on incompatible assumptions. We highlight their quote of Berlin because it provides insight into the strategy Greenberg and Mitchell adopted for their study of psychoanalysis. Berlin said,

These are not two different interpretations of a single concept, but two profoundly divergent and irreconcilable attitudes to the ends of life. It is well to recognize this even if in practice it is often necessary to strike a compromise between them. *For each of them makes absolute claims.*

(cited in Greenberg and Mitchell, 1983, p. 403)

Greenberg and Mitchell maintained that the drive and relational models within psychoanalysis embodied these two major traditions within Western philosophy. Freud's drive model emerged out of the same philosophical assumptions as the concept of "negative liberty" described by Berlin. "The drive model of the mind, like the negative liberty model of the state, takes as its fundamental premise that the individual mind, the psychic apparatus, is the most meaningful and useful unit for the study of mental functioning" (p. 402). In contrast, "within the relational/structure model of the mind and the positive liberty model of the state, human fulfillment is sought in the establishment and maintenance of relationships with others" (p. 403). From this, Greenberg and Mitchell believed, it followed that the drive and relational models were incompatible opposing visions that could not be successfully combined without twisting each of them out of shape. Just as Berlin argued that mixed models in political philosophy had not worked, Greenberg and Mitchell argued that mixed models in psychoanalysis did not work. Mixed conceptual models such as those of Joseph Sandler or Heinz Kohut had failed. "These failures suggest an intrinsic incompatibility between the drive/structure and relational/structure models, one which can be neither overcome nor circumvented" (p. 378).

While Greenberg and Mitchell noted that "human life reflects a paradox—we are inescapably individual creatures; we are inescapably social creatures" (p. 403), they argued that models that tried to build a theory on the basis of the human being as *both* an individual *and* a social animal encountered irreconcilable difficulties, as these were fundamentally incompatible visions of human life and meaning. In their conclusion, they wrote,

The paradox of man's dual nature as a highly individual yet social being runs too deep and is too entrenched within our civilization to be capable of simple resolution in one direction or the other. It seems more likely that both the drive model and the relational model will persist, undergoing continual revision and transformation, and that the rich interplay between these two visions of human experience will generate creative dialogue.

(1983, p. 408)

Greenberg and Mitchell did *not* presume that one theory would win out over the other, but they *did* believe that one had to choose between theories. The theory one chose would depend on one's point of view. In other words, although the relational model would later pride itself on emphasizing a both/and rather than an either/or approach, the very basis for the distinction between drive and relational models was an either/or split, a dichotomy! While Greenberg and Mitchell recognized that the tension between the view of human beings as individuals or as social beings represented a universal paradox, they argued that it was impossible to build a rational theory on the basis of a paradox without having it collapse. Furthermore, since each model could explain it all, and yet neither model could decisively be proven as more accurate or useful than the other, it was unnecessary to combine them, as either one could explain all that needed to be explained. One was left, therefore, to simply choose which model appealed to you as an individual, with no need for holding on to both.

Soon after the publication of this instant classic, Mitchell set out on a highly successful and inspirational mission to champion the relational approach to psychoanalysis. Heated debates ensued over questions such as why the relational model could not make room for the notion of drives. Followers and dissenters argued as though one vision of psychoanalysis could emerge victorious over the other, as though the relational model could defeat the drive model, or vice versa. Greenberg and Mitchell, it should be noted, had not argued that one paradigm could win out over the other. For them, the vision of the human being as individual or social animal was paradoxical, and led to rationally incompatible drive or relational theories that did not need to be reconciled or synthesized. One had to choose. That choice was largely based on one's sensibility; each theory was logically consistent and explained it all. Mitchell himself remained quite cautious about relying on the notion of paradox to build a rational theory. But soon after the establishment of the relational approach, it was commonly asserted that relational theory was based on the acceptance of paradox and the tolerance of ambiguity.

In the last years of his life, Mitchell's energy was diverted to responding to accusations made by his critics, who often reiterated that the main problem with his work was his assumption of dichotomous positions. They wrote of his "reduction of contemporary debates to an either/or choice," "dichotomous thinking" (Richards, 1999, p. 6), and "proclivity to polarization" (p. 9). Mitchell was assailed for perpetuating "sharp polarities" (Smith, 2001, p. 510) and for his tendency to "misrepresent the experience of analysis itself, for the degree to which he [Mitchell] pits one position against another, building his argument on a series of such polarities" (p. 496). He laughed at this representation of himself as "The Dichotomizer," marveling at the irony of being depicted as threatening like "The Terminator," but beneath his good-hearted sense of humor lay a feeling of disappointment at being so misunderstood by his critics.

The "Deconstructor"

Painting a very different portrait of Mitchell, Aron (2003) related Mitchell's work to aspects of his character, demonstrating a unifying theme. Mitchell employed his methodological strategy both in his momentous theoretical breakthroughs and in navigating clinical stalemates. In working out theoretical entanglements, Mitchell first laid out before his readers two contrasting approaches to a problem and then showed how, by examining the problem from a different level of abstraction, one could find a third alternative reconciling the tension between the first two. Similarly, when dealing with therapeutic impasses, Mitchell learned to tolerate, sustain, and identify the entrapped states in which he found himself until he could free his imagination and gradually discover some third avenue along which to proceed. These methodological approaches were central to Mitchell's development of relational psychoanalysis. Mitchell typically presented what seemed like an irreconcilable conflict, but then dismantled this either/or choice by reaching for a third option, by transcending the concrete level of the problem and examining it from a third point of view, which revealed an aspect of truth in both of the original incompatible propositions. He showed that structuring the problem in simple binary terms obscured more than it clarified and impeded the search for a constructive solution.

Mitchell emphasized that when he and Greenberg first introduced the idea of relational psychoanalysis, they were seeking to overcome an unnecessary split in psychoanalytic thinking by bridging the notion of external interpersonal relations with intrapsychic object relations. For Mitchell, the intrapsychic and the interpersonal were mutually constituting transformations of one another. It was precisely because overcoming dichotomization was such a fundamental aspect of his methodological approach that he was so astonished and demoralized when critics accused him of being a "dichotomizer." We understand Mitchell's frustration in light of his overwhelming emphasis on moving beyond forced binary choices, but as we will now show, there was some truth in his critics' accusation, and Mitchell knew that at times one had to make hard choices between incompatible alternatives. In fact, he greatly appreciated the existential value of making such choices.

Just before his untimely death, and in reply to Benjamin's emphasis on the notion of paradox (which we will review shortly), Mitchell (2000b) expressed concern that analysts were overusing the concept of paradox. He was particularly concerned that it could be used to avoid making difficult choices, to rationalize immobilization and remain entrapped in existential fright, restricting the exercise of will in choosing how to live one's life. This was his reaction when he was asked why there was no room in relational psychoanalysis for drive theory. Mitchell always answered that one could construct such a theory, but that he viewed such efforts as attempts to have it all, to refuse to make a clear choice, to avoid taking a stand and renouncing some alternatives. This is an unspoken and under-theorized aspect of relational theory, one that has led to numerous arguments and debates that have left all sides feeling frustrated and misunderstood. Relational theory has championed both/and thinking, for example, in its recognition of the need for both intrapsychic and intersubjective visions, for one- and two-person psychologies. Nevertheless, when it came to the drive versus relational paradigm, Mitchell insisted that it was a dichotomous choice and one had to choose between them. In this particular case, he was not willing to call for a paradoxical acceptance of both/and. He viewed that strategy as a cop-out, which would result in an aesthetically unappealing mishmash of theory.

The centrality of capital "D", "Drive" in Freudian explanations became the single concept that was undigestible in Mitchell's "relational" integration. That this was not inevitable, however, can be seen in recognizing that Jay Greenberg (1991), Mitchell's collaborator in the initial description of the drive/relational divergence, included Drive formulations as central to his own relational approach. In spite of Mitchell's caution with regard to paradox, one way of viewing the emergence of the relational tradition in the 1980s is as a movement toward a theory that contained paradox by emphasizing multiplicity and process over binary choices. This at least opens up the possibility that at some point a new effort to integrate drive and relational theory will emerge, fueled by the very emphasis on dialectic and thirdness that characterized contemporary relational theory following Mitchell.

Paradox in Relational Psychoanalysis

Benjamin (1988) and Ghent (1992) described the longstanding tendency among psychoanalysts to polarize concepts, employ either/or thinking, and resort to reductionism, leading to theoretical schisms. They contended that a more sophisticated contemporary psychoanalytic theory must be able to sustain paradox; in Winnicott's (1971) terms, to allow paradox to be tolerated, respected, and left unresolved. Building on Winnicott, Ghent (1992) joined Mitchell at the NYU Postdoctoral Program in the creation of modern relational theory. He wrote,

> I believe we are witnessing currently an important development in psychoanalysis. Almost since the beginning, our field has been marked by reductionistic dissension of one sort or another: "It's not this; it's that!" As a result there have been innumerable theoretical divergences, dialectical swings. Now, however, I believe there is a chance for a new outlook, one that is built on the capacity for entertaining paradox. I do

not mean synthesis, which ultimately attempts to dispel paradox. Likewise, it is not simply a matter of a dialectical process, nor is it a syncretistic effort to combine theories that are based on different premises and are therefore incompatible.

(1992, p. 156)

Influenced by Thomas Ogden, Irwin Hoffman, and Jessica Benjamin's contributions, Ghent anticipated that the differing concepts of dialectics, paradox, and process would be misunderstood, and so added a footnote in an attempt to clarify his own thinking.

> The argument has been made that my usage of paradox and process is really very close to the notion of the dialectic. Insofar as I see paradox pointing the way to a new level of understanding that is as yet unclear, it begs an understanding of the process that relates the apparent opposites. As this understanding comes about, the paradox gradually vanishes, and is often replaced by a new paradox, a new pointer to the as yet not fully understood. From this perspective, the use of paradox is very much like dialectical thinking, where, indeed, there gradually evolves a synthesis between the opposing pulls. However, there is another perspective, one that is rooted in subjective experience. The value of holding on to paradox in the more static sense, the not precipitously seeking after resolution or synthesis, is exactly what Winnicott is emphasizing—that what is so vitally important is being able, subjectively, to hold on to the apparent contradiction, to live with and gradually integrate it, and not to flee it by rushing into a premature intellectual understanding of the process that underlies it.
>
> (1992, p. 156)

Jessica Benjamin's (1988, 1995) intersubjectivity theory, specifically her conceptualization of "thirdness" (Aron and Benjamin, 1999; Benjamin, 2004), is a compelling effort to move beyond polarized dichotomous positions. Benjamin's theorizing repeatedly attempts to move beyond simple oppositions: subject and object, subjectivity and intersubjectivity, connection and difference, assertion and accommodation, doer and done to. She has been careful not to allow simple reversals to substitute for holding the tension of paradox and struggling for a position of "thirdness" that transcends both polarities (see Aron, 2006).

One of Benjamin's key contributions is the notion of complementarity. Complementarity is characterized by splitting, in which one side takes a position complementary to—the polar opposite of—the other. If one person is experienced as the doer, the other becomes the done to (Benjamin, 2004); if one is the sadist, the other becomes the masochist; if one is the victim, the other becomes the victimizer; if one is male, the other becomes female; if one is active, the other becomes passive. Polarities are split between the two members, and the more each one locks into a singular position, the more rigidly the other is locked into the opposing, complementary position, heightening the split and tightening the polarization. At any time, the split may be reversed without changing the structure of the complementarity. The active member may become passive while the passive member becomes active; their roles are switched, but the dyadic structure remains split between activity and passivity. Benjamin (1988) analyzed this manifest exchange of roles without a change in the underlying relational structure, demonstrating that it constitutes a simple reversal that maintains the old opposition. She developed her initial work in this area in the context of her study of (heterosexual) gender relations, especially in analyzing relations of dominance and submission and the structure of sadomasochism. She later further developed these understandings, applying them to a variety of clinical and social contexts.

Another of the foremost contributors to relational psychoanalysis who has centered his approach on the basis of dialectics is Irwin Hoffman (1998), who elaborated a theory of "dialectical-constructivism." A dialectical relationship exists when there is a tension between two types of experience and yet neither can exist without the other, such that when one is figure, the other is ground, but together they comprise a whole. Central to Hoffman's contribution was his examination of the many dialectical relationships in psychoanalysis, including the interpersonal and intrapsychic; the analyst's visibility and invisibility; analytic discipline and self-expression; analyzed and unanalyzed interactions; associations and interpretations; authority and mutuality; boundaries and intimacy; construction and discovery; conviction and uncertainty; expressive participation and critical reflection; hierarchical and egalitarian relatedness; the individual and the social; initiative and responsiveness; subjectivity and objectivity; meaning and mortality. Having developed a framework that emphasized dialectics over polarization, Hoffman eschewed the sharp differentiation of psychoanalysis and psychotherapy:

> For the kind of analytic-therapeutic process that I am interested in, the distinction between psychoanalysis and psychoanalytic psychotherapy is irrelevant . . . I am proposing a single psychoanalytic modality in which there is a dialectic between noninterpretive and interpretive interventions.
>
> (1998, p. xiii)

In Hoffman's dialectical-constructivist framework, the gold of psychoanalytic interpretation and the copper of interpersonal influence become dialectically enhancing.

Like the other relational theorists we have examined, Harris (2009) suggests "what might characterize the relational turn is the attempt to find a way to go from either/or to both/and" (pp. 370–371). Harris and Aron (1997) traced this approach back to Ferenczi, whose semiotic theory broke down the dichotomy between speech and action. Ferenczi's (1911) early paper on obscene words viewed speaking as a form of action. He contended that speaking a charged set of words promotes regression in both the hearer and the speaker. Harris and Aron wrote,

> Ferenczi suggests that there is a regressive and encapsulated power in obscene words because both the sounds and mode of production are dominated by primary process. The particular graphic term will carry the feelings and experiences of the patient/speaker much more powerfully because the affects and fantasies associated with these words remain remote from more abstract meaning systems.
>
> (1997, p. 528)

Building on this work, Harris writes,

> Embodied cognition, the interdependence of emotion and cognition, the materiality of words and sentences, the transpersonality of mind and subjectivities, the study of intentionality and theory of mind as an outcome of early dyadic life—all these new domains of work and research move us far beyond the old dichotomies. The focus on speech and action, on the embodiment and intersubjectivity of speaking and listening, is at the heart of relational ideas.
>
> (2009, p. 371)

Among the most creative and influential writers in psychoanalysis, Thomas Ogden's (1986) early utilization of dialectical process led to his distinctive notion of "the analytic third" (Ogden, 1994), a central pillar of intersubjectivity theory and one of the richest and most intriguing clinical concepts in contemporary psychoanalysis. Drawing on Kojeve and Hegel, Ogden (1986) defined dialectic as "a process in which each of two opposing concepts creates, informs, preserves, and negates the other, each standing in a dynamic (ever-changing) relationship with the other" (p. 208). According to Ogden, while the dialectical process moves toward integration, the integration is never complete; each integration creates a new dialectical opposition with its own newly emerging dynamic tension. Ogden focused on "the potential space" between the poles of conscious/unconscious, reality/fantasy, and the interpersonal and internal psychological environment, demonstrating that this transitional space constitutes the matrix of the mind.

We will examine Ogden's approach to psychoanalysis in Chapter 18, but here will illustrate his theoretical use of paradox and the centrality of this concept to his thinking. Drawing on Bion, Ogden utilized the notion of "binocular vision" to indicate that in psychoanalysis, truth refers to being able to perceive from multiple perspectives simultaneously. This simultaneity of perception from across multiple angles facilitates the move beyond binary oppositions. For example, whereas psychoanalysts have long debated whether psychoanalytic truths or interpretations were "discovered" or "constructed," Ogden (2005) found a way to view this forced choice in dialectical terms: "What is true is a discovery as opposed to a creation; and yet in making that discovery, we alter what we find, and in that sense create something new" (p. 66). Ogden's vision is paradoxical. Notice that it is not left in terms of an inverse relation: the more discovery, the less creation, and the more creation, the less discovery. Rather, Ogden shows that discovery itself includes an alteration of what is found; discovery and creation constitute and depend on one another.

Psychoanalysis has been hindered by its preoccupation with binaries, polarized between theorists and schools that emphasize drive or culture, self or object, attachment or separation, autonomy or relationship, the individual or the social, the intrapsychic or the interpersonal. In our own dialogue and development, we as psychoanalysts become stuck in impasses and stalemates, locked in heated battles between representatives of these polarized positions. Each school stares across the divide into its mirror image, locked in complementarity. Conceptualizing the third is one attempt to move beyond such oppositions and create triangular space, within which psychoanalysis, too, can think more freely, open dialogue, and grow and develop.

Depths and Shallows

A central polarity that has plagued psychoanalytic theory and practice is the opposition between inner and outer, intrapsychic and interpersonal, or more generally, inner life and outer behavior. This has often been framed in hierarchical terms, in which the inner world is depicted as deeply layered and the outer is associated with the superficial; hence "depth psychology" is equated with inner experience and intrapsychic conflict, and social psychology is disparaged as shallow. Psychoanalysis is characterized as deep because it focuses on the inner world, and psychotherapy is viewed as superficially modifying social behavior. Among the most thorough critiques of this dichotomization, and especially of its limiting clinical implications, has been the lifelong work of Paul Wachtel. Wachtel (1976, 1980) has long argued for a sophisticated and systematic approach to psychotherapy integration, emphasizing that internal and external worlds mutually create one another through processes of assimilation and accommodation, (inner) structure and (interpersonal) transaction.

Wachtel (2009) deconstructs the split between the "inner world" of wishes, fantasies, and affects, and the "outer world" of overt behavior and social reality. For Wachtel, understanding the impact we have on others is central to understanding ourselves, and understanding the impact others have on us requires understanding our own affects and motivations. The inner world is constituted both by our pre-existing structures, past experiences, and dispositions as well as by current life experiences which we shape, and which in turn maintain our inner worlds. We do not simply perceive others based on our inner proclivities. Rather we select others that fit those proclivities, act on them to evoke the responses we anticipate, and then perceive those responses along prescribed lines. Hence others are induced to act as "accomplices" in maintaining our inner structures, not just as "reflections" of those dynamics. We need to understand a person both from the inside out as well as from the outside in, meaning that we need to understand the way the inner world and actual external behavior, structures and transactions, continually recreate and maintain one another. Wachtel's approach does not privilege understanding the person as a center of subjectivity (the inner world) over considering the person as a center of action and agency (in the social world). Rather he advocates,

> [a] dialectical conception in which the seeming contradiction between viewing patient and analyst as centers of subjectivity and viewing them as centers of action is resolved through an understanding of the ways that action and subjectivity constantly and continuously shape and determine each other.
>
> (2009, p. 167)

Self-Interest within Community

Another example of a relational approach based on paradox is Slavin and Kriegman's (1998) use of evolutionary biological theory to describe how our intricate psychodynamic system evolved to guide the ongoing negotiation of the self in the ambiguous, inherently conflicted, relational world. In their view, our minds are shaped within the context of family and the larger culture through interaction with others whose interests inevitably diverge from our own. Within this model of the evolution of mind, dealing with conflict, mutuality, and deception is part of the normal family matrix. For Slavin and Kriegman, self-interest is a natural organizer of human motivation. The patient's skepticism is a natural evolutionary adaptive capacity, functioning in the service of evaluating the degree of overlap and divergence of interests of the patient and the analyst.

This perspective places internal conflict center stage. Resistance becomes an adaptive function that protects one from influence by someone whose interests conflict with one's own. Patients are therefore highly motivated to observe therapists' ways of dealing with their own inevitable conflicts as well as with conflicts of interest between themselves and their patients. Slavin and Kriegman (1998) argue that for an analysis to succeed in helping the patient change, the analyst too needs to change. The analyst's acceptance of his or her vulnerability is essential for patients to recognize their own vulnerability. Therapeutic action requires mutuality—we can expect our patients to reorganize their identities only if we are open to revising our own. Slavin approaches psychoanalysis dialectically, considering meaning and mortality, self and other; he does not oppose the universal to the particular, but rather examines the particular in the context of the universal, and uses the universal to address the role of lived relational experience.

Postmodernism, Feminism, and Deconstruction

Having surveyed the dialectical approach of several contemporary psychoanalytic theorists, we will now highlight the influence of postmodernism and deconstruction, particularly feminist deconstruction, on the current generation of psychoanalytic theorists. Our own approach to deconstructing the binaries that have plagued psychoanalysis has been greatly influenced by the work of Jacques Derrida. For Derrida (1976), Western thought, especially metaphysics, is based on dualistic oppositions that are often value-laden and ethnocentric, and that create a hierarchy that inevitably privileges one term of each pole. The deconstructive strategy does not rest with reversing dichotomies, but rather aims to undermine the dichotomies themselves, and to show that there are "undecidables," items that do not belong on either side of a dichotomy. These undecidables are third terms. Deconstruction contends that in every text, there are inevitably points of undecidability that betray any stable meaning an author might seek to impose. According to Derrida, the dominance of reason, logos, is allied with the archetypically male will to dominate society, which he described as "phallogocentrism."

Feminists such as Helene Cixous (2004) drew upon Derrida's concepts to develop a deconstructive approach to the usual binaries by which men and women, as well as stereotypical male and female characteristics, were polarized, where the male term was always hierarchically positioned superior to the female term, dominating it, with the entire scheme used to dominate women. Cixous argues that masculine sexuality and masculine language are phallocentric and logocentric, fixing meaning through such binary oppositions as father/mother, intelligible/sensitive, and logos/pathos, which rely for their meaning on the primary binary opposition between male and female, phallic and castrated, all reproducing patriarchy and the domination of women. The hierarchization of meaning serves to subordinate the feminine to the masculine. Benjamin (1988) demonstrated that gender was socially constructed, repudiating and splitting off all that was weak and dependent to create femininity.

Modern anthropology and postcolonial studies have also benefited from Derrida's post-structural critique of binary oppositions (Brickman, 2003). Nineteenth-century evolutionary theorists such as Herbert Spencer contrasted primitive savages with civilized Europeans, sorting all of the world's population into one or the other of these two categories. The civilized side of the binary was elevated over the primitive, so that evolutionary theory provided the ideological rationalization used to justify colonialism and other forms of exploitation.

Like Freud, by whom he was profoundly influenced, Derrida always felt himself to be embattled, persecuted by those within and outside of his discipline. Like Freud, Derrida viewed his contribution as a revolutionary force, a dangerous truth that frightened and disturbed the world. He was an outsider, a marginal Jew living in an anti-Semitic world, a leading French public intellectual who always thought of himself, and was perceived as, a Jew from Algiers. As a boy in 1942, without explanation, he was thrown out of school for being a Jew, an event he regarded as a traumatic primal scene (Mikics, 2009). Derrida left Algiers for study in Paris in 1949, but his parents remained until they were forced to immigrate to France after Algeria won its independence and anti-Semitism compelled the Jews to flee.

Derrida's life embodied the paradox of being a modern Jew in modern Europe. Derrida called himself a Marrano (Ofrat, 2001), referring to the Spanish Jews who in response to religious persecution that forced them to convert or die kept their faith while pretending to be Catholic. Their religious identity was indeterminate. It is no coincidence that Derrida, who like Freud experienced himself as on the margins, developed the concept of undecidability. Freud connected the uncanny, that which is both familiar and strange, with ghosts, which were for Derrida a prototype of the undecidable. Neither living nor dead, ghosts don't fit neatly into a category. Derrida himself was uncanny, a quintessential French philosopher who would always be a circumcised Jewish immigrant. To be a Jew is to be a wanderer, never at home, always uncanny, a border crosser, an undecidable.

Derrida's logocentrism refers to the belief dominant in Western philosophy that the spoken word is superior to the written word. The duality spoken/written is based on yet another polarization, that the presence of the speaker in the "logos" or spoken word has special significance, while the written word is devalued by the author's absence. In Christian thought, the same idea was used to devalue Judaism; the presence of the "logos" was contrasted to the rabbinic passion for the written word. Jews were the "people of the book." The dualities of presence and absence thus align with phallic and castrated, Christian and Jew.

According to Derrida, words always mean both more and less than they appear to, to the speaker or listener. Derrida called the gap in meaning "différence," playing on the French word meaning "to defer" and "to differ." Because of this gap in meaning, all meaning is "other," different than anticipated; the meaning of an utterance is inevitably deferred for later. A speaker is not the final authority on the meaning of what they have said. Deconstruction is primarily concerned with what amounts to a critique of the Western philosophical tradition. It seeks to expose and subvert the various binary oppositions that undergird our dominant ways of thinking: presence/absence, speech/writing, male/female.

Western thinking has been founded upon the logic of binary opposi-tions, such as mind/body, rational/emotional, freedom/determinism, man/ woman, and culture/nature. In a manner typical of ideologies, one term is always given a more privileged position than its opposite. The critique of binary oppositions is an important component of feminism, postcoloni-alism, and critical race theory, which argue that the perceived dichotomy between man/woman, civilized/savage, and white/black have perpetuated and legitimized Western power structures favoring "civilized" white men. What is often called paradox Derrida (1992) termed an "aporia," meaning puzzle in Greek. He used the gift as an example. The very giving of the gift can imply the receiver's responsibility to send a thank-you note, thus the gift becomes a debt to return and so is not really a gift. The sharp distinction between giver and receiver, gift and debt, is deconstructed.

Psychoanalysis is replete with just such aporias. As therapists, we accept our patients and ourselves for who we are, even while we can never be satisfied and always want more, both for them and for us. Neither they nor we can change or grow if we don't accept them and ourselves as we are. We must trust ourselves enough to act with some immediacy and spontaneity in the clinical moment, and yet we can't ever take for granted that our motivations and intentions are what they seem to be. We must embrace the paradox of maintaining both a suspicious and accepting attitude toward our patients and ourselves. Freudians have emphasized our suspicious side. Schafer's (1983) analytic attitude stresses an attitude of skepticism— encouraging analysts to always look beneath the surface, listening with what Paul Ricoeur (1970) termed a "hermeneutics of suspicion" (p. 27). In contrast, self-psychology has underscored the need for acceptance, empathy, and validation, listening with something more like what the biblical scholar Tikva Frymer-Kensky (2002) has called a "hermeneutics of grace" (p. 353). While recognizing the importance of the hermeneutics of suspicion, Orange (2011) has argued that in clinical work, it should always be nested within a hermeneutics of trust. Paradox permeates the psycho-therapeutic endeavor. Patients come to us for change, but need to be accepted; they want and need to be believed and yet their most deeply held attitudes and beliefs must be questioned—these are indeed aporias. The idea that we need to change in order for our patients to change begins to break down the sharp polarity of analyst/patient, interpretation/free association, rational/irrational, invulnerable/vulnerable, and objective/subjective.

Derrida's Influence on Feminism

Among the fields most profoundly influenced by Derrida's contributions has been post-structuralist or postmodern feminism. Using Derrida's deconstruction in combination with Michel Foucault's analysis of the relation between knowledge, power, and discourse, third-wave feminists examined the binary oppositions of male/female, man/woman, and masculine/feminine. By reversing the poles of gender and decentering them, they demonstrated that each term was dependent on the definition of the other. Men define themselves in terms of the place of women, such that their power is maintained by keeping women in a powerless position. Gender definitions were viewed as social constructions, contingent rather than natural, although in time, even the binary of contingent versus natural was challenged.

Along with Luce Irigaray and Julia Kristeva, Hélène Cixous, a lifelong friend and collaborator of Derrida's, was known as one of the founders of post-structuralist feminist theory, and was considered by Derrida to be the greatest living writer in French. Cixous and Derrida both grew up as Jews in Algiers, where they each experienced feelings of belonging and exclusion. They were each simultaneously both insiders and outsiders. We would suggest they were optimally marginal. Cixous's (2004) *Portrait of Jacques Derrida as a Young Jewish Saint* explores Derrida's ambivalence about his Judaism and the destabilizing effect of his practice. Toril Moi summarizes Cixous' theories about binary oppositions by presenting a list that includes:

- Activity/Passivity
- Sun/Moon
- Culture/Nature
- Day/Night
- Father/Mother
- Head/Emotions
- Intelligible/Sensitive
- Logos/Pathos
- Nature/History
- Nature/Art
- Nature/Mind
- Passion/Action.

"Against any binary scheme of thought, Cixous sets the *multiple, hetero-geneous difference*" (Moi cited in Grant, 1993, p. 144, additional emphasis added). Influenced by feminism and postmodernism, contemporary relational theorists, especially feminists and queer theorists influenced by post-structuralism, have emphasized multiplicity and difference as a strategy for dealing with problems of identity and its binary other (where there is one there is something other than that one). In fact, as is so often the case, the psychoanalytic literature on multiplicity, which has almost come to define relational psychoanalysis today, is indebted to feminism, but provides little acknowledgment of its influence. Postmodern feminism specifically argues for the diffusion and dispersal of the centered, self-reflective subject among multiple signifying practices. It is often represented by the metaphor of pastiche, a work cobbled together of multiple ingredients. In this vision, there is not dualism of sex but pluralism.

Muriel Dimen (2003), whose academic background is in anthropology, applied her knowledge of social theory and critical feminism to relational psychoanalysis, and vice versa. Bringing into conversation the academic disciplines of biology, psychology, and social theory, her goal is constantly to deconstruct the related dualities of mind/body, body/culture, and culture/mind. In examining the gender normative alignment of mascu-linity with activity and femininity with passivity, Dimen came upon what she called a "whirl of dualisms" that constituted gender as a "force field" (pp. 338–339). For Dimen, dualities lead to reductionism. She points out,

> Many polar pairs line the psychoanalytic landscape—sexuality and aggression, consciousness and unconsciousness, transference and coun-tertransference, analyst and patient, abstinence and gratification, neutrality and participation, intrapsychic and interpersonal, fantasy and reality. Dualism is a problem that therapists know in their bones.
> (Dimen, 2003, p. 6)

We would say that the main argument of our book is to call for the recog-nition that the duality psychotherapy and psychoanalysis must be included on the list of polar pairs that lead to reductionist simplifications.

Similar to Benjamin's (2004) contention that complementarity repre-sents an unconscious symmetry, Dimen (2003) calls duality deceptive: "It looks like two, but behind the two there is really only one; dualism dissolves into monism" (p. 7). Like other feminists influenced by postmodernism, Dimen draws upon both Derrida and Foucault. She writes,

> Dualism's separate-but-equal masks a hierarchy: the one behind the two is always on top. In the table of opposites that have been around since the pre-Socratics—for example, male-female, light-dark,

reason-emotion, mind-body, nature-culture—one term is always implicitly better or higher than the other. Hence the usual deconstructive reading: a binary always conceals a hierarchy.[1]

(2003, p. 7)

Building on Dimen's critique of gender as a whirl of dualisms, Goldner (2011a) identified transgender subjectivities as paradoxical in that they both undermine the gender binary and ratify it. Trans identities may be seen as another example of a Derridean undecidable being used by contemporary critics to deconstruct the binaries of gender and sexuality. Goldner (2003) demonstrates that the gender binary is itself constituted and stabilized by a network of interimplicated and mutually reinforcing oppositions that imply and require one another, and she calls on us to critically deconstruct these dichotomies. In Goldner's view, these binary oppositions are Oedipal formulations; a move to the post-Oedipal entails a shift toward dialectical fluidity.

Dimen argues that intersubjectivity was meant to move beyond the intrapsychic or interpersonal, beyond "one-person psychology" or "two-person psychology." We would clarify that the language of a call for a "two-person psychology" has often been misunderstood in this respect. When Mitchell and Aron (1999) explained their idea of relational psychoanalysis as a "two-person psychology," they clearly stated,

> Relational analysts, in speaking of a "two-person psychology," have never intended to deny that there are two distinct individuals with their own minds, their own histories, and their own inner worlds, which come together in the analytic situation. Rather, the purpose of a "two-person psychology" is to emphasize the emergence of what Ogden calls "the intersubjective analytic third." These emergent properties of the dyad exist in dialectical relation to the individual subjectivities of the patient and the analyst.
>
> (1999, p. xv)

Since its inception, the relational idea of a "two-person psychology" was meant to be a dialectical concept. However, the term "contextual," dialectical," or "field theory" would better capture the intended meaning than does the term "two-person." As Dimen notes, Bromberg's (1996) "standing in the spaces" and Pizer's (1998) "building bridges," are all attempts to move beyond binary thinking toward multiplicity.

Adrienne Harris's (2005) metaphor "gender as soft assembly" utilizes dynamic systems theory and chaos theory to critique and re-envision

---

1 For an overview of feminist poststructuralism, see Weedon (1987); for the application of these ideas to the splitting of autonomy and relationality by gender, see Layton (1998).

developmental theory. She shows that traditional developmental theory, with its "lines of development," is based on the same polarities we have been discussing. Since they are lines, there is no space; one can only move forward or backward in regression or progression (Aron, 2006). The metaphor of lines represents the unity behind polarity. Harris calls for a revised developmental theory that makes room for complexity, contingency, and the nonlinearity that clinicians experience in psychoanalytic work. Harris, borrowing from Lacan, calls gender a "necessary fiction," Benjamin calls it a "real appearance," and Virginia Goldner calls it a "false truth" (all quoted in Dimen and Goldner, 2002, p. xvi). Each of these expressions calls for valuing dialectics, paradox, process, and thirdness. Urging us not to essentialize gender or dematerialize it, they refer to what Dimen and Goldner call "the art of the double take" (p. xvii). Haraway (1991) asks us to imagine a post-gender world in the form of a "cyborg" that features transgendered boundaries and resists gendered norms, perpetually unfixed and contingent. As we have described regarding "trans," the cyborg is another excellent example of Derrida's undecidability, which in Haraway's postmodern feminism becomes an ideal.

This brings us to the contributions of Judith Butler (1990, 2004a, 2004b) whose work, among the most cited in academia, represents a fascinating tour de force of poststructuralist, feminist, queer, postcolonial, and psychoanalytic positions (Layton, 1998). Butler argued that heterosexual subjectivity is constructed upon a culturally mandated taboo against, and an un-grieved disavowal of, same-sex love. Gender is both constituted by and of sexuality. Culture and nature are deconstructed, such that sexuality and gender can no longer be defined and differentiated in relation to their polar opposites. Butler criticizes psychoanalysis for aligning gender, sexuality, and desire when gender does not so much express sexuality but rather functions as a regulatory ideal. Cross-dressing and drag can function as undecidables in breaking up what seem to be clear binary opposites. Following Butler, Domenici and Lesser (1995) attempted to disorient sexuality by examining it from the margins. Corbett (2009) extended Butler's work to show the multiple masculinities among and within homosexual boys, and Reis and Grossmark (2009) have examined multiplicity in heterosexual masculinities.

Brickman (2003) brought together anthropology, postcolonial studies, and psychoanalysis to deconstruct one the most powerful binaries in psychoanalytic thought: primitive and civilized. Brickman demonstrated the long history of racist anthropology that shaped this binary, and the ways in which it was institutionalized in psychoanalysis via concepts such as regression and progression, primitive defenses, primitive pathology, primitive pre-Oedipal dynamics, and unanalyzable patients. Linking race and gender, Brickman demonstrated that primitivity consistently aligned itself with femininity; the repudiation of primitivity and femininity (Black and Jew) established normative subjectivity within Freudian theory. Postcolonial studies apply the same Derrida-inspired critique of binaries. The dualities colonizer/colonized, colonial/postcolonial, dominated/liberated, First World/Third World, are destabilized. However, deconstruction does not abolish these concepts; in fact, they remain the only conceptual tools we have to understand the world. Rather, postcolonial theorists such as Homi Bhabha and Gayatri Spivak have employed these concepts in their deconstructed form (Schwartz, 2000).

We have outlined the ways in which contemporary psychoanalytic theorists have been influenced by currents in postmodernism and feminist deconstruction because much of our own argument will revolve around the deconstruction of polarities and the interconnection among these polarities of sex, gender, race, and other social hierarchies. We hope to demonstrate that an understanding of the relevant dichotomies and how they have structured psychoanalysis is radically liberating. Once we see how these dualities undergird psychoanalytic thought, we are in a much better position to recognize and correct trouble spots in the theory and practice of psychoanalysis. The process involves finding undecidables or thirds and using them to break down polarized thinking. The psychoanalysis/psychotherapy binary is just one example of this approach, but one that is central and has ongoing practical implications. Deconstructing a polarity does not mean eliminating difference. While we argue that psychoanalysis has defined itself and psychotherapy as opposing binaries, we do not assert that there is no difference between psychoanalysis and psychotherapy; instead we advocate that they be viewed dialectically.

Friedman (2006) described psychoanalysis as monstrous in the sense that it does not fit into our usual categories. It is precisely this freakishness that is Freud's great legacy. Just as its founder did not fit into the neat categories of German, Austrian, Jew, or scientist, psychoanalysis does not easily fit into categories such as art, science, or hermeneutics, despite our tendency to simplify, to tame the monster and make it appear more normal. In our view, the single most important way that psychoanalysts tried to preserve simplicity, which they mistakenly confused with purity, was by splitting. The way to tame the monster is to cut him/her up into pieces, operate on the hermaphrodite and separate the male and female elements even if the patient dies in the surgery. The strategy we will examine in depth is the splitting of all that analysts considered primitive onto psychotherapy—dependency, support, nurturance, subjectivity, the maternal, the feminine, the relational. All that our culture deemed feminine was attributed to psychotherapy, whereas all that was marked as masculine—independence, autonomy, individuality, and scientific objectivity—was attributed to psychoanalysis. Thus the monster was made a bit less grotesque.

Chapter 3

Guilt and Shame

Because it is so often concealed from view, shame is considered a hidden emotion. It has also been hidden in a wide variety of psychological and developmental theories (Mills, 2005). An affect spectrum with "many faces" (Nathanson, 1987), shame includes feelings of inadequacy, deficiency, dirtiness, neediness, emptiness, shyness, mortification, embarrassment, humiliation, humility, and disgrace, among others. More than other affects, shame is contagious. It has an inherent tendency to spiral out of control; one is ashamed of being ashamed. In recent years, there has been a fresh focus in contemporary psychoanalysis on shame associated with dissociation, gender variance, sexuality, and clinical impasse. Relational contributions have focused on the analyst as initiator or maintainer of the shame state and on the impact of the analyst's own shame on the analytic process (Harris, 2011c). Bromberg (2011) has highlighted how shame in the clinical situation can escalate out of control through a vicious cycle; the analyst feels ashamed for causing the patient shame, while the patient becomes increasingly ashamed of feeling so ashamed.

The field of psychoanalytic "shame studies" first emerged in full bloom in the early 1970s under the influence of Kohut's investigation of narcissism and the ground-breaking work of Helen Block Lewis (1971), who studied the relationship between shame and guilt in neurosis. Although providing important hints about its central role, Kohut (1971, 1977) did not often use the language of shame, instead speaking of narcissism, disintegration, fragmentation, and the enfeeblement and depletion of the self. Following Kohut's lead, others reworked the psychoanalytic theory of shame in self-psychological terms (Morrison, 1989; Broucek, 1991). Referring to those who studied shame as "shamenicks," herself included, Lewis pioneered the reexamination of the concepts of superego and ego ideal in relation to shame and guilt (Nathanson, 1987, p. xi). A small group of "shamenicks" dedicated themselves to revising the psychoanalytic approach to guilt and shame. In our view, this effort was fueled by a variety of factors: the women's movement and feminism; Heinz Kohut's self-psychology and later developments in intersubjectivity theory; the profound influence of the affect theorist Silvan Tomkins (see Demos, 1995); a renewed focus on trauma, linking it to dissociation and shame; and a shift in the general cultural focus from guilt to shame (Leys, 2007).

As we have noted, we are deconstructing a variety of problematic binaries in the theory and practice of psychoanalysis. In this chapter, we will examine the binary of shame and guilt in order to illustrate several key difficulties caused by this polarization. Within psychoanalytic theory, guilt was long associated with the Oedipus complex, while shame was associated with the pre-Oedipal. Guilt was associated with higher-level, more highly structured, analyzable neurotics, whereas shame was associated with less structured, more primitive, less analyzable patients. It is only a small step to the conclusion that patients struggling with intrapsychic conflict and guilt—in other words, who were analyzable—were ideally treated with psychoanalysis, while immature, primitive patients who experienced too much shame and mortification to examine themselves objectively were best suited for psychotherapy. Thus guilt is to shame as psychoanalysis is to psychotherapy, an example of definition through binary opposition, with the inevitable subordination of one pole to the other.

The hierarchical split between guilt and shame was structured along gender lines. Guilt was associated with masculinity and men, agents and subjects, while shame was attributed to femininity and women, who objectified themselves and were objectified by others. Those at the top of the hierarchy, whether of gender, class, race, or intellectual ability, might feel guilty about being on top at the expense of others, but those below them on the hierarchy were ashamed. Guilt was associated with Whites and shame with minorities. The wealthy felt guilt while the poor felt shame. As we will show, guilt was viewed as an individual, autonomous, deep intrapsychic affect, while shame was associated with the superficially shallow, social, and interpersonal. Within the psychoanalytic situation, guilt was associated with the analyst and shame with the patient. Within the larger therapeutic framework, guilt was associated with psychoanalysis and shame with psychotherapy. These are indeed sweeping generalizations, so we will explain our understanding in further detail.

Freud and Kohut's Jewish Shame

One of the earliest references to shame in Freud's writing is in a letter to his fiancée, Martha Bernays, on September 16, 1883. We highlight this example because it touches on many of the dichotomies we examine, and as we will see in Chapter 12, it is especially relevant to Freud's identity as a Jew and to the binary Christian/Jew. Freud had just returned from a friend's funeral. Dr. Nathan Weiss, assistant at the Neurological Clinic, had hung himself in the public bathhouse. Freud described to Martha his various speculations about what had led to the suicide, including the man's recent unhappy marriage to a woman who had not really loved him. As the coffin was being lowered into the ground, a fight broke out between the two families. Freud wrote,

> Over his corpse began the feud of the families and on his still-open grave there sounded a loud discordant scream for revenge, as unfair and as reckless as if he had uttered it himself . . . A relation and colleague of his old father . . . began to accuse the other family of having dealt the fatal blow. *And all this he spoke with the powerful voice of the fanatic, with the ardor of the savage, merciless Jew.*
>
> *We were all petrified with horror and shame in the presence of the Christians who were among us.* It seemed as though we had given them reason to believe that we worship the God of Revenge, not the God of Love. Pfungen's [an Assistant in Meynert's Clinic] thin voice was lost in the reverberation of *the wild accusation of the Jew.*
>
> (1883, p. 65, emphases added)

We see here and will continue to see the way in which Freud inevitably became trapped in the binaries that circulated around him. It was important to Freud that he *not* feel ashamed of being a Jew. As we will show, shame was marked as feminine. To be ashamed of being a Jew would only legitimize and reinforce the cultural trope that Jewish men were effeminate and homosexual (at this time no distinction was made between sex and gender). Psychologically, Freud needed to feel proud of his Jewishness and to deny a sense of shame. His concern, repeatedly evident in his correspondence, was for Jews not to embarrass themselves in front of gentiles. We can see the binaries foreshadowing much to come in Freud's writing—Christians versus Jews, the God of Love versus the God of Revenge. Freud describes poor, uneducated, religious Eastern Jews as fanatic, wild, merciless, and savage. Hierarchies predominate: East/West, poor/wealthy, rural/urban, primitive/cultured, religious/atheist, and shame/guilt. Consider the following statement by Freud, which illustrates how binaries structured his thinking even when he tried to get past them. He wrote,

> We shall be plunged deep into psychological riddles if we enquire into the origin of the unpleasure which seems to be released by premature sexual stimulation and without which, after all, a repression cannot be explained. The most plausible answer will appeal to the fact that *shame and morality are the repressing forces* and that the neighbourhood in which the sexual organs are naturally placed must inevitably arouse disgust along with sexual experiences. *Where*

there is no shame (as in a male person), or where no morality comes about (as in the lower classes of society), or where disgust is blunted by the conditions of life (as in the country), there too no repression and therefore no neurosis will result from sexual stimulation in infancy.

(Freud, 1892, pp. 221–222, emphases added)

In this early work, we see Freud recognizing the important role of shame and disgust in repression and the etiology of psychopathology. We also see anticipations of civilization on the one side and its discontents on the other. Sexuality/morality, pleasure/unpleasure, indulgence/shame, primitivity/civilization are divided. But what stands out almost unbelievably is Freud's assumption that shame is feminine, like quiche, not tasted by real men, who are regulated by intrapsychic solutions such as guilt and autonomous law! Morality, guilt-based civilization, does not exist among primitives—"the lower classes of society."

The following is not meant to be a comprehensive review of Freud's contributions, but is intended as background for an understanding of how shame was organized hierarchically in relation to guilt, and then aligned with many other binary categories, including gender, race, religion, class, and sexuality. Freud's early work featured shame as a significant clinical phenomenon. In *Studies on Hysteria*, Breuer and Freud (1893–1895) identified "mortification," a type of shame, "an injury that has been suffered in silence" (p. 86), as playing a key role in the formation of hysteria. In *Three Essays*, Freud (1905) spoke of shame and disgust as barriers to instinctual life. Shame was reactive, inhibitory, and prohibitive, exploited by culture and education to oppose the pleasure principle. Freud associated shame with the partial drives of looking and being looked at, scopophilia (voyeurism) and exhibitionism. This marked a shift in emphasis from shame as an affect that initiates defense to shame as a defense against the expression of drives, particularly the visual impulses. Shame was linked to seeing and being seen by others, a social phenomenon.

In *On Narcissism*, Freud (1914) posited the ego ideal, referring to one's aspirations. Self-conscious self-appraisals discrepant with our aspirations generate shame and signal a danger to bonding with needed others. Thus shame is inextricably bound to the problem of narcissism—that is, lovability, acceptability, and selfhood—which depends on acceptance or recognition by the other. After Freud began to appreciate the role of unconscious fantasy, including sexual and aggressive wishes, he developed a model of the mind that pushed anxiety and guilt into theoretical prominence and tended to relegate shame to matters connected with anality and exhibitionism.

In the following notorious passage from his *New Introductory Lectures*, Freud (1933) explained that shame could both express and defend against feelings of inadequacy.

I have promised to tell you of a few more psychical peculiarities of mature femininity, as we come across them in analytic observation. We do not lay claim to more than an average validity for these assertions; nor is it always easy to distinguish what should be ascribed to the influence of the sexual function and what to social breeding. Thus, we attribute a larger amount of narcissism to femininity, which also affects women's choice of object, so that to be loved is a stronger need for them than to love. The effect of penis-envy has a share, further, in the physical vanity of women, since they are *bound to value their charms more highly as a late compensation for their original sexual inferiority. Shame, which is considered to be a feminine characteristic par excellence but is far more a matter of convention than might be supposed, has as its purpose, we believe, concealment of genital deficiency. We are not forgetting that at a later time shame takes on other functions.* It seems that women have made few contributions to the discoveries and inventions in the history of civilization; there is, however, one technique which they may have invented—that of plaiting and weaving. If that is so, we should be tempted to guess the unconscious motive for the achievement. Nature herself would seem to have given the model which this achievement imitates by causing the growth at maturity of the pubic hair that conceals the genitals. The step that remained to be taken lay in making the threads adhere to one another, while on the body they stick into the skin and are only matted together. If you reject this idea as fantastic and regard my belief in the influence of lack of a penis on the configuration of femininity as an idée fixe, I am of course defenceless.

(Freud 1933, p. 132, emphasis added)

Here Freud placed shame in a social context, the wish to hide, to cover oneself up from the view of others. Freud seems torn; on one hand clearly associating shame with femininity, "a feminine characteristic par excellence," but acknowledging that this was more a social convention than an inherent feature of women. We are not sure, he says, what is biologically inherent in sexuality and what is culturally determined. In any event, Freud makes the case that shame is a social emotion, closely tied to the visual, seeing and being seen by others, finding and hiding from others. Shame is a relational affect par excellence—that is what marks it as feminine, and therefore primitive. Autonomy and individuality are identified as masculine and bounded, hence not subject to penetration, permeability, or vulnerability; instead they are subject to guilt and castration anxiety. Shame, on the other hand, will come to be associated with being seen by others, permeability, loss of boundaries, femininity, primitivity, and Jewishness.

Helen Block Lewis was an experienced analyst who was struck by the observation that some of her patients were returning for re-analysis.

Patients who had completed analyses with other analysts were turning to her, because their symptoms had not only returned but had become worse following their analyses. They had become increasingly self-critical and their superegos seemed harsher. Lewis concluded that unanalyzed shame in the patient–therapist relationship was a significant factor in these negative therapeutic reactions, and so she undertook what became her pioneering lifework, a study of shame in psychopathology and psychotherapy.

In her classic *Shame and Guilt in Neurosis*, Lewis's (1971) review of the psychoanalytic literature revealed that there had been a one-sided emphasis on guilt at the expense of shame. The self-punishing functions of the superego had been given attention to the neglect of its self-protective functions. She specifically criticized the unwarranted assumption that shame was a lower-order form of guilt or a precursor to guilt in the development of morality. Instead, she argued that shame and guilt were equal, although they developed along different routes of identification. Essentially, Lewis argued that they were different affects, each of which progressed along separate developmental lines. Identification with the threatening parents stirs an *internalized* threat that is expressed as guilt. In contrast, the ego ideal is based on identification with beloved and admired persons. Failure to live up to these internalized images stirs up shame. In guilt, self-criticism focuses on the behavior or specific activity in relation to a value system, as breaking the laws of morality. In shame, the focus is on the awareness of oneself through the eyes of the (internalized) other. Shame affect is about the whole self, not merely something one has done. In the experience of shame, the other is a prominent and powerful force. For this reason, when feeling shame, a person wants to crawl into a hole or sink through the floor. In contrast, guilt is about behaviors—actions or failures to act in the real world, for which one bears responsibility. Lewis hypothesized that shame is closely associated with sexuality. Absorption in sexual fantasy entails a loss of ego boundaries, and shame serves as a sharp and painful reminder of the other as separate from, and rejecting of, the self. Shame also serves to regulate self-esteem, preventing excessive grandiosity. While Lewis did not use the term dialectic, she argued that shame and guilt reciprocally interacted, such that shame could defend against guilt and guilt against shame. She wrote,

> One may, for example, feel ashamed of some failure of achievement and in the next moment feel guilty for caring about success. Or one may feel guilty for some moral lapse and remain ashamed of "moral weakness" long after the specific lapse has been forgotten.
>
> (1971, p. 27)

In light of all these considerations, Lewis, who was influenced by the second-wave feminism of the 1960s, recognized that women may be more prone to shame than men, and men may be more prone to guilt. Her attempt to equalize the developmental value of guilt and shame may be seen as a feminist effort to treat men and women's psychological experience with greater equality.

In *The Restoration of the Self*, Heinz Kohut (1977) differentiated Guilty Man and Tragic Man to distinguish the two core dimensions of human nature that are the foci of classical psychoanalysis and self-psychology, respectively. He depicted the classical view of Guilty Man as torn by his drives and internal prohibitions, manifesting Oedipal disorders, dominated by the pleasure principle, and bound up in inner conflict. In contrast, he portrayed the self-psychological view of Tragic Man as motivated by a need to fulfill and express his nuclear program and to complete the development of his aims and ideals. In his study of narcissism, Kohut (1971) claimed, "narcissistic personalities are in general not predominantly swayed by guilt feelings (they are not inclined to react unduly to the pressure exerted by their idealized superego). *Their predominant tendency is to be overwhelmed by shame*" (p. 232, emphasis added). In their review of how self-psychologists neglected the role of guilt in psychopathology and treatment, Droga and Kaufmann (1995) call for a dialectical approach that takes into account both Guilty Man and Tragic Man, guilt and shame.

In our view, Kohut was Tragic Man, his life and theory dominated by intense shame and its dissociation. Kohut's central contribution, the study of narcissism, may be understood as having its origins in Kohut's deep feelings of shame and self-hatred regarding his Jewishness and the vertical splitting and dissociation of this aspect of his religious identity. (For a more thorough discussion along the lines briefly developed here, see Aron, 2007.) The study of narcissism may be understood as a reaction to its underbelly, deep feelings of shame (for formulations of the dialectic tension between narcissism and shame see Lewis, 1987; and Morrison, 1989). It is likely that Kohut was among those who experienced profound Jewish self-doubt and self-hatred growing up in the Vienna of the 1920s and 1930s. With childhood conflicts and family dynamics that led him to extreme narcissistic vulnerability and fears of fragmentation, Kohut could not tolerate the shame of his Jewish self. Judaism did not meet his selfobject needs for idealization, mirroring, or twinship. Rather than being lifted up, Jews in Vienna were being knocked down. Rather than admired or idealized, Jews were denigrated and demonized. Rather than feeling connected to others, Jews were the other, less than human. Kohut could not turn to Judaism to meet any of his selfobject needs. He especially could not tolerate being regarded as not human—that, in his own words, was the worst.

Kohut's Jewish self was so shameful that he could not contain it within his identity. He did not just repress it but rather vertically split it off, dissociated it, so that it was "not me." He could never have converted or resigned from the Jewish community because to convert or resign required the recognition that one was Jewish; that would have been the equivalent of repression. Kohut's dissociation could not allow even the acknowledgment of a conversion. It may be accurate to say that Kohut was not conflicted about being Jewish inasmuch as his Jewish identity was dissociated and hence (an awareness of) conflict was not a state he had achieved in this regard (Bromberg, 2003; Stern, 2004). We would add that here, dissociation is differentiated from repressive defenses inasmuch as it results not from anxiety but from the self-annihilating terror evoked in a traumatic situation. Kohut told an interviewer for *The New York Times*, "I've led two totally different, perhaps unbridgeable lives"; it was that disruption, he believed, that made him "alert to the problems of the fragmented self and how it tries to cure itself" (quoted in Marcus and Wineman, 1985, p. 88). Kohut pioneered the investigation of this vertical split in the self, the dissociation of those parts of the self that are so shameful they cause fragmentation and disintegration of the self. His theory of religious experience, on the other hand, reflects his practice as a Christian. It is founded on the experience of God and church as the glue that mends the self, holding the self together and lifting it up by meeting the person's selfobject needs and providing him with meaning beyond his finite existence. It includes the gift of grace and a community of like others, by whom Kohut could feel recognized as a fully human self.

What made Kohut a great psychoanalytic theorist was his ability to transform his own psychological struggles into a theory and treatment approach that transcended the limitations of his own life and that continues to shed light on the tragic and heroic dimensions of all human experience. Given the intensity with which Kohut had to split off or dissociate the shame and indeed the mortification, "an injury that has been suffered in silence," regarding his Jewishness in inter-war Vienna, it makes sense that these dynamics would find their way into his theoretical contributions without being taken up explicitly. The vertical split between guilt and shame was embodied in the polarity of Guilty Man and Tragic Man.

Shame and the Gaze of the Other

Lansky (1994) clarified that shame is the affect that signals the threat of danger to the social bond. Shame results from exposure that challenges the integrity of the self before others. It is tied to human social interactions in actuality or imagination. Lansky made the important point that shame exemplifies Hegel's philosophy that the self is only a self by virtue of being defined as such by the other. Selfhood is always a social phenomenon, dependent on the social bond with others and at risk when the self is not recognized. However, some people have a more immediate, pressing need for ongoing recognition while others have learned to sustain themselves by internalizing this process.

Also emphasizing the social aspects of affect and specifically of shame, Orange (2008) argued that in the analytic system, shame belongs neither to the patient nor to the analyst, but is intersubjectively generated, maintained, exacerbated, and hopefully mitigated within the relational system.

Morrison (1989, 2008a, b), too, emphasized the social, suggesting that shame received little psychoanalytic attention for many years because it was considered "a superficial, strictly social, and interpersonal phenomenon with no special relevance to deep psychoanalytic thought in comparison with guilt" (Morrison, 2008a, p. 76). In contrast to his understanding of Orange, however, Morrison argued that there is no need to do away with the idea of individual subjectivities in order to accommodate a more relational, intersubjective, systemic vision. He differentiated two qualities of subjective experience: the instigation of shame and the actual experienced emotion of shame. Morrison maintains that in most situations, shame arises within the context of intersubjective relational systems. While the social system most often is the initiator of shame, it is the individual subject who actually experiences the emotion.

In a sophisticated study of shame, Broucek (1991) posited that the experience of shame suggests that the self is a relational and contextual structure, dependent on networks of early and recent relationships, conscious and unconscious. Like Mitchell (1988), Stolorow and Atwood (1982), and many other relational and intersubjectivity theorists, he criticized the concept of the atomistic isolated self as a delusion that inappropriately assumed that the mind, like the body, was a container. We can clearly see in Broucek's work the close connection between a shift from a classical to a relational or systems viewpoint and recognition of the role of shame as a clinical phenomenon. Broucek suggested that the classical analytic situation with its use of the couch minimized the patient's shame, thus facilitating free association. Not being in face-to-face contact mitigated or bypassed the patient's feelings of shame. The problem this created was that in bypassing shame, analysis of that shame was also avoided. The analyst's typically silent listening stance could very well also be experienced as shame-inducing. Lack of response can easily feel like a form of rejection; at the very least, it can feel distancing and objectifying. For Broucek, the essence of shame is feeling objectified at a time when you are seeking recognition as a subject. Hence classical technique could induce a surplus of humiliation. Along similar lines, the use of interpretation as the predominant intervention of the analyst is also likely to be experienced by the patient as a form of objectification because it entails a more experience-distant form of relating. More generally, intimacy usually requires a two-way reciprocal process of self-disclosure, because intimacy is based on shared vulnerability. The frustration of complementarity induces shame. The classical stance of neutrality, anonymity, abstinence, and reliance on interpretation deprives the patient of mutuality and can lead to the experience of shame, which is not recognized by the analyst because they have been at least partially responsible for inducing the shame.

Classically trained, her early work on affect most influenced by Joseph and Ann-Marie Sandler, Ruth Stein became increasingly moved by relational and intersubjective theoretical developments. Stein (1997) observed that shame was one of the principal factors contributing to analyst–patient collusions, because in the case of shame, the comfort one usually gets from sharing feelings with another does not apply. She argued that this was a specific feature of shame because recognizing and resonating with the other's shameful feelings can be embarrassing and painful. Sometimes silence is the most empathic route; at other times, suitable words have to be found so as not to withdraw in the face of the patient's shame. Stein pointed out that given the recent attention to the analyst's subjectivity, it was surprising there was such a paucity of literature on the analyst's shame. She wrote,

> There are no descriptions of how it feels for us analysts to really be proven wrong, of the subtle discomfort we feel when we sound off track, of the apprehension and anxiety in appearing ignorant or mistaken, and of having to grope occasionally for the right words, metaphors, and intuitions, only to be corrected by the patient.
>
> (1997, p. 120)

In contrast to guilt, she argued, we still have not incorporated shame into our clinical metapsychology. Beginning with Lewis, "shamenicks" have recognized that shame is contagious. The patient's shame may resonate with the therapist's own sense of failure, inadequacy, and self-deficiency (Morrison, 1989). As contemporary analysts often make use of some selective self-disclosure and may be more revealing than classical analysts were thought to be, one might think they are now more often exposed to the experience of shame. But paradoxically, as analysts feel more comfortable with self-expression and feel less need to be neutral, idealized authorities, they may more easily accept their mistakes and tolerate their shame.

From this very brief review, we can begin to see that the dichotomy of shame and guilt has been reconfigured not only because we have a better understanding of these phenomena through accumulated clinical experience, but also because it takes on a different shape when examined through a broadly relational or intersubjective lens as compared to a classical one. This is no coincidence. The shift from classical to relational theory coincided with the women's movement, the gay rights movement, the civil rights movement, and the cultural challenge to authority that ensued in the 1960s. Guilt was to shame as masculine was to feminine, heterosexual to homosexual, White to Black, and rich to poor. Guilt was the exquisitely internalized emotion, epitomizing developed, structured, internalized conflict. Shame was viewed as a superficial, social, feminine, and immature reaction. Concomitant with the changes in our cultural worldview, all of these hierarchies have been increasingly challenged. In our view, the classical hierarchy in which guilt was privileged over shame was directly related to the general cultural privileging of autonomy over relatedness, agency over communion, and the individual over the social.

In *The Chrysanthemum and the Sword*, Ruth Benedict (1946) popularized her distinction between "guilt culture" and "shame culture." Her identification of Japanese culture as a shame culture was criticized and resented by many Japanese. Many Westerners have also viewed Benedict's distinction as a form of ethnocentric chauvinism. Creighton (1990) argued that these strong reactions against Benedict were based on the idea that Westerners viewed guilt as belonging to a higher level of moral development than shame. Defending Benedict from widespread criticism, Creighton argued that Benedict had not neglected guilt in Japanese culture, had not minimized shame in American culture, and had not maintained that guilt and shame are unrelated. In fact, Benedict had written her book more as a critique of American culture than as a study of Japanese culture. The key point for our purposes is Creighton's argument that shame may be stronger in Japanese culture because of the heavy emphasis placed on acceptance by and living up to the ideals of the group. Creighton argued that the designations "shame culture" and "guilt culture" should not be thought of in pejorative terms, as hierarchical. A person has either shame dominance or guilt dominance much as we are each right- or left-handed, even though it is inappropriate to think of one as better than the other. One of the problems in dichotomizing shame and guilt and then viewing guilt as superior to shame is that it distracts our attention from the fact that each of these affects has its own developmental trajectory, that there are lower and higher developmental forms of shame and guilt. There is a consensus in the contemporary psychological literature that shame gradually evolves into a more complex form as a child develops. It does not evolve into guilt but into higher levels of shame (Mills, 2005)!

In her studies of the intellectual history of trauma and shame, Ruth Leys (2000, 2007) has shown that shame has displaced guilt as the dominant emotional reference in the West. In America, following World War II, there was a cultural paradigm change in the understanding of the self, affect, and personal agency. Leys examined the specific shift from an emphasis on survivor guilt among victims of the Holocaust to a focus on their shame. She noted that the idea of survivor guilt was mistakenly taken to imply that the victims were identified with, and hence complicit with, the perpetrators. This shift from a mimetic to an antimimetic understanding of trauma is part of a larger set of oppositions, including identification versus identity and agency versus victimhood. Leys argued that before World War II most psychoanalysts did not differentiate guilt and shame but in the second half of the century mistakenly treated these affects as binaries. Leys documented the shift in cultural emphasis from guilt to shame as one part of a much broader shift from agency and responsibility to passivity and external imposition. Guilt focused on our actions and our responsibility for those actions, even if they only took place in unconscious fantasy. Shame refers to who we are, to our identity, our difference from others. In this analysis, guilt and shame align with autonomy and relatedness, agency and communion.

Ego or "Wego": Autonomy versus Relatedness

Every human being confronts two fundamental challenges in development. One is to establish and maintain a social world of interpersonal relationships, and the other is to establish and maintain a cohesive, coherent, positively tinged sense of self. These two polarities of human experience have been described in different terms throughout history. Psychologist Sidney Blatt (2004, 2008) studied the dialectical interaction of these two psychological tasks, both clinically and through empirical research in development, psychopathology, and the therapeutic process, referring to these poles as relatedness and self-definition. Early in his career, Blatt discovered two fundamentally different types of depressive experience. One focused on interpersonal concerns such as care, love, attachment, and rejection. Blatt called this "anaclitic depression." The other focused on issues of self-worth, including feelings of failure, worthlessness, and guilt, which he called "introjective depression." While pleased with this discovery, Blatt felt uneasy with these original formulations because they implied that the depressive experiences of women (more often anaclitic) were usually at a less mature developmental level than were the depressive experiences of men (more often introjective), which were thought to be at a developmentally higher level. Subsequently, Blatt and his colleagues conceptualized personality development as involving the dialectic interplay of two fundamental developmental lines, relational and self-definitional.

Western culture has predominantly emphasized self-definition and individualism. Similarly, psychological and psychoanalytic theories traditionally privileged self-definition over interpersonal relatedness. Ego autonomy was the apex of the ego functions within an ego-psychological framework. Non-Western cultures often tend to conceptualize the person as an integral part of his or her relationships. Bakan (1966) referred to these two polarities in terms of agency and communion. Agency refers to feelings of being a separate individual, including self-protection, self-assertion, and self-expansion. Communion refers to merging with, being a part of, blending with others and with the social world. Bakan, and following him Blatt, noted that women tended toward the more communal pole, while men primarily behaved in an instrumental-agentic manner. In short, females emphasized relatedness and males emphasized individuality. Within psychoanalysis, George Klein (1976) called for the need to develop a "wego" psychology to complement our ego psychology (p. 179). He argued for a dialectical model that included both the self's autonomy (ego-psychology) as well as the self-in-relationship (wego psychology). Klein, too, was critical of psychology and psychoanalysis for privileging the ego over the wego, autonomy over relatedness.

Mind and Body

We have reviewed the guilt/shame hierarchy as an illustration of one clinically relevant binary opposition, but we could proceed with numerous other examples: Oedipal/pre-Oedipal, analyzable/unanalyzable, intrapsychic/interpersonal, insight/experience, to name a few. Before turning to the cultural history that shaped the definition of psychoanalysis via binary opposition, we will highlight another set of binary oppositions that have become prominent in recent psychoanalytic discourse, including verbal/ pre-verbal, symbolic/pre-symbolic, words/action, free association/enactment, interpretation/non-interpretive factors, explicit/implicit—which are all deeply rooted in the split between mind and body. As we will demonstrate in Chapter 10, Freud contrasted his own verbal approach of listening to patients with that of his teacher, Charcot, who looked at his patients and observed their symptoms. Even before the invention of psychoanalysis, there was already a divide between images and words, or show and tell. Psychoanalysts have tended to perpetuate this binary, in which speech and language is identified with the intrapsychic model of mind, Oedipal development, the defense of repression, and cure through insight and interpretation. In contrast, the pre-verbal is aligned with the pre-symbolic, unformulated, dissociated, and enacted, and with treatment that emphasizes perceptual and sensory experience, intuition, "now" moments, and intersubjective resonances. Relational and intersubjective approaches are sometimes presented as emphasizing one side of this binary, and classical approaches the other. Lacan and Freud are thought to emphasize the unconscious structured as a language, paying acute attention to the patient's speech, whereas relational analysts are thought to participate in enactments, curing not through verbal insight but through implicit relational knowing.

While these distinctions can be useful, we should be cautious about presenting them as binary oppositions rather than as dialectics. As dichotomies, they are always presented in hierarchical terms with one pole subservient to the other: words are more highly developed than pictures;

interpretation is preferable to other interpersonal interventions. Just as problematic are the simple reversals in which a trans-valuation suddenly occurs: interventions that are beyond interpretation are elevated in status relative to words, which are then devalued as intellectualized; free association is diminished relative to enactment; attunement is promoted as if it were independent of and hierarchically more significant than understanding. Instead, we contend that all show involves tell, and all tell involves show. Words and actions, remembering and repeating, association and enactment, interpretation and non-interpretive interventions are all transformations of each other. They all contain and rely upon one another, and should be thought of dialectically rather than dichotomously.

We have shown that in traditional psychoanalysis, guilt was viewed as hierarchically superior to shame. Guilt was aligned with autonomy and shame with relationality. Guilt and autonomy were viewed as masculine attributes while shame and relationality were viewed as feminine. We briefly touched on issues linking shame and Jewishness for both Freud and Kohut. We reviewed the need for a dialectical model of autonomy and relationality, offering Blatt's work as a model that successfully acknowledges both autonomy and relationality in development, psychopathology, and psychotherapy. Finally, we argued for a psychoanalytic *Weltanschauung* that envisions the human being as both individual and social.

Chapter 4

Treatment versus Care

Psychoanalysis and American Medicine

To set the stage for understanding the current dilemmas in our field, we will provide a brief overview of the history of American medicine. We will examine the development of psychiatry as a medical specialization in the context of that history and of psychoanalysis as a further specialization within psychiatry. The rise in prestige of medicine in America, of psychiatry within medicine, and of psychoanalysis within psychiatry were due to their perceived ability to offer treatment rather than care. As it became aligned with scientific progress and masculine authority, psychoanalysis came to contrast itself with psychotherapy, which it associated with palliative care and the feminine values of support and relationship. For our review of American medicine, we draw primarily from Rutkow's (2010) *Seeking the Cure* to provide the background for understanding how psychoanalysis came to be positioned as a treatment that provided cure rather than care.

"Bleed, Blister, Puke, and Purge"

If you became ill before the 20th century, you were better off not consulting a doctor, as the treatment was often far worse than the disease. More of a trade than a profession, medicine was typically practiced part-time by poorly paid physicians who supplemented their incomes with small businesses or farming, and by clergy who combined healing with preaching. Most doctors called themselves doctors simply because they were "doctoring"—that is, taking care of patients. They had no formal training and little of therapeutic value to offer. In the early 1800s, Benjamin Rush, known as the "American Hippocrates," promoted the elimination of blood and other bodily fluids to decrease congestion. Depletion therapy—bloodletting and forced intestinal evacuation—also known as "heroic therapy," dominated medical treatment. "Bleed, blister, puke, and purge" were medicine's main strategies, as they had been for centuries. Physicians knew nothing of infection or anesthesia and little of anatomy. Hospitals were few in number and poorly managed. Facilities of last resort, they served as shelters for the poor and those with no family to care for them, who went to hospitals to die. Every American doctor was a combination of physician, surgeon, apothecary, and midwife, having obtained no formal education or licensing.

In the mid-19th century, medical schools sprang up around the country as a way for doctors to earn a living by having medical students as paying customers. Admission required neither literacy nor prior educational achievement, and there was no formal medical school curriculum. The country was flooded with professors of medicine, anatomy, and surgery, but the holders of these titles had no academic qualifications whatsoever. Dissatisfied with the harsh treatments in use at the time, unorthodox doctors began to practice "irregular" methods, including vegetarianism and homeopathy, which were gentler than the heroic depletion therapies. Not surprisingly, the public welcomed these irregular treatments as alternatives to bloodletting. To counter the threat posed by the irregular physicians, mainstream doctors established the American Medical Association (AMA) to enforce their professional authority.

While from our modern perspective, the eventual dominance of mainstream medicine might seem like a natural and positive progression, it entailed critical costs as well as benefits. The public liked the irregular doctors because they caused less harm than the regular doctors. Regular doctors, usually middle-class white men, were always more expensive than the irregulars, and only the middle and upper classes could afford their treatment. The irregulars included many women healers and midwives whose interventions were milder than bloodletting. These procedures were safer, less intrusive, and arguably more effective than the regular doctors' treatments (Ehrenreich and English, 1973). Given the major role of women in early pre-professional medicine, it is remarkable that mainstream histories of medicine have still not fully examined the role of these women or incorporated the observations of feminist critics into their studies.

The Rise of Modern Medicine

It was not until the end of the 19th century that regular doctors were able to offer a substantial therapeutic advantage over the irregulars. It took the discovery of bacteriology, immunology, pathology, and physiology, as well as the development of a questioning scientific attitude and the willingness to modify therapeutic practices accordingly, for medicine to modernize. During the 1890s, medicine grew with astonishing rapidity. Scientific advances led to its increasing professionalization, growth in public esteem, and rise in power and prestige.

After the Civil War, America looked toward Germany and Austro-Hungary as centers for the most advanced academic medical study. State-sponsored and well financed, German language universities were regarded as having the most sophisticated medical teaching methods, and American doctors began to flood German-speaking countries in search of better medical education. Returning home with a Viennese medical diploma attested to having received the world's finest medical training. Vienna, with its rich history and numerous medical opportunities, both embraced and exploited these American doctors. Viennese schools offered classes in English, charging higher tuition for this education. When Johns Hopkins Medical School opened in 1893, it was modeled on the German prototype. The first medical school of its kind in America, Johns Hopkins was tied to a hospital and university, and had its own full-time faculty and laboratories. For the first time, American medical students were exposed to basic science laboratory research as well as expanded clinical contact with patients.

By the turn of the 20th century, the revolution in science and technology led to a new confidence in medicine on the part of its practitioners as well as the public. Doctors parlayed their self-confidence into higher incomes, improved social status, and economic and legal power. Reform of medical education became an important part of medical modernization and professionalization. Academic physicians realized that educational reform would create new teaching positions; private practitioners hoped it would decrease competition from those with less education. The Council of Medical Education, a committee of the AMA, prioritized the reform of medical education, using Johns Hopkins, with its German-like standards, as its model. The Carnegie foundation funded a study of American medical education, leading to the Flexner report of 1910, a landmark policy statement that became one of the most decisive documents in the history of American medicine. Flexner recommended closing the proprietary commercial medical schools and retaining only the university-based schools with the highest standards. To anticipate our later argument, we will note here that Freud came to America to speak at Clark University in 1909. Psychoanalysis arrived in America just as American medicine was tightening its controls, eliminating non-professionals, and establishing its authority.

The Flexner report transformed American medical education and significantly contributed to the professionalization of American medicine. By 1920, the number of medical schools fell to 66 nationwide. State medical licensing boards became unwilling to recognize graduates of lower-grade schools and the AMA's Council on Medical Education quickly achieved a monopoly. Medicine became a profession limited to those who could afford a college education and four years of medical school. For the next half-century, the era critical to the establishment of psychoanalysis in America, medicine was the exclusive preserve of upper-middle-class white men; its professionalization had dire consequences for blacks and women. Six out of eight black medical schools and most of the irregular schools, which had been a haven for women seeking a medical education, were closed.

Following Flexner, American medicine was established once and for all as a branch of higher academic education accessible almost exclusively to privileged white men.

On the rise since the 1880s, specialization, which had previously been considered elitist, became increasingly acceptable, a development that was accompanied by the formation of specialized journals and societies. By 1910, the university-affiliated medical schools were oriented toward research. Advances in science and technology heightened the demand for specialists, with surgeons leading the way. By 1927, the AMA expanded its involvement in medical education and postgraduate training and began to publish lists of approved residency programs in medical and surgical specialties, including the specialty of neuropsychiatry.

New state licensing laws were established throughout the country. As feminist historians (Ehrenreich and English, 1973) have documented, a critical next step by the medical establishment was to drive out what remained of the older irregular and folk medicine, namely midwifery. In 1910, midwives, most of them black or working-class immigrants, delivered about half of the number of babies born in America. With the establishment of obstetrics as a medical specialty, the continued use of midwives became intolerable to the medical establishment. Obstetricians launched a public campaign claiming that midwives were incompetent, uneducated, and dirty. While in Europe, midwives were better educated and midwifery was established as an independent profession, in America, state after state passed laws outlawing midwifery. For poor women, this often meant receiving no medical care at all. As we will see in Chapters 7 and 8, lay analysts were similarly excluded by the American medical establishment from practicing psychoanalysis, although they had been allowed to practice psychoanalysis in Europe.

Medicine in Wartime

Advances in medicine have always been facilitated by the exigencies of war. In one of the greatest strategic medical decisions ever implemented by a wartime general, George Washington followed Dr. Benjamin Franklin's advice and inoculated the troops of the Continental Army against smallpox, changing the outcome of the Revolutionary War. Although medicine remained largely ineffective during the Civil War, with no major breakthroughs in treatment, the Civil War gave American doctors unprecedented clinical experience and strengthened their status, setting the stage for the rise of scientific medicine in the late 1800s.

By World War I, American medicine was well enough developed so that for the first time, the United States lost fewer troops to disease than to battle injuries. Sophisticated army hospitals were outfitted with a full complement of medical and surgical capabilities. In World War I, a conflict of attrition, unrelenting bombardment, and deadly new weaponry, "doctors gained unparalleled clinical experience through incalculable human suffering" (Rutkow, 2010, p. 170). Thousands of doctors received a crash course in military medicine. Acute care dominated, and the importance of specialty practice was newly recognized. While the prolonged battle destroyed much of Europe, American medicine stepped up to a position of international leadership. Following developments in science, the repercussions of the Flexner report, and World War I, doctors were positioned to rise to unprecedented levels of power, prestige, and income. By the beginning of World War II, America led the world in many areas of medicine.

As Rutkow (2010) notes, "One of the great ironies of warfare throughout modern history is that the more brutal and widespread the conflict, the higher the casualty count climbs, the greater are the resulting medical advances" (p. 220). More profoundly than earlier wars, World War II transformed American medicine. All wars had provided doctors with practical clinical experience, but World War II began just as American medicine achieved unparalleled prestige and, most importantly, the confidence and support of the government. As we will examine in further detail in the following chapter, among the specialties, psychiatry changed most radically.

During the economic depression of the 1930s, specialization and specialty board certification helped the public and the government to determine what were suitable financial expenditures. However, many doctors continued to view specialists as elitists who did not represent the American tradition of generalist practice. Specialization became firmly established when the U.S. military began to award higher ranks to medical specialists with advanced levels of training and expertise; this included psychiatrists. Those areas of medicine that had not yet set up specialty board certification now did so in order for their members to qualify for the military ranking system. The American government, more than any other government in the world, began to pour money into medical research. This funding led to major advances, including the discovery of penicillin as an antibiotic. By 1943, military doctors routinely treated casualties with penicillin, saving thousands of lives.

In the years following World War II, as the United States entered a long period of economic prosperity, government influence on medical research continued to expand. The government provided abundant funding for scientific research and medical education and instituted health care legislation on a massive scale, giving birth to what would soon become the medical industrial complex. Medicine transformed from being an independent profession largely free of government intervention to being funded and regulated by the government. It became a highly respected and even prized national asset for a prosperous nation that looked up to its healers as heroes. The postwar expansion of the economy brought doctors more patients than ever, and their salaries rose accordingly. It was the era of *Ben Casey*, *Dr. Kildare*, and *General Hospital*. America was the unrivaled global leader in medicine, surgery, medical research, and education.

Excluding the Competition

As medical schools became increasingly competitive, the number of doctors produced did not increase fast enough relative to the population, resulting in an imbalance of supply and demand, and making their value even greater. Nevertheless, the medical establishment remained threatened by the idea of increased competition. Physicians worried that increasing the supply of doctors would compromise their exclusiveness. In their desire to limit competition, they sought to specifically exclude women, Jews, and people of color from the medical profession.

In the early 20th century, millions of Eastern European Jews immigrated to New York and other cities in the United States. Fear of competition from these Jewish immigrants fueled the emergence of traditional anti-Semitic stereotypes and led medical schools and hospitals to create informal quotas limiting the numbers of Jewish medical students and physicians. Educators maintained that Jews were too bookish, aggressive, and greedy. Medical schools deduced applicants' religious affiliation by scrutinizing their names, interviewing them, and asking them directly on medical school applications. At Yale Medical School, applications of Jewish students were marked with an "H" for "Hebrew" (Lerner, 2009). Between 1920 and 1940, the number of Jewish students dropped dramatically. At the Columbia College of Physicians and Surgeons, for example, the percentage of Jewish students fell from 47 to only 6 percent. Quotas were even stricter for doctors, especially for senior physician positions at university-affiliated hospitals. While the quota system eventually began to break down due to the influx of refugee European Jewish physicians fleeing the Nazis in the late 1930s, hospitals continued to discriminate against Jews well into the 1950s (Lerner, 2009).

Women in Medicine

Male doctors associated the entrance of women into the profession with the organized feminist movement, which was stronger in the United States than in other parts of the world. Their dislike of feminism created additional resistance to the inclusion of women. The rare woman who did make it into a regular medical school had to face one sexist hurdle after another to complete her training. Hospitals were usually closed to women, and internships were often denied them. By the 1960s, there was a severe shortage of doctors. Hospitals, needing to fill internship slots, began to hire foreign medical graduates.

At the same time, medical schools came under pressure from social activists, who lobbied congress and sued public institutions, and so began to admit women. Between 1972 and 1980, medical schools increased the number of female students from 15 to 28 percent. By 2005, the number of women medical school students equaled that of men, a 400 percent change in a period of only 35 years. Even now, however, fewer than 10 percent of surgeons are women, and women remain underrepresented in such lucrative specialties as cardiology and gastroenterology. Even more dramatic is the continued problem of racism and lack of access to medical education for people of color. Despite the progress made over the past century, only 2.2 percent of medical students and doctors were African-American in 2006, compared to 2.5 percent in 1910 (Metzger, 2009).

A Mother's Care

In discussing the role of women in medicine, it is important to include the nursing profession and its position in the medical hierarchy. Prior to the founding of modern nursing, nurses were often poor and held in low regard, serving essentially to clean and care for the dying. Some nurses were nuns, drawn from religious orders, and the military often provided nursing-like services to its soldiers. The religious and military roots of modern nursing remain in evidence today in many countries.

The founders of modern nursing were women. They sought to professionalize nursing and raise the class of women who were attracted to the profession. Nursing schools opened in America after the Civil War and attempted to recruit upper-class women as nursing students. Training emphasized character rather than skill; most important was that the nurse be a "lady." Dubbed "The Lady with the Lamp" and "ministering angel" because of her habit of making rounds at night, Florence Nightingale laid the foundation of professional nursing by establishing the world's first secular nursing school in 1860. She authored the first textbook of nursing. Nightingale and the founders of the nursing profession saw it as a natural vocation for women, second only to mothering. Ironically, feminists of the 19th century supported this idea, celebrating the image of the nurse/mother. Idealizing motherhood, the feminists of the time encouraged women to participate in professions that made use of their feminine maternal skills. Although male doctors were at first skeptical of the nursing profession, suspecting that it was just one more way for women to invade medical practice, they were soon won over by the Nightingale nurses' obedient attitudes.

Psychiatry in America

Prior to World War I, psychiatrists worked primarily in psychiatric asylums, which were referred to colloquially as "snake pits." *The Snake Pit*, a 1948 American film depicting a psychiatric asylum, had an enormous impact on the public's opinion of mental institutions. Twentieth Century Fox claimed that 26 of the then 48 states enacted reform legislation because of the movie. While this claim is difficult to substantiate, historians do believe the film led to changes in the conditions of mental institutions in the United States.

When asylums were first built in the early to mid-18th century, it was with the optimistic therapeutic intent of curing the acutely mentally ill. Indeed, despite the lack of effective treatments available to actively treat psychiatric illness, the asylums did achieve a measure of success. Many patients were hospitalized for only three to nine months and were discharged to the community, never to return in need of further hospitalization (Grob, 1994). This success was likely due to several factors, including the relatively high rate of spontaneous remission of acute mental illness and the opportunity for patients to rest and be cared for outside of their possibly stressful home environments.

But by the late 1800s, asylums were transformed into custodial warehouses for the chronically mentally ill, and the optimistic possibility of cure disappeared. As the asylum population increased, the financial burden of their maintenance fell upon local governments, which funded increasingly larger institutions. This led to a vicious cycle, in which wealthy patients sought smaller private settings while asylums became filled with the poor and the elderly. As diagnostic criteria were broadened, an increasing number of the poor were diagnosed with mental illness and assigned to the asylums. The wealthy were treated in private sanitariums, where they were given more benign diagnoses. As the asylums became larger and more populated, their poor and elderly patients met with less staff and increasing pessimism, and ultimately were given up as hopeless, incurable custodial cases. Psychiatrists had always been more interested in treating patients with acute and episodic illnesses, who had a better chance of recovery and cure. Chronic cases were far less attractive to physicians because they were much less likely to improve. The care of these chronically ill patients increasingly became the main function of mental hospitals, frustrating doctors, who were left to provide primarily custodial care.

By the late 1800s, inpatient facilities were populated mostly by the chronically mentally ill. One factor contributing to this development was the rapid growth of the number of patients over the age of 60. Before 1900, the elderly were primarily cared for at home. The increase in individual and family mobility led to smaller families, and the rise of the market economy, involving the separation of the workplace from home, undermined the family's ability to take care of the elderly. The burden thus fell on the publicly supported poorhouses, which were the mainstay of the 19th-century welfare system. In the early part of the 20th century, mental hospitals took in these elderly patients, shifting the financial burden from local communities to the state. Mental hospitals essentially became nursing homes for the aged.

At the same time, these institutions became responsible for the care of tertiary (late-stage) syphilitic patients. Before the availability of antibiotics, insanity resulting from venereal disease accounted for many of the chronic cases admitted to asylums. Paretics, those in the tertiary stage of syphilitic infection, required total care, and increasingly filled the mental hospitals. While hospitals met an urgent social need by caring for the elderly and the syphilitic, physicians did not consider these patients genuine psychiatric cases. The transformation of mental hospitals into old age homes and warehouses for incurable cases led to a depressing environment both for patients and their psychiatrists. By necessarily placing their emphasis on custodial care, the hospitals subordinated physicians' therapeutic goals. Because psychiatrists became associated with an inability to offer treatment or cure, they developed a poor self-image and low morale. Simultaneously, the public valuation of mental hospitals deteriorated, as these institutions became increasingly associated with hopelessness and death.

While other medical specialties were embedded in private practice settings, psychiatry was deeply rooted in an institutional milieu, and the role of the psychiatrist was defined by the custodial practices of the asylum. Toward the end of the 19th and beginning of the 20th century, this professional arrangement began to change. The 19th century brought with it the rise of scientific medicine and exciting possibilities for the treatment and cure of disease. Germ theory, anesthesia, antisepsis, the application of laboratory findings, and the development of new technologies brought medicine into the age of modern science, dramatically raising its prestige. In contrast to other medical specialties, psychiatry appeared backward, tied to the asylum care of chronically dependent patients and preoccupied with managerial and administrative functions rather than with the biological roots of disease and its medical treatment.

For psychiatrists to share in the newly won status of their medical colleagues, they had to essentially reinvent psychiatry, to shift from being asylum superintendents to private clinicians; from treating the chronically and severely mentally ill to practicing prevention and treating problems of middle class living. They needed new theories, rooted in scientific thinking and research. Psychiatry was determined to redefine itself by integrating modern scientific medicine into its practice. As psychiatry's commitment to the mental hospitals began to wane, it sought new possibilities for its practitioners. The introduction from Europe to America at the beginning of the 20th century of the new scientific theory and technique of psycho-analysis offered just such an exciting opportunity.

When Freud came to America in 1909, he landed on fertile soil. With the turn of the century, American psychiatry had entered a new phase, and came to be known as dynamic psychiatry. This was not quite psychoanaly-sis, nor was it at the time just a euphemism for psychoanalysis, which is how the term would be later used. Dynamic psychiatry was a general shift in the field away from the purely organic and biological toward a more psychological and optimistic set of theories. Whereas asylum physicians had sharply distinguished between health and disease, dynamic psychiatry introduced a new model of psychic distress that viewed health and mental illness along a continuum. This model not only blurred the clear demarca-tion between health and disease but also provided the rationale for psychi-atrists to address a wider range of behavior and not limit themselves to treating the pathological extreme. Dynamic psychiatry placed much greater emphasis on the life history and prior experience of the individual. It provided a clear justification for preventive intervention and was the ideology under which psychiatrists could move from the asylums into private practice.

Adolf Meyer's career as a leading figure in the new dynamic American psychiatry spanned just this period from the late 1800s through World War II. Meyer developed an approach he called "psychobiology," which stressed the interaction of the organism and the environment. Meyer was not a sharp theoretician and his concepts were vague and ambiguous: nevertheless he was an enormous influence on the profession. He was eclectic and vigilantly non-dogmatic and so held himself apart from psychoanalysis, but his approach clearly set American psychiatry on a course that was receptive to Freud's ideas, with somewhat of an American twist. Meyer emphasized history-taking and the examination of the details of the patient's life. Even though his broad theory attempted to integrate somatic, constitutional, and genetic factors, his emphasis was on psychology and life history.

William Alanson White was as important and influential a figure in the new psychiatry as Meyer, although today among psychoanalysts he is prob-ably known only for the institute named for him. With a background in neurology, he was influenced by an evolutionary approach that emphasized development from the simple to the complex, as well as the importance of adaptation. While eclectic, White was more positive toward psychoanaly-sis than Meyer and stressed the psychological factors in mental illness. He too shifted his interest from severe and chronic mental illness to the mental hygiene movement. Emphasizing prevention, the mental hygiene move-ment facilitated the growing separation of psychiatry from the mental hospital and the expansion of its authority into the community. For Meyer and White, the mental hygiene movement also served the purpose of connecting psychiatry to medicine, with the shared interest of promoting preventive intervention. Harry Stack Sullivan, whom we will discuss in detail later on, was influenced by this tradition of dynamic psychiatry, particularly by Meyer and White.

We should not give the impression that the 1930s led to an interest only in dynamic psychiatry. Hospital psychiatry continued, as did biological approaches. Psychiatrists working with severe mental illness in the hospitals wanted to align psychiatry with modern scientific medicine, and a variety of new interventions were designed using a biological model. Fever therapy, a variety of shock therapies, and psychosurgery were all utilized in the hope that somatic treatment would lead to radical cures. The spirit of these treatments was very much in line with the desire of psychiatry to be a part of biological medicine. If patients could be cured, they could be released, relieving the severe overcrowding of the mental hospitals. More importantly, psychiatry would be able to provide treatment that worked rather than only custodial care for the hopeless and incurable.

Psychiatry was caught between the medical and welfare systems, which were funded separately, fell under different lines of authority, and had independent priorities. States maintained a variety of mechanisms to regulate mental hospital care. Some utilized the welfare system while others regulated psychiatry under medicine. Would psychiatry have to answer to the medical criteria of success via cure or to the welfare system of care and support? In the modern era, medicine was becoming increasingly valued because of its ability to cure illness. As we all inevitably fall ill at some time or another, we can easily empathize with the sick and enthusiastically support curative treatment. As a society, we are much less tolerant of endless dependency. Medicine, which treats the ill, is usually valued and valorized, whereas welfare for the needy and dependent is often devalued and loathed. Mental hospitals attracted ambivalence in providing some of each—cure and care—but for the doctors themselves, it was to their great advantage to be viewed as providing treatment for the sick rather than custodial care for the hopelessly dependent. This dichotomy of treatment versus care had a significant influence on psychiatry's efforts to raise its social standing and prestige. As we shall see, it also figured into the differentiation of psychoanalysis from psychotherapy.

Careers in hospital psychiatry had become a dead end. Psychiatrists were determined to overcome their inferiority within the rapidly changing field of medicine. The 1921 change in name from the American Medico-Psychological Association to the American Psychiatric Association and of the *American Journal of Insanity* to the *American Journal of Psychiatry* represented the transformation of psychiatry as a profession. The foundations of psychiatry were rapidly falling into line with the newly reorganized, credentialed, and accredited field of medicine. This could not be fully accomplished in the 1920s or 1930s, but awaited the profound revolution brought about by World War II.

Grob (1994) articulated the dichotomous positioning psychiatry adopted in order to distinguish itself from the caring professions and establish itself as an objective science. He demonstrated that the binaries cure/care, scientific/holistic, objective/subjective, and even private practice/hospital work, became aligned with the binary of masculine/feminine. Grob wrote,

> Most psychiatrists rationalized their rejection of a career in mental hospitals by employing professional rhetoric that emphasized a commitment to treatment and a rejection of caring responsibilities. In making such a choice, they had, perhaps unconsciously, embraced a particular concept of medical science that made objective knowledge and biological reductionism its defining elements. The older and more traditional concept, by contrast, had been based on a holistic definition of disease that made sympathy and care central elements of medical practice. By the late nineteenth century objectivity had come to be identified as a masculine attribute and sympathy and care as feminine qualities. The psychiatric rejection of an older tradition that emphasized care, therefore, reflected in part the stratification of occupations along gender lines and the ensuing devaluation of careers that were identified as female in nature.
>
> (1994, p. 233)

There was a clear gender alignment, in which women were reformers and crusaders for social welfare, while medicine retained its position at the top of the patriarchal hierarchy. Cure/care was aligned with masculine/feminine and doctor/nurse. Women employed their mothering skills, while physicians were fathers who knew best. The cure/care split was gendered in such a way that providing treatment was linked with masculine science and progress, whereas providing palliative care was associated with feminine support and dependence.

Psychoanalysis in America

Freud came to America just at the time mainstream American medicine was establishing its professional authority over those it considered charlatans. The professionalization of psychoanalysis was directly influenced by the contemporary agenda of the medical community for credentialing and control. Having been a poor cousin to other medical specialties because it had little to offer in the way of treatment, psychiatry needed to establish its legitimacy and align itself with scientific progress and cure, rather than with custodial care. Doctors wanted to cure, not just provide care. Psychoanalysis arose as a specialty within a specialty just at the time specialization was most highly regarded. As we have shown, the medical profession was predominantly male, while the nursing profession was exclusively female. As masculine scientific treatment and cure was increasingly contrasted with feminine care and support, psychoanalysis came to define itself as a scientific treatment that led to real cure, in contrast to psychotherapy, which provided only a comforting relationship. All that was associated with support, care, and dependence was split off by the psychiatric medical establishment onto the equivalent of nurses—psychotherapists, social workers, and psychologists—all non-MDs. In terms of the dichotomies we explore throughout this book, cure was to care as male was to female, doctor to nurse, autonomy to relatedness, and psychoanalysis to psychotherapy.

Any discussion of the history of psychoanalysis in America must begin with Hale's (1971, 1995) two-volume history. Although weak in its narration of the influence of the theoretical revisionists and the impact of psychoanalysis on psychology, social work, and the humanities, Hale's work remains the definitive history of the psychoanalytic mainstream. As Hale described, Freud's theories appeared on the American scene at the beginning of the century at just the right time, amidst social crises concerning attitudes about sexual morality and dissatisfaction with the then current treatment of nervous and mental disorders. Progressive reformers had been calling for more liberal sexual attitudes, and Freud's ideas about the dangers of sexual repression and the restrictions imposed by "civilized morality" contributed to their critique. Neurologists and psychiatrists were becoming increasingly critical of psychiatry's somatic emphasis. They welcomed Freud's ideas about catharsis, the undoing of repression, the therapeutic value of remembering, and the role of sexuality in neurosis.

Psychotherapy was emerging as a significant force, especially in Boston, where the influence of William James, Pierre Janet, and Morton Prince was prominent. Psychotherapy, hypnosis, and secularized forms of spiritual counseling were practiced. Shortly after Freud's visit to America in 1909, psychoanalytic ideas became increasingly popular. With the founding of the New York Psychoanalytic Society and the American Psychoanalytic Association in 1911, psychoanalysts became the first psychotherapists to establish their own professional institutions devoted to a specific theory and form of practice. It was precisely at this time that American medicine, following the Flexner report, was beginning to accredit its schools and weed out non-physicians from practicing medicine. Several eminent American psychologists and psychiatrists became enthusiasts of Freud's ideas. These included G. Stanley Hall at Clark University, James Jackson Putnam and Smith Jelliffe at Harvard, and Adolph Meyer at Johns Hopkins. Support for psychoanalysis from American academicians stood in marked contrast to Freud's unfavorable reception among his European academic contemporaries.

As it became increasingly associated with psychiatry, psychoanalysis enabled psychiatrists for the first time to establish themselves as the purveyors of office-based psychotherapy. As Shorter (1997) emphasizes, the rise of psychoanalysis as the dominant model of psychiatry was due in large part to the opportunity it created for psychiatrists to enter private practice. While in 1917, only 8 percent of American psychiatrists worked in private practice, by 1970, 66 percent of psychiatrists were full-time private practitioners, with many others supplementing their clinical and hospital income with part-time private practice. This was a dramatic change in the type of work psychiatrists performed, as well as in their lifestyle and income. As we shall see, the later attempt by psychiatrists to protect the domain of private practice played a central role in the narrowing definition of medical psychoanalysis.

Chapter 5

Psychoanalysis in Uniform

Both World War I and II were instrumental in popularizing the therapeutic benefit of psychoanalysis and bestowing international recognition upon Freud's name and movement. In this chapter and the next, we continue our brief historical sketch of the events leading up to the golden age of psychoanalysis in the 1950s in America by reviewing the role of psychoanalysis in wartime. We offer this summary in order to provide the reader with the relevant background for an understanding of the forces that shaped how psychoanalysis in its golden era came to be institutionalized and defined.

Shell Shock

One would assume World War I would have taught military psychiatrists something about shell shock, a condition common to all wars. During the Civil War it was called nostalgia. Later it was called war neurosis, battle fatigue, operational fatigue, combat fatigue, combat exhaustion, and in our time, Post-traumatic Stress Disorder (PTSD). But war is traumatic; its insights are repressed or dissociated and must be rediscovered again and again in an endless repetition compulsion. The immense body of shell-shock literature dealt mainly with chronic cases, not with soldiers in acute distress. What the world's leaders did learn from World War I was that casualties were costly.

During World War I, physicians sympathetic to psychoanalysis held a few influential positions in the armed services medical corps. For a number of victims of shell shock, catharsis proved to be an effective treatment. Physicians began to recognize the role of trauma in symptom formation and the usefulness of catharsis in releasing repressed traumatic memories. In the United States, psychiatrists and neurologists became convinced that dynamic ideas such as repression, trauma, catharsis, conflict, and memory, which were associated with psychoanalysis, were important in treating mental illness. In Europe, World War I presented significant opportunities for psychoanalysis but also exposed important theoretical difficulties that Freud and his colleagues were left to deal with after the war.

The term "shell shock" conveyed a somatic connection between a shell exploding and a shock to the nervous system. This term was misleading, as many soldiers who were not near any physical shell explosion were still susceptible to breakdown. By 1917, the British war office banned the term, reasoning that a diagnosis of shell shock discouraged soldiers from getting better, and substituted the label NYDN (Not Yet Diagnosed Nervous). World War I saw static trench warfare with heavy bombardment. Psychoneuroses accounted for 34 percent of British casualties (Watson, 2000). Allied and Central powers found that officers as well as enlisted men were psychiatric casualties, so they could no longer call these breakdowns "malingering." Clinical services were needed not only at the front but back home because casualties were so widespread and severe. A persistent theme in all modern wars in which psychiatry has played a part has been the conflict for clinicians between protecting the lives and interests of their patients and serving the military purpose of getting the soldiers back to the fight. Diagnosing a soldier's trauma as somatic, the physical result of the actual explosion of a shell, such as a concussion or exploding shell paralysis, made it more likely that the soldier would be treated as a legitimate medical victim in need of evacuation and treatment, deserving of financial compensation or pension. However, the clinician's patriotic obligation was not only to the individual soldier but also to the military and the nation. Diagnoses such as hysteria or traumatic hysteria, which emphasized the psychological rather than the physical, led to the soldier's quicker return to battle and were met with less sympathy and reduced likelihood of financial compensation.

Trauma: Causes and Compensation

In Germany, a professional debate was waged for decades, beginning with concern about the implications of traumatic neurosis brought about by industrial and railroad accidents, and culminating in the trauma suffered by soldiers during World War I. The origins of modern trauma theory can be traced to the railway and industrial accidents of the 19th century. The railroads hired prominent lawyers to argue that they should not be held liable for traumatic neuroses caused by these accidents since the true cause was the patient's neurotic predisposition. The debate revolved around the questions of what caused trauma and who was responsible for its compensation. If the trauma (traumatic neurosis) was physical and caused by an actual train wreck, an argument could be made for holding the railroad company responsible for compensation. If on the other hand, the victim's suffering was a result largely of his own predisposition, for example, because he suffered from a degenerate family constitution, and the train wreck simply triggered symptoms resulting from his neurotic predisposition (as in hysterical neurosis or traumatic hysteria), then the railroad companies could more easily be let off the hook.

Just a few decades later, during World War I, governments followed the railroad companies' rationale, arguing that they should not be held responsible for compensating veterans for their neurotic symptoms. If soldiers suffered a nervous breakdown because of shell shock, the implication being that their disorder was the direct result of a physical war injury, a better argument could be made for the state owing the soldier financial compensation, treatment, and rehabilitation. If the suffering was not a direct result of battle but was brought on by the soldier's nervous predisposition, then the state would be protected from a massive financial obligation. Under these circumstances, the doctor's allegiance could easily be swayed to meet the needs of the state instead of the individual suffering soldier. There are few examples better suited to illustrate the ways in which psychiatric diagnosis can be shaped by political, economic, and social forces. An important aspect of these debates was the frequent latency period from the time of the accident or trauma to the outbreak of symptoms. Freud learned a great deal from these phenomena, working these observations into his theory of trauma, *Nachträglichkeit*, and the latency period of psychosexual development.

Among the Axis powers (Germany, Austria, and Hungary, where many of the leading pioneer analysts lived), maintaining that a soldier's symptoms were psychological implied that he was motivated to be sick in order to collect a financial pension and avoid fighting and working. Psychological symptoms, meriting a diagnosis of traumatic hysteria, were associated with cowardice, the avoidance of responsibility, and the desire to be financially supported, all viewed as unmanly, feminine, or passive homosexual traits. German psychiatrists worried that an outbreak of "pension hysteria" would become a financial drain on the nation's economy.

Paul Lerner (2003) documents the great difficulty German neurologist Herman Oppenheim had in explaining his own position on the matter precisely because it challenged this neat dichotomy. Oppenheim was one of the leading neurologists in Germany and had written the standard text on nervous disease. His life's goal was to establish neurology as a medical specialty. Like Freud, he was frustrated for years by having been denied a full professorship because of anti-Semitism. He was a member of the Central Association for Citizens of the Jewish Faith, an association for strengthening Jewish identity. Oppenheim insisted that traumatic neurosis had legitimate psychological components, was based on actual trauma, and did not simply result from the wish to be financially compensated. In 1889, he published a treatise on traumatic neuroses, claiming that psychological trauma caused organic changes that perpetuated psychic neuroses. Eminent physicians such as Jean-Martin Charcot and Max Nonne harshly criticized this claim.

To anticipate our discussion of later developments, this history is important to keep in mind as we examine what happened during World War II, where at the start, the United States and Britain, following Germany, emphasized careful screening of soldiers in order to avoid psychiatric breakdowns. President Roosevelt feared these breakdowns and subsequent psychiatric hospitalizations would be too costly for the country. A binary split was created between neuroses caused by actual somatic nervous damage, versus hysteria, which had psychological causes, but was attributed by most psychiatrists to what Freud would later call "secondary gain." In other words, omitted from this polarity was the fact that damage could be *both* psychological *and* a direct result of actual trauma. (For an astute analysis of how even today we continue to operate under these polarities, see Hustvedt, 2011.)

Psychoanalytic Formulations of Trauma

Psychoanalysis played a significant but troubling role in this debate during World War I. Its focus on the internal psychological processes of trauma attracted the attention of the German, Austrian, and Hungarian governments, who sent high-level representatives to the Psychoanalytic Congress in Budapest in 1918. One reason for their interest was the hope that psychoanalysis might be an effective treatment for war neuroses. But another reason was purely financial, centered on the issue of who would be held responsible for financial compensation for war injuries and industrial or train accidents.

Many of the early analysts were directly involved during World War I. Sándor Ferenczi conducted what he called the first equestrian psychoanalysis when he analyzed one officer on horseback. Karl Abraham and Max Eitington fought for Germany, Vicktor Tausk and Edward Hitschman for Austria, Ferenczi and Sándor Rado for Hungary. Many physicians made use of psychoanalytic principles in their care of the wounded, which may have meant only that they had read some of Freud's writing. Some of the most effective applications of psychoanalytic ideas to the war neuroses were made not by analysts, but by psychiatrists who used analytic ideas loosely. For example, Berlin physician Ernst Simmel, who was not a trained analyst, reported significant positive results using psychoanalysis on war neurotics. But Simmel used catharsis and abreaction, methods derived from Freud's early work. This left Freud and his colleagues in a bind. They welcomed the publicity Simmel attracted for psychoanalysis, but they also knew that his methods were outdated and contrary to current practice. Yet the fact that psychoanalysis was being used to assist the military was excellent publicity for the psychoanalytic movement. We will soon see just how much this anticipates a similar scenario during World War II.

Freud, Ferenczi, and Abraham did not actually conduct psychoanalyses on war neurotics for both practical and tactical reasons. First, military psychiatry, both then and now, relies on quick methods that can be applied in the field, not on the time-consuming method of formal psychoanalysis. Second, these analysts believed that most soldiers, drawn from the working classes, the uneducated, the poor, the less intelligent, would be less likely to benefit from psychoanalysis. Many doctors experimented with the treatment of war neurotics, using more eclectic and less formal methods, yet were still influenced by psychoanalytic ideas. Freud was eager to benefit from their success, while just as eager to challenge or refine their theoretical conclusions.

Fritz Stern is one example. He wrote the first article describing the psychoanalytic treatment of war neuroses to appear in the German medical press. Stern served in a voluntary war hospital in Berlin-Charlottenberg, overseeing a 300-bed section for nervous illness. He concluded that wartime military life created an atmosphere conducive to hysteria. Having read Freud's *Studies on Hysteria*, he reasoned that under conditions of enemy fire and the need to conform to military standards, the processing of affect became impossible. Thus emotions were converted into hysterical symptoms, which could be treated with a kind of talk therapy that uncovered repressed memories and discharged strangulated affect. Similarly, other psychiatrists such as Willibald Sauer and Fritz Mohr made liberal use of early Freudian ideas to conduct a form of talk therapy emphasizing catharsis and abreaction. Ernst Simmel (1918) detailed his application of psychoanalytic ideas in *War Neurosis and Psychic Trauma*. Simmel's monograph captivated Freud, earning Simmel an invitation to speak at the International Psychoanalytic Conference in Budapest.

Toward the end of World War I, other psychiatric methods for treating the war neuroses came under critical attack, protested by both patients and doctors, to the concern of military officials. These techniques, often known as "active techniques" (note the later use of this term by Ferenczi) or the Kaufmann Cure, after one of its famous advocates, made use of suggestion accompanied by painful electric shocks. A sadistic and highly authoritarian "treatment," electrical stimulation was aimed at "persuading" the soldier to give up his symptoms. (We shall see other applications of electrical stimulation in Chapter 11.) Military officials, seeking more appealing methods of treatment, took a strong interest in Simmel's results and attended the 1918 Budapest Congress. It was not because they were captivated by the fine points of psychoanalytic theory! They had other concerns in mind.

At the Budapest Congress of 1918, there were many reasons for analysts to feel optimistic about the future. Because of the publicity attained in the treatment of war neuroses, the reputation of psychoanalysis was at its height. Freud and Ferenczi had enlisted Anton von Freund to become the first major patron of psychoanalysis. The son of a rich, ennobled industrialist who founded the state brewery, von Freund was analyzed by Freud and became good friends with Freud and Ferenczi. The Lord Mayor of Budapest attended, along with high-ranking military medical officials from Hungary, Austria, and Germany. Having state backing could only help the psychoanalytic cause. Psychiatry, always a marginal medical specialty, was eager to win national and public recognition for its contribution to the war effort. Psychoanalysis was similarly eager for recognition and the funding that would follow. Freud was an outsider, a Jewish private practice neurologist. Acknowledgment from the national government and the military was a significant opportunity for psychoanalysis to win insider status.

But Freud and his followers were faced with a profound dilemma. By World War I, Freud was no longer leading a mixed eclectic group as he had in the first decade of the century. By then, the movement had expunged its dissenters, Jung, Adler, and Stekel. Freud defined Freudian analysis in terms of acceptance of his theories of libido, childhood sexuality, and the Oedipus complex. According to Freudian theory, neurosis is the inevitable result of childhood sexual conflicts, in particular, the Oedipus complex. But the war demonstrated that soldiers broke down due to current military stress. While Freud always reserved a place for the actual neuroses, neuroses caused by current events, this did not seem sufficient to account for the massive outbreak of war neuroses. How could psychoanalysts explain massive war neuroses in terms of infantile sexuality? If war neuroses could be explained as being due to present circumstances or psychological reactions to current events alone, didn't that undermine all of what Freud had been claiming?

Thirty-two members of the International Psychoanalytic Association attended the Budapest Congress, all of them in uniform, except Freud. Sándor Ferenczi, then serving as the chief neurologist at the Maria Valeria base hospital in Budapest, gave the keynote address. Ferenczi began by overstating the case: he distinguished between Freudians, who attended to psychological phenomena, and other psychiatrists, whom he presented as attending only to the somatic. He equated all psychogenic explanations with Freudian psychoanalysis, as if anyone who was not thinking in terms of Freud's ideas was not attending to the psychological at all! Lerner (2003) argues from a historian's perspective that a more balanced view would situate Freud within a general trend toward the psychological. But what much of German psychiatry meant by the psychological was what Freud would have considered secondary gain, namely, becoming symptomatic due to the psychological wish to obtain financial compensation, whereas Freud and Ferenczi were exploring deeper, more conflictual personal motivations and dynamics. Nothing we have seen in the literature of mainstream German psychiatry approaches the sophistication and depth of insight achieved by Freud and his colleagues in the same period.

Ferenczi (1921b) went to great lengths to refute the views of the German psychiatrist Nonne, who raised the critical point that the experience of war neurosis contradicted Freud's ideas about the sexual etiology of neurosis. It seemed obvious that the war neuroses had nothing at all to do with infantile sexuality. This was a major devastating argument against Freud. Ferenczi's reply to Nonne was classic—it became the standard response of analysts for decades to come when confronted with challenges to Freud's libido theory. Essentially, Ferenczi argued that Nonne and others misunderstood the meaning of sexuality within the Freudian system. What Freudians meant by sexuality was far broader than genital sexuality. The reason these psychiatrists did not find evidence of sexual etiology was because they defined sexuality much too narrowly.

Ferenczi stated that Freudian psychoanalysis:

> treats all sensual and affectionate relationships of the individual to the opposite and to the same gender, emotions toward friends, relatives, any fellow person, even the affect relationship to one's own Ego and to one's own body in the rubric of "eroticism" that is, sexuality.
>
> (Quoted in Lerner, 2003, p. 178)

By this definition, what is considered sexual and what is considered relational are identical! In Ferenczi's interpretation, Freud's theory of sexuality was nothing other than a theory of relationships, which took the bodily passions into account! In the war neuroses, the problems were based on issues of narcissistic injury, which from the Freudian point of view, confirmed sexual etiology. Ferenczi added that impotence and other disturbances of libido were common consequences of war and so sexual etiology should not be dismissed too quickly. Furthermore, since all people go through a narcissistic stage, it could be an etiological factor in all traumatic neuroses, no matter the soldier's background. The wish for pensions and fear of the front were secondary gains of illness but not the primary causal agents. That was unconscious sexual conflict, with sexuality broadly defined as including narcissism and all personal relations, including relations to one's self. Ferenczi mounted a formidable defense of Freud's etiological theory. Neuroses might be aggravated by wishes for financial pensions or other entitlements, but they were caused by childhood sexual conflicts, as long as it was understood that the term sexual was being used to cover just about anything relational. We believe that Ferenczi's understanding of the Freudian meaning of "sexuality" is quite remarkable and points to a deconstruction of the binary opposition of Freudian and relational theory.

Karl Abraham followed Ferenczi to the podium. Like Ferenczi, Abraham saw war neurotics as struggling with a regression to narcissism. Based on his clinical findings, Abraham suggested that war neurotics were sexually labile even before the war. After all, why else would some men become neurotic and others not, even if they had experienced the same wartime conditions? Like most German psychiatrists, Abraham traced the onset of war neuroses to the individual's predisposing character—his constitutional deficiencies, not the circumstances of war. Whereas German psychiatrists and neurologists emphasized that these men had always been prone to avoid work, Abraham cast aspersions on their sexuality and masculinity, viewing them as having struggled with their potency, homosexual inclinations, and narcissism even before the war. When war conditions forced these narcissistic and fragile men to put the interests of others ahead of their own self-interest, they broke down.

The third speaker was Ernst Simmel, who, as we have pointed out, was not an analyst. Freud was accepting of Simmel's use of hypnosis under war conditions and had recommended Simmel's book approvingly to Ferenczi and Abraham. Simmel was much more equivocal about sexual etiology than Ferenczi and Abraham, but he did give it some acknowledgment. More importantly, Simmel, unlike Ferenczi and Abraham, had spent the war, day by day, treating war neurotics, and his much greater sympathy for these men was apparent. Whereas the analysts had disparaged the narcissism of the men, Simmel saw them as caught between a conflict of self-preservation and moral obligation to the nation. Rather than focusing on predisposing personality traits and constitutional weakness, Simmel stressed the exogenous, actual, present conditions of war.

During World War I, Simmel had served as military doctor and chief of a hospital for psychiatric battle casualties in Posen. Simmel agreed with Freud that his patients were too uneducated to be properly psychoanalyzed and there was not enough time to conduct a thorough analysis. Simmel had been using hypnosis on the war neurotics and came to believe that psychoanalysis accompanied by hypnosis could be effective and efficient, making psychoanalysis suitable to treat large numbers of patients. But Freud had rejected hypnosis, basing psychoanalysis on eliminating the use of suggestion. Simmel (1921) agreed, condemning such "forcible and restrictive" measures as hypnosis (p. 30). Instead, he advocated a blended analytical-cathartic hypnosis to help the patient free-associate more efficiently in conjunction with analytical conversations and dream interpretation both in the awake and dream state. Simmel's method was psychoanalytic in the sense that he was not using hypnosis to suggest the elimination of symptoms, which he argued led to symptom substitution, but rather to reach the unconscious psychic conflicts through an uncovering expressive form of treatment. He had a genuinely psychodynamic point of view and an excellent record of success. Not only were many of his patients better enough to go home, they were also better enough to return to combat. The military was favorably impressed, ensuring national recognition of the benefits of psychoanalysis.

The psychoanalysts were interested in describing subtle, complex, and deep psychological forces that explained how trauma led to neuroses. But for the government officials, the analysts' arguments dovetailed nicely with their own interest in maintaining that solders suffering from war neuroses had preexisting psychologies leaving them susceptible to becoming neurotic under the conditions of war. If what led to the neurosis was not the actual external traumatic event but intrapsychic dynamics or unconscious narcissistic personality traits, then the state should not be responsible to pay damages. The state would use the new science of psychoanalysis to save a fortune in compensation for disabled veterans. Freud and his analytic colleagues were on the verge of receiving huge grants from the state for research, clinics, and hospitals.

But on November 11th Germany agreed to a ceasefire, and the war ended. Freud (1918c) wrote to Ferenczi,

> Our analysis has . . . had trouble. No sooner does it begin to interest the world on account of the war neuroses than the war ends . . . But hard luck is one of the constraints of life. Our kingdom is indeed not of this world.
>
> (1918c, p. 311)

Psychoanalysis would have to wait for World War II to be given the same opportunity and at that time, be prepared to seize it.

By the war's end, psychoanalysis' reputation had risen in the eyes of the public and the medical profession. In Budapest, Ferenczi was appointed to the world's first professorship of psychoanalysis, although the position would soon be lost, with the rise of the counter-revolutionary and anti-Semitic government. With von Freund's funding, the International Psychoanalytic Press was established in 1919 and the Berlin Polyclinic in 1920. Von Freund died prematurely of cancer in 1920 and the funds he had donated to psychoanalysis became largely worthless after the war. But psychoanalysis had been transformed by World War I, with Freud moving on to articulate the death instinct and the repetition compulsion, develop his ego psychology, and place a new emphasis on aggression.

As we have seen, the analysts recognized that war trauma triggered the outbreak of neurotic reactions. But they deemphasized the external traumatic event, focusing on its meaning rather than on the objective reality. Their emphasis was on the psychology of the soldier, on what the event meant to that individual in the context of his mind, personal history, and dynamic conflicts. All this has often been condensed in psychoanalytic literature under the term "fantasy." The analysts' interest in fantasy did not mean there was no real external objective trauma, but their primary focus was on what the trauma stimulated in the particular individual soldier's mind. What did he do with the trauma? What fantasies did it lead to? What personal meaning did it have and what psychological processes were stimulated by it? While this was a valuable contribution to psychology, it also led, even if inadvertently, to making the actual traumatic event appear irrelevant. Reality and fantasy were historically placed into competitive opposition and treated as binary terms, instead of being viewed dialectically as mutually influencing one another. The legacy of this history continues to confound our modern methods of treatment of the war neuroses, today called "combat-related post-traumatic stress disorder." In a recent review, Carr (2011) asserts, "a combat zone is no place for the intense, prolonged work of psychoanalysis" (p. 472), proposing a short-term treatment for combat-related PTSD, based on Stolorow's inter-subjectivity theory. Carr argues that psychoanalysts have described only the effects of childhood trauma, not the effect of adult traumatic experience given a benign developmental history. Psychoanalytic theories can therefore be perceived as blaming an adult's reaction to trauma on childhood events and experiences. In other words, even after all these years and many devastating wars, psychoanalysis can still be used to locate pathology in intrapsychic dynamics instead of in the subjective experience of present trauma. Of course, we would want to deconstruct this binary of present external experience or intrapsychic internal dynamics. Carr also struggles with the recognition that as soldiers heal from trauma, become more in touch with their feelings, and begin to think more clearly, they may become reluctant to fight and die. This dilemma has been a core conflict among all military psychiatrists throughout history, as Freud (1919a) so clearly described. "The insoluble conflict between the claims of humanity, which normally carry decisive weight for a physician, and the demands of a national war was bound to confuse his activity" (p. 214). The issues at the heart of the debate in 1918 among psychoanalysts studying the war neuroses continue to be of concern to contemporary clinicians.

Simmel went on to undergo a didactic analysis with Karl Abraham in 1919. In 1920, together with Abraham and Max Eitington, he helped establish the Berlin Psychoanalytic Institute, along with its Policlinic, whose purpose was to treat the poor and destitute. Eitington had designed a plan for the clinic based upon his experiences treating the war neuroses of World War I. The goal was to provide the same quality treatment to this population as was being provided for middle-class patients in private practices. The early analysts were politically humanistic in their efforts to provide social services to the masses, including experimenting with treating criminals and juvenile delinquents. Funding was obtained from private philanthropists, and at the Berlin Policlinic, analysts donated their time and 4 percent of their income to treat patients who otherwise could not afford to pay (Hale, 1995). Nevertheless, as Balint (1948) pointed out, while the hopes were great for bringing psychoanalysis to the masses, the only lasting accomplishment of the Berlin experiment was the establish-ment of the tripartite psychoanalytic training system, which came to be known as the "Berlin model."

Simmel fled Hitler, immigrating to America in 1934. He carried with him the prestige of Central European science, bringing Freudian ideas and the lessons of World War I, which later deeply informed American military psychiatry during World War II. Many of the themes we have explored concerning the relationship of psychoanalysis and war were repeated in World War II, but with new twists and a far more dramatic outcome.

Military Screening

We now turn our attention to the role of American psychiatry in World War II. Like Germany and Britain, America learned a critical lesson during World War I about the importance of proper selection of recruits for combat. World War I made clear the extent and costs of what had been mistakenly called shell shock, which had little to do with shells or explosions. The governments were concerned about the financial costs of pensions as well as the enormous loss of soldiers from the fighting. Between the wars, the United States spent almost a billion dollars on the psychiatric problems of veterans. Each psychiatric casualty was estimated to cost the U.S. taxpayer about $30,000 (Shephard, 2001). One solution was to select only those recruits who were psychologically stable enough so they would not break down in combat. The controversial question was whether it was even possible to make such predictions and in a short enough time period to efficiently mobilize for war.

The success of psychiatry in World War I led to its profound growth between the wars. Between 1920 and 1946, membership in the American Psychiatric Association increased from 937 to 4,010, with many joining as a direct result of wartime experience. In these same inter-war years, membership in the American Psychological Association jumped from 393 to 4,427. By the end of World War II, 1,700 psychologists worked directly for the military, with numerous others involved in related research and consultation. Nearly 3,000 psychiatrists participated in the World War II screening program (Herman, 1995). American psychologists were committed to turning psychological expertise into service. Leading up to the war, psychologists had been involved predominantly in administrative and bureaucratic tasks; following the war, they were viewed as wise consultants whose wartime accomplishments deserved generous payoffs in public recognition and funding. The war gave psychology its biggest boost.

During World War I, psychologist Robert Yerkes had directed the military's mental testing program; beginning in 1939, he worked with the Emergency Committee in Psychology to prepare the profession for World War II. Psychiatrists had used their testing skills working with the Public Health Service to screen immigrants for mental illness. In 1921, Yerkes suggested to Congress that the experience of testing recruits could be of direct use in limiting the flow of undesirable immigrants. Maintaining that army intelligence tests documented the association between inferior intelligence and delinquency, Yerkes justified the position of limiting the immigration of the simple-minded and uneducated.

Psychiatric and psychological experience during World War I had led to some disturbing findings. Screening had found mass mental deficiency in the population: two percent of all recruits examined were rejected from the military. Yerkes found more than half of all recruits mentally defective, a virtual epidemic of feeblemindedness. Between 1925 and 1940, neuropsychiatric casualties cost close to a billion dollars in psychiatric services and disability payments. It was repeatedly found that soldiers did not understand what they were fighting for. During World War I, psychiatrists and psychologists were put to work conducting what was called "propaganda" in an effort to destroy the enemy's morale while at the same time bolstering the morale of American troops. During World War II, this was repeated under the rubric of "psychological warfare," the change in name reflecting a broadening of the meaning well beyond the mass communication efforts aimed at enemy troops.

Based on their experience in World War I, psychiatrists set out to be more rigorous in their screening methods. President Roosevelt was worried about the projected high cost of psychiatric hospitalizations. Upon his insistence, the Selective Service Act of 1940 created plans for intensive screening of recruits. Recruits were to be seen in a series of four or five psychiatric evaluations, each of which was to last 15 to 20 minutes. Standardized interviews, administered in private, were intended to gather information about family background and emotional profiles. The rationale was that such careful screening would identify "predisposed" individuals, saving the government the cost of military breakdowns. Along with sample questions for interviewing, guidelines were provided for physicians not trained in psychiatry, who were urged to refer any questionable recruit to a psychiatric specialist. Psychiatric disorders were defined more broadly than they had been in World War I; many more recruits met criteria for psychiatric deferment.

America's entry into World War II began with a massive effort to screen every single one of the 15 million recruits to the armed forces. One-third of the psychiatrists in the United States immediately volunteered to serve in this capacity, but that was hardly enough to screen this many soldiers, and 2,400 non-psychiatric medical officers were rapidly trained, along with many non-medical personnel, including psychologists, social workers, and nurses. The war offered numerous psychologists their first taste of clinical training and practice.

From the beginning, there was controversy as to whether accurate predictions of a recruit's readiness for war could be made on the basis of a 15-minute interview. Abraham Kardiner, a psychiatrist psychoanalyst who had been analyzed by Freud, had an enormous amount of clinical experience interviewing chronic war neurotics who suffered from what later would be called post-traumatic stress. After World War I, he worked at the Bronx Veterans' Bureau Hospital in New York City, where he saw over 1,000 patients suffering from war neuroses. This experience did not lead him to feel optimistic about helping these men, nor did he find it easy to explain their suffering in terms of Freud's model of the mind. In the 1930s, Kardiner went on to work with Freudian revisionists who were actively investigating cultural and social issues. He abandoned libido theory for a more environmentally-oriented approach, but this was difficult for him to acknowledge clearly and directly because of his historical and personal tie to Freud. Kardiner's (1941) book *The Traumatic Neuroses of War* was pessimistically anti-war. Its message that war damaged men was not what the country wanted to hear as it entered World War II. His book was rediscovered in the Vietnam War era, when once again American psychiatry had to deal with war's psychological devastation. Kardiner, highly experienced in selection, was highly skeptical of its effectiveness. He wrote, "I should hesitate to offer any criteria that can be used to predict that a given candidate will have a traumatic neurosis" (quoted in Shephard, 2001, p. 197). Although Kardiner's warnings were prescient, his voice did not win the day in Washington.

In November 1940, when the draft was instituted, Harry Stack Sullivan was made the psychiatric consultant in charge of selection. Herbert "Harry" Stack Sullivan was born on February 21, 1892, in Norwich, New York, a child of Catholic Irish immigrants. He grew up in a rural New York Protestant community known for its intense prejudice toward the Irish. He was the only son of a poor uncommunicative Irish farmer and an extremely unhappy, complaining mother who reportedly showed her son little affection. His childhood experience of social isolation and loneliness might have been the incentive for his later interest in psychiatry. With all of the tensions between native-born and immigrant, rural and urban, Catholic and Protestant, poor and successful, and especially with Sullivan's closeted gay lifestyle, in many ways Sullivan, very much like Freud, lived between worlds and may be considered optimally marginal.

Sullivan received his medical degree from the Chicago College of Medicine and Surgery in 1917. At St. Elizabeth's Hospital in Washington, D.C., he was influenced by psychiatrist William Alanson White, who extended Freud's theories to work with the severely mentally ill. Sullivan helped found the William Alanson White Psychiatric Foundation in 1933 and the Washington School of Psychiatry in 1936, and was already well established before the war began. Sullivan had built his reputation based on his experimental treatment ward for schizophrenics at the Sheppard and Enoch Pratt Hospital, between 1925 and 1929. It has been established that Sullivan was gay, although closeted, and that Sullivan's ward was actually a gay male ward. Many of these young men may have been suffering not so much from schizophrenia as from the difficulties of living as gay men in a homophobic culture (Blechner, 2005; Wake, 2007). The ward had an astonishing 86 percent cure rate for schizophrenics; this was before the advent of neuroleptic medication. Sullivan contributed to the development of milieu therapy and designed every aspect of living in the ward to lessen the patients' anxiety. The staff, hand-picked by Sullivan, was either openly homosexual or extremely easygoing about it. The staff and patients were male. No female nurses were allowed even to enter the ward. Sullivan encouraged physical affection between male patients and male attendants, believing it would free patients from their guilt about their "unconventional" sexuality (Wake, 2007). Sullivan and his colleagues in the 1920s and 1930s tried to help homosexual patients understand how a homophobic environment, rather than homosexuality itself, was responsible for their shame and guilt. In these carefully planned and protective surroundings, these men recovered under Sullivan's care.

In the 1930s, Sullivan pioneered the interdisciplinary exchange between psychiatrists, psychoanalysts, and social scientists. While others in the mental health field were still isolationist, his concern with political issues and events in Europe alerted him to America's need to mobilize for war. When the Selective Service Training and Service Act was passed in 1940, it included the creation of the President's Civilian Advisory Committee on Selective Service (CACSS), which Sullivan soon joined as a psychiatric consultant. The ambitious goal was to eliminate, before induction, all who seemed mentally unfit, that is those likely to develop problems, as well as those who were already deemed sick. The military and government wanted to avoid the expense and disruption of psychiatric breakdown, treatment, hospitalization, and veteran's compensation. But psychiatrists had an additional motivation, which was to demonstrate they could make a useful, expert-based contribution to the war effort. This was a reason so many were eager to volunteer for this task.

Sullivan was one of a group of reform-minded psychiatrists who were attempting to create a healthier society by treating mental illness in its early stages. But there was a fly in the ointment. The military wanted to screen out homosexuals, whom they assumed would not be good soldiers and would disturb military morale. The military feared that recruiting homosexual males would have a devastating effect on the armed forces. Interest in screening out by sexual orientation began in October 1940, when 16 million men registered for the draft. A finding of homosexuality was cause for psychiatric hospitalization, court martial, and dishonorable discharge for thousands of soldiers and sailors.

Sullivan attempted to keep homosexuality from being a disqualifying factor for military service, but in May 1941 the Army Surgeon General's overruled him, and "homosexual proclivities" was added to the screening list. The Selective Service wanted anyone suspected of being homosexual during the screening process to be interviewed in more depth by a psychiatrist, while the Army Surgeon General believed anyone who was homosexual should be rejected as having "psychopathic personality disorders." The Navy issued its own directive declaring as unfit "those whose sexual behavior is such that it would endanger or disturb the morale of the military unit" (Bérubé, 1990, p. 12). Previously, the military had viewed homosexual sex acts as something to be punished, but it had not examined specific individuals or character traits. The focus changed from punishing an explicit sexual behavior to identifying a personality type deemed unfit for combat. The rationale for screening homosexuals out of the military was fiercely advocated by the psychiatrists who taught the screening seminars. According to the published lectures reviewed by Bérubé, it was stated that gay men were either schizoid and paranoid personalities who were too introverted to adjust to military life and thus would be victimized by other soldiers, too effeminate to fight, or sexual psychopaths who would not be able to control their desires and presented a threat to other soldiers.

Because of the severe shortage of psychiatrists, Sullivan developed a plan to provide crash courses on psychiatric interviewing for non-specialist doctors, teaching nine of these two-day seminars across the country. He taught them how to do a psychiatric screening interview in 15 minutes, which he believed was adequate time for him to do these interviews himself. He was, of course, a highly experienced psychiatrist. At first, a medical doctor would screen all recruits as part of the local draft board screening. Later the men would undergo a second interview with a psychiatrist. By 1942, the double-screening process was replaced by a single examination at the induction center, which meant interviewing a staggering number of recruits. The interview was limited to about two minutes. A psychiatrist might examine 200 men per day with no access to background information or personal history (Grob, 1994).

Even at the time, opponents of psychiatric screening delivered devastating critiques of the process, arguing that the selections were arbitrary, capricious, and biased by racial and ethnic considerations, the procedures were unreliable and invalid, and those rejected were left with diminished self-esteem and faced discrimination in civilian life. While the military was determined to screen out homosexuals and soldiers who would break down, they were alarmed that 12 percent of all recruits were rejected on neuropsychiatric grounds.

Sullivan believed a man's body language provided important cues to his ego strength. Often, by the time the recruit arrived at the psychiatrist, he was naked, having seen a line of other doctors. But if he was not naked, Sullivan asked him to undress, because observing the man undress would give him more information about his personality, especially as he would question the man while he was undressing in front of him. Historian Ben Shephard is extremely generous toward Sullivan regarding this procedure. He writes,

How innocent it all was in those days. It's easy to mock Sullivan as a gay doctor rationalizing his own wish to look at a lot of guys' bodies. But Sullivan firmly believed that the ability to coexist easily with other men, to adjust successfully to male groups (and not in any explicitly sexual way) was a vital ingredient of the successful soldier. Anyone who felt inhibited undressing in front of a psychiatrist didn't have what it took; and if he couldn't disrobe and answer Sullivan's questions at the same time, he clearly didn't have much intellectual grasp.

(2001, p. 199)

According to Bérubé (1990), however, it was not Sullivan, but the psychiatrist Dexter Bullard (known to psychoanalysts as the director of his family's famous Chestnut Lodge psychoanalytically-oriented mental hospital), who suggested men be interviewed naked. It was thought that if a man was self-conscious, ashamed of his body, or had a very feminine appearance, he could be gay. The psychiatric term "reverse malingerer" was applied to gay men who faked being straight in order to serve their country (p. 20).

The doctors doing the interviews were usually not psychiatrists and had minimal training, and often asked inappropriate or irrelevant questions. With no opportunity to obtain background information, they often made snap judgments on the basis of how the soldier looked to them. Early on in the draft, the military mandate was to be highly selective and when in doubt, to reject. One out of four white draftees was rejected for nervous or emotional conditions. Often the young man had no idea he had a disability. Rejection from the service on these grounds was a shock to his self-esteem and the nation's pride. To make matters worse, these men's diagnoses and the reason for their rejection was given to their employers, who learned they were "4F," rejected for psychiatric reasons, "idiots," or sexual psychopaths.

Sullivan quit his Selective Service post in 1942 out of frustration with logistical hurdles. He became convinced that the participation of psychiatrists in such a farce would ultimately hurt their reputation as well as impede military effectiveness. He might have resigned because he disagreed with the new director of the Selective Service, Major General Lewis B. Hershey. Hershey believed a standardized psychological examination (Army General Classification Test) at an induction center was more efficient and dependable than psychiatric screening interviews. Other historians suggest Sullivan was fired (Bérubé, 1990).

Psychiatric screening during World War II was the first organized attempt to screen out homosexuals before induction. A fair number of liberal and reform-minded psychiatrists, including Sullivan himself, were conflicted about this. They understood that exclusion from the army was stigmatizing and might cause serious psychological damage. Sullivan believed homosexuals were particularly vulnerable to psychological strain in military life and could rationalize excluding them from service in order to protect their mental health. He was torn between accepting "homosexual proclivities" as a criteria for exclusion from the military to support the war effort in which he passionately believed, and recognizing that including homosexuality in the list of deviations would fuel the prejudice against it. While Sullivan was "a champion of gay rights" well ahead of his time (Blechner, 2005, p. 3), his accommodating approach contributed to the medical and social stigmatization of homosexuals. In 1942, after Sullivan moved on, the National Research Council committee expanded the psychiatric portion of the army mobilization regulations, adding a section called "Sexual Perversions," written by Lawrence Kubie. For the first time, distinctions between "normal" and homosexual persons were articulated. The three signs to watch out for apart from verbal responses to questions were "feminine bodily characteristics," "effeminacy in dress or manner," and "a patulous (expanded) rectum." The lack of a strong critique of homophobia even by liberal psychiatrists suggests how difficult it was to defend homosexuals in public debate. Even now, more than 70 years later, the struggle over gays in the military continues, even beyond "Don't ask, don't tell."

Psychoanalytic Therapy at the Front Lines

Sullivan's screening system got poor results and he regarded his efforts as his first major public failure. By the end of the war, more than 2.5 million men had been disqualified from military service for psychiatric reasons, either through screenings or because of psychiatric breakdown during the war. This figure was high enough to shock the nation into recognizing that emotional disturbance was a significant threat and deserved public attention. The Guadalcanal and North African campaigns confirmed that anyone could break down when subjected to military combat. At Guadalcanal in 1942, 40 percent of those evacuated were neuropsychiatric casualties. Psychiatrists Roy Grinker and John Spiegel concluded that "the realities of war" and "traumatic stimuli" could "produce a potential war neurosis in every soldier" (quoted in Grob, 1994, p. 194). Conducting studies to validate their position, they contended that combat exhaustion could be minimized by limiting the time soldiers were kept on active duty, promoting group cohesion, and providing regular rest periods. When symptoms did occur, they advocated brief interventions using sodium pentothal, a narcotic that brought patients to an altered state of consciousness, along with catharsis to encourage the utilization of less pathological defense mechanisms. They called this treatment "narcosynthesis."

This use of narcosynthesis with catharsis was reminiscent of Simmel's use of catharsis with hypnosis during World War I. Simple interventions seemed to work best in combat conditions. Most treatment on the front lines consisted of nothing more than a mild sedative, a good night's sleep, and warm food. In more serious conditions, a soldier was sent to the rear and given brief psychotherapy, rest, and relaxation. With prompt treatment at the front, nearly two-thirds of cases were returned to duty in less than a week. When sent to the rear, about one-third were well enough to return to combat. The remaining soldiers were sent to VA hospitals back home.

Roy Grinker was a major contributor to psychoanalytic psychiatry. Grinker was born in Chicago in 1900, the son of a famous Jewish neurologist, Julius Grinker, who had himself practiced psychoanalysis as early as 1911 before concentrating on neurology. Graduating from the University of Chicago and Rush Medical School, Roy Grinker became a neurologist and psychiatrist, did postgraduate training in Zurich, London, and Hamburg, and while in his early thirties, wrote what became the standard textbook in neurology. Seeking further training, he went to Vienna in 1933, where he was one of Freud's last patients. Grinker did not particularly enjoy his time in Vienna and resented Freud's negative attitude toward Americans. He recalled that when he entered Freud's waiting room, he was greeted by Freud's large menacing-looking dog, which "would attack me with its snout at the same level as my genitals. So I entered Freud's office with a high level of castration anxiety" (quoted in Shephard, 2001, p. 213). Then Freud's second dog jumped on him, as he lay on the couch! Grinker even complained that Freud himself leaned over and dribbled on him. Nevertheless, Freud ended the analysis by telling Grinker that conducting his analysis had been one of his remaining pleasures, and Grinker returned to the United States with one of the most important credentials any psychiatrist could have: he had been analyzed by Freud himself. Returning to Chicago, he built the Institute for Psychosomatic and Psychiatric Research and Training at Michael Reese Hospital and was Chief Editor of the *Archives of Neurology and Psychiatry* from 1956 to 1976.

As the war approached, Grinker, already well established, negotiated a position as Major with the U.S. Army Air Force. In 1943, psychiatrists were for the first time sent into combat zones. Grinker arranged for his chief resident from Chicago, John Spiegel, to join him in Algiers. Together they treated numerous soldiers and airmen, writing of their experiences in a book called *War Neuroses in North Africa* (1943). Perhaps because they had relatively little personal experience of war trauma, their descriptions were colorfully dramatic and stirring. Their new method of treatment, narcosynthesis, captivated the public's imagination. Patients dramatically reenacted their trauma with Grinker and Spiegel's personal help, and remembered and synthesized their dissociated experiences.

Grinker and Spiegel's work had a huge impact on the military and the public. More than 45,000 copies of *War Neuroses* were distributed within the medical community; it became the bible of military psychiatrists. The treatment was optimistic, dramatic, scientific, and distinctively American. However, the army was not at all sure it worked very well. It seemed to require Grinker and Spiegel's charismatic personalities in order to be effective. The army was concerned that the approach made doctors too sympathetic toward soldiers, and reluctant to send their patients back into battle. Nevertheless, narcosynthesis had a widespread impact on the many new and inexperienced clinicians who joined the military and continued to seek clinical training after the war.

Grinker and Spiegel went on to become major formulators of psychoanalytic thinking about trauma. Their *Men Under Stress* (1945) highlighted the value of a psychoanalytic understanding in the treatment of traumatized military personnel, formulating combat breakdowns as resulting from regression. Their thesis was that in the context of war, the soldier subsumed his own ego into the military superego and thereby regressed. This was a simple application of Freud's idea that in the context of the group, the individual regresses by identifying with the group leader and losing his sense of individuality. But when the group, here the military, lets the soldier down, for example by not protecting him from fear or injury, the soldier in his regressed state breaks down and needs to be comforted like a child. As we saw in the discussions of trauma at the Budapest Congress, the psychoanalytic focus so emphasized the individual's intrapsychic dynamics, childhood history, and predisposing personality traits that relatively little emphasis was given to the objective external reality of actual traumatic events. Yet Grinker and Spiegel's book had a major influence on the popularity of psychoanalysis. In Chapter 9, we will discuss Grinker's influence on his analysand, Rabbi Joshua Liebman, the author of the best-selling *Peace of Mind* (1946).

We have reviewed the troubling intersection of war, trauma, and compensation from its historical origins in legal battles over railroad accident compensation through the First and Second World Wars in Europe and America. War trauma and compensation have continually played a significant role in the development of psychiatry and psychoanalysis. The strategy we have described throughout this chapter is the use of psychiatric diagnosis to demonstrate pre-existing conditions, thereby exonerating employers, including the government, for responsibility to provide compensation. As we were making the final edits on this book, *The New York Times* ran a front-page story entitled, "Branding a Soldier With 'Personality Disorder'" (Dao, February 25, 2012). According to *The New York Times*, even today in our war in Afghanistan,

> The military considers personality disorder a pre-existing problem that emerges in youth, and as a result, troops given the diagnosis are often administratively discharged without military retirement pay. Some have even been required to repay enlistment bonuses. By

comparison, a diagnosis of post-traumatic stress disorder is usually linked to military service and leads to a medical discharge accompanied by certain benefits.

Ironically, trauma, in the form of PTSD, is now associated with service-related injuries entitling the soldier to compensation, whereas personality disorder has become the designated category connoting a pre-existing condition; it is most often associated with femininity, cowardice, degeneracy, childhood development, and in the case reported here, with "histrionic" traits. Binary thinking continues today, albeit with new labels. Psychiatric diagnoses continue to be used for governments' ends. Clinicians in wartime continue to operate under pressure to cut costs, despite the personal cost to the individual soldier under their care.

By 1943, it was clear that concentrating on selection had been a mistake. The little available psychiatric expertise was being wasted on an ineffective process, when what was desperately needed was psychiatric treatment at the front, and back home, following discharge. The Army ordered a major review, censoring information about rejection rates and the mental state of American soldiers. General George Marshall issued a highly critical report, blasting psychiatry as being out of step with the needs of the nation. Army psychiatry might have been wiped out at this point, but one man came along who turned the situation around, making psychoanalysis into a war hero who returned home triumphant. That man was William Menninger.

Chapter 6

Psychoanalysis as War Hero

The first psychiatrist to attain the rank of Brigadier General, William Menninger reshaped Army psychiatry, transforming psychiatry, psychoanalysis, and the mental health professions following the war. Chief of the army's Neuropsychiatric Division, Menninger brought an optimistic American can-do attitude to military psychiatry, focusing on its ability to heal traumatized soldiers. While in the early years of the war a soldier diagnosed as a psychiatric casualty would have been discharged, Menninger's goal was to treat the soldier and get him back to the fight. The belief that treatment could bring about recovery ultimately brought psychotherapy and psychoanalysis into their golden age. This chapter continues the story of the impact of World War II on American psychiatry and psychoanalysis. The historical background of the rise of psychoanalysis to its position of power following the war is essential to an understanding of how psychoanalysis came to define itself in opposition to psychotherapy.

William Menninger was born on October 15, 1899, in Topeka, Kansas. He studied psychiatry at St. Elizabeth's Hospital in Washington, D.C., graduating in 1927. That same year, he returned to Topeka, joining his father and older brother Karl in their medical practice, which by that time specialized in psychiatry. Spurred by William's contributions, the Menninger Clinic evolved into the Menninger Sanitarium, and eventually into the Menninger Foundation, a non-profit organization that provided inpatient and outpatient clinical services and engaged in research, education, and social outreach. At the outset of World War II, Menninger left to become Director of the Psychiatry Consultants Division in the office of the Surgeon General of the U.S. Army. He chaired the committee that produced document "Medical 203," a major revision of U.S. classifications of mental disorders adopted by all the armed services. Following the war, it had a substantial influence on the first mental disorders section of the *International Statistical Classification of Diseases* published in 1949 and on the first *Diagnostic and Statistical Manual of Mental Disorders* (DSM) published in 1952.

William's brother Karl was among the first to introduce Freud and Janet's ideas to clinics in America. Although written when he was a raw beginner with no analytic experience, Karl Menninger's (1930) *The Human Mind* became one of the best-selling mental health volumes in American history, and Karl became American psychiatry's leading spokesman. Karl was the intellectual heavyweight, while William had an easy, warm way with people, inspiring the confidence of military officers and enabling him to raise the funds that fueled the growth of the Menninger empire.

In 1934, William and Karl Menninger traveled to Vienna to study psychoanalysis and meet with Freud. Freud was not fond of America and had little respect for homegrown American psychoanalysts. He was neither impressed by, nor particularly welcoming of, either brother. Karl tried to tell Freud about his famous hospital, but Freud was not a believer in the ability of psychoanalysis to cure psychotics, and so was not appreciative of Karl's attempts. Complicating matters further, Karl was accompanied by his analyst, Franz Alexander, who discouraged Freud from gratifying Karl's narcissism by showing him too much attention! The brothers reacted very differently to Freud's lack of interest. William was turned off by Freud, had great confidence in American psychiatry, and did not feel he had missed anything. Karl, on the other hand, left this 1934 meeting determined to prove himself to Freud, to show Freud that he understood him better than anyone else did, especially the Europeans, and to be invited back to Vienna. That was not to be. In 1938 when Germany invaded Austria and Freud was forced to leave, Karl cabled Freud, inviting him to come to Menninger in any capacity he chose. Freud did not reply.

At the helm of the Menninger Clinic in the 1930s, William Menninger represented the new psychiatry, influenced by Adolf Meyer and his dynamic, broadly psychoanalytic psychiatry. Menninger's hospital was conceptualized as a family, with the doctor, representing the father, at the top of the hierarchy, and the patients at the bottom, viewed as having regressed to a state of childhood. Most doctors were men; the few women physicians were not viewed as equals despite their credentials. In fact, female nurses were more highly regarded. Maintaining that women entered nursing to "sublimate their maternal desires" and "outclass" their mothers (quoted in Friedman, 1990, p. 75), Menninger viewed the nurse as a mother figure whose function was to carry out the physician's orders, an attitude typical of the time. He hired an almost exclusively female nursing staff, strongly discouraging these women from becoming a sisterhood, believing their "enmeshment" would work against their support of the doctors.

Despite the discrepancies in power and authority, the Menninger hospital was progressive for the era, as it included the participation of a diverse staff. Attendants, social workers, and psychologists all had a place in the treatment and care of patients. With Will away at the war, Karl hired these personnel to arrest a potential drift toward the hospital becoming primarily custodial. The war posed a significant problem, because with so many doctors called to service, psychiatric facilities might not have sufficient staff to provide individual treatment, leading to slippage back to the provision of custodial care. The physician shortage was one reason Karl pioneered the development of psychoanalytically oriented group and milieu therapy.

The Rise of Psychodynamic Psychiatry

Menninger shifted psychiatric military efforts away from screening recruits toward psychiatric diagnosis and treatment, but since there were far too few psychiatrists to handle the demand, he emphasized the training of other military clinicians. He made sure that trained psychiatrists worked in induction centers, basic training camps, military hospitals, and hospitals specifically designed to handle neuropsychiatric disorders. But the vast majority of clinicians who had direct contact with the soldiers, almost a million non-medical personnel, had no previous psychiatric training. Menninger developed a system of consultants to provide training and maintain standards of treatment.

Menninger selected psychoanalytically oriented psychiatrists for all key positions, and they proselytized with missionary zeal. Of five civilian psychiatrists appointed to report on the European theater in 1945, four were psychoanalysts, including Will's brother Karl. John Murray, a psychoanalyst from Boston, was made Chief of Air Force psychiatry. The psychoanalyst instructors in the military training programs did not preach psychoanalysis, but taught psychodynamic ideas in the context of general psychiatry. The acceptance of psychoanalysis in the military was really an acceptance of psychodynamics, or very broad psychoanalytically oriented psychotherapy rather than analysis proper. More than 1,000 psychiatrists graduated from these Army training programs and many went into formal psychoanalytic training after the war. In 1944, Menninger issued a bulletin called "Neuropsychiatry for the General Medical Officer," explaining psychiatry to the general Army physician. It explained the causes of symptoms in terms of unconscious childhood conflict and treatment in terms of insight, but it was highly eclectic, mixing psychoanalytic ideas with suggestion and psychoeducation. Menninger's explanations stressed the importance of psychosomatic medicine, incorporating Franz Alexander's psychosomatic theories—recall that Alexander was Menninger's analyst. The shortage of psychiatric personnel provided an ideal opportunity to raise the prestige of psychiatry within medicine and of psychoanalytic thinking within psychiatry. Because so many non-medical personnel were used, excitement about psychoanalysis and clinical work was generated among psychologists and non-medical doctors. The Rockefeller Foundation funded lecture tours by psychiatrists and psychoanalysts to conduct case conferences and train the military. In the idealistic words of Alan Gregg, a Rockefeller Foundation psychiatrist, "the convergent rays of psychiatry, psychoanalysis, and psychology now flood the conduct of man with light as it has never before been illuminated" (quoted in Herman, 1995, p. 91).

The failure of the selection effort clearly demonstrated that constitutional variables were less significant than current experience—the environment mattered! Psychiatrists exposed to psychoanalytic ideas during the war emerged with the conviction that environmental stress was more important than predisposition. The fact that removing the soldier from the stress and providing prompt treatment at the front helped to keep the disorder from worsening was taken as evidence of the critical role of prevention. The optimistic emphasis on prevention and environmental change fit the prevailing zeitgeist of the mental hygiene movement and dovetailed with the political views of the new immigrants, which were at least liberal if not left leaning, social democrat, and socialist.

The economic boom generated can-do optimism and high expectations. "Never in history had the belief that human problems could be solved by throwing money at them been so combined with the money to do it with" (Shephard, 2001, p. 329). The Veteran's Administration, charged with supplying veterans with the best medical care, hired thousands of doctors and launched the largest hospital building campaign in American history. Sixty percent of VA patients were psychiatric cases. In 1945, there were more than 50,000 neuropsychiatric veterans in VA hospitals. By June 1947, almost a half million patients with neuropsychiatric disabilities received pensions from the VA. In 1940, there were 2,423 psychiatrists in the United States; a decade later, there were 5,856, and many were psychoanalytically oriented. By 1944, a division of psychiatry was established in the army's office of the Surgeon General, and in 1946 the National Mental Health Act pumped money into ambitious new psychiatric programs. Menninger estimated that the military trained more psychiatrists during the war than all American medical schools could have produced in a decade.

Clinical psychology grew out of the military's need for trained clinicians. During the postwar period, America trained more mental health professionals than any other country in the world (Herman, 1995), the vast majority male and white. Based on his experience in his family's hospital, Menninger strongly advocated for clinical teamwork, supporting the training of psychologists, social workers, and nurses. In the years after the war, the Menninger Foundation took a leading role in interdisciplinary collaboration and the training of clinical psychologists. Under Menninger's leadership, clinical psychologists were authorized to diagnose patients and conduct individual psychotherapy, in addition to their previous role of performing psychological testing. Nevertheless, Menninger continued to adhere to a professional hierarchy, with the medical doctor on top, insisting that psychiatrists supervise the treatment team.

Psychoanalytic historians have highlighted the impact of World War I on Freud and the development of his theories—his pessimism about the future of civilization, his understanding of trauma, and the death instinct. While Freud did not live to see World War II, we should not underestimate its impact on psychoanalysis, just following the exile and death of its founder. In America, where psychoanalysis was first transplanted after its destruction in Europe, the ravages of war, the Holocaust, nuclear destruction, the Cold War, superpower rivalry, and racial violence all called rationality and ego-autonomy into serious question. It was a perfect storm; these events highlighted the importance of studying the dark forces lurking just beneath the thin veneer of civilization: irrationality, madness, human impulsivity, passion and aggression, precisely those subjects with which psychoanalysis was engaged.

The war significantly raised the profile of American psychiatry. Menninger's genius for publicity ensured its every innovation was presented to the public in the best possible light. Popularizations of army psychiatry projected a heroic picture, depicting psychiatry along psychoanalytic lines, emphasizing emotional catharsis and dream analysis. American doctors returned from the war eager to seek psychoanalytic training, or at the very least, training in psychoanalytically oriented psychiatry. It was clear that technology, which had been critical to America's military triumph, would play a prominent role in its future. Throughout the 20th century, especially after Flexner, medicine had carefully positioned itself as a science employing the most modern technologies. Psychiatry was eager to be associated with medicine's scientific status. Psychoanalysis followed, earnestly seeking to demonstrate that it was a scientific and specialized medical discipline with a technology of its own, "the analytic instrument." Under Franz Alexander's leadership, the field of psychosomatic medicine, based on psychoanalytic conceptualizations, expanded rapidly. Psychoanalysis became tied directly to general medicine, gaining wider exposure and respectability among physicians across medical departments.

The Rise of Psychoanalytic Orthodoxy

American psychoanalysis, as part of the new dynamic psychiatry of the pre-World War II era, had been an eclectic heterodox affair. The analysts who emigrated to America through the early 1930s tended to join in that liberal ecumenical spirit in the hope of expanding psychoanalysis, Americanizing it, and making it suitable for many more patients. But the newer arriving émigrés fleeing Fascism in Europe and Hitler's rise in Germany brought with them a stifling orthodoxy. Between 1933 and 1944, about 4,000 physicians came to the United States from Austria and Germany. Of these, there were fewer than 250 psychiatrists and 50 psychoanalysts. Yet these few played an extraordinary role in the development of American psychoanalysis, a change that transformed the discipline everywhere. Franz Alexander, Sandor Rado, and Otto Fenichel came early in the 1930s. Arriving later were Hermann Nunberg and Felix and Helene Deutsch; after Kristallnacht and the Anschluss, Paul Federn, Heinz Hartmann, Ernest Kris, and Beate Rank. The newcomers were received as stars, idealized for their closeness to Freud, the founder, and became far more orthodox in the United States than they had been in Europe, where psychoanalysis had a more relaxed, coffeehouse salon culture of discussion and debate. As a result of their tragic personal losses, including family trauma, displacement, emigration, and their new status as foreign immigrants, and with the death of Freud, the founding figure, a new orthodoxy prevailed that was quite different from what had been left behind in Europe. In the next chapter, we will explore in detail the impact of these European émigrés and their losses on American psychoanalysis.

In 1953, of 7,000 American psychiatrists, only 500 were psychoanalysts, but many of the others were loosely psychoanalytically oriented. How was psychoanalysis after the war able to exert such an enormous influence on American psychiatry? The numbers do not tell the full story. Though the minority, the analysts became the leaders. They were viewed as intellectuals of profound depth and wisdom. They wrote textbooks, ran psychiatry departments, and sat on examination boards. After the war and through the 1950s, psychoanalytic training became de rigueur for aspiring psychiatrists. By 1948, three-quarters of all committee posts in the American Psychiatric Association were held by analysts, and by the early 1960s, the recommended psychiatric texts were psychoanalytic in orientation. Analytic institutes had more candidates than members, a sign of dramatic growth. By the 1960s in America, psychiatry was equated with psychoanalysis (Stepansky, 2009).

One example of the new orthodoxy can be drawn from the story of Paul Schilder, a member of the Vienna Psychoanalytic Society who immigrated early on to America because anti-Semitism obstructed his opportunities for advancement in Vienna. Schilder had impeccable credentials as a psychiatrist and psychoanalyst, but was rejected for membership by the New York Psychoanalytic Society because he was viewed as too unorthodox. Schilder gave his patients advice and did not see them five times per week on the couch. Nevertheless, Schilder ran a major psychiatry department, influencing a generation of young psychiatrists in psychoanalytic psychiatry. In 1940, William Menninger was prepared to reprimand Eduardo Weiss because colleagues at the Topeka Psychoanalytic Institute accused him of departing from Freudian procedure by seeing patients only three times per week and face-to-face rather than on the couch. Karl objected that their American colleagues barely knew what Freudian analysis was and that it seemed inappropriate for them to be condemning Weiss as not Freudian enough when he was a personal colleague of Freud's, a member of the

Vienna Institute, and had been personally endorsed by Freud to organize the psychoanalytic movement in Italy! We see here the beginnings of the split in America between orthodox versus "unorthodox" psychoanalysis, defined by use of the couch and frequency of sessions, an ongoing theme we return to throughout this book.

At Menninger, Karl recruited analysts who had been victims of anti-Semitism and Nazism. Several of the émigrés came to Topeka to lecture at Menninger's, some staying months or even years. Karl hired all he could to serve as senior consultants and training analysts. Other centers for the new psychiatry, including Chestnut Lodge, Sheppard-Pratt, and St. Elizabeth's, also tried to recruit émigré analysts, and in the 1930s and 1940s these émigré analysts became important leaders and major influences in these organizations. There were significant tensions, however. The émigrés who came to Menninger did not look up to Karl as an intellectual leader or father figure, rejecting his paternal stance as unearned and unwarranted.

Some of the American leaders at Menninger, including William Menninger, John Stone, and Robert Knight, questioned whether they might be better off without these upstart immigrants, but Karl viewed them as indispensible to his agenda. Karl was determined to learn from them, to acquire knowledge of authentic psychoanalysis that he assumed only those close to Freud would have. But equally important, Karl knew that having these émigrés at Menninger would bring the hospital prestige, attracting the best psychiatric residents seeking training analyses and authentic psychoanalytic supervision. William, following his neglect by Freud in his 1934 visit, had no interest whatsoever in bringing European analysts to Menninger. If anything, it seems that at least as of 1934, William believed the Nazis were doing great things for Germany.

Although Will met few of the Jewish psychoanalysts, one whom he did meet was Ernst Simmel, who was among the first of the émigrés to be recruited to Menninger. Karl began systematic recruitment of analysts from Europe in 1936. Simmel was by then a prominent Berlin analyst who escaped Germany and came to Topeka. Based on his World War I experience in treating trauma, he had run a famous psychoanalytic hospital at Schloss Tegel, which had been an inspiration to the Menninger brothers. Simmel told them many more highly regarded and innovative psychoanalysts would soon follow him from Europe. Robert Knight, who would eventually move from Menninger's to Austin Riggs, and became one of the pioneer explorers of the treatment of borderline conditions, was sent to Berlin on a mission to recruit analysts. Knight, like Will, seemed not to understand what the Jewish analysts were up against in facing Hitler. Against Karl's advice, he attended the Berlin Olympic games on his visit to Berlin and stood up to photograph Hitler. Among the analysts recruited to Menninger's were Martin Grotjahn, Bernard Kamm, Eduardo Weiss, Elizabeth Geleerd, and David Rapaport.

By 1939, the Menninger associates had lost their enthusiasm for the immigrants. They found them solemn and disagreeable and possessed of strange habits. They did not fit into the Menninger family. It is not a big surprise that these highly educated, sophisticated, and cultured German-Jewish immigrants, who had just lost everything they had, did not quite fit in to the "cow town" lifestyle of Topeka, Kansas. There seems to have been little understanding of all they had lost and the trauma they had undergone. On top of their cultural differences and difficulties in adjustment, the émigrés believed Menninger was seriously underpaying them. They had come to realize how much more money they might have earned in New York. They were, after all, the most senior analysts in the hospital and they were a huge attraction, bringing in the best students. They knew they would be welcome at other centers. Some had only escaped Europe because they had money; having money had become strongly associated with survival. This led to further conflict, as the émigrés tried to negotiate their salaries, only to have Karl react with agitation, complaining they were being unprofessional for discussing money. On their side, they could not believe a leading psychoanalyst would claim a topic was off limits to discussion!

Soon after this dispute, Karl wrote to his father that he was "not at all adverse to Jews, but I think we must not get too many Jews in the Clinic or it will be bad for them as well as for us" (quoted in Friedman, 1990, p. 118). Karl acknowledged he had learned from Freud's "Jewish science," but then instituted a rule in the Menninger residency program limiting admission to one Jew per appointment date (twice a year). By 1943, Karl once again resumed recruitment of immigrants, but only because the war had so drained Menninger of psychiatric personnel that he was in desperate need.

Whereas earlier émigrés had regarded themselves as avant-garde, humanistic, Freudian intellectuals, those of the postwar years tended to be more conventional. Siding with the conservative forces of the younger American generation, they supported a narrow, medical establishment discipline. As part of this conservative shift, they placed their theoretical emphasis on the ego's adaptation to society. Inclined to be devotional rather than critical, they remained skeptical of new and innovative ideas. While Menninger psychologists under Rapaport experimented with empirical investigations of psychoanalytic concepts, the newer immigrants preferred to concentrate on a careful line-by-line study of Freud's texts. Students learned not to approach these analysts for "new" thinking. By 1951, the émigré analysts had become indispensable to Menninger's. Will found them much easier to like, as they were more conventional, medical and professional. Karl on the other hand, as he felt increasingly confident, liked them less and less, and would have been glad to see them return to Europe.

Psychiatry, Psychology, and Preventive Intervention

Karl Menninger urged the American Psychoanalytic Association to encourage large-scale training of psychiatrists and psychoanalysts. According to Will, the armed forces were discharging 1,000 men per day for psychiatric reasons. Military psychiatrists had concluded that immediate treatment at the front was the most effective form of intervention. It was easy to extrapolate that in civilian life, intervening early in a family and community setting rather than in an isolated institution would be more effective, and that community psychiatry and private practice should replace the previous institutional focus. In the years immediately post-World War II, all medical professionals were eager to expand their authority and jurisdiction. Psychiatrists sought to demonstrate they could provide solutions for civilian life, not only for medical concerns but also for social and political problems.

In 1940, the American Psychiatric Association had only 2,295 members, about two-thirds of whom worked in asylums and were associated with the older biological psychiatry. In December 1941, there were 35 psychiatrists in the regular Army Medical Corps. By the end of the war, under Menninger, there were 2,400 in the army (only 16 were women) and 700 in the Navy. By 1945, there were 1,710 psychologists (40 women, total; 20 women in the military); more than half were doing psychotherapy in addition to diagnostics. Many of these doctors returned to civilian life with the desire to practice psychoanalytically oriented psychiatry and receive specialty training in psychoanalysis. In 1940, psychologists formed the Emergency Committee in Psychology (ECP) to organize psychologists in the war effort. Serving as an employment agency for government and military psychology, the ECP consisted predominantly of academic psychologists and was exclusively male. Despite the objection of women psychologists, military psychology was viewed as a "man's job." It was believed that women should "keep the home fires burning" and "wait, weep, and comfort one another" (quoted in Philipson, 1993, p. 27). Women psychologists were encouraged to serve as volunteers, even though male psychologists were paid for their government and military work. In response to this discrimination, women psychologists formed the National Council of Women Psychologists to support the war effort, but they largely focused on civilian work, and unemployment rates for female psychologists increased during the war.

In Kansas, the Menninger brothers established close relationships with state and federal officials. The federal government became involved in mental health policy and the scope of federal authority dramatically increased. In 1946, President Truman signed the National Mental Health Act, establishing the National Institute of Mental Health in 1949 under the direction of Robert Felix, which supported research, training, and service in mental health. It created legitimacy for psychiatric and psychological services, and supported community-based mental health services. More and more psychiatrists entered private practice, a trend that spread to related mental health professionals, including psychologists, social workers, and psychiatric nurses. Federal money helped train an entire generation of mental health professionals, whose career interests lay in community mental health and private practice settings.

With the influx of federal funding to support research and treatment, the Veteran's Administration established joint training programs with a number of universities to alleviate the severe shortages of professionals available to help the returning GIs, dramatically strengthening the field of clinical psychology. Psychiatrists recognized that psychologists had useful abilities. They were experts in testing and assessment, research, vocational and educational counseling, and group therapy. Psychologists were eager to continue to conduct psychotherapy, for which there was a desperate need. Thus began decades of conflict between psychiatry and clinical psychology. With the potential market for psychological services expanding, psychologists, like other professionals, were eager to expand their scope of practice. Attempting to implement state certification and licensing laws, they fought for the right to do psychotherapy. The American Psychiatric Association insisted that psychotherapy was a medical treatment and that psychologists only be allowed to conduct psychotherapy under medical supervision. Even William Menninger, who had supported multidisciplinary collaboration and clinical psychology during the war, insisted that psychiatrists be the leaders in providing psychotherapy.

The Rise of Talk Therapy

The war led to a normalization of mental troubles, in that psychiatrists and psychologists were no longer dealing only with the severely mentally ill, but with a wide range of problems of living under stressful conditions (Herman, 1995). Military psychiatric experts preached to enlisted men directly and through self-help literature that fear was expectable and normal when it was a response to actual external danger. Under conditions of actual threat, fear mobilized the body's resources to prepare for the emergency. In anticipation of actual combat, it was normal and healthy to be afraid. The handbook issued to all soldiers read: "YOU'LL BE SCARED . . . If you say you're not scared, you'll be a cocky fool. Don't let anyone tell you you're a coward if you admit being scared" (quoted in Shephard, 2001, p. 235). Herman (1995) noted the gendered context of this attitude toward fear, since both soldiers and military clinicians were predominantly men and fear had long been associated with women and hysteria. Historically men, even in combat conditions, had been expected to be brave; it was considered feminine to be anxious and show fear. The psychiatrists of World War II shifted this attitude within a gendered context. Men were now expected to be afraid when facing a perceived actual threat. But this fear was differentiated from the diffuse vague anxiety associated with hysteria in women, which was not associated with a clear danger, and so was considered pathological and typically hysterical, brought on by internal intrapsychic factors. Psychodynamic clinicians used Freud's notion of signal anxiety to articulate the adaptive use of anxiety. The binary differentiation of anxiety and fear was split along gendered lines, with anxiety viewed as primitive, feminine, internal, and pathological, while fear was masculine, adaptive to the external world, and healthy.

Soldiers were also taught it was better to know about this fear rather than not to know about it. A message disseminated during World War II was that insight was useful. A staple of military psychiatry was that psychological self-awareness was an essential element of self-mastery. Soldiers were advised to talk about their feelings. Fear of combat was normal, expectable, adaptive, and masculine. Men should acknowledge and talk to one another about these fears without shame, because insight, self-awareness, and sharing feelings are helpful and not shameful or feminine. This set the stage for the postwar acceptance of the respectability of talk therapy.

Talk therapy was introduced to millions of soldiers for the first time during the war. This was brief psychotherapy, conducted from a broadly psychoanalytic point of view, certainly not psychoanalysis proper. In individual sessions and as part of groups, soldiers discussed their feelings, combat experiences, and personal histories. Psychological awareness and introspection were encouraged in men who previously had no exposure to psychodynamic thinking or practice. For psychiatrists who had worked with the severely mentally ill in asylums, this was a radical change. They now saw how psychotherapy, particularly psychoanalytic insight, was applicable to normal populations under stress. They understood that normality was not neatly separate from psychopathology, but rather that there was a continuum, with people falling somewhere in the middle of the two extreme poles. Psychiatric practice could be normalized, made suitable for a vastly larger population than the mentally ill and applied to everyday life in the community, with seemingly excellent results. Clinicians recognized they had something of value to offer to a new mass market, and a shortage of clinicians made what they had to offer all the more valuable; it also fit the times. It was newly imported from Europe, sophisticated and reliable, the best of modern science. Its practitioners had patriotically served their country and deserved the recognition, acceptance, and funding that the country was now in a good position to bestow. In years when the world appeared dark and irrational, it made sense for the country to turn to psychoanalysts, who understood something about primitive irrational forces.

The new awareness of mental health needs coincided with a booming economy and America's confidence that it could accomplish anything. The American public was exposed to images of psychoanalysts in magazines, newspapers, and movies. In the public mind, the psychoanalyst was the war hero who could bring traumatized men back to life with the use of Freudian-inspired scientific techniques. What remains astonishing is that the public reputation of psychoanalysis was built on the basis of reports of what psychoanalysis had accomplished during the war, even though just about no psychoanalysis proper was done, and relatively little psychoanalytic therapy as we think of it today. Psychiatrists took their inspiration from psychoanalytic concepts and theories, and so psychoanalysis received the publicity and the credit, much as it had after World War I. What was understood to have taken place in the combat aid stations of World War II would transform the profession and the culture.

Chapter 7

Psychoanalysis as Holocaust Survivor

Psychoanalysis should be recognized as a Holocaust survivor. This stunningly compelling observation, recently made by Prince (2009), begs further discussion. The role of persecution, marginalization, and immigration in the development of psychoanalysis has not yet been acknowledged, neither in its founding generation nor as it was compounded in the next generation, après-coup, by the trauma of the Holocaust and the resulting exodus from Europe. For the European émigrés fleeing Hitler, America was not an "average expectable environment" (Hartmann, 1939). The years post-World War I witnessed a rise in American anti-Semitism, which, fueled by economic depression and the prospect of another war, reached its peak during World War II. The émigrés faced an undercurrent of prejudices rooted in beliefs similar to those they had encountered in Europe. Surveys conducted throughout the 1940s and 1950s showed an uninterrupted increase in popular disapproval of Jews in America from the early stages of World War II through the immediate postwar period, with anti-Semitism reaching its highest point in 1946. Jews were described as clannish, pushy, aggressive, and unscrupulous, avoidant of military service, overly influential in government, and wielding excessive financial power.

The first choice for most European Jews fleeing Hitler was immigration to America, which had a flourishing economy and offered boundless opportunity. The United States had the largest community of Jews in the world, comprising 3.5 percent of the American population. The sheer number of Jews in America seemed to the displaced people of Europe to ensure a promise of stability and security. In 1938, the Jewish population of the United States amounted to 30 percent of the world's Jews. By 1955, it had risen to 43 percent. Nevertheless, this figure represented only 3.1 percent of the American population because of the Jews' lower birth rates and the high rate of non-Jewish immigration. Thus while the United States represented the largest absolute number of Jews in the 1950s, the relative number of Jews in America was actually in decline and continued to decline in future decades. By 1986, Jews only represented 2.5 percent of the American population (Hamerow, 2008).

Laws enacted in 1921 and 1924 imposed strict limits on immigration, leading to a drastic reduction in the number of Jews admitted to the country in the following years. As late as 1938, the United States was still suffering from the Great Depression, with millions remaining unemployed. Americans were concerned about economic competition and uneasy about alien political influence. There was also a great deal of ethnic prejudice. Despite popular sympathy for the victims of racist persecution, the American public was opposed to changing the existing immigration laws to accommodate an increase in immigration.

Even before the war, Jews persistently protested the persecution of German Jewry and were vocal opponents of the Third Reich. This advocacy on behalf of their European Jewish brethren only fed into anti-Semitic stereotypes of Jews using their wealth and power to drag the United States into a foreign war and subordinating national interests to ethnic solidarity. As the war went on, American Jews perceived an increase in anti-Semitism at home. Characterized by their countrymen as alarmists who were constantly complaining and at least a bit paranoid, American Jews found themselves in a double bind: their efforts to bring attention to the plight of those being murdered in Europe only aggravated anti-Semitic sentiment.

White, but not Quite

In Europe, the distinction between Aryans and Semites dominated racial discourse, but in America, the dominant binary was White and Black. Although white Americans recognized the existence of numerous racial groups that did not fit neatly into White or Black categories, this did not prevent them from thinking in terms of this binary opposition. African-Americans represented the central paradigm of racial otherness. From revolutionary times through the 19th century, Jews in America were viewed as White. Toward the end of the 19th century, high levels of immigration swelled the Jewish population to unprecedented numbers. Along with social transformations such as industrialization and urbanization, there was a shift in immigration from primarily German Westernized Jews to Jews from Eastern Europe. Jewish race was destabilized and Jews had to fight to maintain their position as whites (Brodkin, 2002; E. L. Goldstein, 2006). Embracing whiteness came with certain costs to Jewish culture and identity. But how could these losses be mourned when what was given up was associated with blackness, femininity, and primitivity—with the abject? And so Jews were left with unmourned losses, a melancholic Jewish-American identity (Butler, 1995).

Because of our affiliation with NYU, we will use it to illustrate the anti-Semitism that was so pervasive at this time. In 1922, NYU had a large Jewish enrollment. Students hung posters warning away "scurvy kikes" and demanding that the administration "Make New York University a

White Man's College" (E. L. Goldstein, 2006, p. 129). There are several things to note about this incident: First, the term "kike" was derived from its use by Western Jews who reproached their Eastern Jewish brethren with the term, since many of those from the East had names ending with "ki." By the 1920s, it had become a popular epithet emphasizing Jewish racial difference. The term itself illustrates how racism is internalized, leading to splitting and fragmentation, with one portion of the colonized identifying with the aggressor and unleashing its contempt on another segment of its own group. Note the confluence of race and gender in the call to make NYU a "White Man's College." Jews were not White and non-Whites were not men. Women were altogether invisible, doubly displaced. It was only in the great social and economic transformation of the post-World War II years that Jews became stably identified as White and stopped describing themselves in racial terms.

American anti-Semitism rose from the 1920s through the late 1940s. Jews continued to be excluded from the elite institutions of non-Jewish society via professional and educational quotas, accompanied by residential segregation, even in the big cities. Many of them the children of Eastern European immigrants, Jews were torn between their empathy for African-Americans and their own continued battle for social equality. This conflict was reflected in their ambivalent relationship with African-Americans, with whom they closely identified as oppressed peoples, but from whom they also wanted to distinguish themselves so as to remain securely on the White side of the racial divide. Jews were caught in an irresolvable contradiction. Given their own history of minority outsider status, pogroms, economic hardship, and residential and occupational restrictions, Jews sought to ally themselves with African-Americans as victims of oppression. However, their experience of anti-Semitism also motivated them to seek the security of being White. They welcomed their White status, even while the racism associated with that position made them uncomfortable.

During World War II, the American military was segregated. Blacks and Asians were kept apart, while Italians, Irish, and Jews were assigned to "White" units, along with mainstream Americans. Roosevelt believed domestic stability and the war effort were best fostered by incorporating immigrants into the "white" population, while reinforcing the sharp divide between Blacks and Whites. Partially in reaction against Nazi racism, the racial categorization of Jews was refashioned in America as ethnicity. Thus Jews could retain some sense of difference and uniqueness as a people while maintaining the dominant racial binary of white and black. Ironically, Jews as a group were often left with nothing in common but religion at a time when they were less religious and less interested in this common denominator. While Jews publicly identified Jewishness as a religious category, many privately considered it a primitive tribal phenomenon.

The categories of race, religion, gender, and sexuality are inevitably and intricately interlinked and interconstructed. The Jewish quest for Whiteness in the 1950s and 1960s was a quest by a Jewish male subject. In the attempt to ensure that Jews would be regarded as White, Jewish women were scapegoated, serving to contain Jewish ambivalence about Whiteness. Stereotypes of the Jewish mother and the Jewish American princess projected this ambivalence onto women. Jewish mothers, not fathers, were anxious and fearful. Jewish princesses, not men, were stereotypically materialistic, concerned with money and accumulation of consumer goods. Whiteness was associated with masculinity, patriarchy, and heterosexuality; misogyny and homophobia projected all that was "abject," the "dark side" onto women and homosexuals (Brodkin, 2002). In this regard, we have come to think of the manic defense as a "manly" defense, with woman the devalued, denigrated, contemptible other. Keep in mind that in the years post-World War II, psychoanalysis was an overwhelmingly White, male, heterosexual, and upwardly mobile middle-class profession.

With the destruction of psychoanalysis in Europe, America became the world center of psychoanalysis. The following statistics are useful in highlighting the dramatic change in professional demographics brought about by the émigré analysts exile to the United States, especially after the Anschluss. In 1938 the American Psychoanalytic Association had 140 members, of whom eighteen were émigrés. In 1937 the New York Psychoanalytic Society had 71 members, of whom five were émigrés. A decade later, in 1948, its membership was 152, with 51, a full third, being émigrés. By 1961, all the officers of the New York Psychoanalytic Society were émigrés. Half of the émigrés (26 of 51) were originally members of the Vienna Psychoanalytic Society, ten of them were from the Hungarian Psychoanalytic Society, and nine were from Berlin. In other words, the psychoanalytic cultures of the three leading European psychoanalytic centers, Berlin, Budapest, and Vienna, were largely transplanted within the New York Psychoanalytic Society and Institute. Many of the émigrés quickly became training analysts and institutional leaders (Thompson, 2012).

Sociologist Louis Coser, himself a refugee who emigrated to the United States in 1941, studied the impact of refugee intellectuals on the social sciences and humanities in America. Coser's (1984) results show that, more than any other group, the European émigré psychoanalysts thrived in America, where they fulfilled a strongly perceived need and encountered an already established tradition with which they felt an affinity. These refugee psychoanalysts significantly influenced the shape of psychoanalysis in America. Coser argues that it is not enough to examine what the émigrés brought with them to America; it is just as important to examine the American context in which they were received and to which they adapted.

Lay versus Medical Analysts

In the 1920s, American analysts opposed Freud's advocacy of lay analysis, which only reinforced Freud's dislike of America. The New York Psychoanalytic Society banned anyone who was not a physician from becoming a member, and even from attending its meetings. This opposition became extremely controversial once the lay European refugee analysts sought to practice in the United States. In 1938, a time of massive immigration by European refugees fleeing Hitler, the American Psychoanalytic Association (APsaA) restricted membership to physicians who had completed a psychiatric residency at an approved institution and tried to enforce this restriction on the European immigrants. In a compromise between the APsaA and the International Psychoanalytic Association (IPA), which had been devastated by the rise of Hitler, the APsaA agreed to grandfather in those analysts who had been trained in Europe prior to 1938, meaning that people who were already established as analysts before the new rules were applied would be allowed to practice as before, in return for gaining control of establishing policy for psychoanalytic training and practice. Lay analysts who were already IPA members were allowed to practice, but no more were permitted to enter training.

Thompson (2012) carefully documents the transformation of American psychoanalysis in this era, and emphasizes the panic that overtook the New York Psychoanalytic Society as the members, then only a small group of 71, were convinced that the European refugees would overwhelm them. The question of lay analysis complicated their feelings, and they attempted to work out an arrangement in which lay analyst refugees would be accepted in a special category as "honorary guests" under the condition that they agree not to train lay analysts in the future.

The decade of the 1930s during the Great Depression witnessed the American "psychoanalytical civil war" (Ernest Jones, cited in Hale, 1995, p. 103). The conflict was between those who wanted to restrict psychoanalysis, to preserve its purity and regulate its training and practice, and those who viewed psychoanalysis more broadly, as a contribution to humanity, social progress, and the mental health field in general. By the end of the 1930s, this battle evolved into a war between orthodox analysts and those who were more eclectic. It is important to recognize the conflation of several independent issues. The professional question of lay versus medical analysis was intertwined with the matter of psychoanalytic theoretical revisionism. Confounding the situation were economic and cultural tensions between American and émigré analysts.

The following letter, written by Anna Freud to Ernest Jones on May 15, 1938, while Anna was still in Vienna, captures the sad stark reality of the times. The Austrian Anschluss had occurred just two months prior. One month later, after being arrested and interrogated by the Gestapo, Anna

Freud fled her home with her father, accompanied by Jones and Princess Marie Bonaparte, with whose help they escaped to England. To anyone familiar with the great Viennese pioneers, it reads like a "Who's Who" of psychoanalysis:

> This morning Kris and Bibrings have left, tomorrow the Waelders depart. Hoffers and Hartmanns have their passports in order and are only waiting their final tax clearance. Jekel's application has also been processed and in a few days he will go to America . . . Federn already has no more money, Steiner and Hitschmann will be penniless the moment they depart; they evidently do not trust themselves to begin a so-called new life. And while I do not find it hard to help the younger people out of their moods, it is of no avail with the others. At most they envy me because I am not yet so old and have more prospects than they. What can one do? It is very sad to be here and to watch it.
> (Cited in Wallerstein, 1998, p. 41)

Anna Freud went on to discuss her concerns about the American refusal to recognize the professional standing of the many lay analysts who had emigrated to save their lives. She specifically mentioned Sachs in Boston, Simmel in Chicago, and Waelder, who would be better off not heading to America.

Some of the European analysts had sided with Freud in support of lay analysis, against what Freud called "the medical fixation" (Wallerstein, 1998, p. 49). But when they came to America, these same prominent analysts switched sides. Among those who changed their positions were Franz Alexander, Sandor Rado, and Grete Bibring. Given all they had lost, the pressure to conform to American standards and fit into the American medical establishment was enormous, turning even brilliant maverick psychoanalysts such as Otto Fenichel, among others, into conservative conformists too afraid to make trouble in their newly adopted country (Jacoby, 1983).

The strategy of defining psychoanalysis in contrast to psychotherapy was established after World War II, and was rooted in the clash between segments of the American and European analysts, aligned by generation. Many of the older generation of American psychiatrists were broadly eclectic, interested in using psychoanalysis to enhance psychiatric treatment in general. They had received whatever training was available in the years before the institutionalization of psychoanalysis. Many of the European analysts who had immigrated to America in the 1920s were similarly broad in their thinking. In contrast, the younger American analysts were preoccupied with establishing a medical specialty that would gain the respect of the increasingly professionalized American medical community. Many of these younger psychiatrists had traveled to Vienna and Berlin for psychoanalytic training. They regarded psychoanalysis as the most scientific of therapies and were determined to restrict training to medical doctors in order to avoid any insinuation of quackery. Having come of age when medicine was militantly regulating itself, they sought to formalize psychoanalytic training so that it was rigorous and disciplined, a proper medical specialty. The young generation of psychiatrists included Lawrence Kubie, Ives Hendricks, and Bertram Lewin, who viewed the older generation with disdain. "To the young, the older generation seemed incompetent, intellectually slack, undisciplined. They could be neither respected nor admired, and thus were inadequate professional father figures" (Hale, 1995, p. 104). To the older generation, including A. A. Brill and Horace Frink, founders of the New York Psychoanalytic Society, the "young Turks" were overly ambitious and narcissistic political manipulators insistent on having their way.

Maintaining the Status Quo

Many of the famous historical splits among the first psychoanalytic institutes involved issues of orthodoxy tied in complex ways to political battles between generations and between the American and newly immigrated European analysts. The situation was complicated even further by the difficulties faced by this new group of European refugee analysts, as they negotiated their personal and professional adjustment in their new and unfamiliar home. The immigrants fleeing Hitler in the late 1930s arrived under very different circumstances from those who had emigrated earlier seeking economic opportunity and greater freedom of expression. Many were not medical doctors, and those who were had difficulty obtaining internships and medical licensing once in the United States. Appreciative of the refuge America had provided them and grateful to the analysts who had supported their entry into the United States, the émigrés were not interested in making trouble by challenging their American hosts. Many joined with the younger generation of more conservative American analysts to create a mainstream psychoanalysis in America that was far more conservative, rigid, and doctrinaire than the psychoanalytic culture they had left behind in Europe. While the émigré analysts had been radical or at least liberal in Europe, when they came to America, they accommodated to their hosts, supporting a conservative, professionalized turn in psychoanalysis as a medical specialty. Fisher (2012) observes that the professionalization of psychoanalysis undermined its revolutionary origins and had the effect of "taming the disturbing truths about our inner world first articulated by Freud and his early analytic cohort." Fisher adds that the bureaucratization introduced by the institutional system and the bias against lay analysis "seriously weakened the dissemination of psychoanalysis into society, limited its creativity, eliminating the rigorous thinking and innovate approaches to be found in non-medical disciplines" (p. 4).

Their conservative turn must also be understood in terms of gender. In this period, to be a man meant to be out in the world making money. Social work was women's work, and social activism was associated with aggressive, moralizing women. In the United States, socially active men, especially immigrant men, would have been perceived as unmanly (Danto, 2009). American mainstream analysts of the postwar years adopted traditional gender norms, using psychoanalysis to rationalize rather than challenge them. It was argued that the analyst was not a political activist and could not change the social conditions in which patients lived, and so the analyst's job was to help the patient come to terms with the surrounding cultural conditions. All of this stood in striking contrast to the pioneering days of European psychoanalysis, when many analysts leaned heavily to the left politically. Following the war, psychoanalysis in America took a decidedly conservative turn, "blunting the revolutionary edge of analysis's destabilizing truths, often co-opting the subversive methods and findings of psychoanalysis" (Fisher, 2012, p. 5). The émigré analysts who had been radical in Europe became depoliticized and conservative so as not to appear subversive or effeminate in their new home.

Esther Menaker was a psychoanalyst social worker who was raised in America and who obtained her doctorate and psychoanalytic training in Vienna in the early 1930s. Menaker described the situation of the refugee analysts in New York City as follows:

> Although they were in no position to oppose the medical community, since they had to focus on survival, they had contributed a very positive intellectual influence, propagating psychoanalysis on a theoretical and academic level that it would never have received from the Americans, who were woefully lacking in knowledge.
>
> (Cited in Aiello, 2009, p. 29)

Menaker's experience confirms reports of other American lay analysts who were trained in Europe. Although it had authorized Menaker's training in Vienna before she went, the New York Psychoanalytic Society would not recognize it upon her return in the mid-1930s, encouraging her instead to relocate to Nebraska (Menaker, 1989). This was not an isolated incident. Lay analysts were prohibited from practice and even from attending the International Psychoanalytic Congress without special written permission, even though they had trained in Vienna! Menaker said that obtaining such permission made her feel "contaminated" (p. 182). The New York psychoanalytic community was concerned about competition. It considered New York to be saturated with analysts, and so was hostile both to lay analysts and to medical émigré analysts – in both cases this would have included many more women analysts then they were used to. Margaret Mahler was told by Adolph Stern, Lawrence Kubie, Sandor Rado, and Clarence

Oberndorf that all émigré medical analysts must first obtain a medical license and then become pioneer analysts in upstate locations, such as Buffalo, Utica, or Syracuse (Mahler, 1988). In fact, before Mahler passed her medical boards (consider the difficulties this posed for new immigrants) she saw a few private analytic patients in order to survive financially, but a member of the New York Psychoanalytic Society threatened to report her to the authorities (Aiello, 2009). Paul Federn's son Ernst was a lay analyst, a social worker from Vienna who escaped to the United States with his father. He contended that by devaluing social work, the medical psychoanalytic establishment displayed a total disregard for social commitment. "The disregard for social issues within the American Psychoanalytic Societies, with the exception of Karl Menninger and a few others, was of course the result of the policy which did not admit non-medical people into the profession" (quoted in Aiello, 2009, p. 32). Many lay analysts were women. In order to support themselves, they worked in child guidance agencies, where they reportedly had the private, necessarily secret, pleasure of reading Melanie Klein.

According to Coser (1984), the refugee analysts "arrived at the right place at the right time" (p. 42). The younger generation of American-born analysts, many of whom had studied with these refugee analysts in Europe, was highly receptive to their ideas and traditions. The "young Turks" were eager to establish their psychoanalytic credentials by ensuring that the psychoanalysis being taught in the institutes was the real thing. They wanted to trace their lineage back to Freud and his circle, and to prove that their extended psychoanalytic training was necessary, warranted, and constitutive of elite status. They were motivated to show that their psychoanalysis was pure and that their training met the highest standards. This was just at the time medicine was standardizing practices and credentialing specialties. The refugees from Berlin, Vienna, and Budapest could not have received a better reception. They were glad to have the opportunity to reestablish something of the tradition and respect they had lost in Europe. Unlike many immigrants of the same era who had difficulty finding academic positions, these refugees were sought after as teachers and practitioners. The demand was so great that they taught and conducted training analyses, despite their thick accents and profound difficulty understanding the English language.

Rudolph Loewenstein, a partner of Heinz Hartmann and one of the major contributors to American ego-psychology, was rescued from Europe late and spoke no English. Nevertheless, having to support himself and his family as a new immigrant in a foreign country, he conducted analyses in English. It is no coincidence that Loewenstein went on to write key papers that emphasized waiting and listening before interpreting. He confessed to Hedda Bolger that he had learned English by silently listening to patients and waiting before making interpretations (Kurzweil, 1996).

In contrast, many of the older generation of American analysts were eclectic, had never been "properly" trained, and had little or no personal contact with Freud and his followers. Some had not even thoroughly studied Freud's work and were not particularly interested in the subtleties of Freud's theories, confusing later psychoanalytic developments with its hypnotic and cathartic origins. Before the 1930s, psychoanalysis in America was at best a watered-down brew. As Kenneth Eisold (1998) has argued, drawing on Hale (1995), the second generation of American analysts, who sought the authority of American medicine and the mantle of "true psychoanalysis," allied themselves with the European émigrés, who were trying to preserve some idealized remnants of what they had lost to Hitler. Together, they overpowered the looser, more eclectic, band of older American psychiatrists. The young generation of American analysts (such as Kubie, Hendricks, and Lewin) teamed up with the European refugees against the older American psychiatrists, who were in turn aligned with the European analysts who had emigrated earlier in the hope of spreading psychoanalysis (Alexander, Rado, Fromm-Reichman, Horney). Together, these groups merged the authority of American medicine with the authority of the recently lost founder of psychoanalysis, Sigmund Freud. It was a powerful coalition and a potent brew, contributing to the erection of what we will show was a formidable manic defense.

Soon the battle lines shifted and the splits were no longer generational or between Europeans and Americans, but between more classical analysts and those who were revisionist and eclectic. The story of the various schisms and alliances and the changing lines of battle is complicated, to say the least. While ideas may be classified into categories, it is always dangerous to sort people into categories. Consider Otto Fenichel. On one hand, Fenichel disliked many who considered themselves "orthodox Freudians;" on the other, he objected to the revisionists, the so-called neo-Freudians, because he felt they had gone too far in deemphasizing drives and sexuality. And so he sided against Karen Horney even though he shared her dislike of the orthodox. Or take Horney herself as an example. She joined with Clara Thompson, Harry Stack Sullivan, and Erich Fromm, who were like-minded in many respects in their critique of the orthodox, but split with them over the issue of lay analysis. In other words, individual analysts did not line up neatly into the various divisions: American/European; medical/lay analysis; pure psychoanalysis/general psychiatry; support/critique of drive theory; political liberals/Marxists; those committed to scientific methodology versus those who put their faith in the findings of the clinical situation.

Immigration, Trauma, and Loss

Hartmann's ego-psychology provided the theoretical scaffolding that justified the exuberant optimism of American psychoanalysis in the postwar years. Ego-psychology's hegemony in American psychoanalysis was matched by America's dominance in the world. The language of American ego-psychology, which dominated the discourse of the 1950s, was meant to sound scientific. It spoke of hypotheses, neutralized energies, neutralization, apparatuses of secondary autonomy, change in function. The language was meant to enhance the scientific status of psychoanalysis and appeal to scientists beyond psychoanalysis as part of the agenda of making psychoanalysis a general psychology. Hartmann and his colleagues wanted to remove psychoanalysis from its intellectual isolation and extend its influence to fields such as biology and sociology. Within the ego-psychological framework, the achievement of autonomy was established as the highest goal for the individual. It was held that the ego could achieve autonomy not only from the drives but also from the environment; this double autonomy provided the ego with the capacity for adjustment and adaptation. Neither enslaved by the drives nor by the environment, the autonomous ego solves problems, makes choices, and permits pleasure. Freud had famously pictured the ego as weak in relation to the drives:

> In its relation to the id it is like a man on horseback, who has to hold in check the superior strength of the horse; with this difference, that the rider tries to do so with his own strength, while the ego uses borrowed forces.

(1923, p. 25)

Freud's stress on drives and constitutional factors envisioned society as restricting human freedom and pleasure, and therefore the goal of psychoanalysis was some small measure of liberation. Hartmann placed more emphasis on how social institutions assist the individual's striving for adaptation. "What to Freud was a coercive force was to Hartmann a benevolent molding institution," says Martin Bergmann (2000, p. 14). Bergmann's retrospective examination of the Hartmann era focused fresh attention on the important role of Jewish émigrés in the establishment of American psychoanalysis, highlighting the role of the Holocaust and its denial as significant factors in this history.

Throughout the first half century after the Shoah, with several notable exceptions, psychoanalysts minimized and even ignored the significance of the Holocaust, both clinically as it affected survivors and their children, and sociologically, in terms of how it affected the profession and the development of psychoanalytic theory. Prince (2009) suggests that the legacy of authoritarianism, intolerance of dissent, and schisms haunting mainstream psychoanalytic institutions can be traced to the wish to reinstate security and lost status and esteem while at the same time re-enacting the legacy of authoritarianism and persecution, and identifying with the aggressor.

Kuriloff (2010) demonstrates that the impact of the Holocaust went largely unspoken; the trauma was silently repeated, enacted in our theories and institutions, rather than remembered and acknowledged. She attributes this to a variety of factors, wisely cautioning that we should not reduce the complexity of this phenomenon to a single explanation. Kuriloff elaborates a multi-explanatory approach and notes, following Anna Ornstein, that not all catastrophic experience leads to pathology and dissociated enactment. She highlights the émigrés' wish for a positivist science with objective standards, which led to a dichotomization of the personal and the professional.

According to Bergmann (2000), as a group, the psychoanalysts were better able to predict what was coming and fled Germany and Austria before it was too late, while other professionals remained. We question whether the analysts had sharper foresight than other professionals. Certainly Freud himself denied what was coming, and he only managed to escape because he had an excellent network of connections that rescued him and Anna after a close call in which Anna was detained by the Gestapo. Bergmann points out that the analysts had an excellent system of international colleagues. Because Jews were excluded from psychoanalysis shortly after Hitler came to power they were motivated to emigrate earlier than those who were more easily able to continue working. Ernest Jones did a good deal to help them escape, and The Emergency Committee on Relief and Immigration of the American Psychoanalytic Association raised funds and assisted immigration and relocation. Yet there was a great deal of ambivalence aroused by the fear of economic competition and professional displacement that would be brought about by incorporating the immigrants into the American scene. From her thorough historical review, Thompson (2012) concludes that while the Emergency Committee, in a very difficult environment, did successfully rescue many European analysts, the battle over lay analysis cast a dark shadow over the committee's humanitarian achievement.

Émigré analysts were often dispersed to less populated areas; this was not unique to the psychoanalytic profession but was true in medicine generally. The horrors of Nazism did not spare physicians: 2,800 of the 3,500 Jewish physicians in Poland were killed in the Holocaust. From 1933 to 1945, some 6,000 European physicians escaped and found their way to the United States. Their plight aroused much indignation among Jews and gentiles, but despite these humane impulses and the relative decline in the number of physicians in the United States, other forces had a countervailing effect. Systematic efforts were made by medical societies to exclude the émigrés from becoming licensed. The real basis for rejecting them was economic. The depression had already cut into the incomes of American physicians. Denied access elsewhere, 65 percent of 1,802 refugee practitioners were concentrated in New York City in 1941 and added to the competitive burden. Most of the analysts who found their way to

America eventually prospered more than they had in Europe before the war, achieving recognition as elder statesman in a thriving profession that welcomed them as pioneers and trailblazers and bestowed heroic status to those who personally knew Freud. Bergmann (2000) suggests that while all of these factors might have contributed to their confidence, their *"optimism"* (p. 7) was due to the Allied victory over Hitler.

Manic Defense: The Repudiation of Vulnerability

What Bergmann describes as optimism is better understood as a manic defense against trauma and loss. We use the notion of manic defense as an organizing framework, not as a single reductionistic explanation; it is a multi-explanatory framework that provides structure to highly overdetermined processes. Manic defense is characterized by denial, omnipotence, disparagement or devaluation, contempt, triumph over the object, and omnipotent control (Klein, 1935; Hinshelwood, 1989). All of these elements were characteristic of American psychoanalysis after the war. Although they escaped with their lives, the émigrés lost a great deal, including family, community, culture, language, institutions, and means of occupation, not to mention a sense of safety and predictability. Many, if not all, worried about relatives and friends and felt guilty for leaving them. Freud's death had a monumental impact; they lost their leader just as they were experiencing their greatest personal and professional vulnerability. Add to this the manic excitement of American psychoanalysis as it overcame its second-rate backwater status compared to European psychoanalysis, dominating the International Psychoanalytic Association just as America was emerging as the dominant world power.

Prince (2009) compares psychoanalytic institutional isolation with that of the survivor family, "a kind of refuge from a threatening world that could be regarded with condescension or contempt" (p. 188). He cites Richards, who described the training analyst system as elevating one to a godlike omnipotent status. Kirsner (2000) describes the "climate of paranoia" (p. 36) that affected psychoanalytic institutes as they tried to mask their fears and insecurities by exerting control and clinging to power.

Makari (2008) argues that before Hitler's rise to power, analysts developed their own theoretical modifications without feeling the need to be narrowly Freudian. But the Viennese analysts who fled Austria following the Anschluss brought with them to America a fetishistic preoccupation with psychoanalytic purity and an idealized version of Freud. Kuriloff (2010) connects the émigrés' longing for purity and orthodoxy to their losses and grief. What was lost became idealized and Freud's name was then thought to carry magical properties. As Hale (1995) has shown, the émigrés allied with younger American analysts searching for psychoanalytic authenticity and lineage to Freud. The tendency toward idealization came from both directions: from the immigrants who romanticized their past and from the young generation of American analysts who were motivated to idealize their old-world teachers and analysts and create a distinguished lineage.

Certainty versus Uncertainty

Whether celebrated or critiqued, the postwar era of ego-psychology, often referred to as the "golden years" or "halcyon days" of psychoanalysis, was a time of great confidence in the profession. Psychoanalysis exuded a sense of certainty and control. Arguing for a darker reading of this period, Adrienne Harris (2011a) suggests that the bedrock of American culture at this time was the evasion of loss and mourning. She describes the dark mood of the Cold War as reflecting a period of fear and constriction, especially under McCarthyism. The certainty of American ego-psychology masked the anxieties and uncertainties that simmered below the surface of American culture—the public face of psychoanalytic theory and practice was a kind of reaction formation. Communist hunters in the McCarthy era were often members of overtly or thinly veiled anti-Semitic groups (Sachar, 2005); most of the people accused of being pro-Communist were Jews. Rather than expressing a confident calm, the nation's paranoid turn reflected simmering conflict, subliminal stirrings of racial, class, religious, sexual, and cultural frustration. We view this paranoia as linked to the pervasive fear that all that was primitive and vulnerable—women, Blacks, homosexuals, Jews—was contaminated. It had to be controlled and kept separate, made "abject." We contend that the certainty and control projected by American psychoanalysis in the 1950s and 1960s was in fact a manic defense, a defense against persecutory and depressive anxieties.

Omnipotence versus Vulnerability

The omnipotence of the era is evident in the attitude promoted by analysts and accepted by the public that psychoanalysis could solve all problems, both on the couch (psychosis, delinquency, and psychosomatics) and in the world (nuclear arms, the Cold War, literature, and philosophy). The denial of vulnerability was pervasive. Especially glaring was the denial of the Holocaust as something to speak about, as a factor in treating other immigrants (Blum, 2010), as a traumatic event in the history of psychoanalysis, and in the history of the analysts themselves. The denial of vulnerability was a denial of the Jewish origins of psychoanalysis, of the analysts' own immigrant status, and of the losses they had suffered. Splitting dominated psychoanalytic thinking: Freudian and neo-Freudian, depth and surface, analyzable and non-analyzable, and eventually psychoanalysis and psychodynamic psychotherapy. Psychoanalysts of the time devalued those who were religious or observant, especially anyone observant of Jewish ritual. Writer Daphne Merkin describes her analyst, Dr. S., as a "deracinated Jew who kept regular hours on Yom Kippur, as if to prove a point" (Merkin, 2010, p. 36). Against Freud's wishes, they held non-medical analysts in contempt. Their omnipotence fed into their entitlement; they expected to earn as much as other physicians, even surgeons. Focusing on a neurotic analyzable elite, they considered themselves heroic for attempting to treat those with weaker egos, a manic idealization of their efforts. In order to protect themselves from experiencing their own vulnerability—their sense of safety had, after all, been shattered—they split off and projected all that was vulnerable onto others. The analyst was presented as invulnerable, rational, and masterful, while all vulnerability, irrationality, and dependency was attributed to the patient. The analyst's neutrality, uncontaminated by suggestion, served to reinforce the boundary between analyst and patient.

It was also in this postwar era that American psychoanalysis elaborated and institutionalized homosexuality as pathology. Freud and his colleagues viewed homosexuality with greater tolerance and less moral opprobrium. Freud had maintained that homosexuals could be trained as psychoanalysts, but in this era in America, those with a homosexual orientation were routinely rejected from institutes. Emphasizing the rigid, authoritarian, and non-scientific culture of the period, Friedman and Downey (1998) also note the grandiosity embodied by the assumption that psychoanalysis could "cure" homosexuality. They ask, "Was the grandiosity of prediction limited to homosexuality, or were psychoanalysts generally promising behavioral change beyond anything that could reasonably be accepted?" They cite the generally accepted belief that psychoanalysis could lead to "total personality reorganization" and Menninger's extravagant description of psychoanalysis as the "supreme paradigm of psychotherapy" (p. 266).

In our view, ego-psychology's championing of independence and autonomy is reflective of a manic defense against vulnerability and loss. As Bergmann remarks, "There is something majestic in Rapaport's description of the autonomous ego and its powers. It reminds one of Nietzsche's superman" (2000, p. 15). Rather than recognize, as Freud had, the relative weakness of the ego, the degree to which the individual could never be autonomous or master of his fate, ego-psychology was adopted by American culture just at the time when the country was at its most omnipotent, riding high from its major military successes and subsequent financial boom. It was a time when America itself wished to avoid the recognition of its own vulnerability, having unleashed nuclear war and faced the horrors of what one nation can do to another. Hartmann's psychology was not only optimistic, but also focused in particular on the neutralization of aggression and on the individual's capacity to gain autonomy over the id. The rider had gained control over the instinctual horse. Life could be experienced as not quite so precarious (Butler, 2004b). This manic attitude perfectly suited an America that was just beginning to come out of the Depression and was experiencing unprecedented affluence. Even the fear of Communism soon gave way to a new mood of American optimism. Medicine and psychoanalysis achieved a significant rise in status, having been recently recognized as war heroes, and Jews were just beginning to feel secure in their standing as White.

Kernberg (Bergman, 2000) suggests that the rejection of the death drive was only one manifestation of a general tendency in ego-psychology to downplay "primitive sexuality" and "primitive aggression" and deny the self-destructiveness of individuals and groups, organizations, and nations. He contends that this "sanitized" version of Freud (p. 145) was suitable to acceptance by the conventional American culture of its day. Kernberg, too, notes that the "optimism" (he puts it in quotes, recognizing that it is an ironic use of the term) associated with "adaptation" came at a time when the world was learning of mass murder both in Nazi Germany and Communist Russia. According to Kernberg, Hartmann underestimated "Freud's discovery regarding the profound self-destructive nature of human beings, the enormous potential for primitive hatred and cruelty underneath the veneer of civilization" (Bergmann, 2000, p. 146). Blum argues to the contrary, that under Hartmann, the aggressive drive was elevated in importance to being co-equal with the libidinal drive in order to compensate for the earlier denial of Nazi aggression. Hartmann acknowledged the centrality of human destructiveness but optimistically argued that it could be neutralized, tamed, channeled, and transformed, all along remaining silent about its impact in the real world.

Kernberg attributed the apparent optimism to denial and to "identification with the aggressor," resulting in the totalitarian ambience of psychoanalysis in the postwar years. "An overarching theory may have reflected a triumphant institutional system" (p. 153). In describing the "average expectable environment," Kernberg says that in hindsight, psychoanalysis conveyed

> an idealized view of the psychosocial environment, the impression of the viewpoint of a privileged class rather than of a generation haunted by the experiences of two world wars, brutal dictatorships, and totalitarian regimes, not to speak of racial and religious persecutions.
>
> (Bergmann, 2000, p. 147)

Blum adds that under the circumstances, the concept of an "average expectable environment" was a wishful fantasy.

A Jewish Science?

In our view, psychoanalysis and historiographers of psychoanalysis have not paid sufficient attention to issues of racism, misogyny, homophobia, and anti-Semitism; to the trauma of immigration and displacement both in Europe and America; to the xenophobia of American postwar culture; to issues of class, the swing from economic depression to affluence; and to related sociocultural changes. Understanding these patterns provides the context for examining the role of race, gender, religion, class, poverty, and sexual orientation in the history of psychoanalysis. We are struck by the fact that when psychoanalysis was in its heyday as part of the mainstream— when it was "civilized"—there was a reluctance to identify it as Jewish, but now that it is considered "primitive," a "dinosaur" profession, historians explain its demise as the passing of a Jewish identity movement (Shorter, 1997). We fear that highlighting the role of the Jewish émigrés can be misconstrued as blaming the excesses of postwar establishment psychoanalysis on the pathology of Jewish survivors. We worry that our argument may be used to attribute the excesses of psychoanalytic rigidity and grandiosity to the pathology of Jewish victims, just as Shorter (1997) attributed the fall of psychoanalysis to Jewish assimilation. We will return to these concerns and to Shorter's arguments in Chapter 16, when we explicitly address the question of whether psychoanalysis should be considered a "Jewish science." But here we would like to underscore our point that the mania, grandiosity, and arrogance of postwar psychoanalysis must be understood as a desperate effort to cope with unmourned losses and profound vulnerability, both on the part of the émigrés and on the part of the American culture that received them, and to which they had to adapt.

Chapter 8

Psychoanalysis versus Psychotherapy

Definition via Binary Opposition

In the heyday of psychoanalysis, its golden age, the psychoanalytic establishment defined psychoanalysis in contrast to psychotherapy. We have provided a brief summary of the events that set the stage for this development. In this chapter, we will review the positions taken by the key players in the formative debates that shaped the definition of the field. As we do so, we recognize that in a profession that is now predominantly female, in a country that has become increasingly diverse—though unfortunately, psychoanalysis still does not reflect that diversity—it can feel off-putting to immerse one's self in what seem to be the professional squabbles of a group of dead white men. Although several famous women stand out as exceptions, such as Anna Freud, Edith Jacobson, Phyllis Greenacre, Clara Thompson, and Frieda Fromm-Reichmann, among others, the power brokers of 1950s American psychoanalysis were predominantly male. Their views will be the primary focus of this chapter, as we examine the 1950s debates that defined psychoanalysis by differentiating it from psychotherapy. Exacerbating the discomfort of reviewing these arguments is that the participants in these debates were full of their own success and power, speaking and writing at a time when psychoanalysis was at its peak in the United States. Masters of the Universe of their day, they had risen to the most prestigious of positions in an exclusive medical specialty just at the height of the country's economic prosperity, following its victory in World War II. These analysts were the recipients of a culture-wide idealized transference; they were the country's wise men. Intellectual and culturally sophisticated, most of them had studied in Europe, carrying the additional mystique of having been analyzed by Freud, members of his circle, or other European pioneer analysts.

As outdated as the debates of the 1950s may seem to us today, it is crucial to examine their arguments in detail in order to understand how psychoanalysis arrived at its current marginalized position. The theoretical concerns debated in the 1950s continue to reverberate in modern times, with implications for how and whom we treat, how frequently we see patients, and how we define our professional identities. In this chapter, we will illustrate the ways in which the cultural, economic, and political factors that shaped psychoanalysts' identities in the 1950s also shaped the theoretical arguments calling for the polarization and bifurcation of psychoanalysis from psychotherapy. We will show that definition via binary opposition was not the only option available to these psychoanalysts at the time, nor were theoretical considerations the sole driving force, and yet these ideas have molded the psychoanalytic educational policies we live by today. We will suggest that these arguments are dangerously anachronistic. To put it bluntly: If we do not change the terms of the debate, psychoanalysis will not survive.

Science, Progress, and the American Way

In the 1950s, psychoanalysis aligned itself with science and progress. The paranoia of the Cold War fueled America's technological race to space and its development of advanced weaponry. There were dramatic breakthroughs in medicine, including the new miracle drug penicillin. Technological inventions were changing Americans' way of life. The analysts whose arguments we will be examining believed that psychoanalysis was an advanced scientific treatment that should be applied only by a highly trained medical expert. Military propaganda had successfully promoted the idea that psychiatry and psychoanalysis had won the war. In the eyes of the public, these psychoanalysts were not merely doctors—they were war heroes! State officials and government agencies called upon them to contribute to a variety of social and political, national and international causes. We see references in the literature to how difficult it was to see patients five days a week when the analyst was busy flying around the country consulting to governors and Congress (Eissler, 1953).

In the 1950s, psychoanalysis was an elite medical specialty, and psychoanalysts made as much money as surgeons. The National Institute of Mental Health (NIMH) funded psychoanalytic research and training, even paying for training analyses. Following the European tradition, psychoanalytic institutes in the United States offered classes in the evening. A young psychiatrist in training could work full time during the day and attend psychoanalytic training in the evening courtesy of the GI bill. For many people, such as federal employees in the Washington, D.C. area and New York City schoolteachers, generous insurance plans paid for 80 percent of psychoanalytic treatment. This meant that a patient in five-times weekly analysis paid for one session and was covered for the other four. An analysis could go on for years, with little financial hardship for the patient. Even mediocre analysts made a good living (Hornstein, 2000). After the war, jobs in VA hospitals opened up to psychologists because psychiatrists no longer wanted these relatively low-paying and unglamorous positions. Is it any wonder we get a sense of these men speaking from positions of power and authority? The tone of the debates often seems elitist, condescending, and exclusivist—imbued with what at the time would have been called "phallic narcissism." As Theresa Aiello (2009) expressed, the "preponderance of white, middle-class men attending medical school at that time" contributed to a "kind of grayness in the writing of theory" (p. 32).

Women in Psychoanalysis

Much of what has been written about the history of psychoanalysis in its golden age in America is based on Nathanial Hale's (1971, 1995) monumental historical account. While Hale's scholarship is authoritative and wide-ranging in scope, he tended to use examples of male leadership to the neglect of women leaders. We would like to take this opportunity to add some details about the position of women in psychoanalysis in order to present a more nuanced historical view. The medicalization of psychoanalysis and accompanying prohibition against lay analysts severely limited the role of women in mainstream American psychoanalysis. In 1958, only 9 percent of all students in institutes of the APsaA were female (Jacoby, 1983), and even that was an increase from prior years. Psychoanalysis was a specialized medical profession, and few women were admitted to medical school. Reluctant to share their power with women, American psychiatrists limited the role of women physicians in institutional psychiatry, virtually assigning them to oblivion.

In contrast, psychoanalysis in Europe had been relatively welcoming of women. While the first analysts in Freud's circle were all men, women soon joined the profession. In a short time, these women gained important institutional positions within the psychoanalytic movement, becoming highly regarded theorists and clinicians. In fact, women were more influential in the field of psychoanalysis than in any other comparable intellectual arena. Of the approximately 653 people who entered the psychoanalytic movement between 1902 and 1930, 133 (about 20 percent) were women, most of whom were medical doctors (Thompson, 1987). From the 1920s through the 1940s, the percentage of women in psychoanalysis in Europe and America was relatively high compared to other professions (Chodorow, 2004). Freud himself recognized the contributions of women analysts; their work was published in the major journals and presented at prestigious professional meetings. Women made significant contributions in the area of child analysis and theories of feminine development, and some were particularly celebrated as gifted clinicians. However, during the 1950s through the 1970s, the proportion of women in psychoanalysis, while remaining high in Europe, "plummeted in the United States, as the émigré analysts began to retire and the medical requirement, unique to the United States, served as de facto discrimination against women" (Chodorow, 2004, p. 116).

At its very beginning in 1911, the APsaA explicitly barred women from membership. The first female members were not admitted until 1926 (McGovern, 1984). A hint of how the male-dominated American psychoanalytic establishment viewed women can be found in a remark made by Clarence Oberndorf (1953) in *A History of Psychoanalysis in America*. "Obey," as his friends called him, was a leader in American psychoanalysis and especially well known in New York, a psychiatrist who had gone to Vienna in the early 1920s to be analyzed by Freud. Obey contended that the greater authority granted to women in America led to neurotic and discontented women seeking independent careers. He was not alone in his view of American women as phallic and aggressive. During Obey's analysis, Freud had told him that American men were too subservient to their women. Europeans of the time generally believed that the boisterous and aggressive behavior of American boys covered up an underlying passivity (Aiello, 2009). Many of the European émigré analysts clung to psychoanalytic orthodoxy, continuing to champion a theory of penis envy that pathologized women's professional aspirations and that was consonant with the gender norms of the 1950s. Somewhat surprisingly, many of these male analysts supported individual women in their professional advancement (many of their own wives were therapists or social workers) even while they perpetuated a misogynistic theory (Menaker, 1989).

Some women, particularly female physicians who trained in Europe, did manage to achieve influential positions in psychoanalysis. Many of the best-known women analysts were émigrés. Between 1911 and 1941, 58 American women joined the psychoanalytic movement; about half had received their training in Europe, and all but five had medical degrees. Some of these talented women gained influence within psychoanalytic societies and institutes as teachers, supervisors, training analysts, and committee members, contributing to theory, clinical practice, and psychoanalytic education (Thompson, 2001). However, women were underrepresented on the editorial boards of the major American psychoanalytic journals and in national organizational leadership. Because it was difficult for women to become physicians, the effort to marginalize and control lay analysts was simultaneously an effort to keep women in their place.

In 1953, the New York Psychoanalytic Society appointed a Committee to Study Unauthorized Training, threatening to expel any member found guilty of educating a non-physician. Anonymous letters were circulated, listing the names of those accused of such heresy, and anyone found providing information to unauthorized groups was subject to expulsion from the Society. Since unauthorized psychoanalytic training was lawless and dangerous to the public, informing on colleagues who assisted such groups was not a violation of free speech. Frieda Fromm-Reichmann, who as we will soon see argued against the sharp distinction between psychotherapy and psychoanalysis, was targeted not only for her unorthodox views, but also because Chestnut Lodge, her clinical home, welcomed psychologists and social workers. As Hornstein (2000) noted, "In McCarthyite America, ferreting out 'radicals' wasn't a job only for the government" (p. 283).

What is Psychoanalysis? Definition via Binary Opposition

Immediately after the war, there was a "gold rush" on psychoanalytic institutes and residencies (quoted in Hale, 1995, p. 211). Waiting lists were long and applications for training numerous. Between 1948 and 1951, the relatively few institutes received 4,066 applications for training from young psychiatrists (p. 222). The sudden popularity of psychoanalysis created several new dilemmas for the growing movement. How to deal with the many patients who sought treatment? How to accommodate the need for more training? How to resolve conflicts between orthodox and more liberal views of psychoanalysis? Although it overlapped with other questions such as theoretical orthodoxy, criteria for analyzability, stringency of training, and medical and lay analysis, the major divide was about whether psychoanalysis should remain a separate, exclusive discipline or become a part of dynamic psychiatry; in other words, whether or not psychoanalysis should be affiliated with psychotherapy. In what follows, the key point we hope to highlight is the way in which this question was definitively answered by the psychoanalytic mainstream. Psychoanalysis would remain a separate discipline, and would define itself not *as* psychotherapy, but *in contrast to* psychotherapy.

William Menninger himself fought this battle immediately after the war. Coming as he did from his family clinic and hospital, which treated psychosis, Menninger deplored the tendency for psychoanalysts to limit their practice to the few "analyzable" patients who were healthy enough to use it and sick enough to need it. Menninger strongly advocated for mass treatment and prevention. Just after the war, at the height of his professional reputation and influence, and as president of the APsaA, Menninger proposed a drastic change in membership criteria that would have allowed more physicians and social scientists to be counted as members. Physicians who had not been analyzed would be admitted as non-voting affiliate members and psychologists would be welcome as research members. This proposal was very much in line with Menninger's broad, "assimilationist" vision of incorporating psychoanalysis into the mental health movement (Hale, 1995, p. 212). Menninger's war experience contributed to his conviction that what psychoanalysis had to offer was much broader and had more far-reaching ramifications than being simply a narrow method of treatment practiced by an elite group of practitioners for a limited number of patients. Yet even at the height of his professional power, Menninger was roundly defeated by those who were identified with psychoanalysis as an elite profession allied with science and orthodox Freudian theory. In fact, the organization voted for even more stringent membership criteria, excluding from membership social scientists and a broader base.

In the 1950s, at the peak of psychoanalysis' rise to power, a series of important panels were convened, focusing on how to define psychoanalysis and how to differentiate it from psychotherapy.[1] Even under the hegemony of a single psychoanalytic theory—ego-psychology—there had been no prior consensus. A committee of the APsaA met between 1947 and 1951 to deliberate this specific issue. Concluding that "it was impossible to find a definition of psychoanalysis that is acceptable to even a large group of members of the American Psychoanalytic Association" (Oberndorf, 1953, p. 234), the committee could not agree on how to differentiate psychoanalysis from other therapies. Discussing the committee's report, Oberndorf expressed his concern that without a definitive definition of psychoanalysis, the door will be open to the untrained to claim that "any flimsy and footloose conversational therapy they elect to employ in their practice may be foisted upon patients as psychoanalysis" (p. 235). The stage was set for American psychoanalysis to define itself with precision. The vignettes that follow are highly condensed and selected highlights of these debates. We begin with Franz Alexander, as his maverick position established him as the protagonist, or perhaps the antagonist, of these debates.

Franz Alexander

Developed in Chicago during World War II and first articulated in *Psychoanalytic Therapy*, published by Alexander and French in 1946, the concept of the "corrective emotional experience" provoked the psychoanalytic establishment to debate the essentials of psychoanalysis and psychotherapy. While Alexander is often criticized for advocating manipulative role-playing, we believe that what analysts objected to was the implication that the analyst

---

1 The widening scope of indications for psychoanalysis (Freud, A. 1954; Stone, 1954); The traditional psychoanalytic technique and its variations (Orr and Zetzel, 1953); Psychoanalysis and dynamic psychotherapy—similarities and differences (O'Neil and Rangell,1954); Some comments on psychoanalysis and dynamic psychiatry (Eissler, 1956); Psychoanalysis and the dynamic psychotherapies (Bibring, 1954); The essentials of psychotherapy as viewed by the psychoanalyst (Johnson and English, 1953); Psychoanalysis and psychotherapy: Dynamic criteria for treatment choice (Johnson and Ludwig, 1954).

was a personal participant in the analysis and that psychoanalysis was a two-person psychology that had to take into account the individuality of the analyst and the fit between patient and analyst. In his shift to a two-person psychology, Alexander paid increasing attention to the interaction between the two members of the dyad. This led him to critique the notion of the blank screen, neutrality and anonymity, and ultimately to downplay the difference between psychotherapy and psychoanalysis. Much of this achievement was obscured, however, by Alexander's advocacy of a positivist epistemology and the remnant of an authoritarian attitude. His position was an awkward mix of elements that reflected his time and circumstances.

Franz Alexander was born in Budapest in 1891. He was his mother's favorite, and was close to his father, who was an academic professor of philosophy. Raised in the humanistic tradition, Alexander remained interested in philosophy and supported interdisciplinary studies throughout his life. He was the brilliant first student at the famed Berlin Psychoanalytic Institute and joined its faculty before immigrating to Chicago in 1930, where he founded the Chicago Institute for Psychoanalysis and pioneered the development of psychosomatic medicine. In Berlin, Alexander had been personally close to Freud, who referred his own son for analysis with him. Alexander first learned about America and its culture through analyzing numerous American visitors to Berlin. In America, he influenced many students, and relevant to our story, was analyst to both Karl and William Menninger, for better and worse! He died in 1964 in California, where he had initiated the research program in psychotherapy at Mt. Sinai Hospital in Los Angeles.

Loyal to Freud's values, Alexander never saw his own work as deviating from the Freudian path. He was committed to psychoanalysis as a science and was among the first psychoanalysts to advocate testing clinical hypotheses with systematic empirical research. He assumed that Freud himself anticipated continued modifications of procedure in psychoanalysis, as in any science. His one significant criticism of Freud was that his "emphasis upon what is and what is not permitted to be called psychoanalysis became a traditional attitude which greatly impeded courageous and free experimentation in this young field so desperately in need of a free spirit of inquiry" (Alexander and French, 1946, p. 2). While the battle was waged over the "corrective emotional experience," another of his tenets, "the principle of flexibility," better captures the heart of what Alexander and his colleagues were promoting.

The crucial therapeutic factor Alexander (1954) recommended was for the analyst to remain objective but at the same time "create a subtle interpersonal climate, preferably the opposite of the original situation" (p. 692). In discussing the rationale for this suggestion, Alexander stated that every neurosis represents an attempt at adaptation to an early family situation—an awkward, unsuccessful attempt to deal with a difficult situation. In the transference, the early situation is replaced by a different interpersonal climate, rendering the old neurotic reaction pointless and confronting the ego with the task of finding a new type of response. In this situation, it is the analyst who creates the "interpersonal climate" by controlling his spontaneous countertransference reactions and replacing them with a consciously adopted attitude. "This is necessary" Alexander suggested, "because the spontaneous countertransference might not be suitable to allow the patient a corrective emotional experience, particularly if it resembles an original pathogenic parental attitude" (cited in Orr and Zetzel, 1953, p. 529). In keeping with Freudian principles, Alexander called on the analyst to frustrate the patient's transference expectations. If the patient was attempting to provoke the analyst into rejecting him, as for example his own father had rejected him, then for the analyst to accept him would be to frustrate his transference wish, although clearly from another perspective, the patient would be gratified by such a response (Smith, 2007). Frustration and gratification are always ambiguous and relative concepts. Pointing out the similarities between these ideas and the work of Weiss and Sampson and their Mount Zion Psychotherapy Research Group, Wachtel and DeMichele (1998) speculate that Weiss and Sampson's lack of reference to Alexander was a way to protect themselves from the accusation of Alexandrian heresy. In the history of psychoanalysis, to be accused of facilitating a "corrective emotional experience" was equivalent to heresy—in other words, it was *not* psychoanalysis.

Alexander's goal was the integration of psychoanalysis into general psychiatry. But in his effort to extend psychoanalysis, he downplayed the difference between psychoanalysis and expressive psychotherapy, and it was precisely this move that elicited the overwhelming opposition of mainstream psychoanalysis. Alexander was always interested in the practical side of treatment and repeatedly observed that while psychoanalysis had made groundbreaking theoretical breakthroughs, little had changed in the way of clinical practice. He believed that analysts were much too conservative about technical experimentation because they were insecure about what they could really offer their patients. He wrote, "If I ask myself what is most disconcerting in my relation to my patients, I can say without hesitation that they expect more from me than I feel I can deliver" (Alexander, 1960, p. 310). As an example, anticipating Kohut's later developments in Chicago, Alexander invested considerable thought with regard to the questions of how much one should tolerate the patient's idealized expectations, how much one should disabuse them of these idealizations, and when and to what degree. He concluded that there was no general answer and that each analyst had to reexamine these clinical questions with each patient. His conviction that each patient–analyst pair must find their own way, and that very little is yet known about what works and for whom, made Alexander a fierce early proponent of empirical psychotherapy research. As we will soon see, it also led him to take a strong position against dogmatic training.

In his championing of the recognition that the analyst brought something unique to the analysis, something that was different from what any other analyst might bring even if using the same theory, Alexander was introducing a variable, the subjective factor, that Freud and classical analysts had been extremely careful to eliminate. Alexander (1958) argued "the therapeutic situation is a highly personal one, in which two unique personalities interact and not as the original model assumes, one real person, the patient, with the therapist, a depersonalized intellect who has mastered psychoanalytic theory" (p. 330). For Alexander, it was precisely the analyst's personal qualities that enabled the patient to recognize that his transference reactions were not appropriate. Even if an analyst could be neutral and objective, according to Alexander, it would not be in the best interest of the analysis of transference.

The question of role-playing on the analyst's part, along with Alexander's blurring of the distinction between psychotherapy and psychoanalysis, were the main focus of the debates of the 1950s. Most analysts responded to Alexander's recommendations by pointing out that to feign a deliberate attitude was artificial, inauthentic, and manipulative. It assumed that the analyst would know precisely what attitude had been pathogenic and what counter-attitude would be beneficial to the patient, and that the analyst would be expert enough to persuasively adopt just that attitude without the patient seeing through this manipulation. In defense of his position, Alexander countered that the traditional posture of neutrality and studied objectivity was also a role adopted by the analyst rather than simply an authentic response. He clarified that he was talking about subtle interpersonal adjustments that were attunements to the other's needs, rather than gross maneuvers and manipulations. The criticism from the mainstream was not that what Alexander was doing was damaging or clinically unhelpful. The objection was predominantly that it was *not* psychoanalysis but psychotherapy.

Alexander pointed to the interpersonal analyst Clara Thompson as being one of the few other analysts who shared his interest in the actual interactions between patient and analyst, which he believed was an underexplored area. Thompson, who had been analyzed by Ferenczi, synthesized Ferenczi's emphasis on the analytic relationship with Sullivan's interpersonal approach of a detailed inquiry. In our view, much can be gained by comparing Alexander to Sullivan, who was actively teaching during this same period. Sullivan's participatory conceptions were radical for their time, and ultimately far-reaching, but they "were only half participatory," one-way only (Fiscalini, 2006, p. 441). For Sullivan, the psychiatrist was a well-trained, expert participant-observer who knew how best to modulate the level of anxiety the patient could tolerate (Green, 1977). As an expert, he could avoid being pulled into the patient's interpersonal entanglements (Hirsch, 1987).

Cooper (2007) highlighted Alexander's technical rationality as well as his epistemological certainty, which led Alexander to be a "practitioner of technical authority" (p. 1087). Cooper argued,

> Alexander stands in almost complete contrast to and antipathy toward interpersonal and relational analytic theories in that he conceptualizes interaction as something that can be controlled; he does not see interaction as growing out of spontaneous and inevitable forms of expression and participation between the personalities of analyst and patient within the ritualized asymmetry of the analytic situation.
>
> (2007, p. 1095)

Smith (2007) suggests that Alexander's paper was ambiguous and contradictory. Alexander kept saying that the analyst's objectivity was a clinical asset, but on the other hand he argued that the objective neutral stance was itself an adopted role. In our view, Alexander was gradually coming to see that the analyst was a personally involved participant. Alexander critiqued the blank screen model because he recognized that the analyst always participates in some form, and so even if successful at appearing like a blank screen, this too was a form of participation, which is what he meant by a studied role. Some of what appears to be ambiguity and contradiction is a result of contemporary analysts reading individual articles by Alexander; a careful reading in sequential order is required in order to see the development of his views.

Alexander had a brilliant insight: he recognized that the analyst was not a blank screen but rather a participant in an interaction who reacted with his or her whole personality. If the analyst is a participant and not a blank screen, Alexander reasoned, shouldn't the analyst's participation be guided strategically by what he knows about the patient? If we are not neutral then shouldn't we respond the way the patient needs us to respond? Here is where Alexander's positivism got him into serious trouble. He believed that an analyst, as an expert in understanding the patient's dynamics, should be able to determine the kind of response the patient needs. Since the analyst was inevitably going to interact as a person in any event, why not interact by providing the patient with precisely the correct kind of emotional experience—a corrective emotional experience.

In directing their criticism at this prescription of a feigned, assumed, inauthentic role, Alexander's critics missed his more decisive contribution, his profound critique of the blank screen and his recognition of the analyst's personal participation. While Hoffman's (1983, 1998) radical critique of the blank screen model did not include a discussion of Alexander, his critique of Sullivan's objectivism is relevant in reconsidering Alexander. It is fascinating to see just how close Alexander's position was to Sullivan's in this same period. Sullivan, too, viewed the analyst as a participant-observer. Sullivan also recognized that the analyst could not and should not be a blank screen. And Sullivan, too, advocated that the psychiatrist respond as an expert in interpersonal relations and participate in the way most useful to the patient, even if it was feigned. And so it is not an accident that the sharp distinction between psychoanalysis and psychotherapy was challenged both by Alexander and by the interpersonalists Thompson and Fromm-Reichmann.

In the matter of psychoanalysis versus psychotherapy, Alexander argued for continuity over polarization:

> Our distinctions of the different kinds of psychotherapies are artificial. In all fields of science, the first inclination is toward distinguishing clear categories. To think in terms of continua requires more sophistication and does not give the type of certainty which Aristotelian dichotomies do: for example, psychoanalysis in sharp contrast to psychotherapy.
>
> (1960, p. 316)

After being repeatedly accused of advocating psychotherapy rather than psychoanalysis, Alexander (1961) wrote, "Anything which deviates from an illusory model—illusory because it is taught but not actually practiced—is rejected with the time-worn formula: 'This may be fine therapy but it is no longer psychoanalysis'" (p. 569). From Alexander's perspective, the urgency to sharply distinguish psychoanalysis from psychotherapy had become an issue due to "the practical consideration that the identity of the psychoanalyst, particularly in the eyes of the public, is threatened by the flexible use of analytic principles." Analysts feared that "psychoanalysis" would be confused with "inferior products which bear the same label" and so became "insistent upon a trademark, i.e., external criteria, to differentiate them" (O'Neil and Rangell, 1954, p. 154).

Alexander's (1961) thinking culminated in a critique of psychoanalytic education. Alexander explained that psychoanalysis was a young discipline, still lacking stringent evidence for fundamental concepts and theoretical generalizations. He believed that practice relied more on tradition and habit than on solid evidence, breeding intolerance against reform and experimentation and encouraging dogmatic allegiance and partisanship. Alexander called for openness to differences of opinion, an experimental spirit, and well-controlled evidence, all of which he believed was lacking because of the insecurity of the new field.

Alexander expressed doubts about the merits of premature standardization of psychoanalytic practice and the enforced indoctrination of students.

He favored precisely the opposite, calling not for "training" but rather for "critical study of the therapeutic process by experimental variation" (p. 573). It was not enough, he said, to train practitioners in a single standard method; institutes should be training in research to investigate the effectiveness of our procedures. Alexander was appalled that while the analytic institutes were not teaching analytically oriented therapy because it was not psychoanalysis proper, their students and graduates were likely to be doing it anyway! This was more than half a century ago. The implication was that analytic training should give increased attention to the candidate's personality as it enters the therapeutic process. Alexander believed that analysts knew this intuitively and made use of it in their clinical practices but were reluctant to acknowledge it publicly.

Alexander argued that nothing was hurting psychoanalysis more than "shrugging off novel therapeutic suggestions by declaring that they may be fine, but are no longer psychoanalysis. If a therapeutic approach in spite of being declared nonanalytic, nevertheless does promote the analytic goal to increase the patient's integrative faculty, then something may be wrong with psychoanalysis. '*In fact, nothing is wrong with psychoanalysis, only with its narrow definition*'" (p. 583, emphasis added).

Leo Stone

Leo Stone was a Brooklyn-born graduate of the New York Psychoanalytic Institute who had studied neurology in Berlin and Vienna. His 1954 contribution to the debates brought him to prominence in psychoanalysis. Stone emphatically denied that the debates were rooted in issues of professional competition, marketing, or questions of economics and status, and accused Alexander of focusing on issues of professional identity and economic factors instead of looking at the "science." He argued that the establishment of "precise operational conditions" and the production of "the powerful dynamic situation of the transference neurosis" were hardly "spurious" considerations. The "routine" of the classical procedure had a definite basis and function in the mobilization and ultimate reduction of the transference neurosis. Stone argued that Alexander made a double error in underestimating the clinical and scientific value of efforts toward detailed classification, and in assigning such efforts "only a practical public relations value, in which most analysts, he believes, are not interested" (O'Neil and Rangell, 1954, pp. 155–156). Stone (1951) freely acknowledged "the great numbers of patients who because of limitations of money or time cannot be analyzed" (p. 224). Nevertheless, in invoking the principle of scientific precision, he insisted that psychoanalysis as a "scientific technology" had to be marked off from psychotherapy. He unreservedly branded the "corrective emotional experience" as constituting "dynamic psychotherapy in contrast to psychoanalysis"(O'Neil and Rangell, 1954, p. 158).

In a review of one of Alexander's books, Stone (1957) called him to task for blurring the distinction between psychotherapy and psychoanalysis. In doing so, he shed some light on the basis of the disagreement. Stone argued that Alexander viewed standard psychoanalysis as "one of many possible applications of psychoanalytic knowledge" (p. 397) that has for historic reasons gained special status. However, for Stone and many of his colleagues, the standard technique was regarded as the pure form of practice, not simply for historical or traditional reasons, but rather because they viewed it as a systematic scientific procedure that best embodied the scientific principles of psychoanalysis as a body of knowledge. It was not that Stone was pushing the scientific metaphor more than Alexander—both viewed psychoanalysis as science—but rather that for Alexander, the clinical application was just one possible way of utilizing the overall theory, whereas for Stone, it had become the single best expression of the theory. Stone disparaged as cliché Alexander's "principle of flexibility," asking who would not endorse flexibility? Comparing psychoanalysis to a surgeon's scalpel, he argued that it was spurious to suggest that analysts should accommodate the treatment to the patient rather than selecting suitable patients; after all, didn't surgeons also select appropriate patients for surgery? Stone was quite satisfied that psychoanalysis worked—he had no question that it was the best method of treatment. It is no accident that he chose surgery as his metaphor. Freud himself had used this analogy. In the 1950s there was no other medical field that had made such dramatic progress or was held in such high esteem—not to mention that was so highly paid. The analytic instrument was modeled on the scalpel.

Unlike Stone, Alexander was dissatisfied with the therapeutic results of standard analysis, as Ferenczi and Rank had been years before. Stone's perspective did not lend itself to a call for empirical research because he already knew that his method worked and was the paramount application of psychoanalytic knowledge. Alexander had no such certainty, believing that analysis needed to continue to explore and test its applications to reach a wider range of patients.

Although Stone (1954) described neutrality as a "mathematical ideal" (pp. 574–575), we do not want to foster the impression that he was rigid or inhumane. Stone's (1961) *The Psychoanalytic Situation* was a dramatic call for the analyst's warm, human, flexible response—most importantly, the analyst's therapeutic commitment to the patient. Stone attempted to maintain a pure and conservative definition of psychoanalysis, to position himself quite clearly as distinct from Ferenczi and Alexander, but also to differentiate himself from the more austere position of Eissler, whom we will discuss shortly.

Max Gitelson

Fiercely orthodox (in the psychoanalytic sense), Max Gitelson was known as the "superego" of the psychoanalytic profession, fighting the good fight against the neo-Freudians, particularly against the Chicago school of the 1940s, which included Alexander and his colleagues. Gitelson's overriding concern was that psychotherapeutic strivings, represented by the mental health movement and organized psychiatry, would destroy the essence of the psychoanalytic process. Gitelson was a purist who wanted to construct a firm barrier between psychoanalysis and psychotherapy. He observed that, just at the time the Nazis were destroying psychoanalysis in Europe, American psychoanalysis developed as an integral part of the rising specialty of psychiatry and, under the banner of "dynamic psychiatry," was prepared to meet the country's wartime needs. "Psychiatry discovered that even with only the rudiments of psychoanalytic theory" it was its most powerful therapeutic tool; "psychiatry without psychoanalysis had become unthinkable" (Gitelson, 1964, p. 468). He bemoaned psychoanalysis' professional tie to psychiatry, suggesting the price of success may have been too high.

Gitelson believed psychoanalysis should remain distinct because it was not predominantly a therapeutic endeavor; rather it constituted its own basic science. It must rely on its own methods and not sell out to public health needs, psychiatry's agenda, or the availability of government money (the NIMH was funding psychoanalytic education and psychiatry programs, which were then heavily psychoanalytic). Gitelson was calling for a return to purity, to the intrinsic goals and methods of psychoanalysis, separate from its psychotherapeutic contribution and from its role in the mental health movement, which he feared had swallowed it up. For example, it was believed that practicing psychotherapy would dilute one's professional identity as a psychoanalyst. Thus for many decades psycho-therapy was not taught at psychoanalytic institutes. Psychiatry and psycho-analysis had been involved in nothing more than "a marriage of convenience," which Gitelson was glad to see dissolve (p. 470). Speaking of Gitelson, Weinshel (1990) wrote that the image of the psychoanalyst was "grossly inflated and almost embarrassingly extravagant. The trouble was that many of the psychoanalysts themselves, as well as conspicuous segments of the general public, fell in love with that image" (p. 280).

Robert Knight

Robert Knight, one of the leaders of psychiatry at Menninger's and soon to be president of the APsaA, was interested in extending psychoanalytic ideas into psychiatry, and championed psychoanalytic therapy as distinct from "orthodox" practice. Whereas Freud had been pessimistic about treating psychotics with psychoanalysis, American analysts, with their optimistic can-do spirit, were more eager to apply psychoanalytic ideas to the treatment of psychosis. Knight's colleagues at the Menninger Clinic, as well as Harry Stack Sullivan, Frieda Fromm-Reichmann, and John Rosen, tried modified forms of psychoanalysis with psychotic patients. This led Knight to be among the first to identify borderline psychopathology and to develop psychoanalytic treatment for borderline patients. Knight's (1949) key differentiation was between "supportive" (which he also referred to as "superficial") therapy and "expressive" therapy. Knight made the explicit assumption that the expressive therapies, with psychoanalysis being the most expressive, require intensive training and experience, whereas the superficial supportive therapies do not. This is ironic, of course, since the healthiest patients, those who were "analyzable," received the most expressive treatments whereas the sickest (and poorest) received superficial treatment. The dominant ideology thus encouraged therapists to pursue the most intensive training to help those who were healthiest, and the least intensive training for patients who might in many ways be more difficult. The ideology stressed training to deal with the depth of the exploration, not the difficulty of the treatment. In his later work on borderline pathology, Knight (1952) revised this opinion and emphasized training for supportive work as well, but this bias has pervaded the field for more than half a century.

Knight (1953) argued that for patients in a borderline state, psychoanalysis proper was contraindicated because free association, the use of the couch, and "the autistic development" that is encouraged cannot be handled by the patient's ego. Instead he recommended a psychotherapy focusing on ego building and strengthening of defenses using a more active, structured, face-to-face method. A dichotomy articulated by Knight was that the difference between psychoanalysis with healthier patients and psychotherapy with more disturbed patients was the analyst's analyzing—and therefore weakening—the defenses of the healthier patients, while strengthening the defenses of the sicker patients.

Lawrence Kubie

Lawrence Kubie was a well-regarded psychoanalyst with a strong track record of publications and a resumé that included working with Menninger on combat exhaustion. He had studied in London for two years in the early 1930s and had been analyzed by Edward Glover, with whom he remained lifelong friends. Like his mentor, he emphasized classical technique and attained a reputation as a heretic hunter. Kubie (1943) differentiated various approaches to psychotherapy, distinguishing between practical support, emotional support, and reorienting education. One of his central distinctions was between palliative and scientific psychotherapy. Palliative treatment consisted primarily of helping patients to live better with their neuroses, whereas scientific psychotherapy, of which psychoanalysis was considered the most important example, was exploratory. The dichotomy between scientific and palliative, interpretation and support, cure and care, science and magic, depth of expression and superficiality, runs like a stream throughout these debates.

Frieda Fromm-Reichmann

Frieda Fromm-Reichmann (1950) was in a unique position to participate in these debates. Born to an orthodox Jewish family, she trained as a psychiatrist and analyst in Germany, and treated brain-injured soldiers during World War I. In the 1920s in Heidelberg, she developed a utopian experiment combining psychoanalysis and Orthodox Judaism, which her friend Gershom Scholem called "the torahpeuticum." She viewed psychotherapy as fulfilling the *mitzvah* of *tzedakah* (the commandment to do justice, charity), talked of "serving people through psychotherapy," and tried to incorporate the mutuality that was being described by her friend, Martin Buber, into her therapeutic relations. Her agenda is best captured in the title of her biography: *To Redeem One Person is to Redeem the World* (Hornstein, 2000). After a dramatic escape from the Nazis, she immigrated to America, and along with her former husband Erich Fromm, aligned herself with Sullivan. In these debates she presented a Sullivanian interpersonal approach, arguing that since she took into account unconscious processes, transference, and resistance, the unconventional treatments she was conducting, including her work with hospitalized psychotic patients, were in fact psychoanalysis. Fromm-Reichmann went so far as to argue that her newer, more interpersonal methods were advantageous even for neurotic patients, who were analyzable by traditional standards. Like Sullivan and Alexander, she minimized, perhaps even obliterated, the differences between psychoanalysis and psychoanalytic therapy.

Interestingly, Wallerstein believes that Fromm-Reichman's argument was based on a new theory—Sullivan's interpersonal approach—while Alexander's was based on Freudian theory. Our reading of Alexander, however, suggests that although believing himself loyal to Freud, he too had modified his theoretical beliefs and now stressed a much more interpersonal "two-person" approach. Alexander, like Sullivan and Fromm-Reichman, had come to the conclusion that the analyst was a personally involved participant. Like Sullivan, Alexander retained a positivist epistemology, believing that the analyst had to participate as an expert, tactically, in the interests of the patient, based on objective, expert observation and deduction. Anna Freud astutely recognized that Alexander was not simply advocating a new technical supplement to psychoanalytic procedure, but rather was basing his recommendations on a new theory.

She observed that it was not simply a matter of the type of disorder treated but "a change in the analyst's outlook and theoretical evaluation of familiar phenomena" (Freud, A. 1954, p. 608).

Phyllis Greenacre

Phyllis Greenacre was an American psychoanalyst and physician who had been influenced by Adolph Meyer. A graduate of the New York Psychoanalytic Institute, Greenacre presented thoughts about variations of method within the framework of classical psychoanalysis. She drew a distinction between analysts who regard transference interpretation as the central core versus those who regard the transference as valuable mainly in setting up the emotional atmosphere in which analysis can proceed (Orr and Zetzel, 1953). Greenacre's position is of great importance, as in later years it was precisely this issue that was used to distinguish psychoanalysis from psychotherapy. Some analysts, following the later Gill, came to define psychoanalysis by its consistent and persistent interpretation of the transference, whereas psychotherapy was defined by the use but not the consistent explication of the transference. It is important to note that at least in this earlier period, not all analysts were in agreement about the priority of interpreting the transference or even of keeping the transference neurosis in the foreground. There were analysts who believed that the transference might often be left in the background and utilized to foster the analytic work of free association. The shift from viewing the methodology of psychoanalysis as being free association to viewing it as being primarily the analysis of transference was slow, inconsistent, and not universally accepted. There were analysts who advocated the classical technique who did not view transference and its systematic interpretation as the defining feature of psychoanalytic technique.

Robert Waelder

Robert Waelder was a Viennese-born psychoanalyst who had training analyses with Hermann Nunberg and Anna Freud and immigrated to America in 1938. He was known for his loyalty to Freudian theory and for being an outspoken critic of Melanie Klein. Waelder believed there was a vital difference between his traditional point of view, which regarded neurosis as a return of the repressed, and Alexander's point of view, which traced the development of neurosis to faulty interpersonal adaptation in childhood. The former traditional point of view implied to Waelder that the main work of analysis consisted of making the unconscious conscious, undoing repression, and reviving the original conflict situation as a necessary precursor to better adjustment. The latter adaptation point of view, since it attributed neurosis to interpersonal relationship, would not necessarily consider the lifting of repression to be essential but could prefer corrective emotional experience to the acquiring of true insight.

Heinz Hartmann

Heinz Hartmann was born in Vienna to an illustrious family known for writing and academics. He was analyzed by Freud and was reportedly one of his favorite students. In 1938 he left Austria with his family to escape the Nazi invasion. He arrived in New York in 1941 and quickly became one of the foremost thinkers of the New York Psychoanalytic Society. Along with Ernst Kris and Rudolph Loewenstein, he is known for the development of ego-psychology. Hartmann agreed that analysis represents a corrective emotional experience, but doubted the value and feasibility of the analyst's taking a deliberate role. He argued that the patient could easily see through repeated changes of attitude on the part of the analyst. Hartmann stressed the scientific value of maintaining a "static situation," suggesting that "the introduction of too many new variables resembles an abandonment of scientific method" and that "significant alteration of methodology would limit the validity of findings" (Orr and Zetzel, 1953, p. 534). In this model, the analyst's participation is kept to a minimum so as not to introduce confounding variables.

Leo Rangell

Leo Rangell was an American-born psychoanalyst, born into an immigrant Jewish family, and raised in Brooklyn. His father and mother were refugees from Russia and Poland, respectively. Rangell interrupted his training at the New York Psychoanalytic Institute to fight in World War II. He graduated from his analytic training just a few years before participating in these discussions, and they helped to establish his professional reputation. Rangell set the stage for these debates by providing historical background, specifically noting that the Committee on Evaluation of Psychoanalytic Therapy, set up within the APsaA in 1947 "was never able to pass the initial and vexatious point of trying to arrive at some modicum of agreement as to exactly what constitutes psychoanalysis, psychoanalytic psychotherapy, and possibly transitional forms" (Rangell, 1954, pp. 734–735). Rangell outlined two schools of thought among analysts about the psychotherapy/psychoanalysis distinction. One group believed there was a continuum, with no discernible or practical line of demarcation between the two disciplines. He saw this view as inherent in Alexander's position. Rangell (1954) went on to make his most memorable statement, expressing his own, and the majority, view:

The other point of view holds that the two are separable and distinct entities and procedures, with delineable borders between them. In this view, the two disciplines, at far ends of a spectrum, are qualitatively different from each other, though there is a borderland of cases between them. An analogous comparison can be made to the fact that conscious is different from unconscious even though there exists a preconscious and different degrees of consciousness. Day is different from night, though there is dusk; and black from white, though there is gray (with no implication as to one being right or wrong, better or worse).

(1954, p. 737)

This was one of the most powerful rhetorical remarks of the debates. It tells us a great deal about the era as well as about what has changed since then. Rangell is saying that there is a continuum, a spectrum of therapies ranging from supportive psychotherapy to expressive psychoanalysis. But in his view, it is misleading to consider them a continuum because to do so would be to overlook that at the extremes they are qualitatively different. Given the choice of viewing the two polar ends as having more or less in common, he made a strategic choice to emphasize their differences. While we do not believe that Rangell intended, even unconsciously, to hint at a racial divide, it nevertheless seems relevant that psychoanalysis was, in fact, racially divided from psychotherapy. The vast majority of psychoanalysts and their patients were white. If any therapy at all was offered to blacks, it was much less likely to be psychoanalysis, if for no other reason than race correlated with class. Rangell continued:

Let us consider that the mental apparatus exerts around it a field of magnetic energy. In psychoanalysis, the therapist takes up his position at the periphery of this magnetic field of his patient, not too far away, so that he is useless and might just as well not be there, nor too close, so that he is within the field interacting with it with his own magnetic field (he can err equally in both directions). Immune from repulsion or attraction (at least optimally, within the limits set by his own unconscious), he sits at the margin, like a referee in a tennis match, so that he can say to the patient, "This is what you are now doing, here is impulse, here defense, here resistance, here compromise formation, here symptom."

In contrast, in doing psychotherapy, the therapist is on the court with his patient, interacting with him, "the two magnetic fields interlocked" (pp. 741–742).

Rangell utilized scientific metaphors about magnetic forces and chemical reactions. We must pay careful attention to this rhetoric, which was so compelling in the 1950s when America had just won the war, not least because of its technical ability. All of these images were designed to make psychoanalysis appear to be a scientific medical procedure. The analyst was to refrain from any personal participation, relying only on interpretation—which was not in itself regarded as participation. Comparing the analyst to the referee of a tennis match, Rangell believed one must remain on the periphery, uninvolved, only making observations.

Since Rangell's position and rhetoric came to dominate psychoanalytic education, we will interrupt the flow of the historical narrative to make some observations about the tennis metaphor from our own current perspective. We are reminded that Stephen Mitchell (1988), who would years later revisit these issues in developing a relational approach to psycho-analysis, was an avid tennis player. In teaching and supervising, Steve would often draw on his experience of playing tennis. In his view, psycho-analysis involved being in the game and playing with the patient in all sorts of ways, becoming engaged very personally and directly with the patient, dancing the patient's dance and being transformed by the patient's entreaties. But that was more than one-quarter of a century later.

While training as a Freudian analyst in the early 1980s, one of us (Lewis Aron) repeatedly heard the following metaphor: Imagine that you are sitting on a lakefront observing the water. You want to throw one pebble into the water at a time so that you can observe the ripples made by the pebbles. If you throw in two or three pebbles you won't be able to keep track of which one caused what effect. Interpretations should always be short and precise so that you can then observe the patient's free associations following the interpretation. If you interpret two conflicts at once, then as the patient associates you won't know whether the emerging resistances were in reaction to one conflict or the other.

When I lecture now, I say that doing analysis feels more like we are in the water together with the patient struggling to stay afloat. A more classical colleague asked, but don't you at least want to have one foot on the ground? Surely, he suggested, we all need to have some grounding, some way to keep our balance. That sounds so reasonable, but it is nothing more than a clever rhetorical remark. Both of us may be fully emerged in the water (that much is mutual or shared) and yet I might be thought to have more experience as a swimmer in treacherous waters (hence the asymmetry). But this is a very far cry from standing on the sidelines only making precise interpretations (Aron, 1996a).

Kurt Eissler

There were many psychoanalysts who held the conviction that Kurt Eissler's (1953) classic, "The effect of the structure of the ego on psycho-analytic technique," which introduced his notion of parameters, was the field's most decisive response to Alexander. This paper became a standard for the teaching of psychoanalytic technique. Eissler was a Viennese psychoanalyst who received an MD and Ph.D. from the University of Vienna and became a member of the Vienna Psychoanalytic Society in 1938 just before fleeing to America. He was little known outside of the psychoanalytic world until Janet Malcolm described him in *The New Yorker*, noting that "Eissler's devotion to Freud . . . was considered a kind of lovable nuttiness" (Malcolm, 1984, p. 14). Masson, whom he had mistakenly chosen as his successor to the Freud Archives, had referred to him as "the pope of orthodox analysis" (Masson, 1990, p. 114).

Eissler's model was based on his assumption that "the living conditions of the patient and the personality of the analyst are both ideal" (Eissler, 1953, p. 105). His positivist strategy is stunning in its scientific-sounding but tautological simplicity. He removed from consideration the psycho-analyst's personality as if it was indeed possible for it to be factored out! Eissler (1956) contended that under "the quasi-laboratory conditions of the psychoanalytic situation" (p. 315) and "exact, scientific methods of investigation" (p. 317), the personality of the scientist shouldn't matter. These analysts were trying their best to make psychoanalysis as close to an exact science as possible. The only way to do that was to factor out the analyst's personality, even if they also realized that the analyst needed to remain a warm and caring physician. It was simply a variable to be factored out through randomization, so theory could be discussed with the assump-tion that the analyst's personality is ideal. That is quite an assumption! Eissler then went on to eliminate from consideration all social, cultural, or historical factors. What difference should it make what culture Newton was part of when he discovered gravity? In science all that should matter is the objective finding.

> Valuable as the sociology of science is, it does not decide which scientific finding is correct and which is not . . . Since it is idle to raise the historical argument in weighing the pros and cons of a scientific proposition, I have omitted the historical factor as one of the variables of psychoanalytic technique to be discussed here.
>
> (Eissler, 1953, pp. 107–108)

Edward Bibring

Edward Bibring, born in Galicia, was analyzed by Paul Federn, and in 1927 became a full member of the Vienna Psychoanalytic Society. Bibring was one of a small group of psychoanalysts close to Freud in Vienna in the inter-war years. In May 1938, following the Anschluss and the rise of National Socialism in Austria, Bibring and his wife Grete immigrated to Great Britain. In 1941, the couple settled in Boston. In yet another pres-entation that became an instant classic, Bibring's paper delineated the purposeful use of suggestion, abreaction, manipulation, clarification, and interpretation. He had a reputation for high standards and for his dedication to teaching a pure form of psychoanalysis.

Bibring explained that in "psychoanalysis proper," all of these therapeutic principles were put to use but formed a hierarchy, such that they were "subordinated to the principle of insight through interpretation" which he viewed as "the supreme agent in the hierarchy of therapeutic principles characteristic of analysis" (O'Neil and Rangell, 1954, p. 161). In his view, Alexander shifted the emphasis from insight through interpretation to experiential manipulation. Bibring (1954) quotes Alexander: "Insight is frequently the result of emotional adjustment and not the cause of it" and "The role of insight is overrated" (p. 768).

Merton Gill

Of all the brilliant, erudite, and persuasive contributions to this debate, it was the words of Merton Gill that most memorably defined psychoanalysis for generations to come. Born in Chicago, Merton Gill did his psychiatric residency at Menninger and graduated from the Topeka Institute. Pursuing research, he very quickly became David Rapaport's right-hand man and went on to become a leader in the field. Gill's (1951, 1954) incisive arguments and definition are especially important to understand because in the decades to come, Gill more than anyone else would systematically examine all of the old points of view and come to disagree with just about all of the arguments made by his younger self and his colleagues at mid-century.

Gill, like many of the other participants, took Franz Alexander as his target, as Alexander blurred the distinction between psychoanalysis and psychotherapy. With Alexander's declaration that the distinction was primarily "for reasons of professional role and prestige," Gill (1954) noted that many of his colleagues "are in sharp, if not heated, disagreement" (p. 772). According to Gill, the dominant point of view among his colleagues was that, "however valuable psychotherapy may be, it cannot do what psychoanalysis can do, . . . it cannot produce intrapsychic or structural ego modifications, can only operate by way of persistent transference effect" (p. 773). Gill argued that psychoanalysis alone would lead to intrapsychic structural change, producing the strongest and most autonomous ego as a result. In contrast, at best, psychotherapy was based on transference cure and strengthening of defenses, leaving the patient more reliant on the analyst, and resulting in a less profound and thorough treatment. Speaker after speaker in these debates kept repeating that they were not claiming that one form of treatment was better than the other. They insisted that some treatments were better for some people and other treatments better for others. But this was a thin defensive protest against the obvious belief that psychoanalysis was the better treatment for the healthier and better-developed patient, who also happened to be the patient more likely to be able to afford such treatment and work within a private practice setting! Still, they heatedly objected to Alexander's attempt to point out the relevance of these social, economic, and professional factors.

While all definitions are structured to differentiate one thing from another, we contend—and this is the main argument of our book— that the definition of psychoanalysis was shaped *specifically* by the way it was contrasted with psychoanalytic psychotherapy in a context where this distinction had taken on all kinds of social, political, economic meanings. In our emphasis on these sociocultural factors, we believe that Alexander was on to something that others wished to play down. The method of definition via binary opposition is evident throughout the debates, and is sharply evident in Gill's writing. Gill alluded to Eissler as suggesting that the better therapy is always called psychoanalytic! Let's look at exactly what Eissler said. Eissler (1950) introduced his idea of parameters as deviations from Freud's model technique in his paper on the implications of ego-psychology for working with delinquents:

> Consequently that technique which, e.g., in the treatment of the delinquencies, achieves its purpose with the smallest possible parameter, should be given the preference among all others and should be called psychoanalytic, although, as is the case of the treatment of delinquents, the deviation necessary at times may be so great that the model technique which it tries to approximate may scarcely be recognizable.
>
> (1950, p. 97)

Yes, astonishing to us today, Eissler's notion of parameter, which later filled analysts with horror because it felt like a sinful deviation, was introduced as a way to extend the reach of psychoanalysis, but it did so by calling whatever was the best technique psychoanalytic even if it was no longer recognizable!

Gill could only object to Eissler's formulation in spite of its orthodoxy precisely for the same reason that he was fighting Alexander for his deviancy: because both approaches blurred the distinction between psychotherapy and psychoanalysis. He disagreed with those who argued that the best kind of therapy possible in any particular case ought to be called psychoanalysis, however much it differs from the classical technique (Gill, 1954). Gill then put forth his carefully worded definition and proceeded to comment on every detail of its wording. "Psychoanalysis is that technique which, employed by a neutral analyst, results in the development of a regressive transference neurosis and the ultimate resolution of this neurosis by techniques of interpretation alone" (p. 775). As Wallerstein (1995) points out, Gill's definition was in substance quite similar to Rangell's (1954) and Stone's (1954). These three leading analysts, who together provided the most specific and oft-cited definition of psychoanalysis, were all American analysts, trained to think of psychoanalysis as a narrow medical sub-specialty. They quite literally defined an American understanding of psychoanalysis that was much narrower and more precise than the definition Freud and the European analysts had used.

Gill clarified that neutrality was not the same as indifference, mechanical rigidity, or the suppression of spontaneity. The analyst should not be a "stick of wood," and he should feel friendly toward the patient, but "he always remains neutral in the basic sense of never trying to mold the patient in his own image" (p. 776). Again taking aim at Alexander, Gill went on to argue for the analyst's use of interpretation alone. "By techniques of interpretation alone" means "not by any other techniques of interpersonal behavior" (p. 780). Here, from our perspective, Gill maintained a polarized stance in which interpretation, verbal understanding and symbolic communication, was contrasted with interpersonal behavior, equated with manipulation. Interpretation and insight were aligned with the inside, depth, and the intrapsychic, while interpersonal behavior was associated with the external, surface, superficial, and social.

Gill acknowledged,

> The analyst's overt behavior toward the patient can more quickly get him to change some aspects of his behavior. But what is the meaning of such a change? It is an adaptation to this particular interpersonal relationship—as it exists between patient and analyst. But this is not the goal of analysis. The goal of analysis is an intrapsychic modification in the patient.
>
> (1954, p. 780)

Why couldn't a patient be affected by both the particular interpersonal relationship *and* the interpretation and understanding that develops within that relationship? Gill, however, was indeed brilliant, and caught himself. He recognized even then that he was trapped in polarization. Demonstrating his apprehension about the exaggerated and unwarranted optimism and grandiosity prevalent at the time with regard to psychoanalysis, he made the following remark:

> It is generally the more experienced analysts who are not so optimistic about the sweeping character changes often hoped for from psychoanalysis. And there is no doubt that we can still recognize our friends

and colleagues, even after they have been analyzed . . . My stress on this point arises from my feeling that discussion of therapeutic results in psychoanalysis and psychotherapy too often views them as *qualitative polar opposites, with psychoanalysis regarded as producing structural changes, and psychotherapy as unable to produce any significant intrapsychic change*, but only altering techniques of adjustment through transference effects or shifts in defensive techniques.

(Gill, 1954, pp. 786–787, emphasis added)

Gill realized that the process of polarizing psychoanalysis and psychotherapy played a role in idealizing the former and denigrating the latter. He wanted very much to correct this, yet he was restrained by his determination to differentiate the two treatments. He wrote, "But again it is possible too easily to set up polar opposites. Transference is not either untouched or completely resolved. There are many points between" (p. 791). Gill acknowledged the tendency toward polarization and called for transcending it, yet his entire argument was built precisely on the series of dichotomies that created it! He would later return to the problem of polarization and try with his collaborator Irwin Hoffman to formulate a more dialectical approach.

It is now Alexander's position that is the more widely accepted. Insight can lead to change, but behavioral change can lead to insight. Internal structure and external behavior are no longer regarded as polar opposites but rather are commonly viewed as transformations of one another. If this is the case, then change can come about from either part of what amounts to a complex system. Alexander was the first to argue this point, and he took the heat. Even back in the early 1950s, there were dissenting voices, and it pays to examine some of them as well.

Adelaide Johnson/Joseph Chassel

Adelaide Johnson, an American analyst best known for introducing the concept of "superego lacunae," presented a paper summarizing the opinion of the panel members on the differences between dynamic psychotherapy and classical psychoanalysis (Johnson and English, 1953). She valuably recorded the opinion of Joseph Chassel, who clearly articulated what was at the time a minority dissenting opinion:

My present thesis is that really psychodynamic psychotherapy is an approach as strong as or stronger than classical psychoanalysis, has increasingly greater range of applicability than classical psychoanalysis; is more inclusive theoretically, and that classical psychoanalysis may turn out to be a special procedure of limited but significant usefulness in certain cases. In short, I would suggest that psychodynamic psychotherapy is a new orientation, based on newer knowledge of "ego psychology" or of the intra- and inter-personal relations of people, and hence is a natural step in our growth as a science. Personally I would prefer that this newer formulated approach also be called psychoanalysis, since it is in the logical line with transference and resistance (and by implication with unconscious processes) while the method described by Freud for the so-called transference neuroses might legitimately be called classical psychoanalysis.

Chassel recognized the dichotomous thinking and the inevitable hierarchy that accompanied it. He noted that historical factors led us to feel that "psychoanalysis is first-class therapy, while psychotherapy is second-class" (Johnson and English, 1953, pp. 550–551).

Anna Freud

In light of Chassel's extremely progressive point of view, this might also be a good time to consider some remarks made by Anna Freud, who largely supported Hartmann, Eissler, and the ego psychologists. Nevertheless, there were some words she felt needed to be said. Let's keep in mind that if they were obvious and everyone knew them, she wouldn't have had to come to America to say them:

> With due respect for the necessary strictest handling and interpretation of the transference, I feel still that we should leave room somewhere for the realization that analyst and patient are also two real people, of equal adult status, in a real personal relationship to each other. I wonder whether our—at times complete—neglect of this side of the matter is not responsible for some of the hostile reactions which we get from our patients and which we are apt to ascribe to "true transference" only. But these are technically subversive thoughts and ought to be "handled with care."
>
> (Freud, A. 1954, pp. 618–619)

Therese Benedek

Therese Benedek was among the most highly regarded analysts in Chicago. Born in Hungary, she became interested in psychoanalysis while in high school, at a time when psychoanalysis was flourishing under Ferenczi's leadership. Benedek had an analysis with Ferenczi that took place in Budapest, probably during the latter half of 1919, shortly after her marriage. Soon after, she fled Budapest because of rising anti-Semitism. Fleeing the Nazis, she emigrated in 1936 and Franz Alexander offered her a position in Chicago. Intimately familiar with the controversies surrounding Ferenczi and Alexander, she was highly sensitive to the question of the analyst's adopting a role and to the problems of excessive therapeutic zeal. Benedek acknowledged that Freud had once stated that psychoanalysis is more of a research tool than a therapy, and had often warned against too great therapeutic ambition in the analyst. Benedek argued that analysts were defensively disclaiming the therapeutic role, thinking of themselves as "not treating, but analyzing." She believed this was a pretense and that analysts were better off acknowledging that they were therapists first and foremost (Johnson and Ludwig, 1954, p. 348).

Edith Jacobson

Edith Jacobson was trained at the Berlin Psychoanalytic Institute and was analyzed by Otto Fenichel. The Nazis imprisoned Jacobson in 1935 because she refused to divulge information about a patient. While hospitalized with Graves' disease, she escaped to Czechoslovakia and emigrated to the United States. Like Stone, Edith Jacobson tried to make room for the analyst's warmth, even while preserving neutrality. Amidst the discussions of technical requirements such as frequency, she observed that in her own clinical experience with depressed patients, for which she was held in high regard, much more depends on the emotional quality of the analyst's responses than on the frequency of sessions. She added that some depressive patients responded better to fewer sessions rather than to more frequent meetings and that it really depended on what the frequency meant to the patient. From trial and error she had learned not to speak too little or too much and to remain empathic. "What those patients need is not so much frequency and length of sessions as a sufficient amount of spontaneity and flexible adjustment to their mood level, of warm understanding and especially of unwavering respect." With an ambivalent nod to Alexander she added,

> Beyond this warm, flexible emotional atmosphere, without which these patients cannot work, supportive counterattitudes and interventions may occasionally be necessary; but they are only a lesser evil for which we have to pay. With these patients we are always between the devil and the deep, blue sea; this cannot be avoided.
> (Jacobson, 1954, p. 604)

"Counterattitudes" referred to Alexander's "manipulations." Note the binary structure and hierarchy inherent in the phrasing "between the devil and the deep, blue sea" and the "lesser evil" of support as opposed to interpretation.

Alexander pointed to the implications of social, professional, ideological, and economic factors for the clinical attitudes being debated. His colleagues at the time insisted on treating the questions as technical and scientific. That their professional identity was being shaped by these external environmental factors seemed to most of them to be a secondary feature, a confounding variable, a distraction from medical and scientific considerations. Looking back at this era, the historian of psychoanalysis Paul Roazen (1990) captured the atmosphere:

> Although it is possible to romanticize the past, Freud and his imme-diate followers were people of imagination and culture; they comprised a remarkable group of nonconformists committed to the life of the mind . . . Once psychoanalysis became part of the American psychiatric establishment, and this conquest was attained shortly after the end of World War II, intellectuality became a threat to the profession's trade unionism.
>
> (1990, p. 133)

Then and Now

The three leading voices in the debates of the 1950s went on to have long and influential careers as leaders in psychoanalysis. In the 1950s, Merton Gill, Leo Rangell, and Leo Stone were in fairly close agreement, although each had somewhat different approaches to the definition of psychoanaly-sis. Yet by 1979, each of the participants had revised his point of view and psychoanalysis had changed considerably. In 1979, the Southern Regional Psychoanalytic Societies sponsored a symposium in Atlanta, Georgia, at which Gill, Rangell, and Stone were invited to update their views on "Psychoanalysis and Psychotherapy, Similarities and Differences, a 25-Year Perspective."

Robert Wallerstein (1989, 1995, 1998, 2000a, b) has carefully recorded the history of how psychoanalysis and psychotherapy were differentiated. He has examined the overlapping issues of medical versus lay analysis, reviewed the conflicting empirical research supporting psychotherapy and psychoanalysis with different patient populations, and explored the issue of theoretical diversification, demonstrating how it affected these definitions. We are indebted to his scholarship. Wallerstein concluded that the consensus achieved in the early 1950s could not be sustained, and that the 1979 discussions testified to the theoretical fragmentation of psychoanalysis. After 25 years, many of the original propositions had been significantly modified, largely in the direction of seeing less distinction between psychotherapy and psychoanalysis than was originally formulated (Wallerstein, 1995, 1998). As Wallerstein's numerous books demonstrate, it would take several volumes to review these issues in their complexity. We will just touch on the highlights, presenting our own conclusions.

By 1979, Leo Stone, the least reformed of the three, had softened his position. While he agreed that attempting to distinguish psychoanalysis from psychotherapy was a worthy effort, he concluded it was not always possible to make clear distinctions or work within such rarefied borders. He acknowledged that support, the hallmark of palliative psychotherapy, was also important in psychoanalysis and that interpretation also played a role in psychotherapy. Stone posited a *dialectical* relationship between the various modes of support and interpretation. The shift from a polarized position to a more nuanced and dialectical one is of course precisely what we are calling for in this book.

In a 2009 interview, near the end of his life, Leo Rangell was asked about his role in these memorable debates. One can still hear the lingering tensions as Rangell commented,

> In looking back, one has to take into account the preoccupation of the times. The main concern of that time was to *preserve psychoanalysis, because the tendency was to dilute it*, and to use analytic principles in all directions. This was actually a laudable thing, but at the same time it was necessary to protect the core itself.
>
> (Rangell and Kalish-Weiss, 2009, p. 110, emphasis added)

Elsewhere, he wrote:

> In the 1930s . . . psychoanalysis was achieving its maturity with the addition of ego psychology to the psychology of the drives. *During that decade the concern was to preserve the identity of psychoanalysis in the midst of derivative schools which emphasized mainly cultural factors at the expense of the internal psychic world.* In the 1940s the success of the newly established discipline came to be widely appreciated in its applicability to emotional disturbances during World War II. In the 1950s, in the flush of its accepted status and now dominant position in Departments of Psychiatry, the task became to facilitate its growth while continuing *to prevent its identity from being blurred*.
>
> (Rangell, 1981, p. 665, emphasis added)

Rangell identified the desire to differentiate mainstream classical and ego-psychologists from the interpersonalists and culturalists; the concern about the widening scope of suitable patients; and the wish to maintain a clear sense of identity. While Rangell was accurate in his depiction of these concerns as having been sequential in emphasis over the decades, we contend that these same considerations were clearly at play during the debates, but at the time, the main protagonists, aside from Alexander, did not want to acknowledge them as relevant.

Looking back, Rangell argued that in 1954, a time when psychoanalysis was being aggrandized and oversold, it was necessary to stress the differences between psychoanalysis and dynamic psychotherapy. However,

In the climate of today, which directs toward psychoanalysis *not a loving engulfment but a rejecting separation, the complementary goal is to point out the links which bridge analytic theory and the multitude of derivative approaches* which are applications of segments of theory geared toward more direct and immediate rewards.

(Rangell, 1981, pp. 666–667, emphasis added)

We believe Rangell was on target. Speaking with great clarity, Rangell identified the key difference between 1954 and 1979 with regard to the definition of psychoanalysis in contrast to psychotherapy. Whereas in 1954, psychoanalysis was being embraced with exuberance, by 1979, that was no longer true. Needless to say, it has gone only further downhill since 1979. We must pause to drive home our point once again: How we define psychoanalysis and psychotherapy is up to us. It is a pragmatic decision. As a profession, we can define psychoanalysis in any way we believe serves the interests of our community and the wider public. There is no "true" definition of psychoanalysis. There is only the manner in which we construct the definition. Rangell was being pragmatic. He was saying that under one set of socio-economic conditions, when psychoanalysis was in high demand, it made more sense to emphasize how psychoanalysis was *different* from psychotherapy. Under circumstances where psychoanalysis is less in demand, it makes more sense to emphasize its *continuities* with other therapies.

Rangell summarized,

> I said then that there is day and night, although there is dusk . . . As a long-range observation over the years, empirically there is in numbers a large borderland in which therapeutic procedures are practiced in a gray area between "psychoanalysis with parameters" and steady intensive psychotherapy which is not quite psychoanalysis. My belief today is that it is still possible to draw a line between the two, although it is also true that in many cases this line is difficult to define. I believe that Gill, Stone, and I are in agreement on the increased effectiveness of deep analytic work in psychoanalytic psychotherapy since our symposium of twenty-five years ago.

(1981, pp. 682–683)

While Rangell still maintained a conceptual difference, the two procedures are not nearly as polarized as they had been 25 years earlier. In other words, now they were differences rather than binary oppositions.

The early polemics regarding psychoanalysis as a form of treatment revolved around the contrast between psychoanalysis and hypnosis or psychoanalysis and suggestion. In the 1950s, the controversy shifted to the contrast between psychoanalysis and psychotherapy. Rangell identified the 1930s as the decade in which ego-psychology had to deal with challenges posed by deviant theories; the 1940s as the decade in which psychoanalysis had to accommodate to a widening scope of patients; and the 1950s as the decade in which, with its absorption into American medicine, psychoanalysis had to fight to maintain its unique identity. We argue that all three of these considerations interacted simultaneously, and the interweaving of these factors often led to confused arguments in which the interlocutors talked past one another.

Having followed all of these earlier debates and their re-examination, Oremland (1991) attempted to sort out the complicated question of whether psychoanalysis was continuous with or disjunctive from psychotherapy. Oremland's answer was to align psychoanalysis with interpretation (of transference) and psychotherapy with interaction. Interpretation was affiliated with understanding, while interaction was viewed as ameliorative. In his review of the history of the debates, Oremland attributed much of the fuss made in the 1950s to the expansion of the therapeutic scope of psychoanalysis following World War II, identifying Harry Stack Sullivan as the most important figure in this expansion. Notice how this begins to blur the distinctions among the three forces identified by Rangell, mixing the issue of theoretical diversification with the widening scope of patients. Keep in mind that Sullivan was making his contributions during each of the three decades identified by Rangell, from the 1930s through the 1950s. Sullivan, Frieda Fromm-Reichman and other interpersonalists did promote the widening scope of patients by treating hospitalized psychotic patients and severe outpatient obsessionals.

The key to the debates, however, was not predominantly this widening scope of patients, but rather the significant challenges posed by interpersonalism to Freudian theory and ego-psychology. Oremland aligned Sullivanian interpersonalism with an emphasis on interaction rather than interpretation, which was precisely the crux of the changes in Alexander's technique. This is exactly why, from a more classical perspective, interpersonal treatment was viewed as psychotherapy rather than psychoanalysis. It was not predominantly because of extrinsic criteria such as frequency or use of the couch. The more significant reason for categorizing the interpersonal approach as psychotherapy was that, similar to Alexander's modified theories, it was understood to emphasize interaction rather than interpretation. Within the structure of this dichotomy, interaction lined up with suggestion and psychotherapy, in contrast to interpretation and insight, which lined up with psychoanalysis. For many years, it was typical for classical analytic authors to align the interpersonalists with superficial, social interaction in contrast to traditional psychoanalysts, who were aligned with deep, intrapsychic interpretation and insight. The controversy regarding theoretical orientation was confounded with the distinction between psychoanalysis and psychotherapy. Obviously, the strategy of defining psychoanalysis in contrast to psychotherapy could only work as long as there was a consensus among psychoanalysts about theory. In other words, defining psychoanalysis by distinguishing it from psychotherapy is only possible if you begin with a single perspective on what psychoanalysis is. The inverse is true as well—you can only maintain a single approach to psychoanalysis by splitting off all other views as being therapy, not analysis. As Wallerstein has emphatically argued, the breakdown of the distinction between psychoanalysis and psychotherapy was intricately tied to the collapse of theoretical consensus among analysts.

Let's examine Oremland's approach a bit more, because we believe it reflects how the more traditional analysts thought about these distinctions, particularly those who had been trained in the era of psychoanalytic medicine. More importantly, it sheds light on how various independent concerns coalesced around the binary of psychoanalysis versus psychotherapy. Oremland wrote:

> Within the psychoanalytic enterprise, a rigid hierarchy of disciplines was soon established with institute-trained psychoanalysts, a small and select group of psychiatrists, at the top. Beneath this elite group were the "dynamic" or "psychoanalytic" psychiatrists, who were partially trained in, or at least considered knowledgeable about, psychoanalysis. This larger group of physicians was followed by a much larger group, the social workers, who abandoning their traditional guidance and case-oriented helping roles, adopted the nonintervening, nondirective, cathartic model that was being touted as psychoanalytic. Operationally, to a large extent the social workers did the clinical work, generally in institutional settings, under the supervision of psychoanalytic psychiatrists, who themselves had been taught, supervised, and treated by the elite psychoanalysts.
>
> (1991, p. 4)

Perhaps the most shocking surprise is that Oremland then wrote, "Although *schematically appealing*, such a hierarchical system could not be maintained because of the varying degree of training and abilities in each of the disciplines" and because of the "nonspecific applications of nonspecific theories to overwhelming problems" (pp. 4–5, emphasis added). "It is little wonder that the Golden Age of psychoanalysis was to dissolve into the interactive excesses and emphasis on spontaneity, intuition, and absence of training that characterized the 'psychotherapeutic' scene in the late 1960s and early 1970s" (p. 5).

Oremland is nostalgic for a Golden Age when there was a clear and distinct hierarchy among the mental health disciplines. Psychology was not even a discipline worth mentioning with regard to 1950s psychoanalysis, as clinical psychology was just beginning to develop and many psychologists were more behavioral and research oriented. Psychoanalysts were on top, psychoanalytically oriented psychiatrists were beneath them, and social workers were on the bottom. Notice the confounding of mental health discipline with the privileged status of the trained psychoanalyst. Oremland, however, also connects the widening scope of patients to increased theoretical diversity. In his view, both led to the breakdown of professional discipline as well as the loss of clear professional identity and definition. By the late 1960s, all three of Rangell's factors intersect, leading to the collapse of psychoanalysis as a profession.

Merton Gill, while agreeing with Oremland about the relevant distinction between interpretation and interaction, astutely called him out on his tendency to get caught up in binary thinking. Gill wrote,

> It is unfortunately easy to fall into a very misleading shorthand and speak of a dichotomy between interaction and interpretation or between interaction and analysis of interaction. Such a shorthand risks abetting the serious error of forgetting that all interventions are interactions, including interventions that aim to analyze interaction.
>
> (1991c, p. 138)

Gill's collaborator Irwin Hoffman (1998) famously went on to make dialectical rather than dichotomous thinking central to his psychoanalytic vision. Gill himself recommended the use of the term "psychoanalytic therapy" for a therapy in which the analysis of interaction is a primary goal, regardless of how ambitious or lengthy the therapy. In other words, Gill no longer believed that one could distinguish a psychoanalytic therapy that did not include interpersonal influence. While analyzing this interpersonal influence had certain advantages, the interpersonal influence in and of itself was also recognized as beneficial and no longer regarded as anti-analytic. Gill reserved the use of the term "psychoanalysis proper" for a psychoanalytic therapy along these lines in which the couch is used along with greater frequency of sessions. In other words, for Gill, the extrinsic criteria were all that were left to distinguish psychoanalysis from a psychoanalytic therapy (1991b, p. 159).[2]

---

2 Examining the changes in Merton Gill's views is particularly complicated for several reasons. Gill went through a series of changes over the years and challenged Wallerstein's reporting of his position. In turn, Wallerstein objected to Gill's portrayal of his formulation. They exchanged public letters (Gill, 1991a, b; Wallerstein, 1991a, b). The conflict continued through Wallerstein's (1995) review of Gill's (1994) last book, and Wallerstein's (1995) further accounts of the debate. One might even say they continued in Wallerstein's (1996) obituary of Gill. Although the intricacies of their dialogue is of interest, we will leave it to readers desiring more detail to review these readily available references. Instead, we present our own reading of Gill's changed position. For a brilliant overview of Merton Gill's contributions, see Hoffman (2000).

Of the three major protagonists, Gill (1984) changed the most in his views. His 1979 position was shaped by the profound theoretical changes he had undergone in recent years. By the late 1970s, Gill had abandoned classical metapsychology and reformulated his understanding of transference. Gill's work startled the analytic world and had a definitive influence on the emergence of relational psychoanalysis. Just as Greenberg and Mitchell (1983) were delineating a relational, in contrast to a drive-structure approach, Gill (1983) similarly proposed a "person" point of view. For Gill, along with his collaborator Irwin Hoffman, the transference was no longer conceived as a spontaneous production of the patient's, but rather a joint formation of two participants in the analytic situation. In this view, transference was a construction, the patient's selective way of structuring experience through the lens of their stereotyped, constricted patterns of relating.

Gill believed the interpretation of transference was the central criterion for psychoanalysis. In 1984, he reviewed the "intrinsic criteria" for psychoanalysis, the same as he set forth in his 1954 article: "the centrality of the analysis of transference, a neutral analyst, the induction of a regressive transference neurosis and the resolution of that neurosis by techniques of interpretation alone, or at least mainly by interpretation" (p. 161). He then assessed the "extrinsic criteria," which were "frequent sessions, the couch, a relatively well integrated patient, that is one who is considered analyzable, and a fully trained psychoanalyst" (p. 161). He concluded that none of the extrinsic criteria could validly delimit a psychoanalytic process, for "no universal meaning of any aspect of the analytic setting may be taken for granted" (p. 174). For example, "while the couch is ordinarily considered to be conducive to regression, it may enable an isolation from the relationship which has a contrary effect" (p. 174). Addressing the possible meanings frequency of sessions might have, Gill stated,

> It would seem obvious that one can accomplish more with greater frequency simply because there is more time to work. But if greater frequency is frightening to a particular patient, frequent sessions may impede the work despite interpretation. One cannot simply assume that more is better.
>
> (1984, p. 174)

In this, as we have shown, Gill was actually following the lead of Edith Jacobson.

Gill (1984) asserted that "the notion of an 'uncontaminated' transference is a myth" (p. 164). Elsewhere he wrote, "there is nothing the analyst says or does which does *not* carry suggestion, whether explicit or implicit" (1994, p. 90). Nevertheless, even in the years after his revolutionary shift to a social perspective, Gill (1984) believed analysis "should be characterized not only by *avoidance of witting suggestion* but also by the analysis of both witting and unwitting suggestion" (p. 177, emphasis added). Gill clearly recognized the tension between the inevitability of suggestion, the fact that all transference is to a certain extent co-created with the analyst, and the need to avoid and analyze suggestion. Yet he could not quite let go of the idea that interpretation could somehow undo the impact of suggestion. He assumed that explicating or interpreting the impact of previous unwitting suggestions would eliminate suggestive effects. This mistakenly assumes that the follow-up interventions would themselves be free of suggestion or could undo suggestion (Mitchell, 1997). Under the impossible ideal of eliminating suggestion, Gill saw no place for the analyst to exert any influence, even in encouraging regression, which he originally assumed was an essential aspect of psychoanalytic methodology (see Aron and Bushra, 1998). Where this left Gill is that in all psychoanalytic therapy, including psychoanalysis proper, influence was inevitable and potentially valuable and therapeutic. It should, however, be unwitting and subject to analysis when possible so that the benefit would generalize beyond the particular therapeutic interaction. There were no differences between kinds of analytic therapy, no interactive or supportive therapy versus an interpretive therapy; rather there was psychoanalytic therapy, with psychoanalysis proper simply being a way to refer to adhering to the more traditional extrinsic criteria.

We have seen that with increasing theoretical diversity came a breakdown in any clear distinction between psychoanalysis and psychotherapy. Years ago, Wallerstein's studies suggested that with increasing pluralism, one person's psychoanalysis became another person's psychotherapy. The schools of analysis, the different theoretical orientations, divided up the psychoanalytic spectrum along diverse lines. Depth and surface were relative to a theorist's orientation and worldview. One person's depth was another person's surface. We went from a single psychoanalysis to multiple psychoanalyses.

Fosshage (1997) argued along similar lines that with the advent of theoretical pluralism in models of development, pathogenesis, and technique, and the expanded application of treatment, the traditional but fragile distinction between psychoanalysis and psychoanalytic psychotherapy has eroded. Pointing to changing market conditions, Fosshage warned that psychoanalysis "can no longer afford to emphasize only its differences from other therapies" (p. 423). Drawing in particular on the dramatic changes introduced by Gill, Fosshage concluded that psychoanalysis was expanding and that its application need not be restricted by what has become known as the extrinsic criteria. In sum, for Fosshage, psychoanalytic therapy *is* psychoanalysis.

Responding from a more conservative perspective, Golland (1999) identified Fosshage as a "leveler," in contrast with a "sharpener," meaning that Fosshage was minimizing differences rather than highlighting them.

The leveling cognitive style exemplified by the Fosshage (1997) thesis asserts, "It's all the same," and, in doing so, proposes to raze (level, demolish) the (admittedly imperfect) theoretical and clinical edifice painstakingly constructed over the past century. Those who applaud the no difference approach forgo the opportunity to learn and practice psychoanalysis.

(Golland, 1999, p. 108)

We believe Golland accurately identified a significant shift—the change in emphasis among analysts from sharpening their differences with other therapists to leveling those differences, although of course this introduces yet another problematic dichotomy. We believe the shift from sharpening to leveling has happened for all of the many social, economic, professional, and cultural reasons we have discussed. Where we disagree with Golland is that this neither demolishes psychoanalysis nor leads to the forgoing of analytic training. Nor do we agree that it eliminates the differences between psychoanalytic therapy and other therapies or the differences between analytic therapy and analysis proper. It simply shifts the discussion to a more balanced account of the similarities and differences and avoids the tendency to dichotomize those procedures rather than see them as existing along a continuum. Eisold (2006) responded to Golland's call to "sharpen" the differences between psychoanalysis and psychotherapy in a manner consistent with our own conclusions.

There are many clinical differences that can be usefully distinguished, and I have no inherent quarrels with many of them. But the point for me is that these clinical differences are interesting and useful in their own ways. They do not warrant the use of the term "psychoanalysis" as opposed to "psychotherapy." Perhaps one might well make the argument that one or the other is superior in certain circumstances or for particular ends. But I do think that we have to put the old polarities behind us. We can no longer take for granted the inherent superiority of any therapeutic technique and privilege it as "psychoanalysis." We are, each in his or her own way, "psychotherapists."

(2006, p. 271)

We conclude this review of the debates of the 1950s and their reexamination by contemporary psychoanalysts with what we think may be surprising to many readers, namely with two voices of mainstream "analytic authority" who actually agree with our radical thesis for reexamining the sharp polarization of psychoanalysis and psychotherapy. We quote them not to rest our case on their authority, but rather because they each point to the social and political agenda behind the distinction and because it is so refreshing to recognize that these disputes cross all party lines. It is one thing to hear these arguments about polarizing psychotherapy and psycho-analysis from a relationalist, an intersubjectivist, or an interpersonalist, but consider the following two points of view.

In a memoir written shortly before his death, Charles Brenner wrote that over and over again he heard his colleagues refer to the difference between psychotherapy and psychoanalysis as if they were two different disciplines. As he did so often throughout his life, Brenner expressed a dissenting, maverick voice. He argued that years ago what people meant by psycho-therapy was not psychodynamic, but today, psychotherapy largely focuses on insight, just as it does in what is referred to as formal psychoanalysis. "There is no distinction between what is called *psychotherapy* and what is called *psychoanalysis* today, as there was many years ago" (2009, p. 669).

Kernberg (1999) called for a "rather strict differentiation of standard psychoanalysis, psychoanalytic psychotherapy, and psychoanalytically based supportive psychotherapy" (p. 1078). He argued that the distinc-tions might be clarifying in their precision, specifying how much each of the procedures makes use of transference analysis and technical neutrality. Yet unlike analysts of the past, Kernberg advocated teaching psychoana-lytic psychotherapy and even supportive therapy within psychoanalytic institutes so as to create a more flexible graduate practitioner, to prevent psychotherapy itself from turning into "wild" psychotherapy, and to help clarify the various procedures and their appropriate range of application. There is just one catch. As Kernberg himself readily acknowledged, he can only accomplish this precision at a cost, namely his definitions will not satisfy the conceptual requirements of the American intersubjectivists, interpersonal analysts, self-psychologists, constructivists, or relationalists. In sum, Kernberg's neat distinctions can only be maintained by excluding what may be the majority of psychoanalysts in the United States.

Kernberg's prominent emphasis on the strict boundaries between psychotherapy and psychoanalysis proper is his usual and best-known stance. However, in less formal discussion of this question, Kernberg said the following regarding his own approach to psychoanalytic therapy with borderline patients:

> I am applying a strictly psychoanalytic technique; it's not standard psychoanalysis. In this country, if I had said, "this is psychoanalysis," I would now be dead. I called it psychoanalytic psychotherapy to survive, and it made no difference how it's called so long as it's clear what the technique is. The Kleinians say "this is not analysis," and they are perfectly right. When I talk to the British independents, they say, "We've done this all the time, this is psychoanalysis." When I talk to the French analysts in a symposium on psychotherapy, they also told me that they do this all the time. One of the most intelligent leading analysts of the French-Canadian group told me, "You're not telling us

anything new." So it could be called psychoanalysis there. The boundaries between psychotherapy and psychoanalysis are affected by ideology and our insecurity. It is also a consequence of the Hartmann era that we are so afraid, so insecure that we have to create very strict boundaries.

(Cited in Bergmann, 2000, p. 336)

Kernberg's honest portrayal brings us right back to Alexander's recognition of the social, cultural, political, and economic forces behind these forced choices and hierarchies. "The boundaries between psychotherapy and psychoanalysis are affected by ideology and our insecurity." Kernberg's statement speaks directly to the heart of our argument. We could not have said it better.

When following World War II and through the 1950s, psychoanalysis was defined in opposition to psychotherapy, the nature of the "ideology" and "insecurity" providing the context for these formulations was of a manic omnipotent defense emphasizing American military, political, and economic power, a masculine protest valorizing autonomy and independence, and a counter-phobic avoidance of influence, permeability, and dependence. It was in this cultural context that relationality was expunged from psychoanalysis and projected onto the psychotherapies.

Chapter 9

Comic Book Crusaders

Psychoanalysis as Superhero

"People Searching for Peace of Mind Through . . . PSYCHOANALYSIS"

What possible connection could there be between psychoanalysis and the comic book genres of gruesome horror stories such as *Tales From the Crypt*, or the adventures of superheroes such as *Superman* and *Wonder Woman*? How are comic book crusaders, caped or otherwise, relevant to our tale of the Golden Age of psychoanalysis in the conservative social and political atmosphere of the 1950s? Stay tuned for the astonishing answer that will be revealed in this chapter . . .

Following World War II, psychoanalysis was accorded public accolades for aiding the war effort. Returning from the front eager for psychoanalytic training, young doctors swarmed the institutes of the APsaA, and psycho-analysis became a dominant force within American psychiatry. A conserva-tive version of psychoanalysis rose to power, blending perfectly with the American 1950s culture of adaptation, conservative politics and gender arrangements, consumerism, and the narrative of scientific progress. In the early 1950s, conservative mainstream psychoanalysis formally distin-guished itself from the dynamic psychotherapies.

In this chapter, we take a brief and hopefully entertaining detour into the world of comic books. We do so in order to provide a more vivid illustration of the role psychoanalysis played in the American popular imagination in the 1950s, the issues psychoanalysis was presented to the American public as addressing, and the larger social and political context in which psychoanalysis rose to power. In a cultural convergence of cosmic, or at least comic, proportions, the Golden Age of psychoanalysis overlapped with the Golden Age of comics, 1933–1955. Our dynamic duo will now reveal the surprising story of *PSYCHOANALYSIS*, the comic book that portrayed the psychoanalyst as superhero, the Superman of the Mind. Published by Entertaining Comics, or EC Comics, best known for its *Tales from the Crypt* horror series and later, *MAD Magazine*, *PSYCHOANALYSIS* was introduced in 1954 as a mass-market comic book. Dramatically capturing the zeitgeist of psychiatry in 1950s America, its complete title read, "People Searching for Peace of Mind through . . . PSYCHOANALYSIS."

We will begin our story by providing some background on the Jewish origins of the comic book industry. At the height of the Great Depression, enterprising American Jews built the comic book industry from the ground up. With most opportunities in commercial illustration closed to Jews due to the infamous anti-Semitic Gentlemen's Agreement made by many advertising agencies, Jewish writers and illustrators entered the comic book field, where Jewish comic book publishers, mostly enterprising marketers, created discrimination-free opportunities. Comics offered Jewish writers and artists a way out of poverty and into a legitimate artistic career. DC Comics, founded in 1934 as National Allied Publications, brought to life the world's most famous superheroes. Storytelling had long been central to Jewish tradition, and the Jewish creators of Superman, Spider-Man, Wonder Woman, and Batman brought a uniquely Jewish perspective to their work.

Consider the Jewish origins of the Man of Steel. Just as Hitler rose to power in 1933 Germany, Jerry Siegel (writer) and Joe Shuster (artist), two prolific, innovative Jews from Cleveland, created the character of Superman. They were unable to convince any newspaper to publish the comic. Max Gaines (born Max Ginzberg), then the print broker for DC Comics, convinced Harry Donenfeld and Jack Liebowitz, DC's publishers, to give it a chance. Actualizing the adolescent power fantasies of his creators—two Jewish Depression kids—Superman emerged as a powerful redeemer capable of liberating them from their social and economic impoverishment. Numerous critics and historians of comics have noted the similarities between Superman and the Golem of Jewish legend, an anthropomorphic being said to have been created by the medieval chief rabbi of Prague, Rabbi Judah Loew, known as the Maharal, to defend the Prague ghetto from anti-Semitic pogroms. Cartoonist and comic book historian Will Eisner views Superman "as a mythic descendant of the Golem and thus a link in the chain of Jewish tradition." He writes,

> The Golem was very much the precursor of the super-hero in that in every society there's a need for mythological characters, wish fulfillment. And the wish fulfillment in the Jewish case of the hero would be someone who could protect us. This kind of storytelling seems to dominate in Jewish culture.
>
> (Cited in Kaplan, 2003)

While some of the greatest comic book arch villains were modeled on the Nazis, the writers and artists made a point of designing the superheroes to look American—in other words, not Jewish.

Max Gaines went on to found his own comic book publishing company, first known as Educational Comics, and later as Entertaining Comics or EC Comics. EC Comics specialized in horror fiction, crime fiction, satire, military fiction, and science fiction from the 1940s through the mid-1950s. When Gaines died in 1947, his son William, who had been planning to become a chemist at NYU, inherited the family business, taking it in a new direction. The comics he published in the 1940s were tame and uncontroversial. But in 1950, *The Crypt of Terror* made its experimental debut, and it quickly became apparent that there was a great demand for horror comics, leading to the development of the successful *Tales from the Crypt* and *The Vault of Horror*. Kaplan (2008) notes that EC Comics distinguished itself from the other 1950s-era comic book publishers by featuring stories about controversial subjects, including racism and anti-Semitism, no doubt inspired by the founders' Jewish backgrounds.

In the early 1940s, comic books were a multimillion-dollar business, but as the decade wore on, the industry became the target of mounting public criticism for the potentially harmful effects of comic books on children. To counter this criticism and distract attention from the horror comics, Gaines, along with editor and author Harvey Kurtzman, debuted *MAD Magazine* in August 1952. From the 1950s through the 1970s, a period gripped by Cold War paranoia and a general culture of censorship, *MAD* filled a gap in political satire. *MAD Magazine* became EC's most enduring legacy.

In 1954, psychiatrist Frederic Wertham wrote *The Seduction of the Innocent*, a study of the negative effects of comic books on children. A German-born Jewish psychiatrist who had chosen his specialty after corresponding with Freud, Wertham condemned the genre, especially crime and horror comics, for contributing to juvenile delinquency, detailing dozens of cases of children who had committed murders, injuries, and suicides after reading the often gruesome and violent stories depicted in comics. He portrayed Batman, Robin, and Wonder Woman as closeted gay and lesbian superheroes, a damning accusation in those homophobic times. In the McCarthy regime, homosexuals were also explicitly linked with Communists, a dangerous connection. Although viewed by many comic book enthusiasts as an arch villain, Wertham was legitimately concerned about the violence, misogyny, and racism endemic in comics and was alarmed by the many advertisements for knives and guns that appeared in the magazines.

According to Kaplan (2003), a writer for *MAD Magazine* and an historian of comics, much of the slander directed against Gaines and his fellow comic-book publishers was motivated by anti-Semitism. A *Hartford Courant* editorial, for instance, referred to comics as "the filthy stream that flows from the gold-plated sewers of New York"—a code phrase for Jewish businesses (cited in Kaplan, 2003). Across the country, comic book burnings became a familiar phenomenon.

Spurred by mounting public criticism, on April 21, 1954, the Subcommittee to Investigate Juvenile Delinquency of the Committee on the Judiciary convened to hear testimony from Gaines. Due to the effects of a strong cold medicine, Gaines' speech was slurred, and his performance on the witness stand less than stellar. "The media jumped on that," said *MAD* cartoonist Drew Friedman of the televised hearings. "They portrayed him as some slovenly Jewish pornographer" (quoted in Kaplan, 2003). At the same time, a federal investigation led to a shake up of the distribution companies that delivered comic books across America. Sales plummeted, and several companies went out of business. Gaines ended publication of the horror stories in September 1954. Many were made into movies in the 1970s. The comic books have been reprinted and cable television companies are now featuring these same tales.

Gaines and his fellow publishers needed to replace the horror stories with a publication that would demonstrate to the public that comics were socially redeeming and contributed a positive message. EC shifted its focus to a line of more realistic comic book titles, the New Direction line, which included *M.D.* and *PSYCHOANALYSIS*. Not surprisingly, the line quickly failed. *PSYCHOANALYSIS* simply could not compete with *MAD Magazine*. In 1999, Gemstone Publishing reprinted the first four original 1955 issues of *PSYCHOANALYSIS* as part of their effort to preserve and promote the history of the comics medium. The reproductions are widely available—we each keep copies in our waiting rooms. We believe we can learn something from examining these 1955 comics. In what follows, we will briefly highlight several themes that dovetail strikingly with our own narrative and thesis.

Each issue of EC's *PSYCHOANALYSIS* featured the ongoing analysis of three patients: Freddy Carter, Ellen Lyman, and Mark Stone. The reader was invited to follow three analyses sequentially as they unfolded over time. Each issue was presented as a single session, so that in total they covered four sessions of each analysis, except for Ellen Lyman, who was cured in only three sessions. One might, if generously inclined, read the stories as condensing a significant amount of analytic work that took place in between publications. The structure of the comic resembles the structure of the recent HBO television series *In Treatment*, in that it exposes the audience to a small sequence of consecutive sessions of a few patients whom it gets to know as their treatments unfold. Despite our concerted efforts, we were unable to speak in depth with anyone who was personally involved with or knew the story of the writing of the *PSYCHOANALYSIS* comic. Thus, while we believe there must have been a psychiatric consultant, we have not been able to locate this information.

The striking cover art of each of the four issues is signed by Jack Kamen, who was most famous for his work on EC Comics and was responsible for all of the artwork in *PSYCHOANALYSIS*. Kamen was particularly known for his "Kamen girls," the voluptuous and cold-hearted bombshells that often appeared in his drawings. True to form, the cover of the first volume depicts a voluptuous blond lying on an analyst's couch. One hand is positioned on her forehead; there is an expression of angst on her face. The other hand holds a tissue; there is a tissue box just under her arm. A wastebasket filled with used tissues stands at the foot of the traditional psychoanalytic couch. Next to her and slightly behind sits the psychiatrist, bearing a striking resemblance to Clark Kent, poised at any moment to turn into Superman. While everywhere else he is depicted smoking a pipe, here the psychiatrist, wearing a suit and tie, cufflinks, and glasses, holds a pen and pad, his cigarette burning in the ashtray beside him. There is no doubt about the message conveyed by the cover photo: Psychoanalysis is heroic. Our superhero is a strong, firm but compassionate man treating a beautiful, erotically charged, helpless and needy young woman. The advertising campaign announcing the upcoming publication of PSYCHOANALYSIS confirms this heroic view. "And now, the most revolutionary idea ever presented in comics! Discover the innermost secrets of people searching for peace of mind in E.C.'s 'New Direction' mag . . ." Clearly, it is not only the magazine that was being presented as revolutionary, but psychoanalysis itself. Psychoanalysis was being sold to the American people as a heroic adventure in which the doctor penetrated the mysteries of anguished minds and successfully cured patients, writing "Therapy Completed" in his charts after just three or four sessions.

In the guise of providing an educational service, a page of each issue was devoted to explaining some aspect of psychoanalytic theory, such as the interpretation of dreams, or giving biographical information about "the Man from Vienna." Here was the Doctor as superhero, slayer of the arch villains of the unconscious mind—but always with a touch of irony and satire. After all, these stories were brought to you by the same people who brought you *MAD Magazine*!

The opening lines of the first issue introduce the doctor and his mission:

> This is a psychiatrist! Into his peaceful, tastefully decorated, subdued office come the tormented and the driven, seeking to unravel the tangled emotional skeins that cloud and knot their broken lives. Skillfully guided by him past the sub-surface reefs of fears and guilts and anxieties, his patients eventually discover for themselves the course to self-understanding, peace, and true personal happiness which like a rich treasure are waiting to be unearthed, and the *map* to this treasure . . . the *key* to its lock. . . . Is *found* through . . . PSYCHOANALYSIS.

In reviewing these stories, we were tempted to do a frame-by-frame analysis because so much is revealed in each frame about 1950s culture, parenting, and economics, as well as about the public perceptions of psychiatry and psychoanalysis. However, we will limit ourselves to brief summaries, in which we highlight only a few central themes relevant to our main thesis.

Making a Man Out of a "Sissy"

Freddy Carter, a 15-year-old boy, is brought to the doctor by his respectable and upstanding parents because he was caught stealing. In the first frame, Mr. and Mrs. Carter are standing in the doctor's office talking to him while Freddy, his face gloomy, is sitting on the couch. All are dressed formally, the men, including 15-year-old Freddy, wearing jackets and ties, the mother wearing a dress with a shawl around her shoulders. The doctor is smoking a pipe. Mr. Carter says that he and his wife have given Freddy every advantage. Mrs. Carter says that she treated him with tender care "as if he were Dresden china." Still in this first frame, the doctor makes his first intervention, responding to Mrs. Carter that perhaps treating him like Dresden china was precisely the *cause* of Freddy's difficulties. By the second frame, the doctor launches into a speech about the parents' overindulgence of their son, spelling out the dangers of excessive gratification of wishes and how it leads to infantilization. Soon he is saying, "I'll be blunt with you both! The trouble with Freddy is *you*! You've *always* been his trouble! You always *will* be." While at first the parents argue with the doctor, they quickly become convinced of the truth of his observations, and Freddy begins his individual analysis. The authoritarian tone and judgmental attitude of the doctor is characteristic of the entire comic book. He is depicted as smart, quick, observant, and insightful. Confrontational and challenging, he speaks with great authority. In our reading, he is also condemning and humiliating, although from his perspective, it is for the patient's own good. In short, this vignette very quickly manages to capture the typical 1950s attitude about medical authority.

Within the first session, Freddy is brought to realize that he has been caught in a tug-of-war between his parents. His father, a hard-driving and domineering engineer, has promoted sports and academics, especially math and science, whereas his sentimental and high-strung mother has encouraged his love for the arts and literature. Freddy stole the watch from his friend because he envied the other boy's peaceful and loving family life. He wanted to steal affection and to shame and humiliate his own parents in order to punish them. It becomes immediately apparent that his father's greatest underlying fear is that Freddie will turn out to be a "sissy" because of his mother's pampering. Clearly, Mr. Carter's goal is for the doctor to make Freddy not only a better student and athlete, but also a real man, not the baby girl his mother had wished him to be.

An important theme, one that arises in all three comic book cases, is that Freddy suffers from asthma and has become something of a hypochondriac. As he comes to learn, his asthma is psychosomatic, meaning imaginary, self-induced so as to get his parents' sympathy and be taken care of like a baby. The doctor is clearly on the side of making a man out of Freddy and fighting off his tendency to regression. When the doctor confronts Freddy with his fear that he could never please his father and so stopped playing football in order to hurt his father out of revenge, Freddy reacts with the observation that the doctor sounds just like his dad talking. To us, this seems perfectly accurate! The doctor, however, confronts this father trans-ference. He says that anything unpleasant *must* sound like his dad talking. "You associate every unpleasurable task, every burden, every average criti-cism, every responsibility with your father." By the end of the third session, Freddy asks to take the sports section of the newspaper home with him from the doctor's office!

All three cases are presented in classical Oedipal terms. By Freddy's last session, he has come to see that his symptoms have resulted from his experience of being passively buffeted about by his parents' conflicts. More crucially, he understands that he has been purposely dividing his parents in order to win his mother's affection, get rid of his father, and then be treated with infantile care by his mother. He needs to realize that such infantile wishes to replace his father and win his mother are typical for male children up to the age of five, and that he now must grow up and renounce them. Freddy's analysis is completed when the doctor refers each of his parents to colleagues, telling the father that he is a neurotic who tyrannizes and dominates his son, and telling Mrs. Carter, "*Your* personality is as sick in *its* way as Mr. Carter's is!" They are referred for psychiatric help! And the doctor returns Freddie to them, saying, "He's all yours!"

In all three cases, we see the same themes. Psychoanalysis and psychiatry are thoroughly identified with one another, with no hint of any distinction between the two. Psychoanalysis *is* psychiatry. Psychoanalysis is a medical procedure and the (male) doctor speaks with the authority and power of the medical establishment at the height of its prestige and status. Medicine at the time, of course, was overwhelmingly male, as was psychoanalysis. The doctor's interventions and interpretations are presented with the dispas-sionate attitude of scientific observation and inference, as if they are completely neutral, and as though there is nothing at all personal or subjec-tive in his judgments. His formulations are based on Oedipal dynamics, which are viewed as central to neurosis; within this framework, his patient's psychosomatics are highlighted.

Keep the timeline in mind. The comics were published in 1955. In 1953 the Academy of Psychosomatic Medicine was formed, and the field seemed to be exploding with knowledge. Franz Alexander's "organ specificity" theory proposed that specific stresses evoke specific unconscious neurotic conflicts that result in specific organic diseases. He maintained that psychosomatic illness depended on constitutional vulnerability, particular personality patterns, and a precipitating stress to produce the pathology. This research reinforced the dominance of the psychoanalytic approach, consolidated the ties between psychoanalysis and medicine, and promoted psychoanalytic treatment. Not surprisingly, each of the cases features psychosomatic symptoms and their cure by psychoanalysis.

Jewish Persecution and Assimilation

We will focus on one more case and touch on the third briefly. Mark Stone, a 28-year-old overweight man who works as a TV writer and advertising executive on Madison Avenue, comes for treatment because he is having what seems to him to be heart attacks. He is afraid he is dying, but the doctors told him his symptoms were due to anxiety and panic. Mr. Stone quickly learns that his symptoms are psychosomatic, resulting from his inner conflict between his longing for material success designed to please his father and his creative and artistic, but less lucrative, endeavors. The doctor challenges Mr. Stone about his excessive overeating. Mr. Stone gains insight into the motivations for his behavior, which include his need for emotional security, his feelings of guilt, and desire for self-punishment. His guilt stems from his feelings of shame about his parents, especially his mother, because she is an immigrant. In fact, one of his first revelations to the doctor is that his name is not really Mark Stone, but Morris Stein, son of Israel Stein, and "we were Jewish." He uses the past tense to describe his religious identity. Mr. Stone insists that he changed his name for business reasons. But his associations recall that his father was persecuted for religious reasons in "the old country." "The Jew by *any name* is hated! *Why* the good Lord gave *all the rottenness in mankind an eternal target . . .* the *Jew*! I remember how the *other* kids *treated* me . . . threw *stones* at me . . ." The name he chose was directly tied to his persecution as a Jew. Morris/Mark was similarly ashamed of his mother, who spoke with a foreign accent. Her accent, speech, and dress all made him "squirm," and he was mortified that she was not an American. When boarding a train for a vacation she asked the conductor, "Man, is this the right train? Maybe we got on the wrong train, heaven forbid? I'm so worried . . . so aggravated! Vacation trips we needed!? A hole in the head I needed!"

Little Morris's father takes pride and some comfort in the fact that the same anti-Semitic neighbors who throw rocks at him will still buy from his store. Morris is ashamed of his father, saying, "But how can you sell to them when they *do* such things? Don't you have any *pride*?" To us, the close parallel between this story and that of Sigmund Freud and his father Jakob is nothing less than uncanny! But perhaps Freud and little Morris were among many little boys who had difficulty understanding their father's accommodations in dealing with violent anti-Semitism. Recall too, that Freud changed his name from Sigismund to Sigmund precisely because Sigismund was a name frequently used in anti-Semitic jokes and comics (Gilman, 1993a; Klein, 1985). It should come as no surprise that in the mid-1950s, a group of Jewish psychoanalytically-oriented writers and artists chose to focus on the problems of immigrant families who had fled violent anti-Semitism in "the old country," portraying the next generation as seeking assistance from psychoanalysis in order to deal with "adaptation." Not surprisingly, Mark Stone develops a negative, hostile transference to the doctor, who interprets it along Oedipal lines. Over the course of the next several sessions, Stone develops the expectable ambivalence and recurrence of anxiety in dealing with termination. His proposal of marriage to a woman is interpreted as an acting out of his transference and dependency longings. But soon the doctor discharges Mr. Stone, pronouncing him a "cured man!" with a clear hint that he is on his way toward true maturity and marriage to an appropriate woman.

The Masochistic Woman

In our final story, Ellen Lyman, the 19-year-old blond bombshell depicted on the cover, suffers from acute migraines. With the doctor's help, she quickly discovers that these headaches were a form of self-punishment for the guilt she feels over competitive and hostile feelings toward her older sister. Behind the conflict with her sister lies the breakdown of her parent's marriage, for which she also feels responsible. Ellen tells the doctor she has been unhappy ever since she was abandoned by a love interest one summer. When Ellen describes what happened and how unhappy she felt, the doctor sharply challenges her, suggesting that in fact she enjoyed this outcome immensely. It allowed her to blame the loved man and her relatives for not loving her sufficiently, to deprive herself of love as punishment for her feelings of responsibility for her parents breakup, and to keep her distance from the possibility of relationship because she is really afraid of love. In order to receive love, the doctor insists, you must be able to give love. Ellen has been rejecting others before they reject her, thus both protecting and punishing herself. Once again, as is true in so many "real" case histories written up in our non-comic-book psychoanalytic journals, the case is terminated on a happy note. Ellen is now capable of giving and thereby receiving love, and a boyfriend is waiting in the wings. "The Ellen Lyman who walked into your office so long ago [three sessions by our count] *no longer exists*! The *slate's* been *wiped clean* . . . and I'm not afraid to write a *new* life-story based upon it! A *happy* story! Good-bye doctor!" Psychoanalysis leads to structural change, not just symptom relief. It is a scientific, rational, deep, inner, thorough cure. "Therapy completed!"

Peace of Mind Through Psychoanalysis

The expression "peace of mind" is used several times in the *PSYCHOANALYSIS* comic, including the title and cover, "People Searching for *Peace of Mind* through . . . PSYCHOANALYSIS." Not coincidentally, *Peace of Mind* was also the name of an extremely popular inspirational book at the time, one with which the Jewish writers and illustrators of the EC series were undoubtedly familiar. Written by Rabbi Joshua Liebman (1946), one of the most successful radio preachers in America, *Peace of Mind* sought to explicitly integrate psychoanalytic ideas with Jewish values. Published by Simon and Schuster just after the war, it reached #1 on the *New York Times* nonfiction best-sellers list on October 27, 1946, holding the top position on the list for 58 non-consecutive weeks. *Peace of Mind* spent more than three straight years on the list; excerpts were published in *Readers Digest*.

Rabbi Liebman received his doctoral degree and ordination from Hebrew Union College and served as a pulpit rabbi in Chicago and Boston. Significantly, Liebman had been analyzed in Chicago by Roy Grinker, who had been one of Freud's last patients, and was one of the most famous psychiatrists in America, having made his reputation in World War II. While *Peace of Mind* was still on the best-sellers list, Liebman tragically died on June 9, 1948 at age 41. Heinze's (2004) *Jews and the American Soul* documents the magnitude of Liebman's impact on popular culture, and is essential reading for those interested in the influence of Jews and Jewish values on the American mental health movement.

Integrating psychoanalysis with Jewish principles, *Peace of Mind* was the first Jewish entry into the inspirational mass market long monopolized by Protestant theologians. Contending that spiritual growth depended on psychological maturity, Liebman argued that Judaism had a particularly valuable contribution to make that was different from Christianity's and more easily integrated with psychoanalysis. Specifically, Liebman maintained that Judaism was based on healthy self-love and self-acceptance, for one could not "love the other as thyself" if one did not first accept and love oneself.

Unlike Christianity, Judaism did not emphasize original sin but rather understood the human being as conflicted, pushed and pulled between the *yetzer hatov* and *yetzer hara*, the good and evil inclinations. The Rabbis understood that all aspects of the human being, including sexuality and aggression, were necessary to life. Without these drives, people would not reproduce or work. And so the Rabbis spoke of "sweetening" the evil impulse by directing it toward life-affirming and spiritual purposes. Liebman argued that Freud's concept of sublimation was in line with this rabbinic tradition. Thus *Peace of Mind* stood as a polemically Jewish text that celebrated the compatibility and mutual reinforcement of psychoanalysis and specifically Jewish spirituality and theology. For Liebman, spiritual accomplishment was equated with psychological maturity, ego-strength, and character integrity.

Liebman was critical of Christianity's emphasis on and encouragement of guilt, arguing that such a focus led to repression and condemnation of natural impulses. Instead of a morbid emphasis on original sin, Judaism was rooted in the fundamental notion that we are created in the image of God. Self-understanding and self-acceptance, rather than self-condemnation, was the end result of psychoanalytic work. Lest this give the impression that Liebman was antagonistic to Christianity, we must add that he dedicated himself to interfaith understanding, praised Christianity for many other contributions to civilization, and maintained close personal friendships with Christian clergy. His overriding message, however, was direct and unapologetic: Judaism was optimistic and life-affirming; human beings are created in God's image and have the potential for good. Our biological drives are not inherently destructive or sinful but can be channeled, sublimated, sweetened, toward the good life.

Liebman's focus on self-acceptance, obtaining "peace of mind," is illustrated throughout the EC Comic series. When the doctor explains to Ellen Lyman that she is judgmental and rejecting of others because she cannot accept herself, he is drawing on one of the most popular ideas in the culture at that time, which was infused with religious tradition: you cannot love another as thyself if you do not love yourself. He asks Ellen how much respect she has for a person named Ellen Lyman. Don't you see, he asks, that your "subconscious" condemning attitude toward others is a reflection of your own self-hatred? You have contempt for yourself, self-loathing, self-blame, look down upon yourself, reject yourself, and so turn this self-hate onto others. "Why continue to *blame yourself* . . . or *judge* people *today* by the *emotional judgments* of your *childhood*? This advice could have been taken right out of Liebman's *Peace of Mind*. Although Liebman's work has been dismissed by history as if it were a simplistic liberal call for self-love, Liebman did not confuse self-love with pathological narcissism; he clearly differentiated the two. For Liebman (1946), narcissism was not self-love or self-acceptance but "a perverted form of self-adoration mixed with and growing out of self-contempt" (p. 43).

We do not have the space to review the arguments stirred up by Liebman's book among both Christian and more conservative Jewish theologians. Nor can we examine the contrasts between Liebman and his fellow inspirational spiritual self-help writers, such as the Protestant Norman Vincente Peale and the Catholic Bishop Fulton Shean. Heinze (2004) covers this ground in splendid detail. Instead, we will focus on two aspects of Liebman's book that are most relevant to our thesis: relationality and binaries.

Written from Liebman's liberal reform Jewish perspective, *Peace of Mind* was the first mass-market book to familiarize the American public with

Jewish religious beliefs. We have reviewed Liebman's depiction of Judaism as fostering self-acceptance and self-love, but an additional religious value highlighted by Liebman and operating together with the first was human mutuality. Loving thyself was a prerequisite to loving the other, but loving the other was equally important and established the value of community. Since Jewish theology placed little importance on the afterlife, it was regarded as this-worldly rather than next-worldly, and in place of immortality, Judaism focused on community and interrelatedness. Judaism emphasized the affirmation of life, this life, in this world.

In writing for the public just after the war, Liebman drew from a wide variety of influences, mostly from other best-selling authors. Heinze (2004) traces the significant influence on Liebman of American pragmatism, James, Dewey, and Mead, as well as Gestalt and field-theorists. Liebman wrote a popular, rather than a technical or medical book. Thus his version of Freudianism was broad and non-doctrinaire. While most frequently citing Freud, he also valued Adler's contributions, which emphasized social feeling and participation within the community. He drew on Menninger, Alexander, Grinker and Spiegel, Fromm, and Horney without entering into theoretical disputes. Much like Harry Stack Sullivan, who was influenced by this same group of social scientists during the same time period, Liebman (1946) emphasized that the self cannot be understood apart from others and that self-realization could only happen in a social context. "The revolutionary clinical work of Freud and his successors emphasizes a new truth in that we are literally *made* by our contacts with others!" (p. 61). Liebman's relational vision of psychoanalysis was prescient. His emphasis on love was a way of talking about relationship, just as Freud often used the sexual drive to speak of any and all intimate attachment.

> The first fundamental truth about our individual lives is the indispensability of love to every human being. By "love" I mean relatedness to some treasured person or group, the feeling of belonging to a larger whole and of being of value to other men.
>
> (Liebman, 1946, p. 60)

Consider his words about individuality and relatedness in terms of contemporary systems theory.

> Science, as a matter of fact, teaches us today that we can understand the universe only in terms of relatedness, that things are nothing in themselves, in isolation, that even the atom has significance only in some pattern of organization . . . Everywhere we turn in the laboratory, whether in physics or chemistry or biology or in psychology, we find that isolation is what is impossible and that relationship is everything.
>
> (1946, p. 61)

Furthermore, the logic of relationality led him inevitably to describe the self as multiple. He argued that we must become pluralistic in thinking about ourselves.

> How easily we accept the fact that this is a varied world, with many races, cultures, mores. In America we rejoice in this diversity, this pluralism, which makes up the rich pattern of our national being. We should try to accept this pluralism in ourselves.
>
> (1946, p. 55)

Liebman continued,

> Man is not a single self. He carries within him many selves . . . Man is like an omnibus with many little egos jostling each other as the vehicle of life hurtles down the highway. The great Jewish philosopher Saadia a thousand years ago pointed out this truth about our inner pluralism.
>
> (1946, p. 186)

A moral writer in the classical Jewish tradition, Liebman read Freud through a Jewish lens. In Liebman's view, Freudian psychoanalysis healed the individual by focusing on intimate relations, what would soon be called object-relations or interpersonal relations. For Liebman, Freud was a relational thinker because Judaism was a relational religion in which man is always embedded in his intimate relations and can only find redemption in and through those relations. Drawing on Martin Buber and Franz Rosenzweig before these names were well known in America, Liebman highlighted I–Thou relations within a community where mutual obligations ruled as a way of life. For a description of Martin Buber's philosophy as anticipating the most significant themes of relational psychoanalysis, see Aron (1996a). Aron describes Buber's concept of the "interhuman," his "I–You" relation, his "category of the between," as well as his emphasis on dialogue and mutuality, as all closely paralleling contemporary relational ideas. In a similar vein, Starr (2008) demonstrates the resonance of relational concepts with themes in traditional Judaism and the Jewish mystical tradition, particularly with regard to the development of the individual within the context of community. Early on, Liebman embraced the ideas of Mordecai Kaplan, the founder of Reconstructionist Judaism, because of Kaplan's optimistic, functionalist, and communally-oriented approach and because he was the first theologian to equate spiritual salvation with psychological self-realization.

The Doctor said to Ellen Lyman, "A person is *not sufficient unto himself*! No one can *exist happily and wholly* without *love* . . . without *giving* it and *receiving* it! You know now that you need *others*." Liebman wrote,

Dynamic psychology indicates today that in the very nature of man there is not only an unconquerable urge to receive love from others, . . . But what is more important, there is an inner necessity to give love and to bestow affection upon the outer world.

(1946, p. 71)

At this time, we are witnessing various claims that psychoanalysis is really a Jewish science, or that there are solid grounds for recognizing its greater Christian influence or its greater compatibility with Buddhism. Hoffman (2011) in particular has made a deeply respectful, sincere, and scholarly case for the Christian influences on Sándor Ferenczi and on relational psychoanalysis specifically. In a moment, we will discuss the need we all feel to move beyond these categorizations, and we know (from personal communication) that Hoffman's intention is similarly ecumenical. But we think it is of historical and scholarly importance to recognize the Jewish-relational tradition that Liebman popularized. Liebman did not view it as a synthesis. He did not believe he was bringing together two independent streams of thought. For him, psychoanalysis, and especially an early relational psychoanalysis, was itself in a direct line of tradition with classic Rabbinic Jewish moral writings and teachings.

So why not stop there? Why do we believe we need to move to a less parochial view? Why not simply accept and be proud of the Jewish heritage that gave birth to psychoanalysis and relational psychoanalysis? While we are certainly proud of that heritage and can easily see the relevant influences, the emphasis we have given to dichotomies and polarities leads us to the concern that in speaking of Jewish and Christian influences, we will get caught up once again in artificial and unnecessarily polarized positions. Just as we do not argue for the elimination of all difference between psychoanalysis and psychotherapy but do not see them as polar opposites, we also do not wish to minimize the differences between various religious traditions, but one can no longer define one in opposition to the other. On the one hand, Judaism and Christianity have common origins and have undergone millennia of mutual influence. It can be challenging indeed to trace whether certain beliefs or practices are "authentically" or originally Christian or Jewish. On the other hand, to merge them into a blended Judeo-Christian tradition minimizes differences that should not be downplayed. A third position is to view them as different but not polarized or defined in opposition to one another. This has been precisely our strategy in arguing that psychoanalysis and psychotherapy are different but not opposites. How do we apply this deconstruction of binaries to our topic? How do we move from either/or to both/and when it comes to religion? Should we? As long as we maintain unnecessary binary thinking, a doer/done-to mentality, a seesaw of me-up/you-down polarities, all we are left with are simple reversals, an endless series of sadomasochistic relations and religious wars. We need not minimize our differences and proclaim a homogenized humanity. We can accept, explore, and enjoy difference without clinging to polarizations.

Consider Joshua Liebman's achievement, or at least his strategy. He argued that Judaism was a religion based on love, including self-acceptance, which led to the love of others, while Christianity traded in original sin and guilt, self-condemnation. But this was a simple reversal. For ages, Christianity presented itself as a religion of love. Man was saved by Christ's love, whereas Judaism was presented as a spiritless legalistic religion that placed its faith in a harsh Old Testament wrathful God. Liebman, who was undoubtedly familiar with Freud's *Moses and Monotheism* (1939), did exactly what Freud did just a few years before. As we will examine in detail in Chapter 14, Freud, too, reversed the commonly held binary in which Jews were thought to be concrete, tied to law and legislation, while Christians were considered spiritual, requiring not observance but faith. Freud showed that it was Jews who invented an abstract God, while Christians accepted the immediate gratification of a wish-fulfilling embodied savior. Liebman did precisely what Freud did, reversing the common traditional stereotype, a simple reversal of the seesaw, such that Jews could argue that they turned out on top.

A classic example of an unnecessary binary was played out in some of the criticisms of Liebman. Will Herberg was an outspoken Jewish critic of Liebman, who dismissed his liberal brand of theology and caricatured him as offering nothing but palliatives of self-love. He argued that his emphasis on communion and partnership with God was an avoidance of full recognition and acceptance of our absolute dependence on and total submission to God. As Heinze (2004) points out, however, Jewish thought accommodates both/and rather than either/or positions, valuing both human dependence on the Divine and human partnership with God. He quotes Rabbi Joseph Soloveitchik (1992) who wrote, "We meet God in the covenantal community as a comrade and fellow member. Of course, even within the framework of this community, God appears as the leader, teacher, and shepherd" (p. 45).

Elsewhere, Aron (2004) took up precisely the same issue in another effort to move beyond binaries. Drawing on his *A Meeting of Minds* (1996a), which differentiated, but did not dichotomize, mutuality and symmetry, Aron attempted to show how his own theology and psychoanalytic metapsychology had mutually shaped one another and became reflections of each other. He wrote that a covenantal relationship requires mutuality, not symmetry or equality, because even though it is clearly hierarchical, it nevertheless must be reciprocal. The centrality of the covenantal relationship implies Judaism's foundations in this mutual relation. If the story of Abraham standing up to God in regard to Sodom illustrates the mutuality of their relationship, then the *Akeda*, the binding of Isaac, depicting

Abraham's silent submission to God's will, is perhaps the quintessential exemplar of asymmetry. The asymmetry is inherent in our transience and nothingness in relation to the Creator; the mutuality derives from our dignity as human beings who are created in the image of the Divine, allowing us to commune with God. In the words of Rabbi Soloveitchik,

> In God, man finds both affirmation of himself as a great being, and a ruthless, inconsiderate negation of himself as nothing. This is the main, the dominant theme of Judaism . . . Finding God is, on the one hand, the greatest victory which man may obtain and, on the other hand, the most humiliating, tormenting defeat which the human being experiences . . . In a word, the dialectical movement of surging forward and falling back is the way of life ordained by God for the Jew.
> (2003, p. 108)

Andrew Heinze demonstrated the central role of Jews and Jewish values in American psychology and psychoanalysis. His research rediscovered the enormous contributions of Joshua Liebman as a popularizer of a psychologized spirituality that followed the trajectory of tradition from the rabbis to psychoanalysis. We have shown that Liebman took for granted that psychoanalysis was a thoroughly relational endeavor, in line with the Jewish emphasis on mutual communal obligations and the commandment to love thy neighbor. In the following chapter, we identify Hippolyte Bernheim as one of the founders of modern psychotherapy and a proto-relational theorist who built on the Jewish values of community to explain mind as a social phenomenon. Liebman was writing in the same period as Zborowski and Herzog (1952), who captured this ethos in their title, *Life is with People*. It was just at this time that Jewish writers, illustrators, and publishers of comic books attempted to popularize psychoanalysis as the most scientific and respectful method of gaining peace of mind. In so doing, they stripped it of any spiritual and theological traces, presented it as thoroughly secular, appealed to a largely Christian readership, presented a wished-for assimilation, and thoroughly ensconced psychoanalysis as a medical specialty. Depicting psychoanalysis as a search for peace of mind and body, they left out the soul.

Chapter 10

Charcot and Bernheim

Origins of Intrapsychic and Relational Models of Mind

While Freud did not distinguish psychoanalysis proper from psychoanalytic psychotherapy, he did distinguish the gold of psychoanalysis from the copper of suggestion. Let's examine the context of this remark, made at the Budapest Congress in 1918, an extremely optimistic moment for psychoanalysis. Psychoanalysis had achieved government recognition for its contributions to the treatment of war neuroses, the central topic of the congress. Speaking about the future of psychoanalysis, Freud (1919d) imagined a time when private and public funding would make the treatment accessible to all. We began this book with this quote from Freud. It is worth repeating here in its entirety, as it is so central to our main thesis.

> It is possible to see that at some time or other the conscience of society will awake and remind it that the poor man should have just as much right to assistance for his mind as he now has to the life-saving help offered by surgery; and that the neuroses threaten public health no less than tuberculosis, and can be left as little as the latter to the impotent care of individual members of the community. When this happens, institutions or out-patient clinics will be started, to which analytically-trained physicians will be appointed, so that men who would otherwise give way to drink, women who have nearly succumbed under their burden of privations, children for whom there is no choice but between running wild or neurosis, may be made capable, by analysis, of resistance and of efficient work. *Such treatments will be free.* It may be a long time before the State comes to see these duties as urgent . . . Probably these institutions will first be started by private charity. Some time or other, however, it must come to this.

Freud's humanistic vision leads him to make the distinction we are now revisiting.

> We shall then be faced by the task of adapting our technique to the new conditions . . . Often, perhaps, we may only be able to

achieve anything by combining mental assistance with some material support . . . *It is very probable, too, that the large-scale application of our therapy will compel us to alloy the pure gold of analysis freely with the copper of direct suggestion; and hypnotic influence, too, might find a place in it again, as it has in the treatment of war neuroses.* But, whatever form this *psychotherapy for the people* may take, whatever the elements out of which it is compounded, its most effective and most important ingredients will assuredly remain those borrowed from *strict and untendentious psycho-analysis*.

(1919d, pp. 167–168, emphasis added)

Freud was not warning about the dangers of mixing gold with copper. Rather, he was envisioning a future in which a pragmatic mix of psycho-analysis with suggestion would be a necessary compromise for a human-istic enterprise. At the time Freud made these remarks, it was precisely this type of compromise that had created worldwide enthusiasm for psychoanalysis. What exactly was Freud trying to differentiate? Not psychoanalysis versus an analytic psychotherapy. Rather, he identified direct suggestion as the antithesis of psychoanalysis, predicting that even suggestion might have to be mixed in as a useful alloy. How had sugges-tion become the "other" of "strict and untendentious psycho-analysis?"

As we saw in examining the heated debates of the 1950s, the main-stream analysts identified transference interpretation as the defining feature of psychoanalysis. Other criteria were viewed as assisting or supplementing this key task of analysis. The main criticism of Alexander's "corrective emotional experience" was that therapeutic maneuvering to be different from the patient's parents interfered with a proper and thorough analysis of the transference, a rationale that in decades to come would be argued even more forcefully and narrowly. Gill (1954) described the elimination of suggestion via transference analysis as the core of his conceptualization of psychoanalysis.

> Psychoanalysis was born out of hypnosis—the technique which, as then employed, maximally used suggestion. Freud's first under-standing of transference came, he tells us, when he saw apparently secure therapeutic results blown away by a change in the patient's feel-ings about him. Ever since, analysis has struggled to develop a treat-ment technique which will be free of the influence of suggestion. A major milestone in this development was Freud's recognition that suggestion operates all through the therapeutic process, but that it can be employed to further the therapeutic work, and be ultimately more or less resolved rather than remain as the precarious underpinning of the therapeutic result. This point of view has lately been reformulated by Edward Bibring in his distinction between technical and

therapeutic devices. The use of transference to further the exploration of unconscious material, for example, is a technical device, while the resolution of transference by its interpretation is a therapeutic device. *The essential difference between psychoanalysis and other psychotherapies has long been seen as consisting precisely in this—that psychoanalysis alone of the psychotherapies attempts to resolve the suggestive influence of the therapist on the patient.* Until recently any innovation introduced into psychoanalytic technique was scrutinized from this point of view—was it introducing a suggestive factor into the treatment?

(1954, p. 790, emphasis added)

Interpretation and resolution of the transference had become for analysts since Ferenczi (1909) the single most important method for eliminating the effects of suggestion. When analysts defined psychoanalysis specifically in terms of analysis of transference, they were insisting that analysis was different from therapy because it strove to eliminate suggestion, whereas psychotherapy did not. Alexander was thought to be advocating psychotherapy rather than psychoanalysis because by manipulating the transference he was not analyzing it; hence he was relying on suggestion, which only worked while the relationship with the therapist was intact. Freud wrote,

> The therapeutic successes that occurred under the sway of the positive transference are open to the suspicion of being of a *suggestive* nature. If the negative transference gains the upper hand, they are blown away like chaff before the wind. We observe with horror that all our trouble and labour hitherto have been in vain.
>
> (1938a, p. 176)

What was so significant about suggestion? Why was it so important for Freud to show that analytic cures were not based on suggestion, even as he repeatedly acknowledged that suggestion had its place within psycho-analysis? Freud readily acknowledged that the patient is motivated to do analytic work out of transference love and the analyst's suggestion. The analyst suggested to patients that they would recall memories of their childhood and must try to overcome their resistance to remembering. In this case, suggestion clearly played a role without seeming to tarnish the pure gold of analysis. Nevertheless, Freud insisted that suggestion was not a factor of psychoanalytic cure. How can this contradiction be reconciled?

There were two major ways in which suggestion was problematic for Freud, aligned with two broad categories identified by Stephen Mitchell (1993) as remaining ongoing problems for psychoanalysis: "What can the analyst know?" and "What does the patient need?" These are problems of epistemology and the understanding of therapeutic action. The epistemological problem of suggestion is: if our findings have been affected by what we have suggested to the patient, how can we trust our results to be anything more than our own preformed biases? If the analyst suggests to the patient that his problems result from an Oedipus complex, and the patient then provides associations confirming an Oedipal etiology, how do we know that the Oedipus dynamic was a cause rather than a reflection of the patient's adoption of the analyst's belief system? In short, the epistemological concern is that suggestion contaminates the data, undermining the scientific basis of psychoanalytic knowledge. The second concern has to do with therapeutic action. If the therapeutic results are due to suggestion, which is based on a positive or loving relationship to the analyst, the therapeutic result is only as good as the relationship while it lasts. The patient remains dependent on the analyst and on their mutual feelings for one another. This is an unstable cure indeed. Furthermore, if this dependence is regarded as infantile, primitive, or neurotic, then the cure has not succeeded in benefiting the patient by helping them become more mature and independent.[1]

In discussing what he calls "the influence taboo," Hoffman (2009) points out that in psychoanalysis, suggestion

> means quite the opposite of what it means in everyday common usage. A "suggestion" in that everyday sense is just that: something for a person to consider, something one could take or leave. But "suggestion" in psychoanalysis is linked to *hypnotic* suggestion, which is largely controlling of the patient's experience and behavior. The transference, moreover, is understood to have inherited the power of suggestion as it functioned in hypnosis and the psychoanalytic process could be

---

1 While it is beyond the scope of this chapter to take up the topic of the nature of therapeutic action from a contemporary point of view, we want to note the almost complete absence of any acknowledgment in the classical discussions that changes are not just internal/intrapsychic but relational/transactional. That is, they reside not just in a state of mind but in a *way of being* with others. Paul Wachtel (1982, 1987, 2009; compare especially to Mitchell, 1997) has given particular emphasis and clarity to the role of feedback and embeddedness in a relational matrix. He identifies the role of vicious circles, accomplices, and action/feedback patterns, implying that change gets consolidated when it is *woven into the person's life*, that is, when it begins to consistently evoke different kinds of responses from people in one's life that in turn keep the changed direction intact because they are consistent with and reinforce the changes. This means one must pay attention not just to the state of the transference but also to the patient's daily transactions in his ordinary life. This relational focus directly addresses the notion that change that is brought about in part by the influence of the relationship can become autonomous of that relationship, because it becomes embedded/entwined with *new* relationships or *new qualities to old relationships* that are themselves a product of (but no longer dependent on) the original relationship with the therapist.

viewed as a kind of "slow motion" hypnotic procedure . . . It's no wonder that many analysts became virtually phobic about being sources of influence in their interactions with their patients beyond promoting, as in Freud, their analysands' efforts to find, and come to grips with, truths about themselves and their worlds.

(Hoffman, 2009, p. 618)

Anticipating Hoffman's critique by close to a century, Freud (1921) explained that the German words *nahelegen* and *Anregung* are both the equivalent of the English "suggestion" and might lead to confusion. He clarified that he was referring to the kind of suggestion where "influence takes place without adequate logical foundation" (p. 90). If we suggest to a patient that they come frequently because the treatment works better that way, and if they follow that suggestion because it seems reasonable and logical, this is the kind of suggestion Freud felt was essential. Similarly, if they accept our explanation of a resistance being due to castration anxiety because they are persuaded of its reasonableness and make it their own, that too is acceptable and unproblematic for Freud.

> The old-fashioned psychotherapist . . . used to suggest to his patient that he was cured, that he had overcome his inhibitions, and so on; while the psycho-analyst, on this view, suggests to him that when he was a child he had some experience or other, which he must now recollect in order to be cured. This would be the difference between the two.
>
> (Freud, 1918a, p. 52)

Only suggestion accepted "without adequate logical foundation" is problematic because it is based on submission to authority, meaning it is irrational. All of these distinctions are based on Enlightenment assumptions about rationality and positivist assumptions about the ability to distinguish truth and fantasy, rationality and irrationality. In our time and culture, the extent to which it is logical and reasonable to accept authority is not what it was in Freud's day. What Freud thought was a patient's reasonable acceptance of an interpretation that he made based on his expertise might seem to us like a submission to Freud's authority. Hence, we would view the interpretation as a form of suggestion in the strict sense. In sum, *the distinction between the gold of psychoanalysis and the copper of suggestion is based on the ability to make a clear distinction between autonomous rational argument and irrational interpersonal influence.*

We will review the historical events and theoretical arguments that left a deep impression on Freud, shaping the intrapsychic focus of psychoanalysis for a full century, and serving as a warning of what might happen if anyone could show his scientific results were based on suggestion. At a decisive turning point in his career, Freud studied with Charcot, whom he revered. Psychoanalytic biographies have not given enough emphasis to the impact on Freud of witnessing the fall of Charcot. Nor have they highlighted the nature of his ambivalent acceptance and criticism of Bernheim, who had challenged and deposed his hero Charcot. Many of Charcot's important findings were thrown into dispute because it was shown that his patients had been unduly influenced by suggestion. Charcot died in disgrace, and Freud learned his lesson.

The Great Charcot

In 1885, Freud was working in Brucke's laboratory, but had been advised by his teacher to abandon his hopes for a career in laboratory research, a path that would have resulted in his hitting a glass ceiling as a Jew in Vienna. As a private practitioner specializing in neuropathology, Freud could support himself and finally get married; by then he had been engaged for three years. He applied for and received a faculty travel grant, which gave him six months of leave. Freud had numerous publications, but they were all on neuroanatomy and not directly helpful in establishing his name as a clinician. He had damaged his reputation with his advocacy of cocaine, which he continued to use, and had just missed an opportunity to discover its clinical use in ophthalmology. As Makari (2008) comments, "It was a good time for him to get out of town" (p. 26). It was also the best professional opportunity of Freud's life. He immediately decided to use the time to study with Charcot, the most renowned neurologist of his day. In the end, this decision changed the direction of his interests from neuroanatomy to psychology, culminating in the creation of psychoanalysis.

Known as "the Napoleon of the neuroses" because it was widely thought he not only looked like the military hero but acted like him as well, Jean-Martin Charcot was the international authority on neurology, consulting physician to kings and princes. A member of the social elite, Charcot lived in a grand house, where he invited acquaintances, including Freud, to extravagant receptions. The Salpêtrière, located in Paris's Left Bank, was the largest medical institution in Europe, possibly the world. A medical warehouse of 5,000 mostly elderly women, the Salpêtrière was a goldmine for Charcot's investigations. He turned it into a state-of-the-art, world-class research center. The Salpêtrière was more of a city-state than a hospital, with 45 buildings, streets, squares, gardens, and a beautiful church. No one was appointed to a faculty position in neurology without the support of Charcot; all the famous names in French neurology were his pupils.

By 1885, Charcot had established his worldwide reputation by making breakthrough discoveries in the "hard" science of pathological anatomy, leading him to be hailed as the "father of modern neurology" (Micale, 1995,

p. 88). He had made important contributions to pulmonary and kidney disease, pioneered the study of geriatrics, identified multiple sclerosis, tabetic arthropathies, localized lesions of the spinal cord, and a clinical syndrome that was called Charcot's disease, amyotrophic lateral sclerosis (ALS), now widely known as Lou Gehrig's disease. Charcot was heavily inclined toward the somatic aspects of neurology. He regarded traumatic shock as causal, but understood it as a strain on the nervous system, believing the trauma could only cause the disturbance because of the patient's hereditary predisposition. Although his theory was a somewhat confused mixture of psychology and neurology, Charcot legitimized the serious study of hysteria by defining it as an inherited neurological disease, not as madness (psychiatry) or malingering (criminal). Most alienists (psychiatrists) were heavily committed to somatic and hereditary assumptions about mental illness and were little interested in mental states (Goetz, Bonduelle, and Gelfand, 1995). While Charcot was interested in heredity, he was also interested in less than fully conscious mental states. Freud's eventual turn away from Charcot was marked by his abandonment of hereditary and somatic assumptions in favor of the psychological, a truly revolutionary approach to the neuroses. But in 1885–86, Freud learned a great deal from the master.

In 1870, Charcot took control of a wing at the Salpêtrière housing large numbers of women suffering from convulsions, and was faced with the diagnostic problem of how to sort out the epileptics from the hysterics. These investigations led him to describe the full blown "grande hystérie." In 1878, Charcot extended his interests to hypnotism, using some of the most gifted female hysterics from the Salpêtrière. Hustvedt (2011) provides a riveting history from the point of view of these celebrity women hysterics. The French medical community had long condemned hypnosis, which was associated with animal magnetism. But because of his reputation, Charcot's presentation of hypnosis from a neurological and hereditary understanding of hysteria gave hypnosis a new dignity, leading to public and professional fascination (Micale, 2008).

Freud lived in Paris between October 1885 and February 1886. He was impressed by everything about Charcot—his scientific achievements, lecturing, commanding presence, and cultural taste. Freud wrote, "Charcot, who is one of the greatest physicians, a genius and a sober man, simply uproots my views and intentions" (quoted in Gay, 1988, p. 49). Historians and biographers note Freud's metaphoric expression of his longing to be impregnated by Charcot: "Whether the seed will one day bring forth fruit, I do not know; but that no other human being has ever acted on me in this way I know for certain" (Gay, 1988, p. 49). Freud aggressively pursued him, finally hitting on the happy scheme of offering to translate Charcot's writings into German.

By 1885, Charcot's interests had shifted to hysteria, hypnosis, and psychological problems, with a concentration on traumatic paralysis.

Charcot focused on male hysteria, a subject of much medical interest (Micale, 2008). Working closely with Charcot's student, Pierre Marie, Freud deeply immersed himself in the study of male hysteria. Between 1886 and 1893, he translated into German more than 33 of Charcot's case histories of male hysteria. Until then, most of the medical community assumed that paralyses were brought about by spinal or brain lesions, although there was no evidence for this. At the Salpêtrière, there were both men and women who had been in accidents and had these symptoms. Charcot demonstrated that he could induce and remove these symptoms using hypnosis, reviving interest in hypnosis as a research tool.

Charcot believed hypnosis could only occur in those with a constitutionally hysterical disposition. If someone could be hypnotized, that proved they were hysterical. The tendency toward hypnoid states was an essential feature of the hysteric and explained why symptoms developed following a trauma. Hysterics were born with a hereditary degenerative constitution, leading them to be highly susceptible to altered states of consciousness. A traumatic event would cause a somnambulistic or dissociated state, enabling the development of an autosuggestion such as, "I'll never be able to walk," a thought that normally would pass because it is connected to many other thoughts, and thus becomes integrated into the mind. But in a dissociative state, the thought quite literally is disassociated, not connected to the stream of thoughts in the mind. It remains isolated in the mind of a patient who is highly susceptible to hypnotic suggestion. Through his use of hypnosis to demonstrate the psychological mechanism of hysterical paralyses, Charcot popularized the notion of an unconscious mind.

By the late 19th century, heredity was the most commonly accepted explanation for neuropathology. Sweeping across Europe was a growing fear of degeneration, a retreat backward in evolution, which was held responsible for a variety of ills, such as poverty, crime, alcoholism, perversion, and political violence. The fear that a degenerate class of people might attack social norms was used to provide a rationale for a strong state that would police degenerates out of existence with the assistance of scientific diagnostic identification. Jews were considered the quintessential example of degeneracy.

Charcot used the notion of the "neuropathic family," developed by his student Charles Fere, referring to disorders that could be traced to a common hereditary origin. When Freud challenged these ideas, Charcot instructed him to study the family of Israelites. Jews were considered the purest example of degeneracy; having married only other Jews for so many generations, they represented a pure sample for studying the influence of heredity. Freud accepted this for a while, writing to his fiancée Martha toward the end of his stay in Paris,

I have to acknowledge to a considerable "neuropathological taint," as it is called. Fortunately, of us seven brothers and sisters there are very few symptoms of this kind to report except that we, Rosa and I (I don't count Emanuel), have a nicely developed tendency toward neurasthenia. As a neurologist I am about as worried by such things as a sailor is by the sea. But you, my darling, must realize that it is your duty to keep your nerves in good condition if the three children, of whom you have been prematurely dreaming, are to be healthy . . . *These stories are very common in Jewish families.*

> (Freud, 1886, p. 210, emphasis added)

Most of the Jewish patients who consulted Charcot were poor and of Eastern European origin, seen in the outpatient clinic at the Salpêtrière, whose opening in 1881 coincided with the mass migration of Russian Jews to the West following the pogroms. Charcot identified one of these Jews as suffering from a distinctly Jewish disorder that he diagnosed in the hope that this new medical diagnosis would replace the label "Wandering Jew," an anti-Semitic slur that we examine in detail in Chapter 14. He diagnosed other Jewish patients with labels such as "wandering hysterical–neurasthenia." In 1889, Charcot examined a Hungarian named Klein who had wandered into Paris on foot, sick and limping, and came to the Salpêtrière for help, complaining of numbness in hand and foot. Charcot told his audience that the patient "is a Jew and has already revealed his pathological drives by his wanderings" (Gilman, 1993b, p. 406). Wandering and limping marked the hysterical Jew as diseased; its etiology was degeneracy brought about through generations of incestuous inbreeding. Charcot supervised a student's dissertation identifying Jewish hysterical feminized men as suffering *vagabondage*, the modern incarnation of the legendary Wandering Jew.[2] According to Charcot, Jews as a race had a high frequency of neuropathology, including the two conditions on which he was the world's leading authority: ataxia and hysteria. He said to the doubting Freud, "take a look (especially in Jewish families, the investigation is easy)" (quoted in Goetz, Bonduelle, and Gelfand, 1995, p. 261).

Freud's professional debut before the Viennese Society of Physicians took place in October. Freud had just opened his practice on Easter Sunday, a public holiday (Jones suggests it was a small sign of rebelliousness). He was newly married and had just completed the translation of Charcot's lectures. Freud (1925a) recalled the chilly reception he received from his Viennese colleagues, a version of events that has become psychoanalytic

---

2 Note Freud's (1920) comment in *Beyond the Pleasure Principle*, acknowledging that his argument is not straightforward, "What we cannot reach by flying we must reach by limping. The Book tells us it is no sin to limp" (p. 64).

lore. It has been generally understood that they objected to Freud's assertion that, based on Charcot's findings, hysteria could be found in men. But this story does not hold together. For one thing, the Viennese medical community did not have a hard time believing men could be hysteric. Most of them knew this quite well, although it was generally considered a rarity. Breger (2000) emphasizes that Freud was caught up in identifying with Charcot's power. Hoping for adulation from his colleagues, he was disappointed by their balanced and skeptical reception.

We think Ellenberger's (cited in Micale, 1993) explanation, that Freud was arguing for the specificity of traumatic hysteria, is more convincing, especially in light of Lerner's (2003) recent historical studies of traumatic hysteria and the pension wars. Charcot was not the first to recognize hysteria in men, and even he thought it was much more common in women. But Charcot found that hysteria in men was often brought about by industrial or railroad accidents, whereas in women it tended to be precipitated by emotionally troubling or stimulating events. What Freud was preaching of Charcot's teaching was more specific. He claimed there was a specific disorder of traumatic hysteria: dynamic paralysis, dynamic amnesia, or dynamic mutism, hysteria caused by some combination of physical and emotional shock to the nervous system that led to somatic symptoms. When the Viennese medical community challenged Freud to produce such a case, they were not generally skeptical about male hysteria, but rather wanted proof that trauma could elicit the somatic symptoms described by Charcot as traumatic hysteria or dynamic paralysis (Ellenberger cited in Micale, 1993). Some of the antagonism toward Freud was part of the nationalistic rivalry between French and German medicine, with Freud recklessly championing the French over his German-speaking teachers. But other serious aspects of this debate were in the background. As we have detailed in Chapter 5, in the late 1800s, many claims were brought about by railroad and industrial accidents, leading to lawsuits against the railroads and the state. Neurologists were often brought in as expert witnesses to testify on behalf of each side.

While the topic of trauma and how it led to neuropsychiatric disorders was highly controversial, and remained so for decades (it is still not well understood), German and Austrian neurologists were skeptical about traumatic hysteria; that is, they were not convinced that the neuroses resulting from trauma were best considered a form of hysteria. Many leaned toward the thinking of Hermann Oppenheim, who argued that trauma led to a specific traumatic neurosis rather than hysteria. There were significant implications to this difference in diagnostic thinking. For most neurologists, hysteria implied a pathological constitution due to degenerative family heredity, whereas Oppenheim's traumatic neurosis placed the cause directly on the trauma itself. If it were a railroad accident or war trauma, the railroad company or government would be responsible for pensions. The debate about the diagnosis of hysteria and traumatic neurosis was fueled by the financial and legal implications of compensation. Charcot showed that trauma played a role in bringing about neuroses, but by diagnosing these disorders as a form of hysteria, he explained them via heredity and degeneracy. It is no accident that Oppenheim, who was Jewish and faced a glass ceiling much like the one Freud faced in Vienna, leaned toward a theory emphasizing environmental factors as leading to these disorders in preference to a theory of degeneration.

The Fall of Charcot

By 1885, challenges were already being raised against Charcot's model of hysteria as well as his methods. Some witnesses of Charcot's performances were skeptical, publishing highly critical accounts of his practices (Ellenberger cited in Micale, 1993). Freud was so impressed with Charcot that he seems to have been oblivious to the strong element of conscious and unconscious suggestion, let alone deception, operating around him. As we will see, Freud always underestimated the role of suggestion operating in the clinical research setting. Charcot's reputation went quickly downhill, and after 1892, Freud's writings took a decisive turn away from him. Charcot was increasingly accused of charlatanism by the medical establishment, and became a subject of public ridicule and scandal. Many of the students who had been loyal to him when he was involved in neuroanatomical research abandoned him when he became involved in hysteria and hypnosis.

Nevertheless, Freud forever treasured his formative experience with the master (1893c). In August 1889, he acquired an engraving of Andre Brouillet's 1887 painting *La Lecon Clinique du Dr. Charcot*, which shows Charcot examining his favorite female hysteric, Blanche Wittman, her blouse loosely falling off her shoulder, as she exhibited the classic grand hysteria to his students and colleagues (see Hustvedt, 2011). Freud hung it in his consulting room where it remained throughout his life. He named his first son Jean Martin, known as Martin, after Charcot. (Freud named all his sons after famous non-Jews, and all his daughters after Jewish women, an example of managing his unconscious ambivalence about his Jewishness, but more on this later.)

Charcot also had to defend himself against Hippolyte Bernheim. In 1882, Bernheim visited the country doctor and hypnotist A. A. Liebault. He became a disciple and proselytizer of clinical hypnotism and the founder of the so-called Nancy school of hypnotism while he was the chair of ambulatory medicine at the department of medicine in Nancy. In 1884 Bernheim published a scathing attack on the Salpêtrière: hysteria and hypnosis were no more than cultural phenomena aroused by the power of suggestion.

Bernheim was a flexible and eclectic practitioner of psychotherapy, a term he himself popularized. Bernheim's theory was that hypnosis did not require a degenerative constitution—it didn't even require an altered state of consciousness. Hypnosis was simply the result of suggestion, and suggestion could affect anyone, since ideas were routinely passed from one mind to another.

Bernheim had become interested in hypnosis as a practical therapeutic tool but also because as a Jew he was concerned with a sensational murder case in which the son of a rabbi had testified that his father participated in the ritual murder of a Christian child, a famous case of "blood libel," an old staple of European anti-Semitism (Kerr, 1993). Bernheim concluded from his study of the trial records that the needed testimony had been suggested to the rabbi's son. It was on the basis of this experience that he inferred that the dramatic symptoms of Charcot's hysteric patients had been induced by suggestion. Bernheim claimed that of the thousands of hysterics he examined, only one passed through all three stages of hypnosis that Charcot claimed, and that patient had been at the Salpêtrière for three years (Ellenberger in Micale, 1993). Bernheim used Charcot and the Salpêtrière as a prime example of gullibility and suggestion, calling it a "culture of hysteria," and showing that Charcot's findings were imaginary rather than carefully proven, rational, and scientific (Makari, 2008, p. 31). We will return to Bernheim as we discuss his influence on Freud, but first will consider how Bernheim's challenge contributed to the fall of Charcot's reputation.

Charcot was a spellbinding lecturer, his presentations grand performances orchestrated for maximum effect. Known for his artistic skills and love of art, he was also known for his penetrating, silent stare as he visually examined patients, making diagnostic pronouncements based on a look. This visual examination of patients well matched his somatic focus. Charcot's case histories were dominated by visual descriptions rather than by emotions or verbalizations. Gilman (1993b) has contrasted Charcot's visual approach with Freud's verbal approach of listening to his patients talk. Charcot drew constantly while traveling, seeing patients, or smoking hashish (Hustvedt, 2011). Let's stop to consider Charcot's visual and atheoretical style in contrast to Freud's emphasis on listening to the patient's story. Notice the visual emphasis in Freud's reminiscences of Charcot:

> He was not unduly reflective, not a thinker: he had the nature of an artist—he was, as he himself said, a "visuel", a man who sees. Here is what he himself told us about his method of working. He used to look again and again at the things he did not understand, to deepen his impression of them day by day, till suddenly an understanding of them dawned on him. In his mind's eye . . . the eye could travel over the long series of ill-defined cases . . . He might be heard to say that the

greatest satisfaction a man could have was to see something new—that is, to recognize it as new; and he remarked again and again on the difficulty and value of this kind of "seeing".

(1893b, p. 12)

The relevance of this emphasis on the visual to our narrative is that Jews were not thought to look like non-Jews, nor were they thought to be able to see the world objectively. Freud was highly identified with the hysteric, for while the hysteric was typically female, at the close of the 19th century, the idea of *seeing* the hysteric, as per Charcot, was equivalent to *seeing* the Jew, the male, circumcised, effeminate Jew. As Gilman (1993b) makes clear, "the face of the Jew became the face of the hysteric" (p. 405). The dilemma for the Jewish doctor was: How do you see the other objectively and scientifically when you yourself have Jewish hysterical eyes? How does this Jew, Freud, see himself—as the doctor identified with Charcot, or as the Jew, deformed, wandering, circumcised, feminized, hysteric, diseased, degenerate?

The opposition of visual to verbal overlaps with the many other binaries we discuss, including speaking/writing, male/female, non-Jew/Jew, and psychotherapy/psychoanalysis. Jews have long been thought of as focused on the written word, not visual images, which violate the commandment against graven images. Scholars have commonly characterized Jewish thought as essentially auditory and verbal, nonvisual, aniconic in its orientation, especially in contrast with the visual Greeks. For the Greeks, God manifested visually, in direct immediate experience; for Jews, God spoke through words in a divine text. Greek truth was visual, Jewish truth was auditory; binaries line up as Greek/Jew, visual/auditory, direct and immediate/delayed and interpreted. Even though modern historical scholarship has demonstrated the overwhelmingly visual nature of religious experience in Jewish spirituality—seeing, not just hearing God, particularly in Jewish mysticism (Wolfson, 1994), Jewish experience has been pervasively characterized as auditory, and so the visual/auditory dichotomy has been culturally at play.

In keeping with his visual bent, Charcot made extensive use of medical photography, a new technological advance. He created a photographic laboratory at the Salpêtrière, in which patients were photographed with a concentration on their face and eyes—he gazed at their gaze. These photographs, which were published regularly in the house periodical, the *Nouvelle Iconographie de la Salpêtrière*, capture the various stages of hysterical fit, with patients undisguised, some naked and in highly sexualized poses. They were in fact poses, as a patient had to hold still for 20 minutes to obtain a clear photograph. Charcot argued that the photographer could capture a precise moment in which one could observe facial expressions, grimaces, or stares. This would serve as an objective record that could be examined; thus photography fit perfectly with an objectivist model of science in which the facts could be captured and recorded and observed by independent outside observers. The methodology of photography highlighted the patient as object and the doctor as objective observer. Charcot's patients at the Salpêtrière were lower class, and were not treated with the respect given his afternoon private patients. Charcot rarely spoke to them, except to fire rapid questions calling for short answers. These patients were specimens used for scientific investigation and dramatic public presentations. Very little is conveyed about them as people, except for their physical features and details of their heredity. For Charcot, the cause of the neurosis was not the traumatic event, but the patient's degenerative heredity.

Pierre Janet examined Charcot's legacy, documenting his teacher's methodological mistakes. Charcot chose model types on which to base his theories. Focusing on patients who had all the symptoms associated with a particular diagnosis, he regarded other patients as having incomplete or less pure manifestations of the disorder. He disregarded his patients' backgrounds, social circumstances, and life conditions, and only saw them during his lectures and exams. By the 1880s, he no longer made rounds and did not speak with them much. Without Charcot's knowledge, his students prepared the patients, examining them repeatedly in preparation for the performance, and hypnotizing them repeatedly, teaching them exactly what was expected. In other words, Janet's findings were all in accordance with what Bernheim had claimed.

Many of the hysterical women were young, attractive, and eager to become star celebrity patients, while Charcot was authoritarian and paternalistic. The Salpêtrière was pervaded by an atmosphere of sexuality. Patients were examined partially undressed and stimulated genitally in public. (We discuss the practice of genital stimulation in the treatment of hysteria in more detail in the next chapter.) Love affairs were common between patients and staff, seemingly not regarded as unethical at the time (Hustvedt, 2011). Some of these women were examined over and over again, in front of doctors and before the public. The staff never contradicted Charcot, who discussed the cases directly in front of the patients themselves. A veritable hothouse of suggestion was created. In the years after Charcot's death, another favorite student, Joseph Babinski, following Bernheim, declared that hysteria was nothing but the result of suggestion and could be cured by persuasion (Ellenberger in Micale, 1993).

Suspicion was raised that Charcot's patients were colluding with him to heighten the dramatic effect of the presentation. Patients were often used to help the doctors transcribe Charcot's notes, and so knew exactly what Charcot expected. Photographs and charts describing in detail the stages of hysterical attack were on display on the walls of the hospital (Gilman, 1993b). Patients knew exactly the sequence of hysterical fit that was expected of them. Charcot's fame and reputation sharply declined toward the end of his life and after his death. His earlier neuroanatomic work retained its standing, but his work on hysteria, hypnosis, somnambulism, amnesia, automatisms, and dissociation was exposed as chicanery. Facing heated criticism from around the world, Charcot retreated from hypnosis, objecting to the sensationalism surrounding the subject, and warning of the dangers to patients and physicians, but it was too late (Goetz, Bonduelle, and Gelfand, 1995). Within a few years of his death, no one took Charcot's psychological research seriously. Breger (2000) summarizes Charcot's genuine contributions, which were considerable. He made the study of hysteria and hypnosis respectable, described and classified syndromes on the basis of symptoms, differentiating neurotic conditions from neurological disorders; documented the existence of male hysteria; disproved the old links between hysteria and the female genital organs; and most importantly, demonstrated the existence of the unconscious mind.

Bernheim's Proto-Relational Theory versus Freud's Theory of Autonomy

We view Bernheim not only as an underappreciated pioneer of psychotherapy, but also as a proto-relationalist in the pre-history of psychoanalysis, espousing a relational point of view against which Freud reacted. Bernheim's theory was that minds were an open system always in interaction with other minds. As Makari (2008) put it, for Bernheim, "The mind's windows were open, taking in commands, suggestions, and ideas from others and then mistaking foreign notions for their own" (p. 30). There was nothing pathological about hypnosis. Minds were always being influenced by other minds; what we think of as our own ideas have regularly been taken in from other minds. For Bernheim, people did not operate rationally; rather the world was dominated by irrationality, credulity, and suggestion. Irrational belief was not unusual, nor did it require altered states of consciousness or hereditary pathology; it was part of normal psychological life. Freud visited Nancy to study with Bernheim in 1889 and translated Bernheim's works into German. As he had also done when translating Charcot's work, Freud included in his translator's commentary his own dissenting point of view, challenging key elements of the text.

During these years, in avant-garde European psychiatry, psychological causation was beginning to displace somatic explanations, including the focus on lesions of the central nervous system. Freud waged an all-out campaign against the commonly accepted belief that hysteria and other nervous disorders were a result of degeneration. By 1896, in his article on hysteria and heredity, in which Freud first used the term "psycho-analysis," he developed a full-blown argument against degeneration theory. Freud did not disregard heredity completely, but made it only one factor among many in the etiology of neurosis. He did away with the notion of nervous pathology passed on through the generations, a notion that had most often been applied to Jewish families. Instead, he began to emphasize sexuality and moved increasingly toward a psychological view of trauma and neurosis.

Makari (2008) convincingly shows that Bernhem's theory challenged not only Charcot's work on hysteria and hypnosis, but represented a challenge to all scientific psychology, because if suggestion was that pervasive and universal then there could be no uninfluenced subject or observer. If minds were intertwined, existing in relation to one another, than there were no clear distinctions between observer and observed, scientist and hysteric. Subject and object could not be clearly distinguished. In other words, even in the pre-history of psychoanalysis, a relational ontology was accompanied by an epistemological challenge to objectivist science! Freud knew Bernheim's challenge had to be answered, especially since he had been building his reputation as Charcot's disciple in Vienna. Freud defended Charcot, asserting that hypnosis was a legitimate subject for scientific examination. But Freud was fighting a losing battle: Bernheim's challenge provoked a great deal of research that supported the finding that anyone could be hypnotized, overthrowing Charcot's descriptions of grand hysteria. Hypnosis was neither a sign of hysteria, nor was it pathological or tied to degeneration.

What did Freud actually learn from his visit to Bernheim in 1889? Freud (1925a) wrote that it taught him the limitations of hypnotic suggestion. The visit to Nancy was pivotal for Freud, because he clearly got the idea from Bernheim, although Bernheim had not yet articulated it in this way—that he could do psychotherapy, which was at the time synonymous with hypnotherapy—without inducing formal hypnosis. A number of things point in this direction. Freud had brought a patient of his (Anna von Lieben) with him to Nancy for Bernheim to hypnotize. Bernheim failed to hypnotize her, telling Freud he had poor results with people in the higher and wealthier classes; hypnosis was easier to induce in people accustomed to passive obedience. The working class and peasantry tended to be in far greater awe of physicians and educated people generally. Liebault, from whom Bernheim had learned hypnotism, was a country doctor whose patients were poor city people and local peasants who paid only what they could afford or nothing at all. Freud was by then in private practice, his clientele predominantly from the upper and upper-middle classes. Freud had to modify his approach to make it useful with these patients. On his visit to Nancy, Freud was impressed with Bernheim's contention that post-hypnotic amnesia, the sine qua non of somnambulism, was not complete; that with concentration, the pressure technique, and skillful questioning, the patient could remember what had occurred even while hypnotized. It struck Freud that one could access the unconscious directly through consciousness, without bypassing consciousness through hypnosis.

Bernheim's theory that hypnotism was nothing more than suggestion eliminated the need to formally induce a hypnotic trance. If hypnosis was not a special altered state, just the product of suggestion, the possibility was opened to use suggestion directly. This was the direction Bernheim ultimately took, making less and less use of hypnosis. By 1892, Bernheim suggested the word hypnosis be dropped in favor of the term "state of suggestion." Years later, Bernheim wrote, "modern psychotherapy, emancipated from hypnotism, is the creation of the Nancy school" (quoted in Ellenberger, 1970, pp. 804–805).

By the time of Bernheim's (1892) next book, which Freud translated (Ellenberger, 1970), Bernheim maintained that therapeutic success was not directly related to the depth of hypnotic sleep. Most subjects remained partially conscious during hypnosis, and most hypnotic phenomena were obtainable with the subject awake. In a lecture of April 27, 1892 to the Viennese Medical Club, Freud espoused Bernheim's view of hypnotism, advising physicians to go to Nancy to learn it (Ellenberger, 1970). As late as 1893, in his paper on clinical hypnotism, Freud (1892–1893) used Bernheim's method rather than catharsis. By pointing out the lack of correlation between hypnotic depth and effectiveness of suggestion, Bernheim made possible the more direct application of verbal psychotherapy in the waking state. By explaining hypnotism in terms of suggestion, Bernheim inadvertently brought the focus of attention onto suggestion itself, a psychological and interpersonal phenomenon. In his preface to the translation of Bernheim's (1892) first book, entitled *Suggestion*, Freud (1888b) offered a penetrating critique of the idea of suggestion. At the end of 1892, when he treated Lucy, and still in 1893, when he wrote the case history, Freud moved back and forth between his use of direct suggestion to eliminate symptoms following Bernheim, his remaining loyalties to Charcot (who died in 1893), and his own development of Breuer's cathartic method.

Having begun with a strong neurological and somatic approach to hysteria and hypnosis, Freud began using hypnotism cautiously, along with the standard and more acceptable treatments of the day. He soon felt increasingly frustrated with these methods—and bored by them as well—since they did not shed any light on the origins or meanings of hysterical symptoms. While it was under Charcot's influence that Freud became seriously interested in the phenomenon of hypnosis and the descriptive diagnosis of hysteria, it was under Bernheim's influence that he began to think psychologically about the dynamics of hypnotism. Once Freud was able to see that hypnosis was largely a psychological phenomenon, he was able to move beyond the induction of a formal trance. Freud was mostly interested in investigating the psychological origins of his patients' symptoms—their memories. Breuer had been lucky in his work with Bertha Pappenheim. As Hirschmuller (1978) emphasizes, it was only after she spontaneously went into trances by herself that Breuer began to induce hypnosis in her. Freud went to Bernheim with the goal of learning how to deepen his patients' trance states so they would talk to him, enabling him to investigate the origins of their symptoms, and eliminate the symptoms through suggestion. Instead, Freud learned that he could accomplish this by having his patients talk with him directly while they were awake.

Freud was one of a number of leading hypnotherapists who were attempting to develop methods of psychotherapy that did not rely upon formal hypnotic induction (Aron, 1996b). Bernheim, by showing that hypnotism was a psychological phenomenon—namely, that it was a form of interpersonal suggestion—created the possibility for the shift from hypnotic suggestion to verbal psychotherapy in the waking state. Bernheim showed that the distinction between states of consciousness was not absolute, and that through an act of will, patients could recall what happened in hypnotic amnesia. But in demonstrating the ubiquity of suggestion, rooted in the connections among minds, Bernheim was also creating the problem that would forever haunt Freud and psycho-analysis: the impossibility of clearly distinguishing one's ideas from another's—the epistemological problem of intersubjectivity. Having been a supporter of Dreyfus, Bernheim attracted considerable anti-Semitic hostility in Nancy and in his final years, he retired to Paris, where he died in 1919.

It is worth considering that as a Jew, Bernheim was drawing on the traditional Jewish view that people are always and inevitably a part of their community, and that individuals could not be understood in isolation from others. The title of the classic work of cultural anthropology examining the Eastern European Jewish shtetl reflects this prevailing ethos: *Life is with People* (Zborowski and Herzog, 1952). In contrast, Freud was impelled to reject this traditional "primitive" and proto-relational view, in favor of the Western, more "civilized" view, that the mature man is an individual, bounded, autonomous agent. After 1888, Freud distanced himself from Charcot, but could not accept Bernheim's claim that suggestion was ubiquitous. Freud had been indoctrinated in the Enlightenment. To accept Bernheim's contention that we are all subject to suggestion was to accept the dominance of irrationality and deny the distinctiveness of indi-viduals. From Freud's perspective, Bernheim's relational description of mind was an accurate description of primitivity, porousness, vulnerability, and lack of boundedness. If minds exist only in relation to other minds, then minds are not autonomous. Freud raised the question against Bernheim: how does suggestion work? How are ideas transplanted from one person into another? Charcot had at least provided some explanation for suggestion. If Charcot's laws were incorrect, what was Bernheim's explanation?

Of course, Freud's challenge to Bernheim only makes sense if one accepts Freud's premise that minds are autonomous entities, and so we need to explain how one mind affects another. But if we begin with the assumption, as Bernheim did, that minds are linked as part of a system, then the fact that minds influence one another is a starting assumption, rather than something that needs explanation. Freud's response affected the entire future of psychoanalysis. Freud began with the starting assumption that minds were isolated, and so suggestion needed explanation. His explanation was that only internal intrapsychic conditions would leave one person susceptible to the influence of another. Freud contended that we should not think of hypnosis as an interpersonal phenomenon occurring between two people, but rather we should examine the intrapsychic conditions in the mind of the subject being hypnotized. For Freud, suggestion only works between people because of autosuggestion. In other words, Freud never accepted interpersonal explanations but always reduced the interpersonal to the intrapsychic. Makari (2008) writes, "This critical strategy allowed Freud to reduce the overwhelmingly complex problems of how two minds interacted, and limit his exploration to the workings of one mind, the patient's" (p. 33). This is the strategy that would dominate psychoanalysis for decades to come. All interpersonal or social phenomena were reduced to understanding the intrapsychic dynamics of one person.

Freud's theory followed Charcot's explanation of dynamic paralysis. Hypnotic suggestions work only because there are prior internal "self-suggestions" in the mind of the subject. Some internal dissociated idea set the stage for a suggestion to take hold. By shifting the site of action from the interpersonal to the intrapsychic, Freud bypassed Bernheim's challenge that all of psychology was contaminated by interpersonal influence. The mind could be studied scientifically because the object being studied was in the mind of one person and so could be studied by an objective other. This was in opposition to Bernheim's view, that what needed to be studied was interpersonal, between the hypnotist and the hypnotized, and therefore the observing doctor could not study it with objectivity. In this deft move, Freud solidified psychoanalysis as the study of the internal workings of the individual mind, eliminating concern about suggestion and the doctor's influence. With this tactic, Freud could join Bernheim in saying that hypnosis and hysteria did not depend on degeneration and thus was not a particularly Jewish defect, while at the same time joining Charcot in believing that hypnosis and hysteria could be studied objectively and scientifically. Freud could side both with Charcot, the highly cultured French master, champion of individuality, autonomy, and rationality, and with Bernheim, the outsider, subjective and irrational Jew, who argued for a community of interconnected minds. It was not the last time that Freud would position himself "between two worlds" (*tsvishn tsvey veltn*).

Suggestion and the Psychoanalysis/
Psychotherapy Binary

Freud rejected Bernheim's ideas about the interrelatedness of minds, insisting that suggestion was not a constant phenomenon but rather a special occurrence that needed explanation in terms of the intrapsychic mind. Soon he provided that explanation in terms of transference. Transference led one person to allow another that kind of penetrating influence. Ferenczi's (1909) paper "Introjection and transference" spelled out Freud's idea that transference was the basis for suggestion, and that analysis of transference would eliminate it as a problem. If suggestion only happened under special circumstances, by eliminating those circumstances, one could retain the objective methodology of a psychological science. But in reducing the role of suggestion to special situations, Freud took a position that was not only clinically problematic, but also ultimately led to the splitting of psychoanalysis from psychotherapy. Psychoanalysis *eliminated* suggestion through *analysis* of the transference, while psychotherapy *used* the transference and so was *based* on suggestion. By viewing suggestion as a discrete occurrence rather than an ongoing process, Freud could allow himself to imagine that it did not contaminate his scientific and objective results. This required a massive self-deception on Freud's part. Early in his work, Freud wrote,

> We learn with astonishment from this that we are not in a position to force anything on the patient about the things of which he is ostensibly ignorant or to influence the products of the analysis by arousing an expectation. *I have never once succeeded, by foretelling something, in altering or falsifying the reproduction of memories or the connection of events*; for if I had, it would inevitably have been betrayed in the end by some contradiction in the material. If something turned out as I had foretold, it was invariably proved by a great number of unimpeachable reminiscences that I had done no more than guess right. We need not be afraid, therefore, of telling the patient what we think his next connection of thought is going to be. It will do no harm.
>
> (1893b, p. 295, emphasis added)

With this background, we can better understand the horror of Freud's reaction when, toward the end of his relationship with his closest friend and collaborator, Wilhelm Fliess, the person who had been his muse and quasi-analyst in writing the *Interpretation of Dreams* and *The Psychopathology of Everyday Life*, confronted Freud with the accusation that his findings were contaminated by his own subjectivity. Freud (1901) wrote in response: "You take sides against me and tell me that 'the reader of thoughts merely reads his own thoughts into other people,' which renders all my efforts valueless" (p. 447). The implication was stark. If suggestion was used, then his findings were scientifically worthless. Freud had to convince himself that he and his fellow psychoanalysts eliminated their subjectivity from the analytic method. Continuing in this vein toward the end of his life, Freud wrote,

> The danger of our leading a patient astray by suggestion, by persuading him to accept things which we ourselves believe but which he ought not to, has certainly been enormously exaggerated. An analyst would have had to behave very incorrectly before such a misfortune could overtake him; above all, he would have to blame himself with not allowing his patients to have their say. I can assert without boasting that such an abuse of "suggestion" has never occurred in my practice.
>
> (1937b, p. 262)

Levy and Inderbitzin (2000), writing in support of what they themselves consider the conservative and classical psychoanalytic position, assert that suggestion has historically been disavowed by analysts and brought to our attention by the relational and intersubjective turn.

> To mitigate its influence, Freud assembled an arsenal of technical devices, including that familiar trio of analytic restraint: abstinence, anonymity, and neutrality. These were to be wielded by a surgically dispassionate, opaquely reflecting objective scientist conducting research on . . . "the patient as cadaver."
>
> (2000, pp. 739–740)

They recognize that no matter how conservatively an analyst practices, suggestion is ubiquitous. "In the sphere of therapeutics aimed at expanding a person's humanness, the irrational persuasion of a personal relation is never absent, even in the austere objectivity some see as the ideal of psychoanalysis" (p. 742). We agree with Levy and Inderbitzin that this remains the central issue that has kept analysts insisting on the opposition between psychoanalysis and psychotherapy, and consequently devaluing the latter.

> The idea that suggestion plays a larger role in dynamic psychotherapy than in psychoanalysis has persisted, and its negative connotation has in some circles diminished the status of psychotherapy, especially as compared to the objective, interpretive purity presumed for psychoanalysis.
>
> (Levy and Inderbitzin, 2000, p. 744)

Psychoanalysis was thought to be pure gold, of greater value, precisely because it eliminated suggestion through the analysis of transference, and thus could maintain the illusion that it isolated the patient's intrapsychic life for scientific examination and analysis. Psychotherapy was devalued as contaminated by suggestion and therefore could only result in social or interpersonal adjustment.

We have now responded to both of Stephen Mitchell's questions. Suggestion was taboo because it interfered with what the analyst could know as objective truth. Suggestion interfered with what the patient needs, because their cure was only as good as the current state of their therapeutic relationship and could easily be lost with the eruption of negativity. In other words, they remained dependent on the therapist. In our view, and in agreement with Levy and Inderbitzin, suggestion is ubiquitous in both psychotherapy and psychoanalysis. It is not a basis for defining one against the other. All psychotherapy relies on interpersonal influence. More importantly, rational influence cannot be so easily distinguished from irrational suggestion.

The Individual and the Group

This brings us to the final section of this chapter, as well as to a central argument of this book. We have been examining polarities, here the dichotomy between interpretation and suggestion, which equates to truth or falsehood, stability and instability, objectivity versus subjectivity, gentile and Jew, male and female. We also claim that it maps onto white and black skins, through one of Freud's major tropes, the dichotomy of civilized versus primitive. Freud (1921) begins *Group Psychology* by deconstructing one of his most significant binaries, the individual and the group.

> The contrast between individual psychology and social or group psychology . . . loses a great deal of its sharpness when it is examined more closely. It is true that individual psychology is concerned with the individual man and explores the paths by which he seeks to find satisfaction for his instinctual impulses; but only rarely and under certain exceptional conditions is individual psychology in a position to disregard the relations of this individual to others. In the individual's mental life someone else is invariably involved, as a model, as an object, as a helper, as an opponent; and so from the very first individual psychology, in this extended but entirely justifiable sense of the words, is at the same time social psychology as well.
>
> (1921, p. 69)

There are several features of this passage worth noting. It is often rightfully cited to show that Freud did not ignore the social realm and recognized the social context of life. Freud was well aware that the individual must be studied in relation to the social surround. As he demonstrated throughout his essay, the individual is strongly affected by group processes. Nevertheless, while Freud argues that individual psychology is social psychology from the start, it is also clear that he begins with the premise of a bounded individual. The social, for Freud, is context, outside of the individual, and the individual remains clearly distinct. This is relevant in light of what we have seen as Freud's response to Bernheim, who believed that minds are interconnected and in ongoing unconscious communication with other minds. That is the essence of the relational position—minds exist, always and already, in relation to other minds. Freud rejects this position.

It is not accidental that Freud refers to individual psychology beginning with a study of the person's fulfillment of instinctual impulses. The drives are what mark the individual as an organism striving for the satisfaction of need. Drive theory and the view of the person as a bounded individual go hand in hand, which is why relational theory has always begun its arguments with a critique of drive theory. From a relational perspective, adding on the realm of the social as the context in which individual drives are gratified does not change the essential nature of the theory into a field theory. Relational theory, like Bernheim, begins with an assumption of minds in relation to other minds.

Freud's discussion of the individual and the group is extremely subtle and sophisticated and cannot be fully reviewed here. But one example of his open-mindedness is apparent when he says:

> As regards intellectual work it remains a fact, indeed, that great decisions in the realm of thought and momentous discoveries and solutions of problems are only possible to an individual working in solitude. But even the group mind is capable of creative genius in the field of intelligence, as is shown above all by language itself, as well as by folksong, folklore and the like. It remains an open question, moreover, how much the individual thinker or writer owes to the stimulation of the group in which he lives, and whether he does more than perfect a mental work in which the others have had a simultaneous share.
>
> (1921, p. 83)

For our purposes, it is important to note that in *Group Psychology*, Freud returns to reconsider the nature of suggestion. No sooner does he raise the problem of suggestion than he associates to memories of Bernheim. We hope this context will provide new meaning to Freud's text:

> We shall therefore be prepared for the statement that suggestion (or more correctly suggestibility) is actually an irreducible, primitive phenomenon, a fundamental fact in the mental life of man. Such, too, was the opinion of Bernheim, of whose astonishing arts I was a witness in the year 1889. But I can remember even then feeling a muffled

hostility to this tyranny of suggestion. When a patient who showed himself unamenable was met with the shout: "What are you doing? Vous vous contre-suggestionnez", I said to myself that this was an evident injustice and an act of violence. For the man certainly had a right to counter-suggestions if people were trying to subdue him with suggestions. Later on my resistance took the direction of protesting against the view that suggestion, which explained everything, was itself to be exempt from explanation.

(1921, p. 89)

This remarkable passage reveals much more than Freud's personal resistance to the idea of being influenced by others. We know that Freud was reluctant to be too influenced by others, preferring to work on ideas in isolation, discussing them only after he had formulated them. He was exceptionally sensitive to issues of priority in giving or receiving credit for an idea. Freud valued individual autonomy over communal group immersion. Freud clarifies his objection to Bernheim: If hypnosis is explained by suggestion, then what explains suggestion? If we could answer for Bernheim, from the relational perspective, if one begins with the starting assumption not of individual autonomy, but that minds exist in relation, then suggestibility does not need explanation in the way Freud expects. Suggestion is the way minds work from the beginning of life to the end. We are influenced. Our communal nature is not added on later as a superficial surface layer, it is life.

Since Freud (1921) begins with individual autonomy, he needs to explain suggestion.

First, that a group is clearly held together by a power of some kind: and to what power could this feat be better ascribed than to Eros, which holds together everything in the world? Secondly, that if an individual gives up his distinctiveness in a group and lets its other members influence him by suggestion, it gives one the impression that he does it because he feels the need of being in harmony with them rather than in opposition to them—so that perhaps after all he does it "ihnen zu Liebe" (for love of them).

(1921, p. 92)

When Stephen Mitchell was asked to explain the "motivation," the force that drives people into relationships, he would say, we don't ask the bees what motivation holds them together in a group; that is just what it means to be a bee. We don't look for a drive that explains why spiders weave a web; that is just what spiders do. We don't seek oxygen because we have a drive to seek it; breathing is just the way we are built. Mitchell did not need to explain the force of attraction to relations because he began with a different assumption, namely that people are interconnected from the start, we are designed to be relational, or as Sullivan (1964) put it, individuality is mythic. Freud gives theoretical preference to the individual's drives. Since the drives are the foundation, the individual is given status above the social, even in an essay that begins by saying it is essential to study both. Mitchell (1997) wrote, "Personal autonomy is not something that antedates interaction with others, but an emergent property of interactive processes, not something that can be sheltered from influence, but something that grows *through* influence" (p. 21). Notice the immediate connection between the relational view that people are built to interpenetrate each other and the shift in the meaning of influence. Influence shifts from interfering with autonomy to being essential to its development.

Freud's monadic view of mind, a "one-person psychology," has dominated Western culture for hundreds of years and is taken for granted. Only recently has it been questioned. Mitchell wrote,

> To argue that we need a concept of drive to describe what the individual seeks in interactions with other people presumes that the individual qua individual is the most appropriate unit of study. It assumes that the individual, in his or her natural state, is essentially alone, and then is drawn into interaction for some purpose or need. I believe that Fairbairn, like Sullivan (1953) was struggling toward a different way of understanding the nature of human beings, as fundamentally social, not as drawn into interaction, but as embedded in an interactive matrix with others as his or her natural state.
>
> (2000a, p. 105)

What drive explained for Freud was for Mitchell fundamental ground. Mitchell is not alone. Intersubjectivity is based on the idea that subjectivity arises from intersubjectivity rather than only the other way around. In our view, there is a great deal of common ground between Mitchell's perspective and that of Stolorow and colleagues. The intersubjective view considers the field created by the mutual influence of each person on the other as the perspective of greater significance, superseding an intrapsychic preservation of the "myth of an isolated mind" (Stolorow and Atwood, 1992). But Freud maintained the Cartesian view, in which he conceptualized the human being first and foremost as an individual organism—even when he paid exquisite attention to the environmental context.

Freud explores ambivalence in couples and groups, addressing what he will call "the narcissism of minor differences" when he writes *Civilization and its Discontents*. It's a concept of critical importance in professional relations, one that all analysts should keep in mind when thinking about or working with members of other schools of thought.

Every time two families become connected by a marriage, each of them thinks itself superior to or of better birth than the other. Of two neighbouring towns each is the other's most jealous rival; every little canton looks down upon the others with contempt. Closely related races keep one another at arm's length; the South German cannot endure the North German, the Englishman casts every kind of aspersion upon the Scot, the Spaniard despises the Portuguese. We are no longer astonished that greater differences should lead to an almost insuperable repugnance, such as the Gallic people feel for the German, the Aryan for the Semite, and the white races for the coloured.

(Freud, 1921, p. 101)

Note Freud's associations to race, which will be extremely important in our analysis. He writes,

So long as a group formation persists or so far as it extends, individuals in the group behave as though they were uniform, tolerate the peculiarities of its other members, equate themselves with them, and have no feeling of aversion towards them.

(1921, p. 102)

Watch how Freud builds his argument. The group represents a threat to individuality, leading to merger, uniformity, and lack of differentiation. Linking the group to the paternal Oedipal family, Freud now explores the role of identification:

We already begin to divine that the mutual tie between members of a group is in the nature of an identification of this kind, based upon an important emotional common quality; and we may suspect that this common quality lies in the nature of the tie with the leader.

(1921, p. 108)

And from group cohesion through identification with the leader, Freud moves back to hypnosis, which he likens to being in love. "There is the same humble subjection, the same compliance, the same absence of criticism, towards the hypnotist as towards the loved object. There is the same sapping of the subject's own initiative" (p. 114).

Freud is describing why groups lead to regression, dissolution of boundaries, loss of individuality and autonomy, masochistic submission: all out of love for the leader, and ultimately out of the masochistic longing to be dominated, to surrender individuality. This, too, is what explains hypnosis and suggestion. Compare a person in Freud's 1921 description of the group to the hysteric or the hypnotized (or as we shall see, to women, children, Blacks, and Jews as viewed by anti-Semites in Vienna):

Some of its features—the weakness of intellectual ability, the lack of emotional restraint, the incapacity for moderation and delay, the inclination to exceed every limit in the expression of emotion and to work it off completely in the form of action—these and similar features . . . show an unmistakable picture of a regression of mental activity to an earlier stage such as we are not surprised to find *among savages or children* (p. 117, emphasis added) . . . The *uncanny* and coercive characteristics of group formations, which are shown in the phenomena of suggestion that accompany them, may therefore with justice be traced back to the fact of their origin from the primal horde. The leader of the group is still the dreaded primal father; *the group still wishes to be governed by unrestricted force; it has an extreme passion for authority; in Le Bon's phrase, it has a thirst for obedience.* The primal father is the group ideal, which governs the ego in the place of the ego ideal. Hypnosis has a good claim to being described as a group of two (p. 127, emphasis added).

We have followed Freud's text and quoted it purposefully to build up to a particular point. Suggestion, for Freud, is "primitive" because it is based on the dissolution of boundaries under the pressure of love and the drive to masochistically submit to the will of the other. Utilizing suggestion clinically is problematic for him precisely because it reinforces this loss of individuality and autonomy. Psychoanalysis had to be scientific and civilized. Onto psychotherapy was placed the copper of suggestion, feminine masochistic longings (in men, among the brothers) to surrender to the will of the primal father.

Our reading of *Group Psychology* has been guided by Celia Brickman's (2003) *Aboriginal Populations of the Mind*. Applying a postcolonial critique to psychoanalysis, Brickman reviews in astonishing detail the way in which Freud, following the anthropology of his time, wove the dichotomy primitive/civilized into the warp and woof of psychoanalytic theory. Although anthropologists have long abandoned the notion of the primitive, psychoanalysts following Freud continue to use the term, particularly in relation to the psychology and psychopathology of regression. Inasmuch as Freud found the primitive in everyone (drives, the unconscious, sexuality and aggression, masochistic longings, infantile desires, childhood beliefs), he universalized the primitive and thus freed it from approbation. The primitive was no longer "other," but all of us. But in pursuing that strategy, Freud also reinforced and perpetuated the alignment in theory of the primitive, the savage, the barbarian, the infantile, the other, the dark continent, the Black, the Eastern Jew, women.

As we shall explore in greater detail in the following chapters, Freud was identified with both sides of all these binaries. As a Jewish man who identified with German culture in fiercely anti-Semitic Austria, as a Western

Jew whose parents immigrated from the East, as a heterosexual man who struggled to conquer his homoerotic longings for Fliess and Jung, as a doctor who was also his first patient, as a universalist and humanist who was also a Jewish particularist, as White but not quite, "Freud's ambivalences became the contradictions of psychoanalysis" Brickman (2003, p. 170). If Freud was correct that it took a Godless Jew to invent psychoanalysis and if Jews have been particularly well suited to be psychoanalysts, it is because of their optimal marginality, their position of being both insider and outsider (Bergmann, 1995). The opposition of psychotherapy and psychoanalysis, of suggestion and interpretation, can only be understood by taking seriously the entire constellation of binaries including civilized/primitive, gentile/Jew, White/Black, male/female. These binaries are all mutually interconnected and interdefining. Gold and copper are not binary opposites. Their compound may be better viewed as a strengthening enhancement rather than as a limitation or unfortunate compromise.

Chapter 11

Women on the Couch

Genital Stimulation and the Birth of Psychoanalysis[1]

Our exploration of the controversy between Charcot and Bernheim and its impact on the development of Freud's early clinical thought led us to emphasize Freud's position as being situated between contrasting and irreconcilable poles. As we continue to examine the early pre-history of psychoanalysis, we repeatedly encounter a series of tensions and polarities with Freud positioned on the border, mediating the binaries of inside and outside, gentile and Jewish, phallic and castrated. In this chapter and those that follow, we will examine in detail the impact on psychoanalysis of Freud's strong identification as a Jew living within a viciously anti-Semitic milieu. We will show how the perception of Freud's Jewish body, as seen by himself as well as through the eyes of his larger cultural surround, reverberated within psychoanalytic theory. Following Dimen (2003), who has articulated the need for a conversation among psychoanalysis, social theory, and feminism in order to rethink our ideas about gender and sexuality, we emphasize an overall cultural history using these approaches. In this chapter, we will examine some of the material realities underlying the dualities masculine/feminine, active/passive, clitoral/vaginal, professional/personal, and doctor/patient. In the process, we uncover a wide range of related variables, including class, race, sexual orientation, and the inevitably associated varieties of classism, racism, anti-Semitism, homophobia, and misogyny. Warning: you might find some of this material shocking, but we do believe you will be stimulated.

Women on the Couch

Psychoanalysis began with Freud's interest in the study of hysteria. A truly revolutionary idea for its time, psychoanalysis was born of Freud's efforts to

---

1 This chapter was adapted from Starr, K.E. and Aron, L. (2011). Women on the couch: Genital stimulation and the birth of psychoanalysis. *Psychoanalytic Dialogues, 21,* 373–392.

explain and treat his patient's symptoms psychologically rather than somatically, as was the traditional medical practice of his day. Since the time of Hippocrates until the early 20th century, hysteria was linked with the pathology of female sexuality and reproduction. Medical intervention focused on the female genitals, which were massaged and electrically stimulated as well as shocked and surgically altered. While all these interventions are relevant to an understanding of the medical approach to hysteria—indeed they are "two sides of the same coin of the patriarchal, medical control of female sexuality" (Warren, 2004, p. 165)—in this chapter, we will focus only on genital stimulation via massage and electricity.

Genital stimulation was a standard practice in the treatment of hysteria, one of several procedures in the medical toolkit of women folk healers and midwives, and later, male physicians and/or their female assistants. What we mean by genital stimulation is the bringing of the female patient to orgasm through the stimulation of the genitals via manual massage, hydrotherapy, vibratory massage, or electrotherapy. Although its use in the treatment of hysteria is well documented in histories of sexuality, electrotherapy, and the history of women's orgasm and the electromechanical vibrator, it is rarely, if ever, mentioned in the major mainstream histories of medicine, psychiatry, or hysteria. It is not, to our knowledge, ever referenced in the history of psychoanalysis, despite its being integral to the context of medical knowledge in which Freud developed his psychoanalytic method.

Freud (1913b) made a point of specifically identifying hypnosis as the antecedent to the use of the couch in analysis. He wrote, "I hold to the plan of getting the patient to lie on a sofa while I sit behind him out of his sight. This arrangement . . . is the remnant of the hypnotic method out of which psycho-analysis was evolved" (p. 133). We contend that the Freudian analytic couch, with its reclining, usually female, patient, is an artifact not only of the practice of hypnosis, as Freud maintained, but also of massage and electrotherapy—that is, the general private practice neurology of Freud's day. Freud's emphasis on hypnosis masked his association with massage, electrotherapy, and the procedure of genital stimulation practiced by his medical colleagues. Freud was German by culture, Jewish by religion or ethnicity, and Austrian by nationality. Freud's position as both insider and outsider—male German scientist and Jew—and his desire that psychoanalysis be accepted as a universal, not a specifically Jewish, science, fueled his efforts to distance his psychoanalytic method not only from hypnotic suggestion, but also from the more prurient practices of his day. Although genital stimulation as a treatment for hysteria was implemented in Europe and North America by both Jewish and non-Jewish practitioners, in the region of Europe in which Freud lived and worked, it was a procedure that was closely associated with Jewish doctors and patients (Jones, 1955).

We are not claiming any direct knowledge that Freud himself practiced genital stimulation. However, we do know that Freud reported doing full body massage as he listened closely to his early patients, owned the best electrical equipment available, and claimed to practice all of the standard treatments of his day (Freud, 1925a), so he may very well have done so, and would certainly have been exposed to it in his years of training. We will show that Freud was knowledgeable about this practice and sought to distance himself and the psychoanalytic method as far away from it as possible. In making our arguments, we are drawing upon a distinguished body of existing historical research; however, our unique contribution as clinicians is to highlight important implications for clinical theory and practice. Specifically, we will demonstrate that the history of genital stimulation provides us with deeper insight into Freud's theoretical emphases on autonomy and individuality, abstinence and the renunciation of gratification, penis envy, clitoral versus vaginal orgasm, mature (genital) sexuality, and the "repudiation of femininity" as the "bedrock" of psychoanalysis. (Freud, 1937a, p. 252)

"Suffocation of the Mother" and Orgasm-by-Proxy

Early medical references to the practice of genital stimulation are quite explicit about the sexual nature of the symptoms and their treatment. Hysteria, derived from the Greek word for womb or uterus, was considered a symptom of woman's insatiable and dislocated sexual desire. Plato described the "wandering womb" as a lustful, angry, and suffocating animal, ravenous for release. Lacking sexual satisfaction, it was thought to pull up into the throat, causing the choking and shortness of breath associated with hysteria. Following Plato's formulation, later writers referred to hysteria as the "suffocation of the uterus" or the "suffocation of the mother" (Jorden, 1603). The ancient Greek physician Galen attributed hysteria to lack of sexual gratification, particularly in passionate women, believing the uterus became engorged with unexpended seed, in need of release through orgasm. Galen documented the treatment of a widow with hysteria by the rubbing of her genitals with ointment until she released a "quantity of thick seed" (cited in Warren, 2004, p. 172), which cured her of her symptoms. The term "Galen's Widow's Treatment" continued to be used as a euphemism for this procedure well into the 20th century.

Accounts of Galen's case history vary in their translation as to who actually did the prescribing and the rubbing—whether it was the widow applying the remedy to herself on the advice of a midwife, a midwife practicing a commonly known folk treatment of the day, a midwife instructed by Galen, or Galen, the male physician, implementing this procedure on his female patient (Warren, 2004). The ambiguity of the practitioner's identity is indicative of the societal discomfort with women's sexuality, the accompanying taboo against masturbation, and the power dynamics surrounding female desire and medical authority embodied by this treatment.

As Ehrenreich and English (1973) have documented, until the formal establishment of an exclusively male medical profession, women folk healers and midwives served as general practitioners to the masses, providing gynecological treatment and treatment for women with hysteria. At the church's behest, these women were rooted out and burned as witches (together with their hysterical patients) specifically because they practiced medicine. Ousted from her role as practitioner, the midwife was relegated to assistant to the male doctor. What had once been an exclusively female domain now required the intervention of the male physician, or, to avoid the condemnation of the church and the "shame of the physician's probing hand," his female assistant (Schleiner, 1995, p. 115).

Islamic physician Ibn Sina, or Avicenna, incorporated "Galen's widow's treatment" into his standard medical corpus. Later medical writers are careful to invoke Galen and Avicenna's authority. Here's an example from a Renaissance medical text:

> When these symptoms indicate, we think it necessary to ask a midwife to assist, so that she can massage the genitalia with one finger inside, using oil of lilies, musk root, crocus, or the like. And in this way the afflicted woman can be aroused to the paroxysm.[2] This kind of stimulation with the finger is recommended by Galen and Avicenna, among others, most especially for widows, those who live chaste lives, and female religious; it is less often recommended for very young women, public women, or married women, for whom it is a better remedy to engage in intercourse with their spouses.
>
> (Cited in Maines, 1999, p. 1)

It is important to note the desexualization, medicalization, and patriarchal medical authority inherently reflected in this prescription. The male physician distances himself from the female patient and from her sexual arousal, not to mention the possibility of his own sexual arousal—an issue not raised in any medical texts—through the introduction of the midwife as an assistant, while maintaining himself as the one in charge. The patient's resulting physical contractions are called a "paroxysm," a term

---

2 The word the author uses in the original is "paroxismo" (cited in Schleiner, 1995, p. 154), a Latin derivative of the Greek "παροξυσμός," or "paroxysm."

that simultaneously medicalizes and desexualizes female orgasm, and which continued to be used in medical descriptions of hysteria well into modernity. This term had a double use, further obscuring what was being done: it was used for both the symptom of hysteria—the attack or fit—and for the orgasmic release caused by the treatment.

Woman's desire and sexual satisfaction are erased. In fact, some medical authors instructed the physician to test the patient for sexual desire by titillating the clitoris first; if the physician detected any sign of pleasure in the patient, the treatment was abruptly stopped (Schleiner, 1995). One can only imagine how these women patients dealt with this paradoxical demand, which seems to have required an interesting reversal of what today we might think of as "faking it." The author restricts the treatment to a subset of unmarried women, while he prescribes married women intercourse with their husbands. Later, as the treatment is further mechanized and de-sexualized through the introduction of electricity, we read of married women regularly visiting spas or being brought by their husbands to physicians' offices for this treatment (Maines, 1999).

In order to guard against the inadvertent titillation of the lay reader, the practice of genital stimulation was often described in medical texts only in Latin; the texts were sold only to doctors and lawyers, and were not available to the public (Furst, 2008; Schleiner, 1995). Although medical practitioners went to great lengths to denude the procedure of its (to us) obvious sexual implications, they still drew moral criticism, often from their own competitors! Dr. Thomas Nichols, who owned a hydrotherapy establishment in New York City in the 1800s, castigated a fellow New York physician, a "mercenary and libidinous wretch" whose medical practice included "manipulations and anointings, managed in such a way as to stimulate the passions and produce a temporary excitement of the organs which his deluded victims mistake for a beneficial result." Nichols noted that this masturbatory cure was "extremely lucrative," attracting "thousands of women" in New York City alone. Nichols own water cure offerings included "local treatment best fitted to give tone to the whole region of the pelvis," including "frequent vaginal injections" and wet bandages "carefully and tightly applied" (cited in Sklar, 1974, np).

"Woman Exists for the Sake of the Womb"

By the 19th century, the euphemistic terminology for genital stimulation reflected the reflex theory of hysteria, which held that hysterical symptoms could result from irritations in any organ or body part. In women, who made up the vast majority of hysterical patients, the ovaries, uterus, or genitals were usually considered the source of the problem (Shorter, 1992). The perils of menstruation, as well as the precarious position of the morbidly mobile uterus, were considered responsible for women's propensity to nervous illness, at double the rate of men's. In 1870, Professor Hubbard of New Haven lectured his medical colleagues,

> The sympathies of the uterus with every other part of the female organism are so evident, and the sympathetic relations of all the organs of woman with the uterus are so numerous and complicated, so intimate and often so distant, yet pervading her entire being, that it would almost seem . . . "as if the Almighty, in creating the female sex, *had taken the uterus and built up a woman around it.*"
>
> (Holbrook, 1875, p. 15)

In combination with reflex theory, the proposed link between the uterus and every other part of the woman's body led to what Shorter (1992) calls a "busybody approach to the vulva" (p. 82) in the treatment of hysteria. These interventions all fell under the category of "local" treatments and ranged from the more benign to the downright sadistic. Genital stimulation via massage and electrotherapy was called "local massage" or "local friction," referring to the application of manual massage, hydro-massage, the mechanical vibrator, or electrical charge directly to the pelvic, genital, or rectal local region responsible for the hysterical reflex. Other, far less pleasant, "local" treatments included leeching, injections, electrical shocks, cauterization, clitoridectomies, and other gynecological surgeries.

Paradoxically, although medical stimulation to paroxysm—desexualized orgasm by proxy—was acceptable, autonomous masturbation was not. Although masturbation in both sexes was discouraged, considered unhealthy and immoral, there was an additional factor for discouraging masturbation in women that was not true for men. Namely, the entire concept of women's sexual satisfaction via the clitoris was intolerable because it had no connection with reproduction and made women seem too much like men—capable of autonomous sexual pleasure without penetration. Women who performed clitoral self-stimulation were considered as wanting to be like men.

Male discomfort with this active (and therefore, "masculine") aspect of female sexuality is evident in the centuries-long lacuna in documented medical information about the clitoris (Blackledge, 2004). Laqueur (1990) notes that while 19th century scientists were well aware of the anatomical role of the clitoris in orgasm, many medical writers claimed that most women *did not feel any sexual pleasure* during clitoral orgasm. Viewed through the lens of a male-centric medical model, women's sexuality was put in its place—in a passive position and dependent on men. Men, in defining their own masculinity—in order to feel themselves "real men"—believed women needed to be passively penetrated in order to achieve sexual satisfaction. Female sexual satisfaction, if it existed at all, was relegated to vaginal penetration via intercourse with a husband, with conception as its aim (Blackledge, 2004). A common prescription for the cure of hysteria was "women married happily and at a sufficiently early age becoming mothers" (cited in Kneeland and Warren, 2002, p. 31). Masturbation in both sexes was considered a moral evil, a source of the genital irritation responsible for hysteria; cauterization and genital surgeries were regularly practiced on children in order to prevent them from masturbating (for a review, see Bonomi, 2009). Immediately following his training with Charcot in 1886, Freud trained in pediatrics with Adolf Baginsky, a German professor of diseases of children, who was well known for identifying masturbation as a main cause of hysteria in both children and adults (Bonomi, 1998). Freud's understanding both of hysteria and of women's sexuality was situated squarely in the midst of this medical and cultural milieu.

"Playing with the Jew"

In late 19th century France, genital manipulation was commonly used both to elicit and stop hysterical fits, a practice Foucault called the "laying on of hands" with regard to Charcot's treatment of women hysterics (Micale, 2008). Although maintaining that hysteria was not exclusive to women, Charcot still retained the gynecological model, transposing it onto men! He applied testicular compression to his male hysterical patients, resulting in the paradoxically male version of "suffocation of the mother"—the sensation of something moving from the stomach toward the neck, creating a sense of suffocation. Not only did Charcot extend what was commonly viewed as the female illness of hysteria to men, but he also applied it in particular to Jewish men, who were considered feminine in the eyes of the larger anti-Semitic European culture, while Jewish women were considered masculine and hypersexual (Boyarin, 1997; Gilman, 1993a). In a perfect blending of anti-Semitic fantasy and pseudo-scientific anatomy, the circumcised penis of the male Jew was equated with the female clitoris; both were considered an inferior penis. In the German vernacular of Freud's day, female masturbation was called "playing with the Jew" (Gilman, 1993a).[3] As an acculturated

3 In response to an early draft of this material, a Viennese colleague, analyst Martin Engleberg commented, "I have to admit I had to check whether the clitoris is really being called 'Jud' in Viennese slang. It is—rather it was—really true but it is not really used anymore, but was used so—definitely in Freud times. Actually I remember, when I was a child, 'Jud' (Jew) would be called a cigarette which was not properly lit—probably referring to a circumcised, i.e. half-cut or so, penis. Then it was also used as an exclamation full of contempt for a shot with a soccer ball which was improperly (and girl-likely) carried out with the tip of the foot—and was therefore often weak and going into a completely wrong direction instead of 'manly' using the back of the foot thus making a very strong shot."

German Jew, well acquainted with his society's anti-Semitic insults, Freud was undoubtedly familiar with this felicitous phrase. In fact, as we shall explore in greater detail in the following chapter, in later developing his theory of castration anxiety, Freud specifically posited a connection between the hatred of Jews and feelings of superiority over women, with circumcision and castration at its root. In a footnote to the case of Little Hans, Freud wrote,

> The castration complex is the deepest unconscious root of anti-Semitism; for even in the nursery little boys hear that a Jew has something cut off his penis—a piece of his penis, they think—and this gives them a right to despise Jews. And there is no stronger unconscious root for the sense of superiority over women.
>
> (1909a, p. 36)

Charcot, who represented the cutting edge of the somatic treatment of hysteria, maintained that Jews had a strong predisposition to hysteria, a fact he attributed to their unwillingness to intermarry. In the medical literature of Freud's day, Jewish endogamous marriage was medicalized as "inbreeding," lending scientific authority to the anti-Semitic characterization of Jews as an incestuous, perverted, and degenerate race (Gilman, 1993b). In a Judaicized variation of the "suffocation of the mother" theme, French historian Leroy-Beaulieu, informed by Charcot's ideas, wrote in his (pro-Jewish) 1895 study of anti-Semitism,

> The Jew is the most nervous of men, perhaps because he is the most "cerebral," because he has lived most by his brain. All his vital sap seems to rise from his limbs, or his trunk, to his head. On the other hand, his overstrained nervous system is often apt, in the end, to become disordered or to collapse entirely.
>
> (1895, p. 168)

Again, we see the male Jew identified with the hysterical woman. Ironically, although Leroy-Beaulieu deplored anti-Semitism, he emphasized that, unlike the other anti-Semitic depictions of the Jew detailed in his study, the foregoing characterization was in fact true.

Western acculturated Jews, including Freud, internalized the surrounding culture's anti-Semitic perception of the Jew as nervous, feminine, depraved, and degenerate, and in turn, placed them squarely upon the Eastern European Jews, from whom they were careful to differentiate themselves (Gilman, 1993a, 1993b). Both the Jewish predisposition to nervous illness and the inherited taint of Jewish degeneracy were commonplaces of the scientific and medical discourse of Freud's time; Freud was particularly sensitive to the argument that hysteria was an inherited disease, because it contributed to this racialized anti-Semitic view (Gilman, 1993a, 1993b).

Freud trained with Charcot in Paris in 1886, an experience that made a lasting impression on him. Charcot, the most famous neurologist of his day, was noted for making valued contributions in the area of local vibratory and electrical treatments and to have owned the latest equipment, including portable vibrators, encouraging his students at the Salpêtrière to experiment with these devices (Didi-Huberman, 2003; Hastings and Snow, 1904). Freud was certainly exposed to these treatments during the time of his training. The standard textbook Freud relied upon for his electrotherapy practice contained explicit instructions on local stimulation of the genitals for the treatment of hysteria and other nervous disorders. In his *Autobiographical Study*, Freud (1925a) wrote, "My knowledge of electrotherapy was derived from W. Erb's text-book [1883], which provided detailed instructions for the treatment of all the symptoms of nervous diseases" (p. 16). Erb, a highly respected German neurologist and the leading electrotherapist of Freud's time, provided detailed instructions on electrical stimulation for the treatment of nervous diseases, noting "the majority of cases also require direct electrical treatment of the genitals" (p. 352). He attributed the nervous disorders in part to a "congenital neuropathic taint" (p. 292), identifying Jews and women as being particularly susceptible.

Such was the context in which Freud opened his neurological practice in Vienna on Easter Sunday 1886, soon after his return from his Paris training with Charcot. Unable to get a university medical appointment because he was a Jew, Freud, like most Jewish doctors faced with the anti-Semitic policies of the Viennese government and a medical establishment that specifically excluded Jews from its ranks, was forced to become a specialist in private practice, a far less prestigious occupation. In fact, because of this institutionalized anti-Semitism, most private practitioners were Jews; they became dermatologists, gynecologists, and neurologists, treating mostly Jewish patients (Killen, 2006). Freud specialized in the treatment of patients with neurological disorders and hysteria. He invested a significant amount of money, borrowed from his childhood friend Ernst Fleischl, to purchase the most up-to-date electrical equipment available for treatment of his almost exclusively Jewish female clientele (Gilman, 2010).[4]

---

4 We are indebted to Gilman's ground-breaking work on Freud and anti-Semitism and his documentation of Freud's use of electrical treatments. We are building on that body of work to consider the prevalence of genital stimulation, which has not been addressed by Gilman.

In addition to electrotherapy, Freud acknowledged employing the other commonly practiced somatic treatments of hysteria, including massage, hydrotherapy, and hypnosis. But he places far greater emphasis on his practice of hypnosis and rejection of hypnotic suggestion when discussing the events leading up to his development of the psychoanalytic method. The narrative history of psychoanalysis has traditionally followed Freud's emphasis, paying no particular attention to *what Freud was actually doing*. But if we keep in mind the context in which Freud was trained, and look closely at Freud's own writing, we realize that not only was he hypnotizing his female patients, he was also electrically stimulating them and giving them full body massages while listening intently to their every word. Freud (1893a) writes in his case study of Emmy von. N, "I shall massage her whole body twice a day" (p. 50), describing Emmy's agitation when "I had to look for the towels needed in massage" (p. 63). While we have no definitive proof that Freud used genital massage—no "smoking gun," so to speak—nevertheless we read, "I therefore asked her in hypnosis why she was so restless this morning . . . she informed me that she had been afraid that her period was going to start again and would again interfere with the massage" (p. 67).

"Thank you, Mr. Edison"

While genital stimulation as a treatment for hysteria was implemented in Europe and North America by both Jewish and non-Jewish practitioners, in Austria and Germany, Jews made up a disproportionately large percentage of the electrotherapists, and most of the illustrious figures in German neurology were Jews (Killen, 2006). There is no doubt that while Freud was massaging Emmy von N., many of his contemporaries, mostly Jewish gynecologists and neurologists, were performing genital stimulation on their female patients, made possible by the discovery of electricity and the invention of the electromechanical vibrator.

Although the salutary effects of vibration on hysteria were known long before the advent of electricity, the available technology was inefficient. Women with hysteria but no husband were often prescribed horseback riding or long and bumpy train and carriage rides, for their rhythmic and erotic benefits (Furst, 2008). Electricity sped the process along considerably. In *The Technology of Orgasm* (1999), historian Rachel Maines compellingly documents the widespread use of the mechanical vibrator in the treatment of hysterical women in the 19th and early 20th centuries. Based on Maines' book, the recent Broadway play, *In the Next Room (or the Vibrator Play)*, portrays 19th-century physicians using vibrators to bring women to orgasm in the treatment of hysteria (*Chicago Tribune*, 2009). Says Dr. Givings, the play's protagonist,

Thanks to the dawn of electricity—yes, thank you, Mr. Edison . . . I have a new instrument which I will use. It used to be that it would take me or it would take Annie—oh—hours—to produce a paroxysm in our patients and it demanded quite a lot of skill and patience . . . but thanks to this new electrical instrument we shall be done in a matter of minutes.[5]

(Ruhl, 2010)

Maines came upon this practice by accident, while researching needle-point in women's magazines, where she came across 1906 advertisements for vibrators, "strongly resembling the devices now sold to women as masturbation aids" (Maines, 1999, p. x). What is particularly interesting is that the sources upon which Maines draws include the same sources used by the more widely known medical histories. A detailed check of these primary sources confirms they indeed include genital stimulation; yet remarkably, this practice has been omitted, or at best, only briefly mentioned, by the better-known texts.

Mechanization made the tedious task of bringing a woman to orgasm less tiring and more efficient, and doctors' private practices far more lucra-tive. Female patients diagnosed with hysteria could return for treatment on a regular basis, be brought to "paroxysm," and leave, satisfied customers. Not having a vibrator in one's arsenal was bad for business. In 1906, physi-cian Samuel Wallian complained about the tedious practice of manual massage, which "consumes a painstaking hour to accomplish much less profound results than are easily effected by the *other* in a short five or ten minutes," the *other* being a mechanical vibrator (cited in Blackledge, 2004, p. 259). Many physicians had vibratory operating rooms like the one shown in Figure 11.1 (Hastings and Snow, 1904, Plate III).

The vibratory operating room shown in Figure 11.1 appears remarkably similar to a psychoanalyst's consulting room, replete with what seems to have been the precursor to the analytic couch. Reduction in battery size and electrification of the home led to the design of portable vibrators suitable for home use. "Aids That Every Woman Appreciates," ran an ad for vibrators, electric mixers, and butter churners in the Sears, Roebuck Catalog (Maines, 1999, pp. 19–20). One brand of vibrators was advertised as "the little home doctor" (Stein and Kim, 2009, p. 50), selling the appliance along, perhaps, with the masturbation fantasy. In the early 1900s these vibrators were not explicitly linked with sex or masturbation. It was only in the 1920s, when they appeared in pornographic films, that the

5 We are indebted to playwright Sarah Ruhl for granting us permission to cite these lines from *In the Next Room (or the Vibrator Play)*.

Figure 11.1 Vibratory operating room.

public readily identified them with sex. Just as doctors split off sexuality and orgasm from paroxysm, advertisers disavowed the vibrator's sexual and orgasmic purpose.[6] Indeed, the portable home vibrator soon put doctors out of business, led to the "rediscovery" of the clitoris, and to the eventual disappearance of hysteria as a diagnosis. Yes, we are indeed asserting that the well-documented disappearance of hysteria was related to the cultural recognition and gradual acceptance of women's sexual pleasure and fulfillment (Stein and Kim, 2009).

"A Construction of Phantasy"

Even while employing electrotherapy as a treatment for hysteria, Freud began to doubt its physical usefulness and to attribute its main curative effect to suggestion. Freud questioned genital irritation as the source of nervous illness, positing a psychic rather than somatic cause. Freud wrote,

> Whether changes in the genitals really constitute so often the sources of stimulus for hysterical symptoms is in fact doubtful . . . Direct

---

6 Advertisers continue to split off the vibrator's orgasmic function when marketing to the public—for a contemporary example, see "Advertising: Trojan Makes Concessions to Place a Suggestive Ad," *New York Times*, September 28, 2010.

treatment consists in the removal of the psychical sources of stimulus for the hysterical symptoms, and is understandable if we look for the causes of hysteria in unconscious ideational life.

(1888a, p. 56)

Freud became disappointed with electrotherapy, and with Erb's electrotherapy textbook, upon which he relied for his practice. In 1925 Freud wrote,

> Unluckily I was soon driven to see that following these instructions was of no help whatever and that what I had taken for an epitome of exact observations was merely the construction of phantasy. The realization that the work of the greatest name in German neuropathology had no more relation to reality than some 'Egyptian' dream-book . . . was painful, but it helped to rid me of another shred of the innocent faith in authority from which I was not yet free. So I put my electrical apparatus aside, even before Moebius had . . . [explained] that the successes of electric treatment in nervous disorders . . . were the effect of suggestion on the part of the physician.

(1925a, p. 16)

Freud discovered early on that suggestion was a principal factor in electrotherapy's effectiveness, and so dismissed it contemptuously as an "Egyptian dream-book." Significantly, this was the same term he later used in reference to *The Interpretation of Dreams* in his letter to Fliess (Freud, 1899a), anticipating the disparaging reception of his work by the German medical community. Clearly, Freud was sensitive to the possibility that psychoanalysis would be linked with suggestion and with the quackery of electrotherapy. By positing a *psychological* cause to hysterical symptoms, Freud positioned psychoanalysis in opposition not only to suggestion, but also to the biologically, usually genitally, based somatic treatments of hysteria practiced by his medical colleagues (Bonomi, 2009; Gilman, 2010). Bonomi (2009) convincingly argues that Freud deliberately avoided any reference to these treatments as well as to his own background in pediatrics in order to disassociate himself and psychoanalysis from the taint of the sadistic, unnecessary, and ubiquitous gynecological surgeries, cauterizations, and castrations that were performed even on young children. Further, there is an added dimension to Freud's rejection of these physical therapies: In opposing psychoanalysis to these treatments, Freud was at the same time distancing himself from the anti-Semitic racialized biological characterization of the Jews as a depraved and incestuous race, genetically predisposed to biologically inherited nervous illness. Freud aspired to separate his psychoanalytic method as far as possible not only from the taint of suggestion, but also from the somatic treatments conducted in the private practices of mostly

Jewish doctors on their mostly Jewish female hysterical patients (Killen, 2006).

Freud's acute sensitivity to the perceived links between psychoanalysis and suggestion and Jews and genital stimulation is vividly apparent in the following anecdote. On March 29, 1910, at a meeting of the Medical Society of Hamburg, Freud presented his psychoanalytic approach to the treatment of hysteria to what turned out to be a hostile and disparaging audience. Describing this contentious meeting, Ernest Jones (1955) reports,

> Weygandt, the gentleman who talked of calling in the police, was particularly virulent. Freud's interpretations were on a level with the trashiest dream books. His methods were dangerous since they simply bred sexual ideas in his patients. *His method of treatment was on a par with the massage of the genital organs* . . . Nonne was concerned about the moral danger to the physician who used such methods . . . Saenger [commented that] fortunately . . . the North German population was very far from being as sensual as that of Vienna.
>
> (1955, p. 130, emphasis added)

Freud, clearly insulted, commented to Jones,

> There one hears just the argument I tried to avoid by making Zurich the centre. Viennese sensuality is not to be found anywhere else! Between the lines you can read further that we Viennese are not only swine but also Jews. But that does not appear in print.
>
> (Jones, 1955, p. 131)

Bristling at the implication of a connection between psychoanalysis and genital massage, Freud reads between the lines of German medical criticism the not-too-subtle anti-Semitic innuendo regarding the depravity of Jewish doctors and their Jewish patients (Vienna was known for its high concentration of Jews). "Making the Zurich the centre" refers of course to Freud's appointment of Jung as the next leader of the psychoanalytic movement in the hopes that having an Aryan at the helm would dispel any notion of psychoanalysis being a "Jewish national affair." And, as Freud had feared 20 years prior, psychoanalysis was indeed likened by his German critics to the "trashiest of dream books," implying not only that it was Jewish and therefore perverted, but also that it employed suggestion and was therefore unscientific.

While Freud rejected the somatic treatments of his day, he still retained the biologically based model of excitation and discharge in his psychological theories; frustration and gratification of libidinal wishes came to dominate his drive theory. Makari (2008) notes that the primary purpose of the clitoridectomies performed by 19th-century gynecologists was to lessen internal stimulation. As we have seen, the goal of genital stimulation was to release tension that had already built up. Although these interventions approached the problem of internal stimulation from opposite sides, they both had the same rationale—the elimination or discharge of tension. Freud psychologized this biological rationale, but never gave up the belief that the regulation of bodily tensions are involved in neurosis. He differentiated the actual neuroses, resulting from built-up sexual tension, from the psychoneuroses, rooted in the patient's early history, psychic conflicts, and repressed sexual impulses (Laplanche and Pontalis, 1967). This was an effort to maintain some rootedness in the body, and in the present contemporary life of the patient, even while his overall emphasis had dramatically shifted to psychical conflicts, personal meanings, and the historical roots of illness.

The actual neuroses had in common their source in contemporary sexual problems of tension regulation. As Makari (2008) documents, while neurasthenia was caused by sexual overindulgence, anxiety neurosis was a disorder of the sexually frustrated—virgins, prudes, abstainers, and those practicing *coitus interruptus* (this would certainly have included Freud). Freud's theory of excess stimulation and release permeated all of his work; much of what would be called the economic point of view, fundamental to Freud's drive theory, was the build-up or release of instinctual tension; hence the overriding importance within drive theory of the object's being either frustrating or gratifying and the consequent emphasis on abstinence. Freud's emphasis was on the idea that the neuroses are precipitated by sexual frustration, leading to the damming-up of libido. This is exactly the rationale in physical terms of the long tradition of inducing paroxysms in hysterical women, although the sexual meaning was repressed or dissociated. We may also speculate that it was the same principle captured by the idea of catharsis or abreaction, the discharge of "strangulated" affect.

"Jewissance"[7]

Although stunning in their originality, Freud's psychological theories were inevitably shaped by the larger context in which they were developed. It is only if we take into account Freud's reaction to anti-Semitism as well as the broader context of 19th-century medicine, that the theoretical underpinnings of psychoanalysis make sense. In the chapters that follow we will elaborate how Freud dealt with his conflicted position as an acculturated German Jew in an anti-Semitic milieu. We will show that he did so in part by appropriating the binaries split by his society between gentile and Jew

---

7 Boyarin (1997, p. xxiii).

and incorporating them into his theories, transforming their biologically racial specificity into psychological universality.

It is much easier to understand why Freud constructed the Oedipus complex as the nucleus of neurosis and castration anxiety as bedrock when we realize that his people, Jews, were accused of being neurotic and perverse because of generations of incest, and that Jewish men were viewed by others and by themselves as castrated and effeminate because they were circumcised. In Freud's transformation, rather than Jews being incestuous, we all have Oedipal desires; it is not Jews who are castrated (circumcised), we all have castration anxiety; rather than Jews being primitive and perverse, we all have these aspects within our unconscious. Unfortunately, in the process of universalizing these dichotomies, Freud projected onto women the negative characteristics attributed to Jews (Gilman, 1993a, b).

There is perhaps nothing in Freud's theorizing more puzzling to the modern reader than the notion of penis envy. The idea set forth by Freud, that girls in their developing sexuality do not discover their own sexual organ and instead, "all the child's interest is directed towards the question of whether it [the penis] is present or not" (Freud, 1926c, p. 212) seems to us today to be preposterously male-centric. But if we consider the context of the 19th-century male-centered medical model of female sexuality, it makes perfect sense. Freud, like his medical colleagues, saw the clitoris not as the locus of female sexuality, but as an inferior penis. He wrote,

> But we have learnt that girls feel deeply their lack of a sexual organ that is equal in value to the male one; they regard themselves on that account as inferior, and this "envy for the penis" is the origin of a whole number of characteristic feminine reactions.
>
> (Freud, 1926c, p. 212)

It's not the vagina Freud is talking about, but the clitoris, the female penis equated by his society with the circumcised penis of the male Jew. Famously referring to adult female sexuality as a "dark continent" (Freud, 1926c, p. 212), Freud equated women's sexuality with dark, uncivilized, primitive, savagery, the same qualities his society projected onto Jews, who were considered primitive, off-white, mulatto (Gilman, 1993a). Brickman (2003) cogently demonstrates just how thoroughly Freud incorporated the colonial dichotomies of primitivity and civilization into his theoretical formulations, viewing psychoanalysis as a civilizing process. Dimen (2003) highlights the psychoanalytic conception of female sexuality as primitive and uncivilized, writing, "the female body, with its savage little clitoris, becomes rather like a wild animal on the outskirts of civilization" (p. 146). While the Aryan was seen as civilized, phallic, male, and autonomous, the male Jew was primitive, castrated (clitoral), female, and suggestible. The clitoris, thought to be a vestigial, and therefore primitive organ, literally had no place in the civilized society of Freud's time; neither, according to anti-Semitic rhetoric, did Jews.

The neglect of the clitoris neither began nor ended with Freud; Freud consolidated into theory a long tradition of devaluing the clitoris, differentiating between paroxysm and orgasm, and limiting the definition of sexual satisfaction to vaginal penetration. However, as Laqueur (1990) notes, it was Freud who actually invented the notion of the vaginal orgasm. Freud's formalization into psychoanalytic theory of the 19th century view of female sexuality perpetuated its detrimental effect on women, especially true believers in psychoanalysis, who were told by their psychoanalysts that they were frigid because they were not having vaginal orgasms. A most extreme example is Princess Marie Bonaparte, Freud's patient and disciple, who had numerous unsuccessful surgeries to move her clitoris closer to her vagina so she could achieve vaginal orgasm (to his credit, Freud tried to dissuade her from doing so) (Appignanesi and Forrester, 1992).

For Freud, the "repudiation of femininity," by which he meant penis envy and castration anxiety, was ultimately a biological fact, the "bedrock" underlying psychic life. Development proceeds through renunciation of infantile wishes, whereas gratification leads only to primitivity. For men, to achieve civilized, masculine, autonomy meant overcoming castration anxiety by giving up feminine passivity in relation to other men, including suggestibility, which was equated with penetration and castration (Freud, 1937a). For women, renouncing penis envy meant accepting their place in a society that equated them with their reproductive function. Women were expected to renounce the desire to be men, and replace it with the desire to have a baby; to renounce autonomous masculinity, as symbolized by the clitoris, and replace it with passive femininity, represented by the vagina in need of penetration; to renounce the phallic desire to participate fully in the world, and accept their passive female position in male-dominated society.

On the surface we are faced with a puzzling inconsistency in Freud's theory—one goal for men, another for women. But if we take into account the anti-Semitic equation of the clitoris with the circumcised penis of the male Jew, the common denominator in Freud's theorizing becomes clear. In this equation, the clitoris, simultaneously representing Jewish female masculinity and Jewish male femininity, must be renounced—both men and women have to give up their "Jew"—in order to have a place in German civilization. In Freud's civilizing project of psychoanalysis, women must relinquish their desire to be autonomous and masculine, while men must surrender their longing to be passive and feminine. As we demonstrate throughout this book, this view continues to have longstanding implications for contemporary psychoanalytic theorizing and practice.

La Petite Mort

Since its inception, the history of genital stimulation as a treatment for hysteria has been fraught with controversy on moral, religious, and professional grounds. We have no record from the patient's point of view about what it was like for the women undergoing this procedure. We don't know if they considered it sexual, if they understood the paroxysm as orgasm, or whether married women told their husbands about what was going on "in the next room." Given what we know about the frequency of childhood sexual abuse, a proportion of these hysterical women likely had actual sexual trauma as the source of their symptoms. One shudders to imagine the impact of these treatments' genital meddlesomeness—gynecological exams, surgeries, cauterizations, and stimulations—on these women who had already been traumatized (J. Davies, personal communication, June 5, 2010).

We do know it was part and parcel of the somatic approach in which Freud was trained and that he used at the beginning of his practice. Although Freud was inevitably shaped by his culture, he was nevertheless far ahead of his time. By proposing a psychological understanding of hysterical symptoms, Freud significantly reduced the likelihood that women with hysteria would be subjected to the genital fiddling of professional medicine. At a time when few, if any, doctors listened to their patients' life stories, Freud took his patients seriously, listened to them carefully, tried to understand the meaning of their lives, and made it possible to talk about sex without shame. Yet we cannot ignore the continued negative ramifications for women of Freud's consolidation into theory of the 19th century medical views of female anatomy. It is only by understanding this background and taking into account Freud's experience as a Jew in a virulently anti-Semitic milieu, which we explore in more detail in the chapters that follow, that we can make sense of his theoretical construct of female sexuality. We hope that by providing this historical context, we will stimulate further discussion and galvanize future research.

Chapter 12

Freud's Anti-Semitic Surround

In his discussion of the case of Little Hans, Freud adds a footnote in relation to Little Hans' discovery that women really do not possess a penis. He writes,

> I cannot interrupt the discussion so far as to demonstrate the typical character of the unconscious train of thought which I think there is here reason for attributing to little Hans. The castration complex is the deepest unconscious root of anti-Semitism; for even in the nursery little boys hear that a Jew has something cut off his penis—a piece of his penis, they think—and this gives them a right to despise Jews. And there is no stronger unconscious root for the sense of superiority over women. Weininger (the young philosopher who, highly gifted but sexually deranged, committed suicide after producing his remarkable book, *Geschlecht und Charakter, Sex and Character* [1903]), in a chapter that attracted much attention, treated Jews and women with equal hostility and overwhelmed them with the same insults. Being a neurotic, Weininger was completely under the sway of his infantile complexes; and from that standpoint what is common to Jews and women is their relation to the castration complex.
>
> (1909a, p. 36)

The implications of this remarkable footnote comprise the subject matter of this chapter. These seemingly incidental remarks, relegated to an aside in Freud's theoretical discussion, offer a window into the impossible double bind of Freud's situation, living as an acculturated Jew in the anti-Semitic milieu of fin de siècle Vienna. At the time Freud made these remarks, fervent hostility toward Jews permeated all aspects of German culture, including the fields of science and medicine. Strongly influenced by evolutionary biology, these disciplines were preoccupied with issues of race and ethnicity. Jews were frequently the object of scientific investigation, at the unflattering center of heated debates about disease, degeneration, character, and sexuality. As a Jew, Freud was subject to this same disparaging scrutiny; as a Jewish scientist, his theories were inherently suspect as being specific to Jews. Desiring to be recognized as an objective observer in the eyes of the German medical community and to have psychoanalysis accepted as a universal, not a specifically Jewish science, Freud occupied the difficult and conflicted position of aspiring to contribute to a discourse in which he himself was a vilified subject.

Freud's commentary on the Case of Little Hans is notable as much for what it obscures as for what it reveals. For although Freud says he does not wish to interrupt his theoretical discussion of castration anxiety for a detour into the unconscious roots of anti-Semitism and misogyny, nevertheless he does. In this brief aside, Freud makes certain links explicit and leaves other important ones out, illuminating the unconscious anxieties and associated defenses of a Jewish scientist presenting his ideas to an increasingly anti-Semitic audience. In referring to Little Hans' unconscious train of thought as "typical," Freud identifies this train of thought as being typical of his time. Indeed, in the prevailing views of the surrounding culture, it *was* typical to consider circumcision a form of castration, a mark of degradation, and a reason to despise Jews. Similarly, the connection to which Freud refers, between the hatred of Jews and feelings of superiority over women, with circumcision and castration at its root, figured prominently in the scientific formulations of his era, as well as in his own. Circumcision represented a clearly feminine trait in the eyes of German society as well as in Freud's cultural unconscious, as he internalized his society's anti-Semitic stereotypes and embedded them in his theories.

For a deeper understanding of how psychoanalysis developed as it did, it is important to attend to what Freud does not mention, in fact specifically omits: He does not reveal that the characters involved in this footnote—the patient Little Hans, the anti-Semitic philosopher Weininger, and the analyst, Freud himself—are all Jewish. Significantly, Freud does not refer to the subjective experience of the assumed-to-be circumcised Jew, who finds himself the denigrated subject of discourse of a society that despised Jews. What Freud couches in terms of what "little boys hear in the nursery," as though referring to little gentile boys conversing amongst themselves about Jews, is in fact what Little Hans, Weininger, and Freud, as Jews, *knew to be true about themselves*: "that a Jew has something cut off his penis" and that for this reason, they themselves were the object of their gentile society's derision.

Throughout Freud's case studies, Freud consistently submerges the facts of anti-Semitism and of his patients' Jewish identities (Blum, 2010). But here, when explicitly making the connection between anti-Semitism and castration anxiety, Freud's omission is particularly striking; it points to the breaking through of Freud's unconscious defensiveness about his own Jewish identity as the object of anti-Semitic scrutiny. Boyarin writes,

In presenting "little Hans" and Weininger as if they were gentiles gazing . . . at the Jewish penis and becoming filled with fear and loathing, Freud is actually . . . representing himself, or at least an aspect of himself, gazing at his own circumcised penis and being filled with fear and loathing.

(1997, p. 234)

Freud is simultaneously insider and outsider, observer and observed, male scientist and circumcised Jew; he cannot bring himself to acknowledge that he is himself the object of the hateful gaze of his beloved German *Kultur*.

We will show that Freud's divided subjectivity contributed to his tendency to think in terms of opposed binary concepts and impacted the ways in which he constructed his theories—in particular, his theories of castration anxiety, penis envy, the Oedipal complex, and the "repudiation of femininity" as the "bedrock" of psychoanalysis (Freud, 1937a, p. 252). Freud dealt with his conflicted position in part by appropriating the binaries split by his culture between Jews and gentiles—feminine/masculine, primitive/civilized, dependent/autonomous, to name only a few—and incorporating them into his theories. In the process, he assigned to women the negative characteristics attributed by his society to Jews. We will return to these ideas, but for now will leave with the following point: Insight into Freud's theorizing requires a careful consideration of Freud's experience as a Jew in a world hostile to Jews, as well as a close understanding of the paradigms inherent in the cultural context in which he strove to make his scientific contributions.

The Promise and Failure of Emancipation

These paradigms were strongly influenced by the political and cultural climate of Europe at the end of the 19th century. After a brief period of relative tolerance toward Jews following Emancipation, Europe was again becoming increasingly publicly anti-Semitic. Based on the ideals of the Enlightenment, Emancipation had earlier in the century newly recognized Jews' rights as individuals, granting them equal citizenship and abolishing discriminatory laws that separated them from the rest of their countrymen. These newfound freedoms led to the increasing integration of Western Jews into modern European society, including the ranks of the educated, where they noticeably distinguished themselves in business, the arts, science, and medicine.

At the same time, Emancipation spurred a flood of immigration by Eastern European Jews, *Ostjuden*, suffering poverty and pogroms to countries offering them better opportunities in the West. Following Austria's

1867 ratification of a constitution implementing democratic reforms and granting Jews full political rights, thousands of Jews fled to Austria from the Eastern parts of the Austro-German Empire, including Galicia and Hungary. Many of these immigrants settled in Vienna, most of them concentrated in Leopoldstadt, the district in which Freud lived and practiced. With only a few exceptions, Jews had been forbidden to live in Vienna since their expulsion in 1669 (Beller, 1991). But in the 1860s alone, the Viennese Jewish population jumped from 1.3 to 6.1 percent; by 1900, Jews made up 8.7 percent of the population (Klein, 1985). The Jews of Vienna were a diverse group, ranging from the orthodox Galician Hasidim to the ultra-assimilated *Hofjuden*, or "court Jews," who played a significant role in Vienna's financial and business affairs (Beller, 1991).

Many immigrants were eager to shed their old traditions in favor of the secular and cosmopolitan ways of the Austrian capital. Others desired a German education and were attracted by the opportunity to attend the University of Vienna. Theodor Billroth, a prominent professor of medicine at the University of Vienna, was incensed by the influx of Galician Jews into the study of medicine. In 1876, he made an incendiary speech ranting against the disproportionate numbers of *Ostjuden* in the medical profession, complaining that they were primitive, uncivilized, and educationally unprepared, and predicting that their social aspirations for assimilation into German society were doomed to failure. Billroth's diatribe reverberated throughout the scientific and medical community, sparking a wave of anti-Semitic riots directed against Jewish students and professors at the University (Levy, 2005).

Yet for three short decades, acculturated Viennese Jews remained hopeful that their patriotic feelings were well-founded, political liberalism would prevail, and they would be accepted as full and equal members of German society. But their recently granted equality was short-lived. Klein (1985) documents the rise to power of the Christian Social Party in the 1890s, led by Karl Lueger, who was confirmed as Mayor of Vienna in 1897. Lueger's platform, with its enthusiastic support of anti-Semitism, paved the way for Hitler's later arrival. In fact, Hitler, who was in Vienna during this time, claimed he learned his anti-Semitism from Lueger. Lueger systematically dismantled the liberal reforms that had benefited Jews in the previous decades, and set the stage for the resurgence of government-sanctioned public anti-Semitism. Capitalizing on the gentile middle classes' discomfort with the financial and professional success of the Jews living in their midst, Lueger reignited the popular anti-Semitism that had been quietly simmering during Vienna's brief period of liberalization. Jews as a group were openly ridiculed in the press, in the government, and in the arts. Barred from prestigious government, university, and hospital appointments, they were prevented from advancing in the civil service, academia, and medicine. At the University of Vienna, classes taught by Jewish professors were boycotted. While Lueger had revived a longstanding tradition of animosity toward Jews, this new wave of anti-Semitism converged with the racial preoccupations of fin de siècle Europe to take a menacing turn for the worse.

From Religious to Racial Difference

Having no national homeland of their own, the Jews had traditionally served in the popular imagination of their European "host" countrymen as a convenient alien "other" against whom identity could be established and clearly defined. Their continued existence and persistent survival as a people despite their lack of a national identity had, throughout history, marked them as different. This difference now became the focus of a Europe in the process of redefining itself for the new century, which projected its anxieties and uncertainties onto the Jew. The modernization of Europe brought with it an ominous change in character of the arguments of anti-Semitism: the hatred that had once been primarily theological in nature was now becoming increasingly biological.

Since medieval times, predominantly Catholic and Protestant Europe had demonstrated a strong antipathy toward Jews based primarily on religious difference. In this theological paradigm, Christianity distinguished itself from Judaism by defining itself against it historically, in terms of no longer being what Judaism was: Judaism was the old practice, Christianity the new. In this model, Judaism, though vehemently rejected, was nevertheless still included within the general conceptual framework of Christianity.

One example of this originally religiously-based hostility was the legend of the Wandering Jew, which began in Germany in the 17th century and then spread rapidly throughout Europe. (Recall Charcot's use of this image in diagnosing his Jewish patients, as we described in Chapter 10. As we will see in Chapter 14, the Wandering Jew is a recurring anti-Semitic trope among both non-Jews and Jews, a restless ghost that refuses to be put to rest.) The tale of the Wandering Jew depicted a fictional Jewish shoemaker named Ahasverus taunting Jesus on the way to the crucifixion and in response, being castigated by him to "go on forever until I return." Enflaming the popular and literary imagination, the image of the Wandering Jew quickly found its way into poetry and literature, including the works of Goethe, Heine, and Hans Christian Andersen. Jews were characterized by the larger society as unrepentant sinners who were doomed to roam without rest. Their seeming immortality as a people and their lack of a homeland were viewed as punishment for their repudiation of Christ. Although the Jews were disparaged as a group and assigned the role of outcast, this marginalized status was originally ascribed to their difference in belief. This meant, ostensibly at least, that Jews could hope to be redeemed and thereby gain acceptance by the Christian majority through the process of conversion.

But with the advent of the modernization of Europe and its increasing secularization, what distinguished the Christian from the Jew was no longer defined in religious terms, as a matter of difference in belief and practice. As religion declined in influence, the traditional theological arguments were secularized, and the difference between Jews and Christians came to be defined in terms of race and biology. Jewishness was no longer a religious category but a racial one, a condition that was permanent, genetically inherited, and could not be modified by conversion. The Jews were now marginalized as the quintessential racial other, who had no homeland because they were incapable of it—they were considered fundamentally physically and psychologically different from non-Jews. Jews were no longer defined in a religious framework as being what Christians used to be and were no longer. In this racial model, the Jew was newly defined as everything the non-Jew "was not, nor would ever be" (Gilman, 1993a, p. 9).

This dangerous shift in anti-Semitic rhetoric had deadly repercussions for European Jewry. As the Aryan defined himself in opposition to the Jew, the Jew in relation to the Aryan became an inferior, damaged being—less than human. The consequence of the dehumanization of the Jews was initially their public humiliation, followed by the call for their expulsion from their "host" countries, and ultimately, their extermination. We find a poignant record of this shift and its outcome, as well as Freud's internalization of his culture's anti-Semitic stereotypes, in Freud's letter to his son Ernst in London, written while Freud was anxiously waiting for an exit permit to flee Nazi-occupied Austria. Freud wrote,

> In these dark days there are two prospects to cheer us: to rejoin you all and—to die in freedom. I sometimes compare myself with the old Jacob whom in his old age his children brought to Egypt. It is to be hoped that the result will not be the same, an exodus from Egypt. It is time for Ahasverus to come to rest somewhere.
>
> (Cited in Jones, 1957, p. 240)

Note that Freud simultaneously identifies himself with the Jewish patriarch Jacob, the father of the Jewish people (Jacob was also Freud's father's name), and with Ahasverus, the legendary character of anti-Semitic fantasy. We can see from Freud's association of these two figures both how strongly he identifies as a Jew and how thoroughly he internalizes the image of the Wandering Jew, applying it to himself and his current situation as well as to his people's ancient history of suffering and exile. Likening England, his hoped-for land of refuge, to Egypt, where Jacob found relief from famine but from which his descendants later fled from slavery, Freud reveals his fear that the legendary anti-Semitic prophecy might be true: there might indeed be no safe haven for him or his progeny. Based not on the fantasy of divine retribution for religious apostasy but on the grim reality of racially based anti-Semitism, Freud's fear was well founded. Thanks to the intervention of his benefactor, Princess Marie Bonaparte, Freud made it safely to England. But many of his close family members were not so fortunate: four of Freud's sisters died in Auschwitz and Theresienstadt (Gay, 1988).

East Meets West

Freud was not alone in his internalization of the views of his surrounding culture. The stereotypical image of the Jew in the cultural imagination not only of gentiles, but also of many assimilated Western Jews, including Freud, was that of the Eastern *shtetl* Jew, or *Ostjude*. The pogroms of the late 19th and early 20th centuries in Eastern and Central Europe led to a stream of Jewish immigration to the West, much to the consternation of the bourgeois, civilized, metropolitan Austro-German population. Among this population, the newly emancipated Western Jews proudly viewed themselves as German nationalists and masters of the German language. Embracing the Enlightenment ideals of universality and equality, they subordinated their identification with Judaism to their wholehearted allegiance to German culture. Both Theodor Herzl and Gershom Scholem noted that many assimilated Jews were more patriotically German and adhered more loyally to the principles of German culture than even the Germans themselves (Klein, 1985).

With the rise of anti-Semitism, the Western Jews became increasingly uncomfortable with the presence of so many of their Eastern European counterparts in their midst. Ashamed of their Eastern European brethren, Western Jews squirmed at the sight of these seemingly alien people, so different in dress and manners, and observant of religious practices they and their families had long abandoned. With anti-Semitism a growing threat to the success of assimilation, the Western Jews were eager to distinguish themselves from the *Ostjuden*, whom they and their countrymen considered to be vulgar and primitive, uncultured, coarse in language and speech, smelly, dirty, and diseased. The *Ostjuden* were viewed as cunning, mendacious, shrewd, and opportunistic, not—as the Western Jews viewed themselves—intelligent and civilized contributors to German culture. As anti-Jewish intolerance intensified, the *Ostjuden* became a growing source of embarrassment and concern to the Western Jews, who became increasingly self-conscious of their own Jewish identity and of any association with "bad" Jewish behavior. Arthur Schnitzler in *The Road to the Open* wrote, "If a Jew shows bad form in my presence or behaves in a ridiculous manner, I have often felt so painful a sensation that I should like to sink into the earth" (cited in Klein, 1985, p. 12). As we saw in Chapter 3, Freud too was ashamed of "bad" Jewish behavior in the presence of gentiles, recounting in a letter to Martha the vituperative speech given by the father of the deceased at his friend Nathan Weiss' funeral. "And all this he spoke with the powerful voice of the fanatic, with the ardor of the savage, merciless Jew. We were all petrified with horror and shame in the presence of the Christians who were among us" (Freud, 1883, p. 65).

Regardless of the actual provenance of the individual exhibiting the behavior in question, the stereotype of the Jew, for both gentiles and assimilationist Western Jews alike, was that of the Eastern Jew. The references to Jews in Freud's early writing fit the model of this stereotype. In a letter to his childhood friend, Emil Fluss, written in 1872 (at age 16), Freud describes, among other unflattering anecdotes involving *Ostjuden*, a conversation between two Eastern Jews, overheard on the train on his return to Vienna from Freiburg, his home town:

> Now this Jew talked the same way as I had heard thousands of others talk before, even in Freiburg. His face seemed familiar—he was typical . . . He was cut from the cloth from which fate makes swindlers when the time is ripe: cunning, mendacious, kept by his adoring relatives in the belief that he is a great talent, but unprincipled and without character. A cook from Bohemia with the most perfect pug-face I have ever seen put the lid on it. I have enough of this lot. In the course of the conversation I learned that Madame Jewess and family hailed from Meseritsch: the proper compost-heap for this sort of weed.
>
> (Freud, 1872, cited in Gilman, 1993a, p. 11)

The irony, of course, is that Freud himself was an Eastern Jew, a fact he did not publicly express until 1925, and for good reason, as identifying himself in the public eye as an *Ostjude* would certainly not have facilitated his professional advancement. In an autobiographical essay he contributed to a professional series about the history of medicine, Freud wrote:

> I was born on May 6th 1856, at Freiburg in Moravia, a small town in what is now Czechoslovakia. My parents were Jews, I have remained a Jew myself. I have reason to believe that my father's family were settled for a long time on the Rhine (at Cologne), that, as a result of persecution of the Jews during the fourteenth or fifteenth century, they fled eastwards, and that, in the course of the nineteenth century, they migrated back from Lithuania through Galicia into German Austria. When I was a child of four I came to Vienna, and I went through the whole of my education there.
>
> (1925a, pp. 7–8)

Freud makes a point of locating his roots in the West, in Germany, and of positioning himself and his family as having *returned* to German Austria, where he was educated in the German system, rather than be associated in the minds of his Austro-German colleagues with the primitive, uncultured Eastern Jewish masses migrating to the West.

Freud's Jewish Identity

Freud was loath to acknowledge his Eastern European roots, presenting himself as an acculturated Western Jew embracing the ideals of the German enlightenment. Calling himself a "godless Jew," (Freud, 1918b, p. 63) Freud made it clear that he rejected the religious tradition of his forebears—his father's family was Hasidic, and his mother's was Orthodox. Although Freud chose as his wife Martha Bernays, who came from a prestigious Orthodox Jewish family—she was the granddaughter of the Chief Rabbi of Hamburg, known as the *Chacham* (Sage) of Hamburg—upon their marriage, and despite her strong protest, he definitively forbade her to light Sabbath candles and to observe the Sabbath or festivals. (After Freud died, Martha resolutely resumed her candle lighting.) It appears that he also did not have his sons circumcised (Gilman, 1993a).

Freud publicly claimed he had little or no knowledge of Hebrew or Yiddish, and that the celebration of the Jewish holidays was foreign to him. However, these claims are contradicted by readily available biographical data and ironically, even by Freud's own writing, most notably his letters to Jewish family, friends, and colleagues, in which he refers to Jewish festival celebrations, uses Yiddish phrases, and adopts a tone of intimacy between Jews living among *goyim*. Although the family in which Freud grew up was not religiously observant, the Freuds did celebrate the High Holy days, Passover, and Purim. Throughout his life, his father, Jakob Freud, continued to study the Talmud, and was admired by his family for his ability to recite the Passover Haggadah service from memory (Klein, 1985, p. 42). Through Jakob, who was his first teacher, Freud developed an early interest in the Bible and its stories, which he freely referenced in his writing, particularly in *The Interpretation of Dreams* (Freud, 1900b).

While it is true that Freud viewed himself as a secular humanist, this self-characterization did not imply his rejection of Judaism; to the contrary, the notion of humanism as integral to Judaism figured prominently in Freud's Jewish education. Leopold Breuer (Josef Breuer's father), a teacher of Jewish religion, was the author of the textbook used in Freud's religion classes at the Gymnasium, where he was taught universalistic Enlightenment values (Rose, 2003). Upon entering the Gymnasium at age seven, Freud studied with Samuel Hammerschlag, whose talent for combining the principles of secular humanism with "the material of Jewish history . . . to find means of tapping the sources of enthusiasm hidden in the hearts of young people" made a lasting impression on Freud (Freud, 1904, p. 255). Viewing humanitarian ideals as central to Jewish teaching, Hammerschlag emphasized the importance of the contribution of the particular individual or group to the universal ideals of mankind (Klein, 1985). He believed that the Old Testament, "the Jewish point of view," was "the root and origin of the theory of the free, autonomous personality and the innate rights of man", maintaining that it continued to serve as an inspiration for realizing these as-yet-unrealized rights in modern times (cited in Klein, 1985, p. 43). Upon leaving the Gymnasium, Freud remained close with Hammerschlag, viewing him as a warm and supportive paternal friend. Freud named his daughter Anna after Hammerschlag's daughter Anna, and upon Hammerschlag's death, wrote a moving and appreciative obituary (Freud, 1904).

Like most Westernized Jews in fin de siècle Vienna, Freud identified with the values of the Enlightenment. Enlightenment thought had led to the opening of the ghetto and promised Jews inclusion in the wider world. Jews hoping to assimilate emphasized their common humanity rather than their particularistic difference. Freud was highly motivated to assert findings that championed universal principles demonstrating that all people are similar, governed by universal laws of the psyche. He was eager to view himself and to be seen by others as having been influenced by the philosophy of Immanuel Kant rather than to appear to the world as regressively Talmudic. Freud's insistence on the universality of his findings and contributions was itself a typically Jewish characteristic, consistent with his Jewish education. (In the 1960s, the American Rabbi Shlomo Carlebach used to joke, "show me a person who emphasizes universal values, and I'll show you a Jew." More on this in Chapter 16.) Like many Jews, Freud's sons enthusiastically enlisted to fight in World War I on behalf of Austria. But Enlightenment did not bring its hoped-for results: the end of the war was accompanied by another strong rise in anti-Semitism and it was this great disappointment that contributed to Freud's pessimism following the war. Anti-Semitism dashed Jewish Universalist aspirations. "Freud's creation became 'Jewish psychology,' Einstein's efforts 'Jewish physics,' and the compositions of Mahler written 'with a Jewish accent.' Interestingly enough, none of the three saw what they had created as particularly Jewish" (Diller, 1991, p. 39).

Throughout his life, Freud never denied, even fiercely defended, his strong Jewish identity, which rather than being dampened by anti-Semitism, appears to have been sharpened by it. In 1926, he told a nationalistic German-American journalist, "My language . . . is German, my culture, my attainments are German. I considered myself German intellectually, until I noticed the growth of anti-Semitic prejudices in Germany and German Austria. Since that time, I prefer to call myself a Jew" (cited in Gilman, 1993a, p. 16). In his *Autobiographical Study* Freud wrote,

> When, in 1873, I first joined the University, I experienced some appreciable disappointments. Above all, I found that I was expected to feel myself inferior and an alien because I was a Jew. I refused absolutely to do the first of these things. I have never been able to see why I should feel ashamed of my descent or, as people were beginning to say, of my "race". . . at an early age I was made familiar with the fate of being in the Opposition and of being put under the ban of the "compact majority". The foundations were thus laid for a certain degree of independence of judgement.
>
> (1925a, p. 9)

In this public declaration of Jewish identity in a professional context, Freud consciously transforms the shame imposed upon him by his anti-Semitic colleagues into a forge for honing the development of his oppositional and independent character. He vocally reports having refused "to do the first"—to feel himself inferior, yet he is strangely silent about the second—the pressure to feel himself "an alien." Through his silent omission, we see that Freud cannot help but acknowledge his experience of being an outsider within the academic establishment, the very environment of German *Bildung* in which he aspired to be a full participant. Even as he publicly described himself to his medical colleagues, he remained the alien in their midst, the Wandering Jew with no permanent home. As we will see in the following chapter, Freud's responses to his culture's anti-Semitism, both conscious and unconscious, not only shaped and refined his Jewish identity over the course of his lifetime, but also greatly influenced the theoretical development of psychoanalysis. In fact, we contend that the impact of Freud's reaction to anti-Semitism continues to reverberate within psychoanalytic theory and practice, even in our contemporary times.

There has been considerable scholarship regarding the question of Freud's Jewish identity, the extent of his Jewish upbringing and education, his relationship with father, the influence of his mother, and the resulting Jewish character, if any, of psychoanalysis. (For an overview, see Salberg, 2010, who draws upon these works to illustrate Freud's complex Jewish identifications). Although we must necessarily limit our attention to our specific focus, we rely heavily on this scholarship throughout this book, particularly on the work of Boyarin (1997), Geller (2007), Gilman (1993a, b), Klein (1985), and Yerushalmi (1991), among others. Freud's relationship to his Jewish identity has frequently been described as "ambivalent," a term that in itself has evoked simultaneous and conflicting feelings as to its appropriateness for capturing the complex texture of Freud's attachment to his own Jewishness. While Loewenberg (1992) pronounces "ambivalence" as "precisely the concept of choice for Freud and his Jewish identity" (p. 511), Yerushalmi (1991), referring to its ubiquitous use in this arena, calls it a "tired and evasive cliché" (p. 6).

Freud first used the term ambivalence in *The Interpretation of Dreams* (1900b), to depict "very intense and often contradictory emotional attitudes" (p. 431); this is certainly true of his relationship to his own Jewishness. Loewenberg (1992) notes Freud's "strong and lifelong attachment to his Jewish heritage," attributing his ambivalence as being "due to his wish to have psychoanalysis, his creature and his 'destiny' . . . thrive as a value-free scientific movement not identified as 'a Jewish national affair' " (p. 511). We do not disagree. Yet a word such as ambivalence, drawn from the terminology of conflict, implies a level of integration and cohesion that does not take into account the process of dissociation, or what some analysts might more traditionally refer to as splitting and projection.

Freud's negative attitudes toward *Ostjuden*, which make their unpleasant appearance throughout his private and public writing in the form of unflatteringly graphic descriptions and cuttingly humorous anecdotes, are completely dissociated from the recognition that he and his family were Eastern Jews. Gilman (1993a) documents the explicit references to *Ostjuden* in Freud's private correspondence, as well as their appearance in a more sublimated form in his later scientific work. Freud refers to the coarse speech, diseased skin, and corrupt nature of the Eastern Jews; he dismisses a new acquaintance as "undoubtedly brilliant, but unfortunately a Polish Jew" (Letter from Sigmund Freud to Eduard Silberstein, June 28, 1875, p. 121) and uses the term *"grobber Jud"* (coarse Jew) (Letter from Sigmund Freud to Eduard Silberstein, August 14, 1878, p. 169) to describe a fellow student at the University. With no conscious awareness that in using these invectives, he was actually referring to himself, Freud adopted his society's negative stereotype of the Jew as his own, and later embedded it in the growing circumcised body of psychoanalysis.

In *A History of Psychoanalysis in America* (1953), the non-Jewish American analyst Clarence Oberndorf told the following story about his own experience in analysis with Freud in the 1930s. Oberndorf had just learned that many analysts took for granted a "second analysis" (*"die Nach-Analyse der Analyse"*). Many patients who had unsuccessful analyses in New York went to Vienna for a second analysis. Often these second analyses fared no better than the first. In other words, by the 1930s, many analysts were recognizing that psychoanalysis was not a miracle cure. Oberndorf brought up this uncomfortable observation with his own analyst, Freud. Freud, who often relied on jokes and stories to make his points as well as his interpretations, told Oberndorf the following joke (keep in mind that Freud's family was from Galicia, Freud himself looked down upon Galicians, Freud loved dogs and kept them in his consulting room while working, and Oberndorf was complaining about the lack of results in analysis):

In a small Galician village where Jews were not allowed to own dogs, a Jewish man came to the rabbi, complaining that his Christian neighbor's dogs were attacking him as he walked down the street. (As we will see in Chapter 14, many roads were blocked to Wandering Jews, who had to find their own "royal road" on which to pass.) The rabbi consulted the Talmud and suggested to the Jew that the next time the dogs attack, he should lie down and play dead. The next time the dogs attacked the Jew, he did exactly what the rabbi had suggested, but still the dogs bit him fiercely. He ran to the rabbi and angrily called him to account for his failed advice. The rabbi said, "You and I both know the way to deceive the dogs, but the dogs don't know it!"

Oberndorf understood Freud to mean that it is difficult to influence the unruly dogs of the unconscious. Just because the ego consciously knows doesn't mean that the unconscious knows. It's just a joke of course, but Freud collected jokes, particularly Jewish jokes, attributing to them great significance. Is it any accident that he modeled the analytic relationship and the therapeutic action of psychoanalysis on the Talmudic advice of the rabbi? Jewish humor, particularly the kind Freud loved, was filled with self-criticism and self-mockery; it was a socially acceptable means of expressing anti-Jewish feelings among Jews. In turning the prejudices into jokes, it both expressed the negative side of the ambivalence about being Jewish while also caricaturing the anti-Semitic slur and mocking it, taking away its sting.

Freud and his assimilated Jewish brethren were caught between two worlds. They desperately wanted to distance themselves from the insularity of the Jewish ghetto and Eastern European orthodoxy. They longed to be accepted as cultivated Germans. They were repeatedly promised entry into German civilization, yet they were repeatedly refused acceptance, reminded always that they were Jews. *"Tsvishn tsvey veltn"*— "Between Two Worlds," is part of the title of the famous Yiddish play, *The Dybbuk*, by S. Ansky. The title captures this sense of many Jews of the period before and during World War I of being torn between worlds (Goldberg, 2006). In Yiddish, the common expression of this is *"nisht ahin nisht aher"*—neither here nor there. This is what Levenson (2001) meant when he said, "Freud . . . wrote Greek and thought Jewish" (p. 378). We contend that it is precisely this position between two worlds that allowed Freud and his Jewish followers to develop a psychoanalytic sensibility. Psychoanalysis requires a position on the border, a position of thirdness, of optimal marginality. Only someone immersed in the culture and yet not subsumed by it is in a position to offer the kind of critique that psychoanalysis offers. The analyst, by necessity, takes a position that is immersed in the subjectivity of the other while also fully utilizing his or her own subjectivity and maintaining boundaries. The analyst is *tsvishn thsvey veltn*—between two worlds, what Buber (1970) alludes to in his dialogical philosophy as the "realm-of-the-between."

White, but not Quite[1]

By the turn of the century, European nations had colonized large parts of the world, with the goal of spreading white civilization to native cultures perceived as dark, savage, and primitive. The hierarchy embedded in this civilizing project was indexed to skin color, with White on the civilized and Black on the primitive end of the spectrum. Coinciding with the dichotomies of this imperialist worldview were the racial demarcations that stratified fin de siècle Europe. The categories of colonialism that were applied globally to deepest Africa, Australia, and the Americas, were applied locally to the Jews (Boyarin, 1997; Brickman, 2003; Cuddihy, 1974). As a race, Jews were not considered White, but were categorized as off-White, swarthy, mulattos. In the medical anthropology of the 19th century, the Eastern Jew was said to have an "African character" and was held up as an example of the dark-skinned races. Not surprisingly, the anti-Semitic literature of the same period portrayed both Jewish and African males as dark-skinned threats to the white Aryan race (Gilman, 1993a, see figure 1, p. 19).

As the increasingly racially-based anti-Semitic rhetoric converged with the epithets of colonialism, Jews were referred to as "white Negros," "Oriental," "barbarians," "primitive," and "a mongrel race." (Brickman, 2003, p. 163; see also Brodkin, 2002 and Goldstein, 2006).

According to the anti-Semitic reasoning of Freud's time, one drop of Jewishness was enough to taint the whole bloodline, leading to the deterioration of future generations. "Jewishness is like a concentrated dye; a minute quantity suffices to give a specific character—or at least, some traces of it—to an incomparably greater mass." Neither intermarriage nor conversion was a solution for removing the dark stain of Jewishness, as "the ancient influences continue to operate" (cited in Gilman, 1991, p. 175). In fact, intermarriage, a Jew marrying a non-Jew, was thought to lead only to the intensification of Jewish blackness in successive generations. The progeny of such crossbreeding were called *Mischling* or "half breeds," and were considered prime examples of racial degeneration. Like the black, the Jew could never hope to disappear into white society. Freud was keenly aware of this truism, incorporating and universalizing the theme of the *Mischling* in his discussion of the dynamics of the unconscious and the preconscious. He wrote,

1 Bhabha (1984); Boyarin (1997).

> We may compare them [the unconscious and preconscious] with indi-
> viduals of mixed race who, taken all round, resemble white men, but
> who betray their coloured descent by some striking feature or other,
> and on that account are excluded from society and enjoy none of the
> privileges of white people.
>
> (Freud, 1915c, p. 191)

The *Michling*, half-breed, or mulatto is precisely what Derrida meant by
the "undecidable," as we elaborated in Chapter 3. In a discussion of
"passing" and performing identity, Leary (1999) argued that the social
construction of gender, sex, and race abrogates simple binaries. For a Jew
to pass as German or for a black to pass as white raises questions
about what it means to be Jew or German, Black or White. Undecidables
introduce complexity.

Further entrapping the Jews in the vise of this racial classification system
was the biological science of the 19th century, which was inextricably
bound with racial theory. Rather than being relegated to the fringe of
pseudoscientific rhetoric, the ideology of race was part and parcel of the
serious scientific discourse of the time. It included wide acceptance, by
Freud and his contemporaries, of a sociocultural evolutionism founded on
the 19th-century ideals of human progress, articulated most prominently
by the English philosopher and social theorist, Herbert Spencer. Setting
forth a prescription for the progression of civilization, this theoretical platform wove together the Lamarckian doctrine of acquired characteristics,
Ernst Haeckel's recapitulation theory, and Darwin's theories of evolution
to explain why the white male European was the most civilized of beings.

The Lamarckian doctrine held that environmental factors influence
genetic attributes, maintaining that characteristics acquired in response to
environmental conditions would be passed on to successive generations as
biologically inherited traits. It implied that parents who inadequately
adapted to the demands of their environment would pass on inferior genetic
material to their progeny; thus a particular individual's—or by extension,
an entire race's—inferior social position could be attributed to its poor
genetic endowment. This principle was combined with Haeckel's famous
proposal, "ontogeny recapitulates phylogeny," the now-discredited evolutionary theory that individual development recapitulates the development
of the species. The development of the human being, like the evolutionary
history of the human race, was envisioned as progressing in stages, from
the primitive to the civilized. Thus "infants recapitulated the earliest
stages of savagery, while savages lived in the infancy of the human race"
(Brickman, 2003, p. 45). Building upon these formulations, Spencer
applied Darwin's theory of "survival of the fittest" to support his reasoning
for why some individuals and cultures were more advanced than, and
therefore superior to, others.

Taken together, these theories formed the basis of the prevailing formulations of cultural difference as tied to the inevitability of genetic inheritance. In these intertwining racial, biological, and colonial paradigms, cultural difference was attributed to varying levels of success in adapting to the environment, leading to subsequent variations in biological legacy. And so, the explanation for why some cultures remained at a "primitive" or undeveloped stage of the evolutionary scale while others progressed toward a more advanced or "civilized" stage lay in their presumed-to-be limited genetic heritage (Brickman, 2003). By extension, the social circumstances in which a particular culture—such as the Jews, for example—found itself were considered to be a direct result of the success or failure of the parents' adaptation to their surroundings. This trope fueled the rhetoric of colonialism, assigning a moral imperative to the civilizing project and holding racial genetics responsible for the success or failure of a cultural group's adaptation to White European civilization.

Brickman (2003) astutely notes the future reverberations within psychoanalytic theory of Spencer's notion that evolutionary progress toward civilization was made possible by the increasing ability, due to greater biological capacity, of the more "highly developed"—White and civilized—races to control their impulses and defer gratification. Spencer wrote,

> The repression of immediate impulsive response was the essential mechanism of evolutionary progress in both the intellectual and the moral sphere . . . Those who were more able to control the forces of nature internal to themselves were also those more able to control the forces of nature that impinged upon them from the outside.
>
> (Cited in Brickman, 2003, p. 46)

Women were not exempt from this biologically based hierarchical system, and did not fare well under it. The application to human beings of Darwin's theories of evolutionary biology, exemplified by *The Descent of Man* (1871), placed men at the top of the evolutionary hierarchy, women at the bottom. Arguing that men exhibited greater variation in form and function than women, Darwin viewed male genetic material as better suited for evolutionary progress. He claimed that men, whose minds and bodies were honed by the struggle for survival, were naturally intellectually and biologically superior to women. As Micale (2008) documents, these notions reinforced the polarization of gender roles at the turn of the century. Threatened by the nascent feminist movement and the challenges of modernization to patriarchal authority, marriage, and family, male-dominated fin de siècle society became increasingly anxious about the destabilizing shift in gender categories. In order to ensure that its men would be men, society needed to keep women in their place. While men were viewed as superior, civilized, progressive, and moral, women were viewed as inferior, primitive, savage, and immoral. As we will elaborate further, these ideas permeated Freud's theorizing, serving as the basis of his social thought and figuring prominently in his metapsychology, most notably in the dichotomous concepts of masculine versus feminine, primitive versus civilized, dependent versus autonomous, gratification versus renunciation, among others, that structured his thinking.

Circumcision as Castration

Intrinsic to the scientific, anthropological, and evolutionary discourse of the time was the racial model of the Jew, who was seen as having innate biological and psychological traits that distinguished him from the non-Jew. The most salient visible characteristic that marked the Jew as racially different was circumcision. Symbolizing the continuity of the Jewish people and inscribed on the body, circumcision had for centuries differentiated the Jew from the Christian—so much so, that all male Jews were assumed by the larger culture to be circumcised, whether they were in actuality or not. Concomitantly, although circumcision was also practiced by many non-Jews, being circumcised had come to be equated—disparagingly—with being Jewish. In the German vernacular of Freud's era, "*judschen*" or "*judischen*", "to make a Jew," was a commonly used metonym for "to circumcise" (Geller, 2007, p. 11). Though it might seem astonishing to us now, in accordance with Lamarckian doctrine, it was a widely held belief that circumcision, which was an acquired characteristic, could become an inherited trait. In fact, circumcision was a favorite topic of controversy in scientific debates about biological inheritance. As anti-Semitism intensified, circumcision, originally a signifier of religious difference, became the centerpiece of discussions about racial difference, including the proclivity to degeneracy, effeminacy, primitivity, and disease.

Vilified by respected scholars of the time who likened it to animal sacrifice, circumcision was associated with depraved sexuality and sexually transmitted disease, and was considered a reflection of the pathological, primitive, and barbaric nature of the Jew. Referring to circumcision, Paolo Mantegazza, a renowned neurologist, physiologist, and anthropologist, and the author of a widely-accepted text on human sexuality with which Freud was most certainly familiar,[2] named the Jews as one of the "savage tribes" performing "genital mutilation." He wrote,

---

2 This was the same book Dora was accused of reading, which convinced Freud of her lack of sexual naiveté.

Circumcision is a shame and an infamy; and I, who am not in the least anti-Semitic, who indeed have much esteem for the Israelites, I who demand of no living soul a profession of religious faith, insisting only upon the brotherhood of soap and water and of honesty, I shout and shall continue to shout at the Hebrews, until my last breath: Cease mutilating yourselves: cease imprinting upon your flesh an odious brand to distinguish you from other men; until you do this, you cannot pretend to be our equal. As it is, you, of your own accord, with the branding iron, from the first days of your lives, proceed to proclaim yourselves a race apart, one that cannot, and does not care to, mix with ours.

(Cited in Gilman, 1993a, p. 57)

With his condemnation of circumcision as a racial signifier, Mantegazza unequivocally transforms religious practice into racial difference. He positions Jews as a primitive and barbaric tribe who insist on isolating themselves as racial outsiders by putting their religious beliefs into practice. The critique that Jewish insularity, cultivated through ritual self-exclusion, is what prevents Jews from joining civilized society was a common anti-Semitic explanation for the pariah status of Jews,[3] here endowed with a racial twist.

Branded by circumcision, Jews were considered by the surrounding gentile community to be castrates, men who were "unmanned," made into women. Given the implications of being a woman in 19th-century male-dominated Victorian society, this was by no means a positive comparison. Women—and Jews—were considered passive, dependent, primitive, hysterical, dishonest, immoral, and incapable of higher intellectual thought. In his book, *Sex and Character* (1906), mentioned in Freud's footnote, Otto Weininger positioned men and women, and Christianity and Judaism as antithetical to one another. He described in great detail the weaknesses of character common to both Jews and women, which he viewed as impediments to the advancement of civilized society.

Born Jewish, Weininger converted to Christianity after completing his degree in philosophy at the University of Vienna. Although he committed suicide shortly after the publication of his book, his work was well received and expressed the prevailing sentiments of his society about Jews, women, and Blacks, all of whom were relegated to a position of inferiority in the hierarchy of White male European civilization. Wrote Weininger (1906),

---

3 Cuddihy (1974), in *The Ordeal of Civility*, uses a version of this formulation as a basis for his arguments. Martin Bergmann (1992) continues to interpret circumcision as derived from child sacrifice, positing that Jews created circumcision as a compromise formation, a smaller sacrifice of their children than incinerating them, as was the practice of the worshippers of Moloch.

"The emancipation of woman is analogous to the emancipation of Jews and negroes. Undoubtedly the principal reason why these people have been treated as slaves and inferiors is to be found in their servile dispositions" and their "many immoral impulses" (p. 338). According to Weininger, neither Jews nor women were capable of autonomy. "Like women, Jews tend to adhere together, but they do not associate as free independent individuals mutually respecting each other's individuality" (p. 308). The circumcised Jew came to signify political powerlessness and physical emasculation, representing that which was "impaired, damaged, or incomplete, and therefore threatening to the wholeness and health of the male Aryan" (Gilman, 1993a, p. 61).

Despite the negative connotations of femininity ascribed to male Jews by the larger culture, symbolized most visibly by circumcision, traditional Judaism did not equate circumcision with castration, nor did it view circumcision as a defect or a sign of weakness or femininity. To the contrary, circumcision was seen as a mark of the covenant between God and His people. It was considered the perfecting of the male organ as well as of the soul (Cohen, 2005).[4]

Boyarin (1997) delineates the different gendering of masculinity and femininity in the pre-modern rabbinic Jewish and gentile worlds. In traditional Jewish culture, that which the *Ostjuden* represented, it was men who most often occupied the internal sphere, staying indoors and studying Torah, while their wives freely engaged with the outside world, running businesses and buying and selling in the marketplace. The ideal of masculinity within traditional Judaism was defined quite differently from, even in opposition to, that of the surrounding society, a "gentle vs. gentile" male ideal. What was considered a womanly trait in the eyes of the gentiles was often valued as manly in the eyes of the Jews. The opposite was true as well—within traditional rabbinic Jewish culture, the private sphere of Torah study was held in higher esteem, and so men who worked in the public sphere of business and commerce were considered to be occupying a feminine position.

According to Boyarin, viewed through the lens of Western Christian culture, traditional Jewish masculinity appeared castrated and feminine

---

4   There are, however, historical Jewish sources that lend support to the idea that circumcision weakened the male organ. No less an authority than Maimonides says that the purpose of circumcision is to weaken the male organ, in order to minimize lust and diminish sexual pleasure. "In other words," writes Shaye Cohen (2005), explaining Maimonides' opinion, "circumcision makes men a little less manly" (p. xiv). This theory, which became popular in the Middle Ages, also provides one rationale for why women were never considered in need of circumcision, namely they already menstruate and do not need to become any more feminized. Nevertheless, it is important to understand that the rabbis did not consciously perceive themselves as feminized because of their circumcision.

precisely because it was not defined by possession of the phallus as a symbolic representation of power. In fact, he argues, traditional Jewish masculinity defined itself in opposition to this idea:

> For Lacan, castration consists specifically of the recognition by all subjects, male and female, that they can never possess the phallus. It nevertheless remains the case that for Lacan, to have the phallus remains the *desire* of all people always and everywhere, male and female, even if "having the phallus" is only an imaginary phenomenon. The phallus is for Lacan a psychic universal, while I avow that the "phallus" is not even so "real" an entity as a psychic universal, however imaginary or symbolic, but a culturally specific representation of human desire and fulfillment, one belonging to the dominant strand of European culture but resisted and refused (albeit not entirely successfully) by a subaltern culture that subsisted within the dominant one, namely the culture of rabbinic Judaism.
>
> (Boyarin, 1997, p. 10)

Traditional rabbinic Jewish culture rejected the phallus—the gentile valorization of power and aggression as attributes of masculinity—in favor of a valuation of *Edelkayt*, literally meaning "nobility," but in Yiddish, "gentleness and delicacy" (p. 23). The ideal male was the *yeshiva bochur*, the scholar who devoted his life to the study of Torah; its secular version was the *mentsh*. While in early modern Europe, gentiles referred to the little finger derisively as "the Jew," this colloquial linguistic stereotyping worked both ways: Jews returned the favor by referring to the thumb in Yiddish as "the goy"! (p. 4) In other words, Boyarin argues, traditional Jewish society defined its own version of masculinity, at least in part, against that of the "goy"—the gentile hypermale. Unlike the Christian view of the male as spirit and the woman as body, the male Jew was embodied, and therefore feminine. Although the Jewish version of masculinity renounced the phallus, it retained the penis. Ideal masculine values included the earthly tasks of satisfying one's wife's sexual desires, providing her with children, and generally being a good-enough husband; the Talmud records the advice of Rav Papa, "If your wife is short, bend down and whisper to her" (Baba Metsia 59a, cited in Boyarin, 1997, p. 119).

At the same time as their husbands were disparaged as being feminine, Jewish women were considered masculine by the standards of the 19th-century European bourgeoisie. Actively participating in the business of the outside world rather than remaining passively at home, Jewish women were seen as engaging in inappropriately aggressive and masculine activities; thus "if the men were read as sissies, the women were read often enough as phallic monsters" (Boyarin, 1997, p. xxii). Rose (2008) notes that the scientific community, which insisted on a clear demarcation of boundaries between the sexes, "regarded Jews as exemplary of the failure to conform to gender roles, because Jewish women supposedly dominated effeminate Jewish men" (p. 144). In describing his grandmother Amalia, Freud's mother, who was born in Galicia, Martin Freud (1958) wrote, "These Galician Jews had little grace and no manners; and their women were certainly not what we call 'ladies'. . . grandmother, a true representative of her race, was no exception. She had great vitality and much impatience" (p. 11). While the ideal passive and delicate woman of Victorian bourgeois society was thought to have little or no sexual desire, the cultivated activity of the Jewish woman was considered unseemly, and led to her being characterized as hypersexual and promiscuous. The dichotomies of active and passive, masculine and feminine, moral and immoral, heterosexual and homosexual, in combination with the image of the damaged and inferior penis, were used to insult both Jewish men and women.

The binaries split between gentiles and Jews in the anti-Semitic formulation were drawn from the same categories Victorian society used to differentiate men from women, even in matters of anatomy and biology. Within the framework of the late 19th and early 20th centuries, the White gentile male was the standard against which both women and Jews were measured. As we have detailed in the previous chapter, in the male-centered model of Victorian medicine, female genitalia were graded against the male sexual organs. The clitoris was considered an inferior penis, and while masturbation was discouraged in both sexes, women who performed clitoral self-stimulation were considered as wanting to be like men. The Jew, like the clitoris, was considered to be primitive, savage, and vestigial, and literally had no place in German civilized society. The denigration of both Jews and women through the equation of their genitalia later became a significant factor in Freud's development of his theory of castration anxiety, penis envy, and the "repudiation of femininity" as the "bedrock" of psychoanalysis.

As Above, so Below

Although the genitals were hidden from view in civilized society, the face was not, and the Jewish nose was touted as a convenient way to discern the Jew from physical characteristics that were openly visible to the outside world. In anti-Semitic caricature, the outward sign of the hooked, bent, and crooked nose was considered an indication of the Jews' inwardly crooked character and depraved sexuality. The "deformed" Jewish nose became an object of preoccupation in the anti-Semitic imagination, a displacement upward of the fantasy of the Jews' damaged phallus, which linked the Jewish male with the feminine (Geller, 2007; Gilman, 1986, 1993a, b).

Following popular folklore linking the size of the penis with the size of the nose, and based on centuries of medical hypothesizing about a biological naso-genital connection (Blackledge, 2004), 19th-century medicine included investigations into the similarities between the anatomical structures of the nose and the genitals, a line of research that Fliess eagerly pursued independently and for a time, in collaboration with Freud. In 1883 the American surgeon John Mackenzie discovered that, like the clitoris and penis, the nose was lined with erectile tissue that responded to sexual excitement with enhanced blood flow (Blackledge, 2004). A "reflex neurosis" was thought to account for the relationship between nosebleeds and menstruation (Bruck, 1910). Conducting gynecological surgeries on the nose, including cauterization with cocaine, Fliess sought to pinpoint the exact locations in the nose that corresponded with zones in the female genitalia and to investigate the connection between menstruation and nosebleeds, which he linked to menstruation and periodicity in men. Through these efforts, Fliess attempted to demonstrate as universal a phenomenon his society linked specifically to Jews (Gilman, 1993b).

The fantasy of male menstruation had a long history in the anti-Semitic characterization of the Jew. Gilman (1993b) documents its roots in medieval Christian tradition, which maintained that Jews were tainted by menstruation, the "Father's Curse," because of their religious apostasy.[5] Stressing the intransigent nature of the Jews, who refused to accept Christ, the image of the Jewish male as a menstruating female was used to link the character of the Jew with the "corrupt nature of the woman (both marked as different by the same sign)" (p. 96). The rumor that only Christian blood could cure diseases specific to the Jews, including male menstruation, provided one of the explanations for the slander of Jewish ritual murder, the "blood libels" accusing Jews of sacrificing Christian children in order to consume their blood.

The fantasy of male menstruation as punishment for the Jews' religious heresy and as a sign of their sexual pathology was further developed in a publication of the 17th-century legend of the Wandering Jew, which was reprinted in 1856. Menstruation was a sign of the overall pathology of the Jews, who, like women, were thought to be highly prone to disease. The sense of smell, thought to be the most primitive and vulgar of the senses, was associated with the Jews, not only because of their damaged noses, but also because Jews were said to smell from this menstruation. Hence to speak of a Jewish odor was to evoke the primitive, the sexual, and the feminine (Geller, 2007). The fascination with male menstruation continued in debates in the 19th century medical literature, fueled by the developing field of sexology, including the work of Magnus Hirschfeld, who posited a

5 Johnson (1998) challenges the myth of Jewish male menses as medieval, but affirms that it was a widespread belief in the modern era.

universal continuum of masculinity and femininity. Hermaphroditic qualities, including male menstruation, were held up as evidence of this continuum, with the implication that Jewish males were firmly positioned at its feminine pole (Gilman, 1993b).

A Case of Male Hysteria

For a time, Freud joined Fliess in his research into the genital/nasal link, as both collaborator and patient. He willingly submitted to cauterizations of his nose, and excitedly reported on his nasal secretions and monthly menstrual cycles, which he believed were marked by an occasional bloody nasal discharge. In what seems to us now to be an astonishing, if not slightly delusional, parallel, Freud linked his menstrual cycle with the flow of his self-analysis! Following is an excerpt from Freud's letter to Fliess on October 15, 1897:

> My self-analysis is in fact the most essential thing I have at present and promises to become of the greatest value to me if it reaches its end. In the middle of it, it suddenly ceased for three days, during which I had the feeling of being tied up inside (which patients complain of so much), and I was really disconsolate until I found that these same three days (twenty-eight days ago) were the bearers of identical somatic phenomena. Actually only two bad days with a remission in between. From this one should draw the conclusion that the female period is not conducive to work. Punctually on the fourth day, it started again. Naturally, the pause also had another determinant—resistance to something surprisingly new. Since then I have been once again intensely preoccupied [with it], mentally fresh, though afflicted with all sorts of minor disturbances that come from the content of the analysis.
>
> (Freud 1897f, p. 270)

It is no coincidence that the excerpt of Freud's letter we cite here, taken from the complete compendium of Freud's letters to Fliess published by Jeffrey Masson (1985), has been redacted in the official version included in 1950 in the *Standard Edition*. Micale (2008) documents that although Ernest Jones claimed only "uninteresting details" had been deleted from Freud's letters to Fliess, a careful comparison of the 1950 and 1985 versions shows that over 130 letters were excluded altogether, and, in the letters that remained, there were two types of information that had been consistently and deliberately excised: Extensive descriptions of Freud's self-analysis, including lengthy reports of his numerous symptoms and considerable neurotic anguish, and those letters and passages that demonstrate Freud's "crypto-homosexual attachment to Fliess" (p. 270). The reason for this censorship is clear: in the 1950s, when psychoanalysis was at the height of its power and influence, the psychoanalytic establishment took great care to present its founder as autonomous, rational, and masculine, even heroic. Freud's enthusiastic declarations of affection for Fliess— which can best be described as homoerotic—as well as his compellingly revealing reports of his neurotic difficulties, paint a rather different, touchingly vulnerable, "feminine" picture of an analyst inhabiting the role of patient. For a strikingly evocative illustration, consider this report to Fliess of Freud's self-treatment:

> The next day I kept the nose under cocaine . . . I repeatedly painted it to prevent the renewed occurrence of swelling; during this time I discharged what in my experience is a copious amount of thick pus; and since then I have felt wonderful, as though there never had been anything wrong at all.
>
> (Freud, 1895a, p. 106)

Keeping in mind the then-current treatments of hysteria (elaborated in the previous chapter) as well as the genital–nasal connection that was the subject of Fliess' research, Freud's report of painting his nose with cocaine and discharging a "copious amount of thick pus," is remarkably similar to the "expelling of thick seed" brought on by genital stimulation—and, presumably, the "wonderful" feeling that followed.

Freud's relationship with Fliess was passionate and intense. They had first met in 1887, when Fliess, who lived in Berlin, visited Vienna. Fliess became Freud's confidante, the sounding board for his personal and professional revelations, including Freud's self-analysis, which he began in 1896, following the death of his father. For 15 years, Freud and Fliess exchanged hundreds of letters, and met whenever they could in various European cities. Freud eagerly anticipated these meetings, expressing desire and longing for their reunion. In unmistakably homoerotic terms, Freud (1896b) wrote to Fliess, "I am looking forward to our congress as to the slaking of hunger and thirst. I bring nothing but two open ears and one temporal lobe lubricated for reception" (p. 193). During their congresses, they usually stayed at the same hotel, often in the same room, while their families were left at home. Fliess' wife Ida was jealous of Fliess' intimate friendship with Freud, while Freud was jealous of Fliess' relationships with other men (Micale, 2008). When years after their friendship ended, Freud fainted in a hotel room in Munich, the site of an argument with Fliess, he confided to Ernest Jones, "There is some piece of unruly homosexual feeling at the root of the matter" (Micale, 2008, p. 267).

Jakob Freud's death profoundly affected Freud, leading him to systematically examine his own unexpected psychological reactions in order to advance his understanding of the universal psychic processes of the mind, an echo perhaps of his teacher Hammerschlag's Jewish emphasis on the value of the contribution of the individual to the larger goals of humanity. Freud described to Fliess the progress of his self-analysis, including his self-torment, depression, doubt, inhibitions, and numerous somatic complaints. He wrote, "I have been through some kind of neurotic experience, curious states . . . twilight thoughts, veiled doubts, with barely a ray of light here or there" (Freud, 1897b, p. 254). This letter was followed two weeks later by "I still do not know what has been happening to me. Something from the deepest depths of my own neurosis set itself against any advance in the understanding of the neuroses." And then, "my little hysteria, though greatly accentuated by my work, has resolved itself a bit further" (Freud, 1897b, p. 261).

During the same period that Freud was his own patient in self-analysis, he was engaged as analyst in an intense analysis with Herr E., a case of male hysteria. Herr E.'s treatment led to a number of advances in Freud's theorizing; but a no less significant aspect of the treatment was that Freud acknowledged that the discoveries brought about by Herr E.'s analysis included insight into Freud's own psychological difficulties! Freud wrote to Fliess of Herr E.,

> he demonstrated the reality of my theory in my own case, providing me in a surprising reversal with the solution, which I had overlooked, to my former railroad phobia . . . For this piece of work I even made him the present of a picture of Oedipus and the Sphinx . . . You will hear more about all of this at our next congress.
>
> (1899b, p. 392)

At the end of the treatment, Freud (1900a) wrote to Fliess, "E. at last has concluded his career as a patient by coming to dinner at my house" (p. 409). One wonders what the American analysts of the 1950s would think of an analyst giving a patient a gift and having him over for dinner with his family as thanks for his role in the analyst's own treatment!

While Herr E.'s treatment was clearly a success for both patient and analyst, and contributed significantly to Freud's psychoanalytic theorizing, Freud chose not to publish this case of male hysteria, restricting his Case Studies to reports of his less than successful treatments of hysterical women. Micale (2008) documents that following Freud's negative reception by the Viennese medical community of his 1886 presentation on male hysteria, Freud suppressed accounts of male hysteria just as Ernest Jones and his daughter Anna later suppressed his.

Freud's infatuation with Fliess ended when Fliess, after reading *The Interpretation of Dreams*, criticized Freud for reading his own thoughts into those of his patients. Fliess' accusation that Freud's subjectivity was influencing his clinical observations was just the thing Freud did not want to hear. It rendered his psychoanalytic discoveries unscientific, implying they were merely the products of suggestion and of the specific subjectivity (Jewishness) of its inventor. Freud (1901) wrote in response, "you take sides against me and tell me that the 'reader of thoughts merely reads his own thoughts into other people,' which renders all my efforts valueless" (p. 447). Freud's defensive response to the painful end of his relationship with Fliess was to valorize the triumph of autonomy over dependence, and masculinity over homosexuality. He announced to Ferenczi in 1910 that with the end of his friendship to Fliess,

> a piece of homosexual investment has been withdrawn and utilized for the enlargement of my ego . . . I feel myself to be a match for anything and approve of the overcoming of my homosexuality with the result being greater independence.
>
> (Freud, 1910c, p. 221)

As we explore in further detail in Chapter 15, Freud would go on to chide Ferenczi for his attachment to him, interpreting his affection for Freud as homosexual. Freud was again a hero.

We have taken a detour into this case of male hysteria (Freud's own) to demonstrate that Freud unconsciously identified with his hysterical patients, adopted a passive, "feminine" role in relation to a man, and even went so far as to keep track of his discharges and menstrual cycles; in short, to demonstrate that Freud unconsciously identified with his society's characterizations of Jews as hysterical, homosexual, feminine, passive, unmanly, menstruating men. In collaborating with Fliess' research, Freud joined him in his attempt to universalize a phenomenon their society ascribed specifically to Jews. It must be emphasized that Freud's insider/outsider position was not only the source of his unconscious conflict, but was, most significantly, also the key to his brilliance. In undertaking his own analysis, in using his subjective experience in order to develop universal theories, Freud was also unwittingly and ironically deconstructing the binaries delineated by his culture with regard to the objective, positivistic basis of scientific knowledge.

Chapter 13

The Right to Pass
Psychoanalysis' Jewish Identity

In this chapter and those that follow, we will explore the impact on psycho-analysis of Freud's Jewish identity and the anti-Semitism that surrounded him. We will show that, influenced by the scientific and cultural paradigms of his day, including most significantly, its anti-Semitic racial characterizations of Jews, Freud developed his psychoanalytic theories around a series of polarities that continue to reverberate within contemporary theory and practice. Freud showed evidence of a particular dissociation linking Jewishness with passivity, femininity, and religious belief, while elevating activity, masculinity, and science. We must emphasize that in making our arguments, we are drawing from a distinguished body of research that thoroughly documents the effects of Freud's cultural surround, including its virulent anti-Semitism, on the polarization of his thought. However, as clinicians who teach and practice psychoanalysis and care deeply about its future, our main focus and contribution is to identify the significant implications of this scholarship for contemporary theory and clinical practice. In our view, these bifurcations, which Freud embedded in his psychoanalytic theories and which continue to operate even today, are responsible for some of the major problems in the history of psychoanalytic ideas and in the clinical practice of psychoanalysis. As we will show, they constitute the underlying binary structure for defining psychoanalysis in opposition to psychotherapy, and contribute to some of its most problem-atic splits, including: analyzable/non-analyzable; phallic/castrated; depth/ surface; rational analyst/irrational patient, among many others.

Freud's Jewish background, and the ways in which Jewish thought and tradition influenced his thinking, have been the subject of considerable scholarly debate examining the Jewish nature, if any, of psychoanalysis. While there have been significant contributions to this discussion by distin-guished psychoanalysts such as Martin Bergmann, Harold Blum, and others, much of the most provocative and compelling scholarship has been conducted outside of the realm of the psychoanalytic community, by histor-ians, anthropologists, and scholars in the fields of Jewish and cultural studies. We build upon the work of these scholars—in particular Gilman,

Boyarin, Brickman, Geller, Van Herik, and Yerushalmi—to address the ways in which Freud's Jewish identity and his desire for psychoanalysis to be accepted as a universal science by the German medical establishment to which he aspired had a significant impact on the way he formulated his psychoanalytic theories. Drawing from existing biographical material, Freud's own writing, and the work of these critical thinkers, we will elaborate how Freud dealt with his conflicted position as an acculturated German Jew in an anti-Semitic milieu by appropriating the binaries split by his society between gentile and Jew, and incorporating them into his theories, transforming their biologically racial specificity into psychological universality; in the process, attributing to women the negative characteristics his society ascribed to Jews. Note that we are not claiming that Freud's Judaism and the surrounding anti-Semitism are the *only* factors that explain why psychoanalysis developed the way it did. Our exploration of the impact of Jewishness and anti-Semitism on Freudian thought is not intended to diminish the overwhelming influence of patriarchy, including the effect of patriarchy on Jewishness and anti-Semitism.[1]

We acknowledge that the question of whether psychoanalysis can or should in any way be considered a Jewish science is, to say the least, a controversial one, and has resulted in sharply conflicting opinions. Consistent with Freud's public presentation, Peter Gay (1987) contended, "The claim for the Jewishness of psychoanalysis based on its materials or its intellectual inheritance have proved to be without foundation . . . Freud . . . was a Jew but not a Jewish scientist" (pp. 147–148). Placing himself in direct opposition to this view, historian Yosef Hayim Yerushalmi (1991) cries out to Freud in imaginary protest that psychoanalysis is "a metamorphosed extension of Judaism . . . psychoanalysis is a godless Judaism. But I don't think you intend us to know this" (p. 99).

We recognize, as did Freud himself, that Jewish pride has often been tempted to claim psychoanalysis as its own. Anna Freud, in her remarks given at the founding of the Sigmund Freud Chair of Psychoanalysis at Hebrew University in Jerusalem (read by her friend Arthur Valenstein), noted that psychoanalysis had been repeatedly rejected by academic institutions, criticized "for its methods being imprecise, . . . for being unscientific, even for being a 'Jewish science.'" To the surprise of the

---

1 See in particular Seidman (1994), who critiques "Gilman's claim that the masculine defines Jewish experience, for both antisemites and Jews," p. 122. See also Rose (2008), who contends that Gilman's explanation does not account for Freud's view of the masculinity complex, or woman as failed maculinity. In other words, why are women masculine and hysterical and masochistic? Rose argues that Freud simply accepted these as characteristics of the "quintessential Jewish woman, counterpart to the feminine Jewish male" (p. 155).

audience, she added, "I believe the last-mentioned connotation . . . can serve as a title of honour" (Freud, A. 1978, p. 148). Anna was 82 years old and had never been to Israel. Reijzer comments on this astonishing remark,

> [Anna Freud] made Jewish history a part of psychoanalytic history and in passing made psychoanalysis a part of Jewish history . . . a completely unexpected step for a woman who had presented herself all her life as a psychoanalyst and had never taken a position as a Jew. Here she came forward as the ambassador of her father: Sigmund Freud, the Jewish atheist.
>
> (2011, p. 85)

We also take serious heed, particularly in light of the Holocaust, of Martin Bergmann's warning that the term "Jewish science" has been used as an anti-Semitic defamation with dire results. Insisting that "psychoanalysis has to be evaluated independent of its author's biography," Bergmann (1979) adds, "The biography of its originator is relevant to his discovery only when it can be shown to distort or limit the validity of the discovery itself" (p.133). While we agree with Bergmann's point that psychoanalysis should not be judged based on Freud's Jewishness or cultural background, we contend that in our contemporary culture, psychoanalysis has already been judged by many as being limited in validity, and has been effectively killed off—sharply criticized, if not rejected outright in many settings and sectors of society. Our aim in examining psychoanalysis' origins and subsequent history is to better comprehend its flaws so they may be corrected. Like any good analysis, one must understand the past, the "genetics," not as an end in itself but as a vehicle for insight and change.

Freud viewed psychoanalysis as an objective science, considering his creation scientifically valid in its own right. Therefore, he did not imagine applying a psychoanalytic investigation to the theoretical formulations of psychoanalysis itself. Ironically, however, this is *exactly* what he proposed with regard to other philosophical systems of thought that are the products of creators of "striking individuality"! In support of our own proposal for gaining deeper insight into the theoretical origins of psychoanalysis through a psychoanalytic understanding of its creator, we feel compelled to quote Freud directly:

> Psycho-analysis enables us to construct a "psychography" of a personality . . . It teaches us to recognize the affective units—the complexes dependent on instincts—whose presence is to be presumed in each individual, and it introduces us to the study of the transformations and end-products arising from these instinctual forces. It reveals the relations of a person's constitutional disposition and the events of his life to the achievements open to him owing to his peculiar gifts. It can

conjecture with more or less certainty from an artist's work the intimate personality that lies behind it. In the same way, psycho-analysis can indicate the subjective and individual motives behind philosophical theories which have ostensibly sprung from impartial logical work, and can draw a critic's attention to the weak spots in the system. It is not the business of psycho-analysis, however, to undertake such criticism itself, for, as may be imagined, the fact that a theory is psycho-logically determined does not in the least invalidate its scientific truth.

(1913c, p. 179)

Our examination of the particularity of the Jewishness of psychoanalysis is not simply an appeal to some national, cultural, or ethnic pride. Rather, our goal is to frame the topic in a universalistic discourse that we believe is not only extremely relevant to an understanding of the current state of clinical theory and practice within psychoanalysis, but is also absolutely critical for re-envisioning its future, if psychoanalysis is to have a future. The Jewishness of psychoanalysis cannot be understood without reference to anti-Semitism, which in turn cannot be separated from homophobia, misogyny, and other forms of racism. Understanding the ways in which the dichotomies underlying these forms of racial and gender prejudice are embedded within psychoanalytic theory will enable us to move beyond this type of polarized thinking, with the goal of re-imagining a psychoanalysis that is more pluralistic, embracing of difference, and universally relevant to our contemporary society. Such a reimagining is crucial if psychoanalysis is to survive.

We must be clear that our intent is not to denigrate Freud or to blame him for the current dire state of the field. To the contrary, our goal is to underscore that both the brilliance of his thinking as well as its flaws were an inevitability of Freud's conflicted position as a Jew in a society that despised him and yet with which he deeply identified. Referring to the generation of writers caught between two worlds—between Jewish and Greek/humanistic, German/*Bildung* culture—Kafka wrote, "their hind legs were bogged down in their father's Judaism, and their front legs could find no new ground. The resulting despair was their inspiration." Kafka famously identified psychoanalysis as the "Rashi commentary" on his generation's struggles (cited in Robert, 1976, pp. 8–9). Drawing on Kafka's observations, Robert (1976) characterized Freud as a "torn-soul" trapped between two cultures, viewing Freud's discovery of psychoanalysis as his attempt at reconciliation.

It was inevitable that the person who created psychoanalysis was on the margins—following McLaughlin (2001), we would say he was optimally marginal. Freud was both insider and outsider; black and white; a Jew who aspired to be German in culture; and a married heterosexual man who had also loved another man, meeting him in congresses and comparing menstrual cycles with him. We contend that it was inevitable that only someone who was both on the inside and the outside, who intrepidly examined his own psyche in order to discern the universal processes of the mind, could have invented psychoanalysis. Inhabiting both sides of the dichotomy of insider and outsider, German and Jew, analyst and patient, Freud left psychoanalysis with a legacy not only of conservatism, of adapting and fitting in to the culture, but also of radicalism, of critiquing the culture as if from the outside.

It is only by taking into account the complexity of Freud's subjective position as well as the larger context in which he lived and worked that we can begin to unpack the ways in which he arrived at his theoretical formulations. Fittingly for a discipline whose universal principles were derived from its founder's willingness to plumb the depths of his unconscious, it is only through an understanding of Freud's subjective experience—both conscious and unconscious—that we can provide an objective critique of his theoretical formulations. It is only when we understand Freud's position as a Jew in an anti-Semitic context that the foundations of psychoanalysis— Freud would call them its "bedrock"—make sense.

Freud strongly identified as a Jew—that is, as an acculturated Western Jew in the Enlightenment tradition. Yet he made a point of dissociating himself from traditional "primitive" and "barbaric" ritual as well as from the *Ostjuden*, the Eastern Jews, who in both the Jewish and non-Jewish imagination, exemplified the racial anti-Semitic stereotypes attributed by the surrounding society to all Jews, including Freud himself. Consciously rejecting the anti-Semitic characterization of the Jew as passive, dependent, and feminine, Freud identified with a masculinized Judaism, a Judaism that was defiant in the face of an opposing majority; that was, like psychoanalysis, abstract, civilized, intellectual, moral, and deep (Van Herik, 1982). Freud envisioned himself as a Jewish hero. He identified with Hamilcar, son of Hannibal, the Semitic general who stood up to the more powerful Romans, and with Moses, a decisive, ruthless man of action. In so doing, Freud was renouncing his father's passivity, and with it, the traditional Jewish understanding of what it meant to be a Jewish man. In the process, he was disavowing his own vulnerability, passivity, dependence, and femininity, a disavowal that was then unconsciously embedded in his psychoanalytic theories.

Yet Freud also identified with another important Jewish biblical figure, Joseph; one who was heroic not because of his brute strength or courage, but because of his particular (might we say particularly Jewish?) ability to interpret dreams, to delve beneath the surface, to perceive what is hidden, and be attuned to deeper meanings. Although Freud called the interpretation of dreams "the royal road to the unconscious," the path of the dream interpreter is not a direct route, but a circuitous wandering beset by "tangles and dream-thoughts which cannot be unravelled" (Freud, 1900b, p. 525). The Wandering Jew, a counterpart to the Oedipal hero, traverses the royal road not by direct confrontation but by unraveling tangled threads, reading hidden signs, and at times, encountering "unplumbable" points that reach down into the unknown, the uncanny, and the feminine; points where even a hero cannot help but turn away.

Freud's response to his culture's anti-Semitism, including his insistence that the "subjective factor," i.e. his Jewishness, had nothing to do with his theories, contributed significantly to his conceptualization of castration anxiety and the Oedipus complex as the universal source of neurosis, as well as to his stress on the analyst's anonymity and neutrality. It is difficult, if not impossible, to understand Freud's theoretical emphases on masculinity, autonomy, and the "repudiation of femininity" without taking into account Freud's disavowal of his own vulnerability, dependence, and "feminine" (read Jewish) qualities. Freud's identification as a Jew in the context of anti-Semitism led to theoretical and clinical developments that continue to be enacted even in our contemporary practice, forming the basis for the split between psychoanalysis and psychotherapy, as well as for the asymmetrical structuring of the psychoanalytic situation between patient and analyst. We will show that in Freud's formulation, to be on the side of health, masculinity, and civilized autonomy, to avoid speaking as a degenerate, feminized, primitive, contaminated, castrate, the analyst had to speak from a position of anonymity, neutrality, and abstinence. In other words, in order to speak from a position of power and authority, the analyst could not, above all, speak as a Jew.

The Right to Pass

A fitting place to begin our discussion of the influence on psychoanalysis of Freud's Jewish identity is at the site of Freud's most intimate public revelation of his private subjectivity. *The Interpretation of Dreams* (1900b) was the product of Freud's self-analysis, precipitated by his father's death, which Freud referred to as a "most poignant loss," "the most important event" "of a man's life" (Freud, 1900b, p. xxvi). A treasure trove of childhood memories, dreams, and self-observations, *The Interpretation of Dreams* is peppered with references to figures from the Old Testament and images from Freud's family's Phillipsohn Bible, an evocative symbol of Freud's Jewish attachment, to which we will return. It is the place where Freud revealed "to the public gaze more of the intimacies of my mental life than I liked, or than is normally necessary for any writer who is a man of science and not a poet" (Freud, 1900b, pp. xxiii–xxiv). It is here that Freud reports the following event from his childhood:

> At that point I was brought up against the event in my youth whose power was still being shown in all these emotions and dreams. I may have been ten or twelve years old, when my father began to take me with him on his walks and reveal to me in his talk his views upon things in the world we live in. Thus it was, on one such occasion, that he told me a story to show how much better things were now than they had been in his days. "When I was a young man," he said, "I went for a walk one Saturday in the streets of your birthplace; I was well dressed, and had a new fur cap on my head. A Christian came up to me and with a single blow knocked off my cap and shouted: 'Jew! Get off the pavement!' " "And what did you do?" I asked. "I went into the roadway and picked up my cap," was his quiet reply. This struck me as unheroic conduct on the part of the big, strong man who was holding the little boy by the hand. I contrasted this situation with another which fitted my feelings better: The scene in which Hannibal's father, Hamilcar Barca, made his boy swear before the household altar to take vengeance on the Romans. Ever since that time Hannibal had had a place in my phantasies.
>
> (Freud, 1900b, p. 197)

Much has been written about this story, focusing on Freud's biography and his various identifications. Daniel Boyarin's (1997) *Unheroic Conduct* is named for this very incident, and we draw liberally upon his work here. But while the aforementioned anecdote has attracted much scholarly attention, we must first attend to its place in Freud's dream book. Freud relates this incident of unheroic conduct as one link in a chain of associations that led him to his longing to visit Rome and to his identification with Hannibal. He writes, "To my youthful mind Hannibal and Rome symbolized the conflict between the tenacity of Jewry and the organization of the Catholic church" (p. 196). Freud claims that his identification with the Semitic general Hannibal, and his sympathy with the Carthaginians over the Romans in the Punic Wars, represented in his own mind his identification with Jewry in the context of racial anti-Semitism. "I began to understand for the first time," he writes, "what it meant to belong to an alien race" (p. 196).

Freud was 10 or 12 at the time he first imagined himself having a different, more manly, Jewish response than his father. He would return to the motif of feeling himself an "alien because I was a Jew" (Freud, 1925a, p. 9), the next time at age 17, upon his entry into the university, when "the anti-semitic feelings among the other boys warned me that I must take up a definite position" (Freud, 1900b, p. 196). The position Freud adopted was most definitively not that of a meek *shtetl* Jew submitting passively to Christian authority; rather Freud saw himself as a defiant Jewish hero taking a stance against the anti-Semitic majority. In stark contrast to the behavior of his unheroic father Jakob, Freud prided himself on his courage in confronting the anti-Semitic threat.

At the age of 27, Freud (1883) related the story of his "first great adventure" (p. 78) to his fiancée Martha. Traveling on a train from Dresden to Riesa and desiring fresh air, Freud opened a window. Several of his fellow passengers asked him to close it, when,

> there came a shout from the background: "He's a dirty Jew!"—And with this the whole situation took on a different color. My first opponent also turned anti-Semitic and declared: "We Christians consider other people, you'd better think less of your precious self," . . . my second opponent announced that he was going to climb over the seats to show me . . . I was not in the least frightened of that mob, asked the one to keep to himself his empty phrases which inspired no respect in me, and the other to step up and take what was coming to him. I was quite prepared to kill him, but he did not step up . . . I felt very ready for a fight . . . I do think I held my own quite well . . . After all, I am no giant, haven't any hackles to show, no lion's teeth to flash, no stentorian roar, my appearance is not even distinguished; all this would have had a lightning effect on that mob, but they must have noticed that I wasn't afraid and I didn't allow this experience to dampen my spirits.
>
> (1883, pp. 78–79)

Freud's behavior on his travels stands in sharp contrast to his father's reaction to the Christian's command, "Jew! Get off the pavement!" Freud makes the point that although (unlike the *goyim?*) he is not particularly strong or physically intimidating, he was "not in the least frightened." Rather tellingly, he later fantasized to his fiancée that his future biography would be called "The Development of the Hero" (Freud, 1885, p. 141). In 1886, he wrote to Martha,

> I was always the bold oppositionist . . . I have often felt as though I had inherited all the defiance and all the passions with which our ancestors defended their Temple and could gladly sacrifice my life for one great moment in history.
>
> (1886, p. 648)

Significantly, the Jewish traits Freud believed he inherited were not the passive, feminine Jewish traits of his father, nor for that matter, of his father's fellow *Ostjuden*, but the masculine courage of his heroic Jewish ancestors. "Once upon a time we were a valiant nation," wrote Freud

(1938b). Although "we Jews have been reproached for growing cowardly in the course of the centuries . . . In this transformation I had no share" (p. 454). Emphasizing the honing of the Jewish character through adversity, Freud (1907) wrote to his Jewish colleague Karl Abraham, "The fact that things will be more difficult for you as a Jew will have the effect, as it has with all of us, of bringing out the best in you" (p. 9).

Freud was reportedly a rather different model to his offspring than his father was to him, as evident from this 1901 incident recalled by his sons, Martin and Oliver. While fishing, they were subjected to anti-Semitic insults from a group of people in the area. "Swinging his stick, [Freud] charged the hostile crowd, which gave way before him, . . . allowing him free passage" (Oring, 1984, p. 46, cited in Blatt, 1988, p. 645). Throughout his life Freud continued to see himself as a defiant, masculine Jewish hero standing up to the forces of anti-Semitism; as we will see, his demand for the right of free passage would continue to reverberate throughout his foundational formulations.

We would like to explicitly draw a connection between Freud's father's being forced off the road and Freud's discovery of his own "royal road," the interpretation of dreams. In 1909, Freud used the Latin expression, *via regia*, which is not reproduced in Latin in the English translation. *"Die Traumdeutung aber ist die Via regia zur Kenntnis des Unbewussten im Seelenleben"* is instead translated as "The interpretation of dreams is the royal road to a knowledge of the unconscious activities of the mind" (quoted in Anzieu, 1986, p. 223). *Via regia* is the Latin term for the King's Highway, referred to in the Hebrew Bible (*Numbers*, Chapter 20, verse 17), in Hebrew as *derech hamelech*. It was on the King's Highway, the main route through the length of the Transjordan, that the Israelites were forbidden passage and were assaulted by the Edomites—"knocked off the road," according to Richard Armstrong (see Gottlieb, 2006, footnote 2, p. 1740). Remember too, that it was on a road, at a crossroads, that a man demanded that Oedipus stand aside so that he could pass, finally hitting Oedipus with his goad. It was upon this provocation that Oedipus killed the stranger who, unknown to Oedipus, was King Laius, his biological father. In sum, Freud was identified with Oedipus, who unlike the Israelites—and unlike his unheroic father Jakob—would not be pushed off the road. And so Freud created his own royal road, the interpretation of dreams, psychoanalysis, upon which he was indeed the hero and where Jews could travel free of attack, covered by the neutrality and anonymity of science.

The Subjective Factor

From the very beginning of his psychological explorations, Freud was plagued by what was not only the concern of a male German scientist in pursuit of objective reality, but also what we consider to be a particular aspect of Freud's Jewish Problem—the problem of suggestion, the dilemma of what Freud often called "the subjective factor." The conundrum Freud faced was this: How could he know, and how could he satisfy his scientific colleagues, that his psychological discoveries about the mind were not simply projections of his own personal experiences or background rather than universal objective findings? Freud made every effort to counter such a possibility, insisting he did not suggest memories to his patients, when we know he did, and asserting that doctors could not possibly suggest false memories, in spite of the vast literature that argued they could do so. Freud wrote,

> The danger of our leading a patient astray by suggestion, by persuading him to accept things which we ourselves believe but which he ought not to, has certainly been enormously exaggerated . . . I can assert without boasting that such an abuse of "suggestion" has never occurred in my practice.
>
> (1937b, p. 262)

As we have demonstrated in Chapter 10, Freud learned a lesson by seeing his idol, Charcot, fall from the heights of world esteem primarily because his discoveries became tainted by suggestion. Freud was determined not to allow his own discoveries to be criticized as being due to suggestion, lest the same fate befall him as Charcot. Makari (2008) documents time after time when just such an accusation was made. Fliess' accusation, "The reader of thoughts merely reads his own thoughts into other people" (Freud, 1901, p. 447) would haunt Freud throughout his life. But suggestion had an additional component for Freud. He feared not only that his accusers would say his findings were tainted by his own subjectivity, but also that they would specifically disparage his entire project as being the imposition of Jewish cultural presuppositions or the result of his studying a primarily Jewish population of patients. Freud was afraid that in either case, whether due to his own Jewish influences or to his database of Jewish patients, his findings would not be considered objective and universal, but rather, subjective and specifically Jewish. In short, Freud feared psychoanalysis would be dismissed as a Jewish theory, using Jewish methodology to study Jewish pathology, leading to discoveries that were, at best, suitable to Jews.

Moreover, we can trace a direct, more disturbing, link between the "subjective factor" (i.e. suggestion) and Jewishness, mediated through the categories of primitivity, degeneracy, disease, contamination, and femininity. As Gilman (1993a, b) has extensively documented, in both the anti-Semitic and scientific formulations of the time, Jews were considered a primitive and degenerate race, due to what was referred to as their practice of "sexual inbreeding." Primitivity implied a lack of individuality, a merger with the masses, the primal horde; to be primitive was to lose one's boundaries and therefore be suggestible. Viewed as castrated by circumcision and feminized in the eyes of their surrounding society, male Jews shared with women many of the insults fin de siècle society cast upon its marginalized members. Note the claim of the anti-Semitic Jewish philosopher Weininger (1906) whom Freud references in his footnote to Little Hans, "Like women, Jews tend to adhere together, but they do not associate as free independent individuals" (p. 308). Jews, like women, were thought to be primitive and suggestible, incapable of (masculine) science, objectivity, abstract thought, and moral judgment. Significantly, as evidenced by the blatant anti-Semitism of the Jewish Weininger, these views were not limited to the surrounding non-Jewish society, but also took shape in the internalized anti-Semitism of many acculturated German Jews, including Freud.

Desiring to be viewed as a "neutral" male scientist capable of objective observation, Freud distanced himself from his society's characterization of the feminized, primitive, suggestible Jew. In the paranoid anti-Semitic rhetoric of Freud's day, Jews were associated with contamination and disease, and Freud sought to dissociate himself from the contamination of suggestion. Freud valorized psychoanalysis as an abstract, intellectual, scientific, moral, and therefore "masculine" discipline. Transforming the rhetoric of race into the rhetoric of gender, he constructed within his psychoanalytic theories an image of the female onto which he projected the degraded qualities of the male Jew (Gilman, 1993a). Himself swimming in the soup of his anti-Semitic milieu, Freud (1915b) would famously refer to women as primitive and immoral, capable only of "the logic of soup, with dumplings for arguments" (p. 167). Paralleling the anti-Semitic view of the hidden sexual nature of the Jew (marked by the hidden sign of circumcision), Freud proclaimed women inaccessible and indecipherable, "owing to their conventional secretiveness and insincerity . . . veiled in an impenetrable obscurity" (Freud, 1905, p. 151). Female sexuality was a primitive, unknowable "dark continent" (Freud, 1925c, p. 244). Elevating masculinity while degrading femininity, Freud attempted to separate himself and his theories from what German society viewed as the feminine and Jewish traits of primitivity, immorality, and suggestibility.

Due to their perceived degeneracy, Jews were thought to be prone to nervous illness, particularly neurological disorders such as hysteria, in which suggestion played a prominent role. We know that Freud himself identified as hysteric, writing to Fliess, "if I succeed in resolving my own hysteria" (Freud, 1897f, p. 262), and regularly reporting on his numerous neurotic symptoms. Boyarin (1997) highlights the fin de siècle representation of hysteria as feminine, and in the case of hysterical men, as homosexual. Freud never forgot the negative reception he received from the German medical establishment in response to his presentation of a case of male hysteria upon his return from his training with Charcot. While we have mentioned other plausible explanations, including German competition with the French and the question of compensation for traumatic injuries, Boyarin contends that it was the presentation of hysteria, a "women's malady," occurring in a man that so incensed the audience, as it raised the specter of the homosexual, feminized man. Further, it was the degenerate male Jew, marked as castrated by circumcision, who typified such a man. Freud was well aware that in the eyes of his surrounding community, he himself fit that configuration.

Gilman (1993b) notes that in the prevailing medical view of the 19th century, degeneration, thought to be a leading cause of obsessional neurosis, was even one of the explanations for the prevalence of Jewish creativity in cultural and scientific fields. Undoubtedly sensitive to the likelihood that he himself would be viewed as a hysterical or obsessional Jewish degenerate, albeit a clever one, a *dégénéré supérieur*, Freud repeatedly repudiated the notion of hereditary degeneracy, emphasizing psychological factors as the source of nervous illness. He commented,

> Psychiatry has found a way out of speaking of *"dégénérés supérieurs."* Very nice. But we have found from psychoanalysis that it is possible to get permanently rid of these strange obsessional symptoms, just as of other complaints and just as in people who are not degenerate. I myself have succeeded repeatedly in this.
>
> (1917, pp. 260–261)

Jews were associated in the popular and medical imagination with sexuality, disease, and madness, all of which were linked to their purported degeneracy. Circumcision marked the Jew as damaged, impaired, and diseased (Gilman, 1993a). Jews were associated with high rates of syphilis, which was sexually transmitted and in its tertiary stage led to madness.[2] Freud's colleague at the University of Vienna, Alexander Pilcz, of the Department of Psychiatry, argued that Jews presented more frequently than any other race with infections of the nervous system due to syphilis. In *Mein Kampf* (1925), Hitler would link the Jews with an epidemic of syphilis, attributing it to their sexually corrupt nature, and accusing the Jews of contaminating the pure, healthy, Aryan nation and weakening the fiber of German society (cited in Gilman, 1993a).

Freud urgently wanted to avoid psychoanalysis being characterized as the product of Jewish degeneracy, the brainchild of a Jewish scientist

---

2 At the same time, there was also an opposite association of Jews and syphilis in the medical literature—in which Jews were linked with *lower* rates of syphilis than the rest of the population (Gilman, 1993a).

incapable of real science or objectivity, capable only of building up false ideas through suggestion in the primitive and suggestible minds of his degenerate Jewish patients. Thus Freud's insistence on eliminating the "subjective factor" that contaminated scientific objectivity was inextricably tied to the subjective fact of his own Jewishness, and to his associated efforts to expunge the taint of primitivity, suggestibility, femininity, contamination, and hereditary degeneration from his psychoanalytic theories.

Freud wished to see psychoanalysis thrive as a value-free science but, as he confided to Abraham, feared it would instead become a "Jewish national affair" (Abraham and Freud, 1965, p. 34). In order to avoid this sectarian fate, Freud sought a non-Jew to take over its leadership, hoping Jung would fulfill that role. Freud envisioned himself as Moses, the leader of the Jewish people, who would bring psychoanalysis to the border of the Promised Land—universal acceptance by the non-Jewish scientific community—although he would not be allowed to enter it. This motif first appeared in *The Interpretation of Dreams*, associated with his longing for Rome, where Freud wrote,

> someone led me to the top of a hill and showed me Rome half-shrouded in mist; . . . There was more in the content of this dream than I feel prepared to detail; but the theme of "the promised land seen from afar" was obvious in it.
>
> (1900b, p. 194)

It reappeared more explicitly in his January 17, 1909 letter to Jung, when he wrote, "We are certainly getting ahead. If I am Moses, then you are Joshua and will take possession of the promised land of psychiatry, which I shall only be able to glimpse from afar" (p. 196). Freud (1907) would yet again refer to himself as alien, writing to Jung, "you are more suitable as a propagandist, for I have invariably found that something in my personality, my words and ideas strike people as alien, whereas to you all hearts are open" (p. 256). That alien "something" in Freud's personality, words, and ideas was the fact of his Jewishness.

In anointing Jung, a non-Jew, as his successor to lead the psychoanalytic movement, Freud had to quell the doubts of his Jewish colleagues, reminding them of the value of putting a non-Jewish face to psychoanalysis. Yet, ironically, in the process of attempting to publicly present psychoanalysis as a universal science, Freud privately gave the impression that both he and his creation were best understood by Jews. Responding to Abraham's doubts about Jung, Freud wrote,

> Be tolerant, and do not forget that really it is easier for you to follow my thoughts than it is for Jung, since to begin with you are completely

independent, and then you are closer to my intellectual constitution through racial kinship, while he as a Christian and a pastor's son finds his way to me only against great inner resistances.

(1908a, p. 38)

Freud's fear that psychoanalysis would be perceived as a Jewish science was soon amplified; Freud discovered that Jung was clearly not suited to be Joshua to Freud's Moses. Freud reacted to this realization by reiterating his insistence on the universality of his creation while at the same time revealing the Jewish identifications of its creator. In a June 8, 1913 letter to Ferenczi regarding Jung's dissension and his statement to the Americans that "psychoanalysis was not a science but a religion," Freud insisted, "there should not be a particular Aryan or Jewish science" (Freud, 1913a, pp. 490–491). Yet ironically, Freud began this letter in the language of one Jew to another, exclaiming, "Our dear Swiss have gone crazy [*meshugge geworden*]," using the Yiddish term instead of the German!

By 1918, Jung elaborated his belief that theoretical divergences were due to national characteristics, pointing to "the specifically Jewish doctrines" of Freud and Adler that reduced motivation to narrow drives for sex and power, a theory "beneficial and satisfying to the Jew, because it is a form of simplification" (Bair, 2003, p. 435). Evoking the anti-Semitic image of the Wandering Jew, Jung maintained that the Jew's nomadic rootlessness made the Jew's creativity, especially in the realm of psychology, of value only for the Jew: "thus it is a quite unpardonable mistake to accept the conclusions of a Jewish psychology as generally valid" (cited in Gilman, 1993a, p. 31). In the mid-1930s, with the Nazis firmly in power, Jung would emphasize and publicize his own belief in the differences between Semitic, Chinese, Swiss, and German psychologies. He wrote,

In my opinion it has been a grave error in medical psychology up till now to apply Jewish categories—which are not even binding on all Jews—indiscriminately to Germanic and Slavic Christendom. Because of this the most precious secret of the Germanic peoples—their creative and intuitive depth of soul—has been explained as a morass of banal infantilism, while my own warning voice has for decades been suspected of anti-Semitism. This suspicion emanated from Freud. He did not understand the Germanic psyche any more than did his Germanic followers. Has the formidable phenomenon of National Socialism, on which the whole world gazes with astonished eyes, taught them better?

(Jung, 1934, p. 166)

Despite Jung's repeated protestations that he was not an anti-Semite, Nazi propaganda used Jung's pronouncements to obliterate the "wholly

Jewish" science of Freud (Bair, 2003, p. 443). As Bergmann (1995) observed, the attempt to hide the discoveries of a circumcised Jew "behind a gentile fig leaf" (p. 246) was ultimately, a devastating failure. Under Nazi pressure, Freud was forced to disband the Vienna Psychoanalytic Society at its March 13, 1938 board meeting, during which it was decided that everyone should flee the country. Faced at the end of his life with the anti-Semitic threat he had most feared, Freud, evoking a critical moment in Jewish history, as he typically did at serious turning points in his life, declared, "After the destruction of the Temple in Jerusalem by Titus, Rabbi Jochanan ben Zakkai asked for permission to open a school at Yavneh for the study of the Torah. We will do the same" (cited in Richards, 2010, p. 3). Vienna was now Jerusalem, psychoanalysis Torah, and Freud, its rabbinic hero, fleeing into exile.

"Unlaid Ghosts" and "Obscure Emotional Forces"

No discussion of either Freud's or psychoanalysis' Jewish identity is possible without acknowledging the powerful role played by the virulent anti-Semitism of Freud's cultural surround in shaping their development. Although Freud's family was of Eastern origin, Freud went to great lengths to distance himself from his culture's characterizations of the *Ostjuden* at the same time as he internalized the anti-Semitic stereotype. Gilman (1993a) documents the contempt Freud showed in his writings for the Eastern Jew, whom he viewed as primitive, diseased, mendacious, and speaking a crude language. Freud was ashamed of his boorish brethren and in comparison, considered himself a member of High German *Kultur*. He made a point of publicly and privately distinguishing himself from this group, disavowing familiarity with their traditions, rituals, and even, rather unbelievably, their language. Although Freud denied knowledge of Yiddish, it is quite likely that his mother Amalia, who moved to Galicia from Vienna only as an adult, primarily—perhaps even exclusively—spoke Yiddish instead of German (Rice, 1990). It is certainly highly unlikely that Freud, who visited his mother almost every Sunday of her life, knew as little of the language as he claimed.

Similarly, while Freud publicly maintained he was "ignorant of the language of the holy writ" and "completely estranged from the religion of his fathers" (Freud, 1913d, p. xv), this claim appears to have been at least somewhat disingenuous. On Freud's 35th birthday, his father gave him the Phillipsohn Bible they had read together when Freud was a child, rebound in leather and inscribed with a *melitzah*, a Hebrew anagram comprised of biblical quotes linked together through complex associations, requiring a thorough knowledge both of Hebrew and of the biblical text. This was a particularly fitting gift from a knowledgeably Jewish father to his psychoanalyst son, for as Yerushalmi (1991) points out, "In *melitzah* the sentences compounded out of quotations mean what they say; but below and beyond the surface they reverberate with associations to the original texts, and this is what makes them psychologically so interesting and valuable" (p. 72).

The Freud family Bible, written side by side in German and Hebrew, was clearly highly meaningful to both father and son, symbolic not only of their relationship to each other, but to each in his own way, their Judaism. In his *Autobiographical Study* Freud (1925a) would acknowledge (but in a sentence only added in 1935), "My deep engrossment in the Bible story (almost as soon as I had learnt the art of reading) had, as I recognized much later, an enduring effect upon the direction of my interest" (p. 8). Calling Freud's postscript an act of "deferred obedience" to his father Jakob, Yerushalmi (1991) notes that Freud was only able to add this sentence after he completed the draft of *Moses and Monotheism*, his "attempt to answer the hitherto unanswerable question of what makes him a Jew" (p. 77). Yerushalmi's detailed explication of the *melitzah* Jakob Freud inscribed to his son indicates that his gift was meant as a "memorial and a reminder of love" (p. 74) and was "a call for Sigmund's return and reconciliation" (p. 73). Yerushalmi's exegesis explains that Jakob Freud was giving his son the Bible for the second time, a striking parallel to the two sets of the Ten Commandment tablets given to Moses, the first of which he shattered in anger. Jakob's *melitzah* indicated that Jakob had stored the "broken fragments" for his son Schlomo (Freud's Hebrew name), in anticipation of his son's hoped-for return to their shared Jewish values.

Despite Freud's rejection of the tradition and religious ritual associated with the Jews from the East, there is no doubt that Freud felt most comfortable among Jews—that is, acculturated German Jews like himself. In contrast to Freud's experience of himself as "alien" in a society that viewed him as such, Freud felt "at home" among intellectual, Westernized Jews who shared his humanitarian Enlightenment ideals. Klein (1985) documents Freud's use of the B'nai B'rith in the early years of psychoanalysis as the primary intellectual forum in which he could present his burgeoning psychoanalytic ideas to a receptive and supportive audience. As Freud (1926a) himself put it in his address to the group many years later, "at a time when no one in Europe listened to me and I still had no disciples even in Vienna, you gave me your kindly attention. You were my first audience" (p. 274).

It was no accident that Freud first joined the B'nai B'rith in 1897, a year of devastating political, professional, and personal disappointments, all due to the revival of official government-sanctioned anti-Semitism. It was the year Karl Lueger was confirmed as Mayor of Vienna, dashing Jewish Enlightenment hopes and leading to a deep sense of despair among Vienna's Jews. It was at this time that Freud, who had been hoping to be appointed to the rank of Professor at the medical school, also found his professional aspirations quashed. Unable to ignore the implications of the rise to political power of the anti-Semitic movement in Vienna and the anti-Jewish sentiment of the university establishment, Freud finally realized that because he was a Jew, he would never be promoted. It was against this backdrop of persecution by anti-Semitic forces more powerful than he that Freud dreamt of Rome, identified with Hannibal, and recounted his boyhood disappointment with his father's unheroic conduct. As Freud himself underscored in his discussion of these matters in *The Interpretation of Dreams*, "the increasing importance of the effects of the anti-semitic movement upon our emotional life helped to fix the thoughts and feelings of those early days" (Freud, 1900b, p. 196).

Having been rejected by the German medical community, and feeling "as though I were despised and universally shunned" (Freud, 1900b, p. 273), Freud withdrew from presenting his ideas at professional or academic conferences, instead finding an intellectual home in this welcoming Jewish brotherhood. It was to this audience, during the period of his self-analysis, sparked by his father's death, that Freud first presented the dream theories that would become the basis for *The Interpretation of Dreams*. As he shared his unfolding theoretical developments in his correspondence with Fliess, he presented them in person to the B'nai B'rith. Both Fliess and the B'nai B'rith provided Freud with a sympathetic audience, serving as substitutes for the less than friendly professional forums of the German medical community.

From 1897 until 1902, Freud was actively involved in the organization, presenting a total of 10 lectures to the group. Freud's personal physician, Ludwig Braun, a fellow B'nai B'rith member, once introduced Freud at a meeting, describing Freud's work as "genuinely Jewish" (Klein, 1985, p. 85). Emphasizing Freud's support of Jewish humanitarian ideals as evidenced by psychoanalysis' effort to discern the universal laws of the psyche that apply to all human beings, Braun asked rhetorically whether anyone could even imagine Freud not being Jewish. Very clearly, to those within the Society, it was unimaginable. Many early proponents viewed psychoanalysis as a redemptive messianic movement that would end anti-Semitism by freeing the world of neuroses produced by sexually repressive Western civilization. Klein (1985) shows that some of Freud's closest associates had a very clearly articulated conception of psychoanalysis as a Jewish mission to the gentiles—what one might view as a modern version of the biblical "light unto the nations" theme of Jewish religious thought very common among adherents of Reform Judaism at that time.

Klein views Freud's activities in the B'nai B'rith as a precursor to the official founding of the psychoanalytic movement. In 1902, aspiring for psychoanalysis to have a more universal breeding ground, Freud turned his attentions away from the B'nai B'rith and founded the Wednesday study group that became the Vienna Psychoanalytic Society, the base for the psychoanalytic movement. Yet for five years, until Jung and another Swiss psychiatrist, Ludwig Binswanger, attended their first meeting in 1907, all of the group's members (by that time, about 20 in total) were Jews.

Upon the occasion of his 70th birthday, Freud once again addressed the B'nai B'rith, repeating his refrain of Jewish defiance in the face of the "compact majority" with which we have become familiar. Yet this time Freud (1926a) also spoke of the "irresistible" lifelong "attraction" for him "of Jewry and Jews", attributing it to "obscure emotional forces, which were the more powerful the less they could be expressed in words" and admitting a "clear consciousness of inner identity, the *heimlichkeit* (hominess) of a common mental construction" (p. 274). As we will explore in greater detail in the next chapter, Freud (1919e) noted in his discussion of "The 'Uncanny'" that "*heimlich* is a word the meaning of which develops in the direction of ambivalence, until it finally coinicides with its opposite, *unheimlich*" (p. 226). Among the meanings of *heimlich* Freud provides in "The 'Uncanny'" is that which is "concealed, kept from sight, so that others do not get to know of or about it, withheld from others" (p. 223). Circumcision is just such an example of *heimlich*. Among the brotherhood of the B'nai B'rith, literally "Sons of the Covenant" (referring to the covenant between God and the Jewish man marked by circumcision), circumcision was the covenant binding them together in *heimlichkeit*, yet in the anti-Semitic view of the surrounding European culture, circumcision was the feminine, uncanny, *unheimlich* signifier of Jewish difference. To the Jews, including Freud, who experienced themselves as objects of the hostile anti-Semitic gaze, the shifting duality of *heimlich/unheimlich* spoke to the simultaneous canniness and uncanniness of their experience of their own Jewishness. It is precisely at the moment that Freud links his experience of Jewishness with the unconscious, the mysterious, and the uncanny, that he loses his fluidity with language; for once, Freud is at a loss for words.

Chapter 14

Universalizing the Jewish Problem

Let us return to the colonial and scientific paradigms of the fin de siècle, which will, in turn, lead us back to Freud's footnote to the case of Little Hans. As we have seen, Jews in the late 19th and early 20th centuries were not considered White, but were viewed as a dark-skinned, swarthy race. Jewish men and women were both perceived as homosexual. While Jewish women were considered aggressive and masculine, Jewish men, marked by circumcision, were viewed as castrated. Jewish men were thought to be passive and effeminate, perverse and degenerate, and since they were like women, hysteric. As we have shown, the characteristics attributed to Jews by the surrounding society were not simply viewed as cultural in nature or as responses to anti-Semitic circumstance, but as being due to racial degeneration, resulting from the Jewish practice of endogamous marriage, characterized as incestuous inbreeding. The biological explanation for Jewish degeneracy dovetailed perfectly with the shift in anti-Semitism away from religious prejudice toward racism.

Given the background of these anti-Semitic paradigms and their specific focus on the castrated, feminized, diseased, and disempowered nature of the circumcised male Jew, we can view Freud's footnote to Little Hans as a window into Freud's unconscious experience, shaped by the paradigms of his time. Freud explicitly links the little boy's fear of castration and anxiety about his own masculinity with the emergence of his hatred of women and Jews.

> The castration complex is the deepest unconscious root of anti-Semitism; for even in the nursery little boys hear that a Jew has something cut off his penis—a piece of his penis, they think—and this gives them a right to despise Jews. And there is no stronger unconscious root for the sense of superiority over women.
>
> (Freud, 1909a, p. 36)

Although its place in a footnote lends Freud's remark about anti-Semitism the air of an afterthought, we read it rather as Freud's compulsion to articulate that which he could not bring himself to say directly in the text. Given his awareness of his society's association of women and Jews and his sensitivity to his position as an "alien" among his own countrymen, there is no doubt that Freud felt himself to be the subject of the anti-Semitic view of the male Jew as castrated and feminine. Yet Freud was unable to consciously acknowledge this. While on the one hand he strongly identified as a Jew, he also strongly identified as a German Austrian and with German *Kultur* in the tradition of Heine and Goethe. Further, Freud fervently desired to be respected as an objective scientist and for his discoveries to be accepted as universally relevant.

The next year, 1910, in his description of the case of Leonardo, Freud (1910a) made a connection explicitly in the text between the boy's concern about his own masculinity and his subsequent feelings of misogyny. He wrote, "he will tremble for his masculinity, but at the same time he will despise the unhappy creatures on whom the cruel punishment has, as he supposes, already fallen" (p. 95). Although it took him nine years to do so, once again Freud was compelled to add to his text a footnote linking anti-Semitism to circumcision and castration. In 1919, he added,

> The conclusion strikes me as inescapable that here we may also trace one of the roots of the anti-semitism which appears with such elemental force and finds such irrational expression among the nations of the West. Circumcision is unconsciously equated with castration. If we venture to carry our conjectures back to the primaeval days of the human race we can surmise that originally circumcision must have been a milder substitute, designed to take the place of castration.
>
> (1919, p. 95)

Finally, at the end of his career, in *Moses and Monotheism* (1939), the culmination of his life's work, Freud explicitly elaborated on the origins of anti-Semitism at length and directly in the text, identifying the equation of circumcision with castration as one important cause of hatred toward Jews. "Further, among the customs by which the Jews made themselves separate, that of circumcision has made a disagreeable, uncanny impression, which is to be explained, no doubt, by its recalling the dreaded castration" (p. 91). Although here Freud makes no explicit mention of misogyny, it reappears in his description of circumcision as "uncanny," which, as we shall see, Freud (1919d) associated with the feminine, the maternal, and specifically, with the female genitals. We can thus trace across the decades Freud's hesitating, yet unambiguous equation of Judaism and circumcision with femininity and castration, all associated with the uncanny.

Reversing the terms of Freud's formula, Boyarin (1997) suggests that for Freud, "it is castration that recalls the dreaded circumcision, dreaded because it is this act that cripples a male by turning him into a Jew" (p. 235). Signifying alien, feminine "otherness," circumcision not only renders the male Jew uncanny to non-Jews, but also—and most significantly for our understanding of Freud in this context—to himself. Let us return again to the Little Hans footnote, where we are provided with just such an example of the uncanny reaction of the circumcised Jew to the reflected vision of himself as castrated:

> Weininger . . . in a chapter that attracted much attention, treated Jews and women with equal hostility and overwhelmed them with the same insults. Being a neurotic, Weininger was completely under the sway of his infantile complexes; and from that standpoint what is common to Jews and women is their relation to the castration complex.
>
> (Freud, 1909a, p. 36)

While Freud evokes Weininger as a "typical" anti-Semite who views Jews as feminine and castrated, he does not mention that Weininger himself was Jewish, instead giving the impression that Weininger was simply a non-Jewish anti-Semite typical of German society. Boyarin marks Freud's omission of Weininger's Jewishness, as well as Little Hans' and his own, as symptomatic of Freud's unconscious acceptance of his society's anti-Semitic stereotypes, "internalized to the point of self-torture" (Stieg, cited in Boyarin, 1997, p. 237). Boyarin argues that, suffering from his own unacknowledged Jewish self-hatred, Freud unconsciously *accepted as true* the anti-Semitic characterization of the male Jew as castrated and feminine; thus, like the little boys he describes as looking in the mirror and feeling contempt for Jews, looking at himself in the mirror produced in Freud the same feeling of uncanniness as that of a non-Jew gazing at a Jew. As we shall elaborate further, something of this experience is captured in Freud's essay "The 'Uncanny'" (1919e), in which he recalls a moment when he saw an unpleasant reflection in a looking-glass and did not recognize it as his own. Building on Gilman's (1993a, b) scholarship, Boyarin identifies Freud's unconscious experience of his own uncanny Jewish femininity as the source of his theorizing that the "repudiation of femininity" is the "bedrock" of psychoanalysis.

In Freud's Oedipal formulation, the qualities of rationality, objectivity, morality, and sincerity are all quite literally associated with phallic masculinity. Freud maintained that the superego emerges from the shattering of the Oedipus complex, which is accomplished only through the experience of the shock of threatened castration. He located the "problem" of femininity in the damaged, already-castrated female genitals, attributing the weak superego of women to their lack of castration anxiety. By this logic, "the logic of soup, with dumplings for arguments" (Freud, 1915b, p. 167),[1] women are—due to the nature of their inferior genitals—emotional, irrational, subjective, and immoral. Freud wrote,

> I cannot evade the notion (though I hesitate to give it expression) that for women the level of what is ethically normal is different from what it is in men. Their super-ego is never so inexorable, so impersonal, so independent of its emotional origins as we require it to be in men. Character-traits which critics of every epoch have brought up against women—that they show less sense of justice than men, that they are less ready to submit to the great exigencies of life, that they are more often influenced in their judgements by feelings of affection or hostility—all these would be amply accounted for by the modification in the formation of their super-ego which we have inferred above.
>
> (1925c, pp. 257–258)

In characterizing women as immoral, unethical, and incapable of objectivity—due to their genital "lack"—Freud—like the "infantile" Weininger—dealt with his internalized feelings of Jewish self-hatred by heaping upon women the same insults his society directed toward him.

Similarly, while disavowing/concealing his own experience of genital deficiency, Freud (1933) characterizes the experience of shame as "a feminine characteristic par excellence," attributing it to the "concealment of genital deficiency." He immediately adds, "If you reject this idea as fantastic and regard my belief in the influence of lack of a penis on the configuration of femininity as an idée fixe, I am of course defenceless" (p. 132). If we take into account Freud's experience of internalized anti-Semitism, we can read this remark ironically, as the breaking through of his unconscious awareness of the defensive function of his idée fixe! For if Freud did not project onto women the genital deficiency attributed to Jews, he would indeed be left defenseless against his own painful feelings of shame and vulnerability.

From Hysteric to Hero

Boyarin (1997) argues that Freud's adoption of the Oedipus complex from his position as a self-diagnosed hysteric was a defensive turn away from his

---

1 Misquoting Heine, Freud used this phrase in his "Observations on Transference-Love" to illustrate the primitive concreteness of some women—"women of elemental passionateness who tolerate no surrogates. They are children of nature who refuse to accept the psychical in place of the material" (Freud, 1915b, p. 167).

seduction theory of hysteria, which emphasized the passive (feminine) sexual position of the child in relation to the adult and therefore would have cast Freud himself as passively feminine—in other words, as homosexual. Freud's "discovery" of the Oedipus complex, which had as its foundation the boy's desire for the mother, enabled Freud to defend against his own unconscious passive (homosexual) desires and to identify himself with active and penetrating heterosexual masculinity. The homoerotic nature of Freud's hysteria was a diagnosis with which the psychoanalytic establishment agreed. In 1951, James Strachey wrote to Ernest Jones, "I was very much interested by your account of the suppressed passages in the Fliess letters. It is really a complete instance of folie à deux, with Freud in the unexpected role of hysterical partner to a paranoiac" (cited in Boyarin, 1997, p. 194). While hysteria was a characteristically feminine neurosis, paranoia was considered a characteristically masculine one, seen as a way of defending against unconscious homosexuality.

In the case of boys, sexual passivity, whether in relation to a male or female seducer, would be read as homosexual. Boyarin points out that this is exactly Freud's logic in relation to the Wolf Man, in which he formulates that female sexual aggression toward the boy, whether real or fantasized, translates into homosexual desire for the father, the desire to be passively penetrated. In the case of the Wolf Man, Freud wrote,

> It looks as though his seduction by his sister had forced him into a passive role, and had given him a passive sexual aim. Under the persisting influence of this experience he pursued a path from his sister via his Nanya to his father—from a passive attitude towards women to the same attitude towards men.
>
> (1918a, p. 27)

Freud (1897f) told a similar story to Fliess of his own childhood seduction by his nanny, writing, "She was my teacher in sexual matters" which accounted for "my own hysteria" and "neurotic impotence" (p. 269). If one applies Freud's formulation of the Wolf Man to Freud himself (as Boyarin suggests Freud did, but then turned away from its homoerotic implications with the creation of his Oedipal theory), the logical conclusion of Freud's childhood seduction by his nurse would be his homoerotic desire for his own father. Yet Freud's revelation to Fliess is immediately followed not by a confession of passive longing for his father, but by a fictional construction of the stirring up of his libido as a child of two or two and a half in response to seeing his mother naked (we must emphasize that this was a hypothesized event, not a recollected one), and his subsequent conclusion that the universal source of neurosis is the boy's Oedipal, heterosexual desire for his mother. Freud wrote,

I can only say shortly that *der Alte* [my father] played no active part in my case, but that no doubt I drew an inference by analogy from myself on to him; that the 'prime originator' [of my troubles] was a woman, ugly, elderly, but clever, who told me a great deal about God Almighty and Hell and who gave me a high opinion of my own capacities; that later (between the ages of two and two-and-a-half) my libido was stirred up towards *matrem*, namely on the occasion of a journey with her from Leipzig to Vienna, during which we must have spent the night together and I must have had an opportunity of seeing her *nudam*.

(1897f, p. 268)

Less than two weeks later, Freud is suddenly certain of his previously hypothesized attraction to his mother, and writes to Fliess that it has dawned on him that the boy's Oedipal desire for his mother and jealousy of his father is a "universal event in early childhood . . . the Greek legend seizes upon a compulsion which everyone recognizes because he senses its existence within himself" (Freud, 1897f, p. 272). Transforming his own boyhood experience of sexual passivity in relation to his nurse into active, masculine desire for his mother, Freud masculinizes—or more accurately, heterosexualizes—the homoerotic passivity he recognized in himself as a self-diagnosed Jewish male hysteric. By placing the boy's incestuous desire for his mother at the centerpiece of his universal theory of normal male development, Freud "obscures his experience as the passively desiring male" (Boyarin, 1997, p. 201), and with it, his own unconscious homosexual identifications. In the process, as Gilman (1993a, b) so cogently demonstrates, Freud is also disavowing his society's characterization of the Jewish male as homosexual, degenerate, and incestuous. By positing the child's incestuous desire for the parent as a universal phenomenon, Freud makes the point that it is not only Jews who are incestuous, "Everyone in the audience was once a budding Oedipus in fantasy" (Freud, 1897f, p. 272).

Boyarin argues that the ambivalent societal gendering of the Jewish male as female and therefore as particularly prone to hysteria was rooted not only in anti-Semitic fantasy, but also in the reality of the traditional masculine ideal of Eastern European Jewry. Seventeenth-century English physician Thomas Sydenham identified the typical male hysterical patient as, "such male subjects as lead a sedentary or studious life, and grow pale over their books and papers" (cited in Boyarin, 1997, p. 211). The pale, gentle yeshiva student who spent his days engaged in Torah study fit just this description, while his wife, typically a robust, energetic woman who ran the household and worked in business and commerce, was a perfect match for Freud's (1910a) description of the women whom he viewed as a root cause of the development of homosexuality in their sons—"masculine women, women with energetic traits of character, who were able to push the father out of his proper place" (p. 99) Of course, this was also a fitting characterization of Freud's own mother, a strong and energetic Galician woman, married to a much older, relatively passive and bookish Eastern European Jewish man.

Boyarin makes the case that the feminized traditional Jewish male ideal, symbolized by the circumcised penis as representing "wholeness" and a covenantal connection with God, was a way in which Jewish men could distinguish themselves—positively—against the non-Jewish, Roman notion of ideal masculinity as powerfully phallic and physically intimidating, and also including contempt for women and fear of the female body. Traditional rabbinic Judaism viewed physical prowess and martial strength disparagingly, referring to it contemptuously as *goyim naches*;[2] in the traditional Haggadah, the wicked son is always shown holding a weapon (see illustrations, Boyarin, 1997, pp. 52, 77). Even as late as 1938, the "wicked son" was portrayed as a muscular man in Roman dress (but wearing a yarmulke!).[3] Boyarin argues that, rather than demonstrating a "primitive" ignorance of "civilized" cultural values, traditional rabbinic Judaism deliberately rejected and reversed these European (originally Greek) cultural norms as a way to set itself apart from the dominant culture.

The New Jewish Man

Yet as Emancipation opened up new possibilities for Westernization and the increasing integration of Jews into the surrounding society, it brought with it what Boyarin identifies as a form of Jewish self-hatred, resulting in the development of the "new Jewish man," personified by Zionist leader Theodor Herzl (who lived just down the street from Freud, at 6 Bergasse), and the "muscle Jew," the invention of Max Nordau, Herzl's second in command. Nordau's vision of a new "muscular Judaism" called for the shedding of the traditional Jewish stereotype of bodily weakness and reliance on intellectuality in favor of a moral self-discipline emphasizing corporeality, physical strength, and agility. Boyarin maintains that the intensifying discourses of homophobia and misogyny at the turn of the century contributed to the already-existing self-consciousness of Westernized Jews, who were seen as feminine and homosexual by the surrounding society. The tortuous, internalized self-hatred experienced by

2 (GOY-em NAH-kes) n. Dubious pleasures; i.e. pleasures (*naches*) experienced by non-Jews (*goyim*).
3 A recent Haggadah published in Israel by a very traditional religious group portrays the wicked son as a soccer player! (Boyarin, 1997, p. 78).

these Jews, who viewed themselves as civilized members of German culture but continued to be disparaged as primitive by their European countrymen, led to the transvaluing of the traditional Jewish values of masculinity into something that was newly perceived as being negative and shameful. In contrast to the *mentsh*, who exemplified the gentle Jewish male ideal of *Edelkayt*, the new "muscle Jew" embodied the physical strength and aggressivity that had been traditionally disparaged by Jews as *goyim naches*. The "muscle Jew" was a phallic Jew, a Jew who would stand up and fight rather than passively submit to anti-Semitic insult. This idea of a new type of Jewish man, vigorously active, physically fit, and fully able to defend himself in a confrontation, was taken up by the Zionist movement in reaction against the perceived passivity of the traditional Jewish response to persecution. It reached its fullest form following the Holocaust, with the image of Jews marching passively to the gas chambers still fresh in the minds of the new Zionist pioneers, who were intent on building a Jewish national home that would be actively governed and defended by Jews.

Following the pogroms in Eastern Europe in the aftermath of World War I, approximately 400,000 Jews fled Galicia, many for Vienna, where, for the most part, the relatively well established, acculturated Viennese Jews received them with contempt. Many of these Eastern European Jewish refugees were captivated by the Zionist vision of the "new Jew," eager for the opportunity to shed the burden of their old identities. A number of early analysts, including Siegfried Bernfeld, Max Eitington, Otto Fenichel, and Paul Federn, among many others, were involved in socialism and Zionism in this context. Liban and Goldman (2000) document the creation of the radical Zionist scouting movement *Hashomer Hatzair*, founded on both Marxist and psychoanalytic principles. Placing Freudian theory at the cornerstone of its educational curriculum, *Hashomer Hatzair* brought European analysts to Palestine to practice "prophylactic" psychoanalysis with the goal of preventing neurosis. Analysts such as Karl Friedjung, who was a member of Freud's Wednesday Psychoanalytic Society, travelled from kibbutz to kibbutz, providing guidance to educators, lecturing to the community, and identifying children at risk. In this way, socially-minded analysts reached a vast number of people who otherwise would not have been exposed to psychoanalysis.

Understanding the revolutionary impulse of the *Hashomer Hatzair* as "a complex mixture of high ideals and self-hatred," Liban and Goldman describe the young pioneers as yearning to "transform themselves into . . . 'new Jews,' who were to become the antithesis of both the despised passive ghetto Jew of the East and the enlightened assimilated Jew of the West" (p. 896). They note that many adherents of the movement identified with revered literary figure Joseph Hayyim Brenner's personal essay depicting his father's response to anti-Semitism in Russia:

> My father was a peddler in the villages. He would cower at the barking
> of the dogs. He feared to pray in public, and lived on paltry hot dishes
> from Sabbath to Sabbath. Weighed down by a heavy load of wares,
> sidecurls cut, "kapota" on his head, he lived his life degraded, down-
> trodden, and full of fear. Once when the "good villagers" pounced upon
> him, he showed no signs of defending himself. He was a fearful man,
> my father. He tried to flee, but was pathetic even in his hasty retreat.
>
>   (Brenner, 1988, p. 597, cited in Liban and
>   Goldman, 2000, p. 897)

How strikingly similar to Freud's recollection of his father's passivity in
the face of anti-Semitic confrontation! Notably, there is no mention in
either of these accounts of the potentially fatal consequences of fighting
back. Both Zionism and Freud embraced the notion of the Jew as a fighter
who is not afraid to defend himself in a confrontation, even in a battle of
one against many.

Boyarin argues that the Zionist movement transformed the political
emasculation of the Jews of the European Diaspora into a power configuration of heteronormative phallic masculinity, which called upon the
European Jews to shed their feminine passivity and physical and emotional
weakness. Yet in Boyarin's view, the Zionist invention of the new Jewish
man was no more than a form of internalized anti-Semitism. It represented
an attempt to overturn the political and cultural characteristics that
marked the Jewish man as queer in the eyes of the larger society by encouraging the full embrace of that society's alien values, in service of the goal
of full Jewish assimilation, which Boyarin reads as annihilation.

Boyarin identifies the shift in Freud's thinking away from the seduction
theory of hysteria and the homosexual implications of its developmental
trajectory, and toward a heterosexually normative Oedipal theory of development, as being the direct result of Freud's subjective experience as a
feminized Eastern European Jew living in the context of fin de siècle society's preoccupation with sexuality during the very period in which the
notion of heterosexuality was invented. He characterizes Freud's adoption
of the Oedipus narrative as "Freud's family romance of escape from Jewish
queerdom into gentile, phallic heterosexuality" (Boyarin, 1997, p. 215).

By repressing his own homoerotic desire, Freud reinvented himself as a
member of the new category of heterosexual man, a category that—unlike
the traditional Jewish idea of masculinity—was predicated on the notion
that no "normal" man would feel desire for another man. Boyarin (1997)
writes,

> In short, not only was the new theory of psychoanalysis essentially an
> act of repression/overcoming, but the Oedipus model itself ought to be
> interpreted as a repression of homoerotic desire. In Freud, the

fundamental ideas of human sexual development are a sort of screen or supervalent thought for a deeper but very threatening psychic constituent that Freud had found in his own hysteria but that had then panicked him: the desire for "femaleness," for passivity, to be the object of another man's desire . . . The analysand in whom Freud came to disbelieve was thus himself.

(1997, p. 208)

Similarly, Feldman (1993) attributes Freud's turn away from the characters of the Hebrew Bible and toward Greek myth for his master account of family relationships to his unconscious discomfort with the same-sex identifications and submissions between fathers and sons that permeate the biblical narrative. Feldman demonstrates that the Hebrew Bible in particular, and Jewish culture in general, offer a model of family dynamics quite different from the intergenerational conflict and rigid gender roles postulated by Freud in his Oedipal master story. The story of Cain versus Abel, the Bible's first murder, does not support Freud's reconstruction of the murder of the father by the primal horde. An act of fratricide, not patricide, is the primal scene of Genesis. Despite the ubiquity of sibling rivalry within the Hebrew Bible, as well as in Freud's own personal life, as evidenced by his well-documented jealousy of his younger brother and the numerous rifts resulting from his intolerance of competing theoretical views, Freud showed very little theoretical interest in the subject.

Feldman notes that the women of Genesis are, in a sense, phallic women. They actively assert their authority, each according to her personality, while the men are often passive and submissive, emotionally attached, providers of nourishment and dwellers in tents. In the Hebrew Bible, gender boundary crossings often line up with the bisexual and homosexual implications of the negative Oedipus complex. Feldman highlights the disparity between the Freudian and biblical characterizations of male and female, active and passive, external and internal. Although the Bible is rife with stories of conflict and aggression, biblical fathers are rarely the ones expressing aggression, and "avoid conflict rather than arousing (and resolving) it" (Feldman, 1993, p. 76). Feldman believes that the negative Oedipus complex, with its bisexual and homosexual implications, was a threatening discovery even for Freud, let alone his (and our) fellow citizens, particularly of the male persuasion. It was probably this threat that delayed his recognition of it, and it may have been one of the reasons for his reliance on Greek drama rather than on biblical narrative.

In selecting the Oedipus myth as his family romance instead of a Jewish narrative, Freud made a concerted effort to shed his identity as Schlomo ben Yakov. By choosing the Greek over the Hebrew, Freud was unconsciously fantasizing that he was no longer Sigismund the son "of the abject

Jakob, but Oedipus, son of Laius, or Hannibal, son of Hamilcar" (Boyarin, 1997, p. 250).

Like Boyarin and Feldman, but from the perspective of a psychoanalyst-clinician, Roy Schafer (1973), too, highlights Freud's neglect of mothers, maternal authority, the pre-Oedipal, and the negative Oedipus complex. Remarking upon "the curious fact of Freud's diffidence with regard to the details of pre-oedipal-pregenital development," Schafer maintains that this diffidence is apparent in the use of the "prefix 'pre' in the words preoedipal and pregenital, as if there is only one real psychoanalytic vantage point, which is the boy's castration anxiety in his sexually rivalrous, fantastically exaggerated and frightening, *oedipal* and *genital* struggle with his father" (p. 277). As Schafer further notes, Freud neglected the negative Oedipal, using the positive Oedipal as his "principal explanatory tool," and viewing the negative Oedipal as a "problematic reversal inspired by defensive needs in the face of castration anxiety, though constructed out of the boy's love of his father" (p. 277). Following Freud, analysts have continued to neglect the negative Oedipal, seeing it either as pathological and/or as a defense against the positive Oedipal. Hence we see that Freud's defensiveness about Jews being passive, feminine, and homosexual has crept into psychoanalytic theory such that there are significant issues we continue to neglect.

The development of the notion of heterosexuality in the fin de siècle and its accompanying homophobia, the thoroughness with which the assumed-to-be circumcised Jewish male was constructed as castrated and queer, and the perception by Jews and non-Jews alike of the *Ostjude* as embodying all that was homosexual and hysterical, meant that for Freud to diagnose himself or any other man as hysteric was tantamount to implying he was not a man. The confluence of these factors, in combination with the invention of the new Jewish man, a masculinized Jew in the gentile phallic tradition, contributed to Freud's abandonment of hysteria and with it, the son's homoerotic fantasies of seduction by the father. Disavowing his own passive, homosexual longings, Freud turned instead toward the positive Oedipal theory, which accounted for the development of "normal" male virility in the boy's desire for the mother and aggression toward the father, and enabled Freud to mask his own homosexual dread.

Further, by universalizing the castration complex as a developmental structure, and by locating its source in the sight of the already-castrated female genitals—and in the case of Little Hans, in his mother's warning—Freud obscured the link between the ideational threat of castration and the reality of the position of the assumed-to-be circumcised Jew in fin de siècle European society. Like Weininger and Little Hans, Freud, too, heard the rumors his society spread about Jews, rumors that referred directly to himself, as well as to the anti-Semitic Weininger and the fearful Little Hans. Geller (2007) points out that in obscuring Little Hans' (Herbert

Graf's) Jewishness, Freud also obscured his role in advising Little Hans' father, Max Graf, to raise his son as a Jew. Max Graf (1942) recalls,

> When my son was born, I wondered whether I should not remove him from the prevailing antisemitic hatred, which at that time was preached in Vienna by a very popular man, Doctor Lueger. I was not certain whether it would not be better to have my son brought up in the Christian faith. Freud advised me not to do this. "If you do not let your son grow up as a Jew", he said, "you will deprive him of those sources of energy which cannot be replaced by anything else. He will have to struggle as a Jew, and you ought to develop in him all the energy he will need for that struggle. Do not deprive him of that advantage."
>
> (Graf, 1942, p. 473)

By advising Max Graf to raise his son as a Jew, Geller contends, Freud assumed the role of the *kvatter* (godfather) who hands the baby over to the *mohel* to be circumcised, thereby binding him to Jewish tradition. Yet Geller notes that in his account of the case of Little Hans, Freud makes no mention either of Little Hans' Jewish identity or of his own contribution to it. While it is clear that the Grafs were conflicted about raising their son as Jewish and of having him circumcised, and that they turned to Freud for advice on these matters, neither these conflicts nor the role Freud played in them appears in the case study. Here we feel compelled to highlight the irony: Freud scrupulously avoids any mention of the issues surrounding circumcision and Jewish identity that were so pervasive in the upbringing of this specifically Jewish little boy *as well as in Freud's relationship to this little boy's family*, and instead uses the case of Little Hans to present his "universal" findings about castration anxiety and Oedipal conflicts! Likewise, Blum (2010) documents that in all of his case studies, Freud avoids references to his own or his patients' Jewish identities and makes no mention of conflicts about Jewishness or anti-Semitism. Patients' internalized anti-Semitism, their shame about being Jewish, conflicts about conversion—all go unreported and un-analyzed in Freud's accounts. To emphasize any of these themes would have made them too specifically about Jews and their neuroses—and indeed, too specifically about Freud himself. Instead, Freud universalizes his Jewish problems by displacing them onto conflicts derived from the Greek Oedipal myth.

Given Freud's understanding of his society's perception of the circumcised Jew as castrated and homosexual, imagine his dismay when instead of finding that Herbert Graf's Jewish upbringing had turned him into a "muscle Jew" prepared to boldly stand up to anti-Semitic insult, Freud was confronted with the reality of the little boy's fear of entering the world of phallic masculinity. Geller argues that, given Freud's internalization of his society's characterization of Jews as homosexual, Freud's anxiety about Little Hans' budding homosexuality, exemplified by the boy's explicitly articulated desire for his father, permeates his analysis of the case. While this anxiety remains for the most part repressed and unarticulated, it makes its startling appearance in the footnote linking Weininger, circumcision, castration, anti-Semitism, and misogyny.

Ken Corbett (2009) uses the case of Little Hans, whom he describes as "the first psychoanalytic boy" (p. 19), to re-examine the canonical psycho-analytic narrative of masculinity. In Freud's account, a boy develops as a boy through his phallic preoccupations and castration anxiety, channeled through his desire for mother and rivalry with father, ultimately consoli-dated through separation from mother and identification with father—the positive Oedipus complex. Corbett convincingly demonstrates that although Freud repeatedly and persistently interprets Hans' desire to have a big penis as an expression of his heterosexual desire for his mother, Hans' associations point in a different direction, almost always to the father—a father who has children and is out in the world. Hans' associations indicate that his longing is "less genital per se than it is generative" (p. 50). Freud's interpretations avoid boys' homoerotic longings and instead accentuate masculinity as developed in contrast to women, their bodies, and affect states. Boys are formed through competition with other men and the repu-diation of homoerotic desire. Building on Butler's (1995) notion of "melan-choly gender," Goldner (2011b) and Harris (2011b) compellingly argue that all gender is based on repudiation and loss. In this vein, we would suggest that in Freud's formulation, masculinity is established precisely through the repudiation of femininity. Phallic primacy means the repudiation of vulnerability, permeability, and penetrability, all of which are threatened by circumcision/castration. Here is a classic example of definition via opposition, in which one pole of the binary—in this case, masculinity—is defined by excluding the other—femininity, vulnerability, penetrability—from its definition.

Further, taking into account the context of homophobia and the rise of heterosexuality in the fin de siècle illuminates another of Freud's case anal-yses and its relationship to his turn toward his Oedipal theory. In the next chapter, we will discuss at length the interpersonal dynamics enacted between Freud and Ferenczi that reflected the themes of homosexuality, homophobia, and paranoia that Freud was developing in his formulation of Schreber. Drawing upon Geller's (1994) research into Freud's analysis of the Schreber case, Boyarin (1997) points out that just at the time Freud was writing about Schreber, he was also involved with his "overcoming" of his homoerotic relationship with Fliess. In 1910 Freud wrote to Ferenczi,

> This need has been extinguished in me since Fliess's case, with the overcoming of which you just saw me occupied. A piece of homosexual

investment has been withdrawn and utilized for the enlargement of my own ego. I have succeeded where the paranoiac fails.

(1910e, p. 221)

Later in the same letter, Freud wrote, "I have certainly not yet written that I worked through Schreber, found confirmation for the kernel of our assumptions about paranoia, and have taken from this all kinds of opportunities for serious interpretations" (p. 222). Identifying a direct parallel between Freud's analysis of the Schreber text via his memoirs and the "text" of Freud's own life, Boyarin identifies the "paranoiac" as Fliess, but also as Schreber. Boyarin interprets Freud's (1911) formulation of Schreber as an autobiographical commentary on Freud's own unconscious processes, inextricably linked with his own internalized homophobia, resulting from Freud's identity as a feminized Jew living in the larger context of an anti-Semitic and homophobic milieu. Freud's recognition of Schreber's desire to be transformed into a woman meant facing his own unresolved feminine desires, which in their society, was equated with homosexuality. Anxious to overcome the pathology of feminization and homosexuality that fin de siècle Europe attributed to Jews, Freud promptly proceeded to pathologize them within his theoretical formulations. It is worth quoting Boyarin's (1997) exegesis at length:

Freud writes that in a homophobic regime, the sentence, I (a man) *love* him (a man)" must be transformed in the following ways: First, "I do not *love* him—I *hate* him"; second "I do not love *him*, I love *her*"; third, "*I* do not love him; *she* loves him." Note what a perfect analogy this provides to the shift from the negative Oedipus to the positive Oedipus complexes. The so-called negative homoerotic desire, "I wish to be penetrated by my father and have his baby" is replaced by "I do not love him (my father); I love my mother and hate my father, even to the point of desiring to kill him, because, after all, it is he whom my mother loves and he who threatens me with castration"—in short, replaced by paranoia! In describing the etiology of Schreber's paranoia in homosexuality—or better . . . in internalized homophobia—Freud was writing, consciously or unconsciously another chapter of his psychosexual-intellectual autobiography.

(1997, p. 219)

Freud would have liked to believe that he had overcome his feminine desire; whether he had been successful in doing so is certainly doubtful. However, Freud *was* successful in transforming his theory of neurosis from one whose male central character was hysteric to one whose protagonist was paranoiac. In his construction of the Oedipal theory as the universal source of neurosis, Freud placed at the center of his thought not the male hysteric, whom his society constructed as homosexual, effeminate, and Jewish, but the Oedipal hero, who was gendered as straight, masculine, and Aryan—an "active, phallic, mother-desiring, father-killing, 'normal' man" (Boyarin, 1997, p. 220). In sum: whereas psychoanalysts, following Freud, would interpret conflict about Jewishness as a displacement of Oedipal conflict, we are suggesting, following Boyarin, that Oedipal conflict was Freud's displacement of his own conflicts over his essential Jewishness.

The Civilized/Masculine/Jewish Ideal versus Primitive/Feminine/Christian Values

In Freud's Oedipal theory, the "ideal" outcome of masculine development is the demolition of the Oedipus complex—the "catastrophe" resulting from the threat of castration, leading to the renunciation of incestuous wishes, the development of conscience and morality, and their institution in the psyche in the form of the superego (Freud, 1925c, p. 257). The superego, by virtue of Freud's formulation of the process of its formation, is thus by definition deficient in women, who are considered already castrated and therefore not subject to the Oedipal shattering prerequisite for the superego's robust development. Freud (1905) noted that most often, it is girls who are held back from progressing through the stages of "normal" development, who never get over their parents' authority, who remain attached to their parents' affection, and persist in their "childish love" long after puberty (p. 227). Due to their customary upbringing, girls are discouraged from being intellectually curious. They are "scared away from *any* form of thinking, and knowledge loses its value for them" (Freud, 1908a, p. 199). Freud likens the restriction of intellect in women to the prohibition of thought necessary to maintain religious faith in God. Aligning himself firmly with the objectivity of the scientific investigator, Freud (1930c) claimed that his use of "terms such as regression, narcissism, pleasure principle are of a purely descriptive nature and don't carry within themselves any valuation" (p. 393). However, it is quite clear that despite his disclaimer of scientific neutrality, these terms are indeed laden with the values of 19th-century European culture in general, and of the colonial enterprise in particular (Brickman, 2003).

As a 19th-century European man, Freud believed that the height of civilization was the achievement of individual autonomy. The civilized male adult was disciplined. He could tolerate delay of gratification, and even renounce it altogether. In contrast, women, children, and primitives sought immediate gratification. Women represent primitive sensuality and fulfillment, family and sexual life; they "come into opposition to civilization and display their retarding and restraining influence" (Freud, 1930a, p. 103). Women are poorly equipped for the instinctual renunciations necessary for the progress of civilization. "The work of civilization has become increasingly the business of men, it . . . compels them to carry out instinctual sublimations of which women are little capable" (p. 103). Freud viewed psychoanalysis as a civilizing project, a process that facilitated the patient's progressive advancement through a series of successive renunciations. As the work of civilization was inherently a masculine enterprise, the "bedrock" of this civilizing project of psychoanalysis was the "repudiation of femininity"—the renunciation of irrational, primitive, feminine gratification, the rejection of wish fulfillment and illusion, in favor of civilized, masculine, abstract rationality.

Analyzing the relationship between Freud's theoretical views on femininity and masculinity and his corresponding attitudes toward Christianity and Judaism, Judith Van Herik (1982) thoroughly documents Freud's repeated association of femininity with passivity, narcissism, vanity, lack of a moral sense or social conscience, intellectual inferiority, arrested psychological development, the pleasure principle, and the gratification of wishes. In Freud's formulations, femininity is inextricably linked with sensuality and with primitive origins, representing "an antagonistic attitude towards civilization as the enemy of family and sexual life" (p. 20). Van Herik demonstrates the connection, pervasive throughout Freud's theorizing, between masculinity, civilization, intellectuality, rationality, abstraction, and renunciation—all of which are held up as positive categories—and all of which Freud attributes to Judaism. These stand in stark contrast to the negative, or relatively devalued, categories of femininity, primitivity, irrationality, sensuality, and wish fulfillment or illusion, on the opposite side of the binary, all of which Freud associates with Christianity!

The polarization of these binaries and their affiliation with the dichotomy of Judaism/Christianity figures prominently in *Moses and Monotheism* (1939) and in *The Future of an Illusion* (1927). In *Moses and Monotheism*, Freud valorizes Judaism as being renunciatory, spiritual, intellectual, abstract, and, in its increasingly renunciatory stages of development, as leading to higher, more progressively advanced forms of morality and intellectual and cultural achievement. In contrast, in *The Future of an Illusion*, Christianity is painted by Freud as being regressive and illusory, rooted in the sensual, intellectually restricted, and functioning as fulfillment of the primitive wish for protection.

In *The Future of an Illusion*, Freud (1927) roots the need for religion in infantile helplessness and the difficulty human beings have in progressing through the developmental stage of renouncing parental authority, as would occur in the ideal trajectory of normal masculine development. Instead, for Freud, religious belief follows along the lines of feminine development, in which the dissolution of the Oedipus complex and its concomitant renunciation of paternal authority are, by definition (by virtue of women being already-castrated) never fully achieved. According to Freud, religious belief in God the Father serves the psychological function of defending against the forces of nature, in the face of which human beings find themselves powerless. Thus Christian belief enables the continuation of the state of infantile helplessness, maintaining the passive, dependent, feminine need for the father's love. The psychological results of this religious situation are exactly those that Freud associates with the typical development of girls and their continuing attachment to their fathers—wishes are fulfilled, thinking is discouraged, and intellect and morality are restricted. Although deference to God the Father is one resolution of the Oedipus complex, it is by no means the ideal one. Childlike wishes for the father's protection are retained in adulthood and are fulfilled via the illusions of safety, security, and justice offered by belief in God. Standing in direct opposition to the reality principle and to rationality, illusion fosters weakness of the intellect. According to Freud, intellect only develops through the renunciation of instinct and the pleasure principle, and through adaptation to the reality principle.

Although Freud declared himself an atheist, a "godless Jew," in *Moses and Monotheism*, written in the final years of his life, Freud unequivocally valorized Judaism as a masculine, civilized, intellectual achievement, the result of instinctual renunciation and the rejection of sensuality. In Freud's framework, Judaism assumes the characteristics of the masculine, civilized, autonomous pole of the binary, while Christianity holds the devalued characteristics of the feminine, primitive, regressed, and dependent pole. Freud (1939) calls Christianity a "cultural regression," contending, "The Christian religion did not maintain the high level in things of the mind to which Judaism had soared." Nor did it eliminate the "superstitious, magical and mystical elements" that Judaism, in its emergence from polytheism, had renounced (p. 88).

In *Moses and Monotheism*, Freud's Moses is a "great man," "ruthless," and a "hero," possessed of a heightened intellectuality and capable of the instinctual renunciations necessary for developing a sublimely abstract and monotheistic conception of God and bringing it to the primitive masses. Freud attributes to Judaism a sublime character, due to its emphasis on ethics, successive instinctual renunciations, exclusive universal monotheistic belief in an abstract God, and its rejection of sensuality, magic, and superstition. Emphasizing the restrictive, demanding paternal qualities of both Moses and his God, Freud describes the Jewish religion as:

> a rigid monotheism on the grand scale: there is only one God, he is the sole God, omnipotent, unapproachable; his aspect is more than human eyes can tolerate, no image must be made of him, even his name may not be spoken.

(1939, p. 18)

Followers of Moses and his God are not passively dependent and intellectually restricted; "instead, they follow the masculine path of oedipal renunciation of instinct under the law of the father, and they achieve its economic
correlates: advance in intellectuality, culture, and morality" (Van Herik,
1982, p. 178).

The trials and persecutions to which the Jewish people were subject
throughout their history served only to sharpen their tenacious character,
while their renunciation of sensuality, and the intellectual acuity required
to worship an increasingly abstract God contributed to the Jews' characteristic "inclination to intellectual interests" (Freud, 1939, p. 115). Freud
writes,

> The pre-eminence given to intellectual labours throughout some two
> thousand years in the life of the Jewish people has, of course, had its
> effect. It has helped to check the brutality and the tendency to violence
> which are apt to appear where the development of muscular strength
> is the popular ideal. Harmony in the cultivation of intellectual and
> physical activity, such as was achieved by the Greek people, was denied
> to the Jews. In this dichotomy their decision was at least in favour of
> the worthier alternative.
>
> (1939, p. 115)

In Freud's framework, circumcision is symbolic of castration—of
submission to the will of the father. Rather than casting the Jews as savage
and barbaric primitives because they were circumcised, as was the anti-
Semitic view of circumcision in his day, Freud contends (as was the traditional Jewish view) that circumcision makes the Jews holy, consecrating
them as God's chosen people. "Those who have adopted circumcision are
proud of it. They feel exalted by it, ennobled, as it were, and look down
with contempt on the others, whom they regard as unclean" (Freud, 1939,
pp. 29–30). Submission to the father is here painful, rather than consoling,
requiring instinctual renunciation; it is therefore ennobling.

In contrast, Freud views Christianity as a regressive return to sensuality,
the mother-goddess, magical belief, and superstition; it is a thinly disguised
polytheism. In Christianity, God has been made incarnate, no longer a
spiritual abstract idea, but embodied in flesh and blood. Wishes have been
fulfilled—the Messiah has come. With the advent of Christianity, the
specificity of the Jewish people is universalized. Rather than remaining a
chosen people consecrated to God because of their willingness to undergo
instinctual renunciations, in the Christian paradigm, Israel becomes all
who accept illusory fulfillment of their wishes through faith.

In *Moses and Monotheism*, Freud reverses the traditional majority
Christian-centric terms of the binary, so that Jews, instead of being
on the negative pole of the dichotomy, come out on top! In the Christian

framework, Jews are concrete and embodied, whereas Christians are spiritually abstract: circumcision is of the flesh (body) and God is served not by faith (spirit) but by the strict observance of commandments (what Christians call Law). But for Freud, it is Jews who are spiritual and abstract, worshipping a God who is not embodied. The Messiah has not yet come but is always deferred until later, a delay of gratification that facilitates frustration tolerance, the hallmark of a civilized people. Freud deftly reversed the power relations inherent in his society's dichotomization of Judaism and Christianity, placing Judaism in the power position! Slavet (2009) points out the startling contradiction inherent in Freud's insistence that Jewish identity is transmitted along masculine, intellectual lines, given that in Judaism, Jewish identity is established via the matrilineal line: a child born of a Jewish mother and non-Jewish father is considered Jewish, while a child born of a Jewish father and a non-Jewish mother is not. Slavet writes that in *Moses and Monotheism*, Freud

> ironically inverts the matrilineal principle of Jewish genealogy, making the matter of biological inheritance a purely *geistig* (intellectual-spiritual) issue based not on material evidence (that is, the identity of the mother) but on hypotheses and inferences (about the identity of the father).
>
> (Slavet, 2009, p. 30)

Jew/Christian was now aligned with masculine/feminine, spirit/body, rationality/illusion, delay/fulfillment, and civilized/primitive. In particular, the binary of civilized versus primitive is so deeply embedded in psychoanalytic theory and so central to its formulations, that it will be of value at this juncture to examine this dichotomy in considerable depth.

Civilized versus Primitive

In *Aboriginal Populations in the Mind*, Celia Brickman (2003) locates the paradigms of colonialism in the origins of psychoanalytic theory, using postcolonial studies to show the influence of evolutionary anthropology on Freud's thinking. Contrasting dark-skinned, primitive savages with white, civilized Europeans, 19th-century evolutionary theorists such as Herbert Spencer sorted all of the world's population into the categories of primitive and civilized, elevating the civilized side of the binary over the primitive, and providing the ideological rationalization used to justify colonialism and other forms of exploitation. Freud read widely in the anthropology and evolutionary theory of his time, and Brickman demonstrates the reverberations within psychoanalytic theory, even unto the present day, of this dichotomization between the categories of civilized and primitive in the scientific and cultural discourse of Freud's time.

In medieval times, the terms pagan, heathen, and infidel were traditionally employed by the Christian church to characterize outsiders to its
community, often in order to justify wars, forced conversion, and religious
persecution of non-Christians. Beginning in the 15th century, these derogatory religious terms were combined with the racialized terms primitive,
savage, and barbarian, and used by European explorers to describe the
indigenous people they encountered in what they referred to as the New
World. Although comprised of culturally and linguistically distinct populations, their European colonizers viewed these religious and racial "others"
as a homogenous entity, grouping them under the category "primitives,"
together with the native peoples of Africa, Australia, and Tasmania,
and other non-European lands, who had already been subjected to
proselytizing, enslavement, and decimation at the hands of the European
civilizing mission.

These "primitive" peoples were, as a group, cast as inferior and
positioned in opposition to "civilized," white European Christians, who
considered themselves to be the acme of human development. In the eyes
of the European colonizers, to be primitive meant to be situated outside of
civilization, external to time and history, living in the "original" and timeless state of nature. To be civilized was to have a history, to live in time,
while to be primitive was to be prehistoric, out of time. Primitivity implied
primeval origins, the primordial "beginning" that occurred prior to the
development of civilization. As the category of the primitive was incorporated into the discourse about the origins of the human race, those people
who were classified as primitive were thought to be contemporary, living
examples of the prehistory of humankind. In the words of John Locke, "in
the beginning all the World was America" (cited in Brickman, 2003,
p. 33). Thus primitive cultures were associated with the childhood of
human civilization, and primitives were considered to be like children.

With the advent of the Enlightenment and the eclipse of religion, a
reversal occurred: prior to this stage, non-Christians had been considered
primitive heathens, but now in civilized circles, adherence to religious
belief and practice was considered primitive—thought to be a superstitious and magical response to fear of the harshness of nature. We highlight
this example in order to demonstrate just how easily a simple reversal of
hierarchies can occur within dichotomous relations, depending on the
context. In the operation of any binary, one can flip the power relations but
maintain and even reinforce the binary structure. With the "advances" of
the Enlightenment, the human mind "matured" into rationality, and
science and reason were valorized over religious faith. Reason and the
capacity for rationality were considered the ultimate in human achievement. As Enlightenment thinkers attempted to theorize the evolutionary
trajectory of the development of the human race, they viewed primitive
cultures as contemporary embodiments of the origins of civilization and

the primitive individual as a living example of the childhood of the universal mind.

Industrialization brought with it the notion that to be civilized meant to be able to delay gratification in order to accumulate wealth and assume political responsibility. Herbert Spencer attributed the progress of civilization to the ability to repress impulsivity, which he viewed as an evolutionary achievement over our animal ancestors. The civilized person had achieved the capacity for restraint and the discipline for work, while the "primitive" not only lived in nature like the animals, but also gave free rein to his animal instincts. To be civilized and adult was to be disciplined and to delay gratification, while primitives were childish and impulsive, seeking immediate gratification.

We can immediately see the influence of these colonial, anthropological, and evolutionary paradigms in Freud's emphasis on the importance of delayed gratification and the renunciation of instinct. Much to his credit, Freud demonstrated that primitivity is universal: each of us has a primitive part of our minds, and so we each carry primitivity within us. This was quite a revolutionary idea at a time when those in his cultural milieu proudly viewed themselves as civilized. Nevertheless, we must emphasize that by arguing that we all have a primitive mind, with primitive drives, Freud was, in the process, also reinforcing his society's cultural and scientific dichotomization of primitivity and civilization.

Recall Haeckel's "ontogeny recapitulates phylogeny," the premise that in childhood, individuals relive the earliest stages of the human past. Following Haeckel, in Freud's formulation, neurosis was a regression to an infantile stage of development, which he equated with a primitive state of mind. In fact, Freud believed that this primitive state of mind reflected not only an earlier stage of human development, but could also be witnessed *in vivo* in the present-day "savages" living in the "wild." Here is Freud's 1913 evolutionary position on the psychology of neurosis, from *Totem and Taboo*:

> There are men still living who, as we believe, stand very near to primitive man, far nearer than we do, and whom we therefore regard as his direct heirs and representatives . . . a comparison between the psychology of primitive peoples, as it is taught by social anthropology, and the psychology of neurotics, as it has been revealed by psychoanalysis, will be bound to show numerous points of agreement and will throw new light upon familiar facts in both sciences.
>
> (1913d, p. 1)

Further, as Brickman (2003) demonstrates, Freud correlated the stages of libidinal development with those of cultural evolution: the omnipotence of thoughts characteristic of infantile narcissism was correlated with the savage's animism; the Oedipal child's infatuation with loving and powerful parents was correlated with the barbarian's worship and appeasement of his all-powerful gods; and the renunciation of Oedipal desires was correlated with the end of religious belief and the attainment of scientific rationality.

All of these stages were indexed to the hierarchy of civilized and primitive, both in the human mind and in the cultural evolutionary scale, which was, in turn, indexed to skin color. The insidiousness of the racialized hierarchy culled from evolutionary anthropology and embedded within psychoanalytic theory cannot be overstated. It is perhaps apt at this point to mention that Freud sometimes referred to his patients as "negroes" (Freud, 1924; Jones, 1957). Brickman documents that in 1914, the *Psychoanalytic Quarterly* published several articles that purported to demonstrate through clinical vignettes that black peoples were arrested at the adolescent stage of development and regressed more quickly to psychotic states; characterized Africans as "the raw material of civilization;" and praised slavery for facilitating the Negro's ability for sustained labor and introducing him to Christianity (p. 87).

According to Freud, the unconscious is the timeless repository of our original primitive natures, existing alongside and often disrupting our complex, more highly refined and civilized conscious minds. "The man of prehistoric times survives unchanged in our unconscious" (Freud, 1915c, p. 296). Brickman writes,

> Freud described the unconscious—as Columbus described the aboriginal Americans he encountered—in terms of lack: the unconscious exhibits a lack of rationality, a lack of relationship to reality, an inability to represent itself in words, a lack of restraint, sexual and otherwise, a lack of morality, and a lack of the sense of time.
>
> (2003, p. 81)

In contrast, consciousness is placed at the civilized pole of the binary, representing autonomy, rationality, and history.

Of course, women did not fare well in these polarizations; it was men who always came out on top. Freud's (1926c) by now famous statement, "the sexual life of adult women is a 'dark continent'[4] for psychology" (p. 212) vividly exemplifies the colonialist context of the hierarchical dichotomies embedded in his theorizing about race and gender. In the psychoanalytic formulation, Freud associates female sexuality with darkest Africa, a metaphor that carries with it all of the connotations ascribed by his colonialist contemporaries to its dark-skinned inhabitants. We can clearly see how the polarities of civilized and primitive were directly lined

---

4 The phrase "dark continent" is written in English in Freud's original German text.

294 Universalizing the Jewish Problem

up with the categories masculine and feminine. Further, we can discern the racial implications of such an alignment: feminine and masculine were indexed to black and white in a hierarchy of inferior and superior, castrated and phallic. In Freud's formulation, because women are already castrated, they are incapable of the moral development that, for men, is a natural byproduct of the shattering of the Oedipus complex. For Freud, women, like primitives and Blacks in the colonialist paradigm, are like children— irrational, narcissistic, concrete, immoral, and impulsive, while men are civilized adults—rational, abstract, moral, and capable of renunciation and delay.

Coming full circle, let us recall that in the anti-Semitic formulations of Freud's day, these same polarities—civilized/primitive, masculine/ feminine, moral/immoral, phallic/castrated, and White/Black—were all mapped onto the binary Aryan/Jew. From the anti-Semitic perspective, Jews were Europe's negroes, a dark-skinned, primitive race possessing all of the negative traits the society attributed to blacks and women. In a brilliant and radical theoretical maneuver, Freud upended all of these binaries by universalizing them! He maintained that we all (including himself and his White, male, civilized, scientific colleagues) carry both the civilized and the primitive within us. All of us are rational and irrational, conscious and unconscious; we each have an ego and an id. Similarly, Freud insisted that we all have bisexual natures; we are each comprised of both masculine and feminine aspects. We all have unconscious perversion and unconscious homosexual inclinations. No matter how civilized we consciously perceive ourselves to be, our unconscious is primitive, unstructured, timeless, unbound, incapable of reason or delay, dark, and feminine. More subtly, and central to the point of our discussion—and this is Gilman's (1993a, b) main argument—Freud skillfully upset the racialized anti-Semitic distinctions that were the preoccupations of the cultural and scientific discourse of his day. In contending that we each have a conscious and an unconscious, an ego and an id, Freud demonstrated that we each have an ego and a Y(id), an Aryan and a Jew. It is not only Jews who are dark, primitive, and feminine—these are universal qualities that exist in each and every one of us.

But while Gilman views Freud's attempt at solving his Jewish problem as relatively successful, Boyarin (2003) disagrees. He emphasizes the ever-present internalized self-hatred that mobilizes the misogynist, homophobic, and racist elements of Freud's theorizing. Following Cuddihy (1974), Boyarin (2003) likens the "civilizing" process of Jewish Emancipation— the Westernization and modernization of Eastern European Jewry—to the larger project of European colonialism. In this analogy, the primitive *Ostjude* was to the civilized Western Jew as the primitive Black was to the White European. However, unlike Cuddihy, who celebrates the West's civilizing mission, Boyarin offers a more nuanced examination of the subjective experience of colonialism on the colonized, which he characterizes as "Janus-like" in its duality. He explicitly identifies Freud's misogyny as a symptom of the divided position of the colonial subject, who has internalized the hatred of his colonizers while at the same time desiring to occupy the colonizing position.

> Freud's essentializing of misogyny was . . . a way to appropriate the phallus for himself as a circumcised male. In other words, Freud's theories allowed him to assert that the "real" difference is not between the Jewish and gentile penis but between having a penis at all and not having one.
>
> (Boyarin, 2003, p. 186)

Similarly, the racist implications against Blacks of the psychoanalytic notion of the primitive can be located at the juncture of the colonialist paradigms and the anti-Semitic characterizations of Jews as off-White, oriental negroes. Comparing the works of Freud and Fanon, Boyarin writes,

> If we see colonized Blacks and Jews as Europeans saw them, that is, as members of a single group, this point is absolutely clear: Freud's racism toward "primitives," as Fanon's toward Jews, should be read precisely (at least in part) as an avatar of self-hatred.
>
> (2003, p. 182)

While Freud postulates the underlying dynamics of Christian anti-Semitism as being due to the unconscious association of circumcision with castration, he is unable to diagnose his own Jewish self-hatred. In other words, by explaining anti-Semitism in terms of the castration complex, as if he were merely a neutral observer, Freud normalized it instead of pathologizing it. Freud was unable to acknowledge the unconscious association of circumcision, castration, and anti-Semitism within his own psyche. It is Ferenczi, not Freud, who makes the link between the negro and the Jew within the primitive unconscious. Without contradicting Freud, Ferenczi *adds* to Freud's formulation by explicitly relating the racism directed at blacks with the anti-Semitism targeted toward Jews, attributing them both to the projection of the unconscious "not me" onto the racial other. In his July 9, 1910 letter to Freud, Ferenczi wrote,

> The persecution of Blacks in America reminds me of the case that Jung so sagely presented, according to which the Blacks represent the "unconscious" of the Americans. Thus, the hate, the reaction formation against one's own vices. Along with the circumcision/castration complex, this mechanism could also be the basis for *anti-Semitism*. The free, "fresh" behavior of the Jew, his "shameless" flaunting of his interest in money, evokes hatred as a reaction formation in Christians,

who are ethical not for logical reasons but out of repression. It is only since my analysis that I have understood the widespread Hungarian saying: "*I hate him like my sins.*"

(Ferenczi, 1910b, pp. 186–187)

Note several ironies here: Without directly challenging Freud, Ferenczi draws upon Jung's ideas to add an alternative and compelling explanation of anti-Semitism to Freud's theoretical contention of a circumcision/castration complex. In the process, he also unwittingly articulates the connection within Freud's own theorizing between the colonially inspired and racially marked characterization of the primitive and *Freud's own Jewish self-hatred*. In Ferenczi's analysis of American racism against the negro, he offers us a cogent explanation for the racism that permeates psychoanalytic theorizing, stemming from Freud's own internalized anti-Semitism. One can easily imagine the saying "*I hate him like my sins*" applied to the Western Jew's contempt for the *Ostjude*, and specifically, to Freud's own contempt for his primitive Eastern origins.

The Uncanny Jew, or Freud's Dybbuk

In his address to the B'nai B'rith upon the occasion of his 70th birthday, Freud (1926a) spoke of the "obscure emotional forces" that tied him to Judaism and to his Jewish identity (p. 274). In equally mystical and irrational terms, Freud (1939) wrote that *Moses and Monotheism*, his attempt to account for the tenacity of Judaism and Jews, "tormented" him like an " 'unlaid ghost' " (p. 103) We contend that, fueled by obscure emotional forces, Freud's Jewish identity, incompletely mourned, haunted him like an unlaid ghost. In fact, we would call it a *dybbuk*, a dislocated soul that cannot rest; an identity that is caught between two worlds; an eternal wanderer who has no home. As Brickman (2011) has convincingly argued, the "unlaid ghost" of Freud's Jewish identity continues to haunt psychoanalytic theory and clinical practice, manifesting as a break with the past that functions defensively as the repudiation of vulnerability. The "more powerful the less it can be expressed in words" (Freud, 1926a, p. 274), the effect of Freud's *dybbuk* can best be described as uncanny, *unheimlich*, a favorite anti-Semitic epithet of the era.[5]

---

5 Freud often spoke of the "daemonic," noting that in Hebrew, uncanny means "daemonic" (Freud, 1919d, p. 221). See also his note on the translation of the motto on the *Interpretation of Dreams*, "*Acheronta movebo*," which Freud (1900b) translates as "stir up the underworld," referring to stirring up the "mental underworld (the unconscious) in order to get a hearing" (p. ix.) In Jewish legend, it was believed that the *dybbuk* could not rest until it told its story; thus the way to exorcise this bothersome, demonic spirit was to "give it a hearing."

During Freud's time, uncertainties about the nature of the Jew were fundamental to debates about whether it was possible for Jews to be integrated into
mainstream European society. Following the anti-Semitic legend of the
Wandering Jew, the image of the Jew as a spectral wanderer who could not
rest because he had no home was pervasive throughout Europe. This ghostly
image haunted the discourse among Jews and non-Jews alike about the pros
and cons of assimilation, the feasibility of Jewish Emancipation, and the
proposal of Zionism as a solution to the so-called "Jewish problem." (Recall
Freud's own identification with the Wandering Jew in the letter he wrote to
his son Ernst in London while waiting to flee Nazi-occupied Austria.)

In an essay remarkable both for the material it touches upon and turns
away from, Freud (1919e) defines "The 'Uncanny'" as "that class of the
frightening which leads back to what is known of old and long familiar"
(p. 220). Strange and frightening precisely because it is already known and
recognized, the uncanny is formulated as the return of that which has become
alienated from the mind through repression, something "which ought to
have remained hidden but has come to light"(p. 241). Freud demonstrates
that the word *heimlich*, which means homey, familiar, belonging, intimate,
wholesome, and comfortable, "develops in a direction of ambivalence, until
it finally coincides with its opposite, *unheimlich*" (p. 226), a word that carries
more sinister meanings, including hidden, concealed, withdrawn from
consciousness, dangerous, haunted, ghostly, undead.

Speaking of himself in the third person, Freud begins "The 'Uncanny'"
with a rather disingenuous disclaimer:

> The writer of the present contribution . . . must himself plead guilty
> to a special obtuseness in the matter . . . It is long since he has experi-
> enced or heard of anything which has given him an uncanny impres-
> sion, and he must start by translating himself into that state of feeling,
> by awakening in himself the possibility of experiencing it.
>
> (1919e, p. 220)

As a male Jew living in anti-Semitic society, Freud was not only well
acquainted with the experience of the uncanny, but also, as Boyarin (1997)
notes, with the experience of *himself* as an uncanny, circumcised, wandering
Jew, as seen through the eyes of his countrymen, as well as through his own
eyes, as he gazed at his reflection in the mirror. Freud is disturbed by his
uncanny "double," the self he sees reflected that is both familiar and
strange, *heimlich* and *unheimlich*, "me" and "not-me." He writes,

> I was sitting alone in my wagon-lit compartment when a . . . violent
> jolt of the train swung back the door . . . and an elderly gentleman in
> a dressing-gown and a travelling cap came in. I assumed that . . . he
> had taken the wrong direction and come into my compartment by

mistake. Jumping up with the intention of putting him right, I at once realized to my dismay that the intruder was nothing but my own reflection in the looking-glass . . . I can still recollect that I thoroughly disliked his appearance.

(p. 248)

Reflecting a process that is enacted at the very same time as it is being put into words, Freud is intruded upon by an image he experiences as alien, but that turns out to be his own familiar reflection. In "The 'Uncanny'", Freud simultaneously acknowledges and turns away from seeing himself mirrored in his society's association of the uncanny with Jews, with uncertainties about their masculinity and femininity, familiarity and strangeness, aliveness and deadness. Having internalized the anti-Semitic characterization of himself as an uncanny, feminine Jew, who on the surface appears *heimlich*, but whose circumcised difference is hidden, concealed, *unheimlich*, Freud turns away from these disliked, uncanny aspects of himself, and transfers them onto the female genitals: They are *heimlich* because they are the entrance to our original home, and *unheimlich*, because they are associated with female sexuality—which is frightening, primitive, a "dark continent" (Freud, 1926c, p. 212)—and also, as we shall see, with death.

Emphasizing his masculinity and disowning his vulnerability, Freud rejects all associations of himself with the feminine and the maternal. Providing exclusively positive Oedipal formulations, he dissociates himself from both pre-Oedipal and negative Oedipal experience, which as Brickman (2011) notes, he characterizes as maternal, primitive, or narcissistic. Recall Freud's comment reported by his patient Hilda Doolittle (1956), "I do not like to be the mother in the transference—it always surprises and shocks me a little. I feel so very masculine" (p. 52). Similarly, Freud (1930c) distanced himself from any connection with the vulnerability of religious experience, tracing his friend Romain Rolland's proposed "oceanic" feeling to limitless narcissism, infantile helplessness, and dependence on the mother, disclaiming, "I cannot discover this 'oceanic' feeling in myself" (p. 65).

In her analysis of the image of the uncanny Jew among 19th- and 20th-century European intellectuals, with whose writing Freud was most certainly familiar, Jewish Studies scholar Susan Shapiro demonstrates that

[the] image of the Jewish people as a 'living corpse' . . . haunts the very formulation of the Jewish Question, not only—but especially in Germany. Can the Jews as a people, as a nation, as a race, and/or as a religion be incorporated into the German nation-state?

(2004, p. 157)

This very question, embodied by Freud's (1925a) characterization of himself as "alien because I was a Jew" (p. 9), and his identification with

Ahasverus, the Wandering Jew, preoccupied him until the end his life, made ever more painful by his love for and identification with German culture.

Let us take a moment to wander off into a closer examination of the figure of the Wandering Jew, whose logic played a central role both in the formulation of the "Jewish problem" as well as in its proposed solutions. The deadliest of these solutions was, of course, the systematic extermination of the Jews at the hand of the Nazis. However, it is important to emphasize that Hitler's Final Solution was rooted in centuries of popular anti-Semitism, and cultivated by the plethora of intellectual debates about Jews in the academic, literary, and philosophical circles of the 19th and 20th centuries. In fact, among many thinkers, even the more benign solutions of assimilation and Emancipation had as their aim the complete eradication of Jews as a separate people. This required the erasure of any visible signs of Jewishness—a process of "dejewification," so to speak. Yet, ironically, as acculturated Western Jews attempted to "pass" in German society, their apparent *heimlichkeit* served only to make them even more *unheimlich* from the anti-Semitic perspective. Writes Shapiro, "It was precisely this effacement and hiddenness of Jewishness that was most threatening for emancipated European Jewish communities" (2004, p. 159).

Unsure of their own identity, for 19th-century Germans, "the Jewish Question was ultimately . . . another way of asking 'What is German': and receiving the satisfying answer—'whatever is not Jewish' " (Rose, cited in Shapiro, 2004, p. 159). Here is yet another classic example of definition via exclusion—what is German is specifically *not* Jewish. As acculturated Western Jews became less distinguishable from their non-Jewish countrymen, they became more threatening to the German's ability to define himself as "not a Jew." The hiddenness of the Jew, accomplished via assimilation, made Jewishness "more threatening because invisible, unlocatable, and, thus, uncontainable" (p. 159). In turn, acculturated Western Jews were threatened by their fellow traditional, mostly Eastern European Jewish brethren, the *Ostjuden*, who were unwilling or unable to make themselves invisible, thus disrupting their attempt to appear like everyone else. In effect, the *Ostjuden* functioned as the repressed, whose return threatens the self. Note the operation of the uncanny in this very dynamic: what appears *heimlich*, homey, familiar, i.e. the person who appears to be like "one of us"—a Western European gentile— is actually *unheimlich*, uncanny, alien—a Jew, that "which ought to have remained hidden but has come to light" (Freud, 1919d, p. 241). In other words, what was frightening to both non-Jews and acculturated Western Jews was the uncanniness of the Jew.

In "The 'Uncanny'", Freud links the attraction to a foreign land with the search for origins, the longing for an original home, which he equates with the desire to return to the maternal genitals. What Freud does not say is

that in the discourse of his time, the eternal search for a home was identified as the crux of the Jewish problem. Having no national home, Jews
were said to be "unwelcome guests or aliens wandering into and within
other peoples' homes, disrupting and haunting them" (Shapiro, 2004,
p. 160). In 1838, Hegelian thinker Karl Gutzkow (whom Freud cites in
"The 'Uncanny'") formulated the Jewish problem as follows:

> Ahasverus is the tragic consequence of Jewish hopes . . . [His] tragic
> fate is . . . his outliving of himself, his obsolescence. Time itself always
> remains young: new peoples arise, new heroes, new empires. Only
> Ahasverus stays on, a living corpse, a dead man who has not yet died.
>
> (Cited in Shapiro, 2004, p. 157)

Philosopher Arthur Schopenhauer's solution to the Jewish problem was
to encourage the disappearance of the Jews through conversion and intermarriage:

> Ahasverus, the Wandering Jew, is nothing but the personification of
> the whole Jewish race . . . It asserts its Jewish nationality with unprec-
> edented stubbornness . . . [but] lives parasitically on other nations . . .
> To bring an end in the gentlest manner to the tragicomedy, the best
> way is for marriages . . . between Jews and gentiles . . . Then, in the
> course of a hundred years, there will be only a very few Jews left, and
> soon the ghost will be exorcized. Ahasverus will be buried, and the
> chosen people will not know where their abode was.
>
> (Schopenhauer, cited in Shapiro, 2004, p. 160)

Schopenhauer's solution of assimilation would put the spectral existence of
Judaism to rest, as all visible evidence of being Jewish would be erased.

Jewish intellectuals internalized this anti-Semitic depiction of themselves even as they responded to it. The proposed solutions to the problem
of Jewish uncanniness on the part of these Jewish thinkers ranged from
Emancipation and assimilation to establishing a national homeland so
that the Jewish ghost could have a final resting place. These intellectuals
included socialist and Zionist theorists such as Moses Hess and Leo Pinsker,
who ardently advocated for a Jewish homeland, as well as members of the
19th-century *Wissenschaft des Judentums*, or Science of Judaism movement,
such as the writers Heinrich Heine and Eduard Gans.

Like Cuddihy (1974) and Boyarin (1997), Jewish Studies scholar
Susannah Heschel (1999) maintains that as Western Europe grappled with
how to integrate what it considered the alien and primitive people living
in their midst, the project of emancipation functioned as a sort of internal
colonization. Judaism functioned as the abject of Christianity, which
defined itself in terms of what Judaism was not: Christianity was new,

while Judaism was old; Christianity was spiritual, while Judaism was concrete; Christianity was moral, while Judaism was immoral. Note once again the hierarchical power relations inherent in this dichotomization, with Christianity on top and Judaism on the bottom.

The explicit aim of the *Wissenschaft* was to upend the power structure of the Christianity/Judaism hierarchy by reversing its terms. Much of the *Wissenschaft*'s scholarship was geared toward demonstrating that the roots of Christianity lay in Judaism—that Judaism was original, while Christianity was derivative. The goal of these Jewish intellectuals was to relocate Judaism from its position of inferiority and obsolescence to one of superiority and originality. They reframed the uniqueness of Judaism as being due to its universality in having given birth to both of the world's major religions, Christianity and Islam, rather than to its difference. We know that Freud was strongly influenced by his close relationship with his teacher and friend, Samuel Hammerschlag, who emphasized the universality of Judaism and Jewish ideals. And as Van Herik (1982) points out, Freud's representation of Judaism as masculine, abstract, and civilized, while Christianity was feminine, concrete, and regressive, was, like the *Wissenschaft*'s, a direct attempt to reverse the power relations of the Christian-dominated discourse of his time.

Yet even while the members of the *Wissenschaft* strove to upend the hierarchy imposed by the Christian hegemony, they were inevitably embedded in its formulations, adopting them within their own intellectual discussions. Heinrich Heine (who was born into a Jewish family, but was baptized as an adult) described the Jews as "the mummy-nation that wanders over the face of the earth, wrapped in its age-old scroll of the law a petrified piece of world-history-a specter" (cited in Shapiro, 1997, p. 67). Jewish philosopher Moses Hess depicted the Jews as "a soul without a body, wandering like a ghost through the centuries" (cited in Shapiro, 1997, p. 64). Like Zionist theorist Leo Pinsker, who called for the establishment of a Jewish nation in Palestine, Hess proposed a Jewish national home as a means to lay the ghost to rest.

Let us now wander back to Freud's essay. Although Freud interprets the *unheimlich* in Oedipal terms, Shapiro (2004) and Jonte-Pace (2001), following Cixous (1976), argue that Oedipal explanations fail to contain the examples of the uncanny provided in this essay. Indeed, we see that the text is disturbed by numerous contradictions and meandering interruptions. At first, Freud acknowledges the work of Ernst Jentsch, who in 1906 published an article about the uncanny. Freud (1919d) states, "Jentsch has taken as *a very good instance* [of the uncanny] 'doubts whether an apparently animate being is really alive; or conversely, whether a lifeless object might not be in fact animate'" (p. 226). In his article, Jentsch uses Hoffmann's tale, "The Sand-Man," to support his contention that the experience of the uncanny stems from intellectual uncertainty about whether something is what it appears to be—in particular, whether it is alive or dead. Jentsch focuses on the character of Olympia, a lifelike doll who appears to be a human being, maintaining that the uncertainty about her aliveness is the central theme of the story and the source of its uncanniness.

Yet Freud later dismisses Jentsch outright, deeming his explanation "irrelevant" (p. 230) to the narrative! Instead, he provides an Oedipal explanation for Hoffman's story, attributing the *sole factor* of its uncanniness to the "universal" fear of castration, symbolized by the threat of the Sand-Man's blinding children's eyes. Freud states emphatically, "Jentsch's point of an intellectual uncertainty has *nothing to do* with the effect"(p. 230). Why this categorical rejection of what is clearly, by Freud's own admission, an uncanny element of the story? The explanation lies further along in the essay, in Freud's description of the double, "the effect of meeting one's own image unbidden and unexpected" (p. 248). He identifies the uncanny as an aspect of the self, the "not-me," that has been repressed and then returns to haunt the ego. In turning away from Jentsch's thesis, Freud is at the same time turning away from his uncanny double—the Jew, who, though he appears on the surface to be identical to the non-Jew, is in fact different; the Jew who, although he appears to be a living being, is in fact an unlaid ghost, a dybbuk, an uncanny spectral wanderer, existing on the border between life and death.

But as Jonte-Pace (2001) notes, Freud cannot completely turn away from the image of the uncanny wandering Jew. He tells us this story:

> As I was walking . . . through the deserted streets of a provincial town in Italy which was unknown to me, I found myself in a quarter of whose character I could not long remain in doubt. Nothing but painted women were to be seen at the windows of the small houses, and I hastened to leave the narrow street at the next turning. But after having wandered about for a time . . . I suddenly found myself back in the same street where my presence was now beginning to excite attention. I hurried away once more, only to arrive by another detour at the same place yet a third time. Now, however, a feeling overcame me which I can only describe as uncanny, and I was glad enough to find myself back at the piazza I had left a short while before, without any further voyages of discovery.
>
> (p. 237)

Freud paints a vivid picture of himself, a Viennese Jew, a stranger in a strange land, wandering through foreign streets, winding his way through a labyrinth of female sexuality, unable to find his way, yet repeatedly, uncannily, returning to the same spot. Freud dissociates his wanderings from those of the uncanny Jew by referring to them as "voyages of discovery," portraying himself as a heroic figure on a quest for self-knowledge. This was a recurring trope in Freud's self-portrayals as well as in his theoretical formulations: the transformation of the internalized image of the uncanny, unheroic wandering Jew into the intrepid, heroic explorer traveling the royal road of the unconscious. Lost in the primitive, "dark continent" of female sexuality, Freud turns himself into an Oedipal hero. What is dissociated—femininity, dependency, and mortality, all associated with vulnerability—is displaced onto the frightening *unhleim-lichkeit* of female sexuality, located at the site of the maternal genitals. The *unheimlichkeit* of the Jew, the abject of Christianity and of anti-Semitism, is displaced onto the feminine, which, repudiated, becomes the abject of psychoanalysis.

According to Kristeva (1982), the abject is that which has been "radically excluded" from consciousness, yet continues to disturb, trouble, fascinate, and challenge from its "place of banishment." Its intrusion is experienced as

> A massive and sudden emergence of uncanniness, which, familiar as it might have been in an opaque and forgotten life, now harries me as radically separate, loathsome. Not me . . . A "something" . . . I do not recognize . . . a reality that, if I acknowledge it, annihilates me.
>
> (1982, p. 2)

Linking fear of the maternal with fear of women's procreative power, Kristeva demonstrates the association throughout the Hebrew Bible of menstruation and childbirth with impurity, pollution, abomination, and defilement. The generative power of female sexuality, like the annihilating finality of its opposite, death, is both fearful and terrifying. As in the rituals relating to death, the rituals surrounding menstruation and childbirth are meant to purify that which is unclean, defiled. Matrilineal authority—the identity of the child established through its mother[6]— threatens the patriarchal order. Kristeva identifies circumcision as a means of separating the child from the abject of the maternal, in order to secure an otherwise tenuous patrilineal authority. From this perspective, circumcision symbolizes the separation of the male child from female impurity by replacing the connection with the mother with a covenant with God. Note the parallel with the cornerstone of Freud's (1937a) theorizing: the "repudiation of femininity" is the "bedrock" of psychoanalysis (p. 252). Freud repeatedly

---

6 In Judaism, Jewish identity is established via the matrilineal line: a child born of a Jewish mother and non-Jewish father is considered Jewish, while a child born of a Jewish father and a non-Jewish mother is not.

likens the work of psychoanalysis to the interventions of the surgeon, who practices his art with precision. In his repudiation of vulnerability, of the abject feminine and the maternal, Freud's analogy most fittingly applies to the surgery of circumcision. Acting as the ritual circumciser, Freud the *mohel* circumcises the male analysand—makes him a real man—through the repudiation of femininity (read vulnerability) and, via the separation from the primitive maternal abject, inducts him into masculinity and the patriarchal order of civilization.

Chapter 15

Freud, Ferenczi, and Schreber

Wandering Jews[1]

Sigmund Freud and Sándor Ferenczi were close friends and fellow travelers, wandering Jews who traveled and vacationed together regularly for many years. As we have seen in the previous chapter, Freud (1919e) equated the love of a foreign place with the search for origins, the longing for an original home. This particular wandering Jew had to overcome a travel phobia, a fear he would miss his train, as well as his phobia of Rome. Join us now, travel with us, all aboard the *Nachträglichkeit* express for a regressive time travel back a century into the uncanny origins of psychoanalysis.

We have been examining the problematic place of binaries in the history of psychoanalysis, focusing in particular on Freud's "optimally marginal" position at the crossroads of his Jewish racial and German cultural identities. Freud's close friend and colleague, Sándor Ferenczi, shared this divided Jewish Enlightenment identity. Freud and Ferenczi, like most of the early analysts, were from Jewish immigrant families who migrated from Eastern Europe, from the periphery to the center, from the *shtetl* or ghetto to the large, cosmopolitan, anonymous city. They were part of a tradition of migration, acculturation, and assimilation (Erös, 2004). For Freud, Ferenczi, and their middle-class colleagues, medicine, particularly private practice, was one of the free professions that allowed upward mobility independent from institutions that would not accept Jews. Before and during World War I, the Jews of Austria-Hungary were intensely loyal to the state, which allowed them to separate political, cultural, and ethnic aspects of their identity. In Austria, Westernized Jews occupied multiple subject positions, sometimes dissociated self-states, thinking of themselves as German by language and culture or *Bildung*, Austrian by political loyalty, and Jewish by race, ethnicity, or religion. In Hungary, Jews were more fully assimilated into the Magyar nation, a process known as Magyarization. They identified as Hungarian, speaking Hungarian and

1 An earlier version of this chapter was presented by Lewis Aron as the Keynote Address to the Spring Meeting, Division of Psychoanalysis (39), American Psychological Association, New York City, April 15, 2011.

German along with Yiddish (Rozenblit, 2001). The Freud–Ferenczi correspondence is filled with Yiddish idioms, such as Ferenczi's (1915) describing his own theory that "all libido is based on '*nachas*'" (pleasure) (p. 80). Thus we might call the pleasure principle the *nachas* principle! In this chapter, we explore the personal and professional relationship between Freud and Ferenczi, two Jewish Enlightenment men—friends, colleagues, and analytic couple—who traveled with, confided in, and collaborated with one another, and who enacted between them dynamics shaped to a great extent by their characteristic reactions to their anti-Semitic and homophobic cultural surround.

Sándor Ferenczi: Progressive Enlightenment Jew

Sándor Ferenczi was born on July 7, 1873, the eighth of 11 children who survived childhood. A twelfth, his younger sister Vilma, died of diphtheria when Sándor was about four. We still await an authoritative biography of Ferenczi as well as a coherent and systematic portrait of his historical–political context (Giamppieri and Erös, 1987), but offer the following as a sketch of Ferenczi's background. His father, known as Baruch Frankel until 1879, emigrated from Poland as part of a large migration of Jews from the East seeking to escape anti-Semitism. Born in Cracow, Poland in 1830, Baruch came from the same sociocultural environment as Freud's father. Over the course of a changing political atmosphere, Baruch Frankel gradually became Bernat Ferenczi. At age 18, he participated in the Hungarian insurrection against Austrian domination. Hungary's Jews had been handicapped by discrimination, particularly by the German guilds in Buda and Pest; thus almost all Jews identified with the Magyar national cause in 1848 and thereafter. At this time, Magyar liberals welcomed Jewish assimilation or Magyarization, as many more people were needed to populate large portions of the Hungarian Kingdom (Lukacs, 1988). The rebellion was suppressed until 1867–68, when it led to the constitution of an independent Hungary and emancipation of the Jews. Bernat Frankel was then offered the name Ferenczy with a "y", a sign of nobility in the new Hungary. (Ennoblement was so widespread in Hungary that these titles did not mean much.) Being a liberal democrat, he refused this status symbol, and in 1879, when Sándor was about six, took the name Ferenci, a commoner's name. Gradually, usage added the letter z (see Fortune, 2002).

By 1900 Budapest was a thriving metropolis in which Jews comprised more than 20 percent of the population and about 40 percent of its voters. Thousands more Jews arrived each year. Their influence in finance, commerce, and culture was even greater than what is indicated by these numbers. Gradually, with their increase in population and prominence, the alliance between Jewish and non-Jewish Hungarians broke down and a new form of modern liberal anti-Semitism began to take hold. The new anti-Semitism was populist and democratic, not religious but racial, and was aimed at assimilated as well as religious Jews, who had acquired power, prosperity, and influence (Lukacs, 1988). This was the Budapest in which Ferenczi lived and worked as an adult. As we will soon see, the years 1918–1920 brought the disintegration of the Austro-Hungarian monarchy and the collapse of the socio-political premises of the pre-war era. This is an important historical distinction to keep in mind in comparing Freud and Ferenczi's experiences with anti-Semitism. In Vienna, the liberal political philosophy promising Jews full emancipation and participation in German culture broke down far earlier than in Hungary. Freud had early in his life become disillusioned, increasingly so with the appointment of Karl Lueger in 1897, and especially after World War I. In contrast, the Hungarian political atmosphere was liberal until 1919–1920, in spite of growing popular resentment toward Jews. At the time Lueger and the Christian Socialists came to power in Vienna, there was a Jewish mayor in Budapest. Lueger referred to Budapest with the derogatory epithet, "Judapest" (Lukacs, 1988, p. 95). Hungarian Jews continued, long after those in Vienna, to seek emancipation and integration into Hungarian society (Sziklai, 2009). By the time Ferenczi faced the loss of his illusion of being a "Hungarian of Jewish faith" (Ferenczi, 1919, p. 365), Freud had already lost his own similar illusions.

Baruch/Bernat became the manager of a bookshop in the center of Miskolc that he purchased in 1856 from Michael Heilprin, a Chasidic scholar who returned to his native America. It gradually became a family business, with the family living in the flat above the store. Soon, Bernat added a printing press and then a concert agency, as the Ferenczis were a musical family. By 1880, he was unanimously elected president of the Miskolc chamber of commerce. The Ferenczi house became a gathering place for artists, musicians, and intellectuals and Sándor was raised in a lively, intellectually stimulating, and politically and culturally liberal environment. Sándor was his father's favorite child, accompanying him on excursions to his vineyard on the hills near Miskolc (Kapusi, 2010). Bernat was an upwardly mobile reform Jew who, along with Sándor, attended the synagogue on Kazinczy Street in Miskolc, a suburb of Budapest. It is the only synagogue that remains standing in Miskolc today.

Sándor's mother, Rosa Eibenschütz, was born in 1840 in Cracow, but her family soon moved to Vienna. Baruch and Rosa married in 1858, likely in Vienna. Over the years, Rosa was busy raising 11 children, and for this reason, she resigned from her prestigious town role as president of the Union of Jewish Women, which she had founded, but whose work required long periods away from home. When Sándor was 15 his father died, and Rosa took over and expanded the business. Very few members of the Ferenczi family survived the deportations of World War II.

Sándor graduated from the Miskolc Calvinist Gymnasium, which would have been the only choice of school for a liberal, enlightened Jewish family. He attended medical school in Vienna, living with his relatives and graduating in 1894, and then left for military service in the Austro-Hungarian army. After his military service, he settled in Budapest, where he began working at the hospice for the poor and the marginal, with prostitutes and society's outcasts. By 1900, he established himself in private practice, as a neurologist at the Elizabeth Hospice, and as a court-appointed forensic neurologist.

Ferenczi maintained a social orientation throughout his medical career, and from the beginning of his involvement with Freud, considered the progressive implications of psychoanalysis. This liberal socialist political leaning was common among the members of Ferenczi's Jewish circle, as they sat and discussed art, science, culture, and politics in the coffee houses of Budapest. After giving a lecture on Freud's *The Psychopathology of Everyday Life* to members of the Galileo Circle on October 30, 1909, Ferenczi wrote to Freud,

> I was happy that I could speak before approximately three hundred young and enthusiastic medical students, who listened to my (or, that is to say, your) words with bated breath . . . The medical students surrounded me and wanted me to promise them, at any price, to tell them more about these things . . . Budapest seems, after all, not to be such an absolutely bad place. The audience was naturally composed of nine tenth Jews!
>
> (Ferenczi, 1909b, pp. 91–92)

As early as 1910, Ferenczi wrote to Freud,

> I would like to recommend to you another point for consideration (in case you haven't come upon it yourself). That is the *sociological* significance of our analyses in the sense that in our analyses we investigate the *real* conditions in the various levels of society, cleansed of all hypocrisy and conventionalism, just as they are mirrored in the individual.
>
> (Ferenczi, 1910a, p. 153)

Ferenczi illustrated this sociological significance with several of his analytic cases, including as examples his analysis of a typesetter described as suffering the "terrorism" of oppressed labor conditions; the analysis of the owner of a print shop who was circumventing union rules to swindle his workers; the "inner hollowness" that analysis uncovered in a young countess and members of her social class; and the sexual masochism that kept a young maid working at lower than necessary wages. As early as 1911, Ferenczi spoke of alcoholism as a symptom of a social neurosis that could only be cured by analyzing its social causation (Nyíri Kristóf, cited in Sziklai, 2009). Ferenczi advocated for the rights of homosexuals and transvestites and wrote about his work with prostitutes and criminals, calling for healthier social conditions and better treatment of the disadvantaged (Gaztambide, 2011). Ferenczi was the Budapest representative of the sexologist Magnus Hirschfeld's "International Humanitarian Committee for the Defense of Homosexuals," founded in 1905 (Stanton, 1991). Hirschfeld's Jewish background led him to fight for the oppressed, and it was he who first coined the term "racism." Hirschfeld's library was among the first to be burned by the Nazis—another wandering Jew forced into exile.

Ferenczi's personality was consistently described by all who knew him as warm, affectionate, caring, enthusiastic, hopeful, empathic, playful, boyish, and above all, accepting and understanding of others. He consistently sought to gain the love and approval of others by opening himself up to them. He found men to whom he could be close as he had been with his father, even if we might speculate that he unconsciously longed for a mother's love. For many years, he had Friday evening Shabbat dinner with his mentor, Miksa Schechter, an orthodox Jew and pioneer of medical ethics. At some point after moving to Budapest, Sándor resigned from the synagogue; we do not know why (Kapusi, 2010). It might have been due to his atheist convictions or to rising anti-Semitism, but most likely it reflected his increasing secularization. It is evident from his correspondence that it did not reflect a disaffiliation with the Jewish community or a diminishment of his Jewish identity.

Freud, Ferenczi, and Schreber: Homoerotic Longings, Homophobia, and Paranoia

As we have discussed, Jewish and German cultural identities carried serious implications with regard to race, gender, sexuality, bigotry, anti-Semitism, and homophobia. In this chapter, we will focus on one incident that occurred in 1910 on Freud and Ferenczi's joint vacation in Palermo as they collaborated on writing the Schreber case. Freud's *Schreber, 'Psychoanalytic notes on an autobiographical account of a case of paranoia'*, was published in 1911. Although developed in collaboration with Ferenczi, it became derailed over a mutual enactment of dynamics related to racism, anti-Semitism, homophobia, and misogyny. The tense interpersonal incident between Freud and Ferenczi both foreshadowed and shaped Ferenczi's personal analysis with Freud as well as their later theoretical and technical divergence.

In the summer of 1910, Freud traveled to Italy via Paris with Ferenczi, who was then 37 years old and single, although involved since 1900 with the married Frau G., Gisella Pallos. Ferenczi's brief and interrupted analysis with Freud would not begin for four more years. They stayed at the Hotel du Louvre, where Freud examined Leonardo's "The Virgin, Saint Anne, and the Christ Child." Freud's paper on Leonardo, emphasizing the connection between "passive homosexuality" and narcissism, had just come out in May. It was Ferenczi's first time in Paris, and Freud served as his guide for a day and a half before moving on to Florence, Rome, and Naples, where they stayed for two weeks. While Freud showed Ferenczi around Paris, he likely recalled his own first visit to Paris when he studied with Charcot, who tried to convince him that hysteria was due to hereditary pathological degeneration, as could be proven by an examination of Jewish family pedigrees, including Freud's own.

Freud and Ferenczi sailed to Palermo. The trip was marred by unpleasant Sirocco winds, but the personal storm was far worse. On Christmas Day 1921, Ferenczi wrote to Georg Groddeck, with whom he engaged in a manner of mutual analysis for much of his life, a revealing self-analytic letter recalling the incident in Palermo.

> I could never be completely free and open with him; I felt that he expected too much of this "deferential respect" from me; he was too big for me, there was too much of the father. As a result, on our very first working evening together in Palermo, when he wanted to work with me on the famous paranoia text (Schreber), and started to dictate something, I jumped up in a sudden rebellious outburst, exclaiming that this was no working together, dictating to me. "So this is what you are like?" he said, taken aback. "You obviously want to do the whole thing yourself." That said, he now spent every evening working on his own, I was left out in the cold—bitter feelings constricted my throat. (Of course I now know what this "working alone in the evenings" and this "constriction of the throat" signifies: I wanted, of course, to be loved by Freud.)
>
> (Ferenczi, 1921a, pp. 8–9)

Comparing Ferenczi's recollections with Freud's contemporaneous description, we can see that both Freud and Ferenczi understood Ferenczi's desires as homoerotic, derivatives of a negative Oedipus complex. From Rome, Freud wrote to Jung, triangulating him with Ferenczi:

> My travelling companion is a dear fellow, but dreamy in a disturbing kind of way, and his attitude towards me is infantile. He never stops admiring me, which I don't like, and is probably sharply critical of me in his unconscious when I am taking it easy. *He has been passive and receptive, letting everything be done for him like a woman, and I really haven't got enough homosexuality in me to accept him as one. These trips arouse a great longing for a real woman. A number of scientific notions I brought with me have combined to*

form a paper on paranoia, which still lacks an end, but takes quite a step forward in explaining the mechanism of the choice of neurosis.

(Freud, 1910b, p. 353, emphasis added)

Although Freud accused Ferenczi of being "infantile," "inhibited," and "dreamy," (Freud, 1910b, p. 215) and of not asserting his equality, according to Ferenczi's account, Ferenczi had stood up for himself as being not a secretary but a collaborator. Ferenczi protested that he wanted a shared collaboration, but Freud accused him of wanting the whole thing. Freud seems to have been unable to collaborate as an equal, interpreting a demand to participate in partnership as a demand to take over the whole. Ferenczi wrote back to Freud, agreeing that he was infantile and inhibited, adding, "On this occasion I have also rather ruthlessly brought to light the resistance against my own homosexual drive components (and the uncommon sexual overestimation of women which goes along with it)" (Ferenczi, 1910c, p. 217). Ferenczi here explicitly understood his own desires for intimacy with Freud to be homosexual, which he homophobically devalued as infantile, even while recognizing that his own heterosexual excess might be a defense against underlying homoerotic desire. Ferenczi (1910c) wrote that he was looking for something more from Freud.

> I did, perhaps, have an exaggerated idea of companionship between two men who tell each other the truth unrelentingly, sacrificing all consideration. Just as in my relationship with Frau G. I strive for absolute mutual openness, in the same manner—and with even more justification—I believed that this, apparently cruel, but in the end only useful, clear-as-day openness, which conceals nothing, could be possible in the relations between two $\Psi\alpha$-minded people who can really understand everything and, instead of making value judgments, can seek the determinants of their $\Psi\alpha$ impulses. That was the ideal I was looking for: I wanted to enjoy the man, not the scholar, in close friendship.
>
> (1910c, p. 218)

In his ongoing idealization of telling the truth at all cost, Ferenczi seemed oblivious to the aggression that could be expressed in this way. He was trapped in these dynamics: while seeing himself as longing for genuine equality and mutuality, he was unable to find a third to either competitive aggression (the positive Oedipal—paranoia) or passive submission (the negative Oedipal—hysteria).

Ferenczi (1910c) went on to mention a dream he had in which he saw Freud standing naked before him. Ferenczi analyzed this dream, deriving two motives. The first was unconscious homosexual tendencies. The second was the "longing for absolute mutual openness" (p. 218). Could Ferenczi's longing for openness from Freud simply be explained on the basis of infantile sexual wishes? While recognizing this motive in himself, Ferenczi also believed that the adult wish for personal contact and relatedness should not be reduced to its genetic origins in infantile longings. He longed for Freud to feel comfortable enough with him to expose himself personally, to speak the truth even if it was unpleasant. Ferenczi wrote,

> Don't forget that for years I have been occupied with nothing but the products of your intellect, and I have also always felt the man behind every sentence of your works and made him my confidant. Whether you want to be or not, you are one of the great master teachers of mankind, and you must allow your readers to approach you, at least intellectually, in a personal relationship as well. *My ideal of truth that strikes down all consideration is certainly nothing less than the most self-evident consequence of your teachings* . . . The final consequences of such insight—when it is present in two people—is that they are not ashamed in front of each other, keep nothing secret, tell each other the truth without risk of insult or in the certain hope that within the truth there can be no lasting insult . . . according to my $\Psi\alpha$. ideal, there are no halfway standards, all consideration for people and conditions disappear beside my ideal of truth. Please don't misunderstand me. I really don't want to "reform" society, *I am not a paranoiac.* I would only like to see thoughts and speech liberated from the compulsion of unnecessary inhibitions in the relations of $\Psi\alpha$.-minded men.— Unfortunately—I can't begin, you have to! After all, you are $\Psi\alpha$. in person!"
>
> (1910c, pp. 219–220, emphasis added)

Freud told Ferenczi that his dreams while they were away together were entirely concerned with Fliess, with which he understood it would be difficult for Ferenczi to sympathize. And here Freud's letter quickly turns to his thinking about Schreber. While there is much that could be said about this letter, we want to highlight Freud's denial of his superhero status as well as its impact on those around him; the intricate connections between themes of homosexuality and paranoia in Freud's personal relationships and collaborative work; and Freud's study of Schreber.

> I am also not that $\Psi\alpha$ superman whom we have constructed, and I also haven't overcome the countertransference. I couldn't do it, just as I can't do it with my three sons, because I like them and I feel sorry for them in the process. Not only have you noticed that I no longer have any need for that full opening of my personality, but you have also understood it and correctly returned to its traumatic cause. Why did

you thus make a point of it? This need has been extinguished in me since Fliess's case, with the overcoming of which you just saw me occupied. *A piece of homosexual investment has been withdrawn and utilized for the enlargement of my own ego. I have succeeded where the paranoiac fails.*
(Freud, 1910d, p. 221, emphasis added)

In this exchange we can see the clash of contrasting visions as they emerge from complementary personalities. In what follows, we will explicate these dynamics. Ferenczi's uncritical idealism about the psychoanalytic value of mutual and reciprocal openness became more central as his own work evolved, and Ferenczi continued to long for Freud's openness and personal closeness. He wrote to Freud that he had not given up hope that Freud would:

let a part of your withdrawn homosexual libido be refloated and bring more sympathy to bear toward "my ideal of honesty." You know, I am an unimpeachable therapist. *I don't want to even give up on the paranoiac as a total loss.* So how can I warm up to the fact that you extend your—in part, justified—distrust to the entire male sex! There is certainly much that is infantile in my yearning for honesty—but it certainly also has a healthy core. *Not everything that is infantile should be abhorred.*
(Ferenczi, 1910e, p. 224, emphasis added)

What Ferenczi expected from Freud, the master psychoanalyst, was precisely what some two decades later he attempted to offer his own patients: mutual openness and honesty. What is additionally fascinating is that Ferenczi did not realize that this was his own innovation, but believed it to be the logical and transparent aim of Freud's teachings. Note also the relation of homosexuality and paranoia hovering in the background of these personal exchanges. As we will elaborate, there was an ongoing tension being played out between Freud and Ferenczi, enacting between them the paired binaries: heterosexual/homosexual, active/passive, positive/negative Oedipus, paranoia/hysteria, male/female. Hence, it is understandable that these forces would become explosive in their attempt to collaborate on these very themes, which were elicited by the Schreber case.

The Eternal, Wandering, "Unmanned" Jew

Freud began his theorizing of the relationship between paranoia and repressed homosexuality in 1908a, in collaboration with Ferenczi, to whom he was introduced by Jung. In 1910, Jung gave Freud a copy of Schreber's *Memoirs of My Nervous Illness*, although he likely knew of the work as early as 1903–1904 (Lothane, 1997). The schism between Freud and Jung that climaxed in 1912 revolved around their differing interpretations of the case of Schreber. Freud used Schreber to highlight the role in paranoia of repressed sexuality, which was central to his theory, and had never been fully accepted by Jung.

In contrast, Ferenczi, who was always ready to understand himself in terms of spiritualized or sublimated homosexuality, argued that what led to paranoia was not homosexuality, but its repudiation. In today's terms, one might read Ferenczi as suggesting that paranoia results from homophobia. Keep in mind that both Freud and Ferenczi's understandings were prior to any formulation of gender identity as distinct from sexuality, and so a man's possession of any culturally designated "feminine" trait was equated with homosexuality. Freud and Ferenczi's works have been used— or rather, misused—for much of the past century, to argue that homosexuality was a pathological and regressed outcome of failed heterosexuality (Phillips, 2003). However, neither Ferenczi nor Freud was moralistic or particularly pathologizing of homosexuality, viewing it as a variation in resolving the Oedipus complex. The pathologizing of homosexuality came later.

Let's return to September 1910 in Palermo, the scene of the primal fight between Freud and Ferenczi. Many of these themes—homoeroticism, homosexuality, homophobia, and paranoia—were brewing in Freud and Ferenczi's minds, leading to this perfect storm. Freud's closeness to and conflict with Ferenczi, his anticipation of Adler's "heresy," his anxious hopes for Jung to become his Aryan successor, reactions stirred by the Wolf Man's analysis, and his preoccupation with Schreber, all stimulated in Freud a recurrence of thoughts about his old close friend, Wilhelm Fliess. Freud announced to Jung in December 1910, "My Schreber is finished," but went on to say that he himself could not judge its objective worth "because in working on it I have had to fight off complexes within myself (Fliess)" (Freud, 1910d, p. 380). Freud anticipated an upcoming schism with Adler, which indeed came to full bloom before *Schreber* was published. Freud wrote to Jung,

> I am very glad that you see Adler as I do. *The only reason the affair upsets me so much is that it has opened the wounds of the Fliess affair.* It was the same feeling that disturbed the peace I otherwise enjoyed during my work on paranoia.
>
> (1910b, p. 382, emphasis added)

Freud later called Adler paranoid, just as he accused Fliess of becoming paranoid following their break. Freud was preoccupied with mastering his homosexual tendencies, writing to Ferenczi, "I feel myself to be a match for anything and approve of the overcoming of my homosexuality, with the result being greater independence" (Freud, 1910e, p. 227). Ferenczi's appeal for Freud's love conjured the Fliess *dybbuk*, as did Freud's deepening homoerotic ties to Jung. Indeed Jung's paranoid collapse may have been triggered by his break with Freud (Lothane, 1997).

Adler's "heretical" theories matched these dynamics in a way that can only be described as uncanny. Breger (2000) argues that Adler's "concept of the masculine protest—that one exaggerates certain culturally defined masculine traits to repudiate threatening feelings of weakness and helplessness that are seen as feminine—fit Freud all too closely" (p. 204). Neither Breger nor Rudnytsky (2002), however, both of whom have astutely clarified the Freud–Ferenczi relationship, take into consideration that this formulation not only fits Freud and Adler in terms of their idiosyncratic psychodynamics, but also captures precisely the Jewish male cultural response to the prevailing anti-Semitic stereotypes in which they were helplessly trapped—regarded as feminine, circumcised, and thus castrated. While Freud's (1937a) notion of "the repudiation of femininity" (p. 252) may seem identical to Adler's "masculine protest," Freud argued from a genitally-derived, biological basis that the masculine protest results from castration anxiety, whereas Adler examined social and cultural forces. All of these currents were in the background, as these two wandering Jews, Freud and Ferenczi, traveled intimately together, writing about homosexuality, paranoia, and Schreber's identification with the Eternal Jew. In writing *Schreber*, Freud had to prove Adler wrong: psychosis was not about social issues but about biology, specifically sexuality, and he had to convince Jung that psychosis was rooted in sexual, not spiritual conflict. If in writing *Schreber*, Freud was overcoming his homoerotic love of Fliess, then he was also simultaneously enacting the relationship with Ferenczi. Recall James Strachey's comment to Ernest Jones about the redacted Freud-Fliess letters, "It is really a complete instance of folie à deux, with Freud in the unexpected role of hysterical partner to a paranoiac" (cited in Boyarin, 1997, p. 194). In Freud's collaboration with Ferenczi, Freud and Ferenczi reenacted the complementary roles of hysteric and paranoiac, but in reverse, with Ferenczi acting as hysterical partner to Freud's paranoiac. The thesis we put forward in this chapter is that Freud and Ferenczi, in a relationship of split complementarity (Benjamin, 1988), divided up between them the two polarized poles of reaction to the anti-Semitism and associated homophobia surrounding them, with Freud reacting along paranoid lines and Ferenczi in his more characteristically hysteric manner. Whereas Freud emphasized his positive Oedipal wishes to repress the negative, Ferenczi highlighted his negative Oedipal wishes, attempting to sublimate them. Whereas Freud tried to emulate the Greek–German ideal of the conqueror-hero, Ferenczi tended toward "ironic obedience," a strategy he would only identify much later (Ferenczi, 1932, p. 19). Let's examine their interrelational dynamics in greater detail.

Ferenczi repeatedly lamented to both Freud and Groddeck that his mother was harsh and severe. Ferenczi's self-analysis convinced him he had been sexually abused by his mother or by nursemaids, as well as threatened with castration for sex play with his sister. Rudnytsky (2002) persuasively argues that Ferenczi's negative transference to Freud was not a paternal but rather a maternal transference to Freud as a depriving mother. More importantly, Ferenczi believed that because of his mother's strict treatment and his father's kindness and warmth, he had experienced a "displacement" of his Oedipus complex, resulting in a "strengthening of homosexuality" (Ferenczi, 1912, p. 452). He associated with an incident when as a boy of about five he allowed a boy who had a larger penis than he to put his penis in his mouth, producing disgust. The association is relevant as we soon turn to one of Ferenczi's theoretical contributions, the notion of introjection and its vicissitudes.

Rudnytsky (2002) contends that Ferenczi's formulation anticipated Freud's later idea of a negative Oedipus complex, which played such a strong role in the Palermo incident. Indeed, the negative or inverted Oedipus is a complex that has not received nearly sufficient historical, scholarly, or clinical study (Jaffe, 1983): Freud and Ferenczi first developed it collaboratively (see Ferenczi, 1914). Ferenczi was familiar with and accepting of his homoeroticism; if anything, he hoped to sublimate it. Freud felt similarly during the years of his relationship with Fliess, but after Fliess, and with the establishment of the Oedipus complex—the positive Oedipus complex—he renounced his homosexuality, claiming to have overcome it. He consistently emphasized the positive over the negative Oedipus complex in healthy development, asserting that the bedrock of psychic life was the repudiation of femininity. Ferenczi's long years of submission to Freud may be usefully understood in terms of the complementarity of their positive and negative Oedipal dynamics.

In Freud's championing of the positive Oedipus and in his "overcoming" of his homosexuality, Freud was also rejecting what his society viewed, and what he internalized, as the stereotypically Jewish, passive, feminine, masochistic, castrated position. This was precisely the role Ferenczi played in exaggerated caricature. The "repudiation of femininity" became "bedrock," and Freud identified with warriors and conquerors, including Moses, whom he transformed from a self-effacing, reluctant leader into a ruthless man of action. While the rabbis emphasized Moses' humility and caretaking, Freud's (1939) Moses possessed "decisiveness of thought," "strength of will," and "energy of action," exhibiting "autonomy and independence" and "divine unconcern which may grow into ruthlessness" (pp. 109–110). While Freud's notion of the heroic culminated in autonomous ruthlessness, Ferenczi's vision idealized mutual openness, surrender, and forgiveness.

As we have seen in the previous chapter, Boyarin (1997) interprets Freud's formulation of Schreber as an autobiographical commentary on Freud's own unconscious dynamics. While Boyarin emphasizes Freud's defensive reaction against his own homosexuality and away from the negative Oedipus, we are expanding Boyarin's analysis by comparing Freud's reactions to those of Ferenczi, who ultimately criticized Freud's "androphile orientation" (Dupont, 1998, p. 187), viewing masculinity itself as an "hysterical symptom" (1998, p. 188). To his patients, Ferenczi directly expressed his pain that as a man, he was taught to suppress his capacities for caretaking and kindness, as these were considered feminine and childish; he held the analyst guilty for his inability to provide maternal care (p. 53). That Freud and Ferenczi differed markedly in their stance toward gender and sexuality is highly significant. Freud and Ferenczi shared the experience of being upwardly mobile, liberal, professional Jews surrounded by a culture of intense anti-Semitism that feminized them, circumcised/castrated them, and rejected them as truly Hungarian, Austrian, or German men. Nevertheless, their individual reactions to these circumstances were dramatically different, because they each had quite distinct childhood experiences with their own mothers and fathers. In other words, their reaction to anti-Semitism is one—but certainly not the only—element involved in shaping Freud and Ferenczi's responses to gender and sexuality and broader aspects of misogyny. To be clear: we are not reducing patriarchy and misogyny to anti-Semitism, but rather are exploring the intersection of misogyny, racism, anti-Semitism, and homophobia. Feminism has exposed the inherent relationship between patriarchy and misogyny, and postcolonial studies have investigated the interrelations between racism, misogyny, and homophobia. A psychoanalytic study of the intersection of anti-Semitism, homophobia, and misogyny enriches the findings of feminism; it does not detract from them. Freud and Ferenczi reacted in opposing ways to their society's anti-Semitism and expectations of normative masculinity; they were both drawn to and made anxious by the other's polar opposite style. This clash of polarities was reflected in their theories and clinical approaches, and in the versions of psychoanalysis that emerged following their work.

The Familiar Stranger

Ferenczi, while loved by Freud, remained enigmatic and exotic (Erös, 2004). Freud emphasized Ferenczi's Hungarian national character. "Hungary, so near geographically to Austria, and so far from it scientifically, has produced only one collaborator, S. Ferenczi, but one that indeed outweighs a whole society" (Freud 1914, p. 33). Later, others, too, highlighted Ferenczi's Hungarian national character and gypsy nature (Thompson, 1988). But as the Hungarian historiographer of psychoanalysis Erös (2004) argues, "Instead of searching for nonexistent Hungarian roots, we should emphasize the ethnocultural and linguistic pluralism in Ferenczi's background" (p. 125). This pluralism was typical of assimilationist, middle-class, upwardly mobile Jewish families, such as Freud and Ferenczi's. Ferenczi was Freud's "familiar stranger" (Erös, 2004, p. 125), both *heimlich* and *unheimlich*. It was not Ferenczi's nationality, language, or culture that evoked this familiar strangeness, but rather his split complementarity with Freud in relation to gender, hysteria, and paranoia. Freud and Ferenczi inhabited the flip sides of positive and negative Oedipal wishes and defenses. Freud's paranoia—his castration anxiety and paternal fear that his sons would band together to kill him—met Ferenczi's hysteria—his excessive "feminine" need to be loved and engaged in direct emotional exchange—even as each unconsciously and ambivalently identified with the other, his uncanny double. Before, during, and after his formal analysis of Ferenczi, Freud repeatedly interpreted to Ferenczi that Ferenczi was trying to obtain the love he missed in childhood from his patients, and via homosexual submission, from Freud. As Ernst Falzeder puts it,

> Freud did not even dream of giving Ferenczi some of this love himself. No, Ferenczi should get a grip on himself, stop acting like an obnoxious child, and should, as Freud admonished him . . . "leave the island of dreams which you inhabit with your fantasy children and mix in with the struggle of men."
>
> (2010, p. 401)

Note the equation of femininity and childishness, accepted by both Freud and Ferenczi until Ferenczi began to challenge this assumption in his final years.

In his analysis of Schreber, Freud focused exclusively on Schreber's dynamic conflicts about his longings for his father's love, the negative Oedipus complex—with not a single mention of Schreber's relation to his mother. As we have seen, the neglect of the maternal is characteristic of Freud's work, reflecting, among other things, his own lack of insight into his conflicts concerning his mother. Not only is the mother neglected, only present as the object of the child's desire, but so too are the loving relations of the boy to his father. Only the competitive and murderous side of the ambivalence is present within the positive Oedipus. Significantly, also neglected in Freud's work was the theme of anti-Semitism, including his society's assumption of the passive, effeminate, perverse, homosexual, castrated nature of Jewish men.

Anti-Semitism raged in Freud's Vienna; it was the backdrop to all of Freud's case histories and is evident throughout his writings and personal correspondence. Yet, as Blum (2010) demonstrates, Freud did not explicitly refer to anti-Semitism in the case histories; in fact, in his clinical writings, Freud was silent on ethnic or national matters and excluded all references to his own or his patients' Jewishness, except in the footnote to Little Hans, in which he explained anti-Semitism in terms of circumcision and castration anxiety. Freud was distinctively trying to establish the etiology of the neuroses on an intrapsychic and universal, not on a hereditary, ethnic, or social, basis (Brunner, 1991). The irony should not be missed that emphasizing universalism was itself a distinctively Jewish tendency! In Little Hans, Freud did not identify Hans and his family as Jews, did not mention his own Jewishness, and also neglected to mention that it was he himself who convinced Hans' father to raise Hans as a Jew. Dora's family and friends, including Herr and Frau K were all Jewish, as were Freud's family, friends, and the members of the early Wednesday Night psychoanalytic society, but Freud never mentioned anything of this Jewishness in the case history, even when he analyzed Dora's interest in and identification with the Madonna. Nor when she dreamt of a burning house did he notice allusions to the burning of Jewish factories in the anti-Semitic rioting of Bohemia, where her father's factories were located. In his study of the Rat Man, with all of the many associations to rats, Freud did not mention the anti-Semitic associations of Jews with vermin, odor, disease, or money. Similarly, Freud never discussed the Wolf Man's anti-Semitism, although when the Wolf Man first consulted Freud in early 1910, Freud wrote to Ferenczi, "A rich young Russian, whom I took on because of compulsive tendencies, admitted the following transferences to me after the first session: Jewish swindler, he would like to use me from behind and shit on my head" (p. 138).

Similarly, Freud made no mention of Schreber's incorporation of the rhetoric of anti-Semitism into his delusional system. Schreber constructed a complex theology involving a divided God with dark and light incarnations, whose "rays" and "nerves" would sexually violate him. Schreber believed that he was being literally "unmanned," an Eternal or Wandering Jew who was being transformed into a woman, so that God could sexually violate him and conceive a new human race. As part of his transformation, he felt his stomach being replaced with an inferior "Jew's stomach." Unmanning and Jewification are equivalent. Examining the margin comments on Freud's copy of Schreber's book, Gilman (1993a) demonstrates that Freud was well aware of this rhetoric. But if Freud commented on Schreber's identification with the Wandering Jew, he would draw attention to the most obvious marker of his own Jewishness, and undercut his credibility as a neutral (non-Jewish) scientist. It was therefore important for Freud to present his data as uncontaminated by anything that might inscribe them as Jewish. The image of the Wandering or Eternal Jew converged with "the eternal feminine"[2] to mark or circumcise the Jew as racially/sexually different (Pellegrini, 1997).

---

2 "The eternal feminine" is a cultural archetype, much invoked by Symbolist artists and writers of the late 19th century, whereby a woman was an instinctual or spiritual being, whether a wicked temptress or a saintly virgin.

Paranoia and anti-Semitism were closely related. In fin de siècle Germany and Austria, paranoia was often centered on the perceived danger of a Jewish conspiracy. Gilman (1993a) contends that Freud displaced the perceived danger from Jews to homosexuals. Similar to his rejection of the hereditary etiology Charcot had championed, Freud rejected Krafft-Ebing's theory that homosexuality, like Jewishness, was an innate biological flaw. Instead, Freud viewed it as a developmental arrest, not as degenerate, but as atavistic or primitive. When Freud and Ferenczi stayed together in Palermo to collaborate on the case of Schreber, the deck was stacked for an enactment of the very content they were immersed in writing about—homosexuality, paranoia, and homophobia. Here were two Jewish men, viewed by their society as castrated, homosexual, and feminine, collaborating together in partnership, writing about the themes that were intensely preoccupying them. Freud was determined not to relive his love of Fliess, while Ferenczi, longing for love and intimacy, dreamt of seeing Freud naked.

Freud's (1911) formulation of Schreber was inextricably linked with his own internalized homophobia, stemming from his identity as a feminized Jew living in the larger context of an anti-Semitic and homophobic milieu, just at a time when homosexuality was being transformed into a distinct identity. Freud's recognition of Schreber's desire to be transformed into a woman meant facing his own unresolved feminine desires, which in their society were equated with homosexuality. Anxious to overcome the pathology of feminization and homosexuality that fin de siècle Europe attributed to Jews, Freud proceeded to pathologize them, or at the very least to characterize them as developmentally primitive.

Whereas Freud began his career focusing on hysteria in men (including in himself), now a new pathology became central—paranoia—and hence a new binary emerged. With paranoia as the new prototype of male psychopathology, hysteria returned to its pre-Freudian position as quintessentially female. Vulnerability was displaced from circumcised Jewish men onto hysterical women and paranoid men—men who were unconsciously homosexual. Hysteria and paranoia, caricatures of femininity and masculinity, were explained by positing universal anxieties: penis envy, castration anxiety, and the repudiation of femininity became psychological bedrock. The negative Oedipus was pathologized and men's wish for penetration was repressed. All differences, including race and religion, became minor differences, except for the one big universal difference—the phallic difference—the difference between the sexes (Pellegrini, 1997). This formulation is not meant to imply that misogyny is secondary to racism or religious hatred; rather, we believe that each of these displaces and disguises the others.

Let's examine how the inventor of the term "introjection" (Ferenczi, 1909) and the first analyst to examine the dynamic of "identification with the aggressor" (Ferenczi, 1933b) dealt with the anti-Semitism that surrounded him. This is a striking illustration of how a colonized people introject the views of the colonizer—how they identify with the aggressor, albeit with disguised ambivalence, or with what Ferenczi (1913) described as "mockery and scorn concealed behind the blind belief" (p. 443). Let's return to Ferenczi's 1921 Christmas day letter to Groddeck, in which he recalled the incident in Palermo.

Georg Groddeck, the self-proclaimed "wild analyst" (Groddeck, 1977, p. 7), was a pioneer in psychosomatic medicine, and practiced at Baden-Baden. After Freud introduced Ferenczi to Groddeck in 1917, Ferenczi became enamored of him and, as was his wont, opened himself up to obtain Groddeck's love. In fact, for the rest of his life, Ferenczi spent summers at Groddeck's sanatorium and the two engaged in something of a mutual analysis. Ferenczi was resentful of Freud because he allowed himself to be pressured by Freud to marry Gizella, a woman older than he who was no longer able to bear children.[3] Ferenczi never felt sexually satisfied in his marriage, writing to Groddeck, "I, my 'It', isn't interested in analytic interpretations, but wants something real, a young wife, a child!" (Fortune, 2002, p. 11). Immediately, Ferenczi shifted to his feelings about Groddeck. "Are you by any chance this female friend for me, or am I using your friendship in a homosexual way to replace her?" (Fortune, 2002, p. 11). Pay attention here to the flow of associations and the emerging themes of heterosexuality and homosexuality, positive and negative Oedipus complex, and Jewishness and anti-Semitism. Ferenczi next told a dream, which he called an "entirely 'Hungarian' dream," illuminating his Hungarian experience and identity. In the dream, Ferenczi was happily singing a Hungarian folksong, the words of which he recalled:

> This is what the old Jew tells me.
> Here!—it's from my market stall.
> I want nothing from your stall,
> I don't want you, old Jew, either.
> This is what Fay Gyula [the name of a dashing man] tells me
> I'll buy you, dearest, dresses, ribbons,
> Don't need your dresses, ribbons, Fay,
> All I want is you.
>
> (Fortune 2002, p. 12)

Ferenczi does not hesitate to provide his associations with the dream. On Christmas Eve, he had a small dinner with his family and there were two

---

3 A review of the Freud–Ferenczi correspondence makes it abundantly clear that even while claiming to remain neutral, Freud admitted to Gizella that he was doing all he could, both in and out of the analysis, to persuade Ferenczi to marry her. For a thorough account of the quadrangle between Freud and Ferenczi, Ferenczi's wife Gizella, and her daughter Elma, see Berman, 2004b.

"servant-girls," sisters, singing and laughing with their friends. The younger one is 16 and has "remarkably red lips." The older is 19 or 20 and Ferenczi writes, "She has, as I was able to establish during the course of a medical examination, remarkably firm, ripe breasts, with enormous nipples which become erect during the examination. Interpretation: these pretty girls didn't want an old Jew like me!" (Fortune, 2002, p. 13.) Ferenczi notices that he is growing grey while a friend of his still has black hair and his wife is a "fresh young blonde."

Ferenczi says that he picked up that folksong as a child when he visited the vineyard with his father and heard the peasant women singing it. Strikingly, Ferenczi recalls that he also heard his own parents sing the song. He remembers yearning for the "earthly charms" of those peasant girls in that vineyard. Ferenczi then adds that the song was somehow "bisexual" and that the "dashing man" Fay Gyula was simultaneously also a beautiful lady.

In our view, the dream reflects Ferenczi's internalization of the anti-Semitism surrounding him, magnified by his identification with his parents' introjections of these same attitudes. That he could happily sing and laugh about these blatantly anti-Semitic images is an illustration of his and his family's identification with the aggressor. It also speaks to their Hungarian nationalism, their longing for acceptance by the culture, and their belief that they would in fact be absorbed as Hungarians of Jewish faith, a hope that would soon be crushed. Perhaps Ferenczi and his parents happily singing this anti-Semitic folksong reveals the workings of dissociation, illustrating Homi Bhabha's (1984) formulation of the ambivalence of colonial mimicry, including the wavering between mimicry and mockery, resemblance and menace.[4] Anticipating Bhabha's insight, Ferenczi contended that identification with the aggressor is never complete (Ferenczi, 1933b, Frankel, 2002). The split-off ego is dissociatively contemptuous and sarcastic, and displays what Ferenczi importantly designated as "ironic obedience." As he elaborated, "The mentally ill person has a keen eye for the insanity of mankind" (Ferenczi, 1932, p. 19).

The Unwelcome Child

The highly successful Budapest Congress of 1918 featured papers on the war neuroses, the importance of which was recognized by the Central Powers for reasons we have explained in detail in Chapter 5. Only a month later, however, the Central Powers lost the war and psychoanalysis lost its opportunity for government support and financing. The Austro-Hungarian Empire was no more, and Europe would never be the same. The end of the

---

4 Thanks to Ann Pellegrini for pointing out the ambivalence within the identification.

war left the Jews in crisis. They had been loyal to the Habsburg monarchy, mourning Emperor Franz Joseph as a *tzaddik*, a righteous man, for whom they said *kaddish*, the traditional prayer for the dead. The Jews attributed to Franz Joseph and to liberalism protection against anti-Semitism, and wondered if the day the monarchy fell would become another Ninth of *Av*, the traditional day of mourning commemorating catastrophes in Jewish history. The Jews had enthusiastically fought in the war both as loyal Austrians and because it was a war against viciously anti-Semitic Russia. With the war's end, anti-Jewish rioting broke out in all of the successor states (Rozenblit, 2001). For Freud and his Viennese Jewish community, the old tripartite identity as German by culture, Austrian by political loyalty, and Jewish by ethnicity was no longer an available option. The death instinct was not simply Freud's response to postwar pessimism; it reflected his reaction to unprecedented levels of anti-Semitism, including thuggish rampages against Jews that raged throughout Vienna. Or, as Ferenczi (1929) later observed, the death instinct is what develops in "the unwelcome child."

In March 1919, Ferenczi was appointed as the first university professor of psychoanalysis. On April 29th, Ferenczi wrote to Freud announcing it as official. The significance of this appointment has been romanticized, as by that time, the independence of the university had been suspended under the Hungarian Republic of Councils (Erös, 2004). With the victory of the counterrevolutionary Horthy regime, there were numerous mass executions and arbitrary arrests. Jews were accused of collaborating with the communists. By August, Ferenczi's professorship was annulled and soon he was also excluded from the Budapest Medical Association (Giamppieri and Erös, 1987). Ferenczi wrote to Freud,

> The ruthless clerical anti-Semitic spirit seems to have eked out a victory. If everything does not deceive, we Hungarian Jews are now facing a period of brutal persecution of Jews. They will, I think, have cured us in a very short time of the illusion with which we were brought up, namely that we are "Hungarians of Jewish faith."
>
> (1919, p. 365)

Ferenczi then added a line that, from our perspective, is bitterly ironic. "I picture Hungarian anti-Semitism—commensurate with the national character—to be more brutal than the petty-hatred of the Austrians." He continued, "Personally, one will have to take this trauma as an occasion to abandon certain prejudices brought along from the nursery and to come to terms with the bitter truth of being, as a Jew, *really* without a country." An eternally wandering Jew. "The blackest reaction prevails at the university. All Jewish assistants were fired, the Jewish students were thrown out and beaten" (pp. 365–366). Freud (1919c) responded with "burning disappointment for you, one which has robbed you of a fatherland" (p. 367). Ferenczi found himself *unheimlich*, uncanny, without a home—a familiar situation for a wandering Jew.

Ferenczi conducted his own psychoanalytic explorations of racism, continuing his early interest in the use of psychoanalysis for socially progressive purposes. Recall that it was Ferenczi who pointed out to Freud the link between the negro and the Jew, between racism and anti-Semitism, attributing them both to the projection of the unconscious "not me" onto the racial other. In his *Clinical Diary*, Ferenczi (1932) wrote, "all hate is projection" (p. 78). Hatred comes about when pain and suffering are inflicted on someone or when they are deprived of love and the person so afflicted cannot bear it, cannot mourn, cannot grieve. By hating the other, one displaces one's own suffering onto them. Ferenczi wrote, "The paranoid mechanism may also manifest itself in the fact that the displacement draws ever wider circles and hatred is extended to a whole family, a whole nation, a whole species" (p. 78). Ferenczi's theorizing on hatred and paranoia also helps explain the racism permeating psychoanalytic theory, as an outward projection of the internalized (dissociated and projected) anti-Semitism of its creator.

Omnipotence versus Vulnerability

Ferenczi never stopped hoping that Freud would cease being the distant and removed father and would allow himself to reveal his own weaknesses and vulnerabilities, to be the castrated son as well as the castrating father. He hoped the two men could genuinely open up to one another, analyze their mutual complicity in the analytic stalemate, and forgive each other for the mutual pain and damage they had caused. This was ultimately Ferenczi's view of analytic process and cure. Until the very end, Ferenczi attempted to get through to Freud, but as Dupont (1988) concluded, Freud interpreted away Ferenczi's complaints, referring them to Ferenczi's intrapsychic dynamics. Freud treated Ferenczi sometimes with friendliness, sometimes with paternal severity, and sometimes with humor, but seems never to have questioned his own position or examined his own contribution to the difficulty between them. In the sometimes odd, third-person style of the *Clinical Diary*, Ferenczi wrote:

> Contrary to all the rules of technique that he established himself, he adopted Dr. F[erenczi] almost like his son. As he himself told me he regarded him as the most perfect heir of his ideas. Thereby he became the proclaimed crown prince . . . The anxiety-provoking idea, perhaps very strong in the unconscious, that the father must die when the son grows up, explains his fear of allowing any one of his sons to become independent.
>
> (1932, p. 184)

Ferenczi's conclusion seems remarkably close to Rank's view that Freud's utilization of the Oedipus myth neglected to take into account parental fears of and hostility toward their children. Like Laius, Freud could not face his mortality, and so threatened his sons (Lieberman, 1985).

Never giving up his love for Freud, in one of his last letters, March 29, 1933, Ferenczi wrote to Freud, "Short and sweet: I advise you to make use of the time of the not yet impending dangerously threatening situation and, with a few patients and your daughter Anna, to go to a more secure country, perhaps England" (Ferenczi, 1933a, p. 448). Freud responded that it was not certain that Hitler will overpower Austria, and if he does it will not reach the level of brutality as in Germany, and in any event his own life is secure, and besides being an immigrant is not easy, and even if they kill you, one kind of death is as good as another!

Written on October 2, 1932, Ferenczi's final entry to his *Clinical Diary* crystallized his self-understanding.

> In my case the blood-crisis {pernicious anemia} arose when I realized that not only can I not rely on the protection of a "higher power" but *on the contrary* I shall be trampled under foot by this indifferent power as soon as I go my own way and not his.
>
> The insight this experience has helped me to attain is that I was brave (and productive) only as long as I (unconsciously) relied for support on another power, that is, I had never really become "grown up." Scientific achievements, marriage, battles with formidable colleagues—all this was possible only under the protection of the idea that *in all circumstances* I can count on the father-surrogate . . . Is the only possibility for my continued existence the renunciation of the largest part of one's own self, in order to carry out the will of that higher power to the end (as though it were my own)?
>
> And now, just as I must build new red corpuscles, must I (if I can) create a new basis for my personality, if I have to abandon as false and untrustworthy the one I have had up to now? Is the choice here one between dying and "rearranging myself"—and this at the age of fifty-nine? On the other hand, is it worth it always to live the life (will) of another person—is such a life not almost death? Do I lose too much if I risk this life?
>
> (Ferenczi, 1932, p. 212)

We would like to imagine that, having attained this degree of insight, Ferenczi put his *Clinical Diary* down with some peace of mind.

If Freud had been disdainful of Ferenczi's efforts at self-analysis, the circle was closed as Ferenczi came to denigrate Freud for relying only on his own self-analysis, which had not penetrated deeply enough. Ferenczi later concluded that Freud could not acknowledge his own vulnerability and

shame, that "he wants to ignore the traumatic moment of his own castration in childhood: he is the only one who does not have to be analyzed"
(Ferenczi, 1932, p. 188). Part of what Freud denied was the humiliation of
his own Jewishness, his circumcision, and hence his vulnerability and
permeability. In a manic reversal he projected this "primitivity" onto
others: Eastern Jews, homosexuals, women. Ferenczi, in contrast, tended to
identify with the most vulnerable. Ultimately, for Ferenczi, psychoanalysis
was a social process through and through, self-analysis was a contradiction
in terms, and mutual vulnerability and mutual forgiveness became the
model of therapeutic action. Following Ferenczi's death, Freud wrote a
rather unenthusiastic obituary for his friend, in which he highlighted
Ferenczi's contributions to bio-analysis and was dismissive of his clinical
innovations. From a long and richly productive dialogue of unconsciouses,
Freud and Ferenczi ended up with a confusion of tongues.

On May 4th, 1933, as he was dying, and with almost no strength left to
hold the pen, Ferenczi wrote to wish Freud a happy birthday. Sándor
Ferenczi died in Budapest on May 22, 1933. Ferenczi's younger brother,
Karoly, and his wife Vilma Klar died in Auschwitz in 1944. His younger
sister Zsofia had an inscription carved in a gravestone in the cemetery of
Miskolc. After their names, it reads, "I will keep hold of your memories for
ever. Your mourning sister."[5]

We are all deeply embedded in social and cultural assumptions and
biases that are well beyond our capacity to observe. These include
prejudices that are unjust and dangerous, and that influence both our
self-understandings and our clinical practices. The Palermo incident and
the history of the Freud–Ferenczi relationship illustrates how these pre-
reflective beliefs and related unconscious dynamics are inevitably enacted
in our relationships, particularly as we actualize the very content we are
formulating in words. Our hope is that this study of the context beyond
the psychoanalytic text will serve as an example of the critical importance
of studying the development of psychoanalytic ideas, including our
fundamental clinical concepts, within the larger framework of the social,
cultural, political, economic, and religious surround.

Following *Schreber*, the "ideal type" of psychopathology shifted from
the hysteric (read feminine) to the paranoid (read masculine); vulnerability
in men was thus doubly and triply displaced onto women, homosexuals,
and psychotics. Throughout this book, we are uncovering and deconstructing binary oppositions. Psychoanalysis itself needs to be understood
as both hysterical and paranoid. Think of the hysteria of catharsis and
emotional abreaction in the early phase and of the "hermeneutics of

---

5 For the tragic story of the anti-Semitic and communist persecutions of Hungarian
analysts throughout the 20th century, see the review by Judit Mészáros (2010).

suspicion" as psychoanalysis developed. Where Freud has been described as having a classical Enlightenment sensibility, Ferenczi has been described as a romantic. If Freud emphasized clinical suspiciousness, Ferenczi championed trust and belief in his patients. Freud advocated neutrality, Ferenczi, warmth and acceptance. Where Freud sought to penetrate the patient, Ferenczi called for the analyst's receptivity and permeability. These binaries, which are all linked to gender and sexuality, race and religion, need careful unpacking. Freud and Ferenczi, along with most of their colleagues, were a generation born of Jewish immigrants, who were very much marginal within the larger culture. Only someone on the margins, between two worlds, was in the position to observe both civilization and its discontents.

Chapter 16

Ethics, Universalism, and the "Jewish Science"

Is psychoanalysis a "Jewish science"? We have shown that as Jews living in an anti-Semitic milieu, Freud and his colleagues were at the margins of society, caught between their German and Jewish identities, situated between two worlds. Bergmann (1995) has argued that only someone on the margins could have invented psychoanalysis, and we have discussed the unique contributions arising from "optimal marginality." Our focus until now has not been on the question of whether there is anything inherently Jewish about Freud's development of psychoanalysis, but rather on the binary structure of German/Jew or anti-Semite/Jew that was at its core. In this chapter, we turn to our remaining question: Is there any truth to the claim that psychoanalysis is a "Jewish science"? More specifically, is there something about Jewishness itself—aside from its marginality, its treatment by non-Jews, or its reaction to anti-Semitism—that contributed to the development of psychoanalysis? Is there anything about psychoanalysis that is inherently Jewish?

We recognize that the question itself provokes discomfort. The label "Jewish science," when applied to psychoanalysis by non-Jews, has always (to Jews) been fraught with anti-Semitic implications, even though it might have seemed acceptable to Freud and his Jewish colleagues to imply as much amongst themselves. Even among Jews, this characterization could be unwittingly fraught with internalized anti-Semitism. Oppenheim, the German neurologist, who was himself Jewish and was the uncle of Karl Abraham's wife, privately observed that psychoanalysis was best suited for the primitive *Ostjuden* who were at the time flooding Berlin (Kerr, 1993).

With regard to the Jewishness of psychoanalysis, we can discern the operation of another set of binaries—private versus public. Despite Freud's concern that psychoanalysis be seen as an objective science in the eyes of the larger scientific community, he privately acknowledged to his Jewish colleagues his expectation that his fellow Jews would understand the theories of psychoanalysis more easily than non-Jews. Freud had hoped to anoint Jung as his Aryan successor precisely in order to avoid the accusation that his creation was particularly Jewish, yet as his relationship with

Jung became increasingly strained, he attributed its failure to the Jewish/ gentile divide. Freud (1912) wrote to Ferenczi, "Jung must now be in a florid neurosis. However this turns out, my intention of amalgamating Jews and goyim in the service of $\Psi\alpha$ seems now to have gone awry. They are separating like oil and water" (p. 399).

In the years before the rise of Nazism, it was not uncommon within public scientific discourse to discuss the notion that a particular psychological system expressed the traits of one ethnic or racial group more than another. In Chapter 13, we described Jung's depiction of "the specifically Jewish doctrines" of Freud's "Jewish psychology" and his implication that Oedipal fixations reflected a particular form of family organization found among Jews. Jung was not alone in his racial views or in his public expression of them. Alphonse Maeder worked in Zürich as assistant physician to Bleuler and Jung, who introduced him to psychoanalysis. Freud had great respect for Maeder until 1912, when Maeder introduced his own dream theories, which contradicted Freud's. Ultimately, Maeder broke away, along with Jung. Speaking for his fellow Swiss colleagues, Maeder protested that his first love had been Jewish and he had many Jewish friends, but it seemed fitting to him that a Jew had discovered psychoanalysis because it was particularly suited to "the Semitic spirit" (Kerr, 1993, p. 424). Theodore Flournoy, a professor of psychology from Geneva, later described the break between the Viennese and Swiss schools of psychoanalysis as being due to a split between Christian and Jewish ideals (Kerr, 1993).

Among the first to openly write about the question "Is psychoanalysis a Jewish science?" was Abraham Aaron Roback (1890–1965) a Jewish Polish-born psychologist. Roback grew up in Montreal, graduated from McGill University and earned a doctorate at Harvard in 1917. He conducted extensive scholarship on Jewish and Yiddish culture. Roback's (1929) book *Jewish Influence in Modern Thought*, which he sent to Freud, included a chapter titled "Is psychoanalysis a Jewish movement?" with a section headed "The Jewish issue openly raised."

Although critical of some aspects of psychoanalysis, Roback was extremely respectful of Freud's contributions. He recognized that therapeutic procedures prior to Freud's were mechanical and relied too heavily on the doctor's authority, while Freud sought to understand his patients. Emphasizing the psychoanalytic use of symbolism, Roback compared it to the Chassidic and Kabbalistic symbolist approaches. While the specifics of Roback's comparisons may be debated, here we would like to focus on his argument for a racial psychology: Roback was convinced that different racial groups had distinctive psychologies, attitudes, and proclivities.

Roback quoted extensively from William McDougall's (1921) *Is America Safe for Democracy?* McDougall, who had been analyzed by Jung, advocated a eugenic approach. He argued that characteristic human traits were due to race, not culture, and explained differences between races as being due to innate differences in particular instinctive endowments. McDougall wrote,

> One of Jung's arguments weighs with me a good deal in favor of his view. He points out that the famous theory of Freud, which he himself at one time accepted, is a theory of the development and working of the mind which was evolved by a Jew who has studied chiefly Jewish patients; and it seems to appeal very strongly to Jews; many, perhaps the majority, of those physicians who accept it as a new gospel, a new revelation, are Jews. It looks as though this theory, which to me and to most of my sort seems so strange, bizarre and fantastic, may be approximately true of the Jewish race.
>
> (1921, p. 127)

We want to highlight Roback's reaction to McDougall's argument and the way he puts it to use. Roback agrees with both Jung and McDougall that racial groups are characterized by certain modes of thought, and concludes that we should attempt to discern those elements that are representative of the Jewish people. "It matters little," writes Roback regarding McDougall, "that there is a disparaging note in the specific application of the hypothesis to Freud's teaching and, indeed, to the Jews in general" (p. 173). Thus Roback, in a book that champions Jewish contributions to civilization, agrees with Jung and McDougall's assumption that each racial group will have its own most suitable psychology. The difference is that Roback values the Jewish psychology of Freud whereas they disparage it. We should remember that Freud himself took racially distinct psychologies for granted, and assumed these were biologically based. He wrote, for example,

> But we shall not overlook the fact that id and ego are originally one; nor does it imply any mystical overvaluation of heredity if we think it credible that, even before the ego has come into existence, the lines of development, trends, and reactions which it will later exhibit are already laid down for it. *The psychological peculiarities of families, races, and nations*, even in their attitude to analysis, allow of no other explanation.
>
> (Freud, 1937a, p. 240, emphasis added)

Roback (1929) begins by reviewing the evidence that Freud suffered from feelings of insecurity and inferiority regarding his Jewishness. He points out that Freud did not emphasize the more positive influence of Jewish thought on his own contributions, but only openly acknowledged that anti-Semitism had led at times to his isolation and lack of recognition. Roback identifies the predominance of Jewish patients and Jewish doctors in psychoanalysis, stating that historians will be able to examine these case histories for evidence of how Jews lived and struggled with the anti-Semitism surrounding them. He points out that the Freudian analysts, especially the international leaders, were predominantly Jews, while the Jungians were largely gentiles. He explains this phenomenon on the basis of racial psychology, writing,

> For this reason, I am disposed to look for the actual causes of the Jewish birth and nursing of psychoanalysis in the *peculiar make-up of the Jew, who is analytical in a psychological sense, and who is constantly reflecting on the Why and Wherefore of everything.*
>
> (Roback, 1929, p. 196)

Roback emphasizes the Jewish inclination toward interpretation and its application to everyday life and to the real, concrete problems of people.

Freud wrote to Roback acknowledging the receipt of the book, but it appears that Freud was so put off by Roback's criticism of his theory that he could not be bothered to read it, or at best, skimmed it. He wrote to Roback,

> It may interest you to hear that my father did indeed come from a Chassidic background. He was forty-one when I was born and had been estranged from his native environment for almost twenty years. My education was so un-Jewish that today I cannot even read your dedication, which is evidently written in Hebrew. In later life I have often regretted this lack in my education. With the expression of that sympathy which your courageous defense of our people demands, I beg to remain . . .
>
> (1930b, p. 395)

Freud was less than eager to be confronted with the Jewishness of psychoanalysis; he was determined for it to have universal applicability. We assert the paradoxical conclusion that Freud wanted to keep out particularistic Jewish elements from being associated with psychoanalysis not only because he was trying to maintain the objectivity of science, but also because his allegiance to the objectivity and universality of science was an expression of the universalist Enlightenment values that were a part of his liberal Judaism. His scientific objectivity had become a religious and particularistic Jewish belief.

Roback's book was published in 1929, just as Hitler and the Nazi party were beginning their rise to power. It was only after the Holocaust that it became explicitly offensive within the scientific community to publicly categorize a psychological system as being better suited to a particular ethnicity or race. With the rise of Nazism, the public declaration that psychoanalysis was a "Jewish science" brought with it brutal racial persecution and ultimately, genocide (Frosh, 2005). We must acknowledge that the question of whether psychoanalysis is a "Jewish Science" is inevitably more provocative in a post-Holocaust world than it was before the rise of Hitler, as it haunted by the resonances of the Nazis cataloguing it as such.

Psychoanalysis is not alone in being haunted by the memory traces of Nazi categorization. In addition to psychoanalysis, Einstein's physics, anthropology and Communism were all "Jewish sciences." The Nazis attacked Einstein's physics as a Jewish theory of relativity. Anthropologist Franz Boas' books were burned because his anthropology challenged racist assumptions. There are remarkable similarities between Boas and Freud. Both were assimilated Jews, born just a few years apart. Both were disappointed by their rejection by German culture, and both believed that anti-Semitism thwarted their academic aspirations. Both viewed science as universal, disallowing any notion of a scientific discipline as being classified as Jewish or German (Frank, 1997). The differences in their trajectories stemmed from Boas' decision, spurred by the rise of racial anti-Semitism in Germany, to immigrate to the United States in 1887.

Anthropologists have had to ask themselves questions very similar to those we are raising here about psychoanalysis and Jewishness.

> There has always been a lively, if sometimes hushed in-house discourse about American anthropology's Jewish origins and their meaning. The preponderance of Jewish intellectuals in the early years of Boasian anthropology and the Jewish identities of anthropologists in subsequent generations have been downplayed in standard histories of the discipline.
>
> (Frank, 1997, p. 731)

As Cuddihy (1974) argued, albeit in an overly reductionistic manner, the "ordeal of civility" de-emphasized the Jewishness of Jews who contributed to Western civilization as part of the price they paid for inclusion. Jewish contributions had to "pass" under the universal values of secular humanism. This was true for anthropology and psychoanalysis, as well as for Marxism and the ideology of the political left, where Jews have always been overrepresented. Jews have been prominently identified with the modern Socialist movement from its very inception and were among the pioneers of the Socialist parties in America. The Universalist message appealed to members of a persecuted minority whose aspirations for emancipation and assimilation had been frustrated by racial anti-Semitism. We have argued throughout this book that Freud and many of the early psychoanalysts were optimally marginal, caught "between two worlds." The anthropologist David Mandelbaum made the identical point about the early Jewish anthropologists. He argued that Jews were born anthropologists in the sense that they acquire sensitivity to cultural differences because of their dual participation in two cultural spheres, Judaism and the surrounding culture (Frank, 1997). The idea of optimal marginality is captured by W. E. B. Du Bois's discussion of double consciousness. "One ever feels his two-ness—an American, a Negro, two souls, two thoughts, two unreconciled strivings; two warring ideals in one dark body" (cited in Frank, 1997, p. 740). Freud, Boas, and Du Bois understood that their insights arose from their double consciousness. The rise of Hitler and Nazism and World War II helped turn the tide in America in favor of Boas' anthropological critique of racial theories, which was then pursued by his students after the war.

Given the recognition, following the Holocaust, of the potential dangers of racial theories, the question of whether psychoanalysis was a Jewish science could barely be raised for discussion. We cannot ignore this history. As a profession, we are understandably still loath to openly consider this characterization. While there is nothing inherently racist in taking into account the ethnic, social, cultural, and economic conditions of a particular group of people in considering their psychology, it remains difficult to do so, even today, without raising the specter of racial prejudice.

Yet we believe there is indeed a great deal about psychoanalysis that is specifically Jewish, even while acknowledging that Judaism is extremely diverse and that what it means to be Jewish is always open to question. Who is a Jew? Still, we contend that psychoanalysis embodies certain Jewish values and methodology. We do not make this argument simply out of Jewish pride, nor do we wish to perpetuate the Jewish ethnicity of the psychoanalytic profession. Rather, we believe that for psychoanalysis to survive, it must become conscious of its Jewish foundations so that it can be self-reflective about these influences. In order for psychoanalysis to be able to adapt to new circumstances and demographics, it must critically evaluate how its original shaping forces continue to structure its theories and practices. Because all that was viewed by psychoanalysis as "not Jewish" was split off into psychotherapy, the only way to move beyond the limitations of psychoanalysis as a "Jewish science" is to deconstruct the psychoanalysis/psychotherapy binary. We recognize that the question of what is Jewish about psychoanalysis has many facets and could in itself be the subject of an entire book. We only touch upon some of them here in a highly condensed and preliminary fashion in order to make several points relevant to our argument for the necessity of deconstructing the psychoanalysis/psychotherapy binary. Our aim in doing so is to pave the way for a progressive psychoanalysis for the 21st century, one that has the potential to truly be a "psychotherapy for the people."

A "Jewish Science"

In *The Impossible Profession*, Janet Malcolm (1982) described the psychoanalytic researcher Hartvig Dahl as the "shabbas goy" of the New York Psychoanalytic Institute. A "shabbas goy" is a non-Jew who regularly assists a Jewish individual or organization by performing certain acts on the Sabbath that are forbidden to Jews under Jewish law. Dahl was following an established tradition, as Jones had long liked to joke that he was the "shabbas goy" among the Viennese (Yerushalmi, 1991, p. 53). That Malcolm so unself-consciously used this analogy in relation to psychoanalysis speaks volumes about the broad-based understanding that psychoanalysis was predominantly Jewish. She immediately added the following parenthetical note:

> The once nastily anti-Semitic characterization of psychoanalysis as "the Jewish science" is today good-humoredly accepted by analysts as an accurate comment on the great predominance of Jews in the profession, and on the parallel between Talmudic and analytic hermeneutics.
>
> (1991, p. 84)

At the height of its success in the 1950s, psychoanalysis was self-identified with masculinity, phallic penetration, and power. It claimed to be deep and complex, capable of comprehensive understanding and cure. Ironically, it was also characterized as Jewish. Jews who, until then, had been identified as weak, passive, feminine, and castrated could, for a time, reverse this bias. They could literally turn passive into active, maintaining that it was the "other," the *goyim*, the non-Jews, who represented a form of treatment—psychotherapy—that was simple and superficial. According to the mainstream analysts of the 1950s, psychotherapy was a behavioral manipulation that did not achieve the deep penetration of psychoanalysis. Just as Freud himself had defined his own Jewish identity as a militant warrior who, unlike his father, would fight back against his enemies, Jewish psychoanalysis in its golden age was, for a brief time, phallic. Castration anxiety was warded off by projecting the castrated state onto superficial, inadequate, and *goyish* psychotherapy. This was a central aspect of what we have described in Chapter 7 as "psychoanalytic mania." Notice how this split actually maintained the very biases Jews wished to negate, promoting the stereotype of Jews as introspective, psychologically convoluted, preoccupied with their internal worlds, and inept at dealing with external practical realities. In other words, underlying the psychoanalysis/psychotherapy binary was the binary of Jewish/gentile. To be Jewish meant to be psychologically locked in an internal world, whereas non-Jews were associated with external reality and pragmatic behavior in the outside world.[1]

In his handbook of psychoanalysis, Lawrence Kubie (1936) took up what was by then an already well-known slogan, that psychoanalysis was a Jewish science (see Alexander, 1936, who addressed this issue in his review of Kubie's text). Kubie discussed this catchphrase in the context of recognizing that analysts themselves were often neurotic and introspective people. He explained that suffering in early life need not lead to pathology but could contribute to the development of an introspective and contemplative nature; the personal difficulties of being a member of a minority group could also lead to psychological-mindedness. Kubie explicitly delineated a connection between Jewishness, minority outsider status, psychological complexity, psychological-mindedness, and psychoanalysis. Whereas historically, especially in Europe, that very binary had gentiles on top and Jews on the bottom, in this postwar period of American history, following America's military victory, economic prosperity, and the emergence of the State of Israel, the usual hierarchy was reversed. No longer willing to view themselves as circumcised/castrated, the Jewish analysts manically positioned themselves as possessing a powerful, phallic "analytic instrument" that could penetrate the depths of the unconscious. Theirs was the most scientific of treatments, held in the highest esteem. Moreover, it was profoundly culturally Jewish, in its emphasis on textual analysis, scholarly debate, interpretation and exegesis, intellectuality, complexity, deep introspection, the internal world, and respect for ambivalence.

In *Hate and the Jewish Science*, Stephen Frosh (2005) contends that psychoanalysis is rooted in Jewish identity and culture, and describes the continuing effect of these origins on the development of the discipline. He writes,

> The claim that psychoanalysis should be considered a "Jewish science" is related to the idea that Jewish thought, Jewish philosophy and Jewish history flooded its foundations, investing it with the specific

---

1 Ernest Jones suggested that one of Freud's most prominent Jewish characteristics was his fondness for telling Jewish jokes, and a book-length study has been done of Freud's jokes and his Jewish identity (Oring, 1984). In his 1915 lecture to the B'nai Brith, "Death and Us," Freud compares the values of non-Jews and Jews. For gentiles he evokes the motto of the Hanseatic League, "It is necessary to sail the seas, it is not necessary to live." He then continues, "In comparison, take what one of our very characteristic Jewish anecdotes expresses: the son falls off a ladder, remains lying there unconscious, and the mother runs to the Rabbi to seek help and advice. 'Tell me', asks the Rabbi, 'How does a Jewish child come to be on a ladder [in the first place]?'" (Freud, 1915a, pp. 16–17). The joke reflects Freud's Jewish anxieties about travel and climbing—the dangers of leaving the Ghetto and aspiring to climb—but it also reflects the stereotype of Jews as less able than gentiles to manage the practical world. Jokes and stereotypes about Jewish husbands who are not handy around the house and rely on non-Jewish handymen continue even today.

inward-consciousness of the Jews, who were newly released in the nineteenth century from the ghettoes and at least some of their traditions. That is, the claim is based on the idea of cultural inheritance: that however atheistic these early psychoanalytic Jews were, they *could not but* pursue a way of looking at things which was "Jewish." What this "Jewishness" consisted in was not a religious perspective—not *Judaism*—but an approach to argument and interpretation established over centuries in which debates over the meanings of texts were the main expression of cultural achievement. The claim is therefore not just a sociological one, that Jews became psychoanalysts because they felt comfortable and familiar in this role, but also an argument about intellectual history: the *reason* they felt so comfortable was that the psychoanalytic world-view was so much like the Jewish one.

(2005, pp. 10–11)

David Bakan's (1958) *Sigmund Freud and The Jewish Mystical Tradition* traced parallels between psychoanalysis and Jewish mysticism. His work initiated a veritable cottage industry of research on Freud's relationship to Judaism and Jewish identity. Bakan attempted to show that Freud was a "crypto-Sabbatean," a follower of the heretical Shabbatai Tzvi (a would be "messiah" in 17th-century Poland). His book drew considerable criticism for being extreme in its claims and virtually devoid of any serious discussion of Kabbalistic ideas. But at the time Bakan wrote his book, the field of contemporary Kabbalah scholarship was in its infancy. Jonte-Pace (2001) points out that although some scholars have supported Bakan's thesis, the consensus is that Freud's contact with Jewish mystical ideas was indirect and that the psychoanalytic technique of interpretation Bakan found so similar to Kabbalistic interpretation is not specific to Kabbalah, but rather was a component of the rabbinic tradition that was broadly shared by European Jews. Jonte-Pace herself concludes that many of Bakan's core observations can be supported.

We ourselves are most moved by Bakan's (1958) general claim about Freud's contribution regarding the relationship between psychoanalysis and interpretation. Harold Bloom (1987) wrote, "Freud's most profound Jewishness, voluntary and involuntary, was his consuming passion for interpretation" (p. 52). It is by now well accepted to think of psychoanalysis, like Judaism and biblical exegesis, as a hermeneutical or interpretive tradition. Bakan persuasively argued that Freud applied to the study of individual behavior the traditional Jewish methodological principle of interpretation, in which every word—even every letter—of the Torah, including the decorative adornments of the letters and the spaces between letters, was assumed to be meaningful and subject to multiple understandings. For psychoanalysts, the human being, created in the image of God, is like a holy text, subject to ongoing and interminable analysis and interpretation. (See Starr, 2008, for an examination of the Jewish interpretive tradition in relation to contemporary psychoanalytic ideas about interpretation.) We have referred to Franz Kafka's identification of psychoanalysis as the Rashi commentary on the struggles of his generation. It is this tradition of textual interpretation transposed onto the interpretation of human beings as living texts that characterizes psychoanalysis.

Whatever one's view of the inherent tie between psychoanalysis and Judaism—whether or not one agrees that Freudian psychoanalysis actually shares a common sensibility with the Jewish textual, ethical, legal, philosophical, mystical, or rabbinic tradition—unquestionably, psychoanalysis has historically been associated with Jews and Jewishness, and has been widely perceived as a Jewish science. Yet the discussion of Jewish involvement in the psychoanalytic movement was until recently, "as though by tacit agreement, beyond the pale" (Yerushalmi, 1991, p. 98). Ostow (1982) wrote that in his years at the New York Psychoanalytic Institute, there was an "unspoken gentleman's agreement" not to discuss Jewishness (p. 150). Ostow courageously attempted to address these difficult issues publicly. For example, he wrote,

> Yet one wonders how similar would the discipline have been if it had been developed by a non-Jew? Is psychoanalysis studied and practiced and developed differently even now by non-Jews as compared with Jews? Is it handled differently in societies most of whose members are non-Jewish as compared with societies with mostly Jewish members? Do the contributions of Jewish psychoanalysts differ from those of their non-Jewish colleagues? If it had been developed by a non-Jew, would exegesis have come to play such an important role in psychoanalysis?
>
> (Ostow 1989, p. 121)

Heinz Reijzer (2011) maintains that psychoanalysis has always been a Jewish affair, but that psychoanalysts have always been afraid of ending up in the position of the "other," the outsider, and thus have distanced themselves from their Jewishness. Reijzer's study is largely limited to psychoanalysis in Europe rather in America, which is our main focus, but his assumptions and observations are still relevant. He clearly acknowledges that no form of science or psychological treatment is either Jewish or non-Jewish. But he argues that the history of psychoanalysis, with its Jewish founders and reputation, invites the conflation of psychoanalysis with Jews, with the result of combining ambivalence toward both. Reijzer contends that analysts tried to distance themselves from their relation to Jewishness by universalizing their discoveries, "even though everything that Freud and the circle around him discovered was the result of what Jewish patients told Jewish psychoanalysts during their treatment" (p. 11). Reijzer establishes that psychoanalysts, especially in Europe, had to distance themselves from appearing Jewish. Jews could, of course, be members of the psychoanalytic movement, but in many countries they had to forget that they were Jews in their identity as analysts. Judaism was thus reduced to nothing but a religion, separated from Jewishness more generally.

As scientists and adherents of the Enlightenment, psychoanalysts had to be rational. They had to examine religion from a distance, not engage in it or identify with it. Reijzer cites as one example Otto Fenichel's (1945) classic work, *Psychoanalytic Theory of Neurosis*, which mentions Christian Science three times but does not refer to Judaism even once. Reijzer tries to persuade his readers that "psychoanalysis has been treated as the Jew among the sciences and that it has tried to escape that stigma by defense and self-cleansing" (p. 27). While not generally discussing American psychoanalysis, Reijzer notes that the situation has been different in New York, where analysts have, for example, felt comfortable speaking out in support of Israel.

How Jewish was psychoanalysis demographically in its heyday and how Jewish is it now? It has been and still is very difficult to assess religious demographics. Professional associations do not generally ask for or report the religious affiliation of their members. Even if they did, self-reports would be quite ambiguous. While many analysts would likely self-report as atheist or unaffiliated, a large percentage of these secularists might have been born into Jewish families. According to Hale (1995), in a 1958 study at Menninger's psychoanalytically-oriented residency program, whose best students went on for analytic training at the Topeka Institute, Jews, who constituted less than 3 percent of the U.S. population, made up one-third of newly trained residents. Catholics, at 20 percent of the population, made up only 8 percent. Half of the residents were Protestant. It was not until the 1970s that non-Jews outnumbered Jews in analytic training institutes, and then, only by a thin margin, even as Jews represented only 3 percent of the population. In a 1971 study, Henry, Sims, and Spray found that 62.1 percent of their sample of American psychoanalysts identified themselves as having a Jewish cultural affinity, compared with only 16.7 percent indicating a Protestant affinity and 2.6 percent a Catholic affinity. An additional 18.6 percent indicated no cultural affinity, a percentage considerably higher than other categories of mental health professionals, suggesting that the proportion of psychoanalysts with a Jewish background was even higher than 62 percent.

It is clear that relative to the general population, Jews have been vastly overrepresented as patients seeking psychoanalytic treatment, accounting for 60 percent of applicants to psychoanalytic clinics in the 1960s (Kadushin 1969). Depicting a Jewish subculture in mid-20th-century America, Glazer and Moynihan (1963) characterize psychoanalysis as a "peculiarly Jewish product" and a "scientific form of soul-rebuilding" (p. 175) that served the same purpose as religion but was divorced from irrational religious ideas. In their view, psychoanalysis served as a central Jewish cultural institution, fulfilling some of the same functions as traditional religious affiliation. One can still see the link between psychoanalysis and Judaism in contemporary popular culture, for example, in the work of Woody Allen, perhaps one of the most famous of modern-day Jewish psychoanalytic patients.

Ethics and Universalism

Philip Reiff (1959) has famously depicted Freud as a moralist, highlighting Freud's ethical and social concerns for humanity. He wrote, "In psychoanalysis, Freud found a way of being the philosopher he desired to be, and of applying his philosophy to himself, humanity, the cosmos—to everything, visible and invisible, which as a scientist and physician he observed" (p. 3). But rather than presenting himself as a philosopher or moralist, Freud desired to be seen as a neutral scientist, and for his discoveries to be accepted by the scientific community as being the result of rigorous and objective scientific observation. In two recent books reviewing Freud's place within science and the humanities, Alfred Tauber (2009, 2010) identifies the assumptions underlying the 19th-century positivism subscribed to by Freud. Predicated on the belief that nature could be observed objectively, free of the distortions of human cognition, positivism presumed that the observer could be separated from the observed, so that no subjective values would be involved in gathering or analyzing the data. The resulting theories would thus not be contaminated by human subjectivity. The findings of objective science were written in a neutral voice and from a universal perspective, possessing no individual viewpoint. Given Freud's positivist vision and scientific aspirations, it is not surprising that he insisted he had made universal discoveries rather than publicly acknowledge any subjective influence, let alone a particularly Jewish one.

Similar to Philip Reiff's (1959) depiction of Freud as a moralist, Tauber (2010) pronounces Freud a "reluctant philosopher." In Tauber's view, psychoanalysis is not so much a science as an interpretive philosophy, a "human science" that is first and foremost a contribution to ethics (p. 216). Surveying the various sources upon which Freud drew in developing his humanistic philosophy, Tauber identifies German Romanticism, the Western literary tradition, the Enlightenment critique of religion, and the Kantian formulation of the autonomy of reason. Yet glaringly omitted from Tauber's list of sources is any attribution of influence from the Jewish tradition. In contrast, recall Joshua Liebman's (1946) *Peace of Mind* (discussed in Chapter 9), which drew a direct link between principles of psychoanalysis and the moral and psychological teachings of the Jewish rabbinic tradition.

Tauber does, however, provide us with one clue pointing in a Jewish direction. He notes that Freud's overall ethical commitment, which emphasized individual freedom arising from and dependent upon the acceptance of one's fate, closely resembled the philosophical system outlined by the Jewish philosopher Baruch Spinoza. Although Spinoza was ultimately excommunicated from the Jewish community for his heretical views, he was well versed in Jewish literature, Bible, and Talmud, and these influences thoroughly permeate his philosophy of ethics. Spinoza may be viewed as the originator of a modern Jewish secular consciousness and can serve as a symbol for the ways in which Jewish universalist ethics have so often been disembedded from their Jewish context and reconfigured as part of Western culture. Indeed, Goldstein's (2006) biography of Spinoza locates the origins of his philosophy in the trauma of the Inquisition's persecution of its forced Jewish converts. The very universality of Spinoza's philosophy, she explains, was necessitated by his psychological need to think of himself as remaining outside the awful dilemmas of his Jewish identity. Many modern Jews, including Freud, followed Spinoza on this secular universalist path as their way of escaping the struggles of Jewish identity in an anti-Semitic Europe. Schwartz (2012) offers a cultural history of the appropriation of Spinoza by a range of modern Jewish thinkers who wrestle with the question of what it means to be a modern secular Jew, and notes how Freud is highlighted as being among Spinoza's descendants.

We believe the same can be said of Freud's incorporation of the Jewish humanist tradition into the body of psychoanalysis. As we discussed in Chapter 12, the notion that humanism was integral to Judaism figured prominently in Freud's Jewish education. Through his close relationship with his Hebrew teacher Samuel Hammerschlag, Freud was steeped in liberal and humanistic Jewish ethical principles. Heinze (2004) notes that, like almost all German and Austrian Jews, Freud's education at the Gymnasium was comprised of "equal parts Kantian philosophy, with its emphasis on the morally free individual, and Jewish exegesis, with its Hebraic constellation of moral heroes." Students were taught "a supremely rationalist monotheism with morality rather than theology at its core. In this way, secular Jews shared fully in the moral though not the dogmatic universe of German Judaism" (p. 72). Similarly, Klein (1985) demonstrates that although Freud rejected Jewish religious ritual, he was inspired by Judaism's support of Enlightenment ideals, particularly "when it taught the love of humanity or fostered unity and freedom among fellow men" (p. 44). In rejecting Jewish religious tradition and embracing Jewish humanism as being concordant with Enlightenment values, Freud's views were similar to those of many of his modern secular Jewish countrymen.

Heinze (2004) observes that the term "secular Jew" fails to capture the complexity and nuance of Jewish intellectual life in turn of the century

Austria. Although they rejected religious ritual and faith in God, even the most secularized Austrian Jews were exposed to Jewish values that were extremely difficult to shed. The secular surrogates that occupied the place of religion—Zionism, socialism, and later, psychoanalysis—were thoroughly imbued with these Jewish values. Writing of these secular Jews, Heinze clearly articulates what we have been calling "optimal marginality":

> Not fully accepted into European society, even when they completely assimilated its customs, they existed always at the margins and developed a uniquely skeptical point of view. Intensely in modern society but not completely of it, Jews were perfectly positioned to create novel critiques of the status quo.
>
> (2004, p. 70)

Unlike the many other minorities living in Austria, Jews had a history of ghettoization. Locked away from the world at large, they primarily focused inward. The life of the mind *was* the Jewish homeland. Jews concentrated on texts and scholarship, family and community. Jewish texts are rife with representations of the intensity and complexity of familial interactions. The Bible depicts family dynamics, sibling rivalries, and the multigenerational transmission of tradition. Midrash and Talmud also focus on family relations. The philosophy of German *Bildung* in which these secular Jews were immersed drew on the Jewish legacy of learning and enculturation but substituted Western texts for Jewish ones. Psychoanalysis also incorporated many of these aspects of Jewish life. It focused inward, on the private sphere of personal relations, on the intricate interactions of family, and on the study of texts and their interpretation.

Critiquing Peter Gay's denial of the influence of Judaism on Freud and the development of psychoanalysis, Heinze (2004) argues that Gay "missed the presence of Jewish moral values in the mind of this secular thinker" (p. 72). We agree with Heinze and extend this critique to Tauber, who despite viewing Freud's contribution as being largely in the realm of ethical philosophy rather than natural science, views him as a secular humanist, thereby missing the profound Jewish influence. Gay and Tauber, following Ernest Jones, read Freud as influenced by universalist values, German *Bildung*, and the Western humanist tradition, omitting the recognition that this very universalism was itself particularly Jewish!

We are not arguing that Freud built particularistic Jewish principles into his theory. Rather, we maintain that the duality of particularism versus universalism calls out for deconstruction. Our point is that in fin de siècle Austria, Jewish particularism *was* universalistic. The elimination of Jewish subjectivity—the drive to transform Jews into universal men and women who would be unmarked, uncircumcised, showing no trace of difference—was a powerful motivating force for these Westernized Austrian/German Jews. Secular Jewish intellectuals were preoccupied with eliminating the supposedly Jewish traits that visibly separated them from their fellow countrymen. In this vein, the rise of Zionism and the formation of Jewish dueling societies can be seen as a simple inversion of the traditional Jewish values of scholarship and intellectuality; an effort to show that Jews could be like everyone else. (Franz Boas had deep facial scars resulting from his dueling.) As we have shown in Chapter 14, while Freud strongly identified as a member of the Jewish people, the very qualities he chose to emphasize as Jewish were precisely those universal traits—German and Western characteristics—that had *not* been at the center of Jewish culture. These included military strength, courage in battle, and various aspects of machismo. Secular Judaism was inherently universalist. To Freud, to be Jewish in the realm of ethics meant to be a humanist—as if Kant were the Jewish lawgiver or, a bit closer to home, Spinoza. Writes Jacqueline Rose,

> Freud offers . . . one of the most striking self-definitions of the modern secular Jew—that is, a Jew for whom shedding the trappings of linguistic, religious and national identity—paradoxically, by stripping away its untenable and, one might say, most politically dangerous elements—does not make him less Jewish, but more.
>
> (2003, p. 71)

The notion that universalism is derived from Jewish particularism is vividly captured in a joke often told by Rabbi Shlomo Carlebach, one of the foremost Jewish teachers and religious songwriters of the 20th century, and a frequent speaker on college campuses in the 1950–70s. Carlebach recounted that if he met a person who said, "I'm a Catholic," he knew he was a Catholic. If he met a person who said, "I'm a Protestant," he knew he was a Protestant. If he met a person who said, "I'm a human being," he knew he was a Jew! In telling this joke, Carlebach was drawing attention to the familiar theme of Jewish universalism. However, in contrast to Rose, who applauds the stripping away of Jewish particularism, Carlebach recognized the Jewish self-hatred, the internalized anti-Semitism, evinced in the disappearance of Jewish self-identification.

For centuries, Judaism has been associated with the idea that Jews are a chosen people in a covenantal relationship with God. This would seem to be a prime example of Jewish particularism, even if we acknowledge that Judaism also comprises universal values. How and why was the particularity of Judaism transformed into universalism? The answer, especially as it shaped Freud and the origins of the psychoanalytic movement, is found in the German–Jewish synthesis, or what Peter Gay has called the Jewish "love affair with German culture" (cited in Klein, 1985, p. 34, n. 34).

The very idea of religion—what we mean by religion today—has largely been shaped by modern Protestant assumptions. Before the modern era, Judaism was not a religion. Batnitzky (2011) has illuminated that prior to Emancipation and the acquisition of citizenship rights for Jews, it was impossible to distinguish between Jewish religion, nationality, and culture. The idea of conceptualizing Judaism as a religion emerged in a German-Jewish context that produced a highly intellectualized tradition of thought developed in response to the German Enlightenment, in a historical context where Jews were promised, but never realized, full integration into German culture.

Batnitzky (2011) traces the origins of modern Judaism as a religion to German-Jewish philosopher Moses Mendelssohn's quest for a German–Jewish cultural symbiosis, in which he defined the Jewish religion as a matter of behavior rather than belief. In freeing Judaism from belief and dogma, Mendelssohn's definition allowed Judaism to exist in harmony with enlightened reason and universal ethics. By the early 20th century, German-Jewish philosopher Hermann Cohen, a founder of the *Wissenschaft des Judentums* movement (see Chapter 14), further advanced the German–Jewish synthesis, rejecting Judaism's particularistic features. Judaism became a universal ethical doctrine, a rational religion of inward faith, inseparable from German *Bildung*, the cultivation of individual character.

Freud's education at the Gymnasium took place during the constitu-tional era in Austria, a time of political liberalism spearheaded by Enlightenment ideals. Jews eagerly anticipated social acceptance and inte-gration into German society. Allegiance to German culture was equated with Enlightenment values, cultural assimilation, and the leveling of social differences. Jewishness might remain a private, subordinated aspect of one's identity, but the ideal was of a neutral, non-particularistic, universal call for common human rights and freedom for all. By supporting the State and identifying with German culture and *Bildung*, Jews attempted to elim-inate the differences that had hampered their equality. Jews tried hard to be German, which meant to be assimilated, universal, a part of the whole. They sought social integration rather than an assertive identity of their own. As we noted in Chapter 12, the assimilation of German Jews was so intense that they often believed that they adhered to German culture more faithfully than the Germans themselves (Klein, 1985). Tragically, the Enlightenment promise was never fulfilled—the doors to equality were opened only for a very short time during Freud's youth. Freud, like his contemporaries, could barely accept—and never really got over—the painful reality that the doors had so quickly shut. They held onto the hope that universal brotherhood of mankind was an attainable ideal.

As Eastern Jews increasingly immigrated to Vienna, Western Jews, self-identified as German, began to distinguish themselves from these immigrants. The large immigration intensified racial hostility and economic competition. By the 1870s, racial anti-Semitism began to stir, and with the economic crash of 1873, intensified. For many German Jews it took decades to recognize that synthesis with German culture was not to be a reality. Denying the level of anti-Semitism that surrounded them, these Jews continued to believe that assimilation could be successful, if only they could be German enough. They thus adhered to principles of German liberalism long after it was dead. Jews then championed the ideal of universalism, as it proposed human rights for all. With the appointment of Karl Lueger and the rise of his Christian Socialist party, by the time Freud began his self-analysis and founded the psychoanalytic movement, the dark reality had set in and the Jews were demoralized. But they continued to dream the dream of their youth, namely that Jews would contribute to a universal message of Enlightenment, rationality, freedom, equal rights, and reason. As Freud realized that his liberal assimilative approach would no longer work he, like many of the liberal Jews of his era, shifted to a more defiant and self-affirmative strategy, one that was originally more natural to the Eastern European immigrants. Asserting his pride in his Jewishness, Freud argued for Jewish superiority, both because he believed that standing up to anti-Semitism strengthened the Jews and because the Jews were the only ones who continued to champion universal Enlightenment values.

Let's consider a few examples of key representatives of this liberal humanistic Judaism who had a direct influence on Freud. (For a thorough scholarly review, see Dennis Klein's (1985) *Jewish Origins of the Psychoanalytic Movement*.) Adolf Jellinek, the Chief Rabbi of Vienna from 1865 until his death in 1893, was an articulate spokesman for this non-particularistic approach to Judaism. He continually championed the universal meaning of the particular laws of Jewish religion. Like Jellinek, Samuel Hammerschlag, with whom Freud studied religion as a child and with whom he later remained close friends, also emphasized Judaism's universal characteristics, far beyond nationalism and dogma. While Hammerschlag himself did not neglect Judaism's particularistic features, such as the Hebrew language, the main thrust of this historical era was toward the universal, and this is certainly what Freud took away from his studies. Joseph Breuer played the largest role in shaping Freud's positive Jewish identity in the years 1883–1886, after the rise of the new racial anti-Semitism. Breuer's father, Leopold, was a student of the *Chatam Sofer*, Rabbi Moses Schreiber, one of the greatest Talmudists of the century. Leopold educated himself in secular studies and became a liberal teacher of religion, writing the Jewish textbook that Freud used in his gymnasium studies, as we noted in Chapter 12. Breuer himself, a father figure to Freud, was a liberal Jew who shared the same universalistic understanding of Judaism and embrace of Enlightenment ideals. From 1873 until his death in 1925, he was a member of the *Chevra Kadisha*

(Holy Congregation), a group that organized charitable and support services for the Jewish community.

We have already described Freud's intense involvement with the B'nai B'rith (see Chapter 13). Solomon Ehrmann, a medical school friend of Freud's from 1874 who was later the president of the B'nai B'rith Viennese chapter and editor of the chapter's *Quarterly Report*, expressed the philosophical hopes of the Viennese chapter of the "Humanitarian Societies of B'nai B'rith" that were so congenial to Freud. "The ideal of humanity was first cogently expressed by the Greeks, revived in the Renaissance, and finally, fully realized in the Enlightenment" (cited in Klein, 1985, p. 78). With their emancipation from the ghetto, the Jews became "the protagonists of genuine humanity as we mean it" (Ehrmann, cited in Klein, 1985, p. 78). Klein (1985) comments, "In their appeal for universal brotherhood and equality, Rousseau, Voltaire, and Lessing were thus the moral ancestors of modern Jewish existence" (p. 78). We want to highlight just how dramatically the modern liberal Judaism embraced by Freud became an expression of humanistic Enlightenment values in which the Greek–German tradition displaced the Jewish rabbinic tradition. With such a displacement, a legitimate question becomes: What is left of Judaism to hold this society together as Jews? Why not simply embrace a humanist society? The answer emerged gradually. The Jews viewed themselves as the last and only "champions of the ideal of humanity" (Ehrmann, cited in Klein, p. 82). The liberal Jews of the B'nai B'rith saw themselves as the only remaining example of universal ideals promising democracy and peace.

One characteristic that Jewish secularists were willing to identify as specifically Jewish was that Jews were naturally prone to civility as gentiles were to violence. As a subscriber to the Lamarckian view that acquired characteristics could be inherited, Freud believed that Jews had inherited an ethical disposition to sublimate the sensual into the abstract and spiritual.[2] Having been too often burned by the mob's turn to irrationality, Jews placed their hopes in rationality. At the same time, Jews recognized that the dark forces of irrationality were always lurking, in need of control. While Freud's morally Stoic attitude is often traced, as he himself wished, to Greco-Roman, Western, and universalist moral traditions, we believe that this emphasis disguises the influence of the Jewish moral philosophy

---

2 Most scholars believe that Freud never abandoned his Lamarckism (Yerushalmi, 1991), even after it had been discredited as a theory of evolution, and he has long been criticized for not keeping up with the science of his day. Bernstein (1998) disagrees with this consensus, arguing that Freud was not so clearly a Lamarckian. Slavet (2008) points out the political implications of the debate over Lamarckism, which had become associated with Jewishness. However, recent scientific research suggests that Lamarck and Freud might not have been entirely wrong (Rechavi, Minevich, and Hobert, 2011).

by which Freud was surrounded throughout his life, both in his family and in his personal and professional community.

In the 19th century, significant developments in Jewish theology produced a number of innovative moral systems emphasizing the importance of the individual within the context of religious life. Heinze (2004) identifies five movements, which amounted to a Jewish moral revolution: Reform Judaism, Ethical Culture, Modern Orthodoxy, the Mussar movement, and Chabad Hasidism. Each of these movements attempted to explain how Judaism could satisfy the psychological needs of the individual. Reform Judaism honed the body of Jewish law into the ethics of interpersonal behavior. Privileging individual needs and rational autonomy, it eliminated required ritual, except for that which felt personally meaningful. Ethical Culture, an American development, eliminated theology altogether, leaving only a moral philosophy. Samson Raphael Hirsch, a student of Rabbi Isaac Bernays—Freud's wife's grandfather—led the Modern Orthodox movement. Hirsch believed that by keeping the laws of Torah, Jews were conveying universal moral principles to the world, fulfilling a spiritual mission to humanity.

In Eastern Europe, where Jews lived under extremely stressful conditions and were isolated from non-Jewish neighbors, two trends emerged: the Mussar movement under Rabbi Israel Salanter, and Chabad Lubavitch Hasidism. The Mussar movement had a significant impact on Jewish education across the spectrum of Jewish denominations. It focused on the moral discipline required to overcome the *yetzer hara*, the unconscious evil inclinations or drives that are always in conflict with our higher inclinations. Only by turning psychologically inward, in necessarily painful self-examination and introspection, could one learn to overcome these unconscious forces. Similarly, Hasidism brought the psychology of the individual into central focus. Unlike other forms of 20th-century mysticism, Hasidism emphasized a strong ethical orientation, in which all of the *mitzvot* (commandments) were understood to have an ethical component. Like the other innovations in Judaism, Hasidism focused both on ethics and on the psychology of the individual, emphasizing meditation, introspection, and struggling with the emotions in order to transform crude elements of the personality into spiritually higher attributes.

In sum, each of these five movements emphasized ethical universals; in particular, the ethics of interpersonal behavior, individual psychology, introspection, emotional regulation, and the control of dark psychological forces. Heinze (2004) makes a strong case that Freud's secular psychoanalysis was a direct extension of these religious innovations. If Tauber is correct in calling Freud a "reluctant philosopher," then it seems to us that it would be more appropriate to characterize Freud as a reluctant Jewish philosopher—specifically, a Jewish moralist.

Modern-day Anti-Semitism and the "Jewish Science"

Given the centuries-long history of popular and institutionalized anti-Semitism and the horrors of the Holocaust, as well as our own subject positions as Jews with a cultural and family history of anti-Semitic persecution, we remain alert to implications of racial prejudice in public scientific discourse, subtle as these undertones may be. Even today, in contemporary scholarship, the characterization of psychoanalysis as a "Jewish science" can still be fraught with insidious anti-Semitic connotations of varying subtlety. We will highlight three examples in which contemporary scholars discuss the Jewishness of psychoanalysis.

In his much acclaimed *A History of Psychiatry*, the eminent social historian Edward Shorter (1997) described psychoanalysis as one of the "dinosaur ideologies of the nineteenth century," an unfortunate hiatus in the evolution of psychiatry toward a biological science of mind and brain. Freud's ideas, he wrote, "are now vanishing like the last snows of winter" (p. vii). According to Shorter's research, by the 1990s, psychoanalysis largely disappeared from psychiatry, having failed to stand the test of time, with a majority of psychiatrists deeming it "scientifically bankrupt" (p. 146).

Shorter's strongly argued characterization of psychoanalysis as nothing but a detour on the road to scientific progress leaves him with the need to solve a two-sided riddle: First, how to explain psychoanalysis' transient success and popularity, a triumph so great that for decades, psychiatry became equated in the public mind with psychoanalysis; second, how to explain the fall of psychoanalysis and account for why psychiatry began to recover from its "analytic infatuation" in the 1970s. Shorter's solution to this riddle brings us right back to our topic: Freud's "Jewish science."

Shorter's (1997) chapter on the history of psychoanalysis concludes with a section entitled "Psychoanalysis and the American Jews." Shorter writes that in both Europe and America, the "misadventure" that was psychoanalysis was based on "the desire of recently acculturated middle-class Jews for some symbol of collective affirmation" (p. 182). While Jews, like many other ethnic groups, had experienced the difficulties of migration, assimilation, and integration, they had also survived the shock of the Holocaust, an event experienced by no other ethnic group. According to Shorter, Jews therefore needed a "special symbol of self-affirmation, a collective badge of pride" (pp. 182–183). Shorter claims psychoanalysis served as that symbol. The initial popularity of psychoanalysis was almost exclusively among middle-class Jews. While in Europe, psychoanalysis gradually lost its Jewish stamp, in America, following the Holocaust and the flood of immigration of Jewish refugee analysts, Jews viewed psychoanalysis as their "healing gift to all the world" (p. 185). Shorter writes, "It is not stretching the facts to refer to psychoanalysis in the middle decades of the twentieth century as a kind of Jewish 'our thing'" (p. 187). In this narrative, Shorter is reprising, although more crudely and without some of the cautions, Cuddihy's (1974) well-known argument that Freudianism was a post-emancipatory ideology designed to transform the social conflicts of the awkward, newly modernizing, Eastern European Jew into scientific problems. Shorter attributes the precipitant decline of psychoanalysis to the increasing social assimilation of American Jews. Jews rapidly assimilated into American culture, as evidenced by a dramatic rise in intermarriage rates after the 1960s and the fact that fewer than half of all Jews belonged to synagogues. The Jewish community was in dissolution and psychoanalysis was no longer needed as a symbol of Jewish solidarity.

The *Journal of the American Medical Association* called this "a splendid book" (McGuire, 1997). The *New England Journal of Medicine* (Pope, 1997) said that Shorter was at his finest in describing the rise and fall of psychoanalysis. The American Psychological Association's *Contemporary Psychology* described Shorter's book as "sublime" (Najavits, 1998, p. 281). No mainstream psychoanalytic journal reviewed the book, nor has it been referred to in the psychoanalytic literature. Of the 20 book reviews we found, although several were critical of various aspects of Shorter's scholarship as well as of his obviously biased account, only one review, in the *Australian and New Zealand Journal of Psychiatry* (Harari, 1999), critiqued Shorter's explanation for the rise and fall of psychoanalysis, namely, its being a Jewish "our thing."

Were Shorter not a celebrated historian of psychiatry and were his numerous historical textbooks not widely used, we might not dwell at such length on his simplistic and reductionist arguments and on his crude caricatures of psychoanalysis. Nevertheless, some interesting considerations are raised by Shorter's otherwise tendentious history. We actually agree with Shorter that psychoanalysis was a Jewish "our thing." He may even be right in proposing that Jewish assimilation has made psychoanalysis less essential as a Jewish contribution. From our point of view, the problem with Shorter's narrative is that he seems so self-satisfied with this result—so pleased that psychoanalysis, this Jewish distraction from "real" scientific progress, has become irrelevant to his history of psychiatry. What marks Shorter's historical presentation as unfriendly to Jews is his lack of appreciation for the viciously anti-Semitic context in which Jewish analysts lived and worked, and in which they constructed their theory and practice. Disdainful of this Jewish "our thing," Shorter is pleased by its decline. There is little expression of appreciation for why Jewish analysts felt it necessary to have a symbol of affirmation. Neither is there any mention of the positive legacy of psychoanalysis, let alone of its continuing usefulness.

Why have no psychoanalytic journals, which have certainly reviewed other books that attack psychoanalysis, even considered Shorter's arguments? Why has almost no one spoken of Shorter's claim that psychoanalysis rose and fell as a Jewish science? Why has psychoanalysis been so relatively weak in contributing to a psychological account of anti-Semitism? Why, even when the International Psychoanalytical Association met in Berlin in 1985 for the first time after World War II, was it so difficult for psychoanalysts to speak directly about the Holocaust and the behavior of analysts during that tragic era (see Frosh, 2005)? We cannot recall any public discussion of the Jewish identity of psychoanalysis within our own institute or professional associations, except for when we raised the issue in preparing for this study. And when we did, we met with a good number of gentile analysts who told us of their resentment of the ways in which Jews dominate the field and take its Jewishness for granted.

If we find Shorter less than friendly, we find other critics of psychoanalysis to be downright anti-Semitic. The fact that Freud and the psychoanalytic movement have been so closely associated with Jews and Jewishness has been used in a way that we do not hesitate to label as such. Kevin MacDonald (2002) proposed a theory that received quite a bit of academic attention, including many glowing reviews, along with criticism that his work is anti-Semitic. MacDonald proposes that Judaism is a group evolutionary strategy to enhance the ability of Jews to out-compete non-Jews for resources. Using the term "Jewish ethnocentrism," MacDonald argues that Judaism fosters in Jews a series of marked genetic traits, including above-average verbal intelligence and a strong tendency toward collectivist behavior. These traits manifest in a series of influential intellectual movements, including, and especially, psychoanalysis. MacDonald describes the psychoanalytic movement as an "intellectual war on gentile culture" (p. 150). We do read MacDonald as trading in anti-Semitism; however, ironically, much of his writing on the history of psychoanalysis is thorough and accurate. In fact, what makes his work so dangerous is precisely that he embeds his anti-Semitic innuendo within a subtle and nuanced presentation of the history of psychoanalysis.

In *The Culture of Critique: An Evolutionary Analysis of Jewish Involvement in Twentieth-Century Intellectual and Political Movements*, MacDonald (2002) includes a chapter entitled "Jewish Involvement in the Psychoanalytic Movement." He writes, "Patients and analysts alike were participating in a secular movement that retained the critical psychological features of traditional Judaism as a separatist, authoritarian, and collectivist cultlike movement" (p. 134). The thesis of this chapter is that

> It is impossible to understand psychoanalysis as a "science," or more properly as a political movement, without taking into account the role of Judaism. Sigmund Freud is a prime example of a Jewish social

scientist whose writings were influenced by his Jewish identity and his negative attributions regarding gentile culture as the source of anti-Semitism.

(2002, p. 109)

It is worth looking closely at this quote. We agree with his analysis, up to a point. We similarly argue that Freud and psychoanalysis were strongly associated with Jews and Jewishness. But notice how Macdonald then adds an emphasis on Freud's negative attitudes toward non-Jews. Here, too, we would agree with MacDonald; we have cited many of Freud's anti-gentile remarks. But MacDonald notably omits any mention of the vicious anti-Semitic culture in which Freud was embedded. This neglect of context has the effect of portraying Freud's own defensive prejudices in a far more negative light. MacDonald then goes on to refer to Freud's negative attitude toward anti-Semitism—as if Freud's attitude toward anti-Semitism should have been neutral!

Macdonald writes,

It is also not surprising, given the clear sense of Jewish intellectual, moral, and, indeed, racial superiority to gentiles that pervaded the early phases of the movement, that outsiders have proposed that psychoanalysis not only had powerful religious overtones but also was directed at achieving specific Jewish interests.

(2002, pp. 144–145)

Macdonald builds a case for psychoanalysis as a cryptic Jewish conspiracy. He actually complains that psychoanalysis has an "overt agenda in pathologizing anti-Semitism" (p. 145). In other words, if psychoanalysis were a real science, if it were objective, then it would treat anti-Semitism as a legitimate and healthy reaction to Jewish behavior! By viewing anti-Semitism as pathological, psychoanalysis displays its own political anti-gentile agenda. This is the essence of MacDonald's anti-Semitic approach. By attributing anti-Semitism to Jewish behavior, he blames the victim, essentially normalizing and rationalizing anti-Semitism as a legitimate response to Jews' pursuit of anti-gentile self-interest. Consider the following quotation, in which MacDonald clearly blames Jewish psychoanalysis for pathologizing anti-Semitism instead of attributing its cause to Jewish behavior. He writes,

As in the case of radical political ideology, psychoanalysis is a messianic universalist ideology that attempts to subvert traditional gentile social categories as well as the Jewish-gentile distinction itself, yet it allows for the possibility of a continuation of Jewish group cohesion, though in a cryptic or semi-cryptic state. Thus although Freud himself believed that Jewish intellectual and moral superiority resulted from Lamarckian inheritance and were thus genetically based, psychoanalysis officially denied the importance of biologically based ethnic differences or indeed the theoretical primacy of ethnic differences or ethnic conflict of any kind. Ethnic conflict came to be viewed within psychoanalytic theory as a secondary phenomenon resulting from irrational repressions, projections, and reaction formations and as an indication of gentile pathology rather than as a reflection of actual Jewish behavior.

(2002, p. 145)

Despite our reluctance to give MacDonald so much free press, we have quoted him at such length in order to highlight the insidious anti-Semitism, masked as scholarship, inherent in characterizing psychoanalysis as a "Jewish science" without providing sufficient context—particularly the context of anti-Semitism in which psychoanalysis was born and raised.

Science historian Jonathan Engel (2008) concludes *American Therapy*, his history of the rise of psychotherapy in the United States, with the following observation:

Psychotherapy has been integrated into the uniquely American ethos of pragmatism. Our can-do nation, often skeptical of intellectualism and scholasticism, was uniquely to embrace an ideology born of fin-de-siècle European angst. *The Jewish science of psychoanalysis, so foreign and distasteful to most Americans of the last century*, has morphed into the eclectic therapy of twenty-first-century social workers, psychologists, and licensed therapists. Their goals are practical: greater emotional well-being, better social adjustment, happier marriages, and more productive lives. Few Americans would argue with these goals.

(2008, p. 261, emphasis added)

We directly acknowledge that all of the major historians of psychiatry agree in reporting on the decline of psychoanalysis. There seems to be no argument on this score. Jonathan Engel has written extensively on the history of American medicine and health policy. In *American Therapy* (2008), he traces the rise of psychotherapy as a profession in the United States. Engel reports, "by 1990 the profession was hitting bottom" (p. 218). He quotes the sociologist Tanya Luhrman, who describes her experience observing the meetings of the American Psychoanalytic Association as like "watching dinosaurs deliberate over their own extinction" (p. 219). Engel attributes the decline predominantly to two factors. First, analysts had priced themselves out of the market. "Considering that analytic training failed to add earning potential for most board-certified psychiatrists, the training was reserved for the independently wealthy or the extraordinarily committed" (p 219). Second, but of greater importance, was "the simple fact that studies repeatedly demonstrated that psychoanalysis did not work" (p. 220). The inefficiency of psychoanalysis, together with its exorbitant prices, led to its extinction.

In an interview for the *Jewish Daily Forward*, Engel highlights the Jewish origins of psychoanalysis and the impact of anti-Semitism and marginality.

> Of the original 13 members of [Sigmund] Freud's circle, Carl Jung was the only one who was not Jewish. That was partially because these physicians were being marginalized in Austrian society because of anti-Semitism. If you wake up one day and realize that there's no room for you in the other guy's club, you start your own club. The patients were also 95% Jewish . . . There were a lot of upper-middle class Jews in Vienna, and analysis was expensive. And, if you think about it, it was really weird to lie down on a couch five days a week and talk about these strange sexual fantasies—especially when you consider the mores of 19th century Victorian society. So this was really counter-cultural. *Maybe the Jews were a little more open to counter-cultural movements because they were socially marginalized.* If people don't like you to start with, there is less at stake.
>
> (Birkner, 2009, np, emphasis added)

When asked by the interviewer "Do you think psychoanalysis will ever rebound?" Engel bluntly replied, "No, it's dead."

The historians of psychiatry are all in agreement that psychoanalysis is in steep decline, if not altogether brain dead. However, they base their conclusions on the study of a very specific subgroup of psychoanalysts, namely medical analysts; in particular, those associated with only the most classical and conservative practices. As we see here, their findings are generally drawn from the observation of members of the American Psychoanalytic Association. They do not include the many actively practicing psychoanalysts from other disciplines such as psychology and social work, who are members of less traditional groups, and who are, in fact, alive and well, thank you. Their dire predictions for the continued vitality of psychoanalysis are understandable to the degree that, as historians of psychiatry and medicine, they are studying the fate of psychoanalysis predominantly within medicine, where it has done the least well.

We would like to highlight an extremely revealing mistake (or re-interpretation), made by the *Jewish Daily Forward*'s editorial staff with regard to Engel's claims. We believe it to be significant. Birkner leads the interview off with a brief introduction to Engel's book. She states, "In the book, Engel explores *America's early affinity for 'the Jewish science of psychoanalysis,'* the subsequent decline of the analytic movement, and the techniques that replaced it" (emphasis added). But note that, as we see in

Engel's quote, his point was precisely the opposite! What he wrote was *"The Jewish science of psychoanalysis, so foreign and distasteful to most Americans of the last century*, has morphed into the eclectic therapy of twenty-first-century social workers, psychologists, and licensed therapists." What happened here? The *Jewish Daily Forward* reported what it wanted to hear from Engel, rather than what he was actually saying! Even in the 21st century, with the substantial assimilation of American Jews, Jews continue to want to claim psychoanalysis as a Jewish science! It was Jews who felt this ready affinity for psychoanalysis; for Jews, it was neither foreign nor distasteful.

Finally—and again, ironically—Engel's major argument falls right in with our line of reasoning. Psychoanalysis, which was a Jewish science, foreign and distasteful to Americans, born in the "angst" and intellectualism of European, misfit Jews, has been replaced by psychotherapy, which is practical, optimistic, and hopeful; red-blooded, familiar, American. In other words, underlying the psychoanalysis/psychotherapy binary we uncover the dichotomy of Jew/gentile. Jews thought of themselves as psychologically deep and introspective; they focused on meaning and interpretation that penetrated beneath the surface. They contrasted this Jewish attitude with gentile (*goyish*) behavioral-oriented therapies that stayed on the surface, looking outward toward external behavior and practical solutions. This brings us right back to the argument with which we began this chapter. Namely, it is only if we deconstruct these binaries—only if we openly examine our discipline's foundational and shaping influences—that we can hope to ensure the continued vitality of psychoanalysis and its relevance to our contemporary culture. Only by acknowledging the attitudes, values, and clinical implications embedded within psychoanalysis' Jewish historical origins can we move beyond these cultural prejudices and begin to make psychoanalysis a psychotherapy for *all* of the people.

Freudian versus Relational: Old Testament versus New Testament

If classical Freudian psychoanalysis is a Jewish science, then is relational psychoanalysis a Christianized version? We have heard this whispered. But we have also seen claims for the Jewishness of relationality. In Chapter 7, we discussed the enormous impact on American psychoanalysis of the arrival of so many Jewish psychoanalysts fleeing Hitler's Europe. Most of these émigrés were, like Freud, secular non-observant Jews whose identification with Western culture added to the traumatic shock of their betrayal by the German culture they had embraced. Following the Holocaust, which caused a crisis of faith even among many traditionally observant Jews, this group of assimilated Jews would hardly be disposed to challenge Freud's view of religion. The émigrés were much more preoccupied with assimilation into American society. They were raised on the same modern Enlightenment and universalist values as Freud. For them, as for Freud, psychoanalysis had replaced religion as a set of beliefs, culture, and ideology—but one that was thoroughly secular and universal. "Psychoanalysis, presenting itself in the U.S. as a medical science with no overt links to Judaism, was a passport to assimilation into one of the higher and more prestigious ranks of American society" (Brickman, 2010, p. 36). Hence for psychoanalysis in its golden years, preponderantly Jewish analysts embraced a secular and universal psychoanalytic vision, just as many other Jews embraced a secular socialist ideology that displaced their Jewish particularistic identity with a universal, idealized, and manic, if not messianic, vision.

In reviewing the contributions to the psychoanalytic study of religion of British object relations theorists such as Winnicott and American self-psychologists following Kohut, Brickman (2010) has proposed that these revisionist approaches constitute a kind of "New Testament" in relation to the "Old Testament" of Freud (p. 35). These theorists softened the psychoanalytic critique of religion by valuing "illusion" as a necessary transitional phenomenon, essential to symbolic expression mediating inner and outer realities. Instead of dismissing religion as narcissistic, these approaches value the healthy developments of narcissism, recognizing the positive value of idealization and mirroring. They do away with "the centrality of the primal crime, the Oedipus complex and the law of the father . . . bringing the good news that psychoanalysis can indeed—against Freud's intentions—be reconciled with religion" (p. 35).

We appreciate Brickman's argument and wish to extend it beyond the realm of the psychoanalytic approach to religion to psychoanalysis in general, and specifically, to its clinical approach. Relational psychoanalysis, in spite of its consistent ideological tendency toward both/and rather than either/or thinking, has ironically defined itself in terms of its opposition to "classical" or "Freudian" psychoanalysis, creating a new binary of Old and New Testaments. In this dichotomization, the Old Testament of classical theory is patriarchal, characterized by the analyst's phallic penetration with interpretations, while the relational New Testament fulfillment/replacement shifts the emphasis to pre-Oedipal maternal holding and containing. Where Freudians have been depicted as rigid, authoritarian, withholding, intellectualized, paternalistic, phallic, and focused on Truth and Insight, relationalists have far too often characterized themselves as democratic, nurturing, optimally gratifying, empathic, holding, containing, maternal, and as highlighting a cure through relationship—love over insight. We keep hearing about the polarities of drive/relations; authoritarian/egalitarian; conflict/dissociation; insight/relationship; repression/dissociation. With all its espousal of postmodern and poststructural deconstruction of binaries, relational psychoanalysis has in fact reinforced and perpetuated all of the problematic binaries in the field. Of course, as we have shown throughout this book, the classical/relational divide parallels and reworks the older psychoanalysis/psychotherapy binary. In its excess, relational theory, instead of deconstructing the binary, makes the mistake of accepting a simple reversal, in which the classical paternal psychoanalysis is now devalued, replaced by relational maternal psychoanalysis—which as we have shown, is what used to characterize psychotherapy.

When Mitchell (1988) developed his version of relational conflict theory he did not propose that analysts gratify instead of frustrate. Rather, he argued that frustration/gratification was only one dimension among many that needed to be considered, and suggested that the overemphasis on not gratifying resulted from Freudian drive theory. As Greenberg (2001) pointed out, relational analysis has tended to shift the analytic goal toward an emphasis on fulfilling the patient's needs rather than on self-awareness and the search for self-knowledge. Freud valued Judaism because of its emphasis on ideas over images, truth over illusion—which led, in his view, to an increase in intellectuality and spirituality precisely because it favored renunciation over fulfillment. Relational psychoanalysis, as it is too often presented, may be viewed as a simple reversal of Freud's thought in that it privileges the analyst meeting the patient's relational needs and thus advocates gratification over frustration, fulfillment over renunciation. In this view the patient suffers from a "basic fault," a deficit, or developmental relational trauma, a "Fall" or "original sin" that can only be healed by the analyst who extends themself, taking on the patient's suffering and providing a new parental experience. In contrast, the classical model is represented as an Old Testament that forced the patient to face his own inner sinfulness, renounce his evil drives, and bear his own guilt. Where classical analysis proposed a cure through knowledge and living with ongoing conflict and renunciation, relational analysis provides what Freud (1921), referring to religion, called, a "crooked cure," a cure through love rather than knowledge and self-struggle (p. 142).

It is not accidental that the New Testament of relational psychoanalysis so closely resembles Christian supersessionist theology. We have even wondered if the battle of a unified mind versus a multiple self-state model of mind is not a reenactment of a battle over radical monotheism. How much is the wish to move beyond Freud a wish to surpass Jewishness with Christianity? But let us be clear, as this is a delicate subject: First, Freud's Jewishness was his particular version of Jewishness—there are indeed many Judaisms. The association of Judaism and the Hebrew Bible with a harsh God of vengeance is itself a misrepresentation of Judaism, as is the assumption, accepted by Freud, that Jewish theology and tradition rejected all visual images and representations of God. Second, we are not in any way discounting or minimizing the contributions and enrichments brought about by the broad spectrum of relational approaches. Indeed, we champion these new approaches. What we object to is the manner in which they are depicted as new, above and beyond a very narrowly portrayed Freudianism. This is Christian supersessionist triumphalism, in which relational psychoanalysis is the fulfillment of, and the replacement for, the Old Testament of Freud. And of course relational theory itself can be and has been claimed as also representing a specifically Jewish version of psychoanalysis. For example, Aron (2004) has suggested that the relational focus on mutuality and asymmetry is consistent with a great deal of Jewish theology emphasizing the mutual covenant between God and Israel, Buber's I-Thou relation. Similarly, Starr (2008) has examined the intersection of relational and Jewish kabbalistic formulations of the mutuality of transformation. We are arguing that in the world of psychoanalysis, these two visions need not be polarized and set against each other hierarchically. We can and must get beyond religious doctrinal disputes, but we can only do this by making them explicit. These visions can—and should—be complementary, paradoxical, and mutually enriching. Only then can psychoanalysis be a "psychotherapy for the people."

Chapter 17

What is Psychoanalysis?

Can you say "Shibboleth"?

In Chapter 8, we reviewed the debates of the 1950s, in which the mainstream analysts of the era defined psychoanalysis by contrasting it with psychotherapy. Throughout this book, we have argued that this method of definition via binary opposition has been detrimental to our profession. This leaves us with the challenge of articulating how psychoanalysis should be defined. In this chapter, we take up this question, which is so central to our profession and our professional identities: "What is psychoanalysis?" We examine several contemporary efforts to define psychoanalysis, and propose our own ideas about how best to go about the process of arriving at a definition that is inclusive of the full range of psychoanalytic therapies. In making our arguments, we keep in mind the words of intellectual historian Dominick Lacapra, "Problematic distinctions are not binary oppositions" (cited in Boyarin, 1999).

We believe we can make reasonable, even if problematic, distinctions between psychoanalysis as an intensive form of psychotherapy, and psychoanalytic therapy that is less intensive, without turning them into polarized dichotomies. We believe it is possible to provide a reasonable, observable definition without positioning psychoanalysis in opposition to some other analytically oriented therapy. We propose that psychoanalysis be defined in an inclusive manner, as a discipline that encompasses the broad range of psychoanalytic theories, methods, and therapies. We do not minimize the impact of frequency of sessions or use of the couch versus face-to-face positions. Nor do we minimize differences based on the analyst's theoretical beliefs or clinical approach. Instead, we argue that the term psychoanalysis should encompass a variety of techniques, theoretical viewpoints, and treatment approaches. While psychoanalysis and psychoanalytic therapy do include a range of differences, these differences should not be cast as binary oppositions, where psychoanalysis is defined as "not psychotherapy". Rather they should be defined dialectically, as each always including the other.

Our view is quite similar to that recently proposed by Steven Cooper (2011). Cooper argues that psychoanalysis should be defined by the analyst's intentions, aims, and actions, not by the patient's response or by external criteria such as frequency or use of the couch. According to Cooper, what distinguishes the psychoanalytic approach is that analysts try to elicit the patient's interest in and curiosity about their unconscious experience. Fromm made this very same argument more than a half century ago, saying that as long as the analyst was trying to help the patient via the understanding of unconscious processes, the analyst was doing analysis. Fromm was a founding faculty member of NYU Postdoc, and a strong influence on Bernie Kalinkowitz, who established the program, as well as on numerous other colleagues. Following Fromm, under Kalinkowitz's leadership and now Lewis Aron's, Postdoc has always downplayed the distinction between psychotherapy and psychoanalysis.

Like us, Cooper does not dismiss the impact of session frequency or the patient's recumbent position. As we do, he generally recommends greater frequency and finds the couch to be of value with many patients. However, for Cooper, the essence of psychoanalysis is not frequency or the patient's position; nor does the designation of analysis hinge on the patient's response. Rather, what makes a treatment an analysis is the analyst's intentions and clinical approach. The patient's increased curiosity or deepening of experience is not the hallmark of an analytic process; it is a desired outcome. This is an important point. If psychoanalysis were to define itself based on the patient's experience of curiosity and increased depth of reflection, then tautologically, a treatment that did not lead to such a desired outcome would not be psychoanalysis. To put it another way: There could never be a "failed psychoanalysis," since by definition, it would not be an analysis! This kind of definition is a blatant example of how psychoanalysis has traditionally been valorized via the denigration of psychotherapy.

In his discerning review of Cooper's book, Waska (2011), who challenges Cooper in many other respects, applauds this position. He writes, "our field will only survive if we stop idealizing our work, promoting a caricature of it that is impossible to obtain, and accept the limits of our value and the value of our limits" (p. 469). We agree with Waska and Cooper that defining psychoanalysis broadly and realistically is essential to our survival, and that to define it narrowly promotes an idealized caricature of what analysts do, while devaluing and denigrating psychotherapy and other psychotherapeutic education.

Let's consider the merits and deficiencies of other approaches to defining psychoanalysis. In a recent interview of Jay Greenberg, conducted by Alex Crumbley for the journal *Psychoanalytic Psychology*, one of the first questions asked was how Greenberg thought about the traditional distinction between psychotherapy and psychoanalysis. A detailed examination of Greenberg's answer brings us right to the heart of the complexity of conceptualizing the distinction. According to Greenberg, the goals of

psychoanalysis are different from the goals of psychoanalytic psychotherapy. Note that for Cooper, the goals are the same in psychoanalysis and
psychotherapy, whereas for Greenberg, they are not only different, but
contradictory and incompatible. Greenberg asserts that in psychotherapy,
the aim is to help the patient feel better and to achieve whatever personal
objectives bring the patient for treatment. In psychotherapy, we are free to
use whatever techniques will be effective in helping a patient feel better at
a particular moment. In stark contrast, "what is unique about psychoanalysis is that it tried to get to *meaning* rather than to *feeling better*" (Greenberg,
quoted in Crumbley, 2011, p. 176). Notice that Greenberg's approach
does not merely claim that there is a difference along a continuum, that one
approach has more of one and the other more of the other quality. His
argument, like the traditional definitions of the 1950s, leads in a different
direction. Namely, one approach pursues meaning, and the other, feeling
better. This is the old dichotomy with which we are long familiar, of delay
and thoughtful reflection, versus gratification and feeling better—the
pleasure principle.

Greenberg suggests that in psychotherapy, the therapist has a roadmap
built on psychoanalytic principles, whereas in psychoanalysis, "There's just
exploration, just the opening of experience as much as possible" (p. 176).
Once again, this is not presented as a matter of emphasis; rather it is
presented as a radical difference. In this polarized account, one side is set
up in opposition to the other, so that the two sides are mutually incompatible. Analysis is equated with exploration, adventure, and openness to
experience, whereas psychotherapy is associated with a preset agenda,
problem solving, and scripted technique.

In our view this is an inaccurate and misleading way to think about
both psychoanalysis and psychotherapy. Is it really true that in psychoanalysis there is no roadmap? Don't analysts use what they have learned
from other patients both when they do psychotherapy as well as when
they conduct analysis? And even in an analysis proper, are there never
times when the analyst attends to problem solving and uses various
techniques to alleviate unnecessary suffering? And when the analyst does
so, does it make good heuristic sense to argue that at such moments
the analyst is not doing psychoanalysis? Really? Even when the research in
this area points to the fact that all psychoanalysis utilizes many of these
so-called psychotherapeutic elements much more than analysts previously
recognized?

We recognize that Greenberg might respond that he is drawing a purely
theoretical distinction, that when he says that psychoanalysis makes no use
of a roadmap, he is describing an ideal analysis. But we question the value
for our field of maintaining this idealized portrait. We think that in all
psychoanalytic therapy, that done once per week face-to-face with a less
traditionally analyzable patient, and that done four times a week on the

couch with someone thought to be analyzable, there will be times when the analyst has more of a feeling that they know where they are going and others when they do not, and that these experiences are both essential to the analytic work. There are times in any analysis when an analyst may be more comforting or soothing, and other times when an analyst may not intervene to ease the patient because they believe at that moment the patient is better off left struggling with something. Both kinds of processes take place across the full range of psychoanalytic therapy.

So what, you might ask, is the problem with calling one approach psychoanalysis and the other psychotherapy? What's wrong with thinking that when an analyst is being comforting or soothing for one reason or another that at that moment we would think of the analyst as using a psychotherapeutic procedure rather than an analytic one? That is a big question! But simply, it seems to us a distortion of how real analysts actually work with real patients. It unnecessarily polarizes the distinction between two approaches that in real life analysts use together harmoniously and even seamlessly rather than in contradiction to one another. It leads to an idealization of one and a devaluation of the other. And worse— it leads to an idealization of those analysts and patients who can work one way, or create the illusion that they work in one way, while devaluing those therapists and patients who are "limited" to working the other way. In addition, this way of defining the difference between psychoanalysis and psychotherapy leads to analysts trying to maintain a kind of "purity" where they eschew therapeutic techniques. It leads to isolating analysts professionally from other therapists and discourages any attempt to draw upon other therapeutic modalities.

Greenberg contends that his presentation is actually not a traditional one, but rather is new and innovative.

> This is a new way of thinking in psychoanalysis, quite in contrast to the way people thought as recently as twenty years ago, when there was much more certainty about what we were looking for and what we were supposed to find. You had to find the inner conflict, you had to find a particular unconscious fantasy, and especially you had to find the Oedipus complex. Whatever your theory, you knew what you were looking for and that's what you had to find. But circa 2010 we are much more open-ended, and so when we start with a patient, we don't know where we're going to end up, or *if* we are going to end up.
>
> (Quoted in Crumbley, 2011, p. 176)

There is something oddly ironic about Greenberg's claim. The distinction he draws between psychoanalysis and psychotherapy is very much in line with the traditional distinctions that have been made throughout psychoanalytic history, from the post-World War II debates onward; yet he claims that the very quality he is using to distinguish psychotherapy from psychoanalysis was not known even two decades ago. It seems to us that Greenberg is mixing together several different kinds of openness here. One kind of openness comes with the recognition of multiple psychoanalytic theories. Multiplicity and pluralism of perspectives has led to a certain kind of openness, in that not all analysts today formulate what they are looking for in terms of drives, drive derivatives, unconscious wishes and Oedipal dynamics. Having multiple theoretical lenses allows an analyst more freedom to draw on various paradigms. But we would argue that this is also true for the full range of psychoanalytic therapies. It is as true in brief analytic once-a-week work as it is for an analysis proper. In today's analytic world, we all have more "freedom" to draw on various roadmaps, and we also all "suffer" from the uncertainty and confusion of these multiple and sometimes contradictory maps.

Greenberg's analogy, drawing on his own personal experience as a father, speaks directly to our point. He recalls comforting his children when they awoke from a bad dream. He would hold them and say, "Don't worry, sweetie, it's only a dream." Greenberg adds,

> You would never say to an analytic patient, "Don't worry, it's only a dream," because you would want them to gain insight into the dream, which is viewed as a vehicle into a certain pain that may be only available through this dream.
>
> (Quoted in Crumbley, 2011, p. 176)

In other words, comforting the patient would shortchange them, deprive them of an opportunity to gain insight and awareness. This illustration is remarkably striking in relation to our overall argument. It is no accident that in comparing a psychoanalytic approach to a psychotherapeutic one, Greenberg associates psychotherapy with support, comfort, reassurance, gratification, and the parenting of an infant or child. Greenberg views psychotherapy as appropriate for those who are infantile, less mature or sophisticated, less civilized. Psychoanalysis is for those who are mature enough to tolerate discomfort, delay, and renunciation, and are therefore able to gain insight, to think, and to symbolize. Psychotherapy is parenting; psychoanalysis is the mature work of civilized adults who can refrain from immediate gratification. As has been argued throughout its history, in psychoanalysis, the analyst does not lead the patient, does not use suggestion, but rather follows the patient's associations; the analytic material emerges and unfolds from within. Greenberg's "no roadmap" is just a variation of the traditional eschewal of suggestion and influence. There is nothing new in this way of distinguishing between psychoanalysis and psychotherapy—it is right in line with the psychoanalytic mainstream of the golden era.

"That's not Psychoanalysis!"

Lest we give the impression that the debates of the 1950s have been laid to rest, we would like to bring your attention to the current debates taking place within the "psychoanalytic mainstream," which seem to us to be disturbingly anachronistic, a throwback to the 1950s. In a forcefully argued article in the *International Journal of Psychoanalysis*, Rachel Blass (2010b) called on her colleagues to take on the "politically incorrect" task of defining the limits of the field by declaring "That's not psychoanalysis!" (p. 81) Blass begins by quoting Freud (1914), who, in describing his purposes in establishing the International Psychoanalytic Association, said, "There should be some headquarters whose business it would be to declare: 'All this nonsense is nothing to do with analysis; this is not psycho-analysis'" (p. 43). For Blass, it is not a question of whether or not to define psychoanalysis, but rather a more specific charge that we define it in such a way so as to delineate its borders, specifically the boundaries between psychoanalysis and psychoanalytic therapy. In an introduction to a symposium on the same theme, Blass (2010a) asks, how does psychoanalytic practice differ from psychotherapy, and what are the implications for practice and training? In our view, the question should not be whether or not we should define psychoanalysis, but rather, should we define it narrowly or more broadly.

We agree with Blass that much of the debate is fueled by the meaning of the terms psychotherapy and psychoanalysis to the professional identity of the practitioner. As Blass suggests, to those who have been part of the broadly defined psychoanalytic community, who have spent years in training, the title "psychoanalysis" continues to be valued, even idealized, associated with the depth and meaningfulness of one's work and of one's life, for that matter. Blass argues, however, that if it means everything, then it means nothing at all, and certainly there is a need to have clear definitions so that we know what analysis is and what it is not. In fact, if we cannot make that distinction, then how can we discuss psychoanalysis in comparison to any other treatment?

It would seem that Freud had the right, if anyone ever has, to declare what is and is not psychoanalysis. In the quote cited by Blass, he explicitly claimed that one of the purposes of establishing the International Psychoanalytic Association was precisely to exercise that right. Remember though, that he wrote this in *On the History of the Psychoanalytic Movement* (1914). At that time, his agenda was to eliminate Jung from the movement once and for all, while also ejecting Adler; he was not at that time differentiating psychoanalysis from psychoanalytic therapy. Freud emphatically remained open to technical variations within the range of what he considered analysis, writing,

> I must however make it clear that what I am asserting is that this technique is the only one suited to my individuality; I do not venture

to deny that a physician quite differently constituted might find himself driven to adopt a different attitude to his patients and to the task before him.

(1912a, p. 111)

Long after 1914, Freud tolerated many technical experiments and modifications of his clinical approach, giving a good deal of rein, for example, to both Ferenczi and Rank in their technical research. What he was describing in 1914 in calling for an agency to protect the title psychoanalysis was neither about differentiating psychoanalysis from analytic psychotherapy, nor was it about regulating the specifics of the technical method; rather it was an effort to dissociate from those who rejected the fundamentals of his theory and substituted their own very different theories and practices.

That leaves us with several questions. First, was that a good move on Freud's part? Was he overly invested in maintaining control of a discipline that in fact had already grown beyond him? Might it not have been better to accept Jung, Adler, and others as psychoanalysts with the acknowledgment that within the discipline of psychoanalysis there would be room for difference and disagreement, even about essentials? In retrospect, the differences between Freud and Adler hardly seem very great in comparison to the differences among analysts in any institute we know of today. Might not psychoanalysis have been enriched if Freud had not only incorporated variations of Adler's ideas such as the masculine protest, inferiority complex, and aggressive drive, but also if he had allowed an association that could house analysts with disparate views, some of which may have turned out to be bad ideas, but some of which might have proven creative and useful?

Whatever answer we have to the question of whether psychoanalysis as a discipline would have been better off had Freud established a broader view a century ago, the question still remains as to what is the impact of trying to force such narrow definitions now, when our analytic organizations are characterized by diversity and multiplicity. Using the rhetoric of a call for "truth," Blass (2010a) argues that we should define psychoanalysis based on its "essence," its "meaning," and its "nature." In contrast, she trivializes the alternative, which she dismisses under the rubric of "postmodernism," "relativism," or "social-constructivism," claiming that these approaches lead to a radical relativism in which we are left with nothing but opinions, one of which is as good as the next, without rational arguments to mediate among them.

But this polarization is itself a misrepresentation and distortion of "truth." Social constructivism does not necessitate relativism. It values rational debate, but does so by taking into account social and pragmatic considerations. To take into account the social context of a concept is not to deny rational debate. In our view, the question is not what is the truth, nature, or essence of psychoanalysis, but rather, what are the consequences of defining psychoanalysis one way or another and to whom? Under what social, economic, cultural, historical, or political conditions does a definition of psychoanalysis lead to benefits or disadvantages to patients, and/or to particular groups of professionals, including those who identify themselves as psychoanalysts of one persuasion or another? One could certainly have rational arguments regarding these questions. Some answers would be better than others—for certain purposes. Context and pragmatic considerations matter.

Blass does not provide her own definition of psychoanalysis in this article; she only asserts the value of doing so. While we cannot, therefore, speak to the implications of her specific definition, nevertheless, she makes clear that she believes it should be narrow enough to exclude large segments of the analytic community as well as numerous individuals who identify as psychoanalysts. She then asks, seemingly innocently, "Why should such a statement be considered to be so disturbing?" (p. 83). Such a question is either unbelievably naïve or completely disingenuous, and in any event does not bring us closer to the truth.

Blass (2010b) caricatures those who fear an authoritarian call for "The Ultimate Truth," claiming she is only calling for rational inquiry. But by isolating the essence of psychoanalysis as if it could be defined independently of people—divorced from social, cultural, political, and economic considerations—she is attempting to establish just that problematic version of The Ultimate Truth. Blass bypasses important questions, which serves to obscure her argument. In calling on us to define psychoanalysis through argued reason, does she really believe that the arguments will be so clear, so persuasively compelling that we will all agree? And if we do not agree on what is and is not psychoanalysis, then who determines which arguments are best? Would it done by majority vote? If so, a majority of whom? Of which group? And if her group ends up in the minority, will she happily call herself something other than a psychoanalyst or would she find it "disturbing"?

We would like to think we understand Blass's concerns, her wish for clarity and truthfulness about what we are doing so that we can compare and contrast one therapy or theory to another with lucidity and without ambiguity. But why can we not compare and contrast a variety of distinct terms, theories, and technical approaches all under the broad heading of psychoanalysis?

Basic Model Technique

As psychoanalysis celebrates its newfound pluralism of perspectives, the foundations of our discipline have come into question, and our once mainstream theory of technique has been challenged. Our increasing emphasis on the subjectivity and intersubjectivity of the psychoanalytic situation has led to some anxiety about standards of practice and how to avoid an "anything goes" approach to psychoanalytic treatment. As we learn to live with the pluralism of contemporary psychoanalysis, what is left of the foundations upon which we may build a theory of psychoanalytic technique?

For many decades, it was common practice among psychoanalytic institutes to teach courses entitled "Standard" or "Basic Model Technique." The phrase "basic model technique" was taken from Eissler's (1953) classic paper, in which he defined parameters in terms of their deviations from an ideal. As Wallerstein (1995) points out, Eissler's basic model technique was widely accepted as "the definitive version of the classical psychoanalytic technique inherited from Freud" (p. 111). Analysts could take this prescriptive theory of technique and apply it to individual patients. Hartmann (1960) referred to clinical psychoanalysis as a technology. There is nothing intrinsically harsh or inhumane about viewing psychoanalysis as a technology, nothing that suggests that the theory must necessarily be applied rigidly or dogmatically. A sensitive and well-functioning psychoanalyst was expected to take the theory, which was intended as a general statement of principles, and apply it to the unique, individual patient with whom that analyst was working at the moment. Hence even the standard or basic model technique—when viewed as a technology—required sensitive, empathic, and individually tailored application. Nevertheless, it was generally accepted that a standard did exist, and its application was viewed rather mechanistically.

The idea of a model technique worked fairly well as long as there was some sense of unanimity in the way psychoanalysis was conceptualized, taught, and practiced. For many decades, almost all psychoanalytic institutes taught only one version of psychoanalysis. Until recently, institutes were exclusively Freudian or Kleinian, Interpersonal or Self-psychological. Yet even within the most mainstream institutes, there was some diversity. There had always been disagreements regarding principles of psychoanalytic technique. One need look no further than Fenichel's (1941) authoritative monograph or the classic collection of 1920s and 1930s papers on controversies in psychoanalytic technique collected by Bergmann and Hartman (1976) to get a glimpse of the rich diversity of opinion regarding psychoanalytic principles of praxis. Nevertheless, even with all of this diversity, there was a clear consensus, within any institute, as to the correct vision of psychoanalysis. Where variance remained, the belief was that one side was right and the other wrong, that one version of psychoanalysis would ultimately prevail as the standard technique and the other approaches would prove to be mere deviations or heresies.

Contrast this with psychoanalysis in our postmodern constructivist age, in which the nature of the analyst's authority (and the teacher's and supervisor's authority) has become less clear. Mitchell (1993) referred to a crisis of confidence in what an analyst can know and in what our patients need from us, and a crisis of authority in our analytic self-image. How can we say to a trainee what the proper psychoanalytic response should be in a given situation, based on the standard psychoanalytic technique, when both we and the student know that there are any number of other analysts and supervisors, often in the same institute or office suite, who would disagree and do things differently? At most, one can say this is what I think I would do with a patient like this, and here is why. But this brings into psychoanalysis what Freud tried so desperately to keep out, what he called in a letter to Ferenczi, "the subjective factor," which he equated with arbitrariness and with the analyst's unresolved personal complexes (letter of January 4, 1928, cited in Grubrich-Simitis, 1986, p. 271). Nevertheless, in the context of reflecting on Ferenczi's clinical contributions, Freud (1937a) wrote: "Among the factors which influence the prospects of analytic treatment and add to its difficulties in the same manner as the resistances, must be reckoned not only the nature of the patient's ego but the individuality of the analyst" (p. 247). Freud recognized that analysts with different personalities would have to adopt distinct methods of practice.

In reevaluating Hartmann's view of clinical psychoanalysis as a technology, Schafer (1997) suggested that one reason Hartmann chose what seems today to be such a "chilling" trope lies in his classicist mentality.

> Classicism valorizes formalization, systematization, thoroughgoing rationalism, and rigorously enforced clarity and consistency. Ideally, classicistic work is so impersonal that contributions can be made with a minimum of individualistic coloring. The ideal does not tolerate self-expressiveness other than a minimum of personal style in the use of one's own reason.
>
> (1997, p. 205)

Because of this mindset, within the long-dominant mainstream analytic school, analysts were thought to be "relatively interchangeable" (Kantrowitz, 1997, p. 127). This was in line with Freud's wish that psychoanalysis be like any other empirical science—it would rely on a standard methodology that yielded replicable results. "Psychoanalysis is a method of research, an impartial instrument, rather like the infinitesimal calculus" (Freud, 1927, p. 36). As we have discussed at length in Chapter 10, this was the main reason he insisted on the elimination of suggestion in psychoanalysis.

In contrast, today, when someone suggests that analytic trainees must begin their education by learning the basic model technique, we become curious as to whose basic model technique they are referring. Systematic and rigorous thinking about psychoanalytic technique remains essential. But it is in the very process of establishing a personal relationship to psychoanalytic theory, a personal approach to the clinical situation, and a personal relation to the profession that one becomes a psychoanalyst. Blass

(2010 a, b) is certainly right that this diversity, with its accompanying complexity, ambiguity, and uncertainty, makes it much more difficult to say, "That is NOT psychoanalysis!"

Shibboleth: The Right to Pass

Blass reminds us that Freud identified several key theoretical principles as essential to psychoanalysis, including the unconscious, dream theory, and the Oedipus complex, each time referring to them as "shibboleth[s]." We will soon return to shibboleths, but will first note that Freud was not referring to technique. In the very same *History*, in which he uses his authority to establish the right to say, "That is not psychoanalysis!" Freud also provides his broadest definition of psychoanalytic method:

> It may thus be said that the theory of psycho-analysis is an attempt to account for two striking and unexpected facts of observation which emerge whenever an attempt is made to trace the symptoms of a neurotic back to their sources in his past life: the facts of transference and of resistance. Any line of investigation which recognizes these two facts and takes them as the starting-point of its work has a right to call itself psycho-analysis, even though it arrives at results other than my own.
>
> (1914, p. 16)

The principles Blass cites are not Freud's markers of psychoanalytic method; rather they are the essentials of his general theory. We will review them in more detail because these principles are the fundamentals of Freud's theory, which he specifically intended to mark the borders between what is psychoanalysis and what is not. In each case, Freud used the word shibboleth, so it behooves us to know what the word means and why Freud might have selected this word from the Hebrew Bible for just this purpose.

In the Book of Judges, Chapter 12, after the Gileadites inflicted a military defeat upon the tribe of Ephraim, the surviving Ephraimites tried to cross the Jordan River back into their home territory and the Gileadites secured the river's fords to stop them. In order to identify and kill these refugees, the Gileadites put each refugee to a simple test:

> Gilead then cut Ephraim off from the fords of the Jordan, and whenever Ephraimite fugitives said, "Let me cross," the men of Gilead would ask, "Are you an Ephraimite?" If he said, "No," they then said, "Very well, say 'Shibboleth' (שיבולת)." If anyone said, "Sibboleth" (סיבולת), because he could not pronounce it, then they would seize him and kill him by the fords of the Jordan. Forty-two thousand Ephraimites fell on this occasion.
>
> (verses 5–6)

A shibboleth is a marker that differentiates a group of people who try to trespass, to cross a boundary; getting it right is a matter of life and death. For Jews like Freud, in a viciously anti-Semitic fin-de-siècle Vienna (and later for Derrida, an Algerian Jew in France), circumcision was the shibboleth. The binaries of life/death, phallic/castrated, male/female, insider/outsider, Jew/German are always in unconscious play when a shibboleth is used to determine if someone has tried to pass, to border cross. With that background, let's examine Freud's uses of the term.

Not surprisingly, the first two usages of shibboleth are also from Freud's *History* (1914). As we pointed out, Freud wrote this history in order to finally divorce himself from Jung and Adler, and so distinguishing features were on his mind. He wrote, "Everything that Adler has to say about dreams, the shibboleth of psycho-analysis, is equally empty and unmeaning" (p. 57). The 1916 version, translated by Brill, puts it as follows: "Just as deplorable and devoid of substance is all that Adler has said about the dream—that shibboleth of psychoanalysis" (p. 446). In a letter to the pastor Oscar Pfister, Freud (1919b) wrote regarding the possibility of a "Jungification" that "the factor of sexuality" was the psychoanalytic society's "shibboleth" (p. 70). In *The Ego and the Id*, Freud wrote:

> The division of the psychical into what is conscious and what is unconscious is the fundamental premise of psycho-analysis . . . at this point some of my readers would already stop short and would go no further; for here we have the first *shibboleth* of psycho-analysis. To most people who have been educated in philosophy the idea of anything psychical which is not also conscious is so inconceivable that it seems to them absurd and refutable simply by logic.
>
> (1923, p. 13)

And then in the *New Introductory Lectures On Psycho-Analysis*, Freud wrote,

> [The theory of dreams] occupies a special place in the history of psycho-analysis and marks a turning-point; it was with it that analysis took the step from being a psychotherapeutic procedure to being a depth-psychology . . . The strangeness of the assertions it was obliged to put forward has made it play the part of a shibboleth, the use of which decided who could become a follower of psycho-analysis and to whom it remained for ever incomprehensible.
>
> (1933, p. 7)

And finally, in a famous footnote added in 1920 to his *Three Essays on the Theory of Sexuality* (1905), Freud wrote, "With the progress of psychoanalytic studies the importance of the Oedipus complex has became more and more clearly evident; its recognition has become the shibboleth that distinguishes the adherents of psycho-analysis from its opponents" (p. 226).

The unconscious, sexuality, the dream theory, and the Oedipus complex were the distinctive principles that Freud believed differentiated psycho-analysis from other psychologies. However, notice that they did not differentiate psychoanalysis from analytic therapy. Presumably, Freud would not have had a problem with classifying Jung's or Adler's theories as psychologies. That is interesting in and of itself. If Adler's theory was wrong, then it was wrong whether it was categorized as psychoanalysis or psychology. Why couldn't Freud imagine that a psychoanalytic theory could be wrong and still be psychoanalysis? The way Freud set it up, only correct theories had the right to use the term psychoanalysis, and so by definition, psychoanalysis was never wrong!

Blass (2010a) points out that many schools of psychoanalysis today would not hold even to the broad concepts Freud identified as shibboleths. For example, she argues, self-psychologists view the Oedipus complex as a break-down product rather than as primary, and relational analysts question the very existence of an internal reality such as the unconscious. That Blass grossly mischaracterizes relational theory should be immediately apparent from the historical consideration that relational psychoanalysis was developed by Greenberg and Mitchell (1983), and later by Mitchell (1988), precisely because they believed that the interpersonal school neglected theorizing unconscious internal psychic structure. They formulated relational theory, linking it with British object-relations, in order to correct this imbalance. In other words, the very point of relational psychoanalysis was to make room for the internal world in dialectical relation to the external world. Blass goes on to say that there are others who would define psychoanalysis narrowly, as a process based on verbal interpretation alone. She readily acknowledges that such an approach would exclude many—we would think most—analysts, including Ferenczi, Balint, Winnicott, Kohut, and just about every American analyst we know, from being defined as psychoanalysts.

In arguing in favor of a definition, Blass (2010a) writes that if psycho-analysis is definable, then some definitions will be better than others and we should debate these proposals. We agree that some definitions will be better than others, but for us, the question is: better for whom and to achieve what purposes? For Blass, the question is which definition is better at grasping the nature and meaning of psychoanalysis. But does psycho-analysis have an independent nature other than the one that groups of psychoanalysts assign to it?

"Go and See What the People are Doing"

The following analogy may seem far-fetched at first, but bear with us, as we will show that it is quite relevant. We are reminded of a frequent strategy used by Talmudic rabbis to resolve questions of Jewish law. During the rabbinic period, the specifics of law were not always established; some were still in flux. When in doubt, the rabbis would from time to time resort to the formula, "Go and see what the people are doing" (Katz and Schwartz, 1998, pp. 64–66). Rabbinic Jewish law in these instances was not settled by theological argument, rational debate, or textual exegisis; rather, at some point, the rabbis turned to the community to see the reality of lived experience. How did people practice Judaism? What the people actually did, how they lived, determined the law. But of course, this raises a critical question. Which people? Whom do you look at? Which community counts as the basis on which to determine the law? Robert Gordis specified as a Jewish community "the body of men and women in the Jewish people who accept the authority of Jewish law and are concerned with Jewish observance as a genuine issue" (quoted in Katz and Schwartz, 1998, p. 65).

We hope you see the problem! If the rabbis are in dispute about the law, they can turn from reason and debate to actually go look at accepted practice, but they then might have to reason and debate about whom to observe and who would count. Yes, only those who accept the authority of Jewish law, but might not there be a variety of communities who accept that authority and yet still have different practices and understandings of the law? The solution works on a practical basis if and only if there is some agreement on who counts as the believing community. We believe there is a very close parallel to the argument we have with Blass. Isn't it possible that we can't agree on definitions, that our premises are incommensurable, because we are living in different communities with different practices, all identified with something known as psychoanalysis?

Nevertheless, there might be some wisdom in the idea of "Go and see what the people are doing", and we will pursue a strategy along those lines. Why not go and see what psychoanalysts actually do in their clinical practice? Why not adopt an empirical strategy, collecting data on what analysts do? For example, if we find that analysts rely exclusively or predominantly on interpretation, then we will know that is how to define psychoanalysis. If we find that dream analysis takes up a substantial amount of time in most analyses, then we will know that analysis should be defined by a focus on dreams. If we can rate analytic content using a variety of scales, then we can determine how much analysts in practice rely on analyzing the Oedipus complex. In sum, why not approach these questions empirically?

Several problems. First, we would have to determine who to count. If we only drew inferences from members of any one organization, then what we would find could only tell us how psychoanalysis is being defined in that community. But much more problematically, some analysts might say that much of what they actually practice is not psychoanalysis but analytic therapy, and therefore only the cases in analysis proper should count. But of course, they are then selecting precisely those cases that would confirm whatever their own definition of analysis dictated. For illustrative purposes, let's say we ask a classical Freudian to tell us which of their cases we should examine to extrapolate principles of psychoanalysis, and they then chose cases they regard as having been in analysis proper. If we then empirically determine that Oedipal themes are frequent, what would that tell us other than that the analyst selected cases with that as part of their criteria? So first we would have to select analysts from the "right" community, and then they would select cases that were analysis "proper."

The fact is that most graduates of analytic institutes in the United States see most of their patients once per week. Well, we say that is a fact, and we think it is a fair statement. But of course it depends on who counts as analysts and which analytic institutes count. Have we included those that are interpersonal or "modern" or Jungian? But a much more difficult problem is that these analysts might regard this work to be *not* analysis but psychotherapy. So the empirical finding that most analysts see their patients once per week does not mean that analysis is done once per week, but rather might mean that most analysts no longer predominantly practice psychoanalysis. In spite of these problems, we propose to use data about what analytic therapists actually do.

Research into Psychoanalytic Practice

While survey research is not common among clinicians, questionnaires have been used in the past to study psychoanalytic practice, going back to the work of Edward Glover (1955), who surveyed 29 members of the British Psycho-analytic Society. Surveys are important because they provide an overall picture of the field so that we can "go see what the people do." Let's begin with a very important study that was conducted in New York City, surveying graduates of the Columbia Center for Psychoanalytic Training and Research in their early postgraduate years (Cherry, Cabaniss, Forand, Haywood, and Roose, 2004). It is significant for several reasons. Columbia is a well-established institute with a superb reputation. It is part of the mainstream American Psychoanalytic Association and is located in New York City, which remains the center of psychoanalytic practice in the United States. The results, therefore, cannot be dismissed as simply reflecting the practices of those on the margins of the profession. This data is based on "mainstream" psychoanalysts. It is also valuable because Cherry and colleagues have continued this research and to update and refine their findings.

They conclude that strikingly little four-times-weekly psychoanalysis is being conducted among analysts who graduated within the last 15 years. The four-time-per-week figure is relevant because at Columbia, that is the minimum frequency used to determine if the treatment is analysis proper.

Interestingly, graduates who have not become training analysts (78 percent of the sample) conduct almost no four-times-weekly analysis once their control cases terminate. Finally, and contrary to the investigators' hypothesis, graduate analysts were found to practice very little twice- or three-times-weekly analytic therapy. On average, they work about 30 hours a week in the office (less if they have another job), with two patients in twice-weekly treatment and zero or one patient in treatment conducted with greater frequency. In other words, graduates of one of the finest institutes in the country, practicing in New York City, see the vast majority of their patients in once-weekly therapy/analysis—depending on your definition! In a follow-up study, Cherry and colleagues report, "Research at the Columbia University Center for Psychoanalytic Training and Research has documented that most graduate analysts practice very little psychoanalysis after their control cases terminate" (Cherry, Aizaga, and Roose, 2009, p. 196). In an independent study, Cherry and colleagues found a similar pattern, in which there was a bimodal distribution. One group continued to sustain at least three ongoing cases in analysis at four-times-weekly frequency. The other half did not maintain this immersion in four-times-weekly treatment; they primarily applied their training to psychotherapy practice (Cherry, Wininger, and Roose, 2009). But again, note that psychotherapy here refers to anything less than four times per week; the bulk of it is actually once per week.

The Division of Psychoanalysis (39) of the APA conducted a survey of its membership in Fall 2008 (Cresci, 2010). Respondents reported seeing a mean of 18 patients per week. The great majority were seen once a week, with only 20 percent of patients seen two or more times per week. Now it is true that members of Division 39 do not have to be psychoanalysts and may not be institute graduates. But before you dismiss the above findings on these grounds, you may want to consider that these same respondents overwhelmingly reported that psychoanalytic training was the single best professional activity that helped them to build their practices! And the single best thing they would advise for others to build their practices was psychoanalytic training! This in spite of the fact that they were actually seeing the vast majority of their patients once per week—whether we call it psychoanalytic psychotherapy or psychoanalysis.

In another study focusing on analysts in New York City, Silver (2003) surveyed analysts from a wide number of institutes. More than half of respondents identified themselves as Freudian analysts. There were extremely few interpersonal analysts, and relational seems to not even have been an available category. For the purpose of her study, Silver considered three times per week as the minimum frequency. She concluded that there was a discrepancy between respondents' desire to engage in psychoanalytic work and their actual practice, which was primarily psychoanalytic psychotherapy. Silver concluded that on average, the number of patient hours spent doing classical analysis had diminished, and that there was a blurring of the theoretical distinction between psychoanalysis and psychotherapy.

Data is difficult to obtain for many reasons. Most studies are conducted by single associations. It is difficult to compare findings across groups, as researchers and their respondents make certain assumptions that other groups might not make, for example, that treatment less than four, or less than three, times per week is psychotherapy rather than psychoanalysis. Blass (2010b) opposes a more catholic definition of psychoanalysis, arguing that such inclusive definitions that focus on common ground among differing perspectives are generally reserved for political and religious definitions. She believes that this kind of definition is inappropriate for psychoanalysis, which is still regarded as a specific approach that demands of its proponents to learn and work together harmoniously. Blass writes,

> Unless some feature uniting all analysts is found and is taken as a shibboleth that separates analysts from those that are not, and unless the differences that exist between analysts beyond this unifying feature are given open and formal expression, then appeal to overarching definitions that are based on common ground is misguided.
>
> (2010b, p. 94)

We strongly disagree with Blass that the need to embrace a multiplicity of viewpoints is limited to religion and politics. In fact, all academic disciplines, including the sciences and humanities, are characterized by diversity, encompassing widely divergent and often contradictory points of view. The obvious example of a discipline meeting the above criteria is not religion or politics, but the science of psychology. Psychology may be defined as the scientific study of behavior. Even that definition can be questioned, as psychologists might not agree about the nature or definition of science, and some might want to include the study of mind along with behavior. Nevertheless, psychologists have enough of a general common ground to identify as psychologists, and psychology very successfully operates as an academic discipline on this basis. This does not preclude psychologists from disagreeing with each other on a wide range of fundamental issues. We do not understand why Blass is so convinced that psychoanalysis should be defined in a more restricted manner than any other science or discipline. If psychology can contain neuropsychologists and phenomenologists, social psychologists and comparative biologists, evolutionary psychologists and postmodern psychologists, then why can't psychoanalysis include Freudians and Kleinians, Kohutians and object-relations theorists, Lacanians and interpersonalists?

Let's once again "go and see what the people do." We believe there is convincing evidence that psychoanalysts and psychoanalytic therapists share common ground. We will use data from research that does not distinguish psychoanalysis from psychoanalytic therapy, but rather looks at psychodynamic psychotherapy very broadly. We propose that the findings of this empirical research are meaningful and that they can go a long way toward helping psychoanalysts regain their focus and come together in a more unified community. We are not suggesting that analysts set aside their differences—it is important to continue debating them. But we believe that agreeing on some basics about a psychoanalytic approach could provide sufficient unity for a respectable professional discipline, with room remaining for conflict and multiple perspectives. Our approach opposes Bass's call for a more limiting definition of psychoanalysis, and argues instead for maintaining a broader definition. We believe, with Wallerstein (1998), that focusing on our common ground will be much better for the future of psychoanalysis than limiting ourselves to doctrinal differences. But unlike Wallerstein, we believe that this common ground is best extended to include psychoanalytic therapy as well as psychoanalysis proper.

In what many analysts consider to be a monumental achievement, Jonathan Shedler (2010) managed to publish a review article on the efficacy of psychodynamic therapy in the APA's flagship publication, *The American Psychologist*. Shedler demonstrated that empirical evidence supports the efficacy of psychoanalytic therapy. He used the terms psychodynamic and psychoanalytic interchangeably, since his focus was on psychoanalytic therapy rather than on psychoanalysis proper, and affirmed that patients who were treated with psychoanalytic psychotherapy not only maintained therapeutic gains, but continued to improve after treatment ended. In fact, he maintained that non-analytic therapies may be effective in part because even non-analytic therapists utilize techniques that are central to the dynamic therapies.

While we have no doubt that Shedler's findings will be challenged and we are not so naïve as to think that his one review article will win the hearts and minds of those clinical psychologists associated with the "empirically-supported" and "evidence-based" medicine movement, nevertheless, Shedler's work has turned the tables and put the challengers of psycho-analysis on the defensive for the first time. However, it is not our intention here to discuss the merits and criticisms of Shedler's review. Instead we want to make use of one research project brought to our attention by Shedler for its use in considering the common ground of the psychoanalytic therapies.

Shedler (2010) writes, "The essence of psychodynamic therapy is exploring those aspects of self that are not fully known, especially as they are manifested and potentially influenced in the therapy relationship" (p. 98). Shedler purposely avoids using the term "unconscious" more than necessary, primarily because he has learned that too many psychologists have been taught to be biased about traditional psychoanalytic terms. He describes psychodynamic therapies with as little jargon as possible.

Shedler reviews the work of Blagys and Hilsenroth (2000), who identified empirical studies comparing the process and technique of manualized psychodynamic therapy with cognitive behavioral therapy (CBT). Seven features reliably distinguished the psychodynamic therapy from other therapies, as determined by empirical examination of actual session recordings and transcripts. It is important to note that these seven items do not identify the underlying concepts being utilized, but rather the processes and techniques used. It also should be clear that these seven characteristics do not comprehensively define the analytic therapies, but rather, it is these seven that differentiate them from other non-analytic therapies. There are very important characteristics that are not included on this list because they are shared by both analytic and non-analytic therapies. Hence there is no mention of maintaining a therapeutic alliance on this list because that is a characteristic of both modalities. Blagys and Hilsenroth have provided a review that relies on a mixed group of studies in which a variety of different coding schemes, methodologies, and treatments (some manualized and some not) were used, and so it is not the final word on the matter. But it offers a very useful starting point for consideration. Let's briefly review the seven items:

1   **Analytic therapists focus on affect and the expression of emotions.** "The therapist helps the patient describe and put words to feelings, including contradictory feelings, feelings that are troubling or threatening, and feelings that the patient may not initially be able to recognize or acknowledge" (Shedler, 2010, p. 99). The psychoanalytically knowledgeable reader will notice how Shedler's phrasing avoids psychoanalytic jargon; in particular, the term unconscious.

2   **Exploration of attempts to avoid distressing thoughts and feelings.** Here Shedler speaks of people doing "things knowingly and unknowingly to avoid aspects of experience that are troubling" (p. 99). He explains the psychodynamic therapist's focus on defense mechanisms, giving as illustrations avoidance, externalization, isolation of affect, and shifts in free association. But he explains all of this without using any technical terms.

3   **Identification of recurring themes and patterns.** The psychoanalytic therapist explores themes and patterns including those that the patient had not noticed or recognized previously. Presumably in exploring the patient's attempts to avoid distressing thoughts and feelings (number 2 above), hidden themes and patterns emerge with greater clarity to both patient and therapist.

4   **Discussion of past experience—a developmental focus.** Exploring affects (number 1) and defenses (number 2) and identifying patterns

(number 3) leads to the exploration of early experiences and "the ways in which the past tends to 'live on' in the present" (p. 99). The focus, Shedler explains, is not on the past for its own sake, but rather on how the past illuminates current issues. The goal is to help patients free themselves from the bonds of past experience in order to live more fully in the present. Notice that Shedler avoids the term "transference," even while obviously describing the historical precedents for the transference, the old object experience. We also want to highlight that this list is not intended to be linear. In other words, the pursuit of developmental issues (transference origins) is itself an aspect of identifying recurring themes (number 3), which would in turn lead to the clarification of feelings (number 1) and to the defenses used to cope with related conflicts (number 2), leading to greater awareness of developmental patterns (transference origins, number 4).

5   **Focus on interpersonal relations**. Psychodynamic therapists are interested in exploring the patient's patterns of interpersonal relations (both internal and external), attachment patterns, and object-relations. Having listed the exploration of the past developmental schemas (number 4), here Shedler lists the exploration of interpersonal patterns in the patient's current life outside of the therapeutic situation. Once again, we would expect that exploring the past patterns will clarify the present and vice versa, and that both will lead to the emergence of affects.

6   **Focus on the therapy relationship**. If the developmental focus (number 4) led to the discussion of past experience and old objects, and the exploration of interpersonal relations (number 5) clarifies patterns of object-relations more generally, then in the specific focus on the therapy relationship (number 6), we get to what is usually described as transference and countertransference. Here Shedler does specify that these are the theoretical terms used by analysts. He is careful to note that explication of the therapy relationship is enormously complex and involves subtle patterns, but that it provides a unique opportunity to explore and rework these often unconscious patterns *in vivo*.

7   **Exploration of fantasy life**. The psychoanalytic therapist uses a less structured approach than other therapists, encouraging "patients to speak freely about whatever is on their minds" (p. 100). Here Shedler is describing what is usually called free association, noting that it is a skill that takes time to learn. As patients learn to free associate, "their thoughts naturally range over many areas of" (often unknown—unconscious) "mental life, including desires, fears, fantasies, dreams, and daydreams."

(2010, p. 100)

Finally, Shedler adds, "the goals of psychodynamic therapy include, but extend beyond, symptom remission. Successful treatment should not only relieve symptoms (i.e. get rid of something) but also foster the positive presence of psychological capacities and resources" (p. 100). Shedler not only assumes a focus on unconscious processes throughout, but also emphasizes that analytic goals are not limited to symptom relief but include more positively stated goals.

> These might include the capacity to have more fulfilling relationships, make more effective use of one's talents and abilities, maintain a realistically based sense of self-esteem, tolerate a wider range of affect, have more satisfying sexual experiences, understand self and others in more nuanced and sophisticated ways, and face life's challenges with greater freedom and flexibility. Such ends are pursued through a process of self-reflection, self-exploration, and self-discovery that takes place in the context of a safe and deeply authentic relationship between therapist and patient.
>
> (2010, p. 100)

We would like to draw attention to the many similarities between Shedler's list, adopted from Blagys and Hilsenroth (2000), and the principles enumerated in the standard textbooks of psychoanalysis. While much of this should be obvious, we point to Karl Menninger's (1958) famous description of "the triangle of insight" (p. 148). His elaboration of psychoanalytic technique highlighted the reciprocal influence and synergy of working back and forth among the triangle of the affects, defenses, resistances, patterns, and fantasies associated with the patient's childhood, contemporary environmental reality, and the analytic situation. These ingredients of psychoanalytic process are quite similar to those described in the classic texts of Fenichel and Greenson, among others.

These seven features of psychoanalytic/psychodynamic therapies may seem so obvious, so much of what we would all teach beginners, that you may wonder why we are bothering to spell them out at such length. We believe these research findings are of substantial significance, more than has been noted by the psychoanalytic community. This is not even the research demonstrating effectiveness—all of this was just preliminary, so as to more accurately identify what constitutes analytic therapy. But we believe that, in some respects, identifying the common ingredients of analytic therapy may be even more important to the analytic community as a whole. In our view, what makes these empirical findings so powerful is that they so closely match what analysts would elucidate on the basis of clinical theories. For example, if the empirical research suggested that analytic therapists focus on interpersonal relations when the analytic community did not believe that, then we would have a serious problem. But these seven characteristics are all remarkably consistent with standard descriptions of the clinical psychoanalytic approach, described clearly and free of jargon.

Our point, the central take-away of this exercise, is that there are at least seven key aspects of how we work that may be used to define an analytic approach in the clinical situation. They are not based on underlying theoretical concepts that are hard to define and measure; rather they are observable and eminently suited to study and teaching. They match very closely with most analysts' clinical self-understandings. They are confirmed by empirical research, providing evidence that this is not just what analytic therapists *think* they do, but rather, it *is* what they do. We believe this kind of exercise, while not the final word, is an exciting and promising approach to help the analytic community focus on what its members have in common—which they too often take for granted.

Now of course, analysts differ among themselves even on these principles. Some schools of analysis place greater weight on interpersonal relations outside of the analytic situation, some lend themselves to a greater focus on the past, and some may emphasize a different approach to the examination or classification of defenses. We can easily generate a list of questions raised by these seven principles and we would expect a good deal of debate about how to implement them. But what strikes us as much more important is that these key characteristics unite the vast majority of analytic therapists. Further, and relevant to our main argument, these seven attributes apply to psychoanalysis proper as well as to psychodynamic therapy. They are true for a full range of psychoanalytically-oriented therapies. Of course, they may be applied differently if one is seeing a patient more frequently or less often. With one patient, the therapist or analyst may start off with an emphasis on the past developmental history, while with another patient, they may spend long periods of time focused on the here and now. The principles must be applied differently by each therapeutic dyad, since each is unique, and patients and therapists may be more drawn to one or the other. Perhaps the use of the couch facilitates a deeper immersion in fantasy, at least for some patients. There will inevitably be a wide range of particularity in implementation. Nevertheless, here we have seven theoretically coherent, historically authentic, and empirically validated components of a definition of psychoanalytic therapy. We have seven shibboleths we can use to distinguish ourselves as members of a profession who work in a particular way, and who cohere as an identifiable group. We contend that for our present purposes—namely for psychoanalysis to survive and once again flourish—we would do well to emphasize our common ground, inclusive of the full range of psychoanalytic therapies. Our commonality provides a "family resemblance" that allows abundant room for difference and disagreement while maintaining a common sensibility. Difference, conflict, and variety may then be studied and contained by the systematic application of "comparative psychoanalysis" rather than by defining psychoanalysis in a way that disowns members of the family.

Another way to think about the definition of psychoanalysis and our identities as psychoanalysts is to borrow from Mordecai Kaplan's (1994) ideas about Judaism as civilization. Viewing Judaism as an evolving civilization that repeatedly adapted to new circumstances throughout its history, Kaplan believed that the foundation and building blocks inherited from the past must be reshaped to fit the needs and value of the current generation, "without altering them in ways that would make them unrecognizable or sap their richness" (Alpert and Staub, 1997, p. vii). Psychoanalysis, too, has evolved over time. We can consider ourselves analysts because we anchor our practice in the long and broad sweep of the living theory and praxis of psychoanalysis as it has evolved over time, rather than because we adhere to the original texts or "basic method" or to other specific moments in that evolution. We view contemporary psychoanalysis as the sum of the conversation within the field up until the present day. We seek out founding principles in the context of the freedom to ground them in the particular historic moment in which we find ourselves, in our contemporary society, and in the needs of the people who come to us for help. In this sense, we are *all* Freudian analysts, in that we all trace our identity and community affiliation to the full sweep of history that originated in Freud's revolutionary insights, even if we are not specifically orthodox. Borrowing again from Kaplan, we believe that the past should inform the present, not unduly constrain it; tradition should have a vote, but not a veto.

Chapter 18

Monsters, Ghosts, and Undecidables

The salient characteristic of a monster is that it does not fit neatly into natural categories. It defies boundaries and thus frightens us, threatening the clarity of our own identities. Larry Friedman (2006) celebrates psychoanalysis as freakish, weird, bizarre, and unnatural—a monster. As a monster, psychoanalysis is neither art nor science, not quite a method of research nor a medical treatment. To insist that psychoanalysis is one thing or another is to tame the beast. Similarly, ghosts are not quite alive but not thoroughly dead. In the anti-Semitic imagination of Freud's day, Jews were viewed as ghosts, a wandering people who had no home. Psychoanalysis is haunted—*heimlich* and *unheimlich*, home and not home—and, as Freud (1918b) proclaimed, could only have been invented by a "godless Jew" (p. 63); that is, by a monster, someone who never fit neatly into standard categories.

Genius that Freud was, he was nevertheless caught in a matrix of binaries that permeated his culture and his very existence. As a Jewish man in Austria, he was regarded by his anti-Semitic countrymen as circumcised, effeminate, and perverse. In this virulently anti-Semitic milieu, Jews were considered immoral and degenerate, tied to the concrete and the body, and incapable of rationality and science. Like all colonized and oppressed people, Freud, to some degree, internalized these attributes (Boyarin, 1997; Gilman, 1993a, b).

Fortunately for psychoanalysis, Freud's thinking was always more complex and nuanced than the binaries in which he was culturally caught. Freud's place on the boundaries was optimally marginal. As both insider and outsider, and neither insider nor outsider, Freud was optimally positioned to appreciate ambiguities. Freud was neither Austrian nor German nor Jew; he was neither White nor Black, as Jews were regarded as mulattos. He was a doctor, but not a real university doctor, as Jews could not obtain those positions. While in many ways conventionally straight and patriarchal—one could say he epitomized patriarchy—from the point of view of his anti-Semitic surround, Freud was not a phallic man, since he was circumcised and therefore castrated and effeminate. Nor was he a woman, onto whom he projected all dependency, shame, and inferiority. Rather, according to the anti-Semitic trope, Freud, like all Jewish men, was effeminate and perverse. As Boyarin (1997) observed, "Gilman has provided a vitally important piece of information by observing how thoroughly Jewishness was constructed as queer in fin de siècle Europe . . . the Jew was queer and hysterical—and therefore, not a man" (pp. 214–215). In some ways, Jewish men were a third sex, leaving Jewish women invisible altogether (Pellegrini, 1997). In short, Freud was a monster: a ghost, queer, an undecidable, mulatto, circumcised, *unheimlich*, a third, while also having the patriarchal advantage of being a man. Who else could discover such a monster as psychoanalysis? Freud was "Janus-like" in his "doubledness" (Boyarin, 1997, p. 244), always on the boundary's edge. Quoting Freud can serve as a basis for drawing diametrically opposed conclusions in support of both conservative and radical projects.

The refusal to fit into neat categories is what gives psychoanalysis its edge, its astute capacity for reflection and critique. But it also creates an uncomfortable tension and anxiety that is too often handled by splitting. In this final chapter, we explore two interrelated binaries: cultural normativity versus the counter-cultural position, and vulnerability versus invulnerability. The relationship between these binaries is complex and nonlinear in that one can maintain both culturally normative or counter-cultural positions in the service of defensive invulnerability, but positioning oneself as either culturally central or on the periphery can accentuate feelings of both vulnerability and invulnerability.

In one vision, psychoanalysis stands outside our culture, providing a needed critique: it is counter-cultural. In fact, psychoanalysis might be said to be the most counter-cultural movement in the contemporary postmodern world. In a society that values speed, instant food, and instant information, psychoanalysis seems to require a great deal of time. Not only does formal psychoanalysis, as it has been traditionally practiced, require multiple sessions per week over many years, but even more importantly, it values the free associative state of consciousness precisely because it is timeless and not governed by the clock (even though individual sessions are literally regulated by the clock). Psychoanalysis values the capacity for reverie, mentalization, and alphabetization, for primary and tertiary process; it attends to conscious and unconscious processes that exist outside of time. In today's economic terms, psychoanalysis violates production norms: it is not cost-effective. Reisman approvingly described Freud as a "rate buster" (cited in Kaplan, 1973, p. 37). How many in our society are successful enough to afford an analysis and have the time to devote to it? It is outright counter-cultural in today's world to suggest that reflection deserves so much time, particularly reflection that seems aimless, as opposed to problem solving, which generates solutions based on rational reasoning. Psychoanalysis encourages a tolerance for living with ambiguity, rather than seeking out quick solutions. Analysts pride themselves on offering this counter-cultural vision. They are invested in representing a version of the good life that is different from the one promoted in today's world. They view psychoanalysis as valuing the uniqueness of the individual, insisting that each person's subjectivity be sufficiently attended to. In this vision, the individual is entitled to lengthy consideration, even if the process is considered by some to be "inefficient" or (mistakenly) thought to be unsupported by empirical research and randomized controlled trials (Shedler, 2010).

To illustrate what we mean by cultural normativity versus the counter-cultural position, we will compare Thomas Ogden's psychoanalytic approach with that put forth by Owen Renik. We must emphasize that neither of these two writers line up in any simple way with the above dichotomy—endorsing the cultural norm or being counter-cultural. Rather, we view their contrasting approaches as dialectic. Each analyst has some tendency to endorse cultural norms and adaptation to social context as well as counter-tendencies that encourage resistance to prevailing norms and values. At our best, we can view these opposing perspectives with binocular vision. We can "build bridges" between them or "stand in the spaces," or find a third voice that allows some paradoxical space for these contrasting worldviews. Ogden and Renik are among the most important contributors to psychoanalysis in recent decades. Their views are much too complex to simply place at opposing poles. But because they are such clear, powerful, and persuasive writers, they are particularly good illustrations of "ideal types." We will begin with Ogden, drawing from his two most recent books (Ogden, 2005, 2009) and at first considering some counter-cultural aspects of his work. Renik's work is largely contained in his clearly articulated and popularly written *Practical Psychoanalysis for Therapists and Patients* (2006). The designation of his approach as "practical psychoanalysis" lends itself to viewing it as embracing our culture's pragmatic and efficient ethos. If Renik's approach is practical, Ogden's might be described as poetic, soulful, even dreamy. For Renik, practical psychoanalysis is located in the pragmatics of symptom relief, while Ogden (2005) believes that psychoanalysis creates "conditions in which the analysand (with the analyst's participation) may become better able to dream his undreamt and interrupted dreams . . . thereby dreaming himself more fully into existence" (p. 2).

Dreaming into Being

Ogden (2005) repeatedly emphasizes his vision of psychoanalysis as a "therapeutic enterprise with the goal of enhancing the patient's capacity to be alive to as much as possible of the full spectrum of human experience" (p. 8). This objective seems remarkably different from that of relieving painful, uncomfortable, or disturbing symptoms. To be alive to the entire spectrum of human experience implies tolerating and fully experiencing pain and discomfort, rather than avoiding it. In what may seem at first to be a non sequitur, Ogden equates coming to life emotionally with the ability to dream one's experience, to dream oneself into existence. Let's pause to reflect on what Ogden means. In our culture, dreaming is not often valued. To dream, even daydream, is to avoid the pressing demands of reality, to waste time, to be unproductive.

Of course, for psychoanalysis, dreaming has special historic significance. Psychoanalysis was dreamt into existence (Aron, 1989) by Freud, whose magnum opus was his dream book (Freud, 1900b). Freud advised aspiring young analysts to analyze their own dreams, as they provided the royal road to the unconscious. There was a time when it was thought to be the height of resistance (used in the pejorative sense) if a patient did not bring a dream to a session. Psychoanalytic institutes offered numerous courses on dreams, and analysts were expected to be competent in dream interpretation. Emphasizing the value of dreams is consistent with the history and tradition of psychoanalysis. But Ogden is also using the idea of dreaming in a different sense.

By dreaming, Ogden does not mean only what we do at night while we sleep. For Ogden (2005), following Bion (1962), dreaming is a mode of thought that goes on continuously—day and night, awake and asleep—in which a person processes his or her experience. "Being alive to one's experience is, as I conceive of it, synonymous with being able to dream one's lived emotional experience" (2005, p. 23). To dream is to do psychoanalytic work, to exercise the "psychoanalytic function of the personality" (Ogden, 2005, pp. 99–100; 2009, p. 104). Dreaming consists of a set of mental operations that allow for the processing and transformation of conscious experience, making it available for unconscious psychological work. Notice this reversal of Freud's classic formulation of the aim of psychoanalysis. Freud calls for making the unconscious conscious, but Ogden reads Bion as reversing figure and ground, making conscious experience available for unconscious processing. To dream is to exercise one's imagination. In the analytic setting, imagination is "sacred" (Ogden, 2005, p. 26), precisely because it is equated with living fully. Psychoanalysis is about care of the psyche, the soul. In our reading of Ogden, psychoanalysis assumes the spiritual aim of preserving the soul.

Ogden is not oblivious to practical goals. For example, he points out that as an analysis reaches a point where a patient feels contained, there is evidence that this containment leads to change. One sign is that the patient may start reporting more remembered dreams to which he can associate and begin to symbolize, a development that may be accompanied by symptom relief or cessation of posttraumatic nightmares. But in Ogden's view, what is of primary significance is the capacity to dream, which includes associating to the dream, experiencing feelings in reporting the dreams, and curiosity about the dream. The sense we get from reading Ogden is that to be overly preoccupied with the diminution of symptoms is to impose an agenda on the patient, even if removing symptoms is what the patient wants. In doing analysis, the analyst is there to respond to who the patient is, to experience their being. It is not simply a matter of understanding the symptom with the idea that once understood, conflicts will be resolved and symptoms will disappear. To experience the patient's being is even more important than understanding the meaning of their symptoms and utterances. Understanding can be a way of avoiding being and experiencing. In an exegesis on Bion, Ogden explicates,

> Thus when the analyst is doing genuine analytic work, he is not "remembering," that is, not consciously attempting to know/understand/formulate the present by directing his attention to the past. Rather, he is experiencing the analysis in a "dream-like" way—he is dreaming the analytic session.
>
> (2005, p. 87)

The analyst's reverie is a waking form of dreaming with the patient, a way of dreaming the patient to life.

Freudian analysts often say that analysis, like the unconscious, needs to be timeless, not measured by hourly productivity. The paradox, of course, is that session length is measured by the clock. The precisely delineated frame provides the necessary background structure for both patient and analyst to enter into a timeless, unconscious state of mind. Ogden builds on this psychoanalytic sensibility, culminating in his advocating the ideal of "wasting time." Speaking about psychoanalytic supervision, but relevant to his thinking about all analytic process, Ogden (2009) writes, "This sense of having all the time in the world, of having time to waste . . . is a necessary element of the emotional background for an important kind of associative thinking" (p. 41). Ogden tells the story of a college professor who only taught classes a few hours per week. When asked by parents of his students what he did the rest of the time, he answered that he was paid to do nothing. Only if he had to do nothing could he just "waste time" reading books that were not considered important or well-known, and how else might he discover unknown authors? For Ogden, an analytic sensibility values a sense of having time to waste. This sensibility is an extraordinarily counter-cultural challenge to our cultural expectations of productivity.

We think it accurate to sum up this aspect of Ogden's message by saying that for Ogden (drawing especially on Winnicott, Bion, and Green), the goal of analysis is the experience of aliveness. Rather than judging the progress of analysis by monitoring symptoms, the key emphasis is placed on the patient and analyst's experience of aliveness and deadness. "The sense of aliveness and deadness of the transference-countertransference is, to my mind, perhaps the single most important measure of the status of the analytic process on a moment-to-moment basis" (Ogden, 2005, p. 43). For Ogden, even the analytic goals of understanding what things mean and resolving conflict are not nearly as important as "talking-as-dreaming" (Ogden, 2009, p. 14). Most important is being fully present with the patient, imagining and dreaming with them until they can dream themself into existence.

When Mitchell and Aron (1999) edited the first volume of *Relational Psychoanalysis: The Emergence of a Tradition*, which included papers by both Ogden and Renik, some members of the relational community questioned why Ogden had been included. They raised the objection that he was not sufficiently "relational" because he tended to work in too "classical" a manner, advocating, for example, that the analyst not use self-disclosure in the way relational analysts proposed it as a legitimate technical option. In 2000, Mitchell and Aron spent the full calendar year teaching the first international online seminar on relational psychoanalysis with participants from 14 countries. It happens that the day before Mitchell's death on December 21, 2000, Mitchell and Aron were teaching the last session of the class, which was a discussion of Ogden's work. In what may have been the last lesson Stephen Mitchell ever taught, he wrote the following email to the class.[1] We believe it beautifully captures Stephen Mitchell's unparalleled ability as a teacher, and presents his own perspective on why he included Ogden in his broad and inclusive approach to relational psychoanalysis, with a "small r."

> I thought it might be helpful to share some of my experiences with interviewing, which I've come to think about a lot in terms of clinical technique, especially in relation to Ogden, but more broadly as well.
>
> When we first started to plan for PSYCHOANALYTIC DIALOGUES back in 1990, we thought about doing interviews & the first person I thought of interviewing was Tom Ogden, because I'd been teaching him for years and had questions I never had had the chance to ask him. So I called & he seemed interested. We agreed that

---

1 Lewis Aron wishes to thank Margaret Black Mitchell for permission to use this previously unpublished email that Stephen posted to our online seminar, Wednesday, December 20, 2000 9:24:42 AM. When Lew first learned of Stephen's passing, one of the first things he did was send this passage to Tom Ogden, telling him the tragic news. It should be noted that Aron and Harris (2011) were delighted to include Ogden once again in *Relational Psychoanalysis (Volume 5): Evolution of Process.*

we would talk on the phone, record the conversation; I'd send him the questions ahead of time to think about, and he could edit the transcript afterward. Something like that. Or, perhaps he would write out the answers & we would go from there.

I got a call from him the next day saying he's changed his mind. He doesn't have lots of time to write, and he was worried the questions I asked might present a detour from the line of work he was pursuing. So, I should send him the questions, but he couldn't guarantee he'd have the time to respond.

This was really disappointing to me, but I sent him the questions and more or less forgot about it—several months passed. Then I got in the mail his incredibly thoughtful replies. He has really deeply engaged the questions & the exchange had advanced his own thinking, he said, so that the material became the last chapter of his next book SUBJECTS OF ANALYSIS.

The meaning of this has grown on me over the years, as I've done interviews with others. For one interview, to enhance "spontaneity," the interviewee thought it best not to have the questions before, and we met in person. But it turned out there was nothing spontaneous at all about that conversation. Each question elicited a canned response that I'd read in his previous books, even when the answers did not exactly fit the questions. There was simply no way to get this man to actually think in our presence, in response to our thoughts. And I began to realize how rare that really is.

Another interviewee actually rewrote our questions into questions he wanted to answer. So, in effect, he ended up interviewing himself.

Looking back, I've come to regard my exchange with Ogden as one of the deepest, most authentic exchanges I've had in the field with anyone. What started out seeming quite controlled and formal, turned out to be profoundly open. I think about this a lot when thinking about Ogden's clinical approach—very formal in certain respects, but generating a situation which allows him to be profoundly engaged with the people he is working with. It's led me to realize how often spontaneity can really be a kind of facile shallowness, and how many different ways there are to structure the analytic situation to provide both the safety and the level of engagement each clinician requires. In that sense, I've come to thinking of the technical implications of relational ideas not at all in terms of an integrated technique but rather a set of ideas for thinking about the work; in engaging those ideas, I think each clinician develops their own clinical methodology.

Mitchell's comments demonstrate his appreciation for the kind of intimacy, depth, spontaneity, and aliveness that Ogden's disciplined approach can generate. We began our own description of Ogden by emphasizing his championing of "dreaming" and "wasting time" and how his approach may thus seem to be outside of and even in opposition to cultural norms of accountability, efficiency, and productivity. The fact that Mitchell and Aron had to justify including Ogden in the relational canon points to the fact that others may have a quite different take on Ogden's approach. Maintaining a dialectical attitude means considering a reversal of the view presented so far. Ogden may, paradoxically and ironically, also be seen as writing from within and endorsing a culturally normative position. For example, one may read Ogden not so much as a critic or dissenter from dominant societal values as a hypertrophy of them. His argument for not imposing an agenda on people by "helping" them or even responding to their explicit manifest requests for help may ironically imply a culturally normative form of authoritarianism in which it is Ogden who decides what kind of help they should get or even really want! Some may believe that because Ogden does not explicitly share his own thoughts and reveries, he is imposing his interpretations on patients in a way that reproduces normative respect for authority and autonomy. Hence a dialectical examination points to aspects of authoritarianism in the very effort to be non-authoritarian and aspects of social conformity even in the most counter-cultural approach.

Practical Psychoanalysis

A former editor of the *Psychoanalytic Quarterly* and program chair of the American Psychoanalytic Association, Owen Renik has been a leader in American psychoanalysis for decades. Yet at first glance, his attack on psychoanalysis is so aggressive, he appears to be an outside critic. Renik (2006) opens his book with a broadside against the way psychoanalysis is generally conducted, which he believes is "extremely impractical" (p. 1). He asserts that psychoanalysis as practiced does not serve the needs of the vast majority of patients. "Most clinical psychoanalysts offer . . . a lengthy journey of self-discovery during which too much concern with symptom relief is considered counterproductive" (p. 1). Calling it a "faith-based movement" (quoted in Wyatt and Yalom, 2008), Renik holds psychoanalysis responsible for its own diminution in status and popular appeal precisely because it has become an impractical and unscientific self-promoting cult.

Renik believes that originally, Freud and the early analysts were focused on symptom relief. As analyses grew longer and analysts increasingly focused on exploration of the mind, they abandoned this practical focus. Not only did this make psychoanalysis less clinically effective, but it also led away from science, since the fluctuation of symptoms was the dependent variable that allowed the analyst to monitor the analytic process with some objectivity. Additionally, not to focus on symptoms is to relieve the analyst of responsibility and accountability, allowing and even encouraging analyses to go on endlessly with no independent measure of progress. For Renik, the goal of analysis is quite simply to help patients feel less distress and more satisfaction. He champions practitioners of "practical psychoanalysis," who

> contrary to the general trend, have more referrals then they can handle—and their practices are filled with patients who are neither analysts in training, nor hapless souls who are encouraged to remain for many years in treatments that produce no significant symptom relief.
>
> (2006, p. 4)

Renik proceeds practically, advising analysts to begin effective analytic work by first establishing with the patient an inventory of symptoms and what would comprise symptom relief. If demonstrable symptom relief does not accompany insight, then the validity of these insights must be questioned, otherwise analysts become complacent about their work. The relationship between patient and analyst is no different from any other relationship, except that an unusual degree of candor is called for on both sides. The analyst is advised to "play his or her cards face up" (p. 59), encouraging the patient to ask the analyst to explain him or herself fully, and the analyst is urged to "keep it real" (p. 63) by placing reality testing at the heart of practical psychoanalytic treatment.

Psychoanalysis or Psychotherapy?

Renik and Ogden seem to put forth two very different conceptions of cure, one situated on the pole of action (specific outcomes of measurable changes in the "real" world) and the other on the pole of reverie (nonspecific outcomes of the capacity to be alive to the full spectrum of human experience). They come from different theoretical traditions, which imply different sets of values, leading to very different decisions about what is attended to and practiced in specific treatments. Thus Renik (2006) finds efficacy in a one-time meeting with a patient who is able to clarify his uncertainty about a career choice, whereas Ogden (2005) can work with a patient for a substantial period of time without any sense of a chief complaint and little knowledge of the patient's immediate circumstances, including his age, the nature of his marriage, or whether he has children.

Ogden's version of psychoanalysis privileges imagination, reverie, and dreaming. Renik's approach is practical, concentrating on reality testing and keeping it real. At first blush they seem diametrically opposed. In at least one central respect, Renik's proposal is aligned with our culture's norms, values, and expectations, whereas Ogden's is counter-cultural. Renik believes we have lost the public's confidence precisely because we have been out of touch with reality, too dreamy, too focused on introspection and self-inquiry, and not attuned to real life problems, eliminating symptoms, and the practical day-to-day reality of relieving distress to improve lives. Ogden crusades for precisely what our society devalues—imagination, dreaming, and the poetic.

For some psychoanalysts, Ogden's approach is the more compelling. It emphasizes those qualities that are traditionally associated with psychoanalysis—dreams and dreaming, association and fantasy. What could be more analytic? Ogden tends to see his patients four and five times per week for many years, usually on the couch. He reveals little about himself directly, preferring to speak "from" the countertransference rather than "of" it. His work seems deep, profound, literary, and intellectual. For some psychoanalysts, Ogden's approach epitomizes authentic psychoanalysis, while they would describe Renik's approach as psychotherapy—perhaps useful, effective, and practical, but geared toward problem solving. He tends to present cases seen for shorter periods of time, less frequently, and one infers, with less use of the couch. Renik's practical psychoanalysis is viewed as being too close to the psychology of consciousness, too social psychological, too commonsensical, much too focused on symptom relief, and therefore too behavioral to be considered psychoanalysis. It is too much aligned with the worst aspect of our culture—its pressures, demands for cost-effectiveness, and lack of tolerance for complexity and ambiguity.

But of course, there are other psychoanalysts who believe Ogden's version is much too austere and impractical. He rarely, perhaps never, describes his patients' struggles to get to him with such frequency or explains how they manage to pay for these intensive analyses over so many years, as if these very practical issues are not relevant to the analytic work. Many readers wonder if only an analyst as famous as Ogden could attract patients to do this kind of work. His emphasis on dreaming and reverie seem impractical, even precious. Where does he get such rarefied patients who have the luxury of spending hours each week discussing their emotional reactions to literature or to the architecture of his waiting room, while he is absorbed in his own reveries? For some, Ogden's approach is counter-cultural to the extreme and does not lend itself to acceptance by the standards of our society. For these critics, Renik's method is a return to Freud's origins as a therapist whose first priority was to bring symptom relief to suffering patients. Renik's approach seems like something they might use with their patients, who most likely are being seen once a week and who press them for practical solutions to real-world problems.

Would the real psychoanalysis please stand up! Which is real and which the imposter? Which is really practical in furthering specifically psychoanalytic goals, whatever they may be? Once again, pluralism in psychoanalysis is managed by splitting, in which one's preferred theory and form of practice is given the honor of being called psychoanalysis, while the devalued other theory and practice is considered "only" psychotherapy.

In thinking dialectically, rather than dichotomously, we might reverse this understanding of Renik's argument. We might consider that it is actually Renik's approach that is more counter-cultural, since he calls for genuinely listening to the patient's point of view about what bothers them and why they are seeking help. Renik's contention is that symptoms are often very important to the patient, and dismissing them as simply manifest content does the patient a disservice and disrespects the patient. But he doesn't see symptoms as the only focus; in fact, what is identified as a symptom continues to evolve through the collaborative work of treatment. In other words, one might well argue that it is Renik's approach that is counter-cultural, in that he believes the patient's self-presentation is meaningful in its own right, while Ogden's focus on dreaming and aliveness can be used to dismiss the patient's subjective presentation of their own distress.

Ideologies can be ambiguous and paradoxical. What appears culturally normative may easily contain within itself the seeds of a counter-cultural vision. Psychoanalysis can be presented as endorsing and perpetuating cultural norms or as a counter-force to the values embraced by society. Ogden can be read as counter-cultural and yet his approach may contain authoritarian and culturally normative ideas about expertise. Renik may seem to be endorsing the culturally normative and even the insurance industry's emphasis on symptom reduction, yet his approach may be seen as radically counter-cultural in its insistence on attending to the patient's own view of the situation.

In the early years of psychoanalysis, the typical analysis was much shorter than it is today. Does that mean the early analysts (including Freud) were not really doing psychoanalysis? Grand (2011) points out that "the former brevity of analysis can be seen as gendered love affair with autonomy and reason; as an over-estimation of insight, ego and interpretation; and as analytic discomfort with affect, inter-dependence, attachment and separation." As psychoanalysis has evolved over time and within new contexts, so must our definition of what is psychoanalysis. Freud was a man on the border, and psychoanalysis is at its best on the margins, reflecting two vertices, looking at the culture from within, as an insider, and from the vantage point of the outside critic. In our view, analysis needs both perspectives so as to not be completely absorbed into promoting adaptation and conformity on the one hand, and on the other, not to become so increasingly irrelevant that it is trivialized and abandoned for its marginality. Splitting off the practical and devaluing it as psychotherapy is problematic, but so is splitting off the realm of dreams, imagination, and reverie and dismissing them as impractical. Psychoanalysis needs to maintain a both/and position without bifurcation. Surface cannot be studied without depth, nor can the unconscious be examined without consciousness. Symptom relief is indeed important, as is imaginative capacity and dreaming. Psychoanalysis may be used short term, to problem-solve, as well as long term, to bring to life someone who is deprived of vitality.

Psychoanalytic Views of the Self: From Adaptation to Authenticity and Authorship

Contrasting the culturally normative with the counter-cultural is closely connected to other binaries that have an important place in clinical psycho-analysis: the patient's adaptation to the culture versus the psychopathology of conformity, and the analyst as participant versus outside observer. Each of these, we believe, is tied to yet another fundamental split: vulnerability versus omnipotence, or guardedness and safety versus exposure and risk.

In the 1940s and 1950s, mainstream American ego psychology placed a premium on adaptation. In the post-1960s world, following Vietnam, Nixon's resignation, the civil rights movement, the women's movement, and the beginning of the gay rights movement, adaptation ceased to be a central cultural value. Indeed, adaptation was derided by the baby boomer generation. Psychoanalysis began to address the psychopathology of social conformity (Kaplan, 1990). Strenger (2005) argued that, influenced by feminism, psychoanalysis took up a Romantic expressivist view of the self, in which the goal of life was to express one's own unique individuality. Authenticity became the new psychoanalytic buzzword, and its focus moved from adaptation toward helping patients develop their own personal idiom (Bollas, 1989, 1992) and enrich their individual subjectivity. Analysts shifted from a focus on normality and pathology to authenticity and personal growth.

Life at the turn of the millennium has changed yet again. Strenger argues that by now, the liberal existential notions of authenticity and psycholog-ical subjectivity have been replaced by a still more radical ethic. Now, life and the self are seen as "design projects" (p. 163). Identity is no longer inherited through ties to family, culture, and religion. Rather, GenXers are more likely to turn to the Internet in an effort to design the self through pastiche. The body and sexuality are viewed as offering unlimited possi-bilities for shaping the self as a perpetual experiment. Pathology is more likely to be seen by analysts in the form of emptiness, created by the endless multiplicity of choices and lack of grounding.

Foucault (1970, 1984, 1988, 1997) questioned the grand historical narratives of medical and psychiatric progress. Rather than a linear line of progress from irrationality to knowledge, Foucault saw hidden forces of power-knowledge shaping human beings to meet society's needs. Postmodernism encouraged living one's life as a work of art with no single ideal of the good life, but with a plurality of styles, a variety of "techniques of the self," according to one's preferred "aesthetic of existence" (Foucault quoted by Strenger, 2005, p. 90). Challenging the concept of authenticity, Foucault encouraged playing with and shaping the self. As Foucault pointed out, this Nietzschean motif of self-creation may well conflict with adaptation, stable relations, and peace of mind. Where does psychoanalysis stand in relation to these quickly shifting societal norms and values? Strenger argues, "both wholesale pathologization and thoughtless celebration of the urban culture of self-experimentation are to be avoided" (p. 22). How will psychoanalysis position itself in relation to the changing cultural trajectory? Will we as psychoanalysts identify with the mainstream culture, feel ourselves to be part of it, endorsing its values? Or will analysts be more likely to see themselves as outside critics, bemoaning the changed norms and identities, and offering a critique and challenge? As Harris (2011b) has pointed out, "we cure with contaminated tools" (p. 709). While psychoanalysis emerged from the radical edge of cultural life, it has also been part of the establishment, shaped by hegemonic ideas of normativity. Will we find a way to remain optimally positioned at the margins, to bring a "binocular vision," to "stand in the spaces," to find a "third" vertex that allows us to sustain the dialectical tension between insider and outsider that was so essential to Freud and his early collaborators?

Omnipotence versus Vulnerability

We bring this book to a close with a meditation on vulnerability and the importance of it being contained and processed rather than dissociated, projected, or enacted. In our view, another binary central to the dichotomous positioning of psychoanalysis versus psychotherapy is invulnerability and vulnerability. In its "halcyon days," psychoanalysis viewed the analyst as well enough analyzed so as not to be vulnerable to the patient's efforts to dislodge the analyst's neutrality and equanimity. In the classic debates about psychotherapy and psychoanalysis in the 1950s, Leo Rangell (1954) said that in psychoanalysis, the analyst sits at the margins like a referee in a tennis match, while in psychotherapy, the therapist is on the court with the patient, interacting. Similarly, Fenichel (1941) wrote that the principal goal in the management of transference is "not joining the game" (p. 73). Well, if you're on the sidelines, not playing the game, then you can't get scored on, and you aren't likely to get hurt; if you are the referee and you call the ball out, then it's out! You are invulnerable. With the relational turn in psychoanalysis, there is increasing recognition of the analyst's inevitable and essential participation, and with that shift has come an acknowledgment of the analyst's vulnerability. Hirsch (1992) has consistently called for an appreciation of the analyst as a "vulnerable co-participant" (p. 739). He recalls that when he once told his interpersonal supervisor, the influential Edgar Levenson, that he felt vulnerable with a patient, Levenson replied that we are paid to be vulnerable.

There is a significant trend among philosophers to ground the philosophy of ethics in the experience of vulnerability. In our view, the ethics and practice of psychoanalysis must also be grounded in the experience of vulnerability. Emanuel Levinas' (1969, 1981) powerful philosophy of ethics begins with recognizing one's responsibility for the vulnerability of the other. Relations to others are the essence of human living. Subjectivity is established—one is born—through accepting one's infinite responsibility to the other. The self's authenticity and morality are mutually constituting. Levinas continually repeats the biblical injunction to serve the poor, the stranger, the widow, and the orphan—those who are most vulnerable. Vulnerability and death cannot be eliminated or denied, but meaning can be affirmed in spite of death through embracing our responsibility for others (Oppenheim, 2006).

Judith Butler (2004b), in *Precarious Life*, builds on Freud's discussion of mourning to argue that mourning entails an acceptance that one is changed by the loss; it is a transformation we cannot fully control, predict, or determine. While in the language of the law, legal rights are argued in terms of bounded individuals and groups—delineated subjects—Butler suggests that this language "does not do justice to passion and grief and rage, all of which tear us from ourselves, bind us to others, transport us, undo us, implicate us in lives that are not our own, irreversibly, if not fatally" (p. 25). In other words, we are not off the field, we are joined in the game, and ethics is grounded in our shared human vulnerability.

Orange (2011) articulates a hermeneutic, intersubjective approach to psychoanalysis that devotes exquisite attention to our receptivity to human suffering. For Orange, following Gadamer, understanding is constituted by receptivity and suffering. Orange writes,

> Not only are we required to witness and to participate emotionally in the suffering of our patients, but, in addition, the process of understanding itself means that we place ourselves at risk and allow the other to make an impact on us, to teach us, to challenge our preconceptions and habitual ways of being, to change us for their sake, even to disappoint and reject us.
>
> (2011, p. 23)

In Orange's psychoanalytic application of Gadamer's hermeneutics, analytic listening means listening in a truly open way, "holding oneself open, vulnerable, to the conversation" (p. 64). Employing Levinas' contributions, Orange places vulnerability at the center of psychoanalysis. Emerging from his Holocaust experience, Levinas' philosophy was rooted in the study of trauma, persecution, and suffering. His "reevaluation of vulnerability is . . . a phenomenology grounded in an optical situation established in Auschwitz, established not by Levinas but by Hitler" (Kugel, cited in Orange, 2011, p. 60n). For Levinas, the suffering of the face of the other places one in contact with the infinite, the sacred, and the holy. In this view, the psychoanalytic vocation of listening to the suffering stranger becomes a sacred calling.

Freud and psychoanalysts following him have long differentiated the primitive from the civilized, including primitive versus mature psychic mechanisms, and primitive populations versus those who with more highly developed, sophisticated mental operations. Celia Brickman (2011) has suggested that what analysts mean by "primitivity" is essentially "vulnerability." For Freud, this was expressed in terms of penetrating and being penetrated. To penetrate was to be phallic, whole, and firm, whereas to be penetrated was to be castrated, permeable, and vulnerable. Martha Nussbaum (2010) in *From Disgust to Humanity* demonstrates that misogyny is rooted in "projective disgust" (p. 15). Males distance themselves from bodily, animal vulnerability by associating women with bodily fluids, and dissociating themselves from their own corporeality. Homophobia is structured along the same lines as misogyny.

> What inspires disgust is typically the male thought of the male homosexual, imagined as anally penetrable. The idea of semen and feces mixing together inside the body of a male is one of the most disgusting ideas imaginable—to males, for whom the idea of nonpenetrability is a sacred boundary against stickiness, ooze, and death.
>
> (2010, p. 18)

Freud (1895b) strikingly attributed ethics to the condition of human vulnerability, writing, "The initial helplessness of human beings is the primal source of all moral motives" (p. 318). Jonathan Schofer (2010), in *Confronting Vulnerability*, argues that vulnerability is the bedrock of classic Jewish rabbinic ethics. Schofer examines how vulnerability organized the structure of rabbinic law. Using a symbol quite similar to Nussbaum's imagery of bodily fluids, he quotes an ethical maxim from *Mishnah Avot*, "Know from where you come: from a putrid secretion" (p. 2). The image of human beings emerging from semen is humbling, capturing the bodily fluidity that Nussbaum highlights, even if it displaces the focus to the man's fluidity. Schofer writes, "Ethics cannot presume a continually healthy, strong, independent agent who encounters weak, needy others" (p. 3). The rabbis emphasize a variety of forms of vulnerability: old age, persecution, drought, poverty, widowhood, orphanhood, being a stranger, and especially death, precisely because we have a tendency to deny our own vulnerability. Schofer maintains, "Confronting vulnerability becomes central to ethical cultivation" (p. 4). While of course the analyst's personal analysis should help the analyst be in touch with their own vulnerability, too often it is used as a rationalization to deny vulnerability and to project all vulnerability onto the patient.

As a 19th-century European man, Freud believed the height of civilization was the achievement of individual autonomy, later theorized as "ego autonomy." Having clear and firm boundaries meant you were independent and whole, phallic and impenetrable. To be merged with another, to experience the "oceanic feeling," fluidity, was to be penetrable, vulnerable to the influence of the other, susceptible to infection. This was primitivity (Brickman, 2003), and as Nussbaum argues, it signified vulnerability and mortality. It was the primitive who was suggestible—the hysteric, the woman, the African, Asian, or Jew, the poor and the uneducated. For the Western Jew, it was the Eastern Jew. Primitivity meant vulnerability to penetration, contamination, and death. In Freud's day, Jews were regarded as contaminated and contagious, an ideology culminating with Hitler's assertion that Jews were "maggots inside a rotting body" (quoted by Nussbaum, 2010, p. 23). As circumcision was the embodied mark of the Jew as feminine and castrated, castration anxiety assumed a central role in Freudian clinical theory and practice. This explains why Freud (1937a) believed that the bedrock of psychoanalysis was "the repudiation of femininity" (p. 252). This was not just a slip or passing sentiment—it was at the core of his values.

From this perspective, to help a patient get better by utilizing suggestion could only reinforce the patient's primitivity, even if it helped them in other ways (so-called transference cures), or was necessary due to practical circumstances such as limited resources. Psychoanalysis proper had to eliminate suggestion; porousness was to be replaced by firm ego boundaries. Certainly it did not eliminate all influence, for how else could you help someone? Freud objected to influence based on the force of one's personality or subjectivity, while accepting that analysis influenced the patient through rational argument. To be influenced by accepting a rational argument means you have used your own reason to evaluate the influence, and so you remain independent and autonomous—that is why in its later formulation, psychoanalysis was supposed to work by interpretation alone (Gill, 1954). In contrast, in hypnotic influence, one is subject to the direct interpersonal influence of the other person. Hypnotic suggestion relies on dependence and merging with the will of the other—penetration and passivity—homosexual submission to the father, and hence is thought to reinforce dependence and "primitive" lack of differentiation.

As we discussed in Chapter 14, Brickman (2003) has demonstrated the influence of evolutionary anthropology on Freud's thinking. The racialized primitive, savage, and barbarian, together with the religious heathen, infidel, pagan, were the outsiders, the "not-us." It is a credit to Freud's brilliance that at a time when those around him saw themselves as civilized, Freud maintained that primitivity is universal: we each carry primitivity within us. We each have an ego and an id, an ego and a Y(id), a German and a Jew. This is consistent with Freud's championing of bisexuality—we each embody male and female aspects. We all have unconscious perversion and unconscious homosexual inclinations. This was truly a revolutionary idea. However, by arguing that we all have primitive minds, with primitive drives, Freud reinforced the hierarchical duality of civilized versus primitive.

In the Middle Ages, religion was dominant and the duality was Christian/heathen. The Enlightenment's emphasis on reason and rationality brought a simple reversal, in which in civilized circles, to be religious was thought to be primitive, superstitious, or magical, while to be civilized meant to be scientific and rational. As we have seen, one can reverse the power relations of the poles of any binary while maintaining the dichotomous structure. Hence while Christian/heathen was originally aligned with right/wrong, heaven/hell, mature/immature, the hierarchy was then reversed, such that the binary became secular/Christian, aligned with rational/irrational, mature/immature. With increasing industrialization, the value of delayed gratification, considered by evolutionary theorists to be the mark of the civilized man, became more prominent. To be civilized and adult was to be disciplined, while primitives were thought to be impulsive and in need of immediate gratification. Adult/child was aligned with civilized/primitive, conscious/unconscious, White/Black, responsible/irresponsible, and culture/nature. To be civilized was to live within the context of historical time, while to be primitive was to be pre-historical, out of time. The unconscious, being primitive, does not know time.

All of these polarities were mapped onto male/female. Men were considered civilized adults, while women were regarded as more like children—irrational, concrete, immoral, and impulsive. If psychoanalysis was about replacing the (Y)id with the ego (and by extension, the superego), it was also about dealing with our femininity. The bedrock answer for both sexes was to repudiate femininity: for men, the fear of castration, and for women, penis envy. Freud noted that in his culture masculinity was active, while femininity was passive. To be a woman (or male homosexual) was to be passively penetrated. The masochistic wish is to be penetrated, just as it is the wish of the primitive to be dominated. To be phallic is to be the active one who does the penetrating/dominating. To be phallic and impenetrable is to be solid, bounded, invulnerable, and autonomous. To be female is to be penetrable, porous, vulnerable, submissive, masochistic, and dependent. To be female is to be embodied and thus vulnerable, while to be masculine is to be cerebral, abstract, disembodied, and therefore invulnerable, not subject to decay, castration, or death.

Ultimately, to be primitive is to be subject to domination and penetration—embodied, and hence vulnerable. In psychoanalysis, this dichotomy positions the patient as primitive and the analyst as civilized. The analyst must be opaque, impenetrable, and courageous, even heroic. The patient is childish, pathological, out of time and history. The dark, feminine, unconscious is penetrated by the "analytic instrument"—the analyst's interpretations. In this binary scheme, the analyst is phallic, abstract, rational, autonomous, disembodied, a blank screen, a surgeon— and therefore not vulnerable, primitive, feminine, dark, Jewish, embodied, or castrated.

Mutual Vulnerability and Thirdness in Relational Theory

With this background set of binaries clarified, let us return to contemporary relational theory, which is an attempt to move beyond these binary oppositions both intrapsychically and interpersonally, itself a binary that requires ongoing deconstruction, or finding a third. Benjamin (2011) has described the "moral third," referring to the sense of lawfulness and trust in re-establishing connection after disruption. Patient and therapist create a rhythm, a steady state. At some point, the rhythm inevitably breaks down and the difference between the two is highlighted. Then comes repair and reestablishment of connection. This is "the law" of intersubjective life, the co-creation and breakdown of patterns of mutual regulation and mutual recognition. Analysis is a study of these configurations as they are relived, reenacted, and reworked while being examined and articulated. Benjamin credits Tronick as well as Beebe and Lachmann, who following Kohut, described this cycle of rupture and repair. Aron (1996a) traces the origins of this approach back to Ferenczi (see especially his *Clinical Diary* (1932) and Aron and Harris, 1993). Ferenczi was explicit in arguing that the analyst would inevitably repeat (we would now say "enact") with the patient the traumatic experiences of childhood, but unlike the earlier objects who denied their participation in the crime, analysts had to take responsibility and acknowledge their participation and guilt.

Benjamin maintains that the analyst acknowledges the rupture, and through this non-defensive validation, re-establishes the steady state, leaving the patient with a feeling of having been recognized. The analyst's acknowledgement shows that the injury is perceived as a violation of an expectable pattern ("the law") and thus it relieves the felt emotional abandonment. Both patient and therapist surrender to the trust that exists between them, trust in the process, trust in love, in faith—some call it God—in something beyond them, to which they both surrender. Thus they are not each submitting to the other so much as surrendering to thirdness, to a moral law, to lawfulness itself—the law that all relationships inevitably are constituted by rupture and repair and can then go on being or be resurrected into new life. By the way, if this sounds suspiciously religious, it is. Benjamin absorbed German idealism, particularly Hegel's. These ideas reverberate with Christian theology regarding the trinity, but can also be traced very clearly to prominent themes in the Hebrew Bible. Marie Hoffman (2011) details the intellectual history in *Toward Mutual Recognition: Relational Psychoanalysis and the Christian Narrative*, while Karen Starr (2008) addresses these themes in *Repair of the Soul: Metaphors of Transformation in Jewish Mysticism and Psychoanalysis*.

Many of us can associate the language of thirdness with centuries of Christian theological controversy concerning the Trinitarian Creed, culminating in the doctrine of the Trinity. God exists as three *persons*, or *hypostases*, but is one being, that is, has but a single divine nature: one in the third and the third in the one. But many of us are less familiar with this theme in Jewish scholarship. Consider one example from medieval Jewish theology that illustrates how closely Benjamin's ideas are to themes in the Jewish tradition. The pre-rabbinic schools of Hillel and Shamai engaged in heated disputes regarding the law, often arguing from diametrically opposed positions. Nevertheless, Jewish tradition has it that a voice from Heaven proclaims, "These and these are the words of the Living God." In other words, the opposing positions are both true! How can this be? Rabbi Judah Loew, known as the Maharal of Prague, was an important 16th-century Talmudic scholar, Jewish mystic, writer, and philosopher. In his work, *Tif'ereth Yisrael* (The Glory of Israel), he describes the mystical power of the number three. "In three, two separate lines are transformed into 'one' through a third line that joins them. Through the Maharal's geometry, three is at the same time *less* and *greater* than two" (Kolbrener, 2011, p. 77). Three represents the paradox of unity and division. The postmodern psychoanalytic conceptualization of the third may be regarded as a theoretical example of Freud's (1905) conclusion about life and love, that, "The finding of an object is in fact a refinding of it" (p. 222).

When patient and therapist are involved in an enactment or impasse, it often takes the form of a clash, a tug of war, a push me-pull you, doer-done to, or sadomasochistic enactment (Benjamin, 1988). This is what Philip Bromberg (2011) refers to as collisions of subjectivity, noting the resonances with Benjamin's theorizing. When in these states, we are often dealing with binaries. Either I am guilty or I am a victim, either you started it or I did, either it's your fault or mine, either you are withholding or I am too demanding, either you really let me down or I expect too much, either you are the best therapist in the world or you suck, either you are crazy or I am. Each of these is a binary. We are talking about splitting, but we are talking about two people who both get caught up in splitting. This is why we call it complementarity—it is complementary splitting or enactment resulting from mutual dissociation.

Benjamin has argued that the therapist must acknowledge the way in which she has hurt the patient, broken the trust or rhythm, how she was un-attuned. Benjamin's perspective is developmental rather than technically prescriptive. She is predominantly focusing on analysts acknowledging to themselves their own participation in enactments and validating their patients' sense of having been injured by them. Aron (2006) emphasized that the therapist must open space within himself to reflect on how he is conflicted or torn, how he can think or feel more than one way about something, and how he can be open to differences within himself—"stand in the spaces" (Bromberg, 1996) or "build bridges" (Pizer, 1998) to his own multiple self-states. For example, the therapist may both be angry with the patient and blaming himself for something. In creating some room for difference within the self, one creates triangular space or thirdness, something like what Bion meant by binocular vision. Rather than being trapped in a polarization, there is some room within which to think and feel. When stuck in impasse or deadlock, the analyst's search for thirdness within himself may pave the way for a shared third. In sum, what Benjamin, Aron, Bromberg and others are calling for is a change in analytic sensibility from opaqueness and impenetrability toward greater interpenetrability and mutual recognition of shared vulnerability. Stated in the more contemporary language that has become associated with relational psychoanalysis and especially with the contributions of Jody Davies, Philip Bromberg, and Donnel Stern, the analyst's acknowledgment of their participation in enactments involves a form of mentalization that creates room for multiplicity and dialogue among multiple self-states within the analyst, the patient, and intersubjectively, in co-created shared space between them.

The dialectics of difference (Bollas, 1989) require permeability; the therapist implicitly or explicitly reveals something about being moved by the patient. The therapist is not masochistic or without boundaries, but is penetrable, movable, and reachable. To work in the way being advocated by these contemporary relational authors entails ongoing self-monitoring and self-scrutiny along with utilizing the patient for feedback, supervision, and mutual regulation. It is not, however, intended to be a simple reversal of authority from the analyst onto the patient, where now the patient is always right in their interpretation of the analyst. As Harris (2011b) notes, extreme forms of self-sacrifice in the service of the treatment can too easily veer into the masochistic, entailing a simple reversal of sadism and masochism between analyst and patient. Analytic vulnerability must be accompanied by self-care, including bodily self-care, as well as by analytic responsibility (Harris and Sinsheimer, 2008). Neither patient nor therapist need be phallic or castrated, civilized or primitive. Meanings and interpretations are not given and received as much as negotiated and co-created. Empathy and even acknowledgment are not given by the therapist but are mutual and bi-directional, even if the therapist tries to lead in some areas of conflict. Thirdness means moving beyond binary oppositions and the inevitable hierarchy that accompanies splitting, thus opening up space to think and feel.

Davies (2010) has described relational practice as characterized by "mutual interpenetrability" and "the acceptance of vulnerability" by both patient and analyst, and by the analyst's "acknowledgment of penetrability" (p. 91). Similarly, I. Z. Hoffman writes,

> Whatever asymmetry of power is optimal for a transformative psychoanalytic conversation, it is accompanied by a more or less conscious undercurrent of mutual identification with respect to the ultimate vulnerability of the participants. When that vulnerability is denied it can fuel subtle abuses of power on the part of the analyst beginning with a refusal to recognize the patient as a fellow caregiver with power to deeply affect the analyst's sense of worth.
>
> (2011, p. 41)

Hoffman (1998) has long emphasized the temptation to deny human vulnerability, particularly focusing on the denial of our mortality.

Building on their earlier presentation of evolutionary biological theory, Slavin and Kriegman (1998) describe how our intricate psychodynamic system evolved to guide the ongoing negotiation and renegotiation of the self in the ambiguous, inherently conflicted relational world. In that world, our minds are powerfully constructed within the family and the larger culture in relating to others whose interests inevitably diverge from our own. Within this model of the evolution of mind, dealing with conflict, mutuality, and deception is part of the normal family matrix. For Slavin and Kriegman, self-interest is a natural organizer of human motivation and the patient's skepticism is a natural evolutionary adaptive capacity. It functions in the service of evaluating the degree of overlap and divergence of interests of the patient and the analyst. This perspective places internal conflict center stage. Resistance is viewed as an adaptive function, which protects one from influence by someone whose interests conflict with one's own. Patients are therefore highly motivated to observe therapists' ways of dealing with their own inevitable conflicts as well as with conflicts of interest between themselves and their patients. Slavin and Kriegman (1998) argue that for an analysis to succeed in helping the patient change, the analyst too needs to change. It is essential to the patient that the analyst is open to change within herself as part of the analytic process. The analyst's acceptance of his own vulnerability is essential for patients to recognize their vulnerability. Self-interest and altruism are both evolutionary adaptations and intimacy is not achievable without mutual vulnerability.

A further caution: the very opposition of binary thinking versus moving beyond binaries is itself a binary; contrasting split complementarity with the third may be read as yet another binary even when it is intended to be dialectical. If it seems that while deconstructing various binaries that we ourselves have become stuck in binary thinking or created yet new opposi-tions, that is inevitable. It is the law, the law of rupture and repair, of deconstruction as an ongoing and always unstable activity, of the third not as some final resolution but as a fleeting moment in an ongoing process. Binaries (and the associated splitting) do have their usefulness, providing stability and structure until such time as integrations of greater complexity can be achieved.

In *A Meeting of Minds*, Aron (1996a) presented relational psychoanalysis as characterized by a variety of forms of mutuality, including mutual influ-ence, mutual recognition, mutual resistances, mutual empathy, the mutual generation of data, and many other dimensions of mutuality, even if also characterized by some aspects of asymmetry in role, function, and respon-sibility. Here we want to add an explicit emphasis on mutual vulnerability. In acknowledging one's own permeability and vulnerability—one's embodiment, mortality, and humanity—one does not need to project all of the conflict, splitting, shame, disgust, animalistic embodiment, penetra-bility, and vulnerability onto the patient. The image that may best capture this mutual analytic vulnerability is drawn from Ferenczi's *Clinical Diary*. Ferenczi wrote,

> Should it ever occur, as it does occasionally to me, that experiencing another's and my own suffering brings a tear to my eye (and one should not conceal this emotion from the patient), then the tears of doctor and patient mingle in a sublimated communion, which perhaps finds its analogy only in the mother-child relationship. And this is the healing agent, which like a kind of glue, binds together permanently the intel-lectually assembled fragments, surrounding even the personality thus repaired with a new aura of vitality and optimism.
>
> (1932, p. 65)

This is the image of mutual vulnerability and bodily fluidity (as we have seen, so often associated with feared, devalued, and contagious femi-ninity) leading not to disgust and shame but transformed, sublimated, and spiritualized into healing. The Yom Kippur liturgy includes the prayer "*mol levavenu*," "circumcise our hearts," along with the commentary "Circumcision creates a wound, and the one who is wounded is vulnerable" (Teutsch, 1999). Here we see that in Jewish tradition, not only is circumcision viewed positively, as a symbol of the desired covenant with God, but also that vulnerability is acknowledged, even valued, as a neces-sary prerequisite for relationship and connection. Intersubjective method-ology might help analysts not only with clinical impasses and stalemates, but with professional, theoretical, sexual, cultural, and historical deadlocks as well. Not only in the clinical interaction, but as a profession and discipline, by owning our vulnerability, attachment, and dependency, by not refuting femininity, psychoanalysis need not split itself off from psychotherapy as its inferior, shameful other. The discipline of psychoanalysis and the psychoanalytic practitioner, in touch with vulnerability, not needing to split off and project it onto others, is capable of mutual recognition, empathy, and moral responsibility. No longer invulnerable, we cannot remain safely behind the couch in our private practices. We must become socially, politically, and environmentally active and bring complexity, depth, dialectics, and dynamic understanding to problems in our communities and in the wider world, as legitimate psychoanalytic praxis. We would invoke Levinas' biblical call to serve the poor, the orphaned, and the widowed, and apply it to Freud's vision of making psychoanalysis a "psychotherapy for the people." No longer dissociating our vulnerability, and without disclaiming our own agency, we can then move toward a progressive psychoanalysis.

References

Abraham, H. C., & Freud, E. L. (Eds.) (1965). *A psycho-analytic dialogue: The letters of Sigmund Freud and Karl Abraham, 1907–1926*. New York, NY: Basic Books.

Aiello, T. (2009). Psychoanalysts in exile. *Psychoanalytic Perspectives*, 6, 8–34.

Alexander, F. (1936). Practical aspects of psychoanalysis. *Psychoanalytic Quarterly*, 5, 283–289.

Alexander, F. (1954). Some quantitative aspects of psychoanalytic technique. *Journal of the American Psychoanalytic Association*, 2, 685–701.

Alexander, F. (1958). Unexplored areas in psychoanalytic theory and treatment. *Behavioral Science*, 3(1), 293–316.

Alexander, F. (1960). Psychoanalysis and psychotherapy. In J. Masserman (Ed.), *Science and Psychoanalysis* (Vol. 3, p. 257). New York, NY: Grune & Stratton, 1967.

Alexander, F. (1961). *The scope of psychoanalysis, 1921–1961: Selected papers of Franz Alexander*. New York, NY: Basic Books, Inc.

Alexander, F., & French, T. M. (1946). *Psychoanalytic therapy*. New York, NY: Ronald Press.

Alpert, R. T., & Staub, J. J. (1997). *Exploring Judaism: A reconstructionist approach*. Wyncote, PA: The Reconstructionist Press.

Altman, N. (1995). *The analyst in the inner city*. Hillsdale, NJ: The Analytic Press.

Altman, N. (2010). *The analyst in the inner city*, 2nd edn. New York, NY: Routledge.

Anzieu, D. (1986). The place of Germanic language and culture in Freud's discovery of psychoanalysis between 1895 and 1900. *International Journal of Psychoanalysis*, 67, 219–226.

Appignanesi, L., & Forrester, J. (1992). *Freud's women*. New York, NY: Basic Books.

Aron, L. (1989). Dreams, narrative, and the psychoanalytic method. *Contemporary Psychoanalysis*, 25, 108–126.

Aron, L. (1996a). *A meeting of minds*. Hillsdale, NJ: The Analytic Press.

Aron, L. (1996b). From hypnotic suggestion to free association: Freud as a psychotherapist, circa 1892–1893. *Contemporary Psychoanalysis*, 32, 99.

Aron, L. (2000). Self-reflexivity and the therapeutic action of psychoanalysis. *Psychoanalytic Psychology*, 17, 667–690.

Aron, L. (2003). Clinical outbursts and theoretical breakthroughs: A unifying theme in the work of Stephen A. Mitchell. *Psychoanalytic Dialogues, 13*, 259–273.

Aron, L. (2004). God's influence on my psychoanalytic vision and values. *Psychoanalytic Psychology, 21*, 442–451.

Aron, L. (2005). On the unique contribution of the interpersonal approach to interaction. *Contemporary Psychoanalysis, 41*, 21–34.

Aron, L. (2006). Analytic impasse and the third: Clinical implications of intersubjectivity theory. *International Journal of Psychoanalysis, 87*, 349–368.

Aron, L. (2007). Reflections on Heinz Kohut's religious identity and anti-semitism. *Contemporary Psychoanalysis, 43*, 411–420.

Aron, L., & Benjamin, J. (1999). The development of intersubjectivity and the struggle to think. Paper presented at the spring meeting of Division 39 (Psychoanalysis) of the American Psychological Association, New York, NY.

Aron, L., & Bushra, A. (1998). Mutual regression: Altered states in the psychoanalytic situation. *Journal of the American Psychoanalytic Association, 46*, 389–412.

Aron, L., & Harris, A. (1993). Sandor Ferenczi: Discovery and rediscovery. In L. Aron & A. Harris (Eds.), *The legacy of Sándor Ferenczi* (pp. 1–35). Hillsdale, NJ: The Analytic Press.

Aron, L., & Harris, A. (Eds.) (2011). *Relational psychoanalysis (volume 4): Expansion of theory*. New York, NY: Routledge.

Bair, D. (2003). *Jung: A biography*. Boston, New York, and London: Little, Brown, and Company.

Bakan, D. (1958). *Sigmund Freud and the Jewish mystical tradition*. Princeton, NJ: D. Van Nostrand.

Bakan, D. (1966). *The duality of human existence: An essay on psychology and religion*. Chicago, IL: Rand McNally.

Balint, M. (1948). On the psychoanalytic training system. *International Journal of Psychoanalysis, 29*, 163–173.

Batnitzky, L. (2011). *How Judaism became a religion*. Princeton, NJ: Princeton University Press.

Beller, S. (1991). *Vienna and the Jews, 1867–1938: A cultural history*. Cambridge: Cambridge University Press.

Benedict, R. (1946) *The chrysanthemum and the sword: Patterns of Japanese culture*. Boston, MA: Houghton Mifflin Company.

Benjamin, J. (1988). *The bonds of love*. New York, NY: Pantheon.

Benjamin, J. (1995). *Like subjects, love objects*. New Haven, CT: Yale University Press.

Benjamin, J. (2004). Beyond doer and done to: An intersubjective view of thirdness. *Psychoanalytic Quarterly, 73*, 5–46.

Benjamin, J. (2011) Beyond doer and done to: An intersubjective view of thirdness, with afterword. In Aron, L. & Harris, A. (Eds.), *Relational psychoanalysis, Volume 4, Expansion of theory* (pp. 91–130). New York, NY: Routledge.

Bergmann, M. S. (1979). Review of the book *From Oedipus to Moses: Freud's Jewish identity*, by M. Robert. *Psychoanalytic Quarterly, 48*, 131–133.

Bergmann, M. S. (1992). *In the shadow of Moloch*. New York, NY: Columbia University Press.

Bergmann, M. S. (1995). The Jewish and German roots of psychoanalysis and the impact of the Holocaust. *American Imago, 52*, 243–259.

Bergmann, M. S. (Ed.). (2000). *The Hartmann era.* New York, NY: Other Press.

Bergmann, M. S., & Hartman, F. R. (1976). *The evolution of psychoanalytic technique.* New York, NY: Columbia University Press, 1990.

Berlin, I. (1966). *Two concepts of liberty.* Oxford: Clarendon Press.

Berman, E. (2004a). *Impossible training.* Hillsdale, NJ: The Analytic Press.

Berman, E. (2004b). Sándor, Gizella, Elma. *International Journal of Psychoanalysis, 85,* 489–520.

Bernheim, H. (1892). *Neue studien uber hypnotismus: Suggestion und psychotherapie* (S. Freud, Trans.). Leipzig: Deuticke. (Original work published in 1891).

Bernstein, R. J. (1998). *Freud and the legacy of Moses.* Cambridge: Cambridge University Press.

Bérubé, A. (1990) *Coming out under fire.* New York, NY: Free Press.

Bhabha, H. (1984). Of mimicry and man: The ambivalence of colonial discourse. *Discipleship: A Special Issue on Psychoanalysis, 28,* 125–133.

Bibring, E. (1954). Psychoanalysis and the dynamic psychotherapies. *Journal of the American Psychoanalytic Association, 2,* 745–770.

Bion, W. R. (1962). *Learning from experience.* London: Tavistock.

Birkner, G. (2009). Psychotherapy's Jewish roots: The author of "American therapy" discusses Freud, Obama. *The Jewish Daily Forward,* February 18. Retrieved from: http://www.forward.com/articles/103139/#ixzz1Sriv90DP

Blackledge, C. (2004). *The story of V: A natural history of female sexuality.* New Brunswick, NJ: Rutgers University Press.

Blagys, M. D., & Hilsenroth, M. J. (2000). Distinctive features of short-term psychodynamic–interpersonal psychotherapy: A review of the comparative psychotherapy process literature. *Clinical Psychology: Science and Practice, 7*(2), 167–188.

Blass, R. (2010a). Affirming "That's not psycho-analysis!" On the value of the politically incorrect act of attempting to define the limits of our field. *The International Journal of Psychoanalysis, 91*(1), 81–89.

Blass, R. (2010b). On The comments of Emanuel Berman, Lewis Aron, Yoram Hazan and Steven Stern. *The International Journal of Psychoanalysis, 91*(5), 1285–1287.

Blatt, D. S. (1988). The development of the hero: Sigmund Freud and the reformation of the Jewish tradition. *Psychoanalysis and Contemporary Thought, 11,* 639–703.

Blatt, S. J. (2004). *Experiences of depression.* Washington, DC: American Psychological Association.

Blatt, S. J. (2008). *Polarities of experience.* Washington, DC: American Psychological Association.

Blechner, M. J. (2005). The gay Harry Stack Sullivan. *Contemporary Psychoanalysis, 41,* 1–20.

Bloom, H. (1987). The strong light of the canonical. *The City College Papers, 20,* 1–77.

Blum, H. P. (2010). Anti-Semitism in the Freud case histories. In A. D. Richards (Ed.), *The Jewish World of Sigmund Freud* (pp. 78–95). Jefferson, NC and London: McFarland & Company.

Bollas, C. (1989). *Forces of destiny.* London: Free Associations.

Bollas, C. (1992). *Being a character.* New York, NY: Hill & Wang.

Bonomi, C. (1998). Freud and castration. *Journal of the American Academy of Psychoanalysis*, *26*, 29–49.

Bonomi, C. (2009). The relevance of castration and circumcision to the origins of psychoanalysis: 1. The medical context. *International Journal of Psychoanalysis*, *90*, 551–580.

Bos, J., Park, D. W., & Pietikainen, P. (2005). Strategic self-marginalization: The case of psychoanalysis. *Journal of the History of the Behavioral Sciences*, *41*, 207–224.

Boyarin, D. (1997). *Unheroic conduct: The rise of heterosexuality and the invention of the Jewish man*. Berkeley, CA: University of California Press.

Boyarin, D. (1999). *Dying for God: Martyrdom and the making of Christianity and Judaism*. Stanford, CA: Stanford University Press.

Boyarin, D. (2003). *Queer theory and the Jewish question*. New York, NY: Columbia University Press.

Breger, L. (2000). *Freud: Darkness in the midst of vision*. New York, NY: John Wiley.

Brenner, C. (2009). Memoir. *Psychoanalytic Quarterly*, *78*, 637–673.

Breuer, J., & Freud, S. (1893–1895). Studies on hysteria. In J. Strachey (Ed. & Trans.), *The standard edition of the complete psychological works of Sigmund Freud* (Vol. 2, pp. 1–311). London: Hogarth Press, 1955.

Brickman, C. (2003). *Aboriginal populations in the mind*. New York, NY: Columbia University Press.

Brickman, C. (2010). Psychoanalysis and Judaism in context. In L. Aron & L. Henik (Eds.), *Answering a question with a question* (pp. 25–56). Boston, MA: Academic Studies Press.

Brickman, C. (2011). *Primitive pasts, civilizing practices: From racialized lives to race in psychoanalytic theory*. Paper presented at the Spring meeting of the APA Division of Psychoanalysis (39). Invited Panel with Lewis Aron, Ph.D., Kimberlyn Leary, Ph.D., MPA, Karen Starr, Psy.D.

Brodkin, K. (2002). *How Jews became white folks*. New Brunswick, NJ: Rutgers University Press.

Bromberg, P. M. (1996). *Standing in the spaces*. Hillsdale, NJ: The Analytic Press.

Bromberg, P. M. (2003). Something wicked this way comes. Trauma, dissociation, and conflict: The space where psychoanalysis, cognitive science, and neuroscience overlap. *Psychoanalytic Psychology*, *20*, 558–574.

Bromberg, P. M. (2011). *The shadow of the tsunami*. New York, NY: Routledge.

Broucek, F. J. (1991). *Shame and the self*. New York, NY: Guilford Press.

Bruck, A. (1910). *The diseases of the nose, mouth, pharynx and larynx*. New York, NY: Rebman Co.

Brunner, J. (1991). The (ir)relevance of Freud's Jewish identity to the origins of psychoanalysis. *Psychoanalytic Contemporary Thought*, *14*, 655–684.

Buber, M. (1970). *I and thou* (W. Kaufmann, Trans.). New York, NY: Charles Scribners's Sons. (Original work published in 1937.)

Butler, J. (1990). *Gender trouble*. New York, NY: Routledge.

Butler, J. (1995). Melancholy gender—refused identification. *Psychoanalytic Dialogues*, *5*, 165–180.

Butler, J. (2004a). *Undoing gender*. New York, NY: Routledge.

Butler, J. (2004b). *Precarious life*. London: Verso.

Carr, R. B. (2011). Combat and human existence. *Psychoanalytic Psychology*, *28*, 471–496.

Cherry, S., Cabaniss, D. L., Forand, N., Haywood, D., & Roose, S. P. (2004). Psychoanalytic practice in the early postgraduate years. *Journal of the American Psychoanalytic Association, 52*, 851–871.

Cherry, S., Aizaga, K.H., & Roose, S. P. (2009). The Columbia longitudinal study of postgraduate career development and psychoanalytic practice: Four years of experience. *Journal of the American Psychoanalytic Association, 57*, 196–199.

Cherry, S., Wininger, L., & Roose, S. P. (2009). A prospective study of career development and analytic practice: The first five years. *Journal of the American Psychoanalytic Association, 57*, 703–720.

Chicago Tribune (2009). North Shore native Sarah Ruhl creates Broadway buzz. *Chicago Tribune*, December 23. Retrieved from: www.triblocal.com/skokie July 5, 2010.

Chodorow, N. J. (2004). Psychoanalysis and women: A personal thirty-five-year retrospect. *Annual of Psychoanalysis, 32*, 101–129.

Cixous, H. (1976). Fiction and its phantoms: A reading of Freud's "Das unheimliche" (The uncanny). *New Literary History, 7*(3), 525–548.

Cixous, H. (2004). *Portrait of Jacques Derrida as a young Jewish saint* (B. B. Brahic, Trans.). New York, NY: Columbia University Press.

Cohen, S. J. D. (2005). *Why aren't Jewish women circumcised?* Berkley, CA: University of California Press.

Cooper, S. H. (2007). Alexander's corrective emotional experience: An objectivist turn in psychoanalytic authority and technique. *Psychoanalytic Quarterly, 76*, 1085–1102.

Cooper, S. H. (2011). *A disturbance in the field*. New York, NY: Routledge.

Corbett, K. (2009). *Boyhoods: Rethinking masculinities*. New Haven, CT: Yale University Press.

Coser, L. A. (1984). *Refugee scholars in America*. New Haven, CT: Yale University Press.

Creighton, M. R. (1990). Revisiting shame and guilt cultures: A forty-year pilgrimage. *Ethos, 18*(3), 279–307.

Cresci, M. B. (2010). Round table discussion: What we are learning from the division's practice survey? *Psychologist–Psychoanalyst, 30*(3), 14.

Crumbley, A. (2011). A conversation with Jay Greenberg. *Psychoanalytic Psychology, 28*, 175–182.

Cuddihy, J. M. (1974). *The ordeal of civility: Freud, Marx, Levi-Strauss, and the Jewish struggle with modernity*. New York, NY: Basic Books.

Cushman, P. (2009). Empathy—what one hand giveth, the other taketh away: Commentary on paper by Lynne Layton. *Psychoanalytic Dialogues, 19*, 121–137.

Danto, E. A. (2005). *Freud's free clinics*. New York, NY: Columbia University Press.

Danto, E. A. (2009). "A new sort of salvation army": Historical perspectives on the confluence of psychoanalysis and social work. *Clinical Social Work Journal, 37*, 67–76.

Dao, J. (2012). Branding a soldier with "personality disorder". *The New York Times*, February 24.

Darwin, C. (1871). *The descent of man, and selection in relation to sex*. New York, NY: Modern Library.

Davies, J. M. (2010) Transformations of desire and despair. In J. Salberg (Ed.), *Good enough endings* (pp. 83–106). New York, NY: Routledge.

Demos, E. V. (1995). *Exploring affect: The selected writings of Silvan S. Tomkins.* Cambridge, England, New York, and Paris: Cambridge University Press.

Derrida, J. (1976). *Of grammatology* (G. C. Spivak, Trans.). Baltimore, MD: Johns Hopkins University Press.

Derrida, J. (1992). *Given time* (P. Kamuf, Trans.). Chicago, IL: University of Chicago Press.

Didi-Huberman, G. (2003). *Invention of hysteria: Charcot and the photographic iconography of the salpêtrière* (A. Hartz, Trans.). Cambridge, MA: The MIT Press.

Diller, J. V. (1991). *Freud's Jewish identity.* Cranbury, NJ: Associated University Presses.

Dimen, M. (2003). *Sexuality, intimacy, power.* Hillsdale, NJ: The Analytic Press.

Dimen, M., & Goldner, V. (Eds.). (2002) *Gender in psychoanalytic space.* New York, NY: Other Press.

Domenici, T., & Lesser, R. C. (1995). *Disorienting sexuality.* New York, NY: Routledge.

Doolittle, H. (1956). *Tribute to Freud.* New York, NY: Pantheon Books.

Droga, J. T., & Kaufmann, P. J. (1995). The guilt of tragic man. *Progress in Self Psychology*, *11*, 259–276.

Dupont, J. (Ed.). (1988). *The clinical diary of Sándor Ferenczi* (M. Balint & N. Z. Jackson, Trans.). Cambridge, MA and London: Harvard University Press.

Ehrenreich, B., & English, D. (1973). *Witches, midwives, and nurses: A history of women healers.* New York, NY: The Feminist Press at the City University of New York.

Eisold, K. (1998). The splitting of the New York Psychoanalytic Society and the construction of psychoanalytic authority. *International Journal of Psycho-Analysis*, *79*, 871–885.

Eisold, K. (2006). Letters to the editors: Reply to Dr. Golland. *International Journal of Psychoanalysis*, *87*, 271.

Eissler, K. R. (1950). Ego-psychological implications of the psychoanalytic treatment of delinquents. *The Psychoanalytic Study of the Child*, *5*, 97–121.

Eissler, K. R. (1953). The effect of the structure of the ego on psychoanalytic technique. *Journal of the American Psychoanalytic Association*, *1*, 104–141.

Eissler, K. R. (1956). Some comments on psychoanalysis and dynamic psychiatry. *Journal of the American Psychoanalytic Association*, *4*, 314–317.

Ellenberger, H. (1970). *The discovery of the unconscious.* New York, NY: Basic Books.

Engel, J. (2008). *American therapy.* New York, NY: Gotham Books.

Erb, W. H. (1883). *Handbook of electro-therapeutics.* New York, NY: William Wood & Co.

Erös, F. (2004). The Ferenczi cult: Its historical and political roots. *International Forum of Psychoanalysis*, *13*, 121–128.

Fairbairn, W. D. (1944). Endopsychic structure considered in terms of object-relationships. *International Journal of Psychoanalysis*, *25*, 70–92.

Falzeder, E. (2010). Sándor Ferenczi between orthodoxy and heterodoxy. *American Imago*, *66*(4), 395.

Feldman, Y. S. (1993). "And Rebecca loved Jacob", but Freud did not. *Jewish Studies Quarterly*, *1*, 72–88.

Fenichel, O. (1939). Problems of psychoanalytic technique. *Psychoanalytic Quarterly, 8*, 57–87.

Fenichel, O. (1941). *Problems of psychoanalytic technique*. Albany, NY: Psychoanalytic Quarterly.

Fenichel, O. (1945). *The psychoanalytic theory of neurosis*. New York, NY: W. W. Norton.

Fenichel, O. (1946). Some remarks on Freud's place in the history of science. *Psychoanalytic Quarterly, 15*, 279–284.

Ferenczi, S. (1909). Introjection and transference. In J. Rickman (Ed.), & J. I. Suttie (Trans.), *First contributions to psycho-analysis* (pp. 35–93). London: Hogarth Press, 1952.

Ferenczi, S. (1910a). Letter from Sándor Ferenczi to Sigmund Freud, March 22, 1910. In E. Brabant, E., Falzeder, & P. Giampieri-Deutsch (Eds. & Trans.), *The correspondence of Sigmund Freud and Sándor Ferenczi, 1908–1914* (Vol. 1, p. 153). Cambridge, MA: Belknap Press of Harvard University Press, 1993.

Ferenczi, S. (1910b). Letter from Sándor Ferenczi to Sigmund Freud, July 9, 1910. In E. Brabant, E., Falzeder, & P. Giampieri-Deutsch (Eds. & Trans.), *The correspondence of Sigmund Freud and Sándor Ferenczi, 1908–1914* (Vol. 1, pp. 186–188). Cambridge, MA: Belknap Press of Harvard University Press, 1993.

Ferenczi, S. (1910c). Letter from Sándor Ferenczi to Sigmund Freud, October 3, 1910. In E. Brabant, E., Falzeder, & P. Giampieri-Deutsch (Eds. & Trans.), *The correspondence of Sigmund Freud and Sándor Ferenczi, 1908–1914* (Vol. 1, pp. 217–221). Cambridge, MA: Belknap Press of Harvard University Press, 1993.

Ferenczi, S. (1910d). Letter from Sándor Ferenczi to Sigmund Freud, October 6, 1910. In E. Brabant, E., Falzeder, & P. Giampieri-Deutsch (Eds. & Trans.), *The correspondence of Sigmund Freud and Sándor Ferenczi, 1908–1914* (Vol. 1, pp. 221–223). Cambridge, MA: Belknap Press of Harvard University Press, 1993.

Ferenczi, S. (1910e). Letter from Sándor Ferenczi to Sigmund Freud, October 10, 1910. In E. Brabant, E., Falzeder, & P. Giampieri-Deutsch (Eds. & Trans.), *The correspondence of Sigmund Freud and Sándor Ferenczi, 1908–1914* (Vol. 1, p. 224). Cambridge, MA: Belknap Press of Harvard University Press, 1993.

Ferenczi, S. (1911). On obscene words. In E. Jones (Trans.), *First contributions to psycho-analysis* (pp. 132–153). New York, NY: Brunner/Mazel.

Ferenczi, S. (1912). Letter from Sándor Ferenczi to Sigmund Freud, December 26, 1912. In E. Brabant, E., Falzeder, & P. Giampieri-Deutsch (Eds. & Trans.), *The correspondence of Sigmund Freud and Sándor Ferenczi, 1908–1914* (Vol. 1, p. 452). Cambridge, MA: Belknap Press of Harvard University Press, 1993.

Ferenczi S. (1913). Belief, disbelief, and conviction. In J. Rickman (Ed.), & J. I. Suttie (Trans.), *Further contributions to psycho-analysis* (pp. 437–450). London: Hogarth Press, 1950.

Ferenczi, S. (1914). The nosology of male homosexuality (homo-erotism). In E. Jones (Ed. & Trans.), *Sex in psychoanalysis* (Vol. 1, pp. 250–268). New York, NY: Basic Books, 1950.

Ferenczi, S. (1915). Letter from Sándor Ferenczi to Sigmund Freud. In E. Brabant, E., Falzeder, & P. Giampieri-Deutsch (Eds. & Trans.), *The correspondence of Sigmund Freud and Sándor Ferenczi* (Vol. 2, p. 80). Cambridge, MA: Belknap Press of Harvard University Press, 1996.

Ferenczi, S. (1919). Letter from Sándor Ferenczi to Sigmund Freud, August 28, 1919. In E. Brabant, E., Falzeder, & P. Giampieri-Deutsch (Eds. & Trans.), *The correspondence of Sigmund Freud and Sándor Ferenczi* (Vol. 2, p. 365). Cambridge, MA: Belknap Press of Harvard University Press, 1996.

Ferenczi, S. (1921a). Letter from Sándor Ferenczi to Georg Groddeck, December 25, 1921. In C. Fortune (Ed. & Trans.), *The Sándor Ferenczi-Georg Groddeck correspondence* (pp. 8–9). London: Open Gate Press, 2002.

Ferenczi, S. (1921b). Symposium on psychoanalysis and the war neurosis held at the Fifth International Psycho-Analytical Congress Budapest, September 1918. *International Psycho-Analytic Library*, 2, 5–21.

Ferenczi, S. (1929). The unwelcome child and his death-instinct. *International Journal of Psychoanalysis*, 10, 125–129.

Ferenczi, S. (1932). *The clinical diary of Sándor Ferenczi* (J. Dupont, Ed., M. Balint & N. Z. Jackson, Trans.). Cambridge, MA: Harvard University Press, 1988.

Ferenczi, S. (1933a). Letter from Sándor Ferenczi to Sigmund Freud, March 29, 1933. In E. Brabant, E., Falzeder, & P. Giampieri-Deutsch (Eds. & Trans.), *The correspondence of Sigmund Freud and Sándor Ferenczi* (Vol. 3, p. 448). Cambridge, MA: Belknap Press of Harvard University Press, 1996.

Ferenczi, S. (1933b). The confusion of tongues between adults and children: The language of tenderness and of passion (M. Balint, Ed.). *International Journal of Psycho-Analysis*, 30(4), 1949.

Fiscalini, J. (2006). Coparticipant inquiry: Analysis as personal encounter. *Contemporary Psychoanalysis*, 42, 437–451.

Fisher, D. J. (2012) Considerations of George Makari's *Revolution in Mind*. Retrieved from: http://internationalpsychoanalysis.net/wp-content/uploads/2012/02/FisherCommentonGeorgeMakari.pdf March 6, 2012.

Fitzgerald, F. S. (1936). The crack-up. In E. Wilson (Ed.), *The crack-up* (pp. 69–84). New York, NY: New Directions Books.

Fortune, C. (Ed.). (2002). *The Sándor Ferenczi–Georg Groddeck correspondence, 1921–1933* (J. Cohen, E. Petersdorff, & N. Ruebsaat, Trans.). New York, NY: The Other Press.

Fosshage, J. L. (1997). Psychoanalysis and psychoanalytic psychotherapy. *Psychoanalytic Psychology*, 14, 409–425.

Foucault, M. (1970). *The order of things: An archeology of the human sciences* (A. Sheridan, Trans.). New York, NY: Random House. (Original work published 1966).

Foucault, M. (1977). *Discipline and punishment*. London: Tavistock.

Foucault, M. (1984). Nietzsche, genealogy, history. In P. Rabinov (Ed.), *The Foucault reader* (pp. 76–100). New York, NY: Random House. (Original work published 1971.)

Foucault, M. (1988). *The care of the self* (R. Hurley, Trans.). New York, NY: Random House. (Original work published 1983.)

Foucault, M. (1997). The ethics of the concern of the self as a practice of freedom. In P. Rabinov (Ed.), *The essential Foucault: Vol. 1, Ethics* (pp. 281–301). New York, NY: Pantheon. (Original work published 1984.)

Frank, G. (1997). Jews, multiculturalism, and Boasian anthropology. *American Anthropologist*, 99, 731–745.

Frankel, J. (2002). Identification and "traumatic aloneness". *Psychoanalytic Dialogues, 12*, 159–170.

Freud, A. (1954). The widening scope of indications for psychoanalysis—discussion. *Journal of the American Psychoanalytic Association, 2*, 607–620.

Freud, A. (1978). Inaugural lecture for the Sigmund Freud chair at the Hebrew University, Jerusalem. *International Journal of Psychoanalysis, 59*, 145–148.

Freud, M. (1958). *Sigmund Freud, man and father*. New York, NY: Vanguard Press.

Freud, S. (1875). Letter from Sigmund Freud to Eduard Silberstein, June 18, 1875. In W. Boehlich (Ed.) & A. Pomerans (Trans.), *The letters of Sigmund Freud to Eduard Silberstein, 1871–1881* (p. 21). Cambridge, MA: Belknap Press.

Freud, S. (1878). Letter from Sigmund Freud to Eduard Silberstein, August 14, 1878. In W. Boehlich (Ed.), & A. Pomerans (Trans.), *The letters of Sigmund Freud to Eduard Silberstein, 1871–1881* (pp. 168–170). Cambridge, MA: Belknap Press.

Freud, S. (1883). Letter from Sigmund Freud to Martha Bernays, September 16, 1883. In E. L. Freud (Ed.), *Letters of Sigmund Freud, 1873–1939* (pp. 58–66). London: Hogarth Press, 1961.

Freud, S. (1885). Letter from Sigmund Freud to Martha Bernays, April 28, 1885. In E. L. Freud (Ed.), *Letters of Sigmund Freud, 1873–1939* (pp. 140–142). London: Hogarth Press, 1961.

Freud, S. (1886). Letter from Sigmund Freud to Martha Bernays, February 10, 1886. In E. L. Freud (Ed.), *Letters of Sigmund Freud, 1873–1939* (pp. 206–211). London: Hogarth Press, 1961.

Freud, S. (1888a). Hysteria. In J. Strachey (Ed. & Trans.), *The standard edition of the complete psychological works of Sigmund Freud* (Vol. 1, pp. 39–59). London: Hogarth Press, 1966.

Freud, S. (1888b). Preface to the translation of Bernheim's suggestion. In J. Strachey (Ed. & Trans.), *The standard edition of the complete psychological works of Sigmund Freud* (Vol. 12, pp. 73–88). London: Hogarth Press, 1961.

Freud, S. (1892). Draft K. The neuroses of defence: From extracts from the Fliess papers. In J. Strachey (Ed. & Trans.), *The standard edition of the complete psychological works of Sigmund Freud* (Vol. 1, pp. 220–229). London: Hogarth Press, 1966.

Freud, S. (1892–1893). A case of successful treatment by hypnotism. In J. Strachey (Ed. & Trans.), *The standard edition of the complete psychological works of Sigmund Freud* (Vol. 1, pp. 115–128). London: Hogarth Press, 1966.

Freud, S. (1893a). Studies on hysteria. In J. Strachey (Ed. & Trans.), *The standard edition of the complete psychological works of Sigmund Freud* (Vol. 2, pp. 48–105). London: Hogarth Press, 1955.

Freud, S. (1893b). The psychotherapy of hysteria from studies on hysteria. In J. Strachey (Ed. & Trans.), *The standard edition of the complete psychological works of Sigmund Freud* (Vol. 2, pp. 253–305). London: Hogarth Press, 1955.

Freud, S. (1893c). Charcot. In J. Strachey (Ed. & Trans.), *The standard edition of the complete psychological works of Sigmund Freud* (Vol. 3, pp. 7–23). London: Hogarth Press, 1961.

Freud, S. (1895a). Letter from Freud to Fliess, January 24, 1895. In J. M. Masson (Ed.), *The complete letters of Sigmund Freud to Wilhelm Fliess, 1887–1904* (pp. 106–107). Cambridge, MA: Harvard University Press, 1985.

Freud, S. (1895b). *Project for a scientific psychology*. In J. Strachey (Ed. & Trans.), *The standard edition of the complete psychological works of Sigmund Freud* (Vol. 1, pp. 281–391). London: Hogarth Press, 1950.

Freud, S. (1896a). The aetiology of hysteria. In J. Strachey (Ed. & Trans.), *The standard edition of the complete psychological works of Sigmund Freud* (Vol. 3, pp. 189–221). London: Hogarth Press, 1962.

Freud, S. (1896b). Letter from Freud to Fliess, June 30, 1896. In J. M. Masson (Ed.), *The complete letters of Sigmund Freud to Wilhelm Fliess, 1887–1904* (pp. 193–194). Cambridge, MA: Harvard University Press, 1985.

Freud, S. (1897a). Letter from Freud to Fliess, June 22, 1897. In J. M. Masson (Ed.), *The complete letters of Sigmund Freud to Wilhelm Fliess, 1887–1904* (pp. 253–254). Cambridge, MA: Harvard University Press, 1985.

Freud, S. (1897b). Letter from Freud to Fliess, August 14, 1897. In J. M. Masson (Ed.), *The complete letters of Sigmund Freud to Wilhelm Fliess, 1887–1904* (pp. 259–261). Cambridge, MA: Harvard University Press, 1985.

Freud, S. (1897c). Letter from Freud to Fliess, August 18, 1897. In J. M. Masson (Ed.), *The complete letters of Sigmund Freud to Wilhelm Fliess, 1887–1904* (pp. 261–262). Cambridge, MA: Harvard University Press, 1985.

Freud, S. (1897d). Letter from Freud to Fliess, October 3, 1897. In J. M. Masson (Ed.), *The complete letters of Sigmund Freud to Wilhelm Fliess, 1887–1904* (pp. 267–269). Cambridge, MA: Harvard University Press, 1985.

Freud, S. (1897e). Letter from Freud to Fliess, October 4, 1897. In J. M. Masson (Ed.), *The complete letters of Sigmund Freud to Wilhelm Fliess, 1887–1904* (pp. 269–270). Cambridge, MA: Harvard University Press, 1985.

Freud, S. (1897f). Letter from Freud to Fliess, October 15, 1897. In J. M. Masson (Ed.), *The complete letters of Sigmund Freud to Wilhelm Fliess, 1887–1904* (pp. 270–273). Cambridge, MA: Harvard University Press, 1985.

Freud, S. (1899a). Letter from Freud to Fliess, August 27, 1899. In J. M. Masson (Ed.), *The complete letters of Sigmund Freud to Wilhelm Fliess, 1887–1904* (pp. 367–369). Cambridge, MA: Harvard University Press, 1985.

Freud, S. (1899b). Letter from Freud to Fliess, December 21, 1899. In J. M. Masson (Ed.), *The complete letters of Sigmund Freud to Wilhelm Fliess, 1887–1904* (pp. 391–393). Cambridge, MA: Harvard University Press, 1985.

Freud, S. (1900a). Letter from Freud to Fliess, April 16, 1900. In J. M. Masson (Ed.), *The complete letters of Sigmund Freud to Wilhelm Fliess, 1887–1904* (pp. 407–408). Cambridge, MA: Harvard University Press, 1985.

Freud, S. (1900b). The interpretation of dreams. In J. Strachey (Ed. & Trans.), *The standard edition of the complete psychological works of Sigmund Freud* (Vols. 4 & 5, pp. 1–715). London: Hogarth Press, 1966.

Freud, S. (1901). Letter from Freud to Fliess, August 7, 1901. In J. M. Masson (Ed. & Trans.), *The complete letters of Sigmund Freud to Wilhelm Fliess, 1887–1904* (pp. 446–448). Cambridge, MA: Belknap Press of Harvard University Press, 1986.

Freud, S. (1904). *Obituary of Professor S. Hammerschlag from Contributions to the Neue Freie Presse. Standard edition, vol. 9*, 255–256.

Freud, S. (1905). Three essays on the theory of sexuality. In J. Strachey (Ed. & Trans.), *The standard edition of the complete psychological works of Sigmund Freud* (Vol. 7, pp. 123–246). London: Hogarth Press, 1961.

Freud, S. (1907). Letter from Sigmund Freud to Karl Abraham, October 8, 1907. *The Complete Correspondence of Sigmund Freud and Karl Abraham 1907–1925* (p. 9). London: Karnac Books.

Freud, S. (1908a). "Civilized" sexual morality and modern mental illness. In J. Strachey (Ed. & Trans.), *The standard edition of the complete psychological works of Sigmund Freud* (Vol. 9, pp. 177–204). London: Hogarth Press, 1959.

Freud, S. (1908b). Letter from Sigmund Freud to Karl Abraham, May 3, 1908. *The complete correspondence of Sigmund Freud and Karl Abraham 1907–1925* (pp. 38–39). London: Karnac Books.

Freud, S. (1909a). Analysis of a phobia in a five-year-old boy. In J. Strachey (Ed. & Trans.), *The standard edition of the complete psychological works of Sigmund Freud* (Vol. 10, pp. 3–152). London: Hogarth Press, 1955.

Freud, S. (1909b). Letter from Sigmund Freud to C. G. Jung, January 17, 1909. In W. McGuire (Ed.), *The Freud/Jung letters: The correspondence between Sigmund Freud and C. G. Jung* (pp. 195–197). Princeton, NJ: Princeton University Press, 1974.

Freud, S. (1910a). Leonardo Da Vinci and a memory of his childhood. In J. Strachey (Ed. & Trans.), *The standard edition of the complete psychological works of Sigmund Freud* (Vol. 11, pp. 57–138). London: Hogarth Press, 1961.

Freud, S. (1910b). Letter from Sigmund Freud to Carl Jung. In W. McGuire (Ed.), *The Freud/Jung letters: The correspondence between Sigmund Freud and C. G. Jung* (pp. 1–592). Princeton, NJ: Princeton University Press, 1974.

Freud, S. (1910c). Letter from Sigmund Freud to Sándor Ferenczi, February 13, 1910. In E. Brabant, E., Falzeder, & P. Giampieri-Deutsch (Eds. & Trans.), *The correspondence of Sigmund Freud and Sándor Ferenczi, 1908–1914* (Vol. 1, p. 138). Cambridge, MA: Belknap Press of Harvard University Press, 1993.

Freud, S. (1910d). Letter from Sigmund Freud to Sándor Ferenczi, January 1, 1910. In E. Brabant, E., Falzeder, & P. Giampieri-Deutsch (Eds. & Trans.), *The correspondence of Sigmund Freud and Sándor Ferenczi, 1908–1914* (Vol. 1, pp. 118–119). Cambridge, MA: Belknap Press of Harvard University Press, 1993.

Freud, S. (1910e). Letter from Sigmund Freud to Sándor Ferenczi, October 6, 1910. In E. Brabant, E., Falzeder, & P. Giampieri-Deutsch (Eds. and Trans.), *The correspondence of Sigmund Freud and Sándor Ferenczi, 1908–1914* (Vol. 1, pp. 221–222). Cambridge, MA: Belknap Press of Harvard University Press, 1993.

Freud, S. (1911). Psycho-analytic notes on an autobiographical account of a case of paranoia (dementia paranoides). In J. Strachey (Ed. & Trans.), *The standard edition of the complete psychological works of Sigmund Freud* (Vol. 12, pp. 1–82). London: Hogarth Press, 1961.

Freud, S. (1912a). Recommendations to physicians practising psycho-analysis. In J. Strachey (Ed. & Trans.), *The standard edition of the complete psychological works of Sigmund Freud* (Vol. 12, pp. 109–120). London: Hogarth Press, 1961.

Freud, S. (1913a). Letter from Sigmund Freud to Sándor Ferenczi, June 8, 1913. In E. Brabant, E., Falzeder, & P. Giampieri-Deutsch (Eds. & Trans.), *The correspondence of Sigmund Freud and Sándor Ferenczi, 1908–1914* (Vol. 1, pp. 490–491). Cambridge, MA: Belknap Press of Harvard University Press, 1993.

Freud, S. (1913b). On beginning the treatment. In J. Strachey (Ed. & Trans.), *The standard edition of the complete psychological works of Sigmund Freud* (Vol. 12, pp. 1–144). London: Hogarth Press, 1961.

Freud, S. (1913c). The claims of psycho-analysis to scientific interest. In J. Strachey (Ed. & Trans.), *The standard edition of the complete psychological works of Sigmund Freud* (Vol. 13, pp. 165–190). London: Hogarth Press, 1961.

Freud, S. (1913d). Totem and taboo: Some points of agreement between the mental lives of savages and neurotics. In J. Strachey (Ed. & Trans.), *The standard edition of the complete psychological works of Sigmund Freud* (Vol. 13, pp. 1–162). London: Hogarth Press, 1961.

Freud, S. (1914). On the history of the psycho-analytic movement. In J. Strachey (Ed. & Trans.), *The standard edition of the complete psychological works of Sigmund Freud* (Vol. 14, pp. 1–66). London: Hogarth Press, 1957.

Freud, S. (1915a). Death and us. In D. Meghnagi (Ed.), *Freud and Judaism* (pp. 11–39). London: Karnac, 1993.

Freud, S. (1915b). Observations on transference-love (further recommendations on the technique of psycho-analysis III). In J. Strachey (Ed. & Trans.), *The standard edition of the complete psychological works of Sigmund Freud* (Vol. 12, pp. 157–171). London: Hogarth Press, 1961.

Freud, S. (1915c). The unconscious. In J. Strachey (Ed. & Trans.), *The standard edition of the complete psychological works of Sigmund Freud* (Vol. 14, pp. 159–216). London: Hogarth Press, 1957.

Freud, S. (1917). Introductory lectures on psycho-analysis. In J. Strachey (Ed. & Trans.), *The standard edition of the complete psychological works of Sigmund Freud* (Vol. 16, pp. 241–463). London: Hogarth Press, 1955.

Freud, S. (1918a). From the history of an infantile neuroses ("Wolf man"). In J. Strachey (Ed. & Trans.), *The standard edition of the complete psychological works of Sigmund Freud* (Vol. 17, pp. 100–122). London: Hogarth Press, 1955.

Freud, S. (1918b). Letter from Sigmund Freud to Oskar Pfister, October 9, 1918. In Psychoanalysis and faith: The letters of Sigmund Freud and Oskar Pfister. *International Psychoanalysis Library*, 59, 61–63.

Freud, S. (1918c). Letter from Sigmund Freud to Sándor Ferenczi, November 17, 1918. In E. L. Freud (Ed.), *Letters of Sigmund Freud, 1873–1939* (p. 311). London: Hogarth Press, 1961.

Freud, S. (1919a). Introduction to psycho-analysis and the war neuroses. In J. Strachey (Ed. & Trans.), *The standard edition of the complete psychological works of Sigmund Freud* (Vol. 17, pp. 205–216). London: Hogarth Press, 1955.

Freud, S. (1919b). Letter from Sigmund Freud to Oskar Pfister, May 27, 1919. In E. L. Freud (Ed.), *Letters of Sigmund Freud, 1873–1939* (p. 70). London: Hogarth Press, 1961.

Freud, S. (1919c). Letter from Sigmund Freud to Sándor Ferenczi, September 5, 1919. In E. L. Freud (Ed.), *Letters of Sigmund Freud, 1873–1939* (p. 367). London: Hogarth Press, 1961.

Freud, S. (1919d). Lines of advance in psycho-analytic therapy. In J. Strachey (Ed. & Trans.), *The standard edition of the complete psychological works of Sigmund Freud* (Vol. 17, pp. 157–168). London: Hogarth Press, 1955.

Freud, S. (1919e). "The 'Uncanny'". In J. Strachey (Ed. & Trans.), *The standard edition of the complete psychological works of Sigmund Freud* (Vol. 17, pp. 219–256). London: Hogarth Press, 1955.

Freud, S. (1920). Beyond the pleasure principle. In J. Strachey (Ed. & Trans.), *The standard edition of the complete psychological works of Sigmund Freud* (Vol. 18, pp. 1–64). London: Hogarth Press, 1955.

Freud, S. (1921). Group psychology and the analysis of the ego. In J. Strachey (Ed. & Trans.), *The standard edition of the complete psychological works of Sigmund Freud* (Vol. 18, pp. 65–144). London: Hogarth Press, 1955.

Freud, S. (1923). The ego and the id. In J. Strachey (Ed. & Trans.), *The standard edition of the complete psychological works of Sigmund Freud* (Vol. 19, pp. 1–66). London: Hogarth Press, 1961.

Freud, S. (1924). Letter from Sigmund Freud to Karl Abraham, June 4, 1924. In E. Falzeder (Ed.), *The complete correspondence of Sigmund Freud and Karl Abraham, 1907–1925* (p. 507). London: Karnac Books, 2002.

Freud, S. (1925a). An autobiographical study. In J. Strachey (Ed. & Trans.), *The standard edition of the complete psychological works of Sigmund Freud* (Vol. 20, pp. 7–74). London: Hogarth Press, 1959.

Freud, S. (1925b). Negation. In J. Strachey (Ed. & Trans.), *The standard edition of the complete psychological works of Sigmund Freud* (Vol. 19, pp. 233–240). London: Hogarth Press, 1961.

Freud, S. (1925c). Some psychical consequences of the anatomical distinction between the sexes. In J. Strachey (Ed. & Trans.), *The standard edition of the complete psychological works of Sigmund Freud* (Vol. 19, pp. 241–258). London: Hogarth Press, 1959.

Freud, S. (1926a). Address to the Society of B'nai Brith. In J. Strachey (Ed. & Trans.), *The standard edition of the complete psychological works of Sigmund Freud* (Vol. 20, pp. 271–276). London: Hogarth Press, 1959.

Freud, S. (1926b). Inhibitions, symptoms and anxiety. In J. Strachey (Ed. & Trans.), *The standard edition of the complete psychological works of Sigmund Freud* (Vol. 20, pp. 75–176). London: Hogarth Press, 1959.

Freud, S. (1926c). The question of lay analysis. In J. Strachey (Ed. & Trans.), *The standard edition of the complete psychological works of Sigmund Freud* (Vol. 20, pp. 177–258). London: Hogarth Press, 1959.

Freud, S. (1927). The future of an illusion. In J. Strachey (Ed. & Trans.), *The standard edition of the complete psychological works of Sigmund Freud* (Vol. 21, pp. 1–56). London: Hogarth Press, 1968.

Freud, S. (1930a). Civilization and its discontents. In J. Strachey (Ed. & Trans.), *The standard edition of the complete psychological works of Sigmund Freud* (Vol. 21, pp. 59–145). London: Hogarth Press, 1968.

Freud, S. (1930b). Letter from Sigmund Freud to A. A. Roback, February 20, 1930. In E. L. Freud (Ed.), *Letters of Sigmund Freud 1873–1939*, 394–395.

Freud, S. (1930c). Letter from Sigmund Freud to Romain Rolland, January 19, 1930. In E. L. Freud (Ed.), *Letters of Sigmund Freud 1873–1939* (pp. 392–393). London: Hogarth Press, 1961.

Freud, S. (1933). New introductory lectures on psycho-analysis. In J. Strachey (Ed. & Trans.), *The standard edition of the complete psychological works of Sigmund Freud* (Vol. 22, pp. 1–182). London: Hogarth Press, 1953–1974.

Freud, S. (1935). Postscript to "Autobiographical Study". In J. Strachey (Ed. & Trans.), *The standard edition of the complete psychological works of Sigmund Freud* (Vol. 20, pp. 71–74). London, Hogarth Press, 1959.

Freud, S. (1937a). Analysis terminable and interminable. In J. Strachey (Ed. & Trans.), *The standard edition of the complete psychological works of Sigmund Freud* (Vol. 23, pp. 216–253). London: Hogarth Press, 1964.

Freud, S. (1937b). Constructions in analysis. In J. Strachey (Ed. & Trans.), *The standard edition of the complete psychological works of Sigmund Freud* (Vol. 23, pp. 255–270). London: Hogarth Press, 1964.

Freud, S. (1938a). An outline of psycho-analysis. In J. Strachey (Ed. & Trans.), *The standard edition of the complete psychological works of Sigmund Freud* (Vol. 23, pp. 139–208). London: Hogarth Press, 1964.

Freud, S. (1938b). Letter from Sigmund Freud to Charles Singer, October 31, 1938. In E. L. Freud (Ed.), *Letters of Sigmund Freud, 1873–1939* (pp. 453–454). London: Hogarth Press, 1961.

Freud, S. (1939). Moses and monotheism. In J. Strachey (Ed. & Trans.), *The standard edition of the complete psychological works of Sigmund Freud* (Vol. 23, pp. 1–138). London: Hogarth Press, 1964.

Friedman, L. J. (1990). *Menninger: The family and the clinic*. New York, NY: Knopf.

Friedman, L. J. (2006). What is psychoanalysis? *Psychoanalytic Quarterly, 75,* 689–671.

Friedman, R. C., & Downey, J. L. (1998). Psychoanalysis and the model of homosexuality as psychopathology. *American Journal of Psychoanalysis, 58,* 249–270.

Fromm, E. (1970). *The crisis of psychoanalysis*. Greenwich, CN: Fawcett Publications.

Fromm-Reichmann, F. (1950). *The principles of intensive psychotherapy*. Chicago, IL: University of Chicago Press.

Frosh, S. (2005). *Hate and the "Jewish science"*. New York, NY: Palgrave, Macmillan.

Furst, L. R. (2008). *Before Freud*. Cranbury, NJ: Lewisburg Bucknell University Press.

Frymer-Kensky, T. (2002). *Reading the women of the bible: A new interpretation of their stories*. New York, NY: Knopf.

Gallop, J. (1982). *The daughter's seduction: Feminism and psychoanalysis*. Ithaca, NY: Cornell University Press.

Gay, P. (1987). *A Godless Jew: Freud, atheism, and the making of psychoanalysis*. New Haven, CT: Yale University Press.

Gay, P. (1988). *Freud: A life for our time*. New York, NY: Norton.

Gaztambide, D. (2011, April 28). "A Psychotherapy for the People": Freud, Ferenczi, and psychoanalytic work with the underprivileged. Paper presented at the Ferenczi Center at the New School for Social Research, New York, NY.

Geller, J. (1994). *Freud v. Freud: Freud's readings of Daniel Paul Schreber's Denkwürdigkeiten eines Nervenkranken*. In S. L. Gilman, J. Birmele, & J. Geller (Eds.), *Reading Freud's reading* (pp. 180–210). New York, NY: New York University Press.

Geller, J. (2007). *On Freud's Jewish body: Mitigating circumstances*. New York, NY: Fordham University Press.

Ghent, E. (1992). Paradox and process. *Psychoanalytic Dialogues, 2,* 135–160.

Giamppieri, P., & Erös, F. (1987). The beginnings of the reception of psychoanalysis in Hungary 1900–1920. *Sigmund Freud House Bulletin, 11*(2), 13–28.

Gill, M. M. (1951). Ego psychology and psychotherapy. *Psychoanalytic Quarterly, 20,* 62–71.

Gill, M. M. (1954). Psychoanalysis and exploratory psychotherapy. *Journal of the American Psychoanalytic Association, 2*, 771–797.

Gill, M. M. (1983). The point of view of psychoanalysis: Energy discharge or person? *Psychoanalysis and Contemporary Thought, 6*, 523–551.

Gill, M. M. (1984). Psychoanalysis and psychotherapy: A revision. *International Review of Psychoanalysis, 11*, 161–179.

Gill, M. M. (1991a) Psychoanalysis and psychotherapy. *International Journal of Psychoanalysis, 72*, 164–165.

Gill, M. M. (1991b). Psychoanalysis and psychotherapy. *International Journal of Psychoanalysis, 72*, 159–161.

Gill, M. M. (1991c) *Indirect suggestion: A response to Oremland's interpretation and interaction.* In J. D. Oremland (Ed.), *Interpretation and interaction: Psychoanalysis or psychotherapy?* (pp. 137–164). Hillsdale, NJ: The Analytic Press.

Gill, M. M. (1994). *Psychoanalysis in transition: A personal view.* Hillsdale, NJ: The Analytic Press.

Gilman, S. L. (1986). *Jewish self-hatred: Anti-semitism and the hidden language of the Jews.* Baltimore, MD: Johns Hopkins University Press.

Gilman, S. L. (1991). *The Jew's body.* New York, NY: Routledge.

Gilman, S. L. (1993a). *Freud, race, and gender.* Princeton, NJ: Princeton University Press.

Gilman, S. L. (1993b). *The case of Sigmund Freud.* Baltimore, MD: Johns Hopkins University Press.

Gilman, S. L. (1993c). The image of the hysteric. In S. L. Gilman, H. King, R. Porter, G. S. Rousseau, & E. Showalter (Eds.), *Hysteria beyond Freud* (pp. 345–452). Berkley, CA: University of California Press.

Gilman, S. L. (2010). Sigmund Freud and electrotherapy. In A. D. Richards (Ed.), *The Jewish world of Sigmund Freud* (pp. 66–77). Jefferson, NC: McFarland & Company, Inc.

Gitelson, M. (1964). On the identity crisis in American psychoanalysis. *Journal of the American Psychoanalytic Association, 12*, 451–476.

Glazer, N., & Moynihan, D. P. (1963). *Beyond the melting pot: The Negroes, Puerto Ricans, Italians, and Irish of New York City.* Cambridge, MA: Harvard University Press.

Glover, E. (1955). Walter Schmideberg. *International Journal of Psycho-Analysis, 36*, 213–215.

Goetz, C. G., Bonduelle, M., & Gelfand, T. (1995). *Charcot: Constructing neurology.* New York, NY: Oxford University Press.

Goldberg, S. A. (2006). Paradigmatic times: An-sky's two worlds. In G. Safran & S. J. Zipperstein (Eds.), *The worlds of S. An-sky: A Russian Jewish intellectual at the turn of the century* (pp. 44–52). Stanford, CA: Stanford University Press.

Goldner, V. (2003). Ironic gender/authentic sex. *Studies in Gender and Sexuality, 4*(2), 113–139.

Goldner, V. (2011a). Trans: Gender in free fall. *Psychoanalytic Dialogues, 21*, 159–171.

Goldner, V. (2011b). Transgender subjectivities: Introduction to papers by Goldner, Suchet, Saketopoulou, Hansbury, Salamon & Corbett, and Harris. *Psychoanalytic Dialogues, 21*, 153–158.

Goldstein, E. L. (2006). *The price of whiteness.* Princeton, NJ: Princeton University Press.

Goldstein, R. (2006) *Betraying Spinoza.* New York, NY: Nextbook/Schocken.

Golland, J. H. (1999). If it's all the same to you . . . The politics of leveling. *Psychoanalytic Psychology, 16*, 103–109.

Gottlieb, R. M. (2006). Review of the book *A compulsion for antiquity: Freud and the ancient world*, by R. H. Armstrong. *International Journal of Psycho-Analysis, 87*, 1740–1744.

Graf, M. (1942). Reminiscences of professor Sigmund Freud. *Psychoanalytic Quarterly, 11*, 465–476.

Grand, S. (2011). Good enough endings: Contemporary perspectives on termination. Paper presented at the meeting of the International Association for Relational Psychotherapy & Psychoanalysis, New York, NY, December 5, 2011.

Grant, J. (1993). *Fundamental feminism.* New York, NY: Routledge.

Green, M. R. (1977). Sullivan's participant observation. *Contemporary Psychoanalysis, 13*, 258–359.

Greenberg, J. (1991). *Oedipus and beyond.* Cambridge, MA: Harvard University Press.

Greenberg, J. (2001). The analyst's participation. *Journal of the American Psychoanalytic Association, 49*, 359–381.

Greenberg, J. R., & Mitchell, S. A. (1983). *Object relations in psychoanalytic theory.* Cambridge, MA: Harvard University Press.

Grinker, R. R., & Spiegel, J. P. (1943). *War neuroses in North Africa: The Tunisian campaign.* New York, NY: Josiah Macy, Jr., Foundation.

Grob, G. N. (1994). *The mad among us.* New York, NY: The Free Press, Macmillan.

Groddeck, G. (1977). The meaning of illness. *International Psycho-Analytic Library, 105*, 1–266. London: The Hogarth Press and the Institute of Psycho-Analysis.

Grubrich-Smitis, I. (1986). Six letters of Sigmund Freud and Sándor Ferenczi on the interrelationship of psychoanalytic theory and technique. *International Review of Psychoanalysis, 13*, 259–277.

Hale, N. G. (1971). *Freud and the Americans.* New York, NY: Oxford University Press.

Hale, N. G. (1995). *The rise and crisis of psychoanalysis in the United States.* New York and Oxford: Oxford University Press.

Hall, A. (1996). Psychoanalysis, psychoanalytic studies, and universities. In M. Stanton, & D. Reason (Eds.), *Teaching transference: On the foundation of psychoanalytic studies* (pp. 69–78). London: Rebus Press.

Hamerow, T. S. (2008). *Why we watched.* New York, NY: Norton.

Hansbury, G. (2011). King Kong & Goldilocks: Imagining transmasculinities through the trans–trans dyad. *Psychoanalytic Dialogues, 21*, 201–220.

Harari, E. (1999). On the history of psychiatry: A special review. *Australian and New Zealand Journal of Psychiatry, 33*(3), 448–455.

Haraway, D. (1991). *Simians, cyborgs, and women.* London: Free Association Books.

Harris, A. E. (2005). *Gender as soft assembly.* Hillsdale, NJ: The Analytic Press.

Harris, A. E. (2009). You must remember this. *Psychoanalytic Dialogues, 19*, 2–21.

Harris, A. E. (2011a). Cold war and postwar: American psychoanalysis in the postwar period. Paper presented at the meeting of the American Psychoanalytic Association, New York, New York, January 17.

Harris, A. E. (2011b). Gender as a strange attractor: Discussion of the transgender symposium. *Psychoanalytic Dialogues, 21*, 230–238.

Harris, A. E. (2011c). The relational tradition: Landscape and canon. *Journal of the American Psychoanalytic Association, 59*, 701–736.

Harris, A., & Aron, L. (1997). Ferenczi's semiotic theory: Previews of postmodernism. *Psychoanalytic Inquiry, 17*, 522–534.

Harris, A. E., & Sinsheimer, K. (2008). The analyst's vulnerability. In F. S. Anderson (Ed.), *Bodies in treatment* (pp. 255–274). New York, NY: The Analytic Press.

Hartmann, H. (1939). Psycho-analysis and the concept of mental health. *International Journal of Psycho-Analysis, 20*, 308–321.

Hartmann, H. (1960). Towards a concept of mental health. *British Journal of Medical Psychology, 33*, 243–248.

Hastings, M. L., & Snow, A. (1904). *Mechanical vibration and its therapeutic application.* New York, NY: The Scientific Authors' Publishing Co.

Heinze, A. R. (2004). *Jews and the American soul.* Princeton, NJ and Oxford: Princeton University Press.

Henry, W. E., Sims, J. H., & Spray, S. L. (1971). *The fifth profession.* San Francisco, CA: Jossey-Bass.

Herberg, W. (1955). *Protestant, Catholic, Jew. An essay in American religious sociology.* Garden City, NY: Doubleday.

Herman, E. (1995). *The romance of American psychology.* Berkley, CA: University of California Press.

Heschel, S. (1999). Revolt of the colonized: Abraham Geiger's Wissenschaft des Judentums as a challenge to Christian hegemony in the academy. *New German Critique, 77*, 61–85.

Hinshelwood, R. D. (1989). *A dictionary of Kleinian thought.* London: Free Association Books.

Hirsch, I. (1987). Varying modes of analytic participation. *Journal of the American Academy of Psychoanalysis, 15*, 205–222.

Hirsch, I. (1992). Extending Sullivan's interpersonalism. *Contemporary Psychoanalysis, 28*, 732–747.

Hirschmuller, A. (1978). *The life and work of Joseph Breuer.* New York, NY: New York University Press.

Hitler, A. (1925). *Mein kampf.* Munich: Franz Eher Nachfolger.

Hoffer, A. (1991). The Freud–Ferenczi controversy: A living legacy. *International Journal of Psycho-Analysis, 18*, 465–472.

Hoffman, I. Z. (1983). The patient as interpreter of the analyst's experience. *Contemporary Psychoanalysis, 19*, 389–422.

Hoffman, I. Z. (1998). *Ritual and spontaneity in the psychoanalytic process.* Hillsdale, NJ: The Analytic Press.

Hoffman, I. Z. (2000). Merton M. Gill: A study in theory development in psychoanalysis. In D. K. Silverman & D. L. Wolitzky (Eds.), *Changing conceptions of psychoanalysis: The legacy of Merton Gill* (pp. 47–87). Hillsdale, NJ: The Analytic Press.

Hoffman, I. Z. (2009). Therapeutic passion in the countertransference. *Psychoanalytic Dialogues, 19*, 617–637.

Hoffman, I. Z. (2011). At death's door: Afterword. In L. Aron & A. Harris (Eds.), *Relational Psychoanalysis, Volume 5: Evolution of process* (pp. 19–44). New York, NY: Routledge.

Hoffman, M. (2011). *Toward mutual recognition: Relational psychoanalysis and the Christian narrative*. New York, NY: Routledge.

Holbrook, M. L. (1875). *Parturition without pain*. New York, NY: M. L. Holbrook, Publisher.

Holt, R. R. (1989). *Freud reappraised*. New York, NY: Guilford Press.

Hornstein, G. A. (2000). *To redeem one person is to redeem the world: The life of Frieda Fromm-Reichmann*. New York, NY: Free Press.

Hustvedt, A. (2011). *Medical muses*. New York, NY: W. W. Norton & Co.

Jacobson, E. (1954). Transference problems in the psychoanalytic treatment of severely depressive patients. *Journal of the American Psychoanalytic Association, 2*, 595–606.

Jacoby, R. (1983). *The repression of psychoanalysis: Otto Fenichel and the political Freudians*. New York, NY: Basic Books.

Jaffe, D. S. (1983). Some relations between the negative Oedipus complex and aggression in the male. *Journal of the American Psychoanalytic Association, 31*, 957–984.

Johnson, A., & English, O. S. (1953). III. The essentials of psychotherapy as viewed by the psychoanalyst. *Journal of the American Psychoanalytic Association, 1*, 550–561.

Johnson, A. M., & Ludwig, A. O. (1954). IV. Psychoanalysis and psychotherapy: Dynamic criteria for treatment choice. *Journal of the American Psychoanalytic Association, 2*, 346–350.

Johnson, W. (1998). The myth of Jewish male menses. *Journal of Medieval History, 24*, 273–295.

Jones, E. (1957). *Life and work of Sigmund Freud, volume three: The last phase 1919–1939*. London: The Hogarth Press.

Jones, E. (1995). *Sigmund Freud life and work, volume two: Years of maturity 1901–1919*. London: The Hogarth Press.

Jonte-Pace, D. (2001). *Speaking the unspeakable: Religion, misogyny, and the uncanny mother in Freud's cultural texts*. Berkeley, CA: University of California Press.

Jorden, E. (1603). A brief discourse of a disease called the suffocation of the mother. In M. MacDonald (Ed.), *Witchcraft and hysteria in Elizabethan London*. New York and London: Routledge, 1991.

Jung, C. (1934). The state of psychotherapy today. In W. McGuire et al. (Eds.) & R. F. C. Hull (Trans.), *Civilization in transition: The collected works of C. G. Jung, Second Edition* (Vol. 10, pp. 157–173). Princeton, NJ: Princeton University Press, 1970.

Kadushin, C. (1969). *Why people go to psychiatrists*. New York, NY: Atherton Press.

Kalish-Weiss, B. (2009). Interview with Leo Rangell. CIPS. Retrieved from: http://www.cipsusa.org/arts-affairs/interview-with-leo-rangell/

Kantrowitz, J. L. (1997). A different perspective on the therapeutic process: The impact of the patient on the analyst. *Journal of the American Psychoanalitical Association, 45*, 127–153.

Kaplan, A. (2003). How the Jews created the comic book industry. Part I: The golden age (1933–1955). *Reform Judaism Magazine, 32*(1). Retrieved from: http://reformjudaismmag.net/03fall/comics.shtml

Kaplan, A. (2008). *From Krakow to Krypton: Jews and comic books.* Philadelphia, PA: The Jewish Publication Society.

Kaplan, D. M. (1973). A technical device in psychoanalysis and its implications for a scientific psychotherapy. *Psychoanalytic Contemporary Science, 2*, 25–41.

Kaplan, D. M. (1990). Some theoretical and technical aspects of gender and social reality in clinical psychoanalysis. *Psychoanalytic Studies of the Child, 45*, 3–24.

Kaplan, M. (1994). *Judaism as civilization.* Philadelphia, PA: The Jewish Publication Society.

Kapusi, K. (2010). Toward a biography of Sandor Ferenczi: Footnotes from Miskolc. *American Imago, 66*, 405–410.

Kardiner, A. (1941). *The traumatic neuroses of war.* New York, NY: Hoeber.

Katz, M., & Schwartz, G. (1998). *Swimming in the sea of the Talmud.* Philadelphia, PA: The Jewish Publication Society.

Kernberg, O. F. (1986). Institutional problems of psychoanalytic education. *Journal of the American Psychoanalytic Association, 34*, 799–834.

Kernberg, O. F. (1996). Thirty methods to destroy the creativity of psychoanalytic candidates. *International Journal of Psycho-Analysis, 11*, 1031–1040.

Kernberg, O. F. (1999). Psychoanalysis, psychoanalytic psychotherapy and supportive psychotherapy. *International Journal of Psycho-Analysis, 80*, 1075–1091.

Kernberg, O. F. (2000). A concerned critique of psychoanalytic education. *International Journal of Psycho-Analysis, 81*, 97–120.

Kernberg, O. F. (2006). The coming changes in pyschoanalytic education: Part I. *International Journal of Psycho-Analysis, 87*, 1649–1673.

Kernberg, O. F. (2007). The coming changes in psychoanalytic education: Part II. *International Journal of Psycho-Analysis, 88*, 183–202.

Kernberg, O. F. (2010). A new organization of psychoanalytic education. *Psychoanalytic Review, 97*, 997–1020.

Kerr, J. (1993). *A most dangerous method.* New York, NY: Alfred A. Knopf.

Killen, Andreas (2006). *Berlin electropolis.* Berkeley, CA: University of California Press.

Kirsner, D. (2000). *Unfree associations.* London: Process Press.

Klein, D. B. (1985). *Jewish origins of the psychoanalytic movement.* Chicago, IL: University of Chicago Press.

Klein, G. S. (1976). *Psychoanalytic theory: An exploration of essentials.* New York, NY: International Universities Press.

Klein, M. (1935). A contribution to the psychogenesis of manic-depressive states. *International Journal of Psycho-Analysis, 16*, 145–174.

Kneeland, T. W., & Warren, C. A. B. (2002). *Pushbutton psychiatry.* Walnut Creek, CA: Left Coast Press.

Knight, R. P. (1949). A critique of the present status of the psychotherapies. *Bulletin of the New York Academy of Medicine, 25*, 100–114.

Knight, R. L. (1952). An evaluation of psychotherapeutic techniques. *Bulletin of the Menninger Clinic, 16*, 113–124.

Knight, R. L. (1953). The present status of organized psychoanalysis in the U. S. *Journal of the American Psychoanalytic Association, 1*, 197–221.

Kohut, H. (1971). *The analysis of the self*. New York, NY: International Universities Press.

Kohut, H. (1977). *The restoration of the self*. New York, NY: International Universities Press.

Kolbrener, W. (2011). *Open minded Torah*. London: Continuum.

Kristeva, J. (1982). *Powers of horror: An essay on abjection*. New York, NY: Columbia University Press.

Kubie, L. S. (1936). *Practical aspects of psychoanalysis: A handbook for prospective patients and their advisors*. New York, NY: W. W. Norton & Co.

Kubie, L. S. (1943). Manual of emergency treatment for acute war neuroses. *War Medicine, 4*, 582–598.

Kuriloff, E. A. (2010). The holocaust and psychoanalytic theory and praxis. *Contemporary Psychoanalysis, 46*, 395–422.

Kurzweil, E. (1996). Psychoanalytic science: From Oedipus to culture. In M. G. Ash & A. Söllner (Eds.), *Forced migration and scientific change: Émigré German-speaking scientists and scholars after 1933* (pp. 139–155). Washington, DC: Cambridge University Press.

Lansky, M. R. (1994). Shame. *Journal of the American Academy of Psychoanalysis, 22*, 433–441.

Laplanche, J., & Pontalis, J. B. (1967). *The language of psycho-analysis*. New York, NY: W. W. Norton.

Laqueur, T. (1990). *Making sex*. Cambridge, MA: Harvard University Press.

Layton, L. (1998). *Who's that girl? Who's that boy? Clinical practice meets postmodern gender theory*. Northvale, NJ: Jason Aronson.

Leary, K. (1997). Race, self-disclosure, and "forbidden talk": Race and ethnicity in contemporary clinical practice. *Psychoanalytic Quarterly, 66*, 163–189.

Lerner, B. H. (2009). In a time of quotes, a quiet pose in defiance. *The New York Times*, May 25. Retrieved from: http://www.nytimes.com/2009/05/26/health/26quot.html November 27, 2011.

Lerner, P. (2003). *Hysterical men*. Ithaca, NY: Cornell University Press.

Leroy-Beaulieu, A. (1895). *Israel among the nations*. New York, NY: Putnam's Sons.

Levenson, E. A. (2001). Freud's dilemma. *Contemporary Psychoanalysis, 37*, 375–390.

Levinas, E. (1969). *Totality and infinity: An essay on exteriority*. Pittsburgh, PA: Duquesne University Press.

Levinas, E. (1981). *Otherwise than being or beyond essence*. Boston, MA: Martinus Nijhoff.

Levy, R. S. (2005). *Antisemitism: A historical encyclopedia of prejudice and persecution, Vol. 2*. Santa Barbara, CA: ABC Clio.

Levy, S. T., & Inderbitzin, L. B. (2000). Suggestion and psychoanalytic technique. *Journal of the American Psychoanalytic Association, 48*, 739–758.

Lewis, H. B. (1971). *Shame and guilt in neurosis*. New York, NY: International Universities Press.

Lewis, H. B. (Ed.). (1987). *The role of shame in symptom formation*. Hillsdale, NJ: Lawrence Erlbaum Associates, Inc.

Leys, R. (2000). *Trauma: A geneology*. Chicago, IL: University of Chicago Press.

Leys, R. (2007). *From guilt to shame: Auschwitz and after*. Princeton, NJ: Princeton University Press.

Liban, A., & Goldman, D. (2000). Freud comes to Palestine: A study of psychoanalysis in a cultural context. *The International Journal of Psycho-Analysis, 81*, 893–906.

Lieberman, E. J. (1985). *Acts of will: The life and work of Otto Rank*. Florence, MA: Free Press.

Liebman, J. J. (1946). *Peace of mind*. New York, NY: Simon and Schuster.

Loewenberg, P. (1992). *Freud's Moses*: Judaism terminable and interminable: By Yosef Hayim Yerushalmi. *International Review of Psycho-Analysis, 19*, 509–512.

Lothane, Z. (1997). The schism between Freud and Jung over Schreber. *International Forum of Psychoanalysis, 6*, 103–115.

Lukacs, J. (1988). *Budapest 1900: A historical portrait of a city and its culture*. New York, NY: Grove Press.

MacDonald, K. (2002). *The culture of critique: An evolutionary analysis of Jewish involvement in twentieth-century intellectual and political movements*. Fairfield, CA: 1st Book Library.

McDougall, W. (1921). *Is America safe for democracy?* New York, NY: Charles Scribner's Sons.

McGovern, C. M. (1984). Psychiatry, psychoanalysis, and women in America: An historical note. *Psychoanalytic Review, 71*, 541–552.

McGuire, M. T. (1997). Review of the book *A history of psychiatry*, by E. Shorter. *Journal of the American Medical Association, 278*, 949–950.

McGuire, W. (1974). *The Freud/Jung letters: The correspondence between Sigmund Freud and C. G. Jung*. Princeton, NJ: Princeton University Press.

McLaughlin, N. (2001). Optimal marginality: Innovation and orthodoxy in Fromm's revision of psychoanalysis. *The Sociological Quarterly, 42*, 271–288.

Mahler, M. (1988). *The memoirs of Margaret Mahler* (P. E. Stepansky, Ed.). New York, NY: The Free Press.

Maines, R. (1999). *The technology of orgasm*. Baltimore, MD: Johns Hopkins University Press.

Malcolm, J. (1982). *The impossible profession*. New York, NY: Vintage.

Malcolm, J. (1984). *In the Freud archives*. London: Jonathan Cape.

Makari, G. (2008). *Revolution in mind*. New York, NY: Harper Collins.

Marcus, P., & Wineman, I. (1985). Psychoanalysis encountering the Holocaust. *Psychoanalytic Inquiries, 5*, 85–98.

Masson, J. M. (1990). *Final analysis*. Reading, MA: Addison-Wesley.

Menaker, E. (1989). *Appointment in Vienna*. New York, NY: St. Martin's Press.

Menninger, K. (1930). *The human mind*. New York, NY: Alfred A. Knopf.

Menninger, K. (1958). *Theory of psychoanalytic technique*. New York, NY: Harper Torchbooks.

Merkin, D. (2010). My life in therapy: What 40 years of talking to analysts has taught me. *The New York Times Magazine*, August 4, 2010. Retrieved from: http://www.nytimes.com/2010/08/08/magazine/08Psychoanalysis-t.html?pagewanted=all February 28, 2012.

Mészáros, J. (2010). Progress and persecution in the psychoanalytic heartland: Anti-semitism, communism and the fate of Hungarian psychoanalysis. *Psychoanalytic Dialogues, 20,* 600–622.

Metzger, J. (2009, February 26). Progress for African-American pioneers in medicine yesterday, today and tomorrow. *Insider: Your College of Medicine News Resource.* Retrieved from: http://news.medinfo.ufl.edu/articles/top-stories/progress-for-african-american-pioneers-in-medicine-yesterday-today-and-tomorrow/

Micale, M. S. (1993). *Beyond the unconscious: Essays of Henri F. Ellenberger in the history of psychiatry* (F. Dubor & M. S. Micale, Trans.). Princeton, NJ: Princeton University Press.

Micale, M. S. (1995). *Approaching hysteria.* Princeton, NJ: Princeton University Press.

Micale, M. S. (2008). *Hysterical men.* Cambridge, MA: Harvard University Press.

Mikics, D. (2009). *Who was Jacques Derrida?* New Haven, CT: Yale University Press.

Mills, R. S. L. (2005). Taking stock of the developmental literature on shame. *Developmental Review, 25,* 26–63.

Mitchell, S. A. (1988). *Relational concepts in psychoanalysis: An integration.* Cambridge, MA: Harvard University Press.

Mitchell, S. A. (1991). Wishes, needs, and interpersonal negotiations. *Psychoanalytic Inquiry, 11,* 147–170.

Mitchell, S. A. (1993). *Hope and dread in psychoanalysis.* New York, NY: Basic Books.

Mitchell, S. A. (1997). *Influence and autonomy in psychoanalysis.* Hillsdale, NJ: The Analytic Press.

Mitchell, S. A. (2000a). *Relationality.* Hillsdale, NJ: The Analytic Press.

Mitchell, S. A. (2000b). Juggling paradoxes. *Studies in Gender and Sexuality, 1,* 251–269.

Mitchell, S. A., & Aron, L. (1999). Editors' preface. In S. A. Mitchell & L. Aron (Eds.), *Relational psychoanalysis: The emergence of a tradition* (pp. ix–xx). Hillsdale, NJ: The Analytic Press.

Molino, A. (Ed.). (1997). *Elaborate selves.* New York, NY: The Hawarth Press.

Morrison, A. P. (1989). *Shame: The underside of narcissism.* Hillsdale, NJ: The Analytic Press.

Morrison, A. P. (2008a). The analyst's shame. *Contemporary Psychoanalysis, 44,* 65–82.

Morrison, A. P. (2008b). Shame—considerations and revisions: Discussion of papers by Sandra Buechler and Donna Orange. *Contemporary Psychoanalysis, 44,* 105–109.

Najavits, L. M. (1998). Psychiatry over time: From care to cure, from Village Green to Park Avenue: A review of *A history of psychiatry. Contemporary Psychology: A Journal of Reviews, 43,* 281–282.

Nathanson, D. L. (1987). *The many faces of shame.* New York, NY: Guilford Press.

Nussbaum, M. C. (2010). *From disgust to humanity.* Oxford: Oxford University Press.

Oberndorf, C. P. (1953). *A history of psychoanalysis in America.* New York, NY: Harper Torchbooks.

Ofrat, G. (2001). *The Jewish Derrida*. New York, NY: Syracuse University Press.

Ogden, T. H. (1986). *The matrix of the mind*. Northvale, NJ: Aronson.

Ogden, T. H. (1994). The analytic third: Working with intersubjective clinical facts. *International Journal of Psychoanalysis*, 75, 3–19.

Ogden, T. H. (2005). *This art of psychoanalysis*. London and New York, NY: Routledge.

Ogden, T. H. (2009). *Rediscovering psychoanalysis*. London and New York, NY: Routledge.

O'Neil, M., & Rangell, L. (1954). Panel reports—annual meeting, 1953—I. Psychoanalysis and dynamic psychotherapy—similarities and differences. *Journal of the American Psychoanalytic Association*, 2, 152–166.

Oppenheim, M. (2006). *Jewish philosophy and psychoanalysis*. Lanham, MD: Lexington Books.

Orange, D. M. (2008). The complexity of shame: Response to Sandra Buechler and Andrew Morrison. *Contemporary Psychoanalysis*, 44, 110–117.

Orange, D. M. (2011). *The suffering stranger*. New York, NY: Routledge.

Oremland, J. D. (1991). *Interpretation and interaction: Psychoanalysis or psychotherapy?* Hillsdale, NJ: The Analytic Press.

Oring, E. (1984). *The jokes of Sigmund Freud: A study in humor and Jewish identity*. Philadelphia, PA: University of Pennsylvania Press.

Orr, D., & Zetzel, E. R. (1953). Panel reports—midwinter meeting, 1952—I. The traditional psychoanalytic technique and its variations. *Journal of the American Psychoanalytic Association*, 1, 526–537.

Ostow, M. (Ed.). (1982). *Judaism and psychoanalysis*. New York, NY: Ktav.

Ostow, M. (1989). Review of the book *A Godless Jew*, by P. Gay. *International Review of Psychoanalysis*, 16, 119–121.

Paris, J. (2005). *Fall of an icon: Psychoanalysis and academic psychiatry*. Toronto: University of Toronto Press, Inc.

Pellegrini, A. (1997). *Performance anxieties*. New York, NY: Routledge.

Philipson, I. J. (1993). *On the shoulders of women*. New York, NY: Guilford.

Phillips, S. H. (2003). Homosexuality: Coming out of the confusion. *International Journal of Psychoanalysis*, 84, 1431–1450.

Pizer, S. (1998). *Building bridges*. Hillsdale, NJ: The Analytic Press.

Pope, H. G. (1997). Review of the book *A history of psychiatry*, by E. Shorter. *The New England Journal of Medicine*, 337, 57–58.

Prince, R. (2009). Psychoanalysis traumatized: The legacy of the holocaust. *American Journal of Psychoanalysis*, 69, 179–194.

Rangell, L. (1954). Similarities and differences between psychoanalysis and dynamic psychotherapy. *Journal of the American Psychoanalytic Association*, 2, 734–744.

Rangell, L. (1981). Psychoanalysis and dynamic psychotherapy—similarities and differences twenty-five years later. *Psychoanalytic Quarterly*, 50, 665–693.

Rangell, L., & Kalish-Weiss, B. (2009). Interview of Dr. Leo Rangell by Dr. Beth Kalish-Weiss, Los Angeles, California, July, 2008. *International Forum of Psychoanalysis*, 18(2), 107–111.

Rechavi, O., Minevich, G., & Hobert, O. (2011). Transgenerational inheritance of an acquired small RNA-based antiviral response in *C. elegans*. *Cell*, 147(6), 1248–1256.

Reeder, J. (2004). *Hate and love in psychoanalytic institutions*. New York, NY: The Other Press.

Reiff, P. (1959). *Freud: The mind of the moralist*. New York, NY: Viking Press.

Reiff, P. (1966). *The triumph of the therapeutic: Uses of faith after Freud*. Chicago, IL: The University of Chicago Press.

Reijzer, H. (2011). *A dangerous legacy: Judaism and the psychoanalytic movement*. London: Karnac Books.

Reis, B., & Grossmark, R. (2009). *Heterosexual masculinities*. New York, NY: Routledge.

Renik, O. (2006). *Practical psychoanalysis for therapists and patients*. New York, NY: Other Press.

Rice, E. (1990). *Freud and Moses: The long journey home*. Albany, NY: SUNY Press.

Richards, A. D. (1999). An intervention in the contemporary psychoanalytic debate. *The Round Robin: Newsletter of Section I, Division of Psychoanalysis (39), APA, 14*, 1–9.

Richards, A. D. (Ed.). (2010). *The Jewish world of Sigmund Freud: Essays on cultural roots and the problem of religious identity*. Jefferson, NC: McFarland & Company.

Ricouer, P. (1970). *Freud and philosophy*. New Haven, CT: Yale University Press.

Roazen, P. (1990). *Encountering Freud*. New Brunswick, NJ: Transaction Publishers.

Roback, A. A. (1929). *Jewish influence in modern thought*. Cambridge, MA: Sci-Art Publishers.

Robert, M. (1976). *From Oedipus to Moses*. Garden City, NY: Anchor Press.

Rose, A. (2008). *Jewish women in Fin de Siecle Vienna*. Austin, TX: University of Texas Press.

Rose, J. (2003). Response to Edward Said. In E. Said (Ed.), *Freud and the non-European* (p. 65). London: Verso.

Roughton, R. E. (2002). Rethinking homosexuality. *Journal of the American Psychoanalytic Association, 50*, 733–763.

Rozenblit, M. L. (2001). *Reconstructing a national identity: The Jews of Habsburg Austria during World War I*. Oxford and New York, NY: Oxford University Press.

Rudnytsky, P. L. (2002). *Reading psychoanalysis*. Ithaca, NY: Cornell.

Ruhl, S. (2010). *In the next room (or the vibrator play)*. New York, NY: Samuel French.

Rutkow, I. (2010). *Seeking the cure*. New York, NY: Simon & Schuster.

Sachar, H. M. (2005). *A history of the Jews in the modern world*. New York, NY: Alfred Knopf.

Salberg, J. (2010). Hidden in plain sight: Freud's Jewish identity revisited. In A. D. Richairds (Ed.), *The Jewish world of Sigmund Freud: Essays on cultural roots and the problem of religious identity* (pp. 5–21). Jefferson, NC: McFarland and Company.

Schafer, R. (1973). Action: Its place in psychoanalytic interpretation and theory. *Annual of Psychoanalysis, 1*, 159–195.

Schafer, R. (1983). *The analytic attitude*. New York, NY: Basic Books.

Schafer, R. (1985). Wild analysis. *Journal of American Psychoanalytic Association, 33*, 275–299.

Schafer, R. (1997). Vicissitudes of remembering in the countertransference: Fervent failure, colonisation and remembering otherwise. *International Journal of Psycho-Analysis, 78*, 1151–1163.

Schleiner, W. (1995). *Medical ethics in the Renaissance*. Washington, DC: Georgetown University Press.

Schofer, J. W. (2010). *Confronting vulnerability: The body and the divine in rabbinic ethics*. Chicago, IL: University of Chicago Press.

Schwartz, D. B. (2012). *The first modern Jew: Spinoza and the history of an image*. Princeton, NJ: Princeton University Press.

Schwartz, H. (2000). Mission impossible: Introducing postcolonial studies in the US Academy. In H. Schwartz & S. Ray (Eds.), *A companion to postcolonial studies* (pp. 1–20). Malden, MA: Blackwell.

Seidman, N. (1994). Carnal knowledge: Sex and the body in Jewish studies. *Jewish Social Studies, 1*, 115–146.

Shapiro, A. E. (1997). The uncanny Jew: A brief history of an image. *Judaism, 46*, 63–78.

Shapiro, S. (2004). The uncanny Jew: A brief history of an image. In L. Erlich & S. Bolozky (Eds.), *Textures and meaning: Thirty years of Judaic studies at the University of Massachusetts Amherst*. University of Massachusetts Amherst (electronic version).

Shedler, J. (2010). The efficacy of psychodynamic psychotherapy. *American Psychologist, 65*(2), 98–109.

Shephard, B. (2001). *A war of nerves*. Cambridge, MA: Harvard University Press.

Shorter, E. (1992). *From paralysis to fatigue*. New York, NY: The Free Press.

Shorter, E. (1997). *A history of psychiatry*. New York, NY: John Wiley and Sons.

Silver, C. B. (2003). A survey of clinicians' views about change in psychoanalytic practice and theoretical orientation. *Psychoanalytic Review, 90*, 193–224.

Simmel, E. (1918). *Kriegsneurosen und Psychisches Trauma*. Munich, Leipzig: Nemnich.

Simmel, E. (1921). Symposium on psychoanalysis and the war neurosis held at the Fifth International Psycho-Analytical Congress Budapest, September 1918. *International Psychoanalysis Library, 2*, 30–43.

Sklar, K. K. (1974). "All hail to pure cold water!" *American Heritage Magazine, 26*(1). Retrieved from: http://www.americanheritage.com, July 5, 2010.

Slavet, E. (2008). Freud's Lamarckism and the politics of racial science. *Journal of the History of Biology, 41*(1), 37–80.

Slavet, E. (2009). *Racial fever*. New York, NY: Fordham University Press.

Slavin, M. O., & Kriegman, D. (1998). Why the analyst needs to change: Toward a theory of conflict, negotiation, and mutual influence in the therapeutic process. *Psychoanalytic Dialogues, 8*, 247–284.

Smith, H. F. (2001). Obstacles to integration: Another look at why we talk past each other. *Psychoanalytic Psychology, 18*, 485–514.

Smith, H. F. (2007). Voices that changed psychoanalysis in unpredictable ways. *Psychoanalytic Quarterly, 76*, 1049–1063.

Soloveitchik, J. B. (1992). *The lonely man of faith*. New York, NY: Doubleday.

Soloveitchik, J. B. (2003). *Out of the whirlwind*. New York, NY: Ktav Publishing.

Stanton, M. (1991). *Sándor Ferenczi: Reconsidering active intervention*. London: Free Association Books.

Stanton, M., & Reason, D. (Eds.). (1996). *Teaching transference: On the foundation of psychoanalytic studies*. London: Rebus Press.

Starr, K. E. (2008). *Repair of the soul: Metaphors of transformation in Jewish mysticism and psychoanalysis*. New York, NY: Routledge.

Stein, E., & Kim, S. (2009). *Flow: The cultural story of menstruation*. New York, NY: St. Martin's Press.

Stein, R. (1997). The shame experiences of the analyst. *Progress in Self Psychology, 13*, 109–123.

Stepansky, P. E. (2009). *Psychoanalysis at the margins*. New York, NY: Other Press.

Stern, D. B. (2004). The eye sees itself: Dissociation, enactment, and the achievement of conflict. *Contemporary Psychoanalysis, 40*, 197–237.

Stern, S. (2009). Session frequency and the definition of psychoanalysis. *Psychoanalytic Dialogues, 19*, 639–655.

Stolorow, R. D., & Atwood, G. E. (1982). Psychoanalytic phenomenology of the dream. *Annuals of Psychoanalysis, 10*, 205–220.

Stolorow, R. D., & Atwood, G. E. (1992). *Contexts of being: The intersubjective foundations of psychological life*. Hillsdale, NJ: Analytic Press.

Stone, L. (1951). Psychoanalysis and brief psychotherapy. *Psychoanalytic Quarterly, 20*, 215–236.

Stone, L. (1954). The widening scope of indications for psychoanalysis. *Journal of the American Psychoanalytic Association, 2*, 567–594.

Stone, L. (1957). Review of the book *Psychoanalysis and psychotherapy: Developments in theory, technique, and training*, by F. Alexander. *Psychoanalytic Quarterly, 26*, 397–405.

Stone, L. (1961). *The psychoanalytic situation: An examination of its development and essential nature*. Madison, CT: International Universities Press.

Strenger, C. (2005). *The designed self*. Hillsdale, NJ: The Analytic Press.

Sullivan, H. S. (1964). *The fusion of psychiatry and the social sciences*, with introduction and commentaries by H. S. Perry. New York, NY: W. W. Norton and Co., Inc.

Sziklai, A. (2009). *The Jewish theme in the relationship of Sigmund Freud and Sándor Ferenczi: between the state and the public sphere* (Vol. 84 of Working paper). Jerusalem: The European Forum at the Hebrew University.

Tauber, A. I. (2009). *Science and the quest for meaning*. Waco, TX: Baylor University Press.

Tauber, A. I. (2010). *Freud, the reluctant philosopher*. Princeton, NJ: Princeton University Press.

Teutsch, D. A. (1999) (Ed.). *Kol Haneshama: Prayerbook for the days of awe*. Wyncote, PA: Reconstructionist Press.

Thompson, C. M. (1988). Sándor Ferenczi, 1873–1933. *Contemporary Psychoanalysis, 24*, 182–195.

Thompson, N. L. (1987). Early women psychoanalysts. *International Review of Psychoanalysis, 14*, 391–406.

Thompson, N. L. (2001). American women psychoanalysts, 1911–1941. *Annual of Psychoanalysis, 29*, 161–177.

Thompson, N. L. (2012). The transformation of psychoanalysis in America: Emigré analysts and the New York Psychoanalytic Society and Institute, 1935–1961. *Journal of the American Psychoanalytic Association, 60*, 9–44.

Van Herik, J. (1982). *Freud on femininity and faith*. Berkeley, CA: University of California Press.

Wachtel, P. L. (1976). Structure or transaction? *Psychoanalytic Contemporary Science*, 5, 101–136.

Wachtel, P. L. (1980). Transference, schema, and assimilation. *Annual of Psychoanalysis*, 8, 59–76.

Wachtel, P. L. (1982). Vicious circles: The self and the rhetoric of emerging and unfolding. *Contemporary Psychoanalysis*, 18, 259–273.

Wachtel, P. L. (1983). *The poverty of affluence*. New York, NY: Free Press.

Wachtel, P. L. (1987). *Action and insight*. New York, NY: Guilford Press.

Wachtel, P. L. (1999). *Race in the mind of America*. New York, NY: Routledge.

Wachtel, P. L. (2002). Psychoanalysis and the disenfranchised. *Psychoanalytic Psychology*, 19, 199–215.

Wachtel, P. L. (2008). *Relational theory and the practice of psychotherapy*. New York, NY: The Guilford Press.

Wachtel, P. L. (2009). Knowing oneself from the inside out, knowing oneself from the outside in. *Psychoanalytic Psychology*, 26, 158–170.

Wachtel, P. L. (2011). *Therapeutic communication*: second edition. New York, NY: Guilford Press.

Wachtel, P. L., & DeMichele, A. (1998). Unconscious plan or unconscious conflict? Commentary on Joseph Weiss's paper. *Psychoanalytic Dialogues*, 8, 429–442.

Wake, N. (2007). The military, psychiatry, and "unfit" soldiers, 1939–1942. *Journal of the History of Medicine and Allied Sciences*, 62, 461–494.

Wallerstein, R. S. (1989). Psychoanalysis and psychotherapy: An historical perspective. *International Journal of Psychoanalysis*, 70, 563–591.

Wallerstein, R. S. (1995). *The talking cures*. New Haven, CT and London: Yale University Press.

Wallerstein, R. S. (1996). Merton Max Gill, M.D. *Annual of Psychoanalysis*, 24, 13–17.

Wallerstein, R. S. (1998). *Lay analysis*. Hillsdale, NJ: The Analytic Press.

Wallerstein, R. S. (2000a). Where have all the psychoanalytic patients gone? They are still here. *Psychoanalytic Inquiry*, 20, 503–526.

Wallerstein, R. S. (2000b). Merton Gill, psychotherapy, and psychoanalysis: A personal dialogue. In D. K. Silverman & D. L. Wolitzky (Eds.), *Changing conceptions of psychoanalysis: The legacy of Merton Gill* (pp. 198–218). Hillsdale, NJ: The Analytic Press.

Warren, C. A. B. (2004). Genital surgeries and stimulation in nineteenth century psychiatry. In M.T. Segal & V. Demos (Eds.), *Gender perspectives on reproduction and sexuality* (Vol. 8, pp. 165–197). Amsterdam: Elsevier Ltd.

Waska, R. (2011). Review of the book *A disturbance in the field*, by S. Cooper. *Psychoanalytic Psychology*, 28, 465–470.

Watson, P. (2000). *The modern mind*. New York, NY: Harper Collins.

Weininger, O. (1906). *Sex and character*. New York, NY: G. P. Putnam's Sons.

Weinshel, E. M. (1990). How wide is the widening scope of psychoanalysis and how solid is its structural model? Some concerns and observations. *Journal of the American Psychoanalytic Association*, 38, 275–296.

Weedon, C. (1987). *Feminist practice and poststructuralist theory*. Cambridge, MA: Blackwell.

Wertham, F. (1954). *Seduction of the innocent*. New York, NY: Reinhart & Company, Inc.

Winnicott, D. W. (1971). *Playing and reality*. London: Tavistock.

Wolfson, E. R. (1994). *Through a speculum that shines*. Princeton, NJ: Princeton University Press.

Wyatt, R. C. and Yalom, V. (2008). Owen Renik on practical psychoanalysis and psychotherapy. *Psychotherapy.net: Resources To Inspire Therapists*. Retrieved from: http://www.psychotherapy.net/interview/owen-renik February 28, 2012.

Yerushalmi, Y. H. (1991). *Freud's Moses*. New Haven, CT and London: Yale University Press.

Zborowski, M., & Herzog, E. (1952). *Life is with people*. New York, NY: International Universities Press.

Index